THE ONE GOD

THE ONE GOD

A COMMENTARY ON THE FIRST PART OF
ST. THOMAS' THEOLOGICAL SUMMA

BY THE
REV. REGINALD GARRIGOU-LAGRANGE, O.P.

TRANSLATED BY
DOM. BEDE ROSE, O.S.B., S.T.D.

B. HERDER BOOK CO.
15 & 17 SOUTH BROADWAY, ST. LOUIS, MO.
AND
33 QUEEN SQUARE, LONDON, W. C.

NIHIL OBSTAT

R. P. *Hieronymus Wespe, O.S.B.*

Censor Deputatus

IMPRIMI POTEST

Thomas Meier, O.S.B.

Abbas

NIHIL OBSTAT

Sti. Ludovici, die 1. Junii, 1943

Gilmore H. Guyot, C.M.

Censor Librorum

IMPRIMATUR

Sti. Ludovici, die 4. Junii, 1943

✠ *Joannes J. Glennon*

Archiepiscopus

To

The Holy Mother of God

The Author

Most humbly dedicates this work

as a

Token of Gratitude and

Filial obedience

TRANSLATOR'S PREFACE

THEOLOGY is the queen of sciences. Many, who are not Catholics, would seriously dispute this statement, and a considerable number perhaps would emphatically deny it. Cardinal Newman, in his *Idea of a University*, declared and proved that no institution of learning can rightly call itself a university unless it teaches theology. St. Thomas Aquinas in the very first question of his admirable *Summa theologica* states and proves that theology is nobler than the other sciences. But his appeal is to men who have the faith, who believe there is a God who will reward those that seek Him, as St. Paul assures us in equivalent words.

There is a crying need at the present day for the civilized nations to give up materialism and return to belief in God and acceptance of His revelation with all that this implies. The words of G. K. Chesterton uttered twenty years ago read now almost like a prophecy. He said: "The age-long struggle of the Church against heresy, in the technical sense of the word, is over. But another great struggle is approaching. I may not live to see it. Hell's next attack will be on that doctrine on which all religion and all morality are based, the existence of a personal, infinite, and eternal God. That effort will be accompanied by a mighty effort to sweep away the standards of Christian purity." What we are experiencing at the present time confirms what Chesterton said.

One of the chief purposes of dogmatic theology is to defend the doctrine of God's existence and His revelation against all adversaries. For all Christians some knowledge of dogmatic theology will prove most beneficial. A knowledge of theology is also of great importance for the spiritual life, especially for a deepening of the interior life of communion with God. There is at the present time, even among devout Christians, too much extroversion and too little introversion. The connection between theology and the interior life is shown by Father Garrigou-Lagrange in the Introduction to his commentary on *The One God*. He points out that there is often too great a separation between study and prayer. He has in mind those who believe in the supernatural, and what he says about study applies not only to theology, but to all branches of knowledge. He sounds a note of warning about sentimentalism in piety, which consists in a certain affected love that is not accompanied by a true and deep love for God and souls. Certainly the emotional element in our nature has its place in the spiritual life, but it must not be allowed to be the standard of judgment in spiritual things. St. Theresa conversed with good theologians, as she says in her *Autobiography*, so as not to stray from the path of truth. She is referring to theologians who sanctified their study of theology by prayer. What Father Garrigou-Lagrange says in his Introduction on the relation between study and prayer is well worth reading. St. Thomas Aquinas realized the importance of prayer in its relation to study. Whenever an intricate problem presented itself either in theology or in philosophy, he did not spend more time in study, but more time in prayer.

It should not be necessary to stress the importance of the study of theology for the clergy. Yet it is to be feared that too often among priests books on dogmatic theology are relegated to the back shelves of oblivion. After their ordination this branch of knowledge tends to become more and more a forgotten science. Undoubtedly a knowledge of dogmatic theology is of great help in preaching, and the reason why some find it difficult to preach is very often that they have forgotten their dogmatic theology. There is also the danger that many seminarians may approach the study of dogmatic theology in a perfunctory manner, viewing it merely as a study required in the seminary course, but as being of no practical value. Moral theology and canon law are considered of more importance. These sacred branches are necessary, but they should never be allowed to usurp the place of dogmatic theology. It must also be said that the study of dogmatic theology, and especially a perusal of this manual, will be of great benefit to the more educated among the laity. How beautifully St. Thomas discusses the mysteries of our faith in his compendious *Summa theologica*. All the fundamental principles of moral theology and canon law are to be found in this work of St. Thomas. There have been many Latin commentaries on the *Summa theologica* of St. Thomas, but it is the opinion of the writer of this preface that there has never been any English translation of any part of any of the Latin commentaries on the *Summa theologica* of St. Thomas. Without a commentary it is often difficult to grasp all that St. Thomas wishes to convey to the student, since at times he expresses his mind on certain points with a brevity that contains richness of thought. It is to be hoped that this English translation of Garrigou-Lagrange's Latin commentary on the first twenty-six questions of the *Summa theologica* of St. Thomas will appeal to many of the clergy, students of theology, and the more educated among the laity.

In conclusion I wish to express my deep sense of gratitude to the Rev. Newton Thompson, S.T.D., for his very careful preparation of my manuscript for the printer, and also for his many valuable suggestions.

CONTENTS

viii CONTENTS

INTRODUCTION

THE IMPORTANCE AND SIGNIFICANCE OF THE THEOLOGICAL SUMMA OF ST. THOMAS

SINCE this volume is an explanation of the first part of the *Theological Summa* of St. Thomas, it is expedient by way of introduction, first to show the importance or value and the significance of this work from two points of view, historical and theoretical. Our reference to the history of theology concerns only those matters about which one is not allowed to plead ignorance.

1) In the history of theology generally three periods are distinguished. First we have the patristic period, which extends from the first century to the eighth, and this is chiefly apologetic, polemic, and positive. Then we have the period of the Middle Ages, from the eighth century to the fifteenth, and this is the scholastic period. Finally there is the modern period, from the sixteenth century to the present time, and this period is chiefly positive and critical.

In each successive age the progress of theology is clearly seen, since, whatever period we take, a certain function of theology comes particularly into prominence, according to the necessities of the times. In this evolution we have the manifestation of something that is truly providential.

Thus in *the patristic period,* theology is primarily apologetic (second century) for the conversion of the world from paganism to Christianity. It afterward becomes chiefly polemic in tone, being directed particularly against the heresies cropping up within the fold of the Church, and these heresies, such as Arianism, Nestorianism and Monophysitism, are concerned with the more important dogmas, such as the Trinity, Incarnation, and Redemption. Theology must then defend the principles of faith from the very sources of revelation, namely, from Holy Scripture and tradition. Thus theology gradually assumes the form which is called *positive,* that is, it gathers together the various points of revealed doctrine as contained in Holy Scripture and divine tradition. But a systematic theology, combining all that is of faith and what is connected with it, so as to form one body of teaching, did not yet exist in the patristic period, except in certain works of St. Augustine [1] and St. John Damascene.[2]

1 Cf. *De Trinitate, PL,* XLII.
2 Cf. *De fide orthodoxa, PG,* XCV.

1

But in the second period, *the Middle Ages,* we find systematic or Scholastic theology definitely established, which didactically and speculatively expounds and defends what is of faith, and which deduces from it theological conclusions. Thus there is gradually formed a body of teaching which, though subordinate to what is strictly of faith, includes the science of theology, as it is commonly accepted in the Church, and which transcends, by reason of its universality and certainty, the various theological systems more or less in opposition to one another. In this age the theological Summae were written, which are so called because each is a complete treatise on all subjects pertaining to theology, and according as these various subjects are considered under the light of the higher principles of faith and reason.

In the third or *modern period,* theology again becomes chiefly both polemic and positive against the Protestants, and apologetic against the rationalists. We may call this third period critical or reflexive, and in this period, too, we see clearly the progress made in theology, since critical reflection normally follows direct knowledge. As St. Thomas says: "human reasoning, by way of seeking and finding, advances from certain things simply understood, namely, the first principles; and again, by way of judgment returns by analysis to first principles, in the light of which it examines what it has found." [3] Thus in this third period, we find developing a more critical knowledge and defense, against Protestants and rationalists, of the very foundations of the faith or sources of revelation, namely, Holy Scripture and divine tradition, and as a result of this we have the fundamental treatises on revelation, the Church, the *de locis* (theological sources), this last being a scientific method of sacred theology.

In this we readily see the progress made in theology which, like a tree, grows and is perpetually renewed as a result of the more diligent efforts made in acquiring a knowledge of the sources, these being, as it were, the roots from which it proceeds.

2) We should note in the history of theology three brilliant epochs, each following immediately the close of an ecumenical council. Thus, after the First Council of Nicaea (325) against Arianism, in the fourth century and the beginning of the fifth century the greater Fathers of the Church flourished. In the East, in the Greek Church, we have St. Athanasius, St. Basil, St. Gregory of Nazianzus, St. Gregory of Nyssa, St. John Chrysostom, and St. Cyril of Alexandria. In the West we have St. Hilary, St. Ambrose, St. Jerome, St. Augustine, and St. Leo the Great.

Similarly, in the second epoch, after the Fourth Lateran Council,

[3] *Summa theol.,* Ia, q.79, a.8.

held in the year 1215 against the Albigenses and Waldensians, the thirteenth century saw the rise of the great theologians St. Albert the Great, Alexander of Hales, St. Bonaventure, and St. Thomas.

Finally, the third brilliant epoch in the history of theology is at the time of the Council of Trent (1545–63). Even before this time there had been some celebrated theologians, such as Cajetan and Sylvester of Ferrara, and during the period of the council and afterward we have Soto, Bannez, Tolet, Medina, the Salmanticenses, John of St. Thomas, and Suarez in speculative theology. But all these theologians are commentators of the Summa of St. Thomas, even Suarez, although he pursues his own eclectic method. During the same period Cano, St. Robert Bellarmine, Natalis Alexander, and Bossuet are prominent in the art of controversy; and in exegesis we have Maldonatus, Cornelius a Lapide, and others.

In like manner, after the Vatican Council (1869–70) there is a revival of theology in the works of Joseph Kleutgen, S.J., Scheeben, Schwane, Hefele; and in the revival of Thomism we have Sanseverino, Cornoldi, S.J., Zigliara, O.P., and others. In several of his encyclicals, especially in the *Aeterni Patris* (1879), Leo XIII highly recommends the doctrine of St. Thomas.

From the fact that these three golden ages of sacred theology follow in the wake of ecumenical councils, it is seen how the Holy Spirit directs, by the living voice of the authoritative teaching of the Church, the progressive knowledge of dogmatic truths with regard to those matters that are of faith, and the progress of theology in questions subordinate to faith. For God, by His special providence, watches over His science, that is, theology, which in the strict sense is the science of God proceeding from divine revelation. On the other hand, in these three generally accepted periods preparations were somehow made for the ecumenical councils then held by reason of the inquiries of the theologians during these times of preparation. Thus human labor is the disposing cause, and God assisting the Church teaching is the principal cause, of the progressive understanding of dogma in matters of faith, and also in consequence of this of the progress itself made in theology.

3) It is to be observed that in each of these three periods there is a time of preparation, a time of splendor, and a stationary time when compendiums and compilations make their appearance. Finally, there is the period of more or less pronounced decline, as in the seventh, the fourteenth, and the eighteenth centuries.

In the time of splendor, the wonderful harmony in the various functions of theology is particularly in evidence, a harmony which the human mind cannot attain suddenly. Generally speaking, during the time of preparation there are two tendencies to some extent opposed to each other, because of a certain excess in each case. Some, for instance, exaggerate the necessity of speculation, as the Alexandrian school does; others devote themselves exclusively to the positive study of Holy Scripture, as the school of Antioch does. Likewise, in the Middle Ages, in the twelfth century, Abélard, assigning too much to the role of reason, falls into many errors, while, on the other hand, several of the school of St. Victor stress too much the mystic element and do not rely sufficiently upon reason.

Contrary to this, in the golden age, especially in the thirteenth century, the doctors succeed in effecting a marvelous reconciliation between the various functions of theology, which is then perfected in its positive, speculative, and even affective aspects. For we then see all the great theologians writing commentaries on Holy Scripture; they have a profound knowledge of the teaching of the Fathers, and they are conspicuous for their wisdom or exalted perception of the mysteries that are most productive of fruit in the Christian life.

This we see is the case in the thirteenth century, in which we detect notable differences as to genius, inclination, and method among the greater theologians.

Thus St. Bonaventure in his works is generally faithful to the teaching of St. Augustine. His preference is for Platonic instead of Aristotelian philosophy, giving precedence to the will over the intellect, and he devotes himself more to mystic contemplation than to speculative theology. At the same time St. Albert the Great, who is profoundly versed in philosophical subjects, purges Aristotelian philosophy of the errors injected into it by the Arabian commentators and accommodates it to the uses of theology as an instrument that is more precise and exact than Platonic philosophy.

Finally, St. Thomas completed what St. Albert had begun. He showed the value of the foundations of Aristotelian philosophy with regard to first ideas and first principles of reason, as also in determining the constitutive principles of both natural things and human nature. Thus he determines more accurately what is the proper object of our intellect and hence what absolutely transcends our natural knowledge, and even the natural knowledge of any created intellect. Better, therefore, than any of his predecessors, St. Thomas distinguished between natural reason and supernatural faith, though he showed how they are interrelated. With wonderful logical order he expounded the various parts of theology according as it treats of God as He is in Himself, how all things proceed from Him, and how He is the final end of all things. Thus he collected all the theological material so as to form one body of doctrine, and this he did by a display of qualities rarely united in one individual, namely, with great simplicity as well as profundity of thought, and also with great rigor of logic as well as with a deep sense of the inaccessibility of the mystery. Therefore his doctrine was praised in the highest terms by the Supreme Pontiffs. Leo XIII wrote as follows: "Among the scholastic doctors, the chief and master of all, towers Thomas Aquinas, who, as Cajetan observes,[4] because 'he most venerated the ancient doctors of the Church, in a certain way seems to have inherited the intellect of all.' The doctrines of those illustrious men, like the scattered members of a body, Thomas collected together and cemented, distributed in wonderful order, and so increased with important additions that he is rightly and deservedly esteemed the special bulwark and glory of the Catholic faith. . . .

"Moreover, the Angelic Doctor pushed his philosophic conclusions into the reasons and principles of the things which are most comprehensive and contain in their bosom, so to say, the seeds of almost infinite truths, to be unfolded in good time by later masters and with a goodly yield. And as he also used this philosophic method in the refutation of error, he won the title to distinction for himself: that single-handed he victoriously combated the errors of former times, and supplied invincible arms to rout those which might in after times spring up.

"Again, clearly distinguishing, as is fitting, reason from faith, while happily associating the one with the other, he both preserved the rights and had regard for the dignity of each; so much so, indeed, that reason, borne on the wings of Thomas to its human height can scarcely rise higher, while faith could scarcely expect more or stronger aids from reason than those which she has already obtained through Thomas." [5]

In the same encyclical various testimonies of the Sovereign Pontiffs are quoted, and we would draw especial attention to the crowning point of these, which is the judgment by Innocent VI, who writes: "His teaching above that of others, the canons alone excepted, possesses such an elegance of phraseology, a manner of statement, and a soundness in its propositions, that those who hold to it are never found swerving from the path of truth, and he who dares to assail it will always be suspected of error." [6] After the thirteenth century scholastic theology gradually begins to decline,

[4] Cf. Cajetan, *Com. in Summam S. Thomae*, IIa IIae, q. 148, a. 4 in fine. (Tr.)
[5] *Aeterni Patris*, Aug. 4, 1879.
[6] Sermon on St. Thomas.

just as following the age of the greater Fathers, after the fourth and fifth centuries, we have that of the minor Fathers, from the sixth to the eighth centuries.

Even after the beginning of the fourteenth century, John Duns Scotus in many of his metaphysical questions receded from the logical method of St. Thomas and established a new school of thought. Duns Scotus disagrees with St. Thomas on two points.

1) He admits a new distinction, namely, an actual-formal distinction on the part of the object, which he considers a possible distinction between the real and the logical, whereas the Thomists say that distinction either precedes the consideration of the mind, and is real, or else it does not, and then it is logical. There is no possible intermediary. Scotus substitutes this formal distinction sometimes for the real distinction which St. Thomas holds, for instance, between created essence and existence, between the soul and its faculties, and between the faculties themselves, and thus he paves the way for nominalism. But sometimes Scotus tends toward extreme realism, substituting the formal distinction for the logical distinction which St. Thomas admits, for instance, between the divine attributes, and between the various metaphysical grades in the created being, for instance, between animality, vitality, substance, and being. Hence being is conceived as univocal, for the distinction between being and the substance of both God and creatures is formal, before any consideration of the mind. This new teaching in metaphysics does not, according to the Thomists, escape the danger of pantheism; for if the created substance and the divine substance are outside of being, since they are formally distinguished from it as objective realities, then they are non-entities, because outside of being is not-being; and so there would be but one thing.[7] Moreover, by such formalism, Scholasticism ends in subtleties and a war of words.

2) Voluntarism is another innovation introduced by Scotus. Thus he maintains that the distinction between the orders of nature and grace depends upon God's free will, as if grace were not supernaturally essential, but only actually so. This same voluntarism makes Scotus affirm that God could have established another natural moral law regulating the duties among human beings, and so He could revoke such precepts as "thou shalt not kill, thou shalt not steal." Thus Scotus paves the way for the contingency and positivism of the nominalists of the fourteenth century.[8]

About the same time Roger Bacon, a prodigy of erudition,

---

[7] Cf. Vacant, *Etudes comparées sur la philosophie de saint Thomas et sur celle de Duns Scot*, 1891, p. 25.

[8] *Ibid.*, pp. 14–16, 19 f.

though not free from rash opinions, here and there in his writings speaks with contempt of Aristotle's philosophy, and of St. Albert and St. Thomas, whom he calls children.

Thomas Sutton, O.P., said to be English by birth (†1310), was one among others who in his commentaries on the four books of the *Sentences* wrote in defense of St. Thomas against Scotus. But Peter Aureolus, O.M., Anthony Andrea, O.M., Richard of Middletown, O.M., took up the defense of Scotus' doctrine, and Gerard of Bonn, O.D.C., strove to reconcile the opinions of each school.

Throughout the fourteenth century and in the early fifteenth century, scholastic theology gradually resolved itself into a war of words, railleries, and useless subtleties. The chief reason for this decline was the revival of nominalism, which maintains that universals are mere concepts of the mind or common names. Hence not even an imperfect knowledge of the nature of things can be acquired, whether of corporeal things or of the soul and its faculties, or the foundation of the natural law, or the essence of grace and the essential distinction between it and our nature.

Thus the advocates of nominalism deny the principle that the faculties, habits, and acts are specified by the formal object. Wherefore nominalists, especially William Ockham, despising the sound and lofty doctrine of their predecessors, prepared the downfall of solid scholastic theology, and prepared for the errors of Luther, whose teachers in the schools of Wittenberg were nominalists.

In the fifteenth century a revival in scholastic theology began with John Capreolus, O.P. (†1444), who is called the prince of Thomists, with Juan de Torquemada, O.P. (†1468), who wrote the *Summa de Ecclesia,* with Cajetan, O.P. (†1534), the distinguished defender of Thomistic doctrine, who was practically the first in the schools to explain the *Theological Summa* of St. Thomas instead of the *Sentences.* In this same period we have Conrad Kollin, O.P. (†1536), who wrote a series of commentaries on the *Summa contra Gentes.* These last mentioned theologians prepared the way for the theology of modern times, which began with the sixteenth century. Its first task was to refute the errors of this time, namely, Protestantism, Baianism, and Jansenism. These attenuated forms of Lutheranism deny the essential distinction between the order of nature and that of grace, and give a distorted notion of predestination and the divine motion.

Most prominent among the controversialists who labored to refute these errors are St. Robert Bellarmine, S.J. (†1621), Cano (†1560), and Bossuet (†1704). Among scholastic theologians, in the Dominican order we have Victoria (†1546), Soto (†1560), Bannez (†1604), John of St. Thomas (†1644), and Gonet (†1681); among the Carmelites we have the theologians of Salamanca, who wrote the best commentaries on the works of St. Thomas. In the Society of Jesus we have Toletus (†1596), Suarez (†1617), Molina (†1600), and Lugo (†1660), who proposed a different interpretation of the Angelic Doctor's teaching. Suarez, the eclectic, sought to steer a middle course between St. Thomas and Scotus, and receded less than Molina did from the Thomistic doctrine on predestination and grace.

Eminent in positive theology during this time are Batavius, Thomassin, Combefis, and others.

In the eighteenth century there was a gradual decline in theology from its former splendor. Yet we still have such Thomists as Charles René Billuart and Cardinal Louis Gotti, who defended the teaching of the Angelic Doctor with clarity and soundness of argument; St. Alphonsus Liguori, who wrote particularly on moral subjects, has received the title of Doctor of the Church.

Finally, after the French Revolution and the Napoleonic Wars, when peace was again restored, the study of both positive and speculative theology gradually began to flourish, and later on a special incentive was offered for the advancement of theology by the Vatican Council in its condemnation of Positivism and agnosticism. The fruits of this were seen in Modernism, condemned by Pius X. This Sovereign Pontiff, like Leo XIII, again highly recommended the study of St. Thomas' works and wrote: "But we warn teachers to bear in mind that a slight departure from the teaching of Aquinas, especially in metaphysics, is very detrimental. As Aquinas himself says, 'a slight error in the beginning is a great error in the end.'" [9]

Finally, the Code of Canon Law, promulgated by the authority of Benedict XV in 1918, says: "Mental philosophy and theology must be taught according to the method, teaching and principles of the Angelic Doctor, to which the professors should religiously adhere." [10] This is stated again in the new law for the doctorate promulgated by Pius XI.[11]

All these testimonies, whether of the Sovereign Pontiffs or of the theologians who always have recourse to the *Theological Summa* of St. Thomas, most clearly proclaim its value and significance. All know of the works that have been written in recent times concerning the *Theological Summa*.[12]

[9] Encycl. *Pascendi* and *Sacrorum antistitum.*
[10] Can. 1366, no. 2.
[11] Encycl. *Deus scientiarum Dominus.*
[12] Consult the commentaries of Father Buonpensiere, O.P., Father del Prado, O.P., Father Billot, S.J., Father Mattiussi, S.J., and others. Many articles have

THE METHOD OF ST. THOMAS
ESPECIALLY THE STRUCTURE OF THE ARTICLES
OF THE THEOLOGICAL SUMMA

Many seem to think that before Descartes wrote his *Discourse on Method,* traditional philosophy was not yet fully and unmistakably cognizant of the rules governing sound reasoning for the construction and teaching of knowledge. Many others, on the contrary, think that Descartes, who despised history and his predecessors, could easily have found out from these latter the true rules of method. Some logicians are even of the opinion that a discourse on method could have been written, more scientific than Descartes', one in accordance with the teachings of Aristotle and St. Thomas. I should like in this article to explain briefly the main features of St. Thomas' method. Let us see first, by way of a statement of the question, what several of our contemporaries have to say about it. Then we shall examine how the Angelic Doctor found the solid foundation of this method in Aristotle's writings and how he made use of *analysis* in inductive inquiry, and also of *synthesis* in demonstration. Finally, we shall see how he closely connected analysis and synthesis in the light of divine contemplation.

ON THE VARIOUS JUDGMENTS ABOUT THIS METHOD

Nowadays there are some who say that the method of St. Thomas is too scholastic and artificial, that it is not sufficiently historical and real. It is, so they say, too much an a priori method, almost always a process of deduction and analysis, or else in the analysis itself there is too much abstraction. It even seems at times to confound logical abstractions with the objectivity of things. Some, though not realizing that they are nominalists, nowadays assert that "St. Thomas speaks sometimes of matter and form, of essence and existence, as if these were distinct realities." [13] To be sure, for the Angelic Doctor, even before any consideration of the mind, matter is not form, created essence is not existence; and therefore,

---

appeared in periodicals, especially in the *Revue Thomiste, Bulletin Thomiste, Revue des sciences philosophiques et théologiques, Angelicum, Gregorianum.* There are also many monographs on some particular part of the *Summa,* and several articles in the *Dictionnaire de théologie catholique* and in other contemporary encyclopedias.

[13] Edgar de Bruyne in his *Saint Thomas d'Aquin,* 1928, p. 99, writes: "If we wanted to remain true to the tradition of the schools we should be led to believe that from the beginning Thomism committed the mistake of confusing the logical and the real. . . . St. Thomas speaks of *essence* as if it were a reality. . . . He reasons about the matter and form of corporeal things as if they were distinct realities that are in opposition."

before any consideration of the mind, matter is distinct from form, and essence from existence. Yet form and essence are not, for St. Thomas, *that which is,* but *that by which* something is; nor does it follow that they are merely logical entities and not realities.[14] But in these days many no longer know how to distinguish between metaphysical abstraction of direct consideration and logical abstraction of reflex consideration.[15] Therefore they think only *that which is* is real, namely, the concrete singular. Hence, for them, the abstract object not only is not concrete, but it is not real. Thus the essence of man, of virtue, of society, and such things, would not be anything real, and the whole of metaphysics, not excepting the principle of contradiction, would be reduced to logic, logical abstractions, logical being, or, as they say, to extreme intellectualism that is without reality and lifeless. They would not dare to say explicitly that the abstract principle of contradiction (that something cannot at the same time be and not be) is not a law of real being but only a logical law governing the operations of the mind, as the laws of the syllogism are. To such an extreme admission, however, is one brought by this silly and at the present day common enough objection.

Moreover, several say that the method of St. Thomas often proceeds, not according to the natural way in which the mind operates, but in the conventional way of the schools of the thirteenth century, namely, by first proposing objections, at least three, which might be proposed afterward with better results; for, placed at the beginning, they are a source of obscurity rather than of light to the mind. Furthermore, it is indeed surprising, some say, that St. Thomas begins by setting forth the errors, introducing them with the formula *Videtur quod non,* and only after this comes the true doctrine, which is proved in very few words by an appeal to authority, more at length, however, in a theoretical manner; and finally the objections are solved.

Therefore some nowadays, in philosophy and also in speculative theology, depart from this method which, so they say, is too scholas-

---

[14] *Summa theol.,* Ia, q.13, a.1 ad 2um; q.54, a.1.

[15] According to the teaching of St. Thomas (I *Sent.,* d.2, a.3, c; *De potentia,* q.7, a.9), the direct consideration of metaphysics, which is called *first intention,* is concerned with the object as conceived by the mind, with the real nature itself of individualized things; as, for instance, the essence of man; whereas the reflex consideration of logic, which is called *second intention,* is concerned with the object only according to the subjective mode of its existence in the mind; thus, for instance, logic considers the formal universality of any predicate or subject, or the laws of the syllogism. Likewise the distinction is said to be real when it precedes the consideration of the mind, and logical when it follows this consideration. In fact, however, before the consideration of the mind, matter is not form; it can even be separated from this latter so as to receive another form.

tic. Already in the time of Pius IX, as is evident from the thirteenth proposition of the *Syllabus*, several said: "The method and principles by which the old scholastic doctors cultivated theology are not at all suitable to the demands of our times and to the progress of the sciences." [16] Some, not considering the profound difference between St. Thomas' method of procedure and the merely a priori or synthetic method adopted by Spinoza, seem to admit that St. Thomas' method and even St. Bonaventure's, from the abuse of philosophical deduction, lead to rationalism and pantheism, as clearly seen from the propositions to which the Sacred Congregation of the Index ordered Augustine Bonnetty to give his assent (1855) in writing.[17]

Now some depart from St. Thomas' method, preferring the historical not only for the useful and necessary investigation in the history of philosophy and theology, but also for a more or less direct knowledge of even philosophical or theological truth. This mode of procedure was indeed already in vogue among the followers of idealistic evolutionism, especially with Hegel, and later on we come across it, though in a modified form, in many works of modern authors. Whatever these modifications may be, this method, so it seems, tends by its very nature to confuse philosophy with the history of philosophy, and thus is established a certain philosophy of the history of doctrines, one that is more or less according to the tenets of evolutionism.

According to this view, which is not infrequent today, among all the systems appearing in the course of time in accordance with the evolution of ideas, no system is absolutely true, but each is relatively true, that is, in opposition to another preceding doctrine, or else to some other brief evolutionary period of the past. They say that, for instance, Thomism was relatively true in the thirteenth century in opposition to the doctrine of certain Augustinians, which it surpassed; but it, too, is not absolutely but relatively false with respect to the subsequent system which, either as an antithesis or as a superior synthesis, is of a higher order in the evolution of ideas. Thus Scotism, coming at a later date, would be truer than St. Thomas' doctrine, and this by the momentum of its progress in the history of philosophy and theology. Then why should not this be so for the nominalism of William Ockham? In like manner, the eclecticism of Suarez, which often seeks to steer a middle course between the system of St. Thomas and that of Scotus, would be a still more perfect synthesis and the beginning of a new process and progress among the modern intellectuals.

[16] Denz., no. 1713.
[17] *Ibid.*, no. 1652.

If it were so, nothing would be absolutely true, not even the principle of contradiction, at least as a law of being and higher reason, as Hegel admits. All the more so, none of the accepted definitions would be absolutely true, and hence from none of them could the true properties of things be deduced. There would be only relative truth, in its reference to the present state of knowledge, and this rather as regards the already superseded past than the unknown future. Even for knowing the relative truth of any doctrine, it would be necessary to have full knowledge of the preceding periods of evolution, which were the prerequisites for the manifestation of its ultimate development. By way of illustration, we may say that for a knowledge of what ought to be our philosophical conception according to the intellectual exigencies of the twentieth century, we would have to go through Kantianism and Hegelianism, and then vitally reconsider Thomism so as to render it truly presentable to modern minds. Yet this new cogitation, as regards the mental attitude of the twentieth century, would not be absolutely but only relatively true, just as the cogitation of St. Thomas was relatively true in the thirteenth century.

This conception of truth, however, does not seem to differ from that of the Modernists, who said: "Truth is no more immutable than man himself is, in that it is developed with, in, and by him." [18] But this proposition, if we wish to consider the question more seriously, presupposes immanence or absolute evolutionism. According to this theory, as Pius IX said in the first proposition of the *Syllabus:* "In effect God is produced in man and in the world, and all things are God and have the very substance of God, and God is one and the same thing with the world, and, therefore, spirit with matter, necessity with liberty, good with evil, justice with injustice." [19] Indeed the charge is made against St. Thomas that his method—as if it did not differ from Spinoza's—leads to pantheism; and now the new historical method, which is evolutional in its tone of thought, leads to the form opposed to it, which is pantheism. Spinoza, indeed, identified all things with the immobile God, while the evolutionists reduce God to universal evolution. According to the evolutionists, God is really in a process of becoming both in man and in the world, and He never will be in the true sense, as Renan said. Thus nothing would be absolutely true and nothing absolutely false. There would be only relative truth and relative falsehood. Only relativity would be absolute.

The above-mentioned confusion between history and philosophy corresponds to the desires neither of the true historian nor of the

18 *Ibid.,* no. 2058.
19 *Ibid.,* no. 1701.

true philosopher. But the true historian seeks to acquire a knowledge of history from the facts, before the uncertain philosophy of history is established. The desire of the true philosopher is, indeed, to acquire an accurate knowledge of philosophy, but he does not consider the temporal sequence of doctrines, as if these were the criterion or sign of their relative truth, and as if this sequence of doctrines were always and necessarily an evolution in the ascendant order, but never a regression and senile decline. From the fact that Scotus came after St. Thomas, it does not follow that his doctrine is truer, and that later on there is greater perfection in the eclecticism of Suarez.

We must use the historical method in the history of doctrines, and this is indeed of great help in understanding the state and difficulty of the question, so as to give us, as it were, a panorama of the solutions of any great problem. But in philosophy we must employ the analytic and synthetic method proportionate to it. In theology, however, we rely first upon proofs taken from the authority of Holy Scripture or divine tradition, or even the writings of the holy Fathers, and in the second place on arguments drawn from reason, while, of course, not neglecting the history of problems and their solutions.

ON THE ARISTOTELIAN FOUNDATION OF ST. THOMAS' METHOD

If we consider, however, the works of St. Thomas, we shall see that the common Doctor of the Church did not despise history, as was the case with Descartes, but, so far as possible in his time, he made use of the history of doctrines, appropriating whatever truth he found in the writings of the ancient philosophers, especially Aristotle, as well as in the works of the Fathers and other Doctors of the Church. Often, too, with very keen mental perception, St. Thomas has recourse to the history of errors in formulating his objections, since Providence permits errors so that the truth may become more apparent, and permits evils so that greater good may result therefrom.

If we consider the general structure of St. Thomas' articles, we detect in it a scientific application of method, which the Angelic Doctor had previously discussed at length in his commentary on Aristotle's *Posterior Analytics*. This work of Aristotle treats of the search for real definition by the division of the genus and the inductive and comparative inquiry into the specific difference; it also discusses a priori and a posteriori demonstrations, and especially the middle term in demonstration.

Some modern writers say that the structure of the *Theological*

Summa is artificial, as in the case of eclectic syncretism in which heterogeneous elements are mechanically and, as it were, accidentally joined together. However, not only all the commentators of the Angelic Doctor, but many contemporary historians (e.g., Father Grabmann [20]) point out that the *Theological Summa* from beginning to end constitutes one organic whole. The orderly arrangement of the three parts, containing thirty-eight treatises (about three thousand articles, almost ten thousand objections), is effected with superb constructive skill. Furthermore, the divisions are not accidental, but have their foundation in the very nature of things. Notwithstanding so great a complexity of questions, the whole doctrinal edifice, as it is well called, is simple in its magnitude, like the Egyptian pyramids or the Gothic cathedrals, not even one column of which can be changed without destroying the perfect harmony of the edifice. But what is the foundation of this method of doctrinal construction?

For a closer inspection of this architecture, attention must be drawn to the general way the articles are composed in accordance with the technique of scholastic exposition, to which St. Thomas adheres, as he didactically proceeds in the *Summa theologica* and the *Quaestiones disputatae*. But he dispensed himself from this in the *Opuscula* and the *Summa contra Gentes*, where he often juxtaposes arguments at the reader's choice, not explicitly distinguishing between direct and indirect arguments, or between those derived from proper and those from common principles.

This art or technique, which to some seems too conventional, truly corresponds to the normal progress of the intellect in the philosophical or theological investigation of truth. Why, in the *Summa theologica*, do we always find at the beginning of each article three objections, which are introduced by the formula, *Videtur quod non?* Why does an article in the *Quaestiones disputatae* often begin with ten objections against one part of the contradiction and ten or twelve against the other?

To some it seems that these objections should follow the demonstration of the truth. On the contrary, according to Aristotle's method and that of almost all the doctors, in the beginning there must be a statement of the question and of what is essentially the point at issue in the difficulty to be solved. It is about this that the methodical doubt is chiefly concerned, and the Stagirite spoke of it long before Descartes, and with shrewder judgment, too, not by doubting the validity of the first principles of reason, but by solving the objections of the skeptics. [21]

20 *Saint Thomas d'Aquin*, p. 41.
21 *Metaphysics*, Bk. IV.

The necessity of this methodical doubt is well shown by St. Thomas. Aristotle said: "With a view to the science which we are investigating, we must first approach the subjects about which it behooves us first to raise doubts. . . . The difficulty to be solved must first be examined." [22] Concerning this the Angelic Doctor says: "Just as he who wishes to free himself from a chain that binds him, must first inspect the chain and the way it binds him, so he who wishes to solve a doubt must first examine all the difficulties and their causes. . . . Those who wish to search for truth, not taking doubt first into consideration, are like those who do not know where they are going . . . hence they cannot go by a direct route, unless perhaps they do so by chance . . . nor can they know when they find the truth sought, and when they do not. . . . Just as in judgments no one can give a decision unless he hears the reasons for and against, so he who has to examine philosophical questions is necessarily in a better position to judge if he has informed himself of practically all the reasons for the doubts raised by the adversaries. On account of these reasons it was Aristotle's custom in almost all his works to prepare for the search or determination of the truth by recounting the doubts raised against it." [23] In this the philosopher's critical spirit manifests itself, nor is it a matter of little importance for one to be well aware of the nature of the difficulty to be solved. Such must be the method of procedure, at least for the great and fundamental questions; otherwise the true difficulty of the problem sometimes remains almost unknown even to the very end of the thesis, or else it receives but a passing comment in the last objection.

But the state and difficulty of the question to be solved are made manifest by the opposite solutions that have already been given by the predecessors, or by the opposing arguments for and against the thesis. This was Aristotle's method of procedure, and St. Thomas followed him, especially in his *Quaestiones disputatae*, in which first he sets forth the opposition, so to say, between thesis and antithesis, the mind being fully aware of the nature of the difficulty to be solved before it proceeds to the development of the superior synthesis. And this is part of the truth contained in the Hegelian method, which Hegel did not retain in its purity of form. Thus the hearers do not let the merits of their case consist in the solution of accidental difficulties, nor do they ask useless questions, which distract the mind from the main point at issue; but at once they go to the very root of the difficulty. Thus the theses must be elaborated in harmony with the teaching of St. Thomas and that is why

22 *Ibid.*, Bk. III, chap. 1, lect. 1.
23 *Com. on Metaphysics*, Bk. III, chap. 1, lect. 1.

they are enunciated in the form of a question by means of the particle "Whether," and not in the form of a positive statement; for the complete solution is to be found only at the end, and often many propositions are required so as fully to express the meaning.

In the *Summa theologica,* because St. Thomas proceeds with more brevity of diction than in the *Quaestiones disputatae,* there are only three principal objections; sometimes they are most striking, gems, and, in opposition to these, there is the counterargument, which generally is taken from authority. St. Thomas does not develop these arguments from authority, but gives only one in each case, sometimes expressed in very few words, because he presupposes what was already said by him in his commentaries on Holy Scripture, especially on the Epistles and Gospels, and also in his *Catena aurea.* Evidently, in our days, these arguments from authority, especially on dogmatic subjects, must be developed, so that whatever is declared by the Church as the proximate rule of faith may be clearly and explicitly known and what is the foundation for this both in Scripture and in tradition.

The body of the article is variously constructed in accordance with the different questions to be solved. But, as the Angelic Doctor explains elsewhere,[24] there are four scientific questions: (1) whether a thing is, for instance, whether God is; (2) what He is; (3) whether He is such by nature, for instance, whether He is free; (4) for what purpose He is such, for instance, for what purpose or why He is free? These four questions are evidently different in nature, notwithstanding the identity of the classical formula in the *Summa theologica:* "Whether this is . . ."

The question *whether a thing is* presupposes what it means in name or the nominal definition, that is, what the name of the thing means according to conventional use. This leads up to the question about what the thing is, just as the third question, whether a thing is of such a nature, leads up to the fourth: for what purpose it is of such a nature. In all these questions, as Aristotle said,[25] the middle term in the demonstration must be the subject of special consideration.

When the argumentative part of the article answers the question, whether a thing is, for instance, whether God is, then, as the Angelic Doctor says: "it is necessary to accept as the middle term the meaning of the word," [26] for instance, this name "God." That is, the name "God" means the first uncaused cause; and the first

---

[24] See his *Commentary on the Posterior Analytics,* Bk. II, chap. 1, lect. 1.
[25] *Ibid.*
[26] *Summa theol.,* Ia, q.2, a.2 ad 2um.

uncaused cause exists, for everything that comes into being has a cause, and there is no process to infinity in directly subordinated causes. Therefore God exists.

It must especially be taken into consideration how St. Thomas answers the question about the quiddity and purpose of things.

ON THE INDUCTIVE SEARCH FOR DEFINITIONS

But when it is asked what a thing is, for instance, what is the human soul, what is charity or faith, it is a question of seeking for a real definition in accordance with laws laid down by Aristotle in one of his works,[27] in which it is shown that the meaning of a definition cannot be demonstrated, unless there are two definitions of the same thing, one of which, obtained by means of final or efficient causality, contains the reason for which of the other, namely, of the essential definition. Thus the circle and its circumference is defined as a figure, every point of which circumference is equally distant from the center, because it is formed by the revolution of a straight line around one of its extremities. But, with the exception of these cases, the definition cannot be demonstrated either a posteriori, as the existence of a cause can be demonstrated from its effects, or a priori, as a property is deduced from the essence; for the definition of a thing is the very means by which its properties are demonstrated, nor is there any process to infinity in this. But if the real definition cannot be demonstrated, it is to be sought for by beginning with the nominal or conventional definition, which determines only what is the subject of discussion. The transition from the nominal to the real and essential definition is effected, as shown in the same work just quoted,[28] by the gradual process of the division of the genera from the highest to the lowest, and by the inductive ascent to the specific difference from a comparison of similar and dissimilar things.[29] This method of finding definitions that truly expresses the reality and essence of things, is most admirably retained by St. Thomas. While several modern authors right at the beginning propose definitions that are some-

[27] *Posterior Analytics*, Bk. II, chap. 8, lect. 7, 8.
[28] *Ibid.*, chap. 12, lect. 13–16.
[29] In this way Aristotle attained to the definition of motion, inasmuch as it has reference to being and to the division of being into potency and act. Thus motion becomes intelligible since it is reduced to being, which is the object of the intellect; whereas, contrary to this, Descartes later on *(Principes,* II, 25) defined motion in reference to rest or cessation of motion, and from this no philosophical and intelligible idea of motion is obtained. By the same method Aristotle defined the soul, the faculties, wisdom, knowledge, prudence, art, the various virtues, and other things.

times very complex, as if they had received them by revelation, often not saying how they obtained them, St. Thomas at the beginning of each treatise inquires throughout several articles into the definition of the thing in question, for instance, the definition of charity, as being a friendship between God and man, and also a special and most sublime virtue. He also inquires into the definition of the four kinds of justice: equalizing, legal, distributive, and commutative, into the definition of prudence, and so on. In these articles there is no inquiry into the middle term of the demonstration, since the quest of the definition is not demonstration; but in this inductive inquiry the holy Doctor often adduces the most appropriate of observations, as Father Simon Deploige observed,[30] for instance, in the case of social matters. Thus the transition is made gradually from natural reason or common sense of mankind to philosophic reason.

This search for the definition is evidently of great importance, for all the demonstrations of the properties of anything have their foundation in its definition. In like manner, the direct division of any whole rests upon its definition; even universal principles are derived from rightly constituted and interconnected primary notions, and these principles, in the metaphysical order, are in every case true. Thus St. Thomas with profound penetration of thought decisively distinguishes between the antecedent and consequent wills from the very definition of the will, the object of which is good, this latter being formally not in the mind but in the things themselves. He says: "The will is directed to things as they are in themselves, and in themselves they exist under particular qualifications (here and now). Hence we will a thing simply, inasmuch as we will it when all particular circumstances are considered, and this is what is meant by willing consequently." [31] On the other hand, as stated in this same article, we will some good antecedently, as long as we will it when all particular circumstances are not considered, but according as it is absolutely good in itself; and this is to will it in a qualified manner and not simply. From these definitions thus established, St. Thomas deduces in the same article

---

[30] Cf. *The Conflict between Ethics and Sociology* (1938), pp. 273 ff. In matters of faith the development of dogma consists in this transition, from a confused to a distinct notion, for instance, from the most confused notion of the human soul to this notion: that the human soul is by itself and essentially the form of the body. This proposition does not enunciate a property but the definition of the soul, which was known before in a confused manner. But if from the definition of man it is demonstrated that he is free, then this enunciates a property of his intellectual nature, and this is a new truth distinct from the definition of man. But often the search for the true definition entails more labor than the deduction of its properties from the same definition.

[31] *Summa theol.*, Ia, q. 19, a. 6 ad 1um.

this most universal principle: "Thus it is clear that whatever God simply wills, takes place; although what He wills antecedently may not take place." But this double proposition virtually contains the whole teaching of St. Thomas about efficacious grace. If, indeed, the above-stated definitions of the consequent and antecedent wills have metaphysical validity, the same must be said of the principle that has its foundation in them. Then not even the least good act and most easy of performance right at the moment happens as dependent solely upon God's antecedent will, or without a decree of His consequent will, the causality of which is infallible, although it most admirably preserves intact human liberty, for, as just stated: "Whatever God simply wills, takes place; although what He wills antecedently may not take place." If any good act, even most easy to perform right at the moment, were to happen without such a decree of the consequent will, then the principle enunciated by St. Thomas would no longer he metaphysically true, and this would mean the complete ruination of his doctrine concerning God's foreknowledge and consequent will. If this principle were of no metaphysical validity, it would amount to nothing more than saying that salutary acts in the majority of cases do not take place unless they have been consequently willed by God, or, in other words, the universal Ordainer did not ordain all good things but only very many. This doctrine would be of no value either philosophically or theologically. But the principles that have been formulated in this order are not metaphysically and universally, or in every case, true unless they have their foundation in the due or correct definition of the subject. In this we clearly see the importance of searching for real definitions.

ON THE MIDDLE TERM IN DEMONSTRATION

From the articles, however, in which a methodical inquiry is instituted into the real definition of anything, we must distinguish and otherwise explain those in which St. Thomas solves the question, whether a thing is of such a nature, and often he solves as one question the composite: For what purpose is it of such a nature? Examples of such are: when he asks whether the human soul is incorruptible (that is, whether and for what purpose it is incorruptible); whether man is free, whether faith is most certain, whether it belongs to God alone to create, whether and for what purpose Christ's passion was the cause of our salvation by way of merit, and other similar questions. In these cases the solution of the question *for what purpose,* refers to a true and indeed a priori demonstration, nor does it mean one derived from common but from proper principles. Hence in these last-mentioned articles that are strictly demonstrative, whether they are deduced from reason alone or from faith and reason, a special inquiry must be made into the middle term of the demonstration, which is, as it were, the golden key of the article.

The title of the article gives the two terms of the conclusion, namely, the minor and the major; the middle term must be assigned by which the other two can be united in a scientific conclusion, and this term assigns "why a thing is and cannot be otherwise than it is." It is the very Aristotelian definition of scientific knowledge.[32]

Sometimes, however, in the composition of the body of these articles, St. Thomas begins with the major and through the minor descends to the conclusion, so that the argument is easily presented in scholastic form as to make it clear what is the middle term in the demonstration. Thus, in the question, "Whether the human soul is incorruptible," [33] the argument may be condensed into the following syllogism: Every simple and subsistent form is absolutely incorruptible. But the human soul is a simple and subsistent form. Therefore the human soul is incorruptible. Likewise, in the question, "Whether it belongs to God alone to create," [34] the argument may be reduced to this syllogism: The most universal effects must be reduced to the most universal and first cause, and that is God. Now being itself, which is absolutely produced in creation, is the most universal of effects. Therefore to produce being absolutely, not as this or that being, or to create, belongs to God alone.

Often, too, St. Thomas begins with the minor, the subject of which is already given in the title and will appear again as the subject of the conclusion. Thus by the minor he ascends from the subject of the title to the middle term in the demonstration. Afterward he enunciates the major, its subject being the same middle term, its predicate being the major term of the title, which in the conclusion must be joined to the minor term. Thus often the process of proof in the article is by the ascent from the minor to the middle term in the demonstration, and by the descent from the major to the conclusion. We have an example of this in the question: "Whether any created good constitutes man's happiness." [35] St. Thomas replies by enunciating first the minor: Happiness is the perfect good, completely lulling the rational appetite which is specified by universal good; now the perfect good, which

---

[32] *Post. Anal.*, Bk. I, chap. 2.
[33] *Summa theol.*, Ia, q.75, a.6.
[34] *Ibid.*, q.45, a.5.
[35] *Ibid.*, Ia IIae, q.2, a.8.

completely lulls the rational appetite that is specified by universal good, cannot be anything created or limited; therefore man's happiness cannot consist in any created good.

If we wish to present the argument in syllogistic form, the major must be enunciated first. In the generality of cases, by retaining the very propositions of St. Thomas, the argument can be reduced to scholastic form. It is better, however, to keep to the Doctor's own terms than to change them so as to follow an excessive logical formalism. Finally, the major or minor must be defended against the attacks made upon it by the opponents of St. Thomas.

In the explanation of the body of the article the middle term of the demonstration must be the subject of diligent inquiry, or, if there are several subordinate middle terms, evidently we must concentrate our attention upon the principal one. The reason is that, as St. Thomas often remarks, "the conclusions are known materially; but the middle terms in the demonstration are the formal cause of our knowledge, and by these the conclusions are known." [36] Thus it is known formally for what purpose a thing is of such a nature, for instance, why man is free. It is because he has knowledge of universal good that his attitude toward some particular good is one of dominating indifference. Or again, why man is a social being; this is because of the requirements of his specific act, which are to know those things which he needs to know. Because of his very limited intelligence he needs the assistance of others.

Thus there is only one formal or proximate middle term, which is the definition of the thing as to its essence, from which the first property is to be deduced, and from this first property the one subordinate to this, and so on in ascending order. Nevertheless, anything that has already been demonstrated directly and from the properties of the thing by means of the formal cause, can still be demonstrated in other ways, for instance, by means of its proper final cause, or even from its common principles, or indirectly either by what signifies it or by the method of reduction to absurdity. Thus St. Thomas in the books of the *Contra Gentes* makes use of these direct or indirect arguments so as to reach the same conclusion and places them together, not giving the reason why they are six or ten in number. But in the *Summa theologica* and the *Quaestiones disputatae* there is usually only one direct argument, which is of the formal kind and is deduced from the properties of a thing, introducing the proximately formal middle term, or if the holy Doctor gives two or three arguments he assigns the scientific reason why and how there are two or three methods of argumentation.

[36] *Ibid.,* IIa IIae, q. 1, a. 1, c.

Therefore the middle term in the demonstration must be clearly presented, which in the syllogism of the first figure is the subject of the major and the predicate of the minor and we know that the modes of the other figures can be reduced to the modes of the first figure.

Therefore this middle term thus clearly stated presents itself as the keystone of the article, inserted in the syllogism as a precious jewel set in a ring. Thus we make use of logic, not indeed for its own sake, but that by it we may acquire a direct knowledge of the middle term or principle in which the truth of the conclusion must be considered, or at least of the main conclusion, if there are several conclusions in the article, as sometimes happens. Having accomplished this task to commit to memory what is of first importance in the article, it is enough to bear in mind the middle term. When the question is again posited, the major and minor terms are included in it; hence in replying to the question it suffices to enunciate the middle term in the demonstration, so that again we may have the demonstration of the conclusion. In illustration of this let us take the question: "Whether the human soul is incorruptible?" It suffices to reply to this: "Every simple and subsistent form . . . Therefore the human soul is incorruptible."

If the middle term in the demonstration of the article is thus carefully taken into consideration, this makes us see more clearly, without the aid of a syllogism, the solution of the objections which were presented in the beginning of the article. As a matter of fact, St. Thomas casts upon the solution of the objections the searchlight of the middle term in the demonstration, and by means of this light the distinction to be made is easily discovered and understood. After this, whatever doubts and corollaries there may be, these can be profitably presented. This method was often adopted by the Salmanticenses.

The stand taken by St. Thomas, if properly understood, is seen to be the just mean and summit between and above the two extremes: on the one hand, of empiric nominalism—which retains a certain objectivity of experience, though denying the necessity and universality of knowledge—and on the other, of the idealism of the conceptualists or subjectivists, which retains a certain necessity and universality of knowledge, although without any ontological validity, that is, without any true objectivity.

Thus St. Thomas' method of procedure in the construction of his articles is far more in accordance with the natural progress of the mind in its search for truth than is the method adopted by several Scholastics of a later date, who in the beginning multiply the preliminary remarks about those things that have already been explained by them and that do not need any further explanation. Often also they materially juxtapose these various preliminary remarks, not showing the essential relation between them, and then they propose the argument in the briefest manner, so that the middle term in the demonstration is not sufficiently clear, and sometimes several arguments in succession are proposed in which the direct formal argument deduced from the properties of a thing is not sufficiently distinguished from the others, or from those derived from the common principles, or from the indirect arguments. This later method is rather mechanical, whereas the method of St. Thomas is organic, according to the natural process of the mind in operation.

Lastly, the importance of the middle term in the demonstration is clearly perceived from the rules to be observed in scholastic disputations. The objector, in accordance with these rules, by clever argumentation, so as to overthrow the conclusion, must attack by three successive objections in scholastic form the middle term in the demonstration, which is, so to speak, the chief point of attack to be defended in the article, and, as it were, the citadel of the defender. But the defender of this citadel must train upon the objector the light of the middle term in the form of a brilliant distinction that is not accidentally but directly and truly to the point. Thus after a well-ordered scholastic demonstration, which is of reasonable difficulty, the truth of the article, having been sifted and freed of all its difficulties, becomes increasingly clear, and is certainly confirmed by this austere criticism which is, as it were, the acid that attacks all metals, gold alone excepted.

ON THE PERFECT UNION OF ANALYSIS AND SYNTHESIS IN THE ANGELIC DOCTOR'S METHOD

In this way St. Thomas perfectly observed the rules of method in general, namely, by always beginning from the more known, by proceeding gradually and not jumping to the conclusion. He never reaches the more remote conclusions before the immediate conclusions are known with certainty. Thus the connection between them is clearly perceived, and all the conclusions make up a truly organic body of doctrine.

In like manner he perfectly applied the rules of the analytic method in the order of finding, especially so, in the direct and not accidental division of the complex subject to be considered, until he reaches the transcendental notions and first principles. Thus, after carefully considering the parts, he arrives at a correct judgment of the whole. He likewise most adroitly made use of the analytic method in the inductive and comparative inquiry into the specific difference of a thing so as to discover the distinct real definitions contained in a confused manner in the nominal ones.

With an equal degree of perfection he employed the synthetic method in his doctrine, both in the questions to be proposed and in the manner of solving them. For in proposing the questions he always begins from the more universal and gradually descends to the less universal, from the essence to the properties, from causes to effects. Likewise, in solving the questions he always starts from principles either revealed or directly known, or derived from experience and from the definition of the thing in question; nor does he depart from the certain principles because of the obscurity of the mystery to which these principles lead, as in the case of the questions on grace and free will. Hence we may say that the element of truth contained in the rules of method as formulated by Descartes, was already perfectly known by the Angelic Doctor.

Thus the *Theological Summa* is a splendid example of this synthetic method in the orderly arrangement of theological knowledge. It first treats of God's existence and His nature, then of His attributes, in the third place of the three Persons, fourthly of God's actions *ad extra,* and so on for the rest. In this orderly arrangement anyone can see that St. Thomas far surpasses the Master of the Sentences, who treats but incidentally of moral theology, discussing faith, hope, and charity on the occasion of the following question: "Whether Christ had faith, hope, and charity," [37] and treating of sin in general when the question of original sin presents itself. [38]

Finally, and this must especially be noticed, the Angelic Doctor succeeded exceedingly well in combining analysis and synthesis, according as ascendant analysis, which terminates in principles and causes, is the principle of descendant analysis. For analysis, having finished with natural philosophy, in ontology ascends to consider the notions of analogous being, act and potency, as also the universal principles of reason and being, which illumine the whole synthesis of general metaphysics. After this the mind ascends to consider the pure Act, the Supreme Being, which is required in the final analysis, the true notion of which is, as it were, the sun of all synthesis in the universality of its scope, which is knowledge of all beings inasmuch as they are beings. [39]

---

[37] Cf. *III Sent.*, d.23.

[38] Cf. *II Sent.*, d.35 f.

[39] See St. Thomas, *Com. on Post. Anal.*, Bk. II, lect. 20; Bk. I, lect. 22 f.; *Com. on Metaphysics*, Bk. I, lect. 1 f.; Bk. IX, lect. 5; also *Summa theol.*, IIa IIae, q.9, a.2; *Contra Gentes*, Bk. I, chaps. 3, 9; *Summa theol.*, Ia IIae, q.112, a.5.

By no means do we find in the system of St. Thomas this abuse of the a priori method which, as clearly seen in the works of Spinoza, excludes by means of mathematics the consideration of efficient and final causes, and hence leads to rationalism and pantheism, as if all things could be deduced from God's nature in a geometrical way.[40] By way of investigation and analysis St. Thomas ascends by the light of the first principles of reason from sensible things and the most certain facts of experience to the supreme and most universal cause who, since He is infinitely perfect and in no way stands in need of creatures, created all things with absolute freedom.[41] Then by the way of synthesis, the holy Doctor judges of all things by means of a lofty principle. As he himself says: "By way of judgment, from eternal things already known, we judge of temporal things, and according to laws of things eternal we dispose of temporal things." [42] In accordance with this union of analysis and synthesis, presented by the Angelic Doctor, as Father del Prado shows,[43] the supreme truth of Christian philosophy, in which the analytic method, or method of finding in the ascending order, terminates, and which is the principle of the synthetic method of judgment, is this: *God is the self-subsisting Being, I am who am.* In other words only in God are essence and existence identical.[44] This is the golden key of the whole doctrinal edifice, which is constructed by the Angelic Doctor with such penetration of thought and fixity of principles that, as Leo XIII testified,[45] no one surpassed him in this. Avoiding both nominalism, which denies the objectivity of metaphysics, reducing it to logic, and the extreme realism of Plato, which on no just grounds considers the universal to exist formally apart from the thing, St. Thomas admirably distinguished between logic and metaphysics, between logical and real being.[46] He clearly shows that, before our mind considers the question, the essence of any finite being is not its existence, and that hence only in God are essence and existence identical.[47] This is the culminating point of the five proofs for God's existence, the terminus in the ascending order by the method of finding, and it is the principle of judgment from the highest cause by the synthetic method.

[40] Cf. Leo Michel, O.P., "Le système de Spinoza au point de vue de la logique formelle" in the *Revue Thomiste,* January, 1898.

[41] *Summa theol.,* Ia, q.19, a.3.

[42] *Ibid.,* q.79, a.9.

[43] *De veritate fundamentali philosophiae christianae* (Fribourg, 1911).

[44] *Summa theol.,* Ia, q.3, a.4.

[45] Cf. Encyclical *Aeterni Patris.*

[46] *Summa theol.,* Ia, q.85, a.2 ad 2um.

[47] *Ibid.,* q.3, a.4.

For many years the more we have studied this *Theological Summa,* the more we have seen the beauty of its structure. The expositions and demonstrations are simple and clear, especially if they are compared with the commentaries on the Sentences of Peter Lombard, and superfluous questions are avoided in accordance with the Angelic Doctor's plan as stated in the Prologue. Likewise, repetitions are eliminated, as much as possible, because subjects are always treated in a general way before they receive special consideration, and St. Thomas does not refer his reader to what is to be said later on. In this simplicity and clarity, the Angelic Doctor evidently far surpasses not only his predecessors, but even Scotus and Suarez.

The perfection of this edifice is in great part due to the consummate skill with which he effects the divisions between the treatises or the questions or the articles or the arguments. These divisions, of course, are not extrinsic but intrinsic, arranged in accordance with the formal point of view of the whole to be divided, and effected by means of members that are truly opposites to each other, so that the divisions are adequate, with subordinate subdivisions; yet all is done with discretion and not by descending to the least details. Thus by a gradual process the light of the principles reaches to the ultimate conclusions that are, nevertheless, still universal—for speculative knowledge does not descend to the particular—and thus it is essentially distinct from experience and prudence.

THE DOCTRINE OF ST. THOMAS PROCEEDS FROM THE FULLNESS OF HIS CONTEMPLATION

In addition to all these considerations, we must finally say that the Angelic Doctor never cherished method for its own sake, but for the purpose of finding out the truth and transmitting it to posterity, especially divine truth to which he especially directed his attention. On the contrary, just as many hunters find greater delight in the sport of hunting than in the game they take, so some evidently have in mind the mode of demonstrating the truth rather than the actual discovery of the truth itself, even when they are investigating things most sublime, such as the infinite value of Christ's merits or the divine processions. This is a deformation of the theologian's profession, when he is not sufficiently contemplative. He then digresses too much and is too much given to argumentation.

Nevertheless, in the hours of study we must give careful consideration to the proper method, which, as we acquire the habit,

we unconsciously make use of little by little, as is the case with a
musician who is practicing to play on the guitar or the harp. Thus
the greater facility gradually acquired in the use of the proper
method disposes a person for a correct knowledge of the different
parts of philosophy and theology, and by this very fact for the contemplation of truth from which proceeds the living doctrine that
illuminates the mind and inflames the heart. The Angelic Doctor
says that doctrine and preaching must "proceed from the fullness of
contemplation." [48] It was so when he taught. Just as only those
musicians make good use of their method who, under the influence
of a certain inspiration, fully penetrate the soul of a symphony, so
St. Thomas employed his scientific method, inspired as it were from
above, illuminated by the light of vivid faith and the gifts of the
Holy Ghost; and this light absolutely transcends all systems and
all knowledge acquired by human efforts. Thus only by this supernatural light does theology attain its end, and then we find verified
in it the words of the Vatican Council: "Reason, indeed, enlightened by faith, when it seeks earnestly, piously, and calmly,
attains by a gift from God some, and that a very fruitful, understanding of mysteries. . . . But reason never becomes capable of
apprehending mysteries as it does those truths which constitute its
proper object. For in this mortal life we are pilgrims, not yet with
God: we walk by faith and not by sight." [49]

Therefore St. Thomas, before he dictated or wrote or preached,
used to recite this prayer: "Ineffable Creator, who out of the
treasures of Thy wisdom hast appointed three hierarchies of angels
and set them in admirable order high above the heavens and hast
disposed the diverse portions of the universe in such marvelous
arrays, Thou who art called the true source of light and superemi-
nent principle of wisdom, be pleased to cast a beam of Thy radiance
upon the darkness of my mind and dispel from me the double
darkness of sin and ignorance in which I have been born.

"Thou who makest eloquent the tongues of little children, [50]
fashion my words and pour upon my lips the grace of Thy bene-
diction. Grant me penetration to understand, capacity to retain,
method and facility in study, subtlety in interpretation, and
abundant grace of expression.

"Order the beginning, direct the progress, and perfect the achieve-
ment of my work, Thou who art true God and man and livest and
reignest forever and ever. Amen."

This prayer was heard; for in the holy Doctor's works on the

48 *Ibid.*, IIa IIae, q. 188, a. 6.
49 Denz., 1796; II Cor. 5: 7.
50 Wis. 10: 21.

logical method is to be seen the light of the gifts of the Holy Ghost as also the gratuitously given grace of the "word of wisdom," [51] as Pope Pius XI says.[52] Therefore, in a certain responsory in the office for the feast of St. Thomas, we read: "There is brevity of style, a pleasing eloquence, sublimity, clarity, and well-founded opinion."

There is *sublimity*, because the knowledge is derived from the highest of causes; there is *clarity*, because by the light of the highest principles he penetrates to the very source of the question; there is well-founded opinion, because "he assigns the cause why the thing is and cannot be otherwise than it is," according to the Aristotelian definition of knowledge.[53] This pleasing eloquence coupled with a brevity of style is the result of a vivid and supernatural contemplation, by which the holy Doctor was conversant not only with the literal but also with the spiritual interpretation of Holy Scripture. He knew, to be sure, that, especially for the discussion of divine subjects, prayer and contemplation were no less necessary than laborious efforts in the pursuit of knowledge; and when difficulties arose, he did not pray less so as to give himself more time for study, but in preference to this he spent more time in prayer. This truth is of great importance for renewing the spirit of study in theology, so that it may be something vital and productive of its due effects. Concerning the holy Doctor's contemplation, Pope Pius XI wrote as follows: "The more readily to obtain these illuminations from above, he would often abstain from food, spend whole nights in prayerful vigil, and, surrendering to a holy impulse, would repeatedly lean his head against the tabernacle and would constantly turn his eyes with sorrow and love toward the image of Jesus crucified. To his friend St. Bonaventure he confided that whatever he knew he had for the most part learned from the book of the crucifix." [54] Christ indeed had said: "The words that I have spoken to you are spirit and life." [55] Of course, books give us the letter, but study without prayer and the interior life does not attain to the spiritual meaning.

Whoever considers the light of divine contemplation from which this great synthesis of St. Thomas proceeds cannot say that this doctrine is extreme intellectualism, devoid of reality and lifeless.

By an intellectual process, as befitting a science, and not according to the tenets of "sentimentalism," St. Thomas treats of God,

---

[51] I Cor. 12: 8.
[52] Cf. Encyclical *Studiorum ducem.*
[53] *Post. Anal.* Bk. I, chap. 2.
[54] Encyclical *Studiorum ducem.*
[55] John 6: 64.

our natural and supernatural states. But he never separates our intellectual life from the influence exerted upon it by the will or even by the sensitive faculties; for he shows to our complete satisfaction the mutual relations between the faculties. He says, indeed: "If therefore the intellect and the will be considered with regard to themselves, then the intellect is the higher power. . . . For the object of the intellect is simpler, and more absolute than the object of the will." [56] Being is prior to and more universal than good; thus the intellect is simpler and higher than the will which it directs. Yet the holy Doctor adds: "But relatively and by comparison with something else, we find that the will is sometimes higher than the intellect . . . thus the love of God (at least in this life) is better than the knowledge of God." [57] The reason is that the intellect draws to itself the thing understood even though this is superior to it, whereas the will is drawn to the thing. Thus charity is the most excellent of all the virtues.[58] St. Thomas also says: "Some are hearers that they may know, and these build upon intellect (only, and not upon charity); and this is building upon sand." [59]

This doctrine is not, indeed, extreme intellectualism. Concerning all these things St. Thomas speaks not oratorically but scientifically, as befitting his scope, which is the search not for the beauty that attracts as in poetic art, but for the truth, without which there cannot be any true goodness or beauty.

St. Thomas excludes the particular from knowledge in the strict sense, since nothing is knowable except by way of abstraction from individualized matter. He certainly affirms that "the knowledge of singulars does not pertain to the perfection of the intellective soul in speculative knowledge"; but he adds immediately that "it pertains to the perfection of the same in practical knowledge," [60] namely, of prudence and the gift of counsel. It pertains also to either external or internal experience, which the Angelic Doctor certainly did not despise. He even asserts that the just person can have by the gift of wisdom "a quasi-experimental knowledge" [61] of the presence of God in the soul and of the mysteries of salvation, according to the following text of St. Paul: "For the Spirit Himself giveth testimony to our spirit that we are the sons of God." [62] He

[56] *Summa theol.*, Ia, q.82, a.3.
[57] *Ibid.*
[58] *Ibid.*, IIa IIae, q.23, a.6.
[59] *Com. in Matt.*, 7: 26.
[60] *Summa theol.*, IIIa, q.11, a.1 ad 3um.
[61] Cf. I *Sent.* d.14, q.2, a.2 ad 3um; *Summa theol.*, Ia, q.43, a.3; IIa IIaC, q.45, a.2.
[62] Rom. 8: 16.

gives this testimony "through the effect of filial love which God produces in us." [63]

The holy Doctor possessed this mystic experience in the highest degree, and it certainly influenced the construction of his theological synthesis, but, as it were, from on high, by conforming and elucidating his faith. But knowledge in the strict sense, whether philosophical or theological, which is acquired by study, is essentially distinct from any individual experience whatever, even the most sublime, and is concerned only with universals either in predication or being or causation.[64]

But the universal in predication is fundamentally in individual things, and expresses what is necessary and negatively eternal in them, namely, what is true not only here and now, but always. It is τὸ τί ἦν εἶναι: the being what is was intended to be.[65] Therefore the holy Doctor says: "So far as universals taken as logical entities are concerned, so far as they are the cause of knowledge and demonstration, they are more truly beings than particulars are, because the former are incorruptible, whereas the latter are not. But as regards natural subsistence, particulars are more truly beings, because they are called first and principal substances." [66] Thus reality is preserved absolutely intact.

Hence in scientific knowledge, and rightly so, St. Thomas reduces all things to universal principles that are fundamental, necessary, and perpetual laws not only of the mind but of being, and of being whether natural or supernatural.

Thus his method is of great help in remedying the defects of modern philosophy, in which the distinction between the internal

---

[63] Cf. St. Thomas, *Com. on Rom.* 8: 16.

[64] *Summa theol.*, Ia, q.1, a.2 ad 2um; IIa IIae, q.45, a.2.

[65] Cf. Aristotle's *Metaphysics*, 1041, a.27. On the etymology of Aristotle's description of essence, Dr. Coffey remarks (*Ontology*, p. 75, no. 1), "that the expression τὸ τί ἦν εἶναι is not easy to explain. He presumes that the phrase τὸ εἶναι supposes a dative understood, such as: τὸ ἀνθρώπῳ εἶναι ("the being proper to man"). To the question τί ἐστι τὸ ἀνθρώπῳ εἶναι ("What is the being proper to man?"), the answer is: that which gives the definition of man, that which explains what he is: τί ἦν. Is the imperfect τί ἦν an archaic form for the present, τί ἐστι; or is it a deliberate suggestion of the profound doctrine that the essence is ideal, or possible, that it is anterior to its actual, physical realization? Commentators are not agreed. Cf. Matthias Kappes, *Aristoteles Lexicon*, p. 25; Mercier, *Ontologie*, p. 30." Father Clarke, S.J. (*Logic*, p. 5, no. 2) remarks: "*Quidditas* is the somewhat barbarous but very expressive equivalent of the Aristotelian phrase τὸ τί ἦν εἶναι. The essence or quiddity of a thing consists in its corresponding to the pattern after which it was fashioned. Hence τί ἦν means, what is its nature? What was it intended to be by the Creator? And therefore τὸ τί ἦν εἶναι means the being what it was intended to be by its Creator." Father Garrigou-Lagrange seems to incline to this latter view. (Tr.)

[66] *Com. on Post. Anal.*, Bk. I, lect. 37.

senses and the intellect, between nature and grace, gradually dis-
appeared. With the elimination of ontological validity from the
first principles of reason there is nothing firm and stable left in
the speculative order and a fortiori in the practical order.[67]

The *Theological Summa* of St. Thomas, constructed as it is according to the above-mentioned method, since it avoids the opposite
extremes of rationalism and fideism, is a work that is both truly
scientific and always elucidated by the light of supernatural revelation. It is, therefore, truly a classical and perennial work, not indeed
of extreme intellectualism, but of "sacred theology" that has been
raised to the status of a true science notwithstanding the obscurity
of faith. It constitutes a really organic body of doctrine, and is truly
a single science, though subordinated to God's knowledge and to
that which the blessed have of Him, and bears, as it were, the stamp
(in us) of the divine science,[68] considering all things under the
formality of God as author of grace and as the ultimate end.

THE RELATION BETWEEN THE STUDY OF THEOLOGY AND THE INTERIOR LIFE

There is often too great a separation between study and the interior
life; we do not find sufficiently observed, that beautiful gradation spoken of by St. Benedict which consists in: reading, cogitation, study, meditation, prayer and contemplation.[69] St. Thomas,
who received his first education from the Benedictines, retained this
wonderful gradation when speaking of the contemplative life.[70]

Several defects result from separating study too much from prayer.
Thus the hardship and difficulty that not infrequently accompany
study are no longer considered a salutary penance, nor are they
sufficiently directed to God. Thus weariness and disgust sometimes
result from study, without any spiritual profit.

St. Thomas speaks about these two deviations [71] when discussing
the virtue of *studiousness* or application to study, which must be
commanded by charity as a check to inordinate curiosity and sloth,
so as to study those things which one ought to study, how, when,
and where one ought, especially with regard to the spiritual end in
view, this being for the acquisition of a better knowledge of God and
for the salvation of souls.

---

[67] A clear and long exposition of this has been given in the books entitled:
*Le sens commun, la philosophie de l'être et les formules dogmatiques; God, His
existence and His nature.* Consult also P. F. Richard, O.P., *Introduction à l'étude
et à l'enseignement de la scolastique* (2d ed.), Part III, chap. 4.

[68] *Summa theol.,* Ia, q.1, a.3 ad 2um.

[69] *Rule of St. Benedict,* chap. 48.

[70] *Summa theol.,* IIa IIae, q.180, a.3.

[71] *Ibid.,* q.166.

To avoid the above-mentioned defects that are opposed to each other, it is good to recall how our intellectual study can be sanctified, by considering first what benefit the interior life receives from a study that is properly directed, and then, on the other hand, what the study of theology can hope to receive in an increasing degree from the interior life. It is in the union of these two functions of our nature that we find the best verification of the principle: "Causes mutually interact, but in a different order." There is a mutual causality and priority among them, which is truly wonderful.

THE INDEBTEDNESS OF THE INTERIOR LIFE TO STUDY

By the study of theology the interior life is especially preserved from the two serious defects of subjectivism in piety and of particularism.

Subjectivism, as it applies to piety, is often now called "sentimentalism." It consists in a certain affected love which lacks a true and deep love for God and souls. This defect arises from the fact that the natural inclination of our sensitive nature prevails in prayer according to each one's disposition. An emotion of our sensitive nature prevails, and this emotion sometimes expresses itself in certain outbursts of praise which are quite without solid foundation in reality. In our days several skeptical psychologists, such as Bergson in France, think that even Catholic mysticism is the result of some prevailing and noble emotion that arises from the subconscious self, and that afterward finds expression in the ideas and judgments of the mystics. But a doubt always remains whether these judgments are true that result from the impulse of the subconscious self and the affections.

Contrary to this, our interior life must be founded on divine truth. It already has this from infused faith that rests upon the authority of God revealing. But study that is properly directed is of great help in fully realizing what the truths of the faith are strictly in themselves, independently of our subjective dispositions. Study is of special help, indeed, in forming a true concept of God's perfections, of His goodness, love, mercy, justice, as also of the infused virtues of humility, religion, and charity, and this without any admixture of emotion that has not its foundation in truth. Therefore St. Theresa says [72] that she received much help by conversing with good theologians, so that she might not deviate from the path of truth in difficult straits.

When our study is rightly ordered, it frees the interior life not

[72] Autobiography, chap. 13.

only from subjectivism but also from particularism resulting from the excessive influence of certain ideas prevalent at some period of time or in some region, ideas which after thirty years will appear antiquated. Some years ago ideas of this or that particular philosophy prevailed, which now no longer find favorable acceptance. It is so in every generation. There is a succession of opinions and events that arouse one's admiration; they pass with the fashion of the world, while the words of God remain, by which the just man must live.

Thus, in truth, study that is well ordered preserves intact the objectivity which the interior life should have above all the deviations of our sensitive nature, and it also preserves the universality of the same which is founded upon what the Church teaches everywhere and at all times. Thus it becomes increasingly clear that the higher, the deeper, and the more vital truths are none other than the elementary truths of Christianity, provided they are thoroughly examined and become the subject of daily meditation and contemplation. Such are the truths enunciated in the Lord's Prayer and in the following words from the first page of the catechism: "What must we do to gain the happiness of heaven? To gain the happiness of heaven we must know, love, and serve God in this world." Equally so it becomes increasingly clear that the fundamental truth of Christianity is: "God so loved the world as to give His only begotten Son." [73]

It is a matter of great importance that these truths profoundly influence our lives, without our deviating into the subjectivism, sentimentalism, and particularism prevalent at some period of time or in some region. In this, however, our interior life is in many ways benefited by good study; and the choicest fruit of penance is to be found in the arduousness of study. It is a fruit much more precious than the natural pleasure to be found in study that may consist in intellectual labor not sufficiently sanctified or directed to God. In diligent study that is commanded by charity, we find pre-eminently verified the common saying: If the roots of knowledge are bitter, its fruits are the sweetest and best. We are not considering here the knowledge that inflates, but that which, under the influence of charity and the virtue of studiousness, is truly upbuilding.

The interior life, which study saves from a number of deviations, therefore remains objective in its tendency and is truly founded on what has been universally and at all times the traditional doctrine. On the other hand the interior life influences the study of theology.

[73] John 3: 16.

WHAT THE STUDY OF THEOLOGY OWES TO THE INTERIOR LIFE

Often this study remains lifeless, whether viewed in its positive, or in its speculative and abstract aspect. Sometimes it lacks the noble inspiration and influence of the theological virtues and of the gifts of understanding and wisdom. Hence theological wisdom is sometimes not that "savory knowledge" which St. Thomas speaks of in the first question of the *Theological Summa*.

At times our mind is occupied too much with dogmatic formulas, in the analysis of their concepts, in the conclusions deduced from them, and it does not by means of these formulas penetrate the mystery of faith sufficiently to taste its spiritual sweetness and live thereby.

Here it is fitting to state that a number of saints, who were incapable of such serious studies as we engage in, penetrated these mysteries of faith more deeply. Thus St. Francis of Assisi, St. Catharine of Siena, St. Benedict Joseph Labre, and many others, who certainly did not attempt to analyze in an abstract and speculative manner the dogmatic concepts of the Incarnation, the Redemption, and the Eucharist, and did not deduce theological conclusions that are known to us. Yet from the fountainhead of these mysteries with a holy realism they drew abundant life for themselves.

Through the formulas they reached by a vital act, in the obscurity of faith, the divine reality itself. As St. Thomas says: "The act of the believer does not terminate in a proposition, but in a thing," [74] in a revealed truth.

Even without the great grace of contemplation, a number of very good Christians, by humility and self-denial, penetrate in their own way the depths of these mysteries. And if this fact is verified in these good Christians among the faithful, with far more reason it must be verified in the religious or priest who has truly understood the dignity of his vocation. Daily the priest must celebrate the Holy Sacrifice with a firmer faith, a more vivid hope, and a more ardent charity, so that his Eucharistic Communion may be almost every day substantially more fervent, and not only preserve but also keep on increasing in him the virtue of charity.

St. Thomas well says: "The more a physical motion approaches its terminus, the more it is intensified. It is just the opposite with a violent motion (the throwing of a stone). But grace inclines in a way similar to that of nature. Therefore (as the physical motion of a falling stone is always accelerated), so for those who are in a state of grace, the nearer they approach the end, the more they

[74] *Summa theol.*, IIa IIae, q.1, a.2 ad 2um.

must increase in grace"; [75] because the nearer they approach God, the more they are enticed or drawn by Him, just as the stone is drawn toward the center of the earth.

If our interior life were to receive such increase of grace every day, it would have a most favorable influence upon our study, and each day this would become more vigorous. Thus study and the life of prayer are causes that interact in beautiful harmony.

THE FRUIT OF THIS MUTUAL INFLUENCE

When the priest's interior life is one of great and solid piety, his theology is always more vigorous. After this theologian has made the descent from faith for the purpose of acquiring theological knowledge by the discussion of particular questions, he desires to return to the source, namely, to ascend from the theological knowledge thus acquired by the discussion of particular questions to the lofty peak of faith. The theologian is like a man who is born on the top of a mountain, for instance, Monte Cassino, and who afterward descends into the valley to acquire an accurate knowledge of individual things. Finally this man wishes to return to his lofty abode, that he may contemplate the whole valley from on high and in a single glance.

There are some men who prefer the plains, but others are more attracted by the mountains: "Wonderful is the Lord on high." [76] So the good theologian must daily breathe the mountain air and derive from the Apostle's Creed an abundance of spiritual nourishment for himself, and also, at the end of the Mass, from the Prologue of St. John's Gospel, which is, as it were, the synthesis of all Christian revelation. Daily, in like manner, he must live his life on a higher plane, directed by the Lord's Prayer, the beatitudes, and the Sermon on the Mount in its entirety, which is a synthesis of all Christian ethics in its wondrous elevation.

When the priest has, as he should have, the spirit of prayer, then his interior life urges him to search more in dogmatic theology and in moral theology for that which savors preferably of vitality and fecundity. For then, under the influence of the gifts of understanding and wisdom, faith becomes more penetrating and savory.

Then the most beautiful quasi-obscurity in Christian doctrine becomes apparent, or the harmonious blends of light and shade which, like chiaroscuro in a painting, hold the intellect spellbound and are the subject of contemplation for the saints. As an example of this, gradually all the great questions of grace are reduced to

[75] *Com. in epist. ad Hebr.,* 10: 25.
[76] Ps. 92: 4.

these two principles: on the one hand, *"God does not command what is impossible,* but by commanding, both admonishes thee to do what thou art able, and to pray for what thou art not able to do,"* as St. Augustine says, who is quoted by the Council of Trent against the Protestants.[77] On the other hand, against the Pelagians and Semipelagians we have: "For who distinguisheth thee? Or what hast thou that thou hast not received?"[78] As St. Thomas says: "Since God's love is the cause of goodness in things, no one thing would be better than another, if God did not will greater good for one than for another."[79]

These two principles taken separately are clear and most certain; but their intimate reconciliation is very obscure, the obscurity resulting from too great a light. To perceive this intimate reconciliation, we would have to see how infinite justice, mercy, and liberty are reconciled in the eminent Deity.

Likewise there is another example; for in proportion as the interior life develops within us, so much the more do we realize the sublimity of the treatise on the Incarnation accomplished for the purpose of our redemption; and we are especially impressed with the motive of the Incarnation of the Son of God, "who for us men and for our salvation came down from heaven and became man."

In the same way, under the influence of a life of prayer, the treatise on the Incarnation is presented to us in a more striking light, and among the various opinions concerning the Sacrifice of the Mass we more and more realize that the teaching of the Council of Trent surpasses them all, when it states: "The victim is one and the same, the same now offering by the ministry of priests, who then offered Himself on the Cross, the manner of offering being different."[80] Increasingly Christ appears as the high priest, "always living to make intercession for us,"[81] especially in the Mass, which is therefore of infinite value. Thus we gradually discover in the councils those most precious adamantine rocks, and likewise in the *Theological Summa* the dominant chapters or the more sublime articles are by degrees made known to us, which are, as it were, the higher peaks by which the whole mountain range is clearly outlined.

If we were to apply ourselves to the study of theology in a true spirit of faith, prayer, and penance, we would find verified in us these words of St. Thomas: "Doctrine and preaching proceed

---

[77] Denz., no. 804.
[78] I Cor. 4:7.
[79] *Summa theol.*, Ia, q.20, a.3.
[80] Denz., no. 940.
[81] Heb. 7: 25.

from the fullness of contemplation," [82] somewhat in the manner of the preaching of the apostles after the day of Pentecost.

Theology, understood in this sense, is of great importance in the ministry of souls. It thoroughly imbues a priest with the spirit of sound judgment according to the mind of Christ and the Church, so that souls are exhorted to strive after perfection in accordance with true principles, by showing one, for instance, that according to the supreme precept, "Thou shalt love the Lord thy God with thy whole heart," all Christians must strive after the perfection of charity, each one, however, according to the manner of his state in life.

And we cannot reach this fullness of perfection in the Christian life unless our lives are profoundly influenced by the mystery of the Incarnation in its redemptive aspect and by the Eucharist, and unless, by faith, enlightened by the gifts of wisdom and understanding, we penetrate these mysteries and taste their sweetness. For this, indeed, the study of theology is of great help provided it be properly directed, not for the satisfaction we get from it, but for the purpose of knowing God better and for the salvation of souls.

Thus these beautiful words of the Vatican Council become increasingly possible of verification in us: "Reason, enlightened by faith, when it seeks earnestly, piously, and calmly, attains by a gift of God some, and that a very fruitful, understanding of mysteries; and this both from the analogy of those things which it naturally knows, and from the relations which the mysteries bear to one another and to the last end of man." [83]

The study of sacred theology, which sometimes is hard and arduous, though fruitful, thus disposes our minds for the light of contemplation and of life, which is, as it were, an introduction and a beginning of eternal life in us.

[82] *Summa theol.*, IIa IIae, q.188, a.6.
[83] Denz., no. 1796.

PROLOGUE TO THE *THEOLOGICAL SUMMA*

IN THIS prologue St. Thomas expresses his intention, namely, to treat of whatever belongs to the Christian religion, in such a way as may tend to the instruction of beginners, because the Catholic doctor must be a teacher to all, even to little ones.

But from the explanation of this purpose it is evident that this work is suitable for beginners, not because it treats solely of the first principles of Christian doctrine, but because all questions are proposed in it according to the order of the subject matter, and not as the occasion of the argument may offer, by which it frequently happens that there are useless questions and repetitions as in many works of preceding authors. Since Holy Scripture includes the order of charity or of the subjection of all affections to God's love, a logical order must also be pursued in the body of Christian doctrine.

Hence this *Summa* of St. Thomas was not meant to be merely an elementary work; for, as Cajetan remarks, all theological problems are here appropriately and clearly treated. Already in this prologue St. Thomas shows himself the great classicist of sacred theology because of his superior simplicity, which is, as it were, a development of common sense and the Christian sense. There is a vast difference between this simplicity and the complicated exposition of Scotus.

As we shall see at the beginning of the second question, the order observed in this work is didactic and strictly theological. St. Thomas adopts a far better method than that of the Master of the Sentences or of Alexander of Hales in the arrangement of the questions, and this not only as to generalities but also as to particulars. In the *Summa* of the Angelic Doctor all questions are considered as they refer to God, who is the proper object of theology, rather than as they refer to man and his liberty. This point of view may be called therefore theocentric but not anthropocentric, as the psychological tendency is of modern times.

CHAPTER I

QUESTION 1

THE NATURE AND EXTENT OF SACRED DOCTRINE

THIS question contains ten articles. It treats (1) of the necessity of sacred doctrine, asking whether it is necessary; (2) of the nature of this sacred doctrine in three articles: whether it is a science; whether it is one science; whether it is speculative or practical; (3) of its excellence compared with the other sciences, in articles five and six; (4) of its subject or proper object; (5) of its method: whether it is a matter of argument, the intrinsic and extrinsic sources being discussed in a general way in this article; there is also an article on the use of metaphor, and the last article concerns the use which theology makes of Holy Scripture.

As to the arrangement of these articles, the objection might be raised that St. Thomas ought to have treated of the subject or object of sacred doctrine before he discussed its nature and excellence, because the nature of a science depends upon its object. In answer to this it must be said that from the very beginning of this question he supposes the nominal definition of sacred doctrine, in which the object of this latter is expressed at least in a confused manner. After this, gradually and methodically, he makes the transition from the nominal to the real and scientific definition, which is completed in the seventh article, in which he speaks explicitly of the proper subject of this science.

Concerning the nominal definition, or the meaning of the words "sacred doctrine," there is a dispute as to what the holy Doctor implies by them. Does he mean faith? or theology? Or does he mean sacred doctrine in general according as it abstracts from faith and theology? Cajetan and several others hold this last view; but John of St. Thomas, Sylvius, and others contend that by these words St. Thomas means theology in the strict sense. This seems to be the true answer, although, of course, the first article is concerned more with sacred doctrine in general. But immediately from the second article it is strictly a discussion of sacred science as distinguished from faith. Gradually St. Thomas passes from the confused to the distinct notion of this science.

WHETHER BESIDES PHILOSOPHY ANY FURTHER DOCTRINE IS REQUIRED [1]

State of the question. Necessity is of many kinds. It is: (a) absolute; (b) hypothetical, which is either physical or moral.

It is a question of hypothetical necessity for the attainment of the end; but it is certainly not a question of absolute necessity that is presupposed by the very nature of the thing independently of the end to be attained, as when we say it is necessary for man to be a rational animal.

We must note that a thing is said to be necessary for the end in two ways. First, as indispensable for the attainment of the end (*ad esse simpliciter*), and this is called physical necessity, as in the case of food for the preservation of human life. Secondly, a thing is said to be necessary for the convenient attainment of the end (*ad bene esse*), as in the case of a horse for a long journey; for otherwise there would be great difficulty in attaining the end, though it would not be a physical impossibility.

The difficulties placed at the beginning of the article by way of a statement of the question, are those which later on were proposed in another form by the positivists and the rationalists. These are: (1) that man must not seek to know those things that are above reason; so say the positive agnostics; (2) now a certain part of philosophy treats of God; so say several rationalists, who seek to reduce theology to philosophy, and they propose a merely natural interpretation of the mysteries of faith, as Spinoza and afterward Hegel did.

In the body of the article there are two conclusions which may be briefly expressed as follows: (1) the divine revelation of supernatural truths is hypothetically necessary, but it is so indispensably (*simpliciter*) or physically; (2) the revelation of certain natural truths that pertain to religion was hypothetically necessary, conveniently so (*ad bene esse*) or morally speaking.

First conclusion. This is proved in the body of the article according to St. Thomas' usual way by beginning with the minor, which is as follows: It is necessary that the end first be made known to men who are to direct their actions to the end. But according to revelation men are ordained to a supernatural end. Therefore it is necessary that the supernatural end first be made known to men by divine revelation.

It is evidently a question of hypothetical, but of indispensable

[1] See also *Contra Gentes*, Bk. I, chaps. 4, 6.

(*simpliciter*) or of physical necessity, because nothing is willed unless it is foreknown. The middle term of the demonstration is: the foreknowledge of the end.

In this argument the major is founded upon reason; the minor is revealed, for the Scripture says: "The eye hath not seen, O God, besides Thee, what things Thou hast prepared for them that wait for Thee." [2] In like manner we read: "But to us God hath revealed them by His Spirit. For the Spirit searcheth all things, yea, the deep things of God." [3] Hence the Vatican Council says that divine revelation is necessary "because God of His infinite goodness has ordained man to a supernatural end, to be a sharer of divine blessings which utterly exceed the intelligence of the human mind." [4] This council likewise declared that the mysteries of faith transcend also the natural powers of the created intellect, which includes even the angelic.[5]

The second conclusion concerns the moral necessity for the revelation of certain truths of the natural order that pertain to religion, such as the existence of God the Author of nature, His universal providence that extends even to the least detail, creation from nothing, the personal immortality of the human soul.

St. Thomas gives the reason for this, namely, that otherwise few there are who would come to know these truths, and this only after a long time, and with a mixture of many errors. This reason is developed by St. Thomas in another of his works,[6] and solemn utterance was given to it in the Vatican Council in the following words: "It is to be ascribed to this divine revelation, that such truths among things divine as of themselves are not beyond human reason can, even in the present condition of mankind, be known by everyone with facility, with firm assurance, and with no mixture of error." [7]

We have the confirmation of this in the history of philosophy, since the Greeks, who were particularly apt at speculation, having spent a long time in this pursuit, did not succeed in acquiring a clear idea of creation from nothing, and they had more or less doubts about the universal scope of Providence and the personal immortality of the soul. In this we clearly see how first of all revelation, even from the very opening words of Genesis in which it

2 Is. 64: 4.
3 I Cor. 2: 10.
4 Denz., no. 1786; see also canons of the same council, *ibid.*, nos. 1807 f.
5 *Ibid.*, no. 1796.
6 Cf. *Contra Gentes*, Bk. I, chap. 4.
7 Denz., no. 1786.

speaks of creation, emphatically confirms from on high the certain findings of philosophy, as evidently is the case in Christian philosophy. This latter surpasses the philosophy of the more profound Greek philosophers, Plato and Aristotle, especially in two respects, namely, as regards the unwavering certainty concerning the most free creation of all things from nothing and the personal immortality of the soul. Thus philosophical speculation directed by faith reaches much loftier heights among the great Christian philosophers.

We have another confirmation of this from the history of modern philosophy, especially from the history of agnosticism, whether of the positivist or idealist type. A third confirmation is found in the history of religions, and of their fluctuating opinions about the great problems concerning God and the soul.

It is not as yet scientific theology but sacred doctrine according as it abstracts from faith and theology that is the subject matter of the body of the first article. There is also a reference to faith inasmuch as faith and not theology is necessary for salvation. Theology as a science is not indeed necessary for any of the faithful, but for the Church collectively, at least according to the ordinary law, since the teaching Church must also make use of human means in the discharge of her office, having recourse to reason in defending what is of faith against the objections of the adversaries.

In the reply to the second objection we find the first mention of theology as distinct from faith. This reply states that there is no reason why theology, guided by the higher light of divine revelation, may not teach those truths which philosophy already teaches us by means of the natural light of reason.

The reason for this is that sciences are differentiated according to the various means through which knowledge is obtained. For it is not the material but the formal object that differentiates the sciences, according as the knowledge is obtained from a different source. Thus the astronomer and the geologist prove that the earth is round in different ways, the former by mathematics, the latter by physics. Thus the distinction between the sciences is the result of the different degrees of abstraction.

Scotus, as Cajetan remarks, attacks this first article since he has a different conception of the distinction between human nature and grace. For Scotus, our soul is by its very nature positively ordained for the beatific vision,[8] the desire for which would be natural and innate, although the soul cannot attain to it without God's help, to which it is not entitled, and which depends upon

---

[8] According to the theory of Scotus, if the soul saw itself directly, it would behold in itself this positive ordination to the immediate vision of God. Cf. Scotus in *Quaestio Ia Prologi Primi Sententiarum*.

God's most free sanction.[9] This theory of Scotus is in harmony with his teaching on being which, he says, applies univocally to God and creatures, and thus the infinite distance between the divine and human natures is not sufficiently safeguarded, as we shall see in question thirteen.

The Vatican Council speaks according to the terminology of St. Thomas when it says: "The Catholic Church, with one consent, has also ever held, and does hold, that there is a twofold order of knowledge, distinct both in principle and in object; in principle, because our knowledge in the one is by natural reason and in the other by divine faith; in object, because, besides those things to which natural reason can attain, there are proposed to our belief mysteries hidden in God which, unless divinely revealed, cannot be known. . . . For the divine mysteries by their own nature [it does not say according to God's free decree] so far transcend the created intelligence that, even when delivered by revelation and received by faith, they remain covered with a veil of faith itself, and shrouded in a certain degree of darkness." [10]

SECOND ARTICLE

WHETHER SACRED DOCTRINE IS A SCIENCE

State of the question. From this title we see that it is now not merely a question of sacred doctrine in general according as it abstracts from faith and theology, but it is a question of theology as a science.

The difficulty is that every science proceeds from principles directly known and evident, whereas sacred theology proceeds from principles of faith, which are obscure and not admitted by all. Moreover, science is not concerned with individual facts but with universal principles, whereas sacred doctrine treats of particulars, namely, of Christ, the apostles, the patriarchs, and the prophets.

The reply of St. Thomas is this: sacred doctrine, that is, sacred theology, is a science, but it is a science that is subordinated to a higher science possessed by God, and in a lesser degree by the blessed. It is proved to be a science in the counterargument from the authority of St. Augustine who says: "to this science alone belongs that whereby saving faith is begotten, nourished, protected,

[9] Concerning this difficulty, see question twelve. In this question it will be necessary to show that the innate desire for the beatific vision would have to be efficacious, otherwise God as the Author of nature would have given a natural inclination to an end to which as Author of nature He could not bring the creature, and thus there would be no proportion between agent and end.

[10] Denz., nos. 1795 f.

and strengthened." [11] In this descriptive definition obtained from
the effects, the divers functions of theology are already to some extent distinguished, for, as theology is somewhat apologetic, by
means of it saving faith is begotten; afterward, by the theological
explanation of sacred doctrine, faith is nourished and is defended
against those denying it, and it is strengthened since the various
points of faith are so arranged as to constitute one body of doctrine, and, like the setting of precious stones in a diadem, its value
becomes increasingly apparent by this orderly arrangement.

Nevertheless the difficulty remains if we contend that theology
is a science not only in the broad sense but in the strict sense; for
science properly so called is certain knowledge of truth that is deduced by demonstration from true and certain principles. Moreover, the certitude of sciences has its foundation in the evidence
of the principles, and, contrary to this, the principles of sacred
theology are not evident.

To solve this difficulty, St. Thomas establishes the second part
of the conclusion: that theology is a science subordinated to the
higher science of God and the blessed. It is proved as follows:

A subordinate science proceeds from principles known by the
light of a higher science, as the science of perspective (optics) proceeds from principles established by geometry. Now sacred theology
proceeds from principles transmitted by God through revelation.
Therefore sacred theology is a science subordinated to the science
of God and the blessed. We say "of the blessed," because they see
God's essence, although in a finite way, a point which we will discuss in question twelve.

Thus in the reply to the first objection the difficulty presented
at the beginning is solved. For the principles of any science are
either in themselves self-evident—and thus a science is not subordinated—or else they are reducible to the conclusions of a higher
science. Hence, too, the conclusions of a subordinated science are
reduced to self-evident principles, but through the intermediary of
a subordinating science.

First corollary. The principles of a subordinated science can be
known in two ways: either by faith and without evidence of reason,
or by a higher science already acquired, and then there is evidence
of reason.

Thus the optician, if he is not a geometer, believes the principles
transmitted by geometry, and then his optics is truly a subordinated science, but as yet imperfect. If afterward this optician becomes a geometer, then his optics will be not only a truly subordinated science, but a perfect one. Likewise, the musician believes

[11] *De Trinitate, PL,* XLII, 1037.

the principles he receives from arithmetic, if he does not know arithmetic; but he can acquire this knowledge.

In the same manner, the theologian who is still a wayfarer, believes the principles transmitted by God revealing and proposed by the Church; and thus his theology is truly a subordinated science, but as yet imperfect. But when this theologian afterward attains to the beatific vision or comes into possession of it, then he not only believes but sees the principles transmitted to him by God through the beatific vision, or in the Word, and he still can, outside the Word, make use of his discursive theology, which then is truly not only a subordinated science, but a perfect one. Thus with the attainment of the beatific vision faith is made void, but not theology. St. Thomas' conclusion concerns sacred theology as it is in itself, and this can be in the theologian either as wayfarer, or as one of the blessed or possessors of God.

Second corollary. The theologian will have the same theological habit in heaven as he now has on earth; just as the optician does not lose his science of optics when he becomes a geometer. So Christ when on earth had acquired knowledge as well as the beatific vision.

Third corollary. Therefore what is substantially a true science is sometimes imperfect under certain conditions. Thus in the theologian as wayfarer, theology is substantially a true science (and is neither opinion nor faith), because its conclusions are reducible to evident principles. But if, in fact, the reduction does not result in actual evidence, this is not owing directly to the defect of this science, but is, as it were, accidentally so, because of the defect in the person knowing, as in the case of the optician who would not know geometry. Hence the theology of the wayfarer is a true science, but it is imperfect *as to its status.*

In other words, a science that is imperfect, not in itself but because it is in the initial stage of its development, can still be called a science, because as such its conclusions are reducible to principles. The optician who is not a geometer has good grounds for thinking that his optics is a science and not merely an opinion.

It must be observed that this distinction between the essence of a science and its state, is of almost similar application in many other problems, and there is a most certain foundation for this. In fact, one as yet merely a boy or even an infant is, as regards his nature, a true human being, but he is in an imperfect state. In like manner, the acquired moral virtues in a sinner can be true virtues, but they are in an imperfect state as regards their disposition. Thus the acquired virtue of true temperance differs from the temperance of the miser which has not as yet reached the perfect state of a virtue that is practically stabilized, but is still in the imperfect state of a fickle disposition.

Likewise the Christian philosophy of St. Thomas does not differ specifically, as regards its formal object, from Aristotle's philosophy; but the difference consists in this, that in Aristotle the habit was imperfect, whereas in St. Thomas it was perfect. Thus Aristotle did not succeed in acquiring a clear idea of creation from nothing, nor of providence that extends even to the least detail, nor was he fully convinced of the personal immortality of the soul. His philosophy never penetrated to such depths as this. In our days some would wish to relegate Christian philosophy to Christian apologetics, which is sacred theology functioning by an appeal to reason. To be sure, the Christian philosophy of St. Thomas did not differ *specifically* from the philosophy of Aristotle except in its circumstances, because it was fortified from on high by divine revelation as its guiding star; because of this positive fortification and the perfection resulting therefrom, it is called Christian.

SOLUTION OF THE OBJECTIONS

Durandus, Scotus, and Aureolus raised objections against the conclusion of St. Thomas. These objections are examined by Cajetan.

First objection. According to Aureolus, since the theologian does not have evidence of the truth of the conclusions, theology is the science of consequences or of logical inferences, but not of the conclusions themselves, or of actual facts. In other words, it would be but a good application of logic to matters of faith.

We reply with Cajetan that from this it follows that theology is a science in an imperfect state, but not that it is not a science. The theologian is not only a logician applying logic to matters of faith, but he must also be a metaphysician, and in addition to this a theologian in the strict sense of the term, treating not only of logical being, or merely of being purely as such, but of the mystery of God's life.

Second objection. A subordinating science states the reason why the principles of a subordinated science are true. But it does not give the reason why the principles of faith are true.

Reply. Wayfarers do not see the reason for this; however there is such a reason. Thus there is a certain reason on account of which God is triune, for He is triune by reason of Himself. Likewise there is a certain reason for the free decree of the redemptive Incarnation.

Third objection. The object of a subordinated science is distinct from that of a subordinating science, as optics with reference to geometry. But theology and the beatific vision have the same object. Cajetan [12] replies to this objection by the following distinction: that theology has the same object *as it is an entity,* this I concede; as it is an object, this I deny; for the object of the beatific vision is God clearly seen, whereas the object of theology is God as revealed, abstracting both from clarity and obscurity. But if, moreover, a subordinating science has a limited object, such as geometry, then the object of the subordinated science, such as optics, is also distinct as an entity.

This distinction between the object *as an entity* and the object *as an object,* is of great importance. Thus God, although He is most simple as an entity, is the object of several specifically distinct habits, namely, of the light of glory, of infused faith, of the gifts of understanding and wisdom, of sacred discursive theology (whether in the blessed or in wayfarers), and of natural theology. And these various habits remain specifically distinct by reason of their object, not as it is an entity, but as it is an object. Likewise man is the material object of various sciences, namely, of biology, psychology, metaphysics, and even theology.

In the reply to the second objection of this article, St. Thomas remarks why sacred theology can treat of individual facts, although science treats of universals. In truth, it treats of these things, namely, of the deeds performed by Abraham, Isaac, and Jacob, not as constituting the principal object but as they are examples, and to establish the authority of those through whom the divine revelation came down to us. But when it treats of Christ, it considers in Him what the redemptive Incarnation is, just as physics or astronomy treats of the sun, considering its influence in the solar system.

First doubt. For true theology is it enough for one to have a knowledge of supernatural things, not through infused faith but through faith acquired by human efforts, such as the formal heretic has? In other words, is infused faith necessary for theology, so that the loss of infused faith through heresy would mean the loss of theology?

Vasquez replies that acquired faith suffices for theology: (1) because theology survives in the heretical theologian; (2) because theology is a naturally acquired habit and therefore does not necessarily depend upon any infused habit. It suffices that the principles of faith be believed by whatever kind of faith.

John of St. Thomas, on the contrary, justly replies that the op-

12 *Com. in Summam S. Thomae,* Ia, q.1, a.2, no. 13.

posite opinion must by all means be held; and he says that it is the one commonly held among theologians, especially the Thomists. This we deduce from the text of St. Thomas who, when comparing the certitude of theological science with other sciences, says: "whereas this derives its certitude from the light of the divine knowledge, which cannot be misled"; [13] and he shows that it is divine revelation which gives to theology its formal aspect.[14]

Now the acquired faith of the formal heretic is uncertain, because he believes by an act of his own judgment and will those truths which he approves of, and rejects others that have been revealed, thus rejecting the formal motive of infused faith, which is the authority of God revealing as regards all revealed truths. Those which he retains are believed on grounds of human reason. Hence the faith of the formal heretic is some kind of opinion from which certainty of conclusions cannot be deduced.[15]

Hence many ideas concerning matters of faith survive indeed *materially* in the theologian who becomes a formal heretic, but there is no longer the formal connection between these ideas, and in the conclusions deduced the word "is" implies an affirmation that is merely an opinion and not a certainty. Hence nothing is left but the corpse, as it were, of theological science in such a person. For science is a habit or simple quality together with subordination of ideas. But this simple quality is specified by the formal object, which in this case is God as made known to us by virtual revelation. Hence, when divine revelation is rejected by formal heresy, this simple quality or theological habit no longer remains, but in its place we have only ideas that are precariously connected under the dominance of a fickle opinion which is the result of the heretic's own judgment and volitional act. Thus the human body, when the soul has departed, is no longer truly a human body; for, lacking what formally connects the various parts, it is but a corpse in the process of corruption or disintegration. The habit of sacred theology implies the presence of a theological bent of mind, and this the heretic, such as Luther or Calvin, no longer possesses.

In reply to Vasquez, it must be said that theology, since it is acquired and not infused, is formally natural, though radically it is supernatural, in that it has its root in infused faith, as we shall state later on. Nor can anyone be said to have acquired a subordinated science who is not certain of having acquired a subordinating science; nor can such a science be acquired by one who accepts from a subordinating science what he approves of and noth-

---

13 *Summa theol.*, Ia, q.1, a.5.
14 *Ibid.*, a.4.
15 *Ibid.*, IIa IIae, q.5, a.3.

ing else, as in the case of the optician who would accept from geometry only those things which he approved of; for he would be accepting these things not on scientific but aesthetic grounds.

Second doubt. With what theological conclusions is this article concerned? It is chiefly concerned with conclusions strictly so called, with those that are inferred by a discursive process which is not only explanatory but also objectively illative, and that establish a *new truth* which is deduced and distinct from the two truths enunciated in the premises. In other words, it is a new truth that is not formally but virtually revealed.

It must be noted that there can thus be several distinct truths of the same thing, even of the same divine reality; because, although God is most simple as an *entity*, yet He can be the *object* of different habits and even more so of different judgments or truths in the same science. Thus three distinct truths are enunciated in the following syllogisms: Every intellectual being is free. But God is intellectual. Therefore God is free.[16] Being is consequent upon person. But in Christ there is only one person. Therefore in Christ there is one being.[17]

These are examples of objectively illative reasoning by which we acquire a new truth. For to say that "God is intellectual," and "God is free," is to enunciate two distinct truths, two true judgments (truth is formally in the mind), although these are enunciated of the same divine reality. If this were not so, we should have to say with the nominalists that the divine names, such as mercy and justice, are synonymous.[18] Father Marin Sola does not stress this point sufficiently in his new theory on the evolution of dogma,[19] about which more will be said later on.

On the other hand, the theological conclusion improperly so called, which is obtained by an explicative process of reasoning is not a new truth but one that has already been revealed and is now more explicitly proposed. Thus the infallibility of the Supreme Pontiff speaking *ex cathedra* is the same truth as that revealed by Christ when He said: "Thou art Peter and upon this rock I will

---

[16] *Ibid.*, Ia, q. 19, a. 1, 10.

[17] *Ibid.*, IIIa, q. 17, a. 2.

[18] *Ibid.*, Ia, q. 13, a. 4.

[19] In *L'Evolution homogène du dogme catholique* (French tr., III, 333), we read: "Two propositions that have the same subject differ or are identical in meaning according to their predicates. If therefore the predicates are really identical, the meaning of the propositions will be also." Although justice and mercy are really identical in God, and not really distinct, the meaning of these two truths is not the same: God is just, God is merciful. This point is of primary importance; if it is denied, we are led involuntarily to the admission of nominalism.

build My Church and the gates of hell shall not prevail against it." [20] In the explicative process of reasoning there may be some inference resulting therefrom which is merely of subjective import, or as far as we are concerned, but in itself it means no addition to knowledge. In this way there is no acquisition of a new truth, but the truth that was formally and implicitly revealed is expressed in another form and more explicitly.

On the contrary, in the objectively illative process a new truth is acquired, which is not formally but virtually revealed, and which is deduced from what has been revealed, as in the proposition: there is one being in Christ. In this we see the specific distinction between theology and faith, which latter is not a discursive science.

Third doubt. When is the discursive reasoning proper or truly illative? It is generally admitted that such is the case when the conclusion is contained in the premises, as the property is contained in the essence, or the effect in its cause. We have an example of this in the following syllogism: every man is free; but Christ is truly a man; therefore Christ has human liberty (which is distinct from His divine liberty). But this truth thus deduced is otherwise revealed in that it has been revealed that Christ freely obeyed and merited for us. Another example is the following: every man can acquire knowledge by experience and observation; but Christ was truly a man; therefore Christ had acquired knowledge (and not only infused knowledge and the beatific vision). A third example would be: it was fitting that Christ, like His apostles, should have the gift of tongues; but this gift presupposes infused knowledge; therefore Christ had infused knowledge.

On the contrary, we have the case of discursive reasoning improperly so called, if the conclusion is contained in the whole, or the singular in the universal, or the implicit in the explicit. The following is an example: all men have sinned in Adam; but Abraham was a man; therefore he sinned in Adam. Likewise in the following syllogism: Christ died for all men; but Abraham was a man; therefore Christ died for him. In the same way it is shown that Christ died for the Blessed Virgin Mary, whom He redeemed, but by preservative redemption.

Fourth doubt. What theological conclusions are definable by the Church as dogmas of faith, such that their contradictory propositions would not only be erroneous but heretical? All know the difference between these two terms: erroneous and heretical. A proposition is said to be erroneous when it is against a theologically certain conclusion, and heretical when it is against the faith.

[20] Matt. 16: 18.

In answer to this we say:

1) All theologians are agreed that the theological conclusion improperly so called is definable as a dogma. The reason is that it
is not a question here of a new truth that has been deduced, but
of a truth that has already been formally but confusedly or implicitly revealed, such as the infallibility of the Supreme Pontiff
when our Lord said: "Thou art Peter. . . ." Then the discursive
reasoning is only explicative, or at most subjectively but not objectively illative. In this case the discursive method explains only
the subject or predicate of the proposition that is expressly revealed. Thus it has been revealed that Christ is truly God and
truly man. But for true humanity a rational soul is an essential
requisite. Therefore Christ had a rational soul. This conclusion
was defined against Apollinaris.[21]

For this same reason particular propositions included in an expressly revealed universal proposition are definable as dogmas of
faith. Thus we conclude that Abraham contracted original sin, for
the universal proposition that has been expressly revealed, "in
whom (Adam) all have sinned," [22] covers all particular cases. This
assertion is generally admitted by theologians.

2) A conclusion deduced even by a truly illative process of reasoning from two principles that are of faith, is also definable as
a dogma of faith.[23] The reason is that, although the conclusion is
reached by the illative process, yet *specifically* as such it is of faith.
It is implicitly revealed, indeed, in the two revealed premises; for
a new idea is not introduced, and the connection between predicate
and subject can be affirmed by reason of the formal revelation. It
is, as it were, the logical explanation of the two propositions taken
together that are of faith.

3) A theological conclusion that is deduced by an objectively
illative process of reasoning from one premise that is of faith, and
another founded on reason, is not of faith in itself, nor can it be
for us defined as a dogma of faith. The reason is that this conclusion is a new truth that is not simply revealed, but is simply deduced
from revelation and is only virtually revealed.[24]

We have an example of this in the following syllogism: being is
consequent upon person, so that there is only one substantial exist-

[21] Cf. John of St. Thomas, *in Iam*, q. 1, disp. 2, a. 4, no. 16.

[22] Rom. 5: 12.

[23] Cf. Salmanticenses, *De fide*, disp. I, dub. IV, no. 127.

[24] So say the Salmanticenses (*ibid.*, no. 124), who quote for this same opinion
such famous Thomists as Cajetan, Capreolus, Bannez, John of St. Thomas, against
Vega, Vasquez, Suarez, and Lugo. Cf. *Dictionnaire de théol. cath.*, art. "Explicite
et implicite"; also art. "Dogme."

ence for each person; but in Christ there is only one person; therefore in Christ there is only one being, namely, the one and only substantial existence for the two natures.[25]

In this discursive method, the major is founded on reason, and the minor is of faith. Hence in the conclusion the connection between the predicate and the subject cannot be affirmed solely on account of the authority of God revealing, but partly because of the revelation contained in the minor, and partly on account of the light of natural reason, by which we are impelled to give our assent to the major premise. Therefore this conclusion belongs directly to theology and not to faith.

In other words, this conclusion is not simply revealed (not even implicitly), but it is simply deduced from revealed principles and is only virtually revealed. Hence if the Church were to propose it as a dogma of faith, the contradictory of which would be heresy, the Church would be uttering what is false, because it would propose as simply revealed and to be believed on the authority of God revealing, what is not simply revealed but merely deduced from what is revealed. But the Church can condemn infallibly as erroneous the denial of such a deduced conclusion.

Another example: infused knowledge is necessary so that the human intellect may not remain imperfect but may know, for instance, various languages not known by one's natural powers; but it was not to be thought of that Christ's human intellect even in this life should be imperfect; therefore Christ even in this life had infused knowledge.[26] This conclusion is not of faith, nor is it definable as a dogma of faith.

In these truly illative processes of reasoning a new truth is inferred in that from the premise known by the natural power of reason (especially if this premise is the major), a new truth is introduced, and we have not merely an explanation of the subject or predicate of the revealed proposition. Such conclusions (if not otherwise equivalently revealed in Sacred Scripture or tradition) are not defined by the Church. But the Church sometimes condemns, and even infallibly, as erroneous, opinions that deny theologically certain conclusions.

For a more complete explanation of the conclusion just stated, we must add that, according to the Vatican Council, "all those things are to be believed with divine and Catholic faith which are contained in the word of God written or handed down, and which the Church, either by a solemn judgment or by her ordinary and universal teaching, proposes for our belief as having been

[25] Cf. *Summa theol.*, IIIa, q.17, a.2.
[26] *Ibid.*, IIIa, q.9, a.3.

divinely revealed." [27] This is the definition of dogma. But that which is only connected with what is revealed, cannot be said to be simply and strictly revealed, but is distinguished from what is revealed as being deduced from it.

Moreover, if the Church defined as a dogma such a conclusion, it would not only be infallibly guarding and explaining the deposit of the faith, but it would be perfecting the teaching that is of faith, and would be establishing new dogmas; for by this definition it would be declaring of faith what before was not of faith, either in itself or for us.

Finally, if the above-mentioned theological conclusions were definable as dogmas of faith, then all theologically certain conclusions, even those most remote, would be equally definable as dogmas, and all conclusions condemned as erroneous could be condemned as heretical in the strict sense of the term. Thus a great part of the *Theological Summa* and, especially so, practically the whole treatise on God and His attributes, rigorously deduced from revealed principles, could become dogmas of faith.

We must therefore carefully distinguish between a theological conclusion that is only virtually connected with what is revealed, and a truth that is formally and implicitly revealed. Yet in individual cases it is not always easy to make this distinction. For what seems to the majority virtually connected with that which is revealed, to one of prodigious and keener intellect appears to be formally and implicitly revealed. There are Thomists who see in the words of St. Paul, "It is God who worketh in you, both to will and to accomplish, according to His good will," [28] a formally implicit revelation that grace is efficacious of itself and not because God foresees our consent. They come to the same conclusion from the following words of our Lord: "My sheep . . . shall not perish forever, and no man shall pluck them out of My hand . . . and no one can snatch them out of the hand of My Father." [29] In accordance with these texts, for many Thomists, an explicative process of reasoning, and one that is objectively illative, suffices to show that grace is of itself efficacious, because it concerns not a new truth that is deduced, but the same truth more explicitly formulated. [30]

[27] Denz., no. 1792.
[28] Phil. 2: 13.
[29] John 10: 27–29.
[30] As for the contrary opinion, namely, that the Church can define as a dogma of faith, theological conclusions in the strict sense of the term, those which are deduced by an objectively illative process of reasoning, cf. Vega, *In Trident.*, Bk. IX, chap. 39; Suarez, *De fide*, disp. III, sect. 11; De Lugo, *De fide*, disp. I, nos. 268–77.

Objection. Father Marin Sola disagrees, saying that at least if it concerns God, a conclusion obtained by a truly illative process of reasoning from one premise that is founded on reason and another that is of faith, is revealed, because it concerns the same most simple divine reality.[31]

We reply to this objection by appealing to the classical distinction given by Cajetan.[32] That the premises of faith and the abovementioned theological conclusion concern the same divine reality, as *an entity,* this I concede; as *an object,* this I deny. For the same divine reality specifies various specifically distinct habits, as it is variously presented to them as object, namely, as clearly seen, or as obscurely believed, or as the object of the gift of wisdom, or as the object of sacred theology, or as the object of natural theology. With greater reason it can be the object of several propositions in the same science, or of several judgments, which are different truths (truth is formally in the mind) of the same divine reality.

For it is evident that, if for the same divine reality there is only one truth for the divine intellect, which by one intuitive act knows the divine essence, for the created intellect, however, and especially for the human intellect, there are several true judgments and truths concerning the same divine reality, as, for example, God is intellectual, God is free, God is just, God is merciful. But it is now a question not of the divine intellect, but of the human intellect with reference to which a distinction must be made between truth that is revealed and truth that is deduced from what is revealed.

[31] Cf. *L'Evolution homogène du dogme catholique,* II, 332 f., where we read as follows: "Under pain of falling into nominalism or the subjective conceptualism of Ockham or Aureolus, we must admit that the validity of a proposition does not depend precisely upon the words but upon their objective meaning, the words being but the material element, whereas their signification constitutes the formal element. Two propositions about God, the predicates of which are identical, are really identical in meaning. Two propositions with the same subject (God), differ or are identical in meaning only by reason of their predicates. If therefore the predicates are really identical, the meaning will be, too, and likewise their doctrine.

Father Marin Sola does not take sufficiently into consideration the fact that in these two propositions, "God is intellectual, God is free," and likewise in these two, "God is merciful, God is just," the predicates are not really distinct, for there is only a virtual distinction between the divine attributes. Nevertheless these four propositions are not the same in meaning, nor do they enunciate the same truth, unless we admit the opinion of the nominalists, that the divine names are synonymous terms, such as Tullius and Cicero. This opinion is refuted by St. Thomas (cf. *Summa,* Ia, q.13, a.4: "Whether names applied to God are synonymous"). From such an admission it would follow that wherever we find "mercy" written, "justice" could be substituted for it, and we could rightly say that God punishes by reason of His mercy. Thus, though his intention is to avoid nominalism, the renowed objector falls into it.

[32] Cf. *Com. in Iam,* q.1, a.3, no. 8.

Moreover, by this method, in seeking to avoid nominalism, the mind would revert to the same, according to the theory that claims divine names to be synonymous terms, a theory which is refuted by St. Thomas.[33] Thus divine mercy and justice would be synonymous and it could therefore be said that God punishes by means of His mercy.

Finally, if the above-mentioned opinion were true, then all conclusions in the treatise on God, even those most remote, provided they are metaphysically certain, could be defined as dogmas under pain not only of error, but of heresy in the strict sense. Thus merely one revealed truth concerning God, namely, that He is the self-subsisting Being, would suffice to render all conclusions deduced from it such that they could be said to be strictly revealed, and to be believed on the authority of God revealing.

This seems to be an inadmissible exaggeration of the powers assigned to theology, or what is called theologism, and consequently it impairs the superiority of faith to theology.

Instance. For anything to be defined as a dogma of faith, it suffices that it is contained actually and implicitly in what is revealed; but any divine attribute whatever is contained actually and implicitly in the divine nature, since this is the self-subsisting Being ("I am who am"); [34] therefore any divine attribute deduced from revelation is a dogma of faith.[35]

Reply. I distinguish the major: provided it is the same truth, this I concede; even if it is a new truth that is deduced, this I deny. And this Father Marin Sola concedes.[36] I contradistinguish the minor: that every divine attribute is actually and implicitly contained in the divine nature, and that each is the same truth for the human intellect, this I deny; that each is a new and deduced truth, this I concede.

Explanation. One divine attribute is actually and implicitly contained in another and in the divine nature, considered reduplicatively as a divine reality, this I concede; considered as an object, so that each is the same truth, again I distinguish: that it is so for the divine intellect, I concede; for the human intellect, this I deny.

Otherwise, as we said, all divine names, for instance, justice and mercy, would be synonymous terms, and it could be said that God punishes by means of His mercy. Moreover, the revelation of merely one proposition about God would be sufficient, namely, that He is the self-subsisting Being, so that from this all the deduced attrib-

---

[33] *Summa theol.,* Ia, q.13, a.4.
[34] Ex. 3: 14.
[35] So says Father Marin Sola, *op. cit.,* II, 342.
[36] *Ibid.,* p. 333.

utes and all the metaphysically certain propositions in the treatise on God could be defined as of faith.

For a dogmatic definition it is necessary that the definition should be the expression of a truth that is the same with what has already been formally and explicitly revealed, and that is not explicitly proposed for our belief. Now even being in general contains *actually* and *implicitly* all the modes of being, for these are not outside of being; and yet, concerning these modes, namely, substance, quantity, and quality, *new truths* are enumerated.

THIRD ARTICLE

WHETHER SACRED DOCTRINE IS ONE SCIENCE

State of the question. The question is whether it is one science reduced to its ultimate species, or whether it is divided into several sciences, just as there are several mathematical sciences, namely, geometry, arithmetic, and several philosophical sciences, as logic, natural philosophy, metaphysics, and ethics.

The difficulty is, as stated in the beginning of the article, that sacred theology treats not only of God, but also of created beings, namely, of angels, of man, or irrational creatures, as also of the morality of human acts. But these various subjects pertain to different philosophical sciences, namely, metaphysics and ethics. Hence it seems that dogmatic theology, which treats especially of God, is a science distinct from moral theology, which is concerned with the morality of human acts. Thus there seem to be several theological sciences, as, among the Scholastics, Vasquez thought subsequent to the time of such nominalists as Durandus and Gabriel Biel.

The answer of St. Thomas is that sacred doctrine is one science. This indeed is what its name, "sacred theology," implies, for it is singular and not plural in form.

The conclusion is proved as follows: The unity of a faculty or habit is gauged by the unity of the formal aspect of its object; but sacred theology considers all things according as they are knowable by revelation; therefore sacred theology is one science reduced to its ultimate species.

The major is philosophically certain. Thus sight is specified by the colored object perceived by the light of the sensitive faculty, logic by being that is a creation of the mind, natural philosophy by mobile being perceived by the light of reason according to the first degree of abstraction, mathematics by quantitative being according to the second degree of abstraction, metaphysics by being as such perceived by the light of reason according to the third degree of abstraction, namely, as removed from all that is material, and ethics is specified by human acts.

The minor. But sacred theology considers everything as it is knowable by revelation. It thus includes all that is formally revealed and believed as of faith, and likewise all that is virtually revealed, which means all that can be deduced from revealed principles. These virtually revealed truths can be said to be, as stated in the body of this article, potentially revealed. They are known by the light not of formal but of virtual revelation. What is formally revealed is the formal motive of faith. But virtual revelation is the light or formal motive why we assent to theological conclusions.

Therefore everything that is considered in theology, namely, God, creatures, morality of human acts, come under the one formal aspect of the object, according as they are considered as included within the scope of virtual revelation, which is the *objectum formale quo* of sacred theology.[37]

1) This conclusion receives its confirmation from the reply to the first objection, which is as follows: "Sacred doctrine does not treat of God and creatures equally, but of God primarily; and of creatures only so far as they are referable to God as their beginning or end. Hence the unity of this science is not impaired."

This reply is concerned with the *objectum formale quod*[38] of

---

[37] By the *objectum formale quo*, or the formal aspect under which or by means of which of any science, is meant in scholastic language, the light inherent in the first principles of such a science by which one is able to reach the conclusions pertaining strictly to such a science. It means the objective evidence of the conclusions borrowed from the first principles of such a science. In other words it is the objective evidence *by which* the conclusions of such a science are made known clearly to all. (Tr.)

[38] A few words of explanation may again be of help to those not well versed in scholastic terminology. There is a distinction between the material and the formal object as such (*objectum formale quod*) of any science. By the material object are meant the realities or entities which constitute the subject matter of a science. The particular point of view from which the subject is discussed constitutes the formal object of that science. An example will help to make this clearer. Thus the extension or extended quantity of cosmic bodies constitutes the material object of geometry. The measure of this continuous extension constitutes its formal object (*objectum formale quod*); for it is the measure of the dimensions of these bodies which is particularly enunciated and considered in the theorems of geometry. Finally, the axiomatic principles of geometry are the source of light by which the theorems are made evident. These are called by the Scholastics the *objectum formale quo* or the *ratio formalis sub qua* of geometry. For these principles constitute formally or actually the object by which, or formally the reason by which, the theorems and conclusions of geometry are made evident. Yet it must be carefully noted that the *objectum formale quo* is what truly and adequately specifies a science, and not its *objectum formale quod*, for this latter may sometimes be the same in different sciences. Thus the measure of extended bodies

sacred theology. This will be more explicitly determined in the seventh article in which the question will be taken up of the proper and formal subject of this science. But even from its nominal definition theology is evidently concerned principally with God and only secondarily with those things that proceed from God, namely, creatures, and the movement of the rational creature toward God. Thus the unity of the science is not impaired. And how this unity of sacred theology depends upon both formal objects, namely, *quo* and *quod,* will be more clearly seen from the explanation of the seventh article. For theology treats of God under the aspect of Deity, in so far as this comes within the scope of virtual revelation. Thus it is distinct from metaphysics, which treats of being as such, and of God as included in the notion of being, in so far as He is known by the light of natural reason.

It is, however, the common teaching in philosophy that the sciences derive their species and unity from the unity of both formal objects *quo* and *quod.* Thus the difference between physics, mathematics, and metaphysics consists in this, that physics treats of mobile being according to the first degree of abstraction; mathematics, of being according to the second degree of abstraction; metaphysics, of being as such according to the third degree of abstraction. Thus any science is specified by its object, not as this latter is an entity, but as it is formally an object, such being the means or precise reason why it can be known.

2) This conclusion is furthermore confirmed by the reply to the second objection, in which it is shown that although there are different philosophical sciences, yet theological science is specifically one. The reason is that the higher science considers its object in its more universal aspect, just as the common sense, which is the lowest of the internal senses and in which the five objects of the external senses are united, attains the visible, the audible, the tangible, and other objects according to the more common notion of the sensible.

So these things discussed by philosophical sciences, namely, by natural philosophy, metaphysics, and ethics, sacred theology can consider under one aspect, inasmuch as they are capable of being divinely revealed, or are virtually revealed, and according as all these are directed to God, as being the principle whom they manifest and the end to whom they tend.

We shall see in the sixth and seventh articles that God in His intimate life can be known only by divine revelation, and this ap-

---

(*objectum formale quod*) is what is formally considered both by geometry and hydrostatics, but the method of approach in each (*objectum formale quo*) is different. (Tr.)

plies equally to those things that participate in God's intimate life, such as grace, the infused virtues, and the gifts. So we shall see that the formal object *quod* and the formal object *quo* in theology are interchangeable, as in the other sciences. The Deity and the divine light are interchangeable, just as being as such and the light of reason in the third degree of abstraction are, just as mathematical quantity and the light of reason in the second degree of abstraction are, just as the colored object and sense perception are.

First corollary. Positive theology and speculative theology are not two sciences, but they are, so to speak, the inductive and deductive parts of the same science. For positive theology brings together the revealed truths by the inductive method from Holy Scripture and tradition. After this, speculative theology takes up the analysis of the concepts of these truths, defending them against opponents by arguments drawn from the analogy of things known by the natural power of reason, and it deduces conclusions that are virtually contained in them.

Second corollary. Positive theology, since it is truly a part of theology, reaches its conclusions under the guidance of the light of revelation, and thus it is distinct from history; but it makes use of history, just as speculative theology makes use of metaphysics.

Third corollary. Specialization is a more difficult process in theology than the other sciences, and this because of its unity. The relationship between moral theology and grace, the infused virtues, the gifts, merit and demerit cannot be fully perceived without a profound knowledge of what dogmatic theology teaches about God's love for us, the divine motion, redemption and its application to us. Hence specialization in theology sometimes leads to a too material and superficial knowledge, which no longer penetrates to the very vitals of this corporate doctrine.

Sometimes specialists in this or that branch of theology have an insufficient knowledge of theology in general, and therefore of those things that are fundamental in theology, so that the branch in which they specialize, for instance, ascetic or mystic theology, is not properly understood by them. Doctors, too, must not be ignorant of the general principles of medical science, otherwise their knowledge of that in which they particularly specialize is deficient.

It is evident from St. Thomas' reply to the second objection that sacred theology, even when discussing man and the morality of his acts, examines in them what is strictly divine, what can be known only by the light of virtual revelation, and what is related to God as such, that is, to His intimate life. In this we see the sublimity of theology, since it considers what is divine in all things by means of the divine light, namely, the various participations of God's intimate life—grace, the virtues, the gifts, their acts, the modalities of these acts, these being meritorious and their opposites demeritorious, in that contraries are governed by the same law.

Just as in the preaching about Christ no distinction is drawn between the dogmatic and the moral parts, but the kingdom of God is spoken of, or God's life as it is in itself and as it is participated in by us, so sacred theology does not consist of two specifically distinct sciences, dogma and moral, but is only one scientific habit, which treats of God as knowable by revelation and of those things that refer to God. Therefore St. Thomas says at the end of the reply to the second objection: "So that in this way sacred doctrine bears, as it were, the stamp of the divine science which is one and simple yet extends to everything." Hence dogmatic theology and moral theology are but branches of the same science, and this applies more so to soteriology, mariology, asceticism, and mysticism.

Fourth corollary. In the human sciences, metaphysics bears a certain relation to theology since it treats of being as such, that is, it treats of supreme generalities and higher principles. Thus it is one and yet it discusses all things from a higher point of view, according as they are reduced to being and to the first principles of being.

Sacred theology considers all things from a higher plane according as these are directed to God, and in this it is guided by the divine light. Hence the unity of this science is perfect, and it thus disposes one for the contemplation enjoyed by the blessed, which is a still more simplified process.

FOURTH ARTICLE

WHETHER SACRED DOCTRINE IS A PRACTICAL SCIENCE

State of the question. It seems that sacred doctrine is a practical science, because its purpose is the regulation of action, namely, direction in the Christian life; and it explains both the Old Law and the New Law, which direct human acts. It is to be noted that according to Scotus, who wrote very extensively on this subject, theology is a practical science because its proper end is action, especially the love of God and one's neighbor, since the whole law and the prophets depend upon these two precepts. Scotus inclines to this view because he thinks that the will is a higher faculty than the intellect, and that all knowledge, even the beatific vision, is ordained to love, as disposing one for a perfection of a higher order.

It must also be noted that we already detect this practical tendency in the writings of the Master of the Sentences, who divided his work, as to the acts of the will, into enjoyment and use, in the following manner:

1) The things to be enjoyed are the Father, the Son, and the Holy Ghost.

2) The things to be made use of for the attainment of eternal happiness are the world and created things.

3) The things to be enjoyed and made use of are the humanity of Christ, the angels, and the saints.

St. Bonaventure said [39] that sacred theology is an affective science, since it is intermediary between speculative theology and practical theology, because contemplation and the performance of good constitute the end in view. St. Albert the Great expresses a similar view at the beginning of his *Summa*. In his opinion sacred theology is an affective study since it is directed to God's love. The nominalists along with Durandus admit that theology consists of two sciences, one of which is speculative and the other practical.

St. Thomas' reply is that sacred doctrine, being one, is both eminently speculative and practical, but it is speculative rather than practical.

1) It is proved in the counterargument from the nominal definition of theology, because it is chiefly concerned with God, who does not come within the scope of things operable, but who is the Being to whom our intentions and actions must be directed.

2) The first part of the conclusion is proved from the intrinsic end of this science in the body of the article as follows: A science which considers things speculative and practical from the same formal point of view, is eminently speculative and practical; but sacred theology considers all things speculative and practical as virtually revealed and directed to God, the first truth and last end; therefore sacred theology is eminently speculative and practical.

The term *eminently* is taken in the sense of formal eminence and not merely of virtual eminence. This means that, just as the absolutely simple perfections are contained in God formally and eminently (which is more than virtually), just as the human soul is formally and eminently sensitive and vegetative, so also, as we shall state farther on, infused faith is eminently speculative and practical, since it is concerned with mysteries to be believed, the precepts, and the counsels.[40] In various passages St. Thomas says

39 *In Proem. I Sent.*, q.3.

40 This distinction between formal and virtual eminence is of great importance. First of all, it must be observed that when we say a being contains some perfection *eminently*, this means that the being in question contains the perfection in a nobler way than it is contained in any being of a lower order. Thus sensation in man is nobler or more refined than in the irrational animals. But when a perfection is contained in a being formally and eminently, this means that the perfection denoted by the concept is contained actually in such a being, though in a nobler manner. Thus human wisdom is contained *formally* and

that the same applies to the gifts of understanding and wisdom.[41]

3) The second part of the conclusion is proved in the body of the article as follows: Sacred theology is more speculative than practical, because, as its name implies, it is more concerned with God than with human acts. God, however, is the object of speculation and contemplation, but He does not come within the scope of things operable, as in the case of ethics that is concerned with things capable of being done, and of the arts that are concerned with things capable of being made. Thus St. Thomas distinguishes better than St. Bonaventure does between theology, which is acquired by human effort, and infused contemplation. This latter is truly an affective and quasi-experimental knowledge that proceeds from the gift of wisdom.[42]

But although theology, which is acquired by human effort, and the gift of wisdom are specifically distinct, yet they are most fittingly united, and this point is clearly exemplified in the great doctors of the Church, as in St. Augustine, St. Thomas, St. Bonaventure, St. Albert, and others. In fact, the Church never declares any servant of God a doctor of the Church unless he has first been not only beatified but also canonized. This means that he must first have been of eminent sanctity, and hence that the gift of wisdom and acquired knowledge are each possessed in a high degree.

Concerning the doctrine of this article, it is important to note here that Scotus denies the possibility of one and the same science being both eminently speculative and practical. To this Cajetan [43] replies that the practical and the speculative are not essential differences of a science, as it is a *science,* but as it is *finite.* The divisions we find in things of the lower order, for instance, in the philosophical sciences, are found united in those of the higher order, as in the case of faith and the gifts of understanding and wisdom. Gonet, too, ably defends the doctrine of this article by considering the loftiness of both formal objects *quod* and *quo* of sacred theology. For the formal object *quod* of theology is not only something speculative, such as being inasmuch as being, nor is it something merely operable, such as human actions about which

---

eminently in the natural wisdom of the angels. When a being possesses the active power that renders it capable of producing a perfection found in other beings, then this perfection is said to be contained in such a being *virtually* and *eminently.* Thus local motion is contained virtually and eminently in the human soul, because through the will it commands the motion of hands or feet. (Tr.)

[41] *Summa theol.,* IIa IIae, q.4, a.2; q.8, a.3; q.9, a.3; q.45, a.3.

[42] *Ibid.,* q.45, a.1, 2.

[43] *Com. in Iam,* q.1, a.4, no. 3.

ethics is concerned, but its object is God considered under the aspect of the Deity, who is the first speculative truth and the last end to be attained and the first rule of our life

Likewise, the formal object *quo* or light of sacred theology is virtual revelation, but it is virtual revelation that has its foundation in both speculative and practical knowledge. Thus formal revelation is the formal motive of faith, which is both speculative or contemplative, and practical according as it is concerned with the belief of mysteries or the fulfillment of precepts. The formal objects *quod* and *quo,* however, are correlatives, in that the latter is the searchlight enabling one to know the former.

Objection. If theology were both speculative and practical, then many of its acts would be both speculative and practical, because of the formal aspect of this science. But this is false; for there are in theology merely speculative conclusions, such as the four relations in the divine Persons, and there are conclusions that are merely practical, such as a particular act to be avoided.

We reply to this by denying the major. Although it is true to say that the rational soul is eminently and formally both vegetative and sensitive, yet it does not follow that its every act must be both vegetative and sensitive. So also each and every act of any science does not extend to everything included in this science. It is not necessary that each and every act totally and adequately share in the formal aspect of a science. Although this latter is formally indivisible, nevertheless it is virtually multiple.

Hence some theologians, such as St. Thomas, excel in dogmatic theology, whereas others, such as St. Alphonsus Liguori, are conspicuous for their knowledge of moral theology. In like manner, although the gift of wisdom is formally and eminently both speculative and practical, some saints, such as St. John of the Cross, are prominent in contemplation; others, however, such as St. Vincent de Paul, distinguish themselves by the wisdom of their direction in works of mercy. In the two saints just mentioned we see the gift of wisdom operating in a high degree; but in the former it manifests itself more in contemplation, whereas in the latter it concentrates rather on those things that pertain to the active life. In the former it is like a searchlight, but in the latter it is like a glow in the heavens that illuminates all things from on high.

From this article as also from the preceding we see that the unity of sacred theology is of a higher order, since it is, as it were, a participation in the science of God and the blessed, a subordinate science, as it were, to this latter science or rather to this higher vision.

WHETHER SACRED DOCTRINE IS NOBLER THAN THE OTHER SCIENCES

State of the question. Our contention so far is that sacred theology is a true science, and indeed one as such eminently speculative and practical. It is one and the same aspect in these three conclusions, namely, that sacred theology proceeds from principles that have been revealed by the higher science of God, a science that is not only most certain but also absolutely one and eminently speculative and practical. Our discussion now centers upon the nobility or excellence of sacred theology with reference to the other sciences, namely, as to the certitude and sublimity of the object.

The difficulty about sacred theology is that it proceeds from principles that are not evident and that are doubted by some. Thus it seems to be inferior to the mathematical sciences. Moreover, theology draws upon the philosophical sciences. Therefore it seems to be inferior to them. St. Thomas accepted several principles from Aristotle.

St. Thomas replies to this, however, as follows: sacred theology transcends all other sciences both speculative and practical. He proves this:

1) By the argument from tradition, in which philosophy and the other human sciences are said to be handmaids of sacred doctrine. He also quotes the following text of Sacred Scripture in support of his doctrine: "Wisdom hath built herself a house . . . and hath sent her maids to invite to the tower, and to the walls of the city." [44] The Supreme Pontiffs have often drawn attention to the dignity of sacred theology.[45]

2) In the argumentative part of the article this twofold aspect of the conclusion is taken up in turn and proved theologically. Among the speculative sciences it is because of the certitude and dignity of the subject matter that one is nobler than the other. Now sacred theology excels the other speculative sciences in both respects. Therefore it is nobler than the others.

The major is evident; for dignity is thus considered from both the objective and the subjective points of view. The minor is no less certain; for sacred theology derives its certitude not from the light of reason but from the light of the divine knowledge, from principles believed by divine faith. But faith in itself is more cer-

[44] Prov. 9: 1–3.
[45] Cf. Syllabus of Pius IX, props. 8, 9, 11, 12, against semirationalism. **Also** especially Leo XIII in his encyclical *Aeterni Patris.*

tain than all the sciences on account of the authority of God revealing.[46] The object of theology has reference to those things which by reason of their loftiness transcend both human reason and the angelic intellect.

Likewise, sacred theology is nobler than ethics and all the practical sciences, because it ordains and directs to a higher end, namely, to the ultimate supernatural end, which is eternal life. Since this latter is essentially supernatural, it surpasses the future life about which the nobler minded among the ancient philosophers spoke.

The argumentative part of the article presents no difficulty about what is meant. The formal aspect is clearly set forth, and is the same as in the preceding articles, namely, that sacred theology proceeds under the guidance of the divine light, and treats of the loftiest object that is both the supreme truth and the ultimate end.

There remains but the difficulty presented in the first objection, namely, that sacred theology, since it argues from principles that are not evident to reason, seems to be less certain than metaphysics, mathematics, and physics.

In the reply to the first objection it is stated that sacred theology is more certain than the other sciences in itself, but not to us. It is more certain in itself on account of its formal motive being higher, for this is virtual divine revelation. It is, however, less certain to us on account of the weakness of our intelligence, "which confronted by the light of those things more intelligible in themselves is as dazzled as the owl is by the light of the sun." [47] Yet, as Aristotle says, "the slightest knowledge that may be obtained of the highest things is more desirable than the most certain knowledge obtained of lesser things." [48] Why is this? It is for the reason that, since knowledge is specified by its object, its worth is estimated more from the object known than from the way in which it is known. Thus the argument of the fittingness about the possibility of the Trinity is of a higher order than the rigorous demonstration of any property of the triangle.

Concerning the distinction made in this reply to the first objection between what is more certain in itself and not to us, and between what is more certain to us and not in itself, we must recall what Aristotle says on several occasions in his Metaphysics, namely, that those things which are more intelligible in themselves, as God, the pure Act, His immutable eternity, are less intelligible to us because they are most remote from the senses; for our human knowledge originates from the senses. On the contrary, motion and time,

[46] *Summa theol.,* IIa IIae, q.4, a.8.
[47] Cf. Aristotle's *Metaphysics,* Bk. II, chap. 1.
[48] Cf. *De animalibus,* Bk. I, chap. 5.

which are to us more intelligible than immobile eternity, are less intelligible in themselves. Eternity is most lucid in itself, for it is the measure of the subsistent Intelligence or of the pure Act, who is pure intellection.

First doubt. Does the greater degree of objective certainty though not of subjective certainty enjoyed by sacred theology over the other sciences apply to this same theology as possessed by us as wayfarers? We answer in the affirmative to this with the Thomists.[49]

Proof. It is repugnant for a formal cause to inform a subject and not give it its formal effect. Thus infused faith by the very fact that it is received in our intellect, notwithstanding the obscurity of the mysteries, imparts to our intellect a firmness or a greater certainty than that enjoyed by any natural science. St. Augustine says: "It would be easier for me to doubt that I am living than to doubt what I have heard (from God) to be true." [50] What indeed Christ says, "Heaven and earth shall pass away; but My word shall not pass away," [51] is therefore most firmly to be held as true. Hence St. Paul says: "But though we, or an angel from heaven preach a gospel to you besides that which we have preached to you, let him be anathema." [52] Hence, according to the teaching of St. Thomas,[53] infused faith, not only as it is in itself, and as if it were in the air, external to us, but as it is in us, is more certain than the first principles of reason, because its formal motive, namely, the authority of God revealing, surpasses in validity the evidence of reason, or the power of the light of reason. But sacred theology, since its motive is virtual revelation, though it is inferior to faith, shares in this certitude of faith which we truly possess.

Nevertheless faith and theology are less certain to us because an obscure object but partially dispels the doubt arising in our mind, but imperfectly corresponds to the connatural mode of knowing by our intellect.[54] St. Thomas says: "Certitude can be looked at in two ways. First, on the part of its cause (in itself); and thus a thing which has a more certain cause, is itself more certain. In this way faith is more certain than those three virtues (i.e., all natural knowledge); because it is founded on the divine truth, whereas the aforesaid three virtues are based on human reason. Secondly, certitude may be considered on the part of the subject (for us), and thus the more a man's intellect lays hold of a thing, the more certain it is. In this way faith is less certain" than the evidence of natural

---

49 Cf. Gonet, *Clypeus theol. thomist.*, I, commentary on this article.
50 *Confessions*, Bk. VII, chap. 10.
51 Mark 13: 31.
52 Gal. 1: 8.
53 *Summa theol.*, IIa IIae, q.4, a.8.
54 Consult the commentaries of Cajetan, John of St. Thomas, and Gonet.

knowledge, because our intellect does not so connaturally and fully attain an obscure as an evident object. Obscure objects do not give us that pleasure and fruition which evident ones do. But St. Thomas goes on to say: "Each thing is judged simply with regard to its cause, but relatively with respect to a disposition on the part of the subject; hence faith is more certain simply, while the others are more certain relatively, i.e., for us." [55] But theology, since the source from which it argues is infused faith, shares in the certitude of faith.

So "we have this treasure (of faith) in earthen vessels," [56] but we have it. It is in us. This means that faith and also theology are more certain in themselves and in us than any natural knowledge whatever, although they are not so to us. Hence, if doubts suddenly arise on account of the obscurity of the object, these are merely subjective, resulting from the weakness of our intellect, but not from the formal motive of the habits of either faith or theology.

In this matter we must therefore take care to distinguish between the two expressions *in us* and *to us*. We have an example of this in the principle of finality. That every agent acts for an end is more certain in itself and in us than the objective existence of colors. Yet this existence of colors is to us (at least for many, for the majority of mankind) more certain than the principle of finality. All see colors by the sense of sight, but all do not perceive intellectually the absolute necessity and universality of the principle of finality. So, in like manner, faith in the Trinity is more certain in itself and in us than the existence of colors, but it is less certain to us. The reason is that the Trinity is the object most removed from the senses, from which our knowledge originates.

On the contrary, some cling most tenaciously to improbable opinions, for example, to political opinions. The formal heretic persists obstinately in his error, which is not in itself anything certain but is something stubbornly inhering in this badly disposed subject. Some do not firmly assent to truths that in themselves are most certain, and others cling most tenaciously either to the poorest of opinions, or to errors. Thus it is quite clear that there is a distinction between what is certain in itself and what is certain for us.

Therefore sacred theology is nobler than all the other sciences. It is so objectively because of the dignity of the object, and subjectively because of the greater certitude accruing to it from the divine light.

Second doubt. How is it that sacred theology is nobler than the sciences from which it accepts anything? It accepts a number of

[55] *Summa theol.,* IIa IIae, q.4, a.8.
[56] II Cor. 4: 7.

principles from metaphysics and therefore seems to be inferior to it; as optics, accepting something from geometry, is inferior to this latter, as being a subalternate science.

In the reply to the second objection it is stated that sacred theology does not accept its principles from other sciences, for these principles are revealed by God; but it accepts from them a certain means for the better manifestation of revealed truths, and thus it makes use of these sciences as being inferior to it and ancillary. It makes use of them, indeed, not because of any defect on its part but on that of our intellect, which is more easily led by means of natural things to acquire a certain understanding of supernatural truths.

This reply is profound and contains several points worthy of note. If sacred theology were to accept its principles from metaphysics, it would be subordinated to this latter, as optics is to geometry. But it accepts them only as the means for the greater manifestation of the revealed truths.

Thus sacred theology makes use of the natural sciences in accordance with the proper meaning of the word "use." In the strict sense of the term, only the superior makes use of the inferior, that is, ordains the action of the inferior in co-operating with the superior's action, which is ordained to a higher end. Thus the writer uses his pen, the painter his brush, the general of the army his soldiers, the finer arts the inferior, as the art of navigation avails itself of the constructive art of shipbuilding. In like manner sacred theology, as the superior science, makes use of metaphysics as the inferior and the handmaid. Thus metaphysics, for instance, the metaphysics of Aristotle, serves a much higher end. The Aristotelian notion of predicamental relation, for instance, is for us instrumental in acquiring a certain knowledge of the Trinity. Aristotle could not foresee so great an honor and glory for his metaphysics that it would serve the uses of the higher science of God. Thus metaphysics is not despised but is honored, just as that citizen is honored who is at the king's immediate disposal; for it is better to obey a king than to rule over a household, and this because of the high end in view for the attainment of which this collaboration is given.

Hence, as John of St. Thomas correctly observes, when sacred theology makes use of natural premises, a metaphysical truth, for example, it makes use of this as a means. But a means, such as a pen or brush, acts in virtue of the power transmitted to it by another, and is at the same time applied to its act and elevated by the motion of the principal agent, so as to produce an effect that transcends its own power. Thus by means of the motion imparted to the pen by the writer, it not only deposits the ink on the paper, but it writes something intelligible; and the brush not only puts the colors on the canvas, but arranges them most beautifully and artistically. In like manner, according to the navigator's instructions, the shipwright constructs a vessel that is seaworthy. So also sacred theology uses the natural premise taken, for instance, from metaphysics. It first approves of the premise for this purpose under the guidance of the divine light of revelation, at least negatively, according as this natural premise is not in opposition to what has been revealed. Then it makes use of this premise not only by a motion that applies the same to act but also by a motion that is instrumental in the attainment of its higher end. This end is a certain understanding of the supernatural mysteries either in themselves (if it is a case of an explicative process of reasoning), or as regards their consequences, corollaries (if it is a case of an illative process of reasoning). Therefore the theological conclusion thus obtained, although it has less certainty than a proposition of the faith, has more certainty than a natural premise as such, because it is deduced from this premise which has been elevated and clarified by a higher light. Thus also in this case, the instrument produces an effect that transcends its own power and it operates by way of disposing for the effect of the principal agent.

It must be noted that great doctors, such as St. Augustine, produced even with a most imperfect instrument, for instance, with Neoplatonic philosophy, a wonderful theological work. It was in this way that St. Augustine wrote his books on the Trinity. Thus great painters sometimes paint a beautiful picture with a most imperfect brush. And besides, in these great doctors, faith, illuminated by the gifts of understanding and wisdom, makes up for the deficiency of the instrument, or of philosophy.[57]

The philosophy, however, to which St. Thomas had recourse was more exact because Aristotle enunciated with great precision the philosophical notions and metaphysical principles, as Euclid did the elements of geometry. Thus St. Thomas excels in both kinds of wisdom, namely, acquired wisdom which is the result of the perfect functioning of reason, and infused wisdom which proceeds according to a connaturalness of judgment with things divine under the inspiration of the Holy Ghost.[58]

In other words, a natural premise is in some way elevated so as to manifest the supernatural order, and it receives a somewhat greater certitude than it would have in its own right; for it is judged by faith and theology, corrected (if it needs to be) and approved by them. Thus St. Thomas in his treatise on the Trinity

[57] Cf. J. Maritain, *Les degrés du savoir*, Part II, chap. 7.
[58] *Summa theol.*, IIa IIae, q.45, a.1 f.

approves of and in some measure corrects the Aristotelian distinction between principle and cause, by showing that in the divine Persons the Father is the principle of the Son but not the cause. We have some evidence of this from experience. We are conscious of assenting with greater certainty to natural truths discovered by us, when we see that they have the approval of the leading doctors, especially when we see that they have divine confirmation and approval.

Even a natural premise which in itself would be only probable would not become certain by reason of its connection with a principle that is of faith, nor would it lead to a theologically certain conclusion; it would only be probable. But if it is certain in itself, it becomes more certain in proportion as it is clarified by a higher light. Thus the philosopher who already has metaphysical certainty of God's existence before he receives infused faith, is after its reception more certain of this truth, since infused faith confirms from on high this metaphysical certitude. These statements are true even for the strictly illative process of reasoning, and more so for the explicative process.

From what has been said it is evident that sacred theology is a science subordinated not to metaphysics but solely to the science possessed by God, and by the blessed; for, as regards its own intrinsic principles, it depends solely upon divine revelation. But theology from its exalted position makes use of natural principles as strangers to it, and it makes use of them not because of any deficiency in itself, but because of the deficiency of our intellect, which is incapable of knowing the truths that are implicitly and virtually contained in the revealed principles solely by the light of faith. Now the angelic intellect, since it is not discursive, does not thus stand in need of this additional natural knowledge so that it may have a certain understanding of supernatural mysteries. For the angel immediately sees the conclusion contained in the principles, the properties in the essence, and thus it immediately knows all the properties of man from the very concept of the human nature. Hence the angel, without any discursive process, immediately understands in this revealed truth, "The Word was made flesh," [59] what we deduce only by a slow process of reasoning.

It follows from this that the certitude of a strictly theological conclusion is less than the certitude of infused faith, but it is greater than the certitude of the natural sciences, even of metaphysics. The certitude of the theological conclusion improperly so called, of the conclusion that is obtained by the explicative process of reasoning, is less than the certitude of faith; but it acquires the

[59] John 1: 14.

certitude of faith, if by the special assistance of the Holy Spirit it is defined by the Church. Then it must be firmly accepted not because it has been proved by an explicative process of reasoning, but because "it hath seemed good to the Holy Ghost." [60]

Objection. The conclusion in a syllogism follows from the weaker premise. But the theological conclusion often results from a premise that is only naturally certain. Therefore then the conclusion is only naturally certain, for it follows from the weaker premise.

We reply with Gonet by distinguishing the major. If the premises equally influence the conclusion, then I concede the major; if one is the instrument of the other under the guidance of a higher light, then I deny it. I contradistinguish the minor: that the theological conclusion often results from a natural premise which is the instrument of another premise that is of faith, under the guidance of a higher light, this I concede; that this natural premise equally influences the conclusion, this I deny. And I deny the consequent and the consequence. Nevertheless, we may still say that the aforesaid logical axiom is in some manner verified since the theological conclusion is not so certain as the premise that is of faith. For to a theological conclusion strictly so called we cannot firmly assent solely on the authority of God revealing, but we assent to it partly on the evidence of reason; although faith makes use of reason in the deduction of this new truth that is only virtually contained in revelation. Such is the case if the natural premise is the major rather than the minor.

Third doubt. Is theology an essentially supernatural habit? It is the common teaching of the Thomists that sacred theology is essentially or intrinsically a natural habit; infused faith, this being however, its extrinsic root, is essentially supernatural. Contenson disagreed with them on this point.

The reason is that theology is a habit acquired by human effort, that is, by natural acts of understanding which are acquired and not infused.[61] Moreover, the formal object *quod* of theology, which is God, specifies it only in that it underlies the formal object *quo*. And this formal object *quo*, or light, is not formal but virtual revelation, which means that it is the light of reason deducing from revelation the conclusions virtually contained in this latter. The object of theology is God not formally revealed but virtually revealed. Nevertheless the extrinsic root of theology is infused faith, and this is essentially supernatural as regards both formal objects *quod* and *quo*; so that, as we said, with the removal of faith by formal heresy, we no longer have theology but merely its corpse,

[60] Acts 15: 28.
[61] See a.6 ad 3um.

because there is wanting that formal connection between the ideas
effected by the principles of faith.

Hence there are some theologians, like St. Bernard, who excel in
faith, this being of a higher order and intense, and these are holier.
Others, like Abélard, excel in dialectic, or in reason or the instrument of faith. There are some saints who have no knowledge of
theology but they have great faith, which means that their lives
are spent in a most profound contemplation of the mysteries of
Christ; the faith of these is most intense and deep. On the other
hand, there are many theologians whose faith is not so intense and
profound, but they have a more extensive knowledge of what has
been defined by the Church and of very many theological conclusions. The intensive increase of faith, however, is of more importance than its extensive increase.

SIXTH ARTICLE

WHETHER SACRED THEOLOGY IS THE SAME AS WISDOM

State of the question. We have seen that sacred theology is a
science subordinated to the science possessed by God, that it is eminently speculative and practical. The question is whether it is worthy
of the name of wisdom, as is the case with metaphysics or first philosophy among the sciences of the natural order.

The difficulty is that: (1) sacred theology borrows its principles
from a higher science, and therefore is subordinate to this science,
whereas "it is for the wise man to direct," [62] and not to be directed;
(2) sacred theology does not prove or defend from on high the
principles of the other sciences, as metaphysics, which treats of
being, does by defending the principles invoked by the other
sciences; (3) sacred theology does not seem to be supernatural wisdom, because this latter is infused, and is not acquired by human
effort.

The reply, however, to this is that sacred theology is wisdom above
all other human wisdom. Sacred doctrine is often called wisdom in
Holy Scripture.[63] St. Paul, comparing God's wisdom with the wisdom of this world, says: "Howbeit we speak wisdom among the
perfect: yet not the wisdom of this world, neither of the princes
of this world that come to naught. But we speak the wisdom of God
in a mystery, a wisdom which is hidden. . . . For the Spirit searcheth all things, yea, the deep things of God." [64] St. Paul speaks in

---

[62] Aristotle, *Metaph.*, Bk. I.

[63] Cf. Deut. 6: 6, quoted by St. Thomas in this article; and especially Wis.,
chaps. 5–7.

[64] 1 Cor. 2: 6 f., 10.

this text, indeed, of revealed sacred doctrine, of faith illuminated by the gifts of the Holy Ghost. But sacred theology, which is acquired by human effort, proceeds from this faith, and thus it participates in the perfection of wisdom.

In the body of the article St. Thomas has recourse to the philosophical notion of wisdom as determined by Aristotle,[65] who shows that metaphysics is not only a science, but wisdom, or the highest of sciences, because it is the knowledge of things acquired not only through their causes, but through the highest of causes. St. Thomas retains this notion of wisdom in the present article and in other parts of the *Summa*.[66]

The doctrine of the article is briefly expressed as follows: Wisdom is the knowledge of things through their highest cause. But sacred theology essentially treats of God, the highest cause, also so far as He is known to Himself alone and to others by revelation. Therefore sacred theology is first of all wisdom, and more so than metaphysics.

The major is the very definition of wisdom established by Aristotle.[67] In this article St. Thomas briefly shows the validity of this real definition, beginning with the nominal. For, according to the nominal definition, wisdom is something of eminence in the cognitive order; thus we have the common saying that it is for the wise man to direct and judge. But a scientific judgment about a thing is obtained through its causes, inquiring what the thing is in itself, what are its efficient and final causes. The highest judgment is therefore obtained through the highest of causes. Thus wisdom surpasses the sciences, since science pure and simple is knowledge through proximate causes, but wisdom is knowledge through the highest of causes. Thus metaphysics treats of being as such through its highest causes, and it therefore does not reach perfection unless it acquires a definite idea of creation or of the production of the totality of finite being from nothing, and of the end of creation, which is the manifestation of God's goodness. Aristotle did not acquire this definite idea that can be known by the natural power of reason, and which, moreover, is equivalently expressed in the first words of the Bible: "In the beginning God created heaven and earth." [68]

The nominal definition of sacred theology and the preceding remarks establish the evidence of the minor. For theology is the knowledge of God derived from revelation. Hence "it essentially

[65] *Metaph.*, Bk. I, chaps. 1 f.
[66] Cf. *Summa theol.*, Ia, q.14, a.1 ad 2um; Ia IIae, q.57, a.2 ad 1um.
[67] *Metaph.*, Bk. I, chaps. 1 f.
[68] Gen. 1: 1.

treats of God viewed as the highest cause," [69] and not only as He is the cause of the being as such of created things, but as He is the cause of grace and glory, that is, as He is the Author of salvation. The reason is that it treats of God not only so far as He can be known naturally from creatures, but also so far as He is known to Himself alone and made known to others through revelation.

In other words, sacred theology not only treats of God as He is the first Being, the self-subsisting Being, and the cause of beings as such, but it treats of God in His intimate life or under the aspect of the Deity. This is what St. Paul said: "But to us God hath revealed them by His Spirit. For the Spirit searcheth all things, yea, the deep things of God," [70] or God's intimate life. That is, the object expressed in this utterance is God under the aspect of the Deity, because the Deity contains formally and eminently all absolutely simple perfections such as being, unity, truth, goodness . . . , in which creatures are naturally capable of participation; whereas the Deity is not capable of participation except by grace, which makes us "partakers of the divine nature." [71] Thus the Deity in a certain manner transcends being and the one, since it contains all these perfections formally and eminently in its higher eminence. It contains them more so than whiteness contains the seven colors of the rainbow, which are included in it not formally and eminently but only virtually and eminently. [72]

Hence sacred theology is especially wisdom because it treats essentially of God, the highest cause, in His intimate life. Nevertheless theology, especially that of the wayfarer, does not attain to a quiddative knowledge of God as He is in Himself; it does not see the Deity, but reaches this in the midst of faith, especially when it discusses the mystery of the Trinity. Thus sacred theology can from on high judge of all created things and of human life, namely, through the highest cause of being and of grace, and through the ultimate end not only natural but also supernatural.

In the reply to the first objection it is stated that sacred theology derives its principles not from any human knowledge but from the divine science, and thus it remains wisdom. Its principles are especially the fourteen articles of faith from which also the other articles of faith can be deduced.

First doubt. How does sacred theology judge of other sciences? In his reply to the second objection St. Thomas says that:

1) "Theology is not concerned with proving the principles of

---

[69] *Summa theol.,* Ia, q.1, a.6.
[70] I Cor. 2: 10.
[71] II Pet. 1: 4.
[72] Cf. *infra,* q.13, a.3, 5.

other sciences," because its proper sphere of action extends to what has been supernaturally revealed, and the principles of the natural sciences are either directly known or are proved in a subalternating science, as geometry proves the principles of optics. In like manner metaphysics defends the first principles of reason.

2) Sacred theology judges, however, of the other sciences, and this in two ways. It judges negatively, because "whatever is found in other sciences contrary to any truth of this science must be condemned as false." Thus many hypotheses that have not been scientifically proved, from the very fact that they are contrary to divine revelation are repudiated by theology. But it positively approves of a certain proposition of metaphysics or of natural philosophy or of ethics, according as it is otherwise revealed, or at least is in conformity with revelation. Thus it approves of propositions about the immortality of the soul or the foundation of moral obligation or the distinction between virtuous, pleasant, and useful good.

Corollary. Thus the legitimate and relative autonomy of the natural sciences is preserved intact according as they proceed from their own naturally known principles and make use of their own method, as the Vatican Council states.[73] But they cannot affirm as a scientific certainty what is contrary to revealed truth, because truth does not contradict itself.[74] Hence the rationalist assertion of the absolute autonomy of reason was condemned by the Vatican Council in the following words: "If anyone shall say that human reason is so independent that faith cannot be enjoined upon it by God, let him be anathema." [75]

Thus there are several declarations of the Church about the benefits of revelation. By means of it reason is freed from error, enlightened and confirmed in truth.[76] It upholds the certainty and purity of natural knowledge; [77] it is the infallible guide of philosophy,[78] and its indispensable norm; [79] not only the philosopher but even philosophy is subject to its teaching authority.[80] In the Syllabus of Pius IX the following proposition is condemned against moderate rationalism: "As the philosopher is one thing, and philosophy another, so it is the right and duty of the philosopher to subject himself to the authority which he shall have proved to be true; but philosophy neither can nor ought to submit to any

---

[73] Cf. Denz., no. 1799.
[74] *Ibid.*, nos. 1797 f., 1878 f.
[75] *Ibid.*, no. 1810; see also no. 1789.
[76] *Ibid.*, nos. 1799, 1807.
[77] *Ibid.*, no. 1786.
[78] *Ibid.*, nos. 1656, 1681.
[79] *Ibid.*, no. 1714.
[80] *Ibid.*, nos. 1656, 1674 f., 1682 f., 1710, 1714, 2073, 2085 f.

such authority." [81] This is practically the same assertion as that condemned as heretical by the Vatican Council, which reads: "Human reason is so independent that faith cannot be enjoined upon it by God." [82] This latter assertion is tantamount to saying that the formal motive of a philosophical admission does not come within the scope of the formal motive of infused faith, namely, the authority of God revealing, and thus in the final analysis the certitude of infused faith would rest not only materially and extrinsically but even formally and intrinsically upon the natural evidence of the signs of revelation. Thus human reason would remain the supreme judge of truth and falsehood. This was the semi-rationalist error of Gunther, Hermes, and the Modernists.

Second doubt. How does theological wisdom differ from the gift of wisdom? St. Thomas answers this question in his reply to the third objection of this article, and more explicitly when he discusses the gift of wisdom. [83] Theological wisdom, which is acquired by human effort guided by the light of divine revelation, judges according to the perfect use of reason, namely, by analyzing the concepts of the principles of faith or of the enunciation of the mysteries, and by deducing the conclusions contained in these principles. Contrary to this, the infused gift of wisdom, under the special inspiration of the Holy Ghost, transcending the discursive method, judges of divine things by way of an inclination or connaturalness for them, and it has its foundation in charity. This connaturalness arising from charity, is a loving sympathy, and by means of this quality the revealed mysteries manifest themselves not only as true, as revealed by God, but as most good since they admirably correspond to our higher aspirations.

So also in the natural order, there are two ways of judging, for instance, in questions of morality. It is accomplished either by way of scientific knowledge, as he judges who is well versed in moral science even though he is not virtuous; or it is accomplished by way of an inclination, as he who is virtuous, who is chaste, for instance, even though he has no knowledge of moral science, judges well of those things that pertain to chastity, because these are in conformity with his virtuous inclination. According to each one's inclination or affection, so does he see the fitness of the end, said Aristotle. Wherefore the prudent judgment is said to be practically true by reason of its conformity with a right appetite, that is, with an upright intention, even though it is speculatively false because of an

[81] *Ibid.*, no. 1710.
[82] *Ibid.*, no. 1810.
[83] Cf. *Summa theol.*, IIa IIae, q.45, a.2.

involuntary error.[84] Thus prudence presupposes all the moral virtues and without it they cannot be virtues. In like manner, knowledge that is the fruit of the gift of wisdom, presupposes charity, whereas acquired theology remains in a theologian who is in a state of mortal sin.

The reply to the third objection of this article must be carefully read and compared with what St. Thomas has to say later on about this subject.[85] Some who read these passages superficially, see in the knowledge resulting from the gift of wisdom but a loving connaturalness for divine things (and this is already present in the act of living faith that is informed by charity, even without the special inspiration of the Holy Ghost). What others perceive is this special inspiration, but they do not sufficiently advert to the fact that the Holy Spirit by means of this special inspiration makes use of the aforesaid loving connaturalness to manifest how excellent are the mysteries of faith, in that they admirably satisfy our nobler aspirations: "O taste and see that the Lord is sweet." [86] If this special inspiration of the Holy Ghost is not considered, one fails to understand why Hierotheus is said "to be patient of divine things."

Great theologians excel in both kinds of wisdom. Thus knowledge that is not discursive and that is the result of the gift of wisdom, illustrates and confirms from on high the discursive knowledge of acquired theology. This is clearly seen in the writings of St. Augustine and not infrequently this reinforcement from on high in some way makes up for the imperfection that is of philosophical formation.

Another corollary. Apologetics is not a science specifically distinct from sacred theology, but it is theology functioning according to the principles of reason, and pertains to it, inasmuch as theology is wisdom and inasmuch as it defends the principles of faith and adheres to the same against those denying them. This has been more fully explained in another of our works.[87] It will be made clearer in the eighth article, in which it is said that theology defends its principles against those who deny them, and it does not leave this defense to another science, because it is wisdom or the highest of the acquired sciences. But in this rational or apologetic function of theology, it makes use of history and philosophy.

[84] *Ibid.*, Ia IIae, q.57, a.5 ad 3um.
[85] *Ibid.*, IIa IIae, q.45, a.2.
[86] Ps. 33: 9.
[87] Cf. *De revelatione*, I, chaps. 2 f.

SEVENTH ARTICLE

WHETHER GOD IS THE SUBJECT OF THIS SCIENCE

State of the question. At first sight is seems that this article comes rather late in the discussion, because a science is specified by its proper object or subject, and from this its definition is derived, its properties are deduced, and its relations are established to the other sciences either inferior or superior.

Nevertheless, if the difficulties propounded at the beginning of this article are carefully considered, we see that it is in the right place here as being a recapitulation of the preceding articles and the goal of the hunt or search for the real scientific definition of sacred theology. The nominal definition of sacred theology, that it is the science of God derived from revelation, sufficed for the preceding articles.

It is now formally and explicitly determined why the subject of sacred theology is not, as some said, either Christ the mediator, or the sacraments, or the public worship due to God, or supernatural being in general, but God Himself in His intimate life.

The difficulty, however, is that every science knows what its subject is by means of the definition of the same, and from this it deduces the properties. Thus mathematics knows what is quantity, either continuous or discrete, namely, magnitude and number. Likewise natural philosophy knows what is mobile being, and metaphysics what is being as such. Contrary to this, sacred theology does not know properly or quiddatively *what God is*. As Damascene says: "It is impossible to say what God is." [88] To say what the Deity is we should have to see it; the beatific vision, however, is not given to one in this life. Moreover, sacred theology treats not only of God, but also of creatures and of human acts.

The reply, however, is that God is the subject of sacred theology.

1) This is already evident from the nominal definition of theology, since the term implies a discussion about God.

2) The direct proof is as follows: The object of a faculty or the subject of a science is that under the aspect of which all things are referred to the faculty or the science; but all things are considered in sacred theology with reference to God under the aspect of God; therefore God under the aspect of God is the subject of this science.

The major distinguishes to some extent between object and subject. The object is that which is presented to the faculty, and is that which the faculty directly and immediately attains, and hence

[88] *De fide orthod.,* Bk. III, chap. 4.

that under the aspect of which it attains all other things. Thus the object of sight is the colored object seen by sense perception; the object of the intellect is being, but the proper object of the human intellect is intelligible being of sensible things. With reference to science, which demonstrates conclusions about some subject (properties of man, for instance, about man), its object is the demonstrated conclusion or conclusions, but its subject is that which is the subject of the conclusions, or that about which the properties are demonstrated. Object and subject are commonly accepted for the same thing. But, strictly speaking, the subject of metaphysics is being as such, because metaphysics demonstrates the properties of being. The subject of natural philosophy is mobile being, and the subject of psychology is the soul. Hence, if metaphysics treats of God in natural theology, it does not discuss Him as the proper subject but as He is the cause of the being as such of various things.

Likewise the subject of medicine is the human body viewed under the aspect of health; and medicine considers all other things as remedies—salts, for instance, medicinal herbs, and such like—and so far as these have reference to the health of the human body. So also psychology considers the various manifestations of the life of the soul, languages, for instance, so far as these refer to the soul. It does not treat of these as the linguist does. Hence, although the object of a faculty may be something common to many sciences, the subject of a science may be something that is restricted.

The minor is: In sacred theology all things are considered with reference to God under the aspect of God. By logical induction this is evident; for it treats either of God Himself, or of those things that refer to Him as the beginning and end of all things Thus sacred theology in the treatises on God as one, as triune, as creator, as Word made flesh, treats of God as the proper subject, not as metaphysics does, which treats of God as He is the cause of the being as such of various things. Moreover, sacred theology treats of God under the aspect of God or of the Deity, and not only as He is the first Being, which metaphysics does. This means that it treats of God in His intimate life, and it is concerned with the "deep things of God." [89] Therefore all the conclusions of sacred theology are derived from a certainty of knowledge of the Deity transmitted through revelation and directed to a greater knowledge of this Deity, just as all the conclusions of metaphysics presuppose the notion of being and are directed to a more profound knowledge of being, and just as all the conclusions of psychology tend to a greater knowledge of the soul. [90]

[89] I Cor. 2: 10.
[90] See Cajetan's commentary on this article, no. 1.

As long as sacred theology treats of creatures it considers them as they refer to God under the aspect of the Deity, just as medicine considers mineral remedies or medicinal herbs so far as they refer to man's health. This means that sacred theology treats of creatures, in that they are vestiges or images of God, and in that the nobler creatures have been admitted to participate in God's intimate life by grace, and are ordained to see God and love Him above all things.[91] Thus God under the aspect of God is the proper subject of theology; or He is the formal object *quod* of theology made known by the light of virtual revelation. St. Thomas had said in the preceding article that it is "God so far as He is known to Himself alone and revealed to others."

This is confirmed by the following argument: A science and its principles have the same subject, since the whole science is virtually contained in its principles; but God under the aspect of the Deity is the subject of the principles of this science, which are the articles of faith; therefore God is the subject of this science.

St. Thomas enumerates the articles of faith.[92] Four of them concern the one and triune God; three refer to Him as He is the cause of creatures, as also of grace and glory; the rest are about the Word made flesh. All the other truths of faith are referred to these articles of faith. As theology is a science deriving its principles from faith, its object is the same as that of faith, though this object is perceived not by the light of formal but of virtual revelation.

We have as yet to consider the difficulty posited at the beginning of this article, which is to the effect that in this life we cannot know what God is or know His essence. The Deity as such or the divine essence is known through the beatific vision. How can it be said, therefore, that sacred theology is the science that treats of God under the aspect of the Deity?

St. Thomas replies to the first objection by saying that, "although we cannot know what constitutes the essence of God, nevertheless in this science we make use of His effects either of nature or of grace, in place of a definition." Thus we say that sacred theology treats of God as the Author of grace, and this means a formal participation in the Deity. We also know the infinite fecundity within the Deity, in that it is manifested to us through the revealed mystery of the Trinity. Thus we have analogical knowledge of the divine Paternity, the divine Filiation, and the divine Spiration.

As Cajetan remarks,[93] God can be considered: (1) under the

---

[91] See reply to the second objection of this article.
[92] *Summa theol.*, IIa IIae, q.1, a.8.
[93] See his commentary on this article, no. 1.

common concepts of being and act; (2) under the relative concept of supreme cause; (3) under the mixed concept (namely, one that is both common and either relative or negative) of pure act, first being; (4) transcending all these modes, however, God can be considered according to His proper quiddity or essence, "which by way of circumlocution we call the Deity." [94]

We have only the name but not the proper concept of the Deity as such. In this life by this name we understand an eminence that contains formally all absolutely simple perfections, such as being, unity, truth. . . . As regards the Deity we are somehow like one who, having seen the seven colors of the rainbow and knowing of whiteness only by name, would understand that by this name is meant the origin of colors. The difference, however, is this, that whiteness contains colors only virtually, whereas the Deity contains absolutely simple perfections formally and eminently.

At the end of the reply to the first objection, St. Thomas remarks that in some philosophical sciences the effect is taken in place of a definition of the cause. Such is the case in a descriptive definition, for it is only descriptively and, as it were, empirically that we define the species of minerals, plants, and animals, man being the exception. We do not know the essence of the rose, the lion, the eagle. This means that we do not know their distinct specific difference, so as to deduce their properties. The reason is that the substantial forms of these plants and animals are immersed in matter. Man alone among animals is properly defined by means of the specific difference, and from this his properties are deduced, because his form, the rational soul, is not immersed in matter, and the power to reason is a mode of intelligence the object of which is intelligible being. Thus by the light of intelligible being man becomes intelligible to himself; he defines his own nature better than that of a lion or eagle, the forms of which do not transcend the material; and just as the specific difference of the lion and eagle is inferior to our intellectual knowledge, so the Deity, which is, as it were, the specific difference of God, is superior to our natural intellectual knowledge. It remains to be said, however, that the Deity is known in the mist of faith as the root of the divine processions manifesting its fecundity, and as the cause of grace and glory, these being properly the formal participations in the Deity as such, since by these gifts "we are made partakers of the divine nature." [95]

In this sense, therefore, we say that the subject of sacred theology is God under the aspect of the Deity, according as He comes within

[94] *Contra Gentes,* Bk. I, chap. 3.
[95] II Pet. 1: 4.

the scope of virtual revelation. But if we distinguish between its object and subject, then the conclusions about God or those things that are directed to Him constitute its object.

First corollary. Even when sacred theology treats of creatures, of the morality of human acts, God is always its subject, that is, God the Creator or God the ultimate end. On the other hand, the subject of ethics is human action. Thus ethics is specifically distinct from moral theology, just as acquired prudence, described by Aristotle as "the right ordering of things to be done," differs from infused prudence spoken of in the Gospels.[96]

Second corollary. Among the various theological systems, that one approaches closer to the perfection of a theological science which has as its germinating idea and, as it were, as its golden key, the exalted notion of God the Author of grace and salvation, rather than the notion of the created will. The reason is that in theology the idea of God is, as it were, the sun illuminating all things, just as in metaphysics this role belongs to the idea of being as such.

Third corollary. From the fact that God is the proper object of theology, this science begins by treating of God as He is in Himself, then of the procession of creatures from God, and finally of the ordaining of created things to God as to their end. Such is the method employed in the *Theological Summa*.[97] It is the synthetic method of descent from God and a return to Him.

Contrary to this, metaphysics is the science of being as such, of being as previously known by us in sensible things, and it begins to treat of the knowableness of extramental being,[98] of being as divided into substance and accident, potency and act, and it discusses God only at the end of the treatise.[99] Moreover, metaphysics, as a general rule, comes after natural philosophy, since the being of sensible things is what is first known by our intellect. The method in philosophy is analytico-synthetic; it ascends to God, and afterward judges of creatures from its lofty standpoint of reference to the first cause.

This difference must be carefully noted. St. Thomas says: "In the doctrine of philosophy . . . the discussion is first about creatures and finally about God; in the doctrine of faith, which discusses creatures only as they refer to God, God is its first consideration, and then creatures; thus it is more perfect, as being more like God's knowledge."[100] Wherefore the philosophical treatise on the

96 *Summa theol.*, Ia IIae, q.63, a.4.
97 See also *Contra Gentes*, Bk. I, chaps. 3, 9; Bk. II, chaps. 4, 46.
98 *Metaph.*, Bk. IV.
99 *Ibid.*, Bk. XII.
100 *Contra Gentes*, Bk. II, chap. 4.

soul begins by discussing the vegetative and sensitive faculties of the soul and ends by discussing the intellective faculties, the spirituality and immortality of which it finally proves; whereas from the very start the treatise on man,[101] considering the soul as coming from God, treats almost immediately of its incorruptibility and its difference from the angelic nature.

EIGHTH ARTICLE

WHETHER SACRED DOCTRINE IS A MATTER OF ARGUMENT

State of the question. The meaning of the title is: Have those things which sacred doctrine teaches the force of conviction? The difficulty is that what is transmitted to us in theology is believed rather than proved. In fact, it seems that proof would lessen the merit of faith. The reply, however, is that sacred theology is a matter of argument, and this for three reasons:

1) That it may prove, not its principles, but the conclusions to be deduced from them.

2) That it may defend its principles from the revealed truths admitted by the opponent.

3) That it may defend its principles by solving the objections of opponents, if they concede nothing at all of divine revelation.

As regards the proof of conclusions, sacred theology is in this respect like all the sciences. As for the defense of its principles, in this it does not differ from metaphysics which, since it is wisdom, defends its own principles against those denying them, solving their objections at any rate, and proving them to be false or at least not convincing.

Thus Aristotle [102] defends the real validity of the first principle of reason, that is, of the principle of contradiction, and also the validity of reason itself. In this process metaphysics, to be sure, makes use of logic, but it does not leave the defense of its principles to logic, for these are concerned not only with logical being but also with real being. It is the privilege of wisdom as such to defend its principles by the analysis of their concepts and the solution of objections, before it proceeds to the deduction of conclusions. So also sacred theology, inasmuch as it is wisdom, before deducing conclusions analyzes the principles of faith, and defends these principles against those who deny them and, by positive and speculative arguments drawn from revelation, solves the objections. In doing so, sacred theology makes use of history and philosophy.

101 *Summa theol.*, Ia, q.75.
102 *Metaph.*, Bk. IV.

As St. Thomas says: "It refutes those things that are said against the faith by showing that they are false or of no consequence," [103] that is, not convincing. Cajetan admirably says: "There is a difference between the solution of an objection and the proof of a thesis. For a proof is drawn from the evidence of argument . . . ; a solution, however, does not require evidence, but simply that the intellect be not compelled. . . . A solution is also obtained from what does not seem to be false, though it may not be known to be true." [104]

We have an example of this in the case of the Trinity. If it is objected that one and the same nature does not belong numerically to several persons, the theologian replies: that this can be said of a finite nature, I concede; of an infinite nature, that I deny. It is not that the theologian positively knows that the infinite nature pertains to several persons; this he believes and consequently maintains that there is no means of proving the impossibility of this in an infinite nature. Thus the possibility of essentially supernatural mysteries is neither proved nor disproved. But we are reasonably persuaded of the same; it is defended against those denying and it is firmly believed. St. Thomas says: "Therefore what is of faith can be proved by authority alone to those who accept the authority; while as regards others it suffices to prove that what faith teaches is not impossible." [105] John of St. Thomas says: "It is not evident to reason that a proposition contradictory to the faith is in itself false, but simply that the arguments by which it is proved are not cogent." [106]

Essentially supernatural mysteries are, of course, likewise supernatural as to their knowableness, for being and truth are one and the same. Therefore not only the existence of mysteries but even their intrinsic possibility is neither proved nor disproved, but we are reasonably persuaded of the same (by an argument of congruence), and it is firmly believed. If, indeed, it were positively proved, for instance, that the Trinity is really possible, then the fact of its existence would be proved because, in necessary things, what is really possible demands of necessity the existence of the same. And if it were positively proved that the beatific vision or eternal life is really possible, this mystery would transcend our naturally acquired knowledge, not because of its essentially supernatural nature but

[103] *Com. in Boetium de Trinitate,* q.2, a.3.

[104] *Com. in a.8,* nos. 4 f.

[105] *Summa theol.,* Ia, q.32, a.1; also *Contra Gentes,* Bk. I, chap. 8. Such is the common teaching of the theologians. Thus Billuart (*De Deo trino,* diss. prooem, a.4) says: 'The possibility of the Trinity is not proved by a positive and evident argument, but by a negative and probable proof.'

[106] *Com. in Iam,* q.1, a.12, nos. 5 f.

because of its contingency, in that it is a contingent future of the natural order which depends upon God's most free good pleasure, just as the last day of this material world does.

From the privilege sacred theology enjoys as wisdom, it follows, as we already remarked, that apologetics is not a specifically distinct science from sacred theology, but is the same science functioning rationally for the defense of the credibility of the mysteries of faith. Just as the critical part of metaphysics defends the real validity of the first principles of reason and of intellectual evidence, and in this it makes use of logic, so sacred theology defends the credibility of the mysteries of faith, and in this it makes use of history and philosophy, presenting from its lofty standpoint, under the direction of faith, arguments drawn from reason as to the demonstrative force, for instance, of miracles and other signs, so that unbelievers may know from these signs that revelation is a fact and may so present unto God "a reasonable service." [107]

What is the mode of argumentation that is pre-eminently proper to sacred theology?

In the reply to the second objection it is stated that the argumentation is from divine authority, for sacred theology proceeds under the guidance of the light of revelation or of the authority of God revealing.

In this reply to the second objection we have the germ, as it were, of the treatise on the theological sources. Melchior Cano, O.P., was the first in this field. The theological sources are divided as follows:

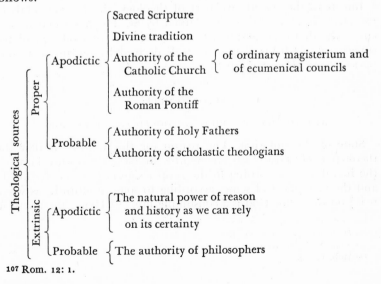

Theological sources	Proper	Apodictic	Sacred Scripture
			Divine tradition
			Authority of the Catholic Church { of ordinary magisterium and of ecumenical councils
			Authority of the Roman Pontiff
		Probable	Authority of holy Fathers
			Authority of scholastic theologians
	Extrinsic	Apodictic	The natural power of reason and history as we can rely on its certainty
		Probable	The authority of philosophers

Cajetan points out [108] that sacred theology makes use of natural or metaphysical reasons, as extrinsic or probable arguments, if these reasons are absolutely considered; it makes use of them as proper and sometimes necessary arguments, if these are considered as ministering to theology, that is, as helping in the deduction of the theological conclusion. But if we use these reasons as persuasive arguments in favor of the possibility of mysteries, then they furnish us with only a probable argument or with one of fitness that may be, however, most profound and always to be examined, but that is not apodictic.

Melchior Cano [109] in treating of history as an extrinsic theological source, holds that, if all the approved and weighty historians concur in admitting the same historical fact, then we have an argument of certainty on their authority.

Hence sacred theology first of all appeals to the argument from authority, and then has recourse to reason for the explanation, defense, right ordering of the authorities, and for the deduction of the conclusions from them.

The method of procedure in sacred theology is explained in the treatise on the theological sources, especially as regards the positive part. It lays down rules for discerning the literal sense of Sacred Scripture, for the discernment of divine tradition, as also for the correct interpretation of the definitions of the solemn utterances of the Church and for the validity of the other decisions. It also decides the doctrinal authority of the Fathers and theologians. It is likewise concerned with the appeal to reason and history.

But as to the speculative part of theology, the fundamentals of the analogical method are explained by St. Thomas when he discusses the divine names; [110] for our knowledge of God and of the supernatural gifts is but analogical, derived by means of a comparison with things in nature.

NINTH ARTICLE

WHETHER HOLY SCRIPTURE SHOULD USE METAPHORS

State of the question. The reason for this inquiry is that the theologian must carefully distinguish in Sacred Scripture between the literal sense according to the proper signification of the words, and the metaphorical sense, according to some similitude, as when it is said that "our God is a consuming fire." [111] Hence the question

[108] *Com. in Iam*, q. 1, a.8, no. 8.
[109] *De locis theologicis*, XI, 4.
[110] *Summa theol.*, Ia, q. 13.
[111] Heb. 12: 29.

is: Why does Sacred Scripture sometimes have recourse to metaphorical language?

The difficulty is: (1) that metaphor fittingly pertains to poetry,
not to the proposition of some truth; and thus it is not allowed in
the sciences; [112] (2) that by metaphors the truth is obscured; (3)
that metaphors taken from corporeal creatures cannot at all represent the purely spiritual life of God.

The answer, however, is: It is befitting Holy Writ to put forward
divine and spiritual truths metaphorically by means of compari-
sons with material things. This is proved in two ways: (1) because
it is natural for man to attain to intellectual truths through sensible objects, and God provides for everything according to the capacity of its nature; (2) because many are unable of themselves to
grasp intellectual things, and Sacred Scripture is proposed to all.
Hence Christ our Lord spoke to the multitude in parables.

Does Sacred Scripture make use of metaphors in the way poetry
does? In the reply to the first objection it is stated that poetry
makes use of metaphors on account of the pleasure derived from
representation, but Sacred Scripture on account of its usefulness.
Farther on,[113] St. Thomas states in substance that poetry makes
use of metaphors because of the lack of appeal on the part of the
object extolled, but theology because of the preponderance of the
divine reality, which cannot be expressed except by way of analogy.

God, however, is analogically made known to us in two ways,
either by proper analogy, as when it is said that God is just; or
by metaphorical analogy, as when it is said that God is angry.[114]

In the reply to the second objection it is pointed out that "those
things which are taught metaphorically in one part of Scripture,
in other parts are taught more openly." Moreover, "the hiding of
truth in figures is useful as a defense against the ridicule of the
impious."

Commenting on the reply to the third objection, regarding metaphors taken from corporeal things, as when it is said that God is a
consuming fire, we say that these are more fitting, in this sense
that they do not permit us to rest the merits of our case in the
similitudes, because God is not a material fire and because this is
said only by way of similitude. On the other hand, when we speak
of the divine perfections in the strict sense, it may be that some
judge of these perfections as being formally and actually distinct
in God as they are in our mind. This would be to detract from
God's absolute simplicity and loftiness of life.

[112] Cf. *Post Anal.*, Bk. II, chap. 12, no. 26.
[113] *Summa theol.*, Ia IIae, q. 101, a. 2.
[114] *Ibid.*, Ia, q. 13, a. 3.

WHETHER IN HOLY SCRIPTURE A WORD MAY HAVE SEVERAL SENSES

State of the question. The special purpose of this article is to distinguish between the literal sense and the spiritual sense in Holy Scripture. The difficulty in admitting several senses is: (1) that many different senses in one text produce confusion; (2) that authors are not fully in agreement about the names to be given to these various senses.

The reply is, however, that in Holy Scripture a word can be used both in the literal or historical sense and in the spiritual sense, which latter is either allegorical or moral or analogical, in accordance with the traditional terminology.

A profound reason is given for this first distinction, namely, that "the Author of Holy Writ is God, in whose power it is to signify His meaning not by words only (as man also can do), but also by things themselves." But what is signified by the words belongs to the literal sense, whereas the signification by which things signified by words have themselves also a signification belongs to the spiritual sense. Thus Job is the figure of Christ suffering, the paschal lamb is the figure of the Lamb who taketh away the sins of the world. Therefore these two senses are fittingly distinguished.

But the spiritual sense (1) is called allegorical so far as the things of the Old Law signify in figure the things of the New Law; (2) it is called moral according as the things done in Christ are types of what we ought to do; (3) it is called anagogical, as the New Law is itself a figure of future glory, as Dionysius says.[115]

So far there is no special difficulty, but St. Thomas furthermore says in the last paragraph of the body of the article: "Since the literal sense is that which the author intends, and since the author of Holy Writ is God, who by one act comprehends all things by His intellect, it is not unfitting, as Augustine says,[116] if, even according to the literal sense, one word in Holy Writ should have several senses." This statement has been and still is a subject of controversy, namely, whether a word can have several senses. St. Thomas seems to affirm this in the passage quoted above,[117] and his leading commentators are generally of the same opinion. Many modern exegetes, however, such as Patrizzi and Cornely, take the opposite view. This question of the many different literal senses in Holy

---

[115] Cf. *Coel. Hier.*, Bk. I, chap. 5.
[116] *Confess.*, Bk. XII, chap. 31.
[117] See also II *Sent.*, d.12, q.1, a.2 ad 7um; *De potentia*, q.4, a.1.

Scripture is explained at length by Father P. V. Zapletal, O.P.[118]
When it is said, for instance, "God created heaven and earth," [119]
the word "heaven" would mean, so says St. Augustine,[120] both the
material heaven and the angels. Or again, when it is said: "Give
us this day our daily bread," this would mean both the ordinary
bread and the supersubstantial bread, explicitly so named in the
Gospel.[121] Let us see first the replies to the objections that are advanced in argument by those who deny the many different literal
senses in Holy Scripture.

In the reply to the first objection it is stated that: "The multiplicity of these senses does not produce equivocation . . . seeing
that these senses (namely, these about which the objection is concerned, the literal sense, and the threefold division of the spiritual
sense) are not multiplied because one word signifies several things,
but because the things signified by the words can be themselves
types of other things."

Some say that in this passage St. Thomas seems to deny the
multiplicity of the literal sense. Many Thomists reply that such is
not the case, because St. Thomas would then contradict himself.
He is now speaking, they say, only of the quadruple sense about
which the objection was concerned, the literal sense, namely, and
the threefold spiritual sense.

In the same reply to the first objection it is furthermore remarked
that: "In Holy Writ no confusion results, for all the senses are
founded on one (the literal) from which alone can any argument
be drawn . . . and nothing necessary to faith is contained under
the spiritual sense which is not elsewhere put forward by the Scripture in its literal sense."

In the reply to the second objection, St. Augustine's terminology
is explained, who called the spiritual sense, for instance, allegorical.

In the reply to the third objection it is stated that the literal
sense is either proper or parabolical, that is, metaphorical. Thus
when God's arm is mentioned, the literal sense is to be taken metaphorically as expressing God's power.

There is still a doubt whether there are not several literal senses
in some texts of Holy Scripture.[122] St. Augustine answers in the
affirmative. Summing up the question, he writes: "When it is said
'In the beginning God created heaven and earth,' it is revealed
that God did not create from eternity and at one and the same time

[118] Cf. *Hermeneutica biblica*, pp. 26–36.
[119] Gen. 1: 1.
[120] *Confess.*, Bk. XII, chaps. 26–32.
[121] Matt. 6: 11.
[122] Cf. P. V. Zapletal, O.P., *loc. cit.*

both the material heaven and the angels, both visible and invisible things; for this truth is afterward held as certainly revealed." [123] St. Augustine remarks that if we perceive this twofold sense, why is it that Moses, guided by the light of inspiration, did not perceive it? St. Gregory the Great says the same.[124]

St. Thomas, says Father Zapletal, frequently speaks of the literal sense in a favorable manner, as he so does at the end of the argumentative part of this article. Likewise in another of his works he writes: "It is not incredible that Moses and other authors were granted by God knowledge of various truths capable of perception by man, and that the one statement of words denotes these truths, so that any one of them may be the meaning intended by the author." [125]

Thus it is not incredible that Moses, inspired to write: "In the beginning God created heaven and earth," understood not only the material and visible heaven, but also the invisible angels, as Augustine says.[126] In like manner, our Lord Jesus, saying that thus we must pray: "Father . . . give us this day our daily bread," [127] could have had in mind both the ordinary bread and supersubstantial bread. The opponents say that this second sense is not literal but spiritual. But it is evidently not so, for the actual words of the first Evangelist are: "Give us this day our supersubstantial bread." [128] Perhaps Jesus said to the multitude "daily bread," and to the apostles "supersubstantial bread."

St. Thomas, who is conservative in his statement, writes: "it is not incredible. . . ." [129] He would have more to say if it were a question only of the spiritual sense, because this latter is quite evident. Hence he is speaking of the twofold literal sense. The majority of the commentators of St. Thomas, as Father Zapletal points out, admitted the multiplicity of the literal sense. Among these are Cajetan, Cano,[130] Bannez, Sylvius, John of St. Thomas, and Billuart.[131] Against this multiplicity of senses are quoted, among the earlier

[123] St. Augustine, *loc. cit.*
[124] Cf. *in Ezech.* 3: 13.
[125] *De potentia*, q.4, a.1.
[126] St. Augustine, *loc. cit.*
[127] Luke 11: 2–3.
[128] Matt. 6: 11.
[129] *De potentia*, q.4, a.1.
[130] *De locis theol.*, Bk. II, chap. 11 ad 7um, arg. ad 3am rationem.
[131] Many of them, such as Bannez, quote as example the following verse: "In the beginning God created heaven and earth." They say that the words *"in the beginning"* mean: (1) in the beginning of time, so that the world is not eternal; (2) it was created before all things, which means that the angels were not created before the material world. Billuart discusses this point in his treatise *De regulis fidei*, diss. Ia, a.8.

theologians, Alexander of Hales, St. Bonaventure, and St. Albert the Great who said: "Theology gives one meaning to a word." [132] Of the same opinion are most of the modern exegetes, who bring forward the objection that, if there were several literal senses, the result would be confusion and equivocation. This is their chief reason.

In reply to this we say that if the names used were equivocal, as in the case of dog used to denote the terrestrial animal and the heavenly constellation, then I concede the assertion; but if the names are analogous, then I deny it. Thus heaven denotes both the starry firmament and the angels, and bread is understood in the ordinary sense of the term and it also means the Holy Eucharist. But if it is a case of two subordinated analogates, or of two that are co-ordinated under a higher, and if no false sense arises from this, then there is no equivocation. [133]

It is still a disputed question. The following argument may be advanced in favor of those who admit a twofold literal sense. If men can utter words that have a twofold literal sense and that are most intelligible to an intelligent hearer, much more so can God do this, who is the author of Holy Scripture. But intelligent men frequently utter words that have a twofold literal sense and that can easily be understood. Thus at a certain banquet a prelate who was a moderate Thomist said to another prelate who was of the rigid type: "Do you want a little water in your wine?" The rigid Thomist perceived quite well the twofold literal sense in the words, the first being a reference to the mixing of water with the wine, the other to the moderation of Thomism. His answer therefore was: "I admit only one drop of water in the wine of the Mass." There was likewise in these words a twofold literal sense: (1) the obvious sense; (2) the metaphorical literal sense, the one however primarily meant, namely, that there must be no mitigation in the soundest of doctrine. Thus it is said that W. Goethe sometimes assigned a twofold literal sense to his verses, so that at least the more intelligent readers might perceive this second sense. This frequently is the case when persons of great culture converse.

[132] *Summa theol.*, I, tr. 1, q.5, memb. 2 ad 5um.
[133] John of St. Thomas (*in Iam*, disp. 12, a.12) says: "Nor does it follow that there is equivocation or confusion from such plurality of senses, and this for two reasons: (1) because there is often a certain similarity or order among these senses, for where there is order, there is no equivocation; (2) because a multiplicity of senses results in equivocation when it is the occasion of deception, or when there is a possibility of falsity in the other sense. But when each sense is true, as must be the case by the very fact that it is said of God in the literal sense, then there is no occasion either for equivocation or deception. It is due, however, to the element of mystery and the excellence of the speaker that he can in one utterance include and denote several senses."

But if men can so express themselves, why could not God, and even Moses, have attached a twofold sense to the words: "In the beginning God created heaven" (namely, the material heaven and the angels). And why could not these words, "Give us this day our daily bread," have a twofold literal sense, the one referring to ordinary bread and the other to supersubstantial bread?

But the opponents would say that in these examples one of the senses is literal (as in the case of ordinary bread and the material heaven), whereas the other sense is spiritual, since bread in the usual sense of the term is the symbol of the other kind, and since the material heaven is the quasi abode of the angels. Hence it is not quite clear that there are two literal senses; but neither is the contention of the opponents an established fact. It is therefore a probable opinion, if the question concerns the presence of a two-fold literal sense in certain texts, and a more than probable opinion if it is a question of the possibility of these two senses.

As for the words, "In the beginning God created heaven and earth," it is not quite clear that there are two literal senses. However, the Fourth Lateran Council discovers two truths in this text, namely, that God did not create the world from eternity, and that "He created out of nothing, from the beginning of time, both the spiritual and corporeal creature, to wit, the angelic and the mundane," [134] which means that the angels were not created before corporeal creatures. Hence this council seems to understand, as St. Augustine did, that the words, "In the beginning God created heaven," mean that He created at one and the same time, the heavenly bodies and the angels.

We must conclude that the possibility of a word having two literal senses appears to be a certainty, but that there are actually two senses is but a probability. Therefore St. Thomas says: "It is not incredible that Moses and other authors were granted by God knowledge of various truths capable of perception by man, and that one statement of words denotes these truths, so that any one of them may be the meaning intended by the author." [135]

Thus we bring to an end the question on sacred doctrine, a question in which the holy Doctor determined the nature and dignity of sacred theology, effecting this by an examination of its object and of the light from which it proceeds. He also determined its method of argumentation and the various senses of Holy Scripture.

[134] Denz., no. 428.
[135] *De potentia, loc. cit.*

CHAPTER II

THE prologue to this question is concerned with the orderly arrangement of the whole *Theological Summa*. The definition of sacred theology, however, is the foundation for this division; for it is the knowledge of God as such, as acquired by the light of revelation. Hence it follows that theology must treat: (1) of God in Himself,[1] and as He is the principle of creatures, especially of rational creatures; (2) of the rational creature's advance toward God as its end; (3) of Christ, who as man, is our way to God. Thus there are three parts to the *Theological Summa*.

It must be noted that the order is not philosophical but strictly theological. St. Thomas says: "For in the teaching of philosophy, which considers creatures in themselves and leads us from them to the knowledge of God, the first consideration is about creatures, and the last about God; whereas in the teaching of faith, which considers creatures only in their relation to God, the consideration about God takes the first place, and that about creatures the last. And thus it is more perfect as being more like God's knowledge; for He beholds other things by knowing Himself." [2]

This theological order is known as the synthetic order. It begins by considering the higher and more universal things in causation, and it descends to the lower and less universal; and this is in accordance with the very order of nature and causality.

Moreover, in this order, those things that are necessary receive first consideration, which, in the first and second parts of the *Summa,* are God and created natures, especially human nature. These are considered before the great contingent fact of the Incarnation of the divine Word for the redemption of the human race in accordance with the following statement in the Apostle's Creed: "Who for us men and for our salvation came down from heaven."

---

1 The prologue says: "God, as He is in Himself," that is, as He is the principle and end of creatures. This expression, however, does not mean "just as He is," because it is only in the beatific vision that God is known "just as He is."

2 Cf. *Contra Gentes*, Bk. II, chap. 4, § 3.

Finally, this order is of the nature of a complete revolution, in that its starting-point is God, the beginning of all things; and in the treatise on the last things it returns to this same starting-point, which is God, the ultimate end of all things. Thus it embraces everything, and for this reason the work is truly a *Summa* in which the dogmatic and moral parts of sacred theology are united under one formal aspect.

It is not exactly the same order that is observed in the *Summa Contra Gentes,* because in that work St. Thomas proceeds by the apologetic method. Yet it is not a philosophical summa that begins with a consideration of creatures, for it begins with a consideration of God Himself. In the first three books, however, God and creatures are considered according to what can be known of these by reason alone, whereas in the fourth book strictly supernatural mysteries are discussed, such as the Trinity and the Incarnation.

Although St. Thomas proceeds by the synthetic method in these two theological works, nevertheless, in beginning the treatise by considering the question of the demonstration of God's existence, he brings together arguments which had been given by Aristotle.[3] Thus he makes use of them, as was said, "not because of the defect or insufficiency of sacred theology, but because of the defect of our intelligence, which is more easily led by what is known through natural reason (from which proceed the other sciences), to that which is above reason, such as are the teachings of this science."[4] It is, indeed, under the guidance of a higher light that this assembly of philosophical arguments concerning God's existence is effected, and by this means certitude rests on more solid grounds.

There is a threefold division in the first part of the *Summa.* Here are considered: (1) whatever pertains to the divine essence, or *de Deo uno;* (2) whatever pertains to the distinction of Persons, or *de Deo trino;* (3) whatever pertains to the procession of creatures from God, or *de Deo creante et elevante.*

The treatise on the one God is likewise divided into three parts. First, whether God exists (q. 2). Secondly, the manner of His existence, or rather, what is not the manner of His existence. This is discussed from the third question to the end of the thirteenth, in which the metaphysical attributes of God are considered, many of them expressed in the negative form, such as the simplicity, the perfection, the infinity, the immutability, and the unity of God. These pertain to God as He is in Himself, and are considered from the third question to the end of the eleventh. Then in the twelfth

---

[3] *Physics,* Bk. VIII; *Metaph.,* Bk. XII.
[4] *Summa theol.,* Ia, q. 1, a. 5 ad 2um.

and thirteenth questions God is discussed in His relation to us, how He is known and named by us. The analogical method is employed here, namely, the method of speculative theology. Thirdly, whatever concerns God's operation is discussed from the fourteenth question to the end of the twenty-sixth. In these questions the knowledge, life, will, love, justice, mercy, providence, predestination, power, and beatitude of God are considered.

From this division it is already apparent that the theological treatise on the one God is concerned with several truths that cannot be known by reason alone. Such are the beatific vision (q. 12), God's providence even as it concerns those creatures that are of the supernatural order, or predestination (q. 23). These must be the subject of special consideration, because there are other attributes that have already been discussed by philosophy in their metaphysical aspect.

It must be pointed out that this order proposed by St. Thomas is a great improvement upon the order established by Peter Lombard in the *Books of the Sentences.* This theologian, as we remarked, divides the subject matter not as it refers to God (the subject of sacred theology), but as it refers to the human will, the two acts of which are enjoyment and use. Thus his treatise is concerned first of all with those things in which we must find our delight, with those things that bring us happiness, namely, with the Father, the Son, and the Holy Ghost, or, with the triune God. Then he discusses the knowledge, power, and will of God. He afterward comes to a consideration of those things which we must make use of, namely, creatures; in other words, angels, man, and grace. Original sin and actual sin are here discussed. Afterward he takes up the consideration of those things that must be the object both of our enjoyment and of our use, namely, Christ as man, and the virtues. Finally he discusses the sacraments and our last end.

In this division a discussion of the moral part of theology is not directly intended, but only as the occasion requires, as in the third book of the *Sentences,* although the division of the entire treatise gives one the impression that it is concerned more with moral questions, namely, with those things that can be the object of our enjoyment and use.

Several modern authors, such as Scheeben, after the treatises on the one and triune God, and on creation, begin at once with the treatise on Christ before discussing grace and the infused virtues. Thus grace is presented more in its Christian aspect; but, on the other hand, grace must be considered as it existed even in the state of innocence and in the angels, who were not redeemed by Christ.

THE EXISTENCE OF GOD

THERE are three articles to this question: (1) whether the existence of God is self-evident; (2) whether it can be demonstrated that God exists; (3) whether God exists. Thus three possible standpoints are considered. (1) There is the standpoint of those who, like St. Anselm, say that God's existence is self-evident; (2) then there are those who, like the agnostics, hold that God's existence is neither self-evident, nor possible of demonstration; (3) and we have the stand taken by St. Thomas, who shows that God's existence can be and is demonstrated by a consideration of existing effects.

John of St. Thomas asks why St. Thomas treats in theology of God's existence. He replies that the reasons given by sacred theology in proof of the existence of God as the Author of nature, are not its own but are taken from metaphysics. These reasons, however, are corrected and perfected by theology guided by the light of revelation, which says those men are inexcusable [5] who, from the orderly arrangement of all things in the world, did not know that there is a supreme Ordainer. This constitutes the preamble to the faith. It is also of faith that God exists as the Author of grace and salvation; and this is not proved but supposed by sacred theology, and is afterward explained and defended by it.

This question begins by taking for granted what is meant by the name God or the nominal definition, namely, that by this name men generally understand the intelligent and supreme Cause of the universe, which He has designed. Hence the question is, whether this highest and most perfect cause truly exists as really and essentially distinct from the world. Thus any demonstration of God's existence begins by some nominal definition of God, and the existence is proved of the first Mover, the first Cause, the first necessary Being, and the supreme Ordainer.

FIRST ARTICLE

WHETHER THE EXISTENCE OF GOD IS SELF-EVIDENT

State of the question. That proposition is self-evident which, as soon as the terms are known, and without the medium of demonstration, is known as true and necessary. Such are the first principles of reason, which are immediately evident and which therefore cannot be demonstrated except indirectly or by a reduction to absurdity. Is the proposition, *God is,* self-evident; is it evident from the terms alone?

[5] Rom. 1: 20.

In the state of the question St. Thomas first gives the reasons for affirming this. (1) Damascene says: "The knowledge of God is naturally implanted in all," [6] and therefore the proposition seems as self-evident as the first principles of reason are. (2) St. Anselm's argument [7] is proposed by the following syllogism: Nothing greater can be thought of than what is signified by the word "God"; but what exists actually and mentally is greater than what exists only mentally; therefore, as soon as the word "God" is understood, it evidently follows that God exists not only mentally but also actually. This argument was later on revived by Descartes, Leibnitz, and the ontologists. It was admitted even by Spinoza, but according to the pantheistic type of ontologism. (3) It is evident that truth exists, says St. Thomas (for if it is said that truth does not exist, then it is true that truth does not exist); but God is truth; therefore God exists.

It must be noted that St. Anselm's argument, as de Wulf [8] relates, was admitted by William of Auxerre, Richard Fitzacre, and Alexander of Hales. St. Albert the Great seems to be of the opinion that this argument appeals to philosophers. It is rejected, however, by St. Thomas, Robert Middleton, Scotus, and many Scholastics. Among modern intellectuals it is rejected by Kant who, moreover, in accordance with his subjectivism, maintains that St. Anselm's deceptive argument, which he calls the ontological argument, is implied in all the classic proofs of God's existence. In this difficult question that must be carefully considered, as we shall at once see, there are three systems of thought that are in opposition to one another, namely, the exaggerated realism of St. Anselm and the ontologists, the subjective conceptualism of Kant, and the moderate realism of St. Thomas, this latter being, so to speak, the just mean and summit between the other two.

The reply. That God exists, is not self-evident, at least to us.

1) The indirect proof is given in the counterargument as follows: no one can mentally admit the opposite of what is self-evident (e.g., of the principle of contradiction, or of causality); but "the fool said in his heart, there is no God"; [9] therefore, that God exists, is not self-evident.

To this the followers of St. Anselm reply: This proposition, "God is," is self-evident only to the philosophers, as this other, that "incorporeal substances are not in space." It is not self-evident, however, to those whose intelligence is obscured by reason of inordinate

---

[6] *De fide orthod.,* Bk. I, chap. 1.
[7] *Proslogium,* chap. 3.
[8] *History of Medieval Philosophy* (4th ed.), p. 335.
[9] Ps. 52: 1.

passions, and who, therefore, do not consider what is signified by
this name God. Truly this indirect argument does not seem to be
apodictic. On the contrary, what is said in the body of the article
constitutes a cogent argument for St. Thomas.

2) The direct proof is then given. The entire argumentation has
its foundation in the distinction between "what is self-evident in
itself and to us," and "what is self-evident in itself, but not to us,"
and is reduced to this conclusion: A proposition is self-evident in
itself, but not to us, when the predicate is included in the essence
of the subject, the essence of either subject or predicate being unknown to us. Now in this proposition, "God is," the predicate is
included indeed in the essence of the subject (for God is His own
existence), but we do not know the essence of God. Therefore this
proposition is self-evident in itself, but not to us, not even to
philosophers; it needs to be demonstrated by things that are more
known to us, though less known in their nature, namely, by effects.[10] The major is evident; but the difficulty is in the minor, as
regards the words, "we do not know God's essence." For a better
understanding of this difficulty the objections of St. Anselm's followers must be presented as they increase in urgency.

The followers of St. Anselm object that we have not the quiddative knowledge of God which the blessed enjoy in heaven, which
means that we do not know the Deity as it is in itself; but we do
know what is meant by the name God, namely, that if God exists,
then He is the first Cause and the most perfect Being; and this
suffices.

St. Thomas would reply to this, as he points out in the reply to
the second objection of the following article, by saying: The names
given to God are derived from His effects (as first Cause, most perfect Being), and this point will be more clearly explained later on
in the first article of the thirteenth question in which the analogy
between names taken from creatures as applied to God is discussed.
"Consequently, in demonstrating the existence of God from His
effects, we may take for the middle term the meaning of the word
God." [11] In other words, the nominal definition of God does not
include actual existence, and from this definition all that can be
concluded is that God is self-existent and independent of any other
being, *if He exists*. It follows then that God's existence must be

[10] As Cajetan observes, although a proposition that is self-evident in itself excludes an a priori middle term of demonstration, it can admit with reference to
us an a posteriori middle term; that is, a middle term by which we acquire a
greater knowledge of the subject. Scotus objects, saying that a proposition self-
evident in itself and not to us, is not a proposition. In reply to this we say that
St. Thomas has in mind the fundamental aspect of the proposition.

[11] *Summa theol.*, Ia, q.2 ad 2um.

demonstrated a posteriori, that is, from those effects already known to us. This is just what is said in the reply to the second objection of this article.

The followers of St. Anselm again object that, even apart from the effects, we at once know God's essence, namely, that He is the primal Truth and the supreme Good. And it is at once evident that truth exists, especially primal Truth; and it is likewise evident that good exists, especially the supreme Good.

In the reply to the third objection of this article, we read: "The existence of truth in general is self-evident; but the existence of a primal Truth is not self-evident to us." This is proved indeed a posteriori in the third article by the fourth way as follows: "Among beings there are some more and some less good, true, noble, and the like. But 'more' and 'less' are predicated of different things, according as they resemble in their different ways something which is the maximum . . . and consequently something which is uttermost being."

Likewise in the reply to the first objection of this article, we read: "Man naturally desires happiness (or to be happy), and what is naturally desired by man must be naturally known to him." Thus he has a confused knowledge of the supreme good. "This, however, is not to know absolutely that God exists; just as to know that someone is approaching is not the same as to know that Peter is approaching, even though it is Peter who is approaching; for many there are who imagine that man's perfect good, which is happiness, consists in riches, and others in pleasures, and others in something else."

From these replies to the first and third objections, we see that St. Anselm's argument would be valid and fundamentally true if absolute realism were true, that is, if the formal universal had objective existence, as Plato, the Platonists, the ontologists, and Spinoza thought, though the latter applied this theory only to the notion of substance. Even long ago Parmenides formulated the principle of contradiction in accordance with the theory of absolute realism, when he said: "Being exists, non-being does not exist." The principle of contradiction would be then not only an abstract principle (abstracting from actual existence), but also a judgment pertaining to the order of existence. Contrary to this, Aristotle formulated this principle in the abstract by saying: "Being is no. non-being"; something cannot at the same time be and not be.

But if absolute realism were true, that is, if the universal existed not only fundamentally, but formally apart from the thing, then being in general would be identical with the divine being, as Parmenides maintained, later on Spinoza, and also the ontologists, though with some modifications. That such is the conclusion of their teaching is clear from their condemned propositions. These are: "An immediate and at least habitual knowledge of God is essential for the intellect, so that without this there is no possibility of its acquiring any knowledge since this is intellectual light itself. That being which is in all things and without which nothing is perceived by the intellect, is the divine being. There is no real distinction between universals considered apart from things and God. All other ideas are but modifications of the idea by which God as being is simply understood." [12]

Hence, whereas St. Thomas says: "What first comes to our mind is intelligible being" of sensible things, these extreme realists say that what first comes to our mind is the divine being. In other words, the ontological First or the first Being is what is first known by our mind. But in this case being in general is identified with the divine being, as Parmenides maintained among the ancient philosophers and Spinoza among the moderns. Evidently, if this extreme realism were true, St. Anselm's argument would be valid and undoubtedly a fundamental truth even in the order of invention (like the principle of contradiction). But this absolute realism leads to pantheism and is without any foundation; for what is first known is intelligible being of sensible things, and this will be more clearly seen later on.[13] Sometimes we have a superficial refutation of St. Anselm's argument. Its true refutation does not leave out of consideration the problem of universals.

Several followers of St. Anselm object that, even independently of absolute realism, God's essence is sufficiently made known to us by the name God, so that we can at once affirm that God is not a stone, or a man, but that He is "the greatest being that is possible of conception." It is especially this that the philosophers understand the name implies. But the greatest being possible of conception must exist not only mentally but also actually; otherwise it would be possible to conceive a greater being, namely, one that would exist both mentally and actually. Thus God's existence is demonstrated, but by an a priori proof derived from the notion of God.

About the end of the reply to the second objection of this article the minor of the preceding syllogism is denied, for we read: "Nor can it be argued that this being actually exists, unless it be admitted (by the adversary) that there actually exists something than which nothing greater can be thought." In other words, the atheist or the

---

[12] Denz., nos. 1659 f.

[13] *Summa theol.,* Ia, q.88, a.3: "Whether God is the first object known by the human mind."

agnostic will say: Most certainly God is self-existent and is independent of any other being, if He truly and actually exists; but
it must be proved that He actually exists. This is not proved from
merely the abstraction of God, a notion that does not include actual
existence. In other words, if extreme realism is untrue, in this argument given by St. Anselm there is an unwarranted transition from
the ideal order of essences to the real order of actual or de facto
existence. Against the proof of the minor it must be said that
neither God existing is greater than God viewed as possible as
regards His essence, to which the nominal definition refers; but in
addition to this He has actual existence, and this cannot be proved
merely from the abstract notion of God.

To state the case more briefly, in the ideal order of essences conceived by us there cannot be anything greater than the most perfect being; [14] but in the order of real and de facto existence, a fly
that really exists is greater as regards actual existence than a creatable angel, and even than the most perfect being that is conceived
as merely possible of existing. From this we more clearly see what
St. Thomas meant when in the body of the article he said: "We
do not know the essence of God."

Similarly, St. Thomas had said in the prologue to this second
question: "We must consider whether God exists and the manner
of His existence, or, rather, what is not the manner of His existence"; this means that He is not finite, not mobile, not corporeal,
and so forth. To know positively what God is would be to have a
proper and positive knowledge of the Deity, and not a knowledge
that is analogical and as it refers to creatures. In this case, the
proposition, "God is," would be self-evident, as St. Bonaventure
says, who, on this point, does not seem to differ from St. Thomas.

If we had an intuitive and quiddative knowledge of the Deity,
then we would see actual existence in the same, because God is
His existence.[15] But we know God's essence only in an abstract and
analogical way, and essential existence is of course included in this
abstract notion, but not actual existence. In other words, it is in-

---

14 Cajetan says in his commentary on this article: "The reason for this sur-
passing excellence is the nobility of the thing signified in itself," and there is no
contradiction implied when we say, *"Existence is not,"* but only when we say,
"What exists is not." The whole of Cajetan's commentary on this article should
be read.

15 In God, as He is in Himself, there is no distinction between essence and
existence, not even between the ideal order and that of actual existence. *I am who
am,* or *Who is,* each is a judgment that pertains both to the essential and to the
existential order. Identity of the two orders (the ideal and the real), which Hegel
posited as the foundation of his system, is found only in God. See *Summa theol.,*
Ia, q. 12, a. 2 (end).

deed a priori evident that, if God exists, He is self-existent and independent of any other (this being a hypothetical proposition that concerns essential existence); but it is not a priori evident solely from the abstract notion of God, that He truly and de facto exists.

This already virtually excludes the opinion of those who posit either some impressed or expressed species in the beatific vision. From this species we would have only an abstractive and analogical knowledge of God, and we would not know God just as He is. As St. Thomas says: "The essence of God, however, cannot be seen by any created similitude representing the divine essence as it really is," because the essence of God is the self-subsisting Being. We cannot know of God what He is, unless we directly see the Deity, without the intermediary of any created species or representation. We shall then at once see not only that God is self-existent if He exists, but that He is actually self-existent, existing as such externally to the soul.[16]

In other words, as with our abstract notions, so our abstract and analogical notion of the most perfect Being does not include actual existence, but abstracts from it. It differs, however, from our notions of contingent beings, such as of an angel or a stone, in that it includes essential existence. Thus we already have evidence of the truth of the hypothetical proposition that, if God exists, then He is self-existent.

THE ONTOLOGICAL ARGUMENT AND THE OPINIONS OF MODERN PHILOSOPHERS

Several modern philosophers sought to confirm St. Anselm's argument by a consideration of the objective validity of our intellect. Descartes says: Whatever is contained in the clear and distinct idea of anything, the same is true; but real existence is contained in the clear and distinct idea of God; therefore God exists.[17]

We reply to this by distinguishing the major. In the ideal order of essences known by abstraction, whatever is contained in the clear idea of God is true, this I concede; in the order of real and actual existence, this I deny. We contradistinguish the minor in like manner; for our idea of God is, like our other ideas, an abstract one and, moreover, is analogical, derived from creatures.

Leibnitz says: For the argument of Descartes to be valid, this

---

[16] St. Thomas says (De veritate, q. 10, a. 12, the end): "But in heaven, where we shall see God's essence, His essence will be far more self-evident to us than the following truth is now self-evident to us: that affirmation and negation of a thing are not both true."

[17] Méditations et réponses aux objections.

must prove that it is really possible for God to exist objectively, or outside the mind. His argument is as follows: If God is really possible, He exists, because His essence implies existence; but it is a priori manifest that God is really possible, for neither contradiction nor negation is implied in the idea of God; therefore God exists.[18] Father Roselli, O.P., incautiously admitted this argument.

We reply to this by neither affirming nor denying the major, because in absolutely necessary things, existence that is necessary and not contingent follows from real possibility. Thus if the Trinity were proved a priori to be really possible, then its existence would follow from this. We distinguish the minor. That it is a priori manifest that God is really possible, and that this is negatively apparent, I concede; positively so, this I deny. This means that we do not see the existence of the most perfect Being to be an impossibility; but neither can this be positively proved a priori. Why so? It is because, as St. Thomas says, in the body of the article, we do not know God's essence; we have not a positive and proper knowledge, but only an analogical knowledge of the Deity. In a relative and negative sense we know that God is the supreme Being, the principle of other beings. In other words, because we do not know God's essence, we cannot know a priori whether He is capable of existing. Moreover, it is difficult to reconcile certain absolute perfections that are clearly properties of the most perfect Being, such as God's absolute immutability and His liberty. It is also difficult to reconcile the free act which, as an act, could be non-existent in God, with His absolute immutability and necessity. Likewise, the intimate reconciliation between the omnipotent God's mercy and justice, as also between His goodness and permission of evil, these are hidden from us. They do not indeed impair the forcefulness of the a posteriori demonstration of God's existence, but they do not allow of an a priori demonstration.

But Leibnitz objects that there is nothing of negation implied in the idea of God. Therefore it evidently excludes contradiction, for this latter is the result of some negation.

In reply to this we say that concealed contradiction can be the result only of the association of two ideas for which there is no foundation. Thus there is no negation involved in the idea of the swiftest motion; yet it implies contradiction because it is always possible to think of a swifter motion, just as the sides of a polygon inscribed in a circle are always divisible. So also there is no negation involved in the greatest possible creature, but it implies a contradiction because "God can make something else better than

18 *Monadologie,* § 45; *Méditation sur les idées,* p. 516.

each thing made by Him." [19] Likewise, there is perhaps no foundation for the union of the two concepts of being and infinite.

Hence we cannot positively affirm a priori the possibility of God's existence. For a positive knowledge of the analogical validity of our ideas of being, goodness, and the like, as these relate to God, this postulates God as the cause of finite beings from which our notions of being, goodness, and the like, are abstracted; for between the cause and its effects there is a certain similarity, at least that of analogy.[20]

Being is that the act of which is to exist (whether it be self-existent or dependent upon another for existence), and it is only from the similitude of the inferior analogate previously known to us that we can know the supreme analogate of being; but this similitude has its foundation in causality,[21] and from the existence of the effect we conclude the actual existence of the cause.

In more recent times Father Lepidi [22] sought to revive the ontological argument by having recourse to the principle of the objective validity of our intellect. His argument is as follows: The intellect clearly makes known to us that being is either logical or real; there is no intermediary. But the objective idea of the most perfect and infinite Being clearly represented in our mind is not a logical being. Therefore it is a real being. Yet it is not, as is self-evident, being that is possible of realization, existing potentially in its cause. Therefore it is actually existing real being.

We reply to this by conceding the major. Concerning the minor, we say, please prove it. Probable reasons, to be sure, are advanced, just as persuasive reasons are given to show the possibility of the Trinity; but they have no demonstrative value. It is not positively proved a priori that God is really possible or that the Trinity is really possible. This possibility is neither efficaciously proved a priori, nor is it efficaciously disproved by unbelievers.

But Father Lepidi persists in his objection by proving the minor as follows: Logical being is that which in no way exists in itself, nor can it so exist, but exists only in the mind. Because logical beings are not in the true sense entities, they are absolute non-entities, squared circles or negations, as a not-man, or privations, such as blindness. But, on the contrary, the most perfect Being is conceived as having plenitude of being. Therefore the idea of the most perfect Being is not the idea of a logical being, but of a real being, and it is not only possible of existence, but it also actually exists.

[19] *Summa theol.*, Ia, q.25, a.6.
[20] *Ibid.*, q.4, a.3; q.88, a.3.
[21] *Ibid.*, q.4, a.3; q.13, a.5.
[22] *Revue de phil.*, December, 1909; *Ontologia*, pp. 90 f.

In reply we say that this proves only that we do not see the impossibility of the most perfect Being existing; in fact, we are persuaded of the same (just as we are persuaded of the possibility of infinite internal fecundity), but we have no positive proof of the same. The atheist can say: Perhaps there are no legitimate grounds for uniting in one concept the notions of being and infinity. An infinite man implies a contradiction; infinite being does not seem, indeed, to imply a contradiction; but yet we do not know a priori whether the notion is correct that has reference to something extramental. It may be like the notion of a supreme and infinite possible being, which at first sight does not seem to imply a contradiction, and yet it does if "God can make something else better than each thing made by Him." [23]

Finally, Father Lepidi objects that the aforesaid argument presupposes the five a posteriori proofs given by St. Thomas; but these are required only for acquiring the true notion of the most perfect Being, and from this correct notion, due to the objective validity of our intellect, the existence of this most perfect Being is proved. Thus the five proofs would serve as the ladder of ascent to the roof of the edifice, and after we have reached the roof, the ladder is no longer necessary.

We reply to this with the following distinction: If this notion of the most perfect Being were univocal or at least of itself immediately referred to God, as our notion of being of sensible things has immediate reference to the being of sensible things, then I agree. But this notion is analogical and for this reason does not bring us to a knowledge of God, the first analogate, except by the way of causality, by beginning from the previously known inferior analogate, which is finite being. By reason of the principle of causality, when imperfections have been removed from the absolutely simple perfections in which finite beings participate, these are attributed to God, the first Cause. Hence the five classical proofs of God's existence, as we shall see farther on, are not only guides but are truly a posteriori demonstrations. They would be merely guides if our intellect had a confused intuition of God, as the ontologists contend, in accordance with the realistic tendency of Plato.[24]

Yet there is an element of truth in what Father Lepidi and others of like mind say, for it will be more clearly seen later on that the

[23] *Summa theol.*, Ia, q.25, a.6.

[24] Father Lepidi admitted a certain naturally innate idea of God, inasmuch as the soul, since it is according to God's image, received, at the moment of its creation, a certain irradiation from God, or a confused notion of the Creator. But this is not proved, nor can it be proved. Moreover, according to the principles of Thomism, all our ideas are the result of abstraction from sensible things (cf. *Summa*, Ia, q.84, a.3, 6).

five classical proofs are in some way co-ordinated since they all
have their remote foundation in the notion of being and in the
principle of contradiction or of identity (of being with itself, in
that it is opposed to not-being), and their proximate foundation is
in the principle of causality.

Thus we construct the following apodictic but a posteriori argument: Because of the objective validity of our reason, the principle
of contradiction or of identity is the fundamental law not only of
reason but of extramental being. But, if such is the case, the fundamental or supreme reality must be one of absolute identity, which
means that it is not composite but is most simple and immutable,
so that it is its being and its act, which means that it is the self-
subsisting Being. Therefore the most simple and immutable self-
subsisting Being exists above all composite and mutable beings.

This proof is apodictic but a posteriori. It is, as it were, a combination of the five classical proofs, clearly setting forth the opposition that prevails between the principle of identity and the
changeableness of the world (first three proofs), and its composition
(fourth and fifth proofs). Thus, by reason of this opposition, it
would make it at once evident, at least for the philosophers, from
the very fact that the world is composite and changeable, that it is
contingent, which means that it is not self-existent. From this, too,
the immediate conclusion is that the self-existing Being must be to
existence, as A is to A, that it must be identical with it, so that He is
the self-subsisting Being.

In other words, at the beginning of our discovery by the way of
finding, it is first of all apparent, by reason of the real validity of the
principle of contradiction or of identity, that being is being, non-
being is non-being, or being is not non-being. And at the end of our
discovery by the way of finding, due to the same principle of identity, it is evident that the supreme reality is absolutely identical with
itself, without composition and change, that it is the self-subsisting
Being: "I am who am." In this, indeed, we have the refutation of
pantheism, since the most simple and unchangeable self-subsisting
Being is really and essentially distinct from every composite and
changeable being.[25] But this distinction is clearly seen only after a
profound penetration of the five a posteriori proofs.

God's existence is known not a priori solely from the notion of being, as the followers of St. Anselm declare; but a posteriori from
the notion of being and its first principles by means of the light reflected in the mirror of sensible things.

Confirmation of this proof. The existence of God who transcends
the world cannot be denied without denying the real or ontological

[25] *Ibid.*, q.3, a.8, "Whether God enters into the composition of other things."

validity of the principle of contradiction or of identity. We already have precise evidence of this in the ancient teaching of Heraclitus, and more so in Hegelianism, which declares that the principle of contradiction is only a grammatical law and at the same time a law of the lower reasoning faculty, but not the supreme law of the higher or intuitive reason and of reality. Instead of the most simple and immutable God we then have universal pantheistic evolution; for the denial of the existence of the immutable and self-subsisting Being means that the creative evolution of itself or universal becoming is the only fundamental reality, in which being and not-being are identified, since what is becoming does not as yet exist and still in some way does exist. But if this becoming is its own reason for such becoming and needs no extrinsic cause, then we have the denial of the principles of efficient and final causality and hence of the real validity of the principle of contradiction or of identity. For if evolution is creative of itself, that is, if this becoming is its own reason for such becoming, then it is without an efficient cause, and so in evolution of this kind the greater proceeds from the less. It is likewise without a final cause, because this evolution lacks a directing agent; it has no material cause and is like a flux without a fluid, because this evolution is not in any subject that is distinct from it and that would necessitate being moved by another; it is without formal cause, for "in effect, God is produced in man and in the world, and God is one and the same thing with the world, and therefore, spirit with matter, necessity with liberty, good with evil, justice with injustice." [26] In all this we have the very negation of the real validity of the principle of contradiction, which would be merely a grammatical law of speech, and a law of logic governing the discursive process of the lower reason, but it would not be a law of the higher intellect directly perceiving the universality of this flux.

Hence if Hegelianism were non-existent, the theologians could devise it as a means of proving by the method of absurdity God's existence and His distinction from the world. Thus we pass from the criticism of St. Anselm's argument, which in our opinion is insufficient, to the a posteriori proofs of God's existence.

THE DECLARATIONS OF THE CHURCH ABOUT ONTOLOGISM

A decree of the Holy Office (September 18, 1861) condemned seven propositions of the ontologists, stating that the propositions cannot be safely held.[27] In this decree it is not the ontological or a priori argument, or its possibility that is rejected; but the doctrine

[26] See *Syllabus of Pius IX*, Denz., no. 1701.
[27] Denz., nos. 1659-65.

is condemned which states that "the immediate knowledge of God, at least habitual, is essential for the human intellect, so that without it the intellect can have no knowledge of anything; since it is intellectual light itself." The following two propositions are also condemned: "That being which is in all things and without which there is not anything we do understand, is the divine being. Universals objectively considered are not really distinct from God." Ontologism confuses being in general with the divine being, and thus would end in the pantheistic ontologism of Spinoza.

Equally condemned is the ontologism of A. Rosmini, who declared that "being, which is the object of man's direct perception, must of necessity be something of the necessary and eternal being." [28] We say that the intelligible being of sensible things is the proper object of our intellect, and the ontologists apply this to the divine being about whom we have a confused knowledge.

SECOND ARTICLE

WHETHER IT CAN BE DEMONSTRATED THAT GOD EXISTS

State of the question. Posited that God's existence is not self-evident to us, the question is whether it can be demonstrated. The difficulty is threefold: 1) that God's existence is the first article of the Creed, "I believe in God," and it is not the articles of the faith but only the preambles to the articles that are demonstrated; (2) that the medium of demonstration is the essence of a thing, and we do not know God's essence; (3) and that God's existence cannot be demonstrated from effects, for there is no proportion between the finite effect and the infinite God.

This last difficulty is variously proposed by modern agnostics, whether they are positivist empiricists such as Stuart Mill and Spencer, or idealists such as the Kantians. According to the positivists, we have indeed knowledge only of phenomena, and of their laws or constant relations. According to Kant, the theoretical reason cannot prove God's existence, because the principle of causality is only a subjective law of our mind; at least it is not clearly seen to be a law of real being, for the notion of causality seems to be a subjective category of our understanding, useful indeed for the subjective and for us necessary classification of phenomena, but without any ontological validity, and a fortiori without any transcendent validity for acquiring a knowledge of the transcendent Cause.

According to Kant only the practical reason proves God's existence with a certainty that is objectively insufficient but subjectively sufficient, namely, from the postulates of moral action. Kant indeed

---

[28] *Ibid.*, no. 1895.

says: It is a synthetic a priori or subjectively necessary principle that the just person is deserving of happiness. But the just do not enjoy permanent happiness in this life. Therefore God the rewarder must exist, who is the only one who in the other life can effect a permanent union between virtue and happiness. This is not theoretically demonstrated, but it is reasonably believed by moral faith.

Likewise the traditionalists or fideists, condemned in the year 1855,[29] held that reason left to itself (without the aid of primitive revelation handed down by traditions among the nations) cannot demonstrate God's existence. Already in the Middle Ages Nicholas of Ultricuria [30] upheld fideism, denying the real validity of reason, especially the real validity of the principle of causality.

The reply is that God's existence can be demonstrated by effects known to us.

1) The authority of Scripture is proof of this, for we read: "The invisible things of Him from the creation of the world are clearly seen, being understood by the things that are made." [31] But this would not be the case if, by the things that are made, God's existence could not be demonstrated. All Scholastics, except such radical nominalists as Nicholas of Ultricuria, so understood this and similar texts of Holy Scripture.[32] The above-mentioned text from the Epistle to the Romans is quoted by the Vatican Council in defining against traditionalists, fideists, Kantians, and positivists that "the same Holy Mother Church holds and teaches that God, the beginning and end of all things, may be known for certain by the natural light of human reason by means of created things; for the invisible things of Him from the creation of the world are clearly seen, being understood from the things that are made." [33] The same is defined in the corresponding canon.[34]

Moreover, there is a better explanation of this text against the agnostics of our times in the antimodernist oath that expresses the faith of the Church in the following words: "I (name) firmly hold as true and accept everything which the infallible teaching authority of the Church has defined, maintained, and declared, especially those points of doctrine which are directly contrary to the errors of the present time. And first of all I profess (profiteor) that God, the beginning and end of all things, can be known for certain and proved by the natural light of reason, that is to say, through the visible works of His creation, just as the cause is made known to us

[29] Ibid., nos. 1649–52.
[30] Ibid., no. 553 f.
[31] Rom. 1: 20.
[32] Wis., 13: 1–5.
[33] Denz., no. 1785.
[34] Ibid., no. 1806.

by its effects." [35] The word "profiteor" in the Latin of this oath expresses a profession of faith, and this is especially evident from what is stated a little farther on, for we read: "Thirdly, I firmly believe that the Church was instituted by the true and historic Christ." We have elsewhere fully examined each word of the above quoted dogmatic definition of the Vatican Council, which is explained by this oath.[36]

In the definition as explained by the oath we have the condemnation of the fideism of the traditionalists whose theses had already been proscribed.[37] Kantianism is likewise condemned.[38] Moreover, the Church declares that God's existence can be proved not only from the postulates of practical reason, but from the visible effects. Nor is the proof founded in the primacy of the immanent method of sufficient weight, because the proof does not give us objectively sufficient certitude. This has already been shown at length in another work.[39]

Hence the Church in some measure gives her approbation to the validity of the a posteriori traditional proof of God's existence, but she neither approves nor condemns St. Anselm's argument and Descartes' theory of innate ideas.

Moreover, the above-quoted definition as given by the Council is concerned with "the existence of the true God, the beginning and end of all things." [40] It is not, however, formally defined that reason can demonstrate creation out of nothing, but that it can demonstrate the existence of God, the first Cause, and that the divine attributes of infinity, eternity, supreme wisdom, providence, and sanctity are included in this notion. To avoid the charge of heresy, therefore, it would not suffice to say with several agnostics that reason can demonstrate the existence of some first eternal cause, which however is perhaps an immanent principle in the world,

---

[35] *Ibid.*, no. 2145.

[36] See *God, His existence*, I, 8–39.

[37] Denz., nos. 1622, 1650.

[38] Cf. *Acta Concilii, Collectio Lacencis*, VII, 130, which explains the word *"certo."* The council is speaking of objectively sufficient certainty and not solely of subjectively sufficient certainty, as Kant said it was.

[39] Cf. *God, His Existence*, I, 40–60. Maurice Blondel in his *"L'Action,"* pp. 437 f., writes: "The knowledge which before option was purely subjective and propulsive, after the choice becomes privative and constitutive of being (according as the free choice is good or bad). . . . The second kind of knowledge . . . is no longer merely a subjective state of mind; for instead of positing the problem in the practical order . . . it directs the attention to what is an accomplished fact (in the free choice), to that which is. Thus it truly is an objective (but practical) knowledge, even though it is obliged to admit a deficiency in action." But quite recently Blondel made a retractation of this last chapter of his first work, and he is now more in agreement with the traditional teaching.

[40] Denz., no. 1785.

neither transcendent nor personal, that is to say, intelligent and free. This would not be proving the existence of the true God.

It is not defined whether reason alone can deduce explicitly the proper attributes of the true God, especially infinity. However, Bautain had to acknowledge his acceptance of the following proposition: "Human reasoning can with certainty prove the existence of God and the infinity of His perfections. Faith, being a supernatural gift, presupposes revelation, and hence cannot be consistently invoked to prove the existence of God against an atheist." [41] Hence, if the denial of the demonstrability of God's infinity is not heretical, it is at least erroneous.

Finally, the aforesaid definition is concerned not with the fact but with the possibility of proving God's existence. It is defined to be physically possible even in the state of fallen nature.[42] Moral possibility, however, or a possibility that presents no great difficulty, is proximate to the faith, this being the common teaching of the theologians; otherwise the Scripture would not have said: "But all men are vain, in whom there is not the knowledge of God: and who by these good things that are seen could not understand Him that is, neither by attending to the works have acknowledged who was the workman." [43] At least from the order to be seen in the world there is no difficulty in concluding as to the probability of a supreme Ordainer, and then man is bound to make further inquiries. If he does not do so, his ignorance is not entirely involuntary or invincible. Therefore theologians commonly reject the possibility of invincible ignorance about the existence of God as the author of the natural moral law. The first principle of this law, namely, "good must be done, evil must be avoided," [44] is known without difficulty; and there can be no law without a lawgiver, nor can there be any passive designing without active designing, or without a supreme Designer.

Hence the following proposition was condemned as temerarious and erroneous, namely, the proposition about a philosophical sin that would be against right reason and yet not an offense against God, because it would be committed "by a man who either has no knowledge of God, or does not advert to Him." [45]

Revelation is morally necessary, however, as the Vatican Council says: "that such truths among things divine as of themselves are not beyond human reason can, even in the present condition of man-

[41] *Ibid.*, no. 1622.
[42] Cf. Vacant, *Etudes sur le Concile du Vatican*, I, 28, 289, 673.
[43] Wis. 13: 1.
[44] *Summa theol.*, Ia IIae, q.94, a.2.
[45] Denz., no. 1290.

kind, be known by everyone with facility, with firm assurance, and with no admixture of error." [46] These are the principal arguments drawn from authority.

2) The conclusion is proved by reason. In the body of the article St. Thomas: (1) distinguishes between two kinds of demonstration, one being a priori, the other a posteriori; (2) he shows that the demonstration a posteriori, or from the effect, is valid; and (3) he shows how this applies to the demonstration of God's existence.

1) Demonstration is of two kinds. The a priori demonstration is through the cause, and it assigns the reason for which of the thing demonstrated. Each of the four causes can give us this kind of demonstration. Thus the spirituality of the soul is assigned as the reason for its incorruptibility (formal cause); likewise, man is mortal from the fact that he is composed of contraries (material cause); also that we are free is proved from the fact that we are endowed with reason and have knowledge not only of particular but also of universal good (directive formal cause). In like manner, the necessity of the means is demonstrated a priori from the end; thus grace is necessary for the supernatural vision of God. The same is true of the efficient cause. Given the cause in the act of causing, as in the case of the sun illuminating, then the effect follows. Thus this kind of demonstration can be effected by means of the four causes.

Demonstration through the effect, however, is called a posteriori, because the effect is something posterior to the cause; but sometimes it is previously known to us. This demonstration shows that the cause is, *quod vel quia est,* for in the Latin terminoloy of the Scholastics, *quia est* means the same as *quod est.* Thus it is called *demonstratio quia* in opposition to *demonstratio propter quid.* It is therefore a demonstration by means of those things that are previously known to us. The order of invention is then ascendant, whereas the order of things is descendent.

It must at once be noted from the reply to the second objection that, "in demonstrating God's existence from His effects, we must take for the middle term the meaning of the word 'God.'" This means that we must begin with the nominal definition of God, since by the name "God" is understood the supreme Cause, the most perfect Being, the supreme Ordainer, and the question is whether the supreme Cause exists.

2) The reason for the validity of the demonstration from the effect and the kind of demonstration required. It is valid in virtue of the principle of causality, for, as St. Thomas says in the body of

---

[46] *Ibid.,* no. 1786. For an explanation of this, consult author's commentary on q.1, a.1.

the article, "since every effect depends upon its cause, if the effect exists, the cause must pre-exist."

But this principle of causality must be properly understood. The Positivists understand it as referring only to the phenomenal order, since every phenomenon presupposes an antecedent phenomenon. Thus if we have expansion of iron, this presupposes the phenomenon of a greater degree of heat, because heat expands iron. If such were the case, this principle would hold good only in the order of phenomena, and as an experimental law but not as an absolutely necessary law. But a miracle would be out of the question, because a miraculous phenomenon does not suppose an antecedent phenomenon, but proceeds from God's exceptional intervention as first Cause, operating beyond the ordinary course of nature. Nor does it suffice, as the Kantians say, that the principle of causality should be a subjectively necessary law of our mind for the necessary subjective classification of phenomena. To prove the existence of the transcendent Cause, this principle must have, moreover, ontological validity as regards extramental being; in fact it must have transcendent validity.

As a matter of fact, this principle is commonly formulated not only in the phenomenal but also in the ontological order, and not only does it state that "every phenomenon supposes an antecedent phenomenon," but it also says: "Everything that comes into being has a cause"; or rather, to express it more universally, every contingent being is efficiently caused by another. Even if *de facto* this contingent being eternally existed, it would still need a productive and conservative cause, because a contingent being is not its own reason for existence.

Nor need we be surprised that this principle is thus formulated with reference to extramental being and not only to phenomena, because the proper object of our intellect, as distinct from the object of either the external or internal senses, is not only color, sound, extension, hardness, and such like, but it is the intelligible being of sensible things. Whereas the object of sight is colored being considered as colored, the object of the intellect is colored being considered as being; and at once our intellect perceives the truth of the first principle of contradiction or of identity, that "being is being, not-being is not being," or "no being is not-being." This pertains to the ontological order, which is above the order of phenomena.

Moreover, one cannot deny the principle of causality without denying the principle of contradiction. This is evident from an analysis of the terms, for this principle of causality is immediately evident without any middle term of demonstration; but it can, moreover, be demonstrated indirectly by the method of reduction to absurdity, as all Scholastics admit.

In fact, uncaused contingent being is repugnant to reason. In other words, nothing is what results from nothing, without a cause nothing comes into being. Parmenides already expressed the same in the negative form (for it was the negative formula of the principle of causality, in which the efficient cause was not as yet sufficiently distinguished from the material cause). Why is an uncaused contingent being repugnant to reason? It is because a contingent being is that which can either exist or not exist (this being its definition). Therefore it is not self-existent, and must be dependent upon another for this; otherwise, if it were neither self-existent nor dependent upon another for existence, it would have no reason for existing, and so would be the same as nothing. "Nothing is what results from nothing." To say that from nothing, or that from no cause either efficient or material, something comes into being, is a contradiction.

It is not, indeed, so clearly and directly contradictory, as if one were to say, "the contingent is not contingent"; but to say, "something that is contingent is not caused," is to deny a property of the same that directly enters into its definition, and indirectly this means to nullify its definition.[47] Such would be the case if Lucifer were to say: "Therefore I came forth from nothing, not having been caused." To say, "Something contingent exists that is not caused," is to affirm a positive relation of agreement between two terms which are in no way related to each other. Most certainly nothing comes into being without a cause.

Hence the ontological validity of the notion of being and of the principle of contradiction or of identity being admitted, this means that the ontological and not only the phenomenal validity of the notion of cause and of the principle of efficient causality must be admitted. The experimental law that heat expands iron pertains to the order of phenomena, and is hypothetically necessary, which means that if heat exerts its influence, the expansion of iron is the result; but this does not exclude the possibility of this expansion being produced by a higher cause beyond the ordinary course of nature. On the contrary, the principle of efficient causality is a law of the ontological order and is of absolute necessity; we cannot conceive of even a miraculous exception, for nothing comes into being without a cause. This formula extends to every cause whatever, whether the proximate and lowest, or the supreme cause.

It must be noted that for our demonstration it is not absolutely

[47] For a more complete explanation of this, consult, *God, His Existence*, I, 181–91.

necessary to prove that the notion of cause is not innate to us, but that it is abstracted from sensible things. Even if it were innate to us, it could and would have not only phenomenal but also transcendent and ontological validity; for it manifests to us something deeper than phenomena, namely, the dependence of contingent being upon another being, for that which is not self-existent is dependent upon another for its existence.[48]

St. Thomas says: "From every effect the existence of its proper cause can be demonstrated." Why does he say "the proper cause"? It is because, if it is not a case of the proper cause, then the demonstration is invalid. Thus the following inference is valueless: this man exists, therefore his father exists, and yet the father is the cause of the son. Very often the father dies before the son. Likewise, very often the antecedent phenomenon disappears when the subsequent phenomenon makes its appearance, as in the case of the local motion of rubbing the hands together by which heat is produced. Hence the agnostics would merely say that "from every effect it can be demonstrated, not that its cause does exist, but that it did exist." Thus heat is produced by local motion, and this latter presupposes heat, and so on indefinitely. In like manner, rain comes from the clouds, the clouds from the evaporation of the water, the evaporation is caused by the heat of the sun, and so on indefinitely, so that there was never a first rain, or a first evaporation. The case is the same in the series of generations of plants, animals, and men. There was never a first oak or a first lion or a first man. In fact, even Aristotle admitted that the world and generations are eternal, yet according to a certain mysterious dependence on the pure Act.

St. Thomas would reply that we are concerned with the proper cause, whereas the proposed difficulty does not refer to the proper cause.[49] What is the proper cause? It is the cause on which the effect absolutely first of all, or necessarily and immediately, depends, as Aristotle said, just as the property depends on the specific difference, for instance, the faculty of reasoning on the ability to reason. The proper effect is like a property manifested *ad extra* in its relation to the proper cause about which we are concerned in this article.

St. Thomas presupposes from the works of Aristotle [50] the philosophical and profound notion of the required proper or absolutely first cause. Of the four modes of per se predication, the fourth pertains to causality, as the killer kills, light illuminates, the sculptor is

---

[48] In Adam, since he was created an adult in the state of innocence, with his ideas, the idea of cause was *per accidens* infused, or innate; in us it is acquired by abstraction as the notion of being is. Cf. *Summa*, Ia, q.84, a.6.

[49] This is explained more fully in *God, His Existence*, pp. 71–81.

[50] *Post. Anal.*, Bk. I, lect. 10; *Metaph.*, Bk. V, chap. 2, lect. 3.

the cause of the statue.[51] St. Thomas also examines more closely this notion of cause in his discussion of creation.[52] The most universal effect (that is, being inasmuch as this term applies to all existing things) must be reduced to its most universal cause, as the proper effect of this cause. St. Thomas again refers to this causality when treating of the conservation of all things by God.[53] These articles constitute the most sublime comment on the doctrine of the present article, and this because they treat of the same relation of causality, but they do so by starting from above, from God already known, and not by ascending to Him as we do here by the way of finding out.

For a more profound understanding of the proper or proximately direct cause, that is, of the one that is necessarily and immediately required, we must recall the five evident propositions taken from the *Metaphysics* of Aristotle. In this we see the methodical transition from the natural reason or the common sense to the philosophical reason, in accordance with Aristotle's accustomed way, who thus gave metaphysics its elements as Euclid did to geometry.

1) The proper cause must be the direct or necessarily required cause,[54] and not the accidental cause. We have an example of a direct cause in the following: a man generates a man, or the man generating is the direct cause of the generation of the man. An accidental cause would be: Socrates generates a man; because for a man to be generated it is not necessary that the one generating be Socrates or Plato. A fortiori, it is accidental that the musician generates a man, because it is accidental for the one generating to be a musician. In like manner and with far greater reason, the grandfather is the accidental cause of the generation of the grandson, for he is not directly concerned in it, and often he is already dead. His son generates inasmuch as he is a man, and not inasmuch as he is the son of another man, as St. Thomas says.[55] Hence a series of past causes, as grandfather, great-grandfather, and so on, is a series of accidental causes and in Aristotle's opinion was infinite in the past, that is, there was no first generator; but, according to St. Thomas, this is not repugnant to reason, as we shall state farther on.[56] We

---

[51] The first mode of *per se* predication is the definition of the thing; the second is the property that is necessarily connected with the essence of the thing; the third is the first substance, which exists in itself; the fourth is the necessarily required cause.

[52] Cf. *Summa*, Ia, q.45, a.5.

[53] *Ibid.*, q.104, a.1.

[54] It is said to be necessarily required, rather than necessary, because it can be a free cause. Thus we speak of God.

[55] *Summa theol.*, Ia, q.46, a.2 ad 7um.

[56] *Ibid.*

maintain it to be of revelation, however, that the world had a beginning, and Adam the first man was able to generate because, as
we have said, man generates inasmuch as he is of adult age, and not
inasmuch as he is the son of another man.

2) The proper cause must be not only direct, but proximately or
immediately required for its proper effect, as the specific difference
is the cause of the property that is derived from it. Thus to say
that an animal generates a man, is to assign the direct cause, but
not the proximately direct cause, not the proper cause. We must
say that a man generates a man.

3) Hence a most particular or singular cause is the proper cause
of a most particular effect. Thus Socrates is the proper cause of the
generation, not of a man, but of this man, his son. St. Thomas
says: "Of two things in the same species (as a father and son), one
cannot directly cause the other's form as such, since it would then
be the cause of its own form, which is essentially the same as the
form of the other; but it can be the cause of this form for as much
as it is in matter, in other words, it may be the cause that this
matter receives this form." [57] Thus Socrates is said to be the proper
cause of the generation not of a man but of this man.

4) The most universal cause is the proper cause of the most universal effect. As St. Thomas says: "For the more universal effects
must be reduced to the more universal and prior causes. Now
among all effects, the most universal is being itself. Hence it must
be the proper effect of the first and most universal cause, and that
is God." [58] Thus only God can create or "produce being absolutely,
not as this being (for instance, this wood), or such being (for instance, wood rather than stone)." [59] In like manner, "this movement is produced by this mover," [60] for example, the movement of
the carriage by the horse; but if motion taken in the absolute sense
is not its own reason for existence and needs a cause, we must reduce motion taken in the absolute sense and hence all motions to
a higher universal cause, namely, to the first mover, who will be the
proper or proximately direct cause, not of this particular motion,
but of motion itself taken in the absolute sense (as it is a universal
effect); and hence this first mover, the cause of all motions, will be
immobile, at least as regards local motion. In fact, if immobility is
a requisite for the mover not only of bodies but also of spirits,
whatever kind of motion this may be, then our soul is mobile, not

[57] *Ibid.*, q.104, a.1.
[58] *Ibid.*, q.45, a.5.
[59] *Ibid.*
[60] Likewise my will is the proper cause not of the free choice, but of my free
choice as being mine.

by way of local motion, but because of the discursive and delibera-
tive process of its reasoning faculty.

5) Finally, we must distinguish between the proper cause of
the beginning of the effect and the proper cause of the being of the
effect.[61] Thus the builder is the proper cause of the building of the
house, and when the actual construction of the house ceases, then
its construction in the passive sense also ceases; but the builder is
not the proximately direct cause of the being of the house, for its
being does not depend on the being of the builder; in fact, when
the builder dies the house continues in its being. Likewise, Socrates
is the cause of his son as to his becoming, or as to his passive generation, but not as to his being; for the son's being is independent
of the father's being; in fact, whereas the father dies, the son continues to exist.

On the other hand, the illumination by the sun is the cause of
the air being illuminated, and when the sun ceases to illuminate,
then the air is no longer illuminated. In like manner, the object
seen is the objective cause of the seeing, so that the seeing ceases
with the removal of the object. Likewise the evidence of the principles is the cause of the evidence of the conclusion, not only as
to its becoming, but also as to its being. Also the attraction of the
good that is desired is the cause of the desire not only as to its
becoming, but also as to its being and continuance in being.

These five subordinate propositions not only give us a more profound insight into the meaning of the proper or proximately direct
cause as understood by Aristotle and St. Thomas, but they also explain the following words of this article: "From every effect the
existence of its proper cause can be demonstrated," and not only
that it did exist.

This is the same as saying with Aristotle,[62] that the positing of
the cause (as it is the cause) means the positing of the effect, and,
on the other hand, the removal of the cause means the removal of
the effect. Thus the positing of a potential cause means the positing of a potential effect; for instance, the builder can build, and
the house can be built. The positing of the cause in the act of
causing the becoming of the effect means the positing of this becoming (the one who builds, is building); the positing of the cause
in the act of producing the being of its effect means the production
of this being. Thus, as long as the sun illuminates the atmosphere
by its presence, this latter remains illuminated.

It is now easy to explain the end of the argumentative part of
this article, which is but the application of the preceding to the

[61] *Summa theol.*, Ia, q.104, a.1.
[62] *Metaph.*, Bk. V, chap. 2, lect. 3 (end).

proof of God's existence. This means that, if there are in the world effects proper to God, the supreme Cause, then God's existence can be demonstrated a posteriori from them, and, indeed, by an absolutely necessary metaphysical demonstration, if these effects pertain to being, inasmuch as it is the being of created things. But these effects proper to God are investigated in the following article.

Already from the aforesaid it is clear that these effects must be universal, since the most universal effects are the proper effects of the most universal cause, as being by participation is the proper effect of Him who is essential being. Thus our conclusion will be that this motion is caused by this previous motion; but if motion taken absolutely in its generic sense is not its own reason for existence, then we must seek for the proper cause of motion in the generic sense, and of all motions.

So we shall conclude: (1) that the proper cause of all motions is the first and immobile Mover (first way); but that it does not follow immediately from this that the first Mover is infinite and intelligent; (2) likewise that the proper cause of all caused causality is the first uncaused Cause (second way); (3) that the proper cause of all contingent being is the necessary Being (third way), and this necessary Being will manifest Himself to us as the cause not only of the becoming but also of the being of contingent beings; (4) that the proper cause of those things that admit of greater and less in being, in truth, and in goodness, is the greatest in being, in truth, and in goodness (fourth way); (5) finally that the supreme and intelligent Ordainer of all things is the proper cause of the ordaining of all things. This means that the supreme Ordainer is the absolutely first cause of the ordaining and preserving of all things in the world, just as the sculptor is the proximately direct cause of the formation of the statue as to its becoming (but not as to the being of the statue, for this continues in existence after the sculptor's death).

First doubt. The question is whether the aforesaid demonstration from effects ought to have its foundation in a series of accidentally connected causes, or in a series of actually existing and essentially connected causes.[63]

This difficulty arises from another general principle that together with the principle of causality is included in all proofs of God's existence. The principle is that we cannot proceed to infinity in a series of subordinated causes. Therefore we must come to a first uncaused cause. What sort of subordination are we concerned with here?

Some, having failed to grasp the meaning of St. Thomas in the

[63] This has been more fully explained in *God, His Existence*, I, 77–84.

following article, think that he considers an infinite series of accidentally subordinated causes to be a contradiction in terms, so that this necessarily implies that creation was not eternal, which means that there must have been a first man, a first lion, and no series of eternal generations of men, animals, and plants. But afterward, these same persons find St. Thomas, in the article in which he asks whether it is of faith that the world began, writing as follows: "But it is not impossible to proceed to accidental infinity as regards efficient causes," [64] in a series, for instance, of past generations. This shows that they misunderstood the proofs of God's existence.

We find the solution to the doubt precisely in the complete reply of St. Thomas from which the above-mentioned quotation is taken. He writes: "In efficient causes it is impossible to proceed to absolute infinity; for example, there cannot be an infinite number of causes that are absolutely required for a certain effect; for instance, that a stone be moved by a stick, the stick by the hand, and so on to infinity. But it is not impossible to proceed to accidental infinity as regards efficient causes; as for instance, if all the causes thus infinitely multiplied should have the order of only one cause, their multiplication being accidental; as an artificer acts by means of many hammers accidentally, because one after the other may be taken. It is accidental, therefore, that one particular hammer acts after the action of another; and likewise it is accidental to this particular man as generator to be generated by another man; for he generates as a man, and not as the son of another man. For all men generating hold one grade in efficient causes, namely, the grade of a particular generator. Hence it is not impossible for a man to be generated by man to infinity; but such a thing would be impossible if the generation of this man depended on this man, and on an elementary body, and on the sun, and so on to infinity." [65]

Hence the ancients said that "man and the sun generate man," which means man acting in conjunction with the general agents actually existing; for, if there were a cessation of solar heat on the earth, this would mean the end of the generations of animal and plant life. But the influence of the sun directly depends on the actual influence of a higher cause, and we cannot proceed to infinity in a series of directly subordinated efficient causes; as Aristotle said: ἀνάγκη στῆναι, or we must come to a first in this series. Otherwise all movers would be moved and no reason could be as-

[64] *Summa theol.*, Ia, q.46, a.2 ad 7um.
[65] *Ibid.*

signed for the being or cause of motion itself. We must therefore come to a first cause that is its own principle of action.[66]

In accordance with the modern physics of our times, we may express the series of directly subordinated efficient causes as follows: the ship supports the sailor, the sea enables the ship to float, the earth holds the sea in check, the sun keeps the earth fixed in its course, and some unknown center of attraction holds the sun in its place. But we cannot proceed to infinity in this series; otherwise all movers would be moved, and so we could not assign any cause for motion itself, which needs a cause, since it is not its own principle of motion. Hence we must come to the supreme Mover that is not of the past but is actually existing, who is His own action and His own being, because operation follows being, and the mode of operation the mode of being.

Similarly there may be many wheels in a clock, but we must come to that part of the mechanism whose elasticity, whether you call it tension or weight, is the cause of the local motion of the wheels and of the index hand of the hours. Thus local motion originates from some force, from some dynamic influence that must be explained by some higher cause.

In the opinion of St. Thomas, that creation was not eternal but took place in time, so that there was a first day, a first revolution of the sun, is dependent on God's most free will and is known only by revelation.[67]

So also Aristotle,[68] although he admits the eternity of motion, proves the existence of a supreme and immobile mover who does not need to be premoved so as to act. In fact, he says that the greatest motion must be infinitely powerful to move in an infinity of time (that is to say, eternally).[69] In like manner, from the fact that act is prior to potency, Aristotle seeks to prove the perpetuity of eternal generation. Hence he concludes that the first Mover is permanently unmoved.[70] Indeed he shows that there is no process to infinity in any genus of directly subordinate causes.[71]

---

[66] Of course the Augustinians generally rejected, as St. Bonaventure did, the possibility of eternal creation, whereas, contrary to this, the Averroists held with Aristotle that the world actually is eternal, being somehow dependent, however, in the order of causality, on the pure Act. St. Thomas holds in all his writings that eternal creation is not repugnant to reason, and that temporal creation is an article of faith, which cannot be demonstrated.

[67] *Summa theol.*, Ia, q.46, a.2; *Contra Gentes*, Bk. II, chap. 38; *De potentia*, q.3, a.14. *Quodl.*, XII, q.6, a.1; *Opusc.*, 27, *De aeternitate mundi*.

[68] *Physics*, Bk. VIII (lect. 9, 21, 23 of St. Thomas' commentary).

[69] *Ibid.*, lect. 21.

[70] *Metaph.*, Bk. XII, chap. 6 (lect. 6).

[71] *Ibid.*, Bk. II.

1) In the genus of material cause we must admit the presence of first matter, namely, some first material subject; otherwise there would be no second matter or what is disposed to receive this or that form. In such a case there would be no earth, air, water, fire, or bodies composed of elements. To deny first matter would be to do away with the material cause, which is a necessary requisite as constituting the subject of alteration.

2) In the genus of formal cause there must be a substantial form underlying the accidental forms, and also in the category of substance, as in the categories of quantity, quality . . . we must come to the supreme genus, for without this there would be no directly subordinate genera, and so there would be nothing definable and nothing intelligible. Thus the supreme genus of substance is divided into corporeal and incorporeal substances; the corporeal are divided into non-living and living; the living into non-sensitive and sensitive; the sensitive into irrational and rational. Likewise there is no proceeding indefinitely in a series of demonstrations, but we must come to those first indemonstrable and to us self-evident principles.[72] It is always a case of ἀνάγκη στῆναι (necessity of a first).

Similarly, in the genus of efficient cause there is no proceeding indefinitely in a series of directly connected causes, although there may be such a series of accidentally connected past causes. Thus, as Aristotle says, man is moved to take off his clothes when it is warm, but this happens because of the sun, but now the sun is moved by a superior force, and we cannot proceed to infinity in this series of directly connected causes; otherwise there would be no cause for movement as such or in the absolute sense (and not merely as it is this particular motion). But motion needs a cause, because it is not its own principle of motion; it is not as A is to A in its reference to being, that is to say, it is not identical with its being.

Lastly, in the genus of final cause there is no process to infinity in a series of directly subordinated ends, otherwise there would be no final causality. As St. Thomas says: "Absolutely speaking, it is not possible to proceed indefinitely in the matter of ends from any point of view. For in all things whatever there is an essential order of one to another, so that if the first is removed, those that are ordained to the first, must of necessity be removed also. . . . In ends, that which is first in the order of intention, is the principle as it were, moving the appetite. Consequently, if you remove this principle, there will be nothing to move the appetite (that is, attract it). . . . But since accidental causes are indeterminate . . .

[72] *Post. Anal.*, Bk. I, lect. 35.

it happens that there is an accidental infinity of ends and of things ordained to the end." [73]

There is direct subordination when it is said that we walk so as to keep in health, and that we seek health for the sake of happiness. But if we were to say that happiness is sought for some other reason and so on indefinitely, then this would do away with all finality and hence with every desire and action. The ultimate end, considered at least under the aspect of happiness in general, is prior in intention. Thus all men wish to be happy, although many do not know what truly constitutes happiness.

Hence in the four kinds of causes there can be no process to infinity in a series of directly connected causes, otherwise this would do away with every kind of cause. Thus we see that this principle of the impossibility of proceeding indefinitely in such a series of causes is, as it were, the corollary of the principle of causality; in fact, it is the corollary to the commonly accepted principle of causality according as this latter is proportionately or analogically verified in the four kinds of causes.

Corollary. But if the process were to infinity in a series of accidentally connected past causes, as regards generations of men, animals, and plants, then the first Cause would have only a priority of dignity and causality in its relation to the world. This will be more clearly explained farther on when we show that there is no necessity for a first man, a first lion, a first day, or a first revolution of the sun.[74] So it would have been if God had most freely willed an eternal creation; yet in this case He would have priority of causality as regards the created world, just as the foot would have with reference to its imprint or trace left in the sand, if the foot were eternally implanted in the sand. Hence in the proofs for God's existence, we must not proceed according to a series of past causes, but we must get away from this series and rise above it to an actually existing higher cause. For it is evident that any contingent being, such as Abel the son of Adam, does not necessarily require another contingent being as cause, but they both postulate the necessary Being as higher cause.

Second doubt. What is to be our method of procedure as regards agnosticism, in showing the ontological and transcendental validity of the ideas and principles from which the proofs for God's existence are deduced?

This question has been fully discussed by us elsewhere,[75] and only the outstanding principles will be discussed here. Agnosticism

[73] *Summa theol.,* Ia IIae, q.1, a.4.
[74] *Ibid.,* Ia, q.46, a.2, c. ad 6um et 7um.
[75] See *God, His Existence,* I, 111-242.

in general rejects the demonstrability of God's existence because it denies the ontological and transcendental validity of first ideas and principles of reason, especially the principle of causality. For their formula of the principle of causality is not: every contingent being has an efficient cause; but they say: every phenomenon presupposes an antecedent phenomenon, and so on indefinitely. Hence, by virtue of this principle thus formulated in the order of phenomena, it is impossible to transcend this same order.

These agnostics are either of the empirical or idealist type. The empiricists, such as the Positivists, reduce the principle of causality to an experimental law which is repeatedly confirmed and corroborated by heredity; but in their opinion we do not know whether the law applies beyond the scope of our experience. Perhaps, beyond the limits of our experience, there is a phenomenon without one preceding it, or perhaps something comes into being that is not caused. But this is contrary to common sense or natural reason, for something to come into being that is not caused.

The idealist agnostics, however, such as Kant, seek somehow to explain this intimate persuasion of the common sense and of the absolute necessity and universality of the principle of causality. But they say that this necessity is subjective, and is the result of the subjective application of the category of our mind, namely, of the category of causality as regards phenomena. Thus they say that it is for us unintelligible for something to come into being that is not caused; but perhaps this is not absolutely impossible outside our mind.

But we cannot in the course of this theological treatise engage in a lengthy and philosophical discussion of this question, which we have done in another of our works as above mentioned. It suffices to point out the fundamentals, the ignorance of which does not excuse one.

The ontological validity of first ideas and of the first principles of reason is shown inasmuch as these ideas and correlative principles do not express sensible phenomena but being that is in itself intelligible and accidentally sensible, and also the first modes of being. Hence they are said to have not merely phenomenal validity, as the ideas of color, heat, or sound have, for these express phenomena; but their validity is ontological since by means of them we acquire a knowledge of being that underlies the phenomena.

Of such a nature are the ideas of being, substance, and also of causality. For causality is not anything directly sensible (either the proper sensible, as color or sound; or the common sensible that affects several senses, such as extension or figure); but it is the accidentally sensible and directly intelligible which, as St. Thomas says, "is apprehended by the intellect immediately that the object of sense perception is presented to it; just as, when I see someone speaking or moving, I apprehend by the intellect (without any illative process of reasoning) that there is life; hence I can say that I see him living," [76] although life is not directly sensible as color is. Just as only the intellect, reading what is within, can directly apprehend being, and substance or substantial being, so only this faculty is able directly to apprehend efficient causality and finality. For efficient causality is the production or realization of actual being, and this realization is apprehended only by the faculty whose object is real being. It is not apprehended by sight which is specified by the colored object, or by hearing which is specified by sound. But, whereas sight apprehends the colored being as colored, the intellect apprehends colored being as being and, if this being undergoes a change, the intellect apprehends its passive and active realization. Likewise, whereas the sense of touch is aware of the extension and hardness of bodies, the intellect knows that the passive pressure produced upon us by the resistance of bodies is a reality.

Hence St. Thomas says: "Understanding implies an intimate knowledge, for *intelligere* (to understand) is the same as *intus legere* (to read inwardly). This is clear to anyone who considers the difference between intellect and sense, because sensitive knowledge is concerned with external sensible qualities (or phenomena), whereas intellective knowledge penetrates into the very essence of a thing (at least the intellect has a confused knowledge, which means that it penetrates to the intelligible being of sensible things). The object of the intellect is what a thing is, as stated in *De anima* (Bk. III, chap. 6). . . . Thus, under the accidents lies hidden the nature of the substantial reality (and only the intellect knows the difference between the natures of a stone, a plant, and an animal); under words lies hidden their meaning . . . and effects lie hidden in their causes, and vice versa." [77] In like manner, St. Thomas shows that although the irrational animal knows by sense perception the thing toward which it tends as its prey, yet it does not see in it the idea of an end as such, or the reason for the existence of the means. These cannot be apprehended except by the faculty whose object is intelligible being and the reasons for the existence of things.[78]

Nor can it be said that the idea of causality is merely a subjective category of the mind, the sole purpose of which is to express something mental or logical being; for this idea, just as that of

[76] *Com. on De anima*, Bk. II, chap. 6, lect. 13.
[77] *Summa theol.*, IIa IIae, q.8, a.1.
[78] *Ibid.*, Ia IIae, q.1, a.2.

extramental being, is a representation that is essentially related to
the thing represented. As St. Thomas says: "That which is primarily understood is the object, of which the species is the likeness."
Just previous to this he had said: "But since the intellect reflects
upon itself, by such reflection it understands both its own act of
intelligence, and the species by which it understands." [79] Similarly
he writes: "Yet it is the stone which is understood, not the likeness
of the stone, except by a reflection of the intellect on itself; otherwise the objects of sciences would not be things, but only intelligible species." [80] That the sciences are concerned with things is a
truth held by all men as in accordance with natural reason. Thus
these sciences are distinct from logic, which is concerned with mental being. Otherwise we should have to identify direct with reflex
understanding; yet the two are distinct, because the latter presupposes the former.

Confirmation. The ontological validity of the first ideas of reason
and of the correlated principles is admitted by all as naturally
evident, even by the agnostics when they are not actually defending
their own opinion, which is a denial of this validity. Thus all men
are convinced that even in some world of which we know nothing
it is absolutely impossible that anything should come into being
without a cause. Therefore, in opposition to empiricism, we say
that this principle transcends experience. Even the idealist agnostics hold that they are really the authors of their books; hence they
admit that causality expresses a reality, and not only what is merely
subjective. Otherwise we should have to say that the murderer was
not really the cause of death, and that he does not deserve really
to be punished; but we must say that he was the cause of death
only in the manner in which we conceive of it. In like manner,
we should have to say that Kant was not really the author of the
Critique of Pure Reason, but is said to be the author of this work
as we conceive of it. According to this opinion there would be no
real relation of dependence of the creature on God, but only a
logical relation, just as we conceive it to be in God with reference
to creatures.

Hence to deny the ontological validity of the first ideas of our
intellect is to deny that the object of the intellect is intelligible
being.[81] In other words, this means that intelligible being is reduced

[79] *Ibid.,* Ia, q.85, a.2; cf. ad 1um, ad 2um et ad 3um.
[80] *Ibid.,* q.76, a.2 ad 4um; consult also *Com. on De anima,* Bk. III, lect. 8.
[81] It is self-evident that the object of the intellect is intelligible being. This
truth is established from the operations of the mind by an inductive process
of reasoning; for every conception or idea presupposes the idea of being (and is
concerned with the modes of being). The formal element in every judgment consists in the final analysis in the verb "is." ("Peter runs" is equivalent to "Peter

either to the order of sensible phenomena that are the objects of
the external or internal senses, or else to that of mental being which
is the object of logic, and thus there would no longer be any distinction between logic and the other sciences. Hence this question
in its final analysis is one that concerns the problem of universals.
Empirical agnostics, like all sensualists, are nominalists. For such as
these the idea is but a certain composite and confused image of the
imagination accompanied by a common name. The idealist agnostics are subjectivist conceptualists, and for these every idea is but
an expression of mental being. Contrary to this, traditional realism
holds that the proper object of our intellect is the intelligible being
of sensible things which "the intellect apprehends immediately that
the object of sense perception is presented to it," previous to any
illative process of reasoning.[82]

But the transcendent validity of the first principles of reason and
of their correlated principles consists in this, that by them we acquire certainty of knowledge as regards the first transcendent cause,
or, in other words, of the Cause that is really and essentially distinct from the world. Taken in this sense, the transcendent validity
of these ideas is clearly seen from the fact that these ideas express
perfections which, in what is formally denoted by them, imply no
imperfection. Hence the analogical but proper attribution of these
ideas in an eminent degree to the supreme Being implies no contradiction, and they are actually attributed to Him, if the world
demands a supreme cause having these perfections.

Such are the ideas of being, unity, truth, goodness, causality . . .
for these are already analogically predicated of various finite beings; analogically, to be sure, but properly and not merely metaphorically. Thus being is first of all predicated of substance and
then of accidents, of a stone, for instance, and then of its size, qualities, and other notes. In like manner, goodness is already predicated
analogically but properly of a good stone, a good fruit, a good horse,
of a virtuous and generous man. Moreover, these ideas are not only
predicated analogically of finite beings, but they imply no imperfection in what they formally denote, although the way in which
they are predicated of creatures does imply perfection. Thus wisdom, as found in human beings and even in angels, is imperfect;
but wisdom as such is not, for it means the knowledge of all things
by the highest of causes. Hence there is no repugnance in the idea
that these perfections, which in themselves imply no imperfection,

---

is running"). Every process of reasoning gives either the reason for the existence
of the thing demonstrated (in a priori demonstrations), or for affirming the
existence of the thing (in a posteriori demonstrations).

[82] Cf. St. Thomas, *Com. on De anima*, Bk. II, chap. 6, lect. 13.

should be attributed analogically and in a most eminent degree to the most perfect Being. And they must actually be attributed to Him if the world requires these perfections.

Thus the idea of cause, unlike the idea of being, is not absolute, but is relative to the thing caused. It therefore admits the possibility of our raising the mind to God and of actually attributing to Him the aforesaid perfections. But before doing so we see no repugnance in this kind of attribution, since these ideas, analogical as they are in the created order, imply no imperfection.

We must therefore stress especially the transcendent validity of the idea of cause, inasmuch as it is already analogically but properly predicated in the created order and implies no imperfection in what it formally denotes. For it is quite clear that the word "cause" is predicated analogically but properly of the four kinds of causes. The intrinsic causes (the material and the formal) of course denote imperfection, especially matter which is able to be actuated and perfected, and also the form, which is a component part, something that is participated and limited by the matter in which it is received. But extrinsic causes (efficient and final) imply no imperfection, and are *de facto* predicated analogically but properly in the created order. Thus the efficient cause is *de facto* predicated of the principal cause, which operates in virtue of its own power, as in the case of a writer, and the same applies to the instrumental cause, which acts in virtue of another power, as a pen is moved by the hand of a writer. Hence it is not repugnant to the idea of efficient causality that it should be attributed analogically but properly to the most perfect Being. And it must *de facto* be attributed to Him, if the world requires the presence of a most perfect Cause. But the proper or uncreated mode of the divine causality will not be for us positively knowable in this life but only negatively (saying that it is the uncaused cause, not premoved), and relatively (as when we call it the supreme, most eminent, absolutely transcendent cause).

St. Thomas does not here take up professedly this question of analogy, but explains it at length later on.[83] Why is this? It is because he proceeds as a theologian, by the synthetic method, starting from the divine Being and His knowableness by us, and not by the analytical method of investigation, as the philosophers would, inquiring step by step into the foundations for the demonstrability of God's existence.

However, St. Thomas points out what is necessary for this in his reply to the second and third objections of this article. This dif-

[83] *Summa theol.,* Ia, q. 13.

ficulty is presented in the second objection as follows: The middle term of demonstration is the essence, or what is called the definition; but we cannot know what constitutes God's essence; therefore we cannot demonstrate that God exists.

The reply may be expressed in scholastic form by saying: I distinguish the major. That the middle term of demonstration is the essence in a priori demonstrations, this I concede; thus the immortality of the soul is demonstrated from its spirituality. But in a posteriori demonstrations, I subdistinguish: that the middle term is the real definition of the cause, this I deny; that it is the nominal definition, this I concede. Therefore it can be demonstrated a posteriori that God exists, taking as a prerequisite for this the nominal definition of God, which states that He is the supreme and most perfect Cause; of course this definition derives its force from its reference to God's effects, and it suffices, although God's nature or His intimate life is hidden from us.

The third objection may be expressed equivalently by the following syllogism: A cause can be demonstrated only by an effect that is proportionate to it; but God's effects are finite, and hence they are not proportionate to Him, since He is infinite; therefore God's existence cannot be demonstrated a posteriori from His effects.

The reply of St. Thomas is that from the effects we cannot have a perfect knowledge of the first Cause, but its existence is proved. There is also the possibility of a distinction as regards the word "proportionate" in its application; for God's effects are proportionate to Him, the proportion not being of perfection but of causality, and this suffices for an a posteriori demonstration. For there is a proportion of causality between the proper cause and its proper effect, although this latter is less perfect. Thus, just as we say that light illuminates, fire heats, so we say that the first Mover moves all things, the supreme Ordainer has ordained all things in the world, the most real Being "realizes" or produces and preserves all things in being. This proposition pertains to the fourth mode of direct predication between the effect and its proper, necessarily and immediately required, cause.

This a posteriori knowledge of God from finite effects will indeed be very imperfect, namely, analogical; but the knowledge acquired will apply properly and not merely metaphorically to God, as will be stated farther on.[84] For, whereas God is said metaphorically to be angry, inasmuch as anger is a passion and not an absolute perfection, it is without any use of metaphor that justice,

[84] *Ibid.*, a.3.

and a fortiori the supreme Cause, the most perfect Being, and other such terms are predicated of God.

Final doubt. In the first objection of this article a difficulty of a different kind is presented, which may be expressed by the following syllogism: The articles of faith are not demonstrated; but that God exists is an article of faith, for we say, "I believe in one God"; therefore that God exists is not demonstrated.

In the reply to this first objection it is remarked that God's existence, so far as it is known by natural reason, is not an article of faith, but is a preamble to the faith. In other words, the major is conceded, and the minor is denied. But St. Thomas adds: "There is nothing to prevent a man, who cannot grasp a proof, accepting, as a matter of faith, something which in itself is capable of being scientifically known and demonstrated."

Two objections are raised against this reply. The first is as follows: No one can accept revelation as the motive for believing in the existence of God as the author of nature; for the act of faith presupposes the evidence of credibility, and this has its foundation in the principle that God's veracity is infallible and that He has confirmed this revelation by divine signs.

Reply. That the existence of God as the author of nature cannot begin to be known by revelation, in a rudimentary and confused manner, let this pass without comment; that we cannot have a more explicit and more certain knowledge of the same by revelation, this I deny. All men have, practically by natural instinct, a confused knowledge of God's existence as the Ordainer of the world and the Lawgiver; for when human beings come to the full use of reason, they have knowledge at least of the first precept of the natural law, which is that "we must do good and avoid evil"; the natural law, however, like the order prevailing in the world, presupposes clearly enough a supreme Ordainer. This truth not only is known as the result of a scientific or philosophic process of reasoning, but it also arises as it were spontaneously from the rational faculty, as when we say: "The heavens show forth the glory of God." [85]

But, if afterward men doubt God's existence, influenced by their unrestrained passions and the objections of materialists and skeptics, this truth can be manifestly made known to them by revelation and confirmed by some divine sign; for, as the Vatican Council declares: "the miracle is a clear indication of God's omnipotence and liberty." [86] Thus certain materialists, who believed in the absolute determinism of the laws of nature, when confronted by what

[85] Ps. 18: 1.
[86] Denz., no. 1790.

was manifestly a miracle, acknowledged God's existence and liberty, and accepted the Christian revelation.

They had already given their assent to the hypothetical truth that, if there is a God, He cannot lie. This suffices in conjunction with some clearly enough divine sign for the evidence of credibility that is a prerequisite to the act of faith elicited on the authority of God revealing.

For this reason we said in the reply, let the major pass without comment, rather than conceding it; for God's existence as the Author of nature can be made known to one, if not by revelation itself, at least by some manifest and divine sign that confirms the revelation. This sign suffices in conjunction with the hypothetical truth that, if there is a God, then He cannot but say what is true. It was by this method that certain Positivists were converted. Certainly God can, if He so wills, clearly manifest Himself to unbelievers.

Second objection. The Vatican Council seems to infer that all the faithful, even philosophers and theologians, must believe in God's existence from a supernatural motive. Therefore this truth is "an indemonstrable article of faith" and not merely a demonstrable preamble to the faith. For the Vatican Council says: "The Holy . . . Church believes that there is one God. . . ."; [87] and the principal attributes of the true God are enumerated. Farther on we read: "All those things are to be believed with divine and Catholic faith which are contained in the word of God, written or handed down, and which the Church . . . proposes for belief as having been divinely revealed." [88] But St. Paul says: "He that cometh to God must believe that He is, and is a rewarder to them that seek Him." [89]

It is the common teaching of the theologians that at least these two primary truths can be the subject matter of belief, and that they always were necessary as means for attaining salvation.[90] Therefore all, even Christian philosophers, must believe God's existence and say, by reason of belief and not of knowledge, "I believe in one God."

We are confronted by two difficulties (1) the article of faith in itself, as it is distinct from the preamble to the faith, cannot be demonstrated; (2) for us, at least according to the teaching of St. Thomas,[91] one and the same thing cannot be both known (or

---

[87] *Ibid.*, no. 1782.
[88] *Ibid.*, no. 1792.
[89] Heb. 11: 6.
[90] *Summa theol.*, IIa IIae, q.2, a.5.
[91] *Ibid.*, q.1, a.4 f.

evident) and believed (or obscure) by the same person. We do not believe what we already see, for the evident object is already sufficient of itself to move the intellect. I do not believe, but I see the presence of the pen which I hold in my hand.

Certain theologians, as Mazzella and Didiot, thought it impossible, after the declaration of the Vatican Council, for the Thomists to continue to defend the thesis that, one and the same thing cannot be the object of science and of belief for the same person. On the contrary A. Vacant,[92] although he himself does not admit the Thomist thesis, shows that it was not condemned by the Vatican Council, and, in fact, that it is more easily reconciled with the declarations of the Council.

What is the more common opinion among the Thomists? They say that all the faithful, even philosophers, who know the demonstration of God's existence as the Author of nature, must believe God's existence as the Author of grace or salvation. This is what St. Paul has in mind in the following text: "He that cometh to God must believe that He is, and is a rewarder to them that seek Him." [93] The reference is certainly to a supernatural rewarder, otherwise the believer would not have a supernatural end in view, since he would not have even a confused knowledge of this. There is also reference in this text, as in the parallel texts of the Council, to God's existence as the Author of salvation and grace. This truth is an indemonstrable article of the faith, and is something more than a preamble to the faith. God, the Author of salvation, is called the God of Abraham, Isaac, and Jacob in the Old Testament, and the heavenly Father in the New Testament.

On the other hand, God's existence as the Author of nature is a demonstrable preamble to the faith, as St. Thomas stated in his reply to the first objection. Thus it remains true that the same thing, taken in the same sense, is not for the same person both known (or evident) and believed (or obscure). God as the Author of nature is not called either the God of Abraham, Isaac, and Jacob, or the heavenly Father, but the first Mover and Ordainer of the world, pure Act.

Moreover, according to the teaching of the Thomists, when the Christian philosopher is not actually considering the demonstration of God's existence as the Author of nature, it is possible for him to believe the same, and he actually does, as included in the belief of God's existence as the Author of grace. Finally, infused faith confirms from on high the certitude resulting from a philo-

92 Cf. *Etudes sur le Concile du Vatican*, I, 169; II, 132, 200 f.
93 Heb. 11: 6.

sophical demonstration, since it is the same faculty and is concerned with the same object, considered not in its formal but in its material aspect.[94]

This view, which is the one more commonly held among the Thomists, is more in harmony with the Vatican Council, which says: "The Church believes that there is one God . . ." (then His attributes are enumerated).[95] Certainly the whole of this previous declaration pertains directly to the faith, if the reference is to God as the Author of salvation and His supernatural providence. But from this it does not follow that God's existence as the Author of nature must be strictly believed by Christian philosophers. Likewise, when the Council says: "All those things are to be believed by faith which are contained in the word of God, written or handed down . . . , and which the Church proposes for belief," [96] this does not militate against the general principle that some of the faithful are ignorant of certain dogmas that are necessary for salvation, and that Christian philosophers may hold it to be true that God exists as the Author of nature, and this solely for the reason that they have proved the same, and while they are actually considering this proof.

The foregoing suffices to establish the demonstrability of God's existence.

THIRD ARTICLE

WHETHER GOD EXISTS

State of the question. From the difficulties presented by St. Thomas at the beginning of this article, it seems that he had in mind the principal objections raised by both the pessimists and the pantheists against the true God.

The first difficulty, which has often been formulated, is taken from the fact that physical and moral evil are in the world. It seems from this that the world has not been produced by a perfect cause, by one of infinite goodness whose works exclude all that is evil.[97] Thus among modern philosophers, Stuart Mill admitted that God is finite, because He cannot prevent all evils. This same point of view accounts for the pessimistic doctrine of Schopenhauer and Hartmann. The second difficulty is as follows: What can be ac-

---

[94] *Summa theol.*, IIa IIae, q.1, a.4 ad 3um.

[95] Denz., no. 1782.

[96] *Ibid.*, no. 1792.

[97] This objection is developed in the treatise on Providence; cf. *Summa theol.*, Ia, q.22, a.2; *De malo*, Ia, q.49, a.2.

counted for by a few principles is not produced by many; but natural things can be reduced to one principle, which is nature; and voluntary things can be reduced to one principle, which is human reason or will; therefore it is not necessary to admit the existence of a first transcendent cause that is distinct from the world.[98] This difficulty is later on developed in its pantheistic aspect.[99]

From what is said in the present article, some have made the unwarrantable assertion that St. Thomas did not consider the pantheistic hypothesis and therefore did not refute it, and that his five ways of proving God's existence are of no validity in disproving the pantheism of Spinoza, who admitted in some sense the existence of a first Mover, a first Cause, a first necessary Being, a supreme Being, even to some extent a first Ordainer, but a being who is not really and essentially distinct from the world. If such were the case, the Angelic Doctor would have been ignorant of this question as it was discussed even in his time.

In answer to this we say that the pantheism of several ancient as well as of certain medieval philosophers was not unknown to St. Thomas. In fact, he has this error in mind in the second objection of this article, and he alludes to it more explicitly farther on.[100] He certainly knew from the works of Aristotle about the two principal forms of monism, or the pantheism of antiquity, that is, the static monism of Parmenides, and the absolute evolutionism of Heraclitus. In the former case, the material things of the world are absorbed in the one and only immobile Being, and it is a sort of acosmism. In the latter case, and in contradistinction to the former, God is absorbed in the evolution itself of the world; God becomes in the world, and this pantheism is a sort of atheism. Pantheism must of necessity always fluctuate between atheism and acosmism.[101] Spinoza is of the school of Parmenides in the application of his absolute realism to the notion of substantial being. Hegel's evolutionism, on the contrary, is developed more in conformity with the views of Heraclitus.

St. Thomas was acquainted, moreover, with the pantheism of certain medieval philosophers. In a certain article he does indeed refute the materialistic pantheism of David of Dinant as well as

98 This is the principle of economy.

99 *Summa theol.*, Ia, q.3, a.8: "Whether God enters into the composition of other things"; also Ia, q.19, a.3: "Whether whatever God wills, He wills necessarily."

100 *Ibid.*, Ia, q.3, a.8; q.19, a.3.

101 The identification, to be sure, of God with the world means ultimately one of two things: either the absorption of God in the world, or the absorption of the world in God.

the pantheistic theory that God is the formal cause of all things.[102] He even refuted the pantheistic emanationism of the Neoplatonists who, to some extent, adopted the views of the Averroists.[103] The latter taught that God operates externally by reason of the necessity of His nature or of His wisdom, and that there is only one intellect for all human beings.[104]

As a matter of fact, St. Thomas radically refuted pantheism by showing that there can be no accident in God, [105] that the world postulates God as its extrinsic, most simple, and absolutely immutable cause, whereas the world is essentially composite and mobile,[106] that nothing is predicated univocally of God and creatures,[107] and that creation is a most free act.[108] But all these statements have at least their philosophical foundation in the five proofs which we shall now set forth in detail, since they refer to the efficient Cause, which is extrinsic to the world, and which is absolutely simple and immutable, and therefore really and essentially distinct from the world that is changeable and composite.

Certainly the Angelic Doctor had all these points in mind when he wrote the five proofs, which we shall now carefully consider. We must preface our examination of each of the five proofs in detail by a more general statement regarding their universality and order. Are the five proofs included confusedly in this most general of demonstrations?

THE UNIVERSALITY AND ORDER OF THESE PROOFS

The five proofs given by St. Thomas are most universal in scope, being deduced from the highest metaphysical principles. The starting point, which is also the minor, and which is previously enunciated in each of these proofs, is the fact as established in any created being whatever, namely, the fact of corporeal or spiritual motion, of causality, of contingency, of composition and imperfection, and of ordination in the passive sense. But the principle or the major in each of these a posteriori demonstrations is the principle of causality with its corollary: that there is no process to infinity in directly subordinated causes. The first proof is concerned

---

[102] *Summa theol.*, Ia, q.3, a.8; also *Contra Gentes,* Bk. I, chaps. 17, 27, 28.

[103] *Summa theol.*, Ia, q.90, a.1; *Contra Gentes,* Bk. II, chap. 85.

[104] *Summa theol.*, Ia, q.19, a.3; q.76, a.2; *opusc. de unitate intellectus; Contra Gentes,* Bk. I, chaps. 26, 27, 32, 50, 65, 81, 82, 88; Bk. II, chaps. 23–27; 31–37, 73, 76, 78, 85, 87.

[105] *Summa theol.*, Ia, q.3, a.6.

[106] *Ibid.,* a.1–8.

[107] *Ibid.,* q.13, a.5 f.

[108] *Ibid.,* q.19, a.3.

with the supreme and efficient cause of motion, the second with conditioned causality, the third with contingency, the fourth with composite and imperfect being, and the fifth with the orderly arrangement of things in the world. The fourth and fifth proofs treat also, and especially so, of the supreme and exemplary directive cause. The terminating point of these five proofs is the existence of the self-subsisting Being, who is absolutely simple and unchangeable, and hence really and essentially distinct from the world that is composite and changeable. The ultimate objective, indeed, of no matter which of these proofs we take, is the establishing of some divine attribute, and this latter can be predicated only of the essentially self-subsisting Being.[109] The five proofs reach this summit, as constituting the supreme truth in the order of finding, from which afterward the divine attributes are deduced. This highest truth, which is also revealed ("I am who am"), is, so to speak, the golden key to the entire treatise on the one God. It is the culminating point in the way of finding and the beginning in the way of judgment, and in this transcendent truth are contained the supreme reasons of things.[110]

This must be carefully noted, because several theologians, such as Suarez,[111] not understanding these five proofs, so changed them as to deprive them of all demonstrative validity.

All these proofs are deduced from the laws of finite or created being, considered as such, inasmuch as any finite being whatever, ranging from stone to angel, in accordance with these five general aspects, is dependent on the first Cause. There is not one of these proofs that is deduced from objects of the sensible or physical order, although examples are given from objects of sense perception, since these are more known to us. This means that the starting point of these five proofs can also be facts pertaining to the intellective life, according as these are in our soul and also in the angels, that is, from intellectual and volitional movements, from their causality, from the contingency of mind, its composition and imperfection, and from the fact that either our mind or the angelic is ordained to something else as its universal truth and its universal good.[112]

---

[109] *Ibid.*, q.3, a.4: "Whether the essence and existence are the same in God."
[110] *Ibid.*, q.79, a.9.
[111] Suarez (Disp. Met., XXIX, sec. 1, no. 7), in rejecting the necessity of the divine premotion for our will to act, does not admit the universality of the principle that whatever is set in motion, is set in motion by another. Also in not admitting a real distinction between created essence and existence, he likewise failed to understand the other proofs of St. Thomas, especially the third and fourth. It is the opinion of the Thomists that Suarez deprives these proofs of their demonstrative value.
[112] See the answer to the second objection of this article; also Ia, q.79, a.4.

The universality of these proofs may be expressed as follows:

Every finite being is ⎰

mobile	and is dependent on the first immobile Mover
caused in causing	and is dependent on the first uncaused Cause
contingent	and is dependent on the first necessary Being
composite and imperfect	and is dependent on the most perfect and most simple Being
ordained to something	and is dependent on the supreme Ordainer

⎱ the self-subsisting Being

THE ORDER IN WHICH THESE FIVE PROOFS ARE PRESENTED

These proofs start from the more evident signs of contingency and proceed to discuss those of deeper significance, namely, from the very beginning of motion, which obviously is contingent, and they proceed to discuss the composition and imperfection even of beings that existed before our time, for instance the stars and the whole world of physical entities, or else they proceed to discuss the composition of any finite being whatever, even if it had no beginning. The ordaining of any finite being whatever to some end is also considered, for instance, even of any finite intelligence whatever, whose object is truth.

As regards the terminus of these five proofs, they manifest: (1) the necessity of a first cause, as first mover, first uncaused cause, first necessary being; (2) the perfection of the first cause, as most perfect, most simple, and the ordainer of all things to an end. Hence these five proofs start from the more elementary principles, from those already known to us, and they proceed gradually to a consideration of those that are of deeper significance and of greater perfection. This will be more clearly seen in the exposition of the proofs. The orderly arrangement of these proofs excels by far that presented by the theologians who preceded St. Thomas.

We shall see farther on that the other traditional proofs are easily reduced to these five, particularly the proof based on the contingency of mind, which refers back to the third way; and to the fourth way are referred the proof based on the eternal verities leading up to the maximum in truth, and the proof based on the natural desire for the sovereign good leading up to the maximum in good. Also the proof based on moral obligation that leads to the admission of a supreme Ordainer and Lawgiver refers back to the fifth way.

IS THERE A MOST GENERAL PROOF THAT INCLUDES CONFUSEDLY THESE FIVE PROOFS?

There is indeed a general proof which is readily understood by the natural reason or the common sense, and which includes confusedly the other proofs. It has its foundation in the principle that is derived from the principle of causality, namely, that the greater or more perfect does not come from the less perfect, but the imperfect comes from the more perfect. This principle, especially as expressed in its primary negative form, is self-evident, even for the common sense, and it concludes confusedly the principles of the five typical proofs. For the principles of the first three proofs show clearly the necessity of a first mover, a first uncaused cause, a first necessary being, and the principles of the other two proofs clearly denote the perfection of the first cause, since the imperfect is evidence of the most perfect Being, and the orderly arrangement of things of a supreme intelligence.

Hence this general demonstration, although in itself somewhat vague, is very strong, for it contains virtually the probative force of the five typical proofs. The natural knowledge of God's existence finds expression in it, and the spontaneous certitude resulting from it, which is prior to strictly philosophical certitude is confirmed by this latter. It holds its own against objections, even though it may not give a direct answer to particular difficulties.

This most general proof may be presented in the following form: The greater does not proceed from the less, the more perfect from the less perfect, but contrariwise; but men, who contingently exist, have being, life, intelligence, morality, and sometimes holiness; therefore there must be a first Cause which possesses, by reason of itself and eternally, these perfections of existence, life, intelligence, and holiness. Otherwise the greater would come from the less, as the proponents of absolute evolutionism are obliged to admit, and it is by recourse to this method of absurdity that God's existence is proved, who is absolutely perfect and distinct from the world.

The principle of this general demonstration refers back to the negative formula of the principle of causality, long ago expressed by Parmenides, who said: "Nothing is made from nothing," which means that without a cause nothing comes into being. But if the greater or more perfect were to come from the less perfect, then this greater degree of being would be without a cause. Hence it is the common saying that after creation we have not more of being but more beings. This means that we have not more of being by way of intensity, or more of perfection, because whatever of perfection there is in the world pre-existed in God in a more eminent way.

The minor of this proof is a fact admitted by all. The principal perfections in the world are existence, life, and intelligence; and these are found in human beings. But evidently human beings are contingent, because they are born and die.

Hence the conclusion is, that there is an eternally existing being, life, and intelligence; more than this, there is an externally self-existing Being, Life, and Intelligence. Otherwise, if there were only eternally existing contingent beings, since these have not in themselves the reason for their existence, they would have no reason for existing. Any contingent being does not necessarily require another contingent being as its cause, but they both of necessity require the necessary Being.

This demonstration is therefore most forceful, even though it still fails to give a definite answer to the particular difficulties that we shall afterward have to examine. This explains why the certitude either of natural reason or of the common sense persists, even though it may be incapable of giving a definite answer to all the objections. In this sense the saying is true, that a thousand difficulties do not make one doubt, provided they do not destroy the middle term in the demonstration of the declared conclusion, or its principle, but are, as it were, from some extrinsic source.

We have elsewhere examined these five proofs,[113] which St. Thomas has expounded in various works of his.[114] We shall now, however, briefly consider them as they are given in the *Theological Summa,* and as they are further elucidated in the subsequent articles of the same work.

Each of these proofs starts from some established fact (of motion, of conditional causality, of the presence of contingent beings, their imperfection, of order in the world), and it ascends to God by the principle of causality and its corollary, namely, that there is no regress to infinity in a series of directly subordinated causes.

THE FIRST PROOF: FROM MOTION

The fact: "It is certain and evident to our senses, that in the world some things are in motion." It is a question of motion or change taken in its widest sense, first, indeed, of physical change (whether substantial, local, qualitative, or quantitative), which

---

[113] See *God, His Existence and His Nature,* I, 242–372.

[114] Cf. *Com. in Physicam Aristoteles,* Bk. VIII, lect. 9 f.; *in Metaph.,* Bk. XII, lect. 5 f.; *Contra Gentes,* Bk. I, chaps. 13, 15, 16, 44; Bk. II, chap. 15; Bk. III, chap. 64; *De verit.,* q.5, a.2; *De pot.,* q.3, a.5; *Compend. theol.,* chap. 3.

latter is by way of augmentation. We are also concerned, as is evident from this article,[115] with the spiritual motion of our intellect and our will.

The principle: "Now whatever is in motion is put in motion by another." This principle is necessary and most universal. For motion is the transition from potentiality to actuality, or from indetermination to determination. "But nothing can be reduced from potentiality to actuality except by something that is in actuality . . . ; now it is not possible that the same thing should be at once in actuality and potentiality in the same respect." In the same being, to be sure, one part of it can move the other, as in the case of living beings. But if the part that moves, is itself moved, by a motion of the higher order, then this requires an external and higher mover.[116]

Moreover, there can be no regress to infinity in a series of essentially subordinated movers. We are not concerned with past movers, as in the series of generations either of animals or of men; for these movers are accidentally and not essentially subordinated, and their influence as such has ceased. "Hence it is not impossible," says St. Thomas, "for man to be generated by man to infinity." [117] But it is contrary to reason for the absolutely sufficient reason or first cause

---

[115] *Summa theol.*, Ia, q.2, a.3 ad 2um; cf. Ia, q.79, a.4; q.82, a.4 ad 3um; q.105, a.2–5; Ia IIae, q.9, a.4.

[116] Cf. *ibid.*, Ia, q.105, a.5. In this article the relation between cause and effect is considered in the inverse order. Many agnostics object to this principle, that whatever is in motion, is set in motion by another. They say that it has its foundation in a spatial image; mover and moved are conceived as being spatially distinct; but the mover may be a certain immanent force, as in the case of living beings.

Our reply is that this principle has not its foundation in a spatial image, but in the very idea of motion, whether this is local, or quantitative, or even of the spiritual order, as pertaining to the intellect and will that transcend space. Likewise the distinction between potentiality and actuality is not spatial, but ontological and necessary, in order that motion, even that which is spiritual, may be made intelligible with reference to being, which is the first intelligible. From nothing, of course, nothing is made, and being does not come from what is (already determined) actual being; a statue does not come from what is already a statue. Therefore something comes from undetermined or potential being, for example, the statue is made from the wood.

Nor can it be admitted that becoming itself is simply as such prior to being, for that which becomes is less perfect than that which is, and the greater or more perfect is not produced from the less.

Nor does the argument of the first way advance the supposition against pantheism, that there are several substances distinct from one another; even though there were *only one* substance that is in motion, we should still have to say that, whatever is in motion, is set in motion by another, or by a part of itself; and if this part is itself moved, then this requires a mover that is not spatially, but qualitatively and by its nature, of a higher order.

[117] *Summa theol.*, Ia, q.46, a.2 ad 7um.

of motion to be explained by this past and even infinite series of movers, which also themselves are moved. If this series is eternal, it is an eternally insufficient explanation of motion, and is not its own reason for this.

We are concerned, therefore, with a series of actually and essentially subordinated movers. St. Thomas says farther on: "It would be impossible to proceed to infinity, if the generation of this man depended on that man, and on an elementary body, and on the sun, and so on to infinity." [118] Thus we say that the moon is attracted by the earth, the earth by the sun, and the sun by another center of attraction. But in this ascending series there can be no process to infinity. For if all the essentially subordinated movers receive that impulse which they transmit, so that there is not a prime mover which imparts movement without receiving it, then motion is out of the question. So a clock, even if you increase the number of wheels, will never run without a spring, or without the ductility or elasticity of some metal, or without some weight that acts as its driving power.

Therefore it is necessary to arrive at a first mover, which is set in motion by no other; and this everyone understands to be God as He is nominally defined. The first mover is immobile, not with the immobility of inertia or of passive potency, which implies imperfection and is inferior to motion, but with the immobility of actuality, who does not need to be premoved so as to act. In other words, we must come to a first mover, who acts by himself, who is his own action,[119] and consequently his own being, for operation follows being, and the mode of operation the mode of being.[120] The prime and most universal mover of bodies and of spirits must, therefore, be pure Act, without any admixture of potentiality, both with regard to action and with regard to being; and hence, as will be clearly seen farther on,[121] He must be the self-subsisting Being.[122]

---

[118] *Ibid.*

[119] *Ibid.*, q.3, a.6; q.9, a.1; q.25, a.1 ad 3um; q.54, a.1.

[120] *Ibid.*, q.25, a.2.

[121] *Ibid.*, q.3, a.4.

[122] *Objection.* According to the principle of conservation of energy, the quantitative totality of (actual and potential) energy remains constant throughout its various transformations. But, by reason of the influx from the first mover who is distinct from the world, there would be a change, that is, an increase, in this quantitative totality. Therefore, this influx is not admitted.

Reply. I distinguish the major: that the quantitative totality of energy remains constant equivalently so, this I concede; that it is absolutely identical, this I deny. The minor is distinguished in the same way. In other words, the quantitative totality of energy remains constant inasmuch as a certain motion (for example, the local motion of my hands) ceases, and an equivalent motion is produced (for example, the equivalent heat in my hands); but the prior form of energy is only

And so it is evident that this prime mover absolutely transcends the changeable world.[123] We shall see farther on [124] that the first Cause is free, and that when it wills, a new effect is the result of its eternal action, and that this has been eternally decreed by it.

Thus absolute evolutionism is refuted, according to which becoming or creative evolution, which underlies the phenomena, is the principle of all things. This is impossible, since becoming is not its own reason for this; for it includes a new element that is not the effect of its action, otherwise the greater would come from the less, being from nothing. This absurdity must be acknowledged by all who believe in a progressive evolution, in the course of which the more perfect is always produced by the less perfect.[125]

---

the secondary cause of the other form, and produces it under the invisible influx of the prime mover.

Moreover, from the very fact that there is transformation of energy, evidently it is not absolutely the same. Only in the cause that is its own action and its own being, and hence is not transformed, is there absolute identity. Likewise the quantitative totality of human energy remains about the same in the world, yet human beings undergo a change. In fact, it is the general rule that "the generation of one thing means the corruption of another." Finally, the principle of conservation of energy would not exclude the invisible influence either of our free will or of the first Cause, unless it were proved that the world is a closed system, constantly the same and removed from the invisible influence of a higher Cause. But this cannot be proved. Experience furnishes us only with an approximate proof that the productive energy and the produced energy are equivalent. Hence this principle no more conflicts with the conclusion of this first proof than does the old established principle that "the generation of one thing means the corruption of another."

[123] *Summa theol.*, Ia, q.3, a.8.

[124] *Ibid.*, q.19, a.3; q.25, a.2 ad 3um.

[125] Suarez (*Disp. Met.*, 29, sect. 1, no. 7) objects to this first proof, giving as his reason that, although a mere potentiality cannot pass from this to actuality unless it is premoved, yet, in his opinion, virtuality or virtual act can reduce itself to actuality without being premoved. But our will is not mere passive but active potentiality, and is virtual act. Therefore it does not need to be premoved so as to act. Hence the principle of the first proof is not so universal and necessary as stated.

Reply. This objection is examined by John of St. Thomas (*in Iam*, q.2, disp. 3, a.2, no. 6). It is easy enough to solve the objection. St. Thomas, too, admits with Aristotle an intermediary between even active potency and its act or action. As examples of this we have artistic, scientific, or virtuous habits, which constitute the first actuality of potency. Therefore the question is whether this first actuality can reduce itself to second actuality without being premoved by a higher cause. St. Thomas denies this, because the first actuality is in potency as to its second actuality, as to something new and more perfect; for when the second actuality makes its appearance there is some becoming, something new that is coming into being. This becoming presupposes an active potency which was not its own activity, not its own action, in fact a potency which immediately before was not in action, but was only capable of action. Therefore this first actuality, which can

THE SECOND PROOF: FROM THE NATURE OF
EFFICIENT CAUSE

The fact, which is the starting point of this proof, is expressed as follows: "In the world of sense we find that there is an order of efficient causes," for instance, of those things that are necessary not only for the production but also for the conservation of vegetative and sensitive life on the face of the earth. And from conditional causality the mind soars to the unconditioned first Cause, that is necessary not only for the production but also for the conservation of things in being.[126] Hence this proof is of somewhat deeper significance than the proof from motion, but the method of procedure is about the same. It is made clear from what St. Thomas says in the two subsequent articles,[127] about God's preservation of things in being. This same relation of dependence is considered in these articles, though the consideration is of the transcendent order, not by way of finding but of judgment, the descent being from God to creatures.

The minor of our proof, previously enunciated in the first way, is: We find that there are in the world essentially subordinated causes. For instance, there are all the cosmic causes, which are necessary not only for the production but also for the conservation of animal and plant life. Thus we have the chemical activity of the air, the atmospheric pressure according to its determinate degree, solar heat. . . . But causes of this kind presuppose a first unconditioned cause. For, on the one hand, it is impossible for "anything to be the efficient cause of itself, for in this case it would be prior to itself." On the other hand, in actually and essentially subordinated causes, it is impossible to go on to infinity, as was already shown in the first way. Therefore, apart from and transcending the series of mundane and efficient causes, there is a first cause that is not caused, or an unconditioned cause that is absolutely independent of the others. But the unconditioned cause must be its own action, and even its own being, because operation follows being, and the mode of operation the mode of being. In fact, this cause is the self-subsisting Being, a point that will be more clearly

---

be called the virtual act (or the virtuality spoken of by Leibnitz), cannot bring itself into action without being premoved by an agent of a higher order.

From this objection it is evident that Suarez, in rejecting the divine premotion as regards the act of our will, fails to perceive the probative force of St. Thomas' first proof. If now the will does not need to be premoved for it to act, then the greater proceeds from the less, the more perfect from the less perfect.

[126] *Summa theol.*, Ia, q. 104, a. 1 f.
[127] *Ibid.*

established farther on.[128] Hence this cause merits the name God, since it corresponds to the nominal definition of God. Thus an absolutely unconditioned Cause is required, who transcends the physical energy of heat or of electricity or of magnetism, and of whom the liturgy says:

"God, powerful sustainer of all things,
Thou who dost remain permanently unmoved." [129]

THE THIRD PROOF: FROM THE CONTINGENCY OF THINGS IN THE WORLD

This third proof, like the others, starts from a fact of experience, which serves as the minor in the demonstration, and is as follows: We find in nature certain things that manifestly are contingent, which means that it is possible for them to be and not to be. Daily indeed we see plants and animals being generated and perishing, or ceasing to exist. It is indeed a fact attested to by science, that there was a time when there were no plants, animals, or men on this earth, when the heavenly bodies did not exist as they now do, but only in a nebulous state. This fact of the contingency of corruptible things is illustrated by the following principle.

Contingent beings, however, since they have not in themselves the reason of their existence, of necessity presuppose the necessary self-existent Being. Otherwise nothing would have existed. If at any time the necessary Being had not existed, then nothing would exist. Therefore there must be something the existence of which is necessary.

Moreover, if something is only hypothetically or physically and not absolutely and metaphysically necessary (as cosmic matter is necessary for all changes), "it has its necessity caused by another." But it is impossible to go on to infinity in necessary things which have their necessity caused by another. Therefore there is required, as the cause of all other things, the existence of a being that is not hypothetically but absolutely necessary.[130]

The difficulty is that perhaps this necessary being is in the world as its immanent principle, and so is not God. We say in reply that this necessary being is not: (a) an aggregation of contingent beings, even though it were infinite in time and space, because to increase the number of contingent beings still leaves the series contingent, and no more constitutes a necessary being than a numberless series of idiots results in an intelligent man; (b) it is not the law governing contingent beings, since the existence of this law depends on

[128] *Ibid.,* q.3, a.4.
[129] See Roman Breviary, hymn assigned for None.
[130] *Summa theol.,* Ia, q.44, a.1.

the existence of contingent beings; (c) it is not the common substance of all the phenomena, for this substance would be the subject of motion (first proof), and susceptible to perfection. Thus at
any moment it would be deprived of some contingent perfection,
which it could not give itself, because its being and perfection can
never be more than it previously had. The necessary being can indeed give, but not receive; it can determine, but not be determined; it must have, however, of and by itself, and eternally, whatever it can have.[131]

From this very fact that the necessary Being is self-existent, it
follows that His essence is not only something capable of existing,
of receiving and limiting existence, but that this necessary Being
is the self-subsisting Being. This point will be made clearer in the
next question.[132]

THE FOURTH PROOF: FROM THE GRADES OF
PERFECTION IN BEINGS

The perfection of the First Cause is what is particularly made
manifest in this proof, which is as follows: Among beings there are
some more and some less good, true, noble. This means that being and its transcendental and analogous properties (unity, truth,
goodness, beauty) are susceptible of greater and less, which we do
not find to be the case with specific and generic perfections. Thus
goodness is predicated of the stone, the fruit, the horse, the professor, the saint, on various grounds and in varying degrees. In
like manner the unity of the soul excels that of the body; there
is a greater degree of truth in principles than in conclusions, and
in necessary propositions than in those that are contingent. So also
life is found in varying degrees according as it is vegetative, sensitive, intellective, moral; and the highest degree of the moral life
is sanctity. This fact of the inequality of perfection in beings is
illustrated by the following principle.

More and less are predicated of different things according as they
resemble in their different ways something which is the maximum
and which is the cause of the others. To understand this principle,
its terms must be explained.

1) It is a case of different things. But a multiplicity of things
different in themselves does not explain the unity of similarity that
is found in these things. To express this more briefly: multitude
does not give the reason for the unity in which it participates. Ele-

---

131 *Ibid.*, q.3, a.6, where it is stated that in God, the necessary Being, there
cannot be any accident.
132 *Ibid.*, a.4.

ments that are different in themselves, do not of themselves coalesce to form some sort of unity. As St. Thomas says: "Multitude itself would not be contained under being, unless it were in some way contained under one." [133] Thus those things that are many numerically, are one specifically; and those that are many specifically are one generically; and there are many processes of reasoning that are one in principle. Our first conception is of being, then of nonbeing, of division of being, of indivision or of unity of being, and finally of multitude, which last is logically and ontologically posterior to unity.[134]

2) We are concerned with the absolute perfections of being, truth, goodness predicated of different things in varying degrees, which means that they are predicated of finite beings in an imperfect manner. But the imperfect is a composite of perfection and of a limited capacity for perfection. Thus goodness is found in varying degrees in the stone, the fruit, the horse, the good professor, the saint; and in all of these it is found in a finite manner, although this goodness in itself is not limited, for what is formally denoted by the concept implies no imperfection.

But the composite of perfection and of a limited capacity for the same needs a cause, for, as St. Thomas says, "things in themselves different (perfection and limited capacity for this) cannot unite unless something causes them to unite." [135] The reason is that the union of several things presupposes unity. Multitude does not explain the reason for the unity that is imperfectly contained in it. Union that is effected according to either composition or similitude presupposes a unity of a higher order. It is a question of the exemplary cause and also of the efficient cause, because the exemplary cause without the efficient does not actually produce anything. "Consequently there is something that is truest, something best, something noblest, and something that is uttermost being; for those things that are greatest in truth are greatest in being." So says St. Thomas in this article. But why does he add: "Now the maximum in any genus is the cause of all in that genus"? He does so to show that the greatest in truth, in goodness, and in being is the true equivalent of the nominal definition of God, or of the supreme Being, and of the cause of all beings. Therefore he concludes by saying: "And this we call God." If this greatest in being were not the cause of all beings, it would not correspond to the nominal definition of God.

Some were of the opinion that, previous to the introduction of

---

[133] *Ibid.*, q. 11, a. 1 ad 2um.
[134] Consult St. Thomas' *Com. on Metaph.*, Bk. IV, lect. 3.
[135] *Summa theol.*, Ia, q. 3, a. 7.

this causal element, this proof does not proceed by the way of causality. But there is no other way of proving God's existence, as was previously stated,[136] and we must not only come by this proof to the ideal conception of the supreme Good, conceived by us as the exemplar in this order, but also to the supreme Good as truly existing outside the mind, and as truly and actually the cause of other beings.

This interpretation is confirmed by what St. Thomas says in another of his works: "If one of some kind is found as a common note in several objects, this must be because some one cause has brought it about in them; for it cannot be that the common note of itself belongs to each thing, since each thing is by its very nature distinct from others, and a diversity of causes produces a diversity of effects. . . .

"(Moreover), if anything is found to be participated in various degrees by several objects, it must be that, starting with the one in which it is found in the highest degree, it is attributed to all the others in which it is found more imperfectly. For those things that are predicated according to more and less, this they have by reason of their greater or less approximation to one of some kind; for if any one of these were to possess this perfection in its own right, then there is no reason why it should be found in a higher degree in one than in the other."[137] St. Thomas also says: "What belongs to a being by its very nature, and not by reason of any cause, cannot be either partially or completely taken away."[138]

This argument differs entirely from St. Anselm's, for it does not start from the idea of perfect being, but from the real grades of perfection as found in the world. Therefore, by means of the proof based upon exemplary and efficient causality, the most perfect Being is established, since actually existing imperfect beings originate from the real fount of perfection.

We find the same argument in the *Theological Summa,* but the order is reversed. The descent is from God, since the same relation of dependence can be considered by starting from the lowest or from the highest in the grades of being. The passage from the above-mentioned work reads as follows: "Whatever is found in anything by participation must be caused in it by that to which it belongs essentially, as iron becomes ignited by fire. Now it has been shown above (q. 3, a. 4) that God is the essentially self-subsisting Being; and it was also shown (q. 11, a. 3, 4) that subsisting being must be one; as, if whiteness were self-subsisting, it would be one,

136 *Ibid.,* q. 2, a. 2.
137 *De pot.,* q. 3, a. 5.
138 *Contra Gentes,* Bk. II, chap. 15.

since whiteness is multiplied by its recipients. . . . Therefore it must be that all things which are diversified by the diverse partici- pation of being, so as to be more or less perfect, are caused by one first Being, who possesses being most perfectly. Hence Plato said that unity must come before multitude." [139]

Thus this fourth way proves the necessity of a maximum in being, unity, truth, and goodness; in fact, it proves the necessity of the most pure Being that is not a reality considered as distinct from the limited capacity in which it would be received. Thus the maximum in being must be to being as A is to A. It must be the self-subsisting Being.[140] And so it is quite clear that this supreme Being by reason of His absolute identity, which excludes composi- tion, imperfection, and changeableness, completely transcends the world, which is essentially composite and imperfect.[141]

St. Thomas applies this proof to the intellect, truth, goodness, and the natural law.

1) The application to our intellect. "What is such by participa- tion and what is mobile and imperfect, always requires the pre- existence of something essentially such, immovable and perfect. Now the human soul is called intellectual by reason of a participa- tion in intellectual power; a sign of which is that it is not wholly intellectual but only in part. Moreover, it reaches to the under- standing of truth by arguing, with a certain amount of reasoning and movement. Again, it has an imperfect understanding. . . . Therefore there must be some higher intellect by which the soul is helped to understand." [142] And this higher intellect must be the self-subsisting Being.[143]

2) Application to eternal truths. We perceive by the intellect truths that are at least negatively eternal, absolutely necessary and universal, such as the principle of contradiction. But the absolute necessity of these, which is the rule of every finite intellect and of every possible and actual contingent being, calls for an actually existing and necessary foundation. Therefore this necessary and eternal foundation exists, and it is the necessary and the eternal intellect.

St. Thomas says practically the same in the following passage: "From the fact that the truths understood are eternal as regards what is understood, it cannot be concluded that the soul is im- mortal, but that the truths understood have their foundation in

[139] Summa theol., Ia, q.44, a.1.
[140] Ibid., q.3, a.4.
[141] Ibid., a.8.
[142] Ibid., q.79, a.4.
[143] Ibid., q.14, a.4.

something eternal. They have their foundation, indeed, in the first Truth as in the universal Cause that contains all truth." [144] This means that, in accordance with the fourth proof, they have their foundation in the maximum truth.

Obviously the absolute necessity of the principle of contradiction, which is the law governing every real being, whether possible or actual, has not its foundation in either contingent being or in the different natures of contingent beings; multitude does not explain the reason for unity. There is required a supreme truth. Likewise the first principle of ethics, good is to be done and evil to be avoided,[145] has its proximate foundation in the nature of virtuous good to which our will is ordained, and its ultimate foundation is in the supreme Good and in the maximum Truth.

Thus the natural law in the rational creature is "the participation of the eternal law." [146] This is confirmed by the fifth proof, since the passive ordination of our will to do what is virtuously good presupposes the active ordination of the supreme Ordainer or Lawmaker.

3) Application to the natural desire in us for universal good. More and less are predicated of different goods, according as these approximate in varying degrees to the highest goods. It follows psychologically from this that, in conceiving universal good, we naturally desire a non-finite good (in virtue of the principle of finality: every agent acts for an end). And this desire, being natural, cannot be to no purpose. We are not concerned here with the conditional and inefficacious desire for the beatific vision, but with the natural desire for natural happiness, which no finite good, but only the supreme Good naturally known and loved can satisfy. Hence St. Thomas says: "That good which is the last end, is the perfect good fulfilling the desire. Now man's appetite, otherwise the will, is for the universal good. And any good inherent to the soul is a participated good, and consequently a portioned good. Therefore none of them can be man's last end." [147] And farther on he says: "Hence it is evident than nothing can lull man's will except the universal good. This is to be found not in any creature, but in God alone, because every creature has good by participation." [148]

This may be expressed more briefly as follows: If there is a natural appetite for universal good in the things of nature, since good is not in the mind but in things, then it must be the universal or

[144] *Contra Gentes*, Bk. II, chap. 84.
[145] *Summa theol.*, Ia IIae, q.94, a.2.
[146] *Ibid.*, q.91, a.2.
[147] *Ibid.*, q.2, a.7.
[148] *Ibid.*, q.2, a.8.

most perfect good. Otherwise the existence of this appetite or natural desire would be a psychological contradiction. In such a case
the tendency of this natural desire would be and would not be for
infinite good.

This is an apodictic argument at least for philosophers, and it
must be most clear to the angels. It is an application of the fourth
proof in conjunction with the principle of finality: that every agent
acts for an end, and that a natural desire cannot be purposeless.
The fifth proof confirms this argument, since the passive ordination of our will to non-finite good presupposes the supreme Ordainer.

THE FIFTH PROOF: FROM THE ORDER OR
THE GOVERNANCE IN THE WORLD

We see that things lacking intelligence act for an end. Not only is
this an established fact, but it is the minor of this demonstration.
Indeed we notice that there is a wonderful order and finality prevailing in the strikingly regular courses of the heavenly bodies. The
centripetal and centrifugal forces are so regulated that the heavenly
bodies move in their orbits with enormous speed and in perfect
harmony. More striking are the unity and variety that we behold
in the organic structures of plants, animals, and man. Finality, or
the relation to an end, is clearly seen in the evolution of the primitive embryonic cell, which in its simplicity virtually contains all
that belongs to the determinate organism of this particular species
rather than of a certain other, of a lion, for instance, rather than
of a dog. This evolution manifestly tends to a determined end.
Hence Claude Bernard spoke of "the directive idea" of this evolution. There is something truly wonderful in this. In like manner
the organs of animals are adapted to this particular function rather
than to a certain other, such as the eye with its multiplicity of
visual conditions and its cells is adapted to this most simple operation of seeing, and the ear to that of hearing. Similarly the instinct
and activities of animals are directed to certain determined ends.
Thus the activities of the bee are for the building of its hive and
the making of honey.

What particularly manifests this finality, as St. Thomas notes, is
the fact that natural agents of the irrational order "always or nearly
always act in the same way, so as to obtain the best result." [149] If
God had created but one eye for the evident purpose of seeing,
this would already be something wonderful. This best result, which
is the terminus of action, is strictly entitled to the name of end;

[149] *Ibid.*, Ia, q.2, a.3.

for the end is the good in view of which an agent acts. In fact, before God's existence is proved, the principle of finality, "every agent acts for an end," is an evident truth. As St. Thomas says: "An agent does not move except out of intention for an end (unless it do so at least unconsciously). For if the agent were not determined to some particular effect, it would not do one thing rather than another. Therefore, in order that it produce a determinate effect, it must of necessity be determined to some certain one, which has the nature of an end." [150]

It will not do to have recourse to chance, for chance is an accidental cause, and hence is not the cause of what happens always and according to nature. Otherwise the accidental would no longer be accidental but essential; instead of being something which accrues to the essence, it would be its foundation, and in that case the essential would be subordinate to the accidental, and this would be unintelligible and absurd. The wonderful order existing in the universe would be the result of no order, the greater would proceed from the less. Neither will it do to appeal solely to the efficient cause, and to reject the final cause. For in that case we could not give any reason for the action of an agent: why, for instance, a certain organ has a certain determinate tendency; nor could we say why an agent acts instead of not acting. There would be no raison d'être for the action. The active potency or the inclination of the agent tends essentially toward something, just as the imperfect tends toward the perfect. "Potency refers to act." For instance, the faculty of sight is for seeing. Therefore, we cannot doubt the existence of finality in the world, the order of which is the suitable arrangement of means in view of an end.[151] Now the existence of order or finality in the world is illustrated by the following principle which is the major of this demonstration.

Irrational beings cannot tend toward an end, unless they are directed by some supreme Intelligence. In fact, to be directed presupposes a directing cause, which is an act that pertains to the intellect and not to the imagination. "It is for the wise man to direct." Why? Because an intelligent being alone perceives the raison d'être of the means. "Irrational beings," says St. Thomas, "tend toward an end by natural inclination; they are, as it were, moved by another and not by themselves, since they have no knowledge of the end as such." [152] Animals have a sensitive knowledge of the thing which constitutes their end, but they do not per-

[150] Ibid., Ia IIae, q.1, a.2; also Ia, q.44, a.4; Contra Gentes, Bk. III, chap. 2.
[151] See Aristotle, Physics, Bk. II, chaps. 8 f., and the Commentary of St. Thomas, lect. 7–14.
[152] Summa theol., Ia IIae, q.1, a.2.

ceive the formal end as such in this thing. If, therefore, there were no intelligent designer directing the world, the order and intelligibility in things would be the effect of an unintelligible cause, and our own intelligences would originate from a blind and unintelligible cause, and again we should have to say that the greater comes from the less, which is absurd. This was understood to be so by Anaxagoras, and he was very much praised by Aristotle for having made this assertion.[153] There is, therefore, a supreme intelligent Being, who directs all things in nature to their respective ends.

Kant objects that this argument proves only the existence of some finite intelligence. We reply to this by saying that it is not enough for the first Ruler to have, like ourselves, an intellectual faculty directed to intelligible being, for this would at once demand the presence of a designing intelligence of a higher order. The supreme Designer cannot be designed for any other purpose. Therefore He must be the self-subsisting Intellection and self-subsisting Being, and this will be more clearly seen in subsequent articles.[154]

This proof, like the preceding proofs, is most universal in scope. It takes in anything whatever that denotes design, and from this it rises up to the supreme Designer. Thus it starts with equal force either from the fact that the eye is for seeing, and the ear for hearing, or that the intellect is for the understanding of truth, or the will for the willing of good.

Viewed under this aspect, there are two proofs for God's existence that are referred back to this fifth way. One is the natural tendency of our will to do what is good and avoid what is evil; the other is the natural desire of the will for happiness, or for unlimited good, which is found only in God, who is the essential Good.

Evidently this twofold ordination of the will presupposes a supreme Ordainer, just as the ordination of sight to seeing does. This proof must be most convincing for the angels; by the very fact that they see that their will is directed to universal good, at once without any discursive process they see that passive ordination presupposes the active ordination of a supreme Ordainer. "There is no ordination without an ordainer." [155]

This fifth proof, since it starts from the consideration of the order prevailing in the world, the harmony, for instance, in the movements of the heavenly bodies, is readily understood at least

153 *Metaph.*, Bk. I, chap. 3.
154 *Summa theol.*, Ia, q.3, a.4; q.14, a.1, 4.
155 *Contra Gentes*, Bk. III, chap. 38.

in a confused way by the natural reason. Hence it is said: "All men are vain in whom there is not the knowledge of God, and who by these good things that are seen could not understand Him that is. Neither by attending to the works have acknowledged who was the workman." [156] Hence the Psalmist says: "The heavens show forth the glory of God." [157]

THE ONE END TO WHICH THESE FIVE PROOFS CONVERGE

We have already pointed out at the end of each of these five proofs that the result of each is to move us to admit the existence of a divine attribute which can be predicated only of the self-subsisting Being, as will be explicitly proved by St. Thomas.[158] The article referred to serves the double purpose of pointing out to us what is the terminus in the ascending order in the process of reasoning or the terminus by way of finding in proving God's existence, which rises from sensible things until it reaches the supreme cause, and it is also the principle in the descending or synthetic process, by which reason deduces the divine attributes, and judges of all things by the highest cause.[159]

In fact, the prime mover must be his own action, and, therefore, his own existence, and the same must be said of the first uncaused cause, of the necessary being, of the most perfect being, and of the ruler of the universe. Thus the supreme truth of Christian philosophy, or the fundamental truth by way of judgment, is that "in God alone essence and existence are identical." God is "He who is." [160] This is the golden key to the whole treatise on the one God, and its dominating principle.

These are, therefore, the principal metaphysical proofs to which all others are reduced. If we study them carefully, we see, contrary to the assertions of modern agnostics, that the existence of God, who transcends the world, cannot be denied without denying the principle of causality, namely, that "every being which is contingent, changeable, composite, imperfect, and relative, is caused," and so requires a first and unchangeable being, one that is absolutely simple and perfect. Now, the principle of causality cannot be denied or doubted without denying or doubting the principle of contradiction, for "a contingent and uncaused being" would exist neither of itself nor by reason of another, and consequently could

[156] Wis. 13: 1.

[157] Ps. 18: 1. On the natural knowledge of God's existence, cf. *Contra Gentes,* Bk. III, chap. 38.

[158] *Summa theol.,* Ia, q.3, a.4.

[159] *Ibid.,* q.79, a.9.

[160] Ex. 3: 14.

not be distinguished from nothingness, since it would have no reason for existing. This would mean the subversion of the principle of contradiction, that "being is not non-being," and of the principle of identity, that "being is being, non-being is non-being."

If, on the contrary, the principle of contradiction or identity is the supreme law of reality and of our reason, then the supreme reality must indeed be the identity of essence and existence, or self-subsisting Being. Thus the five ways of proving God's existence unite in the wonderful opposition prevailing between the principle of identity and the changeableness and composition of the world. From this opposition it is at once evident that the world is contingent and depends on the immutable and pre-eminently simple Being whose name is "I am who am." [161]

It is, therefore, absolutely necessary to choose between the existence of God, who transcends the world, and the denial of the real validity of the principle of contradiction. Absolute evolutionism denies this validity, maintaining that motion or becoming is its own reason for such,[162] and hence that the more perfect comes from the less perfect, and that contradictories are identified in a universal process of becoming. Thus we see in absolute evolutionism an incontestable proof, by *reductio ad absurdum* of the true and transcendental God, since this existence cannot be denied without denying the real validity of the first principle of reason, and without positing a fundamental absurdity as the principle of all things. For if God is truly the absolutely necessary being, then the denial of His existence means the positing of a fundamental absurdity as the principle of all things.

We see the radical absurdity of this system in the first of the propositions condemned in the Syllabus of Pius IX, which reads as follows: "There is no supreme Being, who is all-wise, ruler of the universe and distinct from it; God is identical with the nature of things, and is, therefore, subject to changes; God really becomes or begins to be in man and in the world, and all things are God and have the same substance with Him; thus God and the world, spirit and matter, necessity and liberty, truth and falsehood, goodness and evil, justice and injustice, are all identified in the one same and only reality." [163] If absolute evolutionism were true, then nothing would be stable, and therefore we should have to say that there is nothing but relative truth. In such a state of knowledge the antith-

161 *Ibid.*
162 For this reason Heraclitus is said to have denied the real validity of the principle of contradiction, reducing it to a grammatical law. See Aristotle's *Metaphysics*, Bk. IV, chaps. 3-8.
163 Denz., no. 1701.

esis would always be truer than the thesis and then there would be a synthesis of a higher order, and so on indefinitely. Contradictories would be identified in the very process of becoming, which would be its own reason for such.

To avoid this absurdity we must affirm the existence of God, who, as the Vatican Council says, "being one, sole, absolutely simple [164] and immutable [165] spiritual substance, is to be declared as really and essentially distinct from the world (which is composite and subject to change), of supreme beatitude in and from Himself, and ineffably exalted above all things which exist or can be conceived beside Himself." [166]

St. Thomas gives us in merely a few words his solution to the objection raised against God's existence because of the prevalence of evil in the world,[167] because he intends to examine this problem more at length farther on in this treatise.[168] But we now merely call to mind the solution of the problem of evil given by St. Augustine, who says: "Since God is supremely good, He would not at all permit any evil in His works if He did not have power and goodness enough to draw good out of evil." [169] Thus in the physical order He permits the death of some animal for the preservation of another, of a lion, for instance; and in the moral order He permits persecution for this greater good, namely, the constancy of the martyrs. Similarly, St. Thomas says: "God allows evils to happen in order to bring a greater good therefrom. Hence it is written (Rom. 5:20): 'Where sin abounded, grace did more abound.' Hence, too, in the blessing of the paschal candle we say: 'O happy fault that merited such and so great a Redeemer.' " [170]

Reply to the second objection. Nature is not the first cause of those things that are done in a natural way, because, "since nature works for a determinate end under the direction of a higher agent, whatever is done by nature must needs be traced back to God, as to its first cause. So also whatever is done voluntarily," as all mobile and defectible beings must be traced back to some first immobile and essentially necessary being.

This suffices for the proofs of God's existence, which we have expounded more philosophically in another work.[171]

[164] See the fourth and fifth proofs as above explained.
[165] See the first, second, and third proofs of St. Thomas.
[166] Denz., no. 1782.
[167] *Summa theol.,* Ia, q.2, a.3 ad 1um.
[168] *Ibid.,* q.22, a.2 ad 2um; q.48, a.2 ad 3um.
[169] *Enchiridion,* chap. XI.
[170] *Summa theol.,* IIIa, q.1, a.3 ad 3um.
[171] See *God, His Existence and His Nature.*

CHAPTER III

QUESTION 3

INTRODUCTION

ON GOD'S NATURE AND HIS ATTRIBUTES IN GENERAL

BEFORE we come to consider God's various attributes, we must discuss His nature as conceived by us, and His attributes in general. This especially applies here, because from the very end to which the five proofs converge, which is the self-subsisting Being, there arises the question whether what formally constitutes God's nature, according to our conception of it, is self-subsisting Being, from which perfection all the other attributes are afterward deduced.

WHAT FORMALLY CONSTITUTES GOD'S NATURE ACCORDING TO OUR CONCEPTION OF IT

State of the question. We are not concerned here with God's nature as it is in itself and as it is seen by the blessed; for what formally constitutes the divine nature as it is in itself, is that most proper and most eminent formal concept of the Deity, which contains actually and explicitly (and not merely implicitly) all God's attributes, which are truly identified in the absolute simplicity of the Deity, and which are seen in it by the blessed without any deductive process.

It is our analogical and very imperfect knowledge of God's nature that concerns us here, and the question is whether among all the divine perfections there is one that is, as it were, the source of the others, just as in the human nature rationality is the source of the various properties in man. Then the divine nature, when so viewed, according to our imperfect mode of knowing it, is virtually distinct from the divine attributes. This means that it contains them actually and implicitly, but not explicitly; for these attributes are afterward explicitly derived from it.

Billuart and certain other Thomists make another addition to the state of the question, but, unless I am mistaken, on insufficient grounds. Billuart is of the opinion that it is not a question of the divine nature as expressed by the most common and transcendental concept of *uncreated being*, which applies to all the divine attributes, just as the concept of created being applies to all the differences found in creatures.

There seems to be no foundation for this distinction between what is common and special in God, for God is not in any genus, not even according to our mode of conceiving Him. We can indeed distinguish in any creature the transcendentals that are common to all the genera and the species. But this distinction is of no value in God, since God is not in any genus, and transcendentals, such as being, unity . . . , are verified in God in a most special manner, that is, by reason of Himself. Hence it is not repugnant on a priori considerations for what constitutes the divine nature to be the *self-subsisting Being,* this constituting the terminus of the five proofs in the ascending order and the principle for the derivation of the attributes.

THE VARIOUS OPINIONS AS TO WHAT CONSTITUTES THE DIVINE NATURE

1) The nominalists reply that God is an accumulation of perfections, and there is no need of our inquiring into the logical priority of one perfection over the others. It would be a useless question. In fact, the nominalists said that the distinction between the divine attributes was a purely mental one (*rationis ratiocinantis*), a verbal distinction, such as we have between Tullius and Cicero, and from this it would follow that the divine names are synonymous.[1] This opinion of the nominalists leads to agnosticism, for it could just as well be said that God punishes by His mercy and forgives by His justice. This would mean the end of all knowledge about God, and for this reason the nominalists were formerly expelled from the University of Paris.

2) On the other hand, Scotus admitted an actual and formal distinction between the divine attributes, a distinction that is actual from the nature of the thing, and which is prior to the consideration of our mind, and which gives us the answer to the question as to what constitutes the divine nature, by saying that it is radical infinity, demanding as such the various divine attributes.

In reply to this, the Thomists say that radical infinity, or the exigency of all perfections, does not constitute the divine nature, but is presupposed by it and has its foundation therein. It is indeed the very essence of God that demands all the perfections which are derived from it. Moreover, God's infinity is deduced from the fact that He is the self-subsisting Being.[2] Besides, infinity is a mode

---

[1] *Summa theol.*, Ia, q. 13, a. 4.
[2] *Ibid.*, q. 7, a. 1.

of each of the divine attributes. Finally, the Thomists say that the actual and formal distinction of Scotus, by the very fact that it is prior to our consideration of it, is already a real distinction, however slight this may be, and hence it is excluded from God by reason of His absolute simplicity in whom, as the Council of Florence says, "all things are one and the same where there is no opposition of relation," [3] and this opposition is to be found only between the divine Persons.

3) Several Thomists of the seventeenth century and later, such as John of St. Thomas, the Salmanticences, and Billuart, hold that subsistent intellection is what constitutes the divine nature. Their principal argument is as follows: The supreme degree of being is that which must constitute the divine nature; but the various grades of being are existence, life, and intellection; therefore subsistent intellection is what constitutes the divine nature.

Hence in their opinion "self-subsisting Being" is in God to be taken as something transcendental and not specific. But, as we have pointed out in the state of the question, there seems to be no foundation for this distinction in God between what is common and what is specific; because God is not in any genus, not even according to our mode of conceiving Him.

4) Many other theologians, several of them being Thomists, hold that self-subsisting Being is what constitutes the divine nature. Among the Thomists holding this opinion we have Capreolus, Bannez, Ledesma, Contenson, Gotti, and more recently del Prado and Father Billot. We find this view expressed in the twenty-third proposition of the Thomistic theses approved by the Sacred Congregation of Studies (1914): "The divine essence, in that it is identical with the actuality of the divine being in act, or in that it is the self-subsisting Being, is proposed to us as constituted, as it were, in its metaphysical aspect, and by this same furnishes us with the reason of His infinite perfection." [4] But Suarez says that it is better to posit the fact itself of aseity as the principle from which the divine attributes are derived.

Others reply to this, and justly so, that the reason for this fact is that only in God are essence and existence identical, or that God alone is the self-subsisting Being. But Suarez expresses a different view, because he does not admit a real distinction between created essence and existence.

As we shall at once see, it seems that our preference must be for

[3] Denz., no. 703.

[4] Cf. Guido Mattuissi, S.J., *Le XXIV tesi della filosofia di S. Tomasso d'Aquino approvate dalla S. Congregazione degli studi*. Roma, 1917, pp. 260–76.

this opinion, on the supposition, however, that God is not a body but pure spirit. But it is especially because God is He who is [5] that He transcends all spirits. Before we prove this fourth opinion, mention must be made of two other views proposed by those outside the Catholic schools of theology.

Fifth opinion. There are those who maintain that essential goodness is what formally constitutes the divine nature. Thus Plato was of the opinion that the supreme reality is the idea of Good transcending essence and intelligence.[6] In like manner Plotinus considered that the supreme reality is the One Good transcending intelligence. We still find some traces of this theory in the writings of several Augustinians although they do not explicitly examine this question. Thus Peter Lombard divided the subject matter of his *Book of the Sentences* with reference to enjoyable and useful good, namely, to those things that can be enjoyed, especially God, usables or creatures, inasmuch as they are means for the attainment of the supreme Good.

To this opinion the Thomists reply in the words of St. Thomas,[7] that, as being is absolutely prior to the good, God, prior to being conceived as the supreme Good, is conceived as the supreme Being existing of Himself; in fact, God is the supreme Good only because He is the plenitude of being. In other words, the idea of being is more absolute, simple, and universal than the idea of good, and good can be conceived only as being that has reached its final stage of perfection, and that is capable of appealing to the appetitive faculty and perfecting it. Hence God is the supreme Good inasmuch as He is the plenitude of being.

But it must be conceded [8] that in a certain sense, that is, not in order of being but of causality, good is prior to being, since the end is first among causes, attracting the agent, and the agent educes the form from the matter for the production of the causated being. Hence, for us, God is first of all considered as the supreme Good, our ultimate end; but in Himself, God is first of all the self-subsisting Being, and would be so even if He had not created anything, and were not the end of any creature.

Sixth opinion. It is that of certain modern philosophers, such as Secrétan and J. Lequier, who believed in voluntarism and absolute libertism. These maintained that divine liberty is what formally constitutes the divine nature, for God is His own reason for what

[5] Ex. 3: 14.
[6] *The Republic,* Bk. VII.
[7] *Summa theol.,* Ia, q.5, a.2.
[8] *Ibid.*

He is. But there is nothing, they say, that is more its own reason for what it is than liberty, which determines itself as it wills. Hence God would be absolute liberty, and most freely would have determined all things, even those that pertain to His intimate life. Wherefore, according to Secrétan,[9] the definition of God is not "Who is" or "I am who am," but "I am that which I most freely will to be."

The writings of Descartes revealed a tendency to accept this theory. In his opinion, eternal truths, even the truth of the principle of contradiction, depend upon God's free will. Ockham had said something similar to this in maintaining that God could have commanded us to commit murder and even to lead an irreligious life; to which Leibnitz replied that "God would then no more be, according to His nature, the supreme Good than the supreme evil of the Manichaeans."[10] St. Thomas likewise said: "To say that justice depends simply upon the will of God, is to say that the divine will does not act according to wisdom; and this is blasphemy."[11]

This libertarian theory cannot be admitted, because freedom of choice presupposes deliberation on the part of the intellect, otherwise it would be the same as chance. But chance is an accidental cause, and so cannot be the first cause; for the accidental presupposes the essential. If anyone digging a grave, did not intrinsically as such dig, the treasure would not accidentally be found. Hence it is most manifest that the first liberty presupposes the supreme Being and the first Intellect.

Besides these six opinions, it is difficult to conceive or think of any other ways of solving this problem. Priority is given either to Being or to the Good or to the Infinite or to Intellection or to liberty. Whether we consider in God what is subjective or what is objective, no other answers than these can be found.

We have already stated why the last two opinions cannot be admitted, nor the opinion of the nominalists nor that of the Scotists. Therefore we have but two opinions left to consider, namely, whether self-subsisting Being is what formally constitutes the divine nature, or whether it is self-subsisting intellection.

Solution. From the teaching of St. Thomas we see that the formal constituent of the divine nature is self-subsisting Being, which is the view held by several Thomists above mentioned, although not all are of this opinion.

We are at least persuaded of this for three reasons: (1) because of the order observed by St. Thomas in this treatise on God; (2)

9 *La philosophie de la liberté*, I, Bk. XV, pp. 361–70.
10 *Theodicée*, II, §§ 176 f.
11 *De veritate*, q. 23, a. 6.

from his teaching on this point; [12] (3) from the solution of the difficulties proposed against this opinion.

1) The order observed in the treatise is evidence of this. In fact, according to this order, by means of the five proofs, we advance in knowledge to the establishing of this supreme truth: "God is the self-subsisting Being," [13] and the divine attributes are afterward derived from this supreme truth.

Thus from the beginning of the third question to the end of the fourth article the mind continually advances in knowledge, for the first article establishes that God is not a body; the second, that God is not composed of matter and form; the third, that God is not a composite, consisting of His nature and the principle of individuation. From this we conclude that God is a pure spirit. But a pure spirit can be a created being; hence to distinguish God from even the noblest of creatures, it is established in the fourth article that God is the self-subsisting Being, since He is the first efficient cause, pure act, and essential being.

This is the culminating point in the ascendant order or by the way of finding, and the principle in the descendent process or by the way of judgment, of wisdom, which judges of all things by the highest of causes. Thus from the fact that God is the self-subsisting Being is deduced the real distinction between God and the world, [14] and from this the divine attributes are afterward deduced, such as goodness (plenitude of being), [15] infinity (being not received in anything is infinite), [16] immutability, eternity, and other attributes. Likewise the divine intellection is deduced from the immateriality of the divine being, and omniscience from the fact that God is the self-subsisting Being. Hence it is only in the fourteenth question that the divine intellection is discussed. In fact, the opening words of the prologue to this question are: "Having considered what belongs to the divine substance, we have now to treat of God's operation." Being is prior to truth and intellection, for intellection is predicated only of the subject and as this latter is related to intelligible being as the object.

Such is the order observed in this treatise on God. From this we see that the formal constituent of the divine nature is stated before the fourteenth question, in the fourth article of the third question, where it is shown that only in God are essence and existence identical. As Father del Prado [17] with good reason shows, this prop-

[12] *Summa theol.,* Ia, q.13, a.11.

[13] *Ibid.,* q.3, a.4.

[14] *Ibid.,* a.8.

[15] *Ibid.,* q.5.

[16] *Ibid.,* q.7.

[17] *De veritate fundamentali philosophiae christianae.*

osition constitutes the fundamental of Christian philosophy, fundamental indeed not by way of finding but by way of judgment, since wisdom judges of all things by the highest cause, or by reason.

2) This opinion is equivalently what St. Thomas said: "This name, *He who is,* is most properly applied to God for three reasons. First, because of its signification . . . , since the existence of God is His essence itself. . . . Secondly, on account of its universality . . . to designate by this the infinite sea of substance. . . . Thirdly, from its consignification, for it signifies present existence, and this above all applies to God, whose existence knows not past or future." [18]

Thus, when Moses asked God His name, "God said to Moses: I am who am. He said: Thus shalt thou say to the children of Israel: He who is hath sent me to you." [19] The Hebrew word "Yahweh" (from which the word Jehovah is derived, which is written with the vowel signs of Adonai) is the equivalent of "He who is." It is known as the Tetragrammaton, a word of four letters, and is God's proper name in the strictest sense.

3) This opinion receives its confirmation from the solution of the principal difficulty proposed by other Thomists who hold a different opinion. This difficulty is enunciated as follows: The highest degree of being is what constitutes the divine essence. But this highest degree is intellection; for, in the ascendant order of the grades of being we have: existence, life, intellection. Therefore intellection is what constitutes the divine nature.

St. Thomas replies to this by distinguishing between participated being—which can be without life and intelligence—and self-subsisting being, which is the fullness itself of being, including all other perfections actually and implicitly. In the passage referred to, St. Thomas says: "Although therefore existence does not include life and wisdom, because that which participates in existence need not participate in every mode of existence, nevertheless God's existence includes in itself life and wisdom, because nothing of the perfection of being can be wanting to Him who is subsisting being itself." [20] Similarly, from the work just quoted, we read: "Being taken simply, as including all perfection of being, surpasses life and all that follows it." [21]

[18] *Summa theol.,* Ia, q. 13, a. 11.

[19] Ex. 3: 14.

[20] *Summa theol.,* Ia, q. 4, a. 2 ad 3um.

[21] *Ibid.,* Ia IIae, q. 2, a. 5 ad 2um; see also I *Sent.,* d. 8, q. 1, a. 1, 8; *De potentia,* q. 7, a. 2 ad 9um; cf. Gotti, O.P., *De Deo,* tr. II, dub. 3, § 3; Contenson, O.P., *De Deo,* diss. II, c. 2, spec. 2.

The theologians of the sixteenth and seventeenth centuries usually discussed this question at the beginning of their treatise on God. St. Thomas discusses it in a special manner in the thirteenth question, in connection with the divine names, and rightly so, because the divine being is first considered by him, and then our possibility of knowing it.

Nevertheless the different views about these attributes as presented by nominalism, the formalism of Scotus, and the moderate realism of St. Thomas, oblige us to insert this introduction, which serves as material for reflection upon this treatise, and which was ideally present to the mind of St. Thomas as he was assigning in orderly arrangement the various parts of this treatise.

In this question of the divine attributes, all theologians distinguish between absolutely simple perfections, which imply no imperfection (such as intellection) and relative or mixed perfections, which denote imperfection even in their formal signification (such as reasoning). But certain theologians do not sufficiently distinguish the divine attributes or the absolutely simple perfections from God's free action and the divine persons; for, although the latter do not imply any imperfection, yet they are not absolutely simple perfections in the strict sense.

HOW THE DIVINE ATTRIBUTE IS DEFINED

To avoid the above-mentioned confusion we must define the expression "divine attribute," as the Thomists usually do, by saying that it is an absolutely simple perfection which exists necessarily and formally in God, and which is deduced from what we conceive as constituting the divine essence.[22]

Explanation of this definition.

1) We are concerned with what is an attribute in the strict sense of the term, for sometimes the term refers in an improper sense to all that is predicated even not necessarily of God (as the divine free act) or else relatively (as the relations of paternity, filiation, passive spiration, by which the divine persons are constituted).

2) It is called an absolute perfection, not to the exclusion of perfections that are named with reference to creatures, such as providence, mercy, justice, omnipotence, but to the exclusion of the divine relation, to which the term "attribute" does not apply since

---

[22] Cf. Damascene's *De fide orthodoxa*, Bk. I, chap. 12; *Summa theol.*, Ia, q.3, a.3 ad 1um; q.13, a.4 ad 2um, 3um.

the relations are not common to the three Persons; for the attribute is a property of the nature and is common to the three Persons.

3) It is called an absolutely simple perfection so as to exclude relative or mixed perfections, which essentially imply imperfection, such as rationality. But what in the strict sense is an absolutely simple perfection? It is that perfection which in its formal concept implies no imperfection, and which it is better for one to have than not. Many add these last words to the definition, and rightly so, because the divine free act and the divine relations, although they imply no imperfection, yet are not absolutely simple perfections, at least in the strict sense. For it is not better for God to have the creative act than not, and there would have been no imperfection in God if He had not created, no matter what Leibnitz said about this; nor does it add to God's perfection that He most freely wills to create the universe. In like manner the Father, to whom the opposite relation of filiation does not apply, would be lacking in some absolutely simple perfection if the relation of filiation were an absolutely simple perfection, as if it were superadded to the infinite perfection of the divine nature, which is common to the three Persons. Hence neither the divine relations nor the divine free act are absolutely simple perfections, at least in the strict sense. But the contrary of this is true as regards liberty and omnipotence, for God would be free and omnipotent, even if He had not created anything.

4) It is said to be necessarily existing in God, which means that it is like a property of the divine nature, so that God's free acts such as creation, are excluded by these words.

5) It is said to be formally existing in God so that also mixed perfections may be excluded; for these are only virtually in God, since He can produce them in creatures. Thus life is formally attributed to God, but not animal or rational.

6) It is said, "as derived from the essence," so as to exclude the prior concept of the divine nature. Thus the divine attribute is accurately defined.

HOW THE DIVINE ATTRIBUTES ARE CLASSIFIED

The theologians are not altogether in agreement concerning this classification. Some stress too much the attributes as they relate to us in the classification; others prefer to discuss the attributes as they relate to God as He is in Himself.

Suarez and several other theologians, discussing the attributes more as they relate to us, classify them into positive attributes, such as goodness, wisdom, justice, and negative attributes, such as incorporeity, infinity, immutability, ineffability. They also point out that very many negative attributes, such as infinity and immutability, are incommunicable, or cannot be participated in.

A difficulty presents itself in this classification, inasmuch as certain attributes expressed in a negative form, such as infinity, are in themselves positive, just as incorporeity in itself denotes spirituality,[23] and immutability in itself expresses stability in the highest degree, the positive form of which is eternity. Hence this Suarezian division stresses too much the *quoad nos* element in the attributes.

St. Thomas, however, in considering the attributes as they relate to God as He is in Himself, seems to have devised a better classification, by distinguishing between those that pertain to the divine substance and those that refer to the divine operation.[24] In the first class of attributes we have simplicity, perfection, goodness, infinity, immensity, immutability, eternity, unity, invisibility, and ineffability. In the second class, however, we have knowledge, will, and love, and subordinate to these are justice, mercy, and providence, as virtues residing either in the will or in the intellect. Finally, as regards virtually transient operations, we have the creative, conservative, and directive powers.[25] This division is primary and fundamental, because it stresses more God as He is in Himself, and not so much as we are related to Him. The classification proposed by Suarez is more of the nature of a subdivision, and St. Thomas refers to it as such.[26]

HOW THE DIVINE ATTRIBUTES ARE DISTINCT FROM ONE ANOTHER AND FROM THE DIVINE ESSENCE

There are three leading opinions, and they are the result of the different ways of solving the twofold problem about universals and the analogy of the divine names.[27] Let us first consider the extreme views that are fundamentally in opposition.

1) The nominalists admitted only a mental distinction between the divine attributes, like the verbal one between Tullius and Cicero, or between Cicero the subject of some proposition and Cicero the predicate of another proposition.

[23] On the contrary, for the angels who have a positive and intuitive knowledge of spiritual things, corporeity is the negation of spirituality.

[24] *Summa theol.*, Ia, prologue to q.3 and especially to q.14.

[25] *Ibid.*, q.25.

[26] *Ibid.*, q.13, a.2. In this same article St. Thomas notes another subdivision, since certain divine names are predicated absolutely (as perfection, simplicity), whereas others are predicated relatively as referring to creatures (such as providence, mercy, justice, omnipotence).

[27] This has been more fully examined by us in *God, His Existence*, II, 203-46.

They give two reasons for this opinion: (1) The universal is not even fundamentally present in things; only individuals exist, and in these there is no true, essential, and unchangeable similarity according to the species, the genera, and the transcendentals; (2) hence not even analogically can anything be predicated of God and creatures at least in the proper sense, but only metaphorically or symbolically.[28] Hence to say, "God is just," would no more properly belong to Him, than to say "God is angry." To say that "God is just" would not mean that He is so substantially but only causally, inasmuch as He is the cause of justice in creatures just as He is the cause of life in animals.[29]

Criticism. From this opinion it follows that the divine names are synonymous and that, contrary to reason, Scripture, and tradition, it can be said therefore that God punishes by means of His mercy and pardons by means of His justice; for, as the nominalists say, there is only a verbal distinction between these two attributes as between Tullius and Cicero, and wherever we find the name Tullius written the name Cicero can be written for it. Thus this opinion leads to pure agnosticism, which would result in God being absolutely unknowable, the treatise on God an absolute impossibility, and all the definitions of the Church about the divine attributes would be identical in meaning. As St. Thomas remarks: "If the words 'God is good' signified no more than 'God is the cause of good things,' it might in like manner be said that God is a body, inasmuch as He is the cause of bodies." [30] In the next two articles of this question he observes that not all the names applied to God are metaphorical in meaning, for some are applied properly although analogically (as in the case of "God is just"), and not all the divine names are synonymous.[31] The nominalist view destroys the analogy of being, and leads to equivocality of being.[32]

2) Scotus admits, however, that the divine essence is distinct from the attributes and the Persons, and he posits an actual and formal distinction pertaining to the nature of the thing, between the divine

---

[28] Concerning the philosophical errors of the nominalists, see Denzinger, nos. 553-70. The following philosophical errors of Nicholas of Autrecourt are condemned: (1) "That we can have no certainty from the natural appearances of things," which is practically a denial of the ontological validity of primary ideas; (3) "There is absolutely no difference in meaning between the propositions: God is, God is not." This is a denial of the transcendent validity of the notion of being in acquiring a knowledge of God, and so being is equivocal or is used in absolutely different senses, if its affirmation and negation are no different in meaning; (32) "God and the creature are not anything."

[29] *Summa theol.*, Ia, q.13, a.2.

[30] *Ibid.*, q.13, a.2.

[31] *Ibid.*, a.3 f.

[32] *Ibid.*, q.13, a.5, for a refutation of this view.

attributes, which is previous to our consideration of them, as already stated. Only in this way, according to Scotus, it can be affirmed that God punishes by His justice and not by His mercy. This necessitates that these two attributes be formally and actually distinct in God, previous to our consideration of them, about the same way as, in our soul, the intellect and the will are formally and actually distinct.[33]

This theory has its foundation in the extreme realism advocated by Scotus, who contends that already in created beings there is an actual and formal distinction between the metaphysical degrees of anything whatever, as, for instance, in Peter, between humanity, vitality, substantiality, and entity. From this it follows that being is predicated univocally of God and creatures, as Scotus explicitly maintains. Nor is it to be wondered at that being is univocal, if, previous to the mind's consideration, it is formally and actually distinct from substantiality, vitality, that is, from the modes of being.

Criticism. (a) This actual and formal distinction, devised by Scotus, if it is truly more than virtual, that is, as we remarked, if it truly exists in the thing before the mind's consideration, is already a real distinction, however slight it may be,[34] and then it is opposed to God's absolute simplicity; for, as the Council of Florence says: "In God all things are one and the same where there is no relation of opposition." [35] In other words, in this way Scotus ends in extreme realism and in a certain anthropomorphism, since he posits in God a distinction that exists only in the mind. This theory is the absolute reverse of nominalism and agnosticism. Thus Scotus does not sufficiently recede from the exaggerated realism of Gilbert de la Porrée, which was condemned in the Council of Reims as contrary to God's absolute simplicity.[36]

b) The metaphysical degrees are not actually distinct in a thing before the mind's consideration, as, for instance, in Peter, animality, vitality, rationality, and substantiality; for these are reduced to the same concept of humanity, of which animality is the genus, and rationality is the specific *differentia*. Thus they correspond to the same reality that is in itself one but virtually multiplex.[37]

c) Moreover, if being is formally and actually distinct from its

[33] Consult Scotus in *I Sent*, d.3, q.1, 3; d.8, q.3; d.5, q.1.

[34] There is no intermediate distinction between the real and the virtual or that distinction which has its foundation in the thing, because there is no intermediate step between what precedes the mind's consideration and what does not.

[35] Denz., no. 703.

[36] *Ibid.*, no. 391.

[37] Cf. Goudin, *Metaphysica*, disp. I, q.3: "De distinctione quo gradus metaphysici distinguuntur."

modes, then these modes would be outside being, and therefore non-entities. There is danger of pantheism in this, for if being were univocal, there would be but one being, because the univocal is not differentiated except by differences extrinsic to it, and what is not being is a nonentity. Truly the modes of being are included in the concept of being, and are contained in it actually and implicitly. Therefore being is not univocal (like a genus, the *differentiae* of which are extrinsic to it), but analogical. Being expresses something that is not absolutely but proportionately the same in self-existing Being, in created substantial being, and in accidental being. Finally, this doctrine of Scotus does not seem to be in conformity with the teaching of the Fourth Lateran Council, in which we read: "So great similarity cannot be detected between the Creator and the creature that we do not have to take note of a greater dissimilarity between them." [38] This is practically a definition of analogy, since the analogical aspect in God and creatures is not absolutely but proportionately the same, as with wisdom which in God is the cause of things and in us is measured by things.[39] Hence, while the nominalists tend toward equivocation of being, Scotus maintains the univocation of being. The two opinions are fundamentally in opposition.[40]

3) The common opinion of the theologians mediates, so to speak, between nominalism and exaggerated realism, and towers above them. This opinion, the source of which is the moderate realism of St. Thomas, is commonly formulated by the Thomists and a great number of theologians as follows: There is a minor virtual distinction between the divine attributes and God's essence, between the divine attributes, and likewise between the divine persons and the essence.

St. Thomas uses simpler terminology, saying that God's essence is distinct from the attributes and the divine Persons "not really but logically." [41] He is speaking of the logical distinction that is founded on reality, which subsequently is commonly called virtual; and this calls for an explanation.

a) The virtual distinction is a distinction founded on reality, which means, contrary to Scotus' theory, that it is non-existent previous to the mind's consideration, and it does not destroy God's absolute simplicity. Against the nominalists and agnostics, however,

[38] Denz., no. 432.

[39] Cf. *infra*, q.13, a.5.

[40] Nevertheless, when Scotus substitutes his formal distinction for St. Thomas' real distinction, for instance, between the faculties of the soul, he paves the way for nominalism.

[41] *Summa theol.*, Ia, q.28, a.2.

it is said to be "founded on reality," since the different absolute perfections found in creatures are equivalently expressed in the eminence of the Deity.[42] St. Thomas says expressly: "To the various and multiplied conceptions of our intellect there corresponds one altogether simple principle, according to these conceptions, imperfectly understood." [43] The eminence of the Deity is most simple, but it is virtually multiple, and all absolutely simple perfections are contained in it formally and eminently. This must now be briefly explained, and more fully in the thirteenth question.

Formally: This means substantially and properly; not merely metaphorically, but analogically and properly.[44]

Eminently: How the perfections are contained is mysterious; but the divine attributes are so identified in the most eminent and formal concept of the Deity as not to be destroyed by it. They are contained formally in it, and yet they are not formally distinct. In fact, they are found in their purest state, without any imperfection, only in the Deity.

More briefly, absolute perfections are in God more so than the seven colors are in the white light; for these seven colors are only virtually present in whiteness, whereas the divine perfections are formally distinct from one another. For, whereas whiteness is not blue, one and true are predicated of the Deity.[45]

b) The distinction between the divine attributes is called a minor virtual distinction. For the major virtual distinction is that which is of the nature of excluding and excluded, as in Peter the genus of animality is distinct from rationality, which is the *differentia* extrinsic to it, and there is a real foundation for conceiving it as in potentiality for this latter, as being susceptible of further perfection by something extraneous to it. But there is no real foundation for conceiving anything in God as in potentiality for some further perfection by the addition of something extraneous to Him. Whatever is conceived in God, must be conceived in Him as purest act. Hence there is a minor virtual distinction between the divine attributes, and between these and the divine essence. This means that the distinction is not of the nature of excluding and excluded, but of implicit and explicit. In other words, God's nature as we conceive it (the self-subsisting Being) contains the attributes more so than virtually, more so than the genus contains the differences extrinsic to it, for they are contained actually and implicitly in it; but dis-

---

[42] *Ibid.,* q.13, a.4, 5; *I Sent.,* d.2, q.1, a.3.
[43] *Summa theol.,* Ia, q.13, a.4.
[44] *Ibid.,* a.1–5.
[45] See Cajetan's *Commentary in Iam,* q.13, a.5, no. 7.

cursive reasoning is necessary for their explicit deduction from the divine nature. But the Deity, as it is itself, contains them actually and explicitly. Thus the blessed no longer need to have recourse to discursive reasoning so as clearly to see God's attributes in the Deity. Hence all the attributes mutually include one another, or each contains the others actually and implicitly.

Moreover, this minor virtual distinction properly applies only to those attributes that are differentiated specifically and that pertain to different orders, as, for instance, between intellection and volition, justice and mercy; but there is no such distinction between attributes which, as found in creatures, differ only as potency and act do, such as between essence and existence, intellect and intellection. There is only an extrinsically virtual distinction between these, which means that the foundation for this distinction is not in the divine reality but in creatures. Otherwise it would have to be said that our conception of God includes the presence of something potential in Him for which there is a foundation in the divine reality. St. Thomas, as we have remarked, makes use of simpler terminology, and says that the distinction between the attributes and the Persons and the divine essence is "not real but logical." [46] Moderate realism and the doctrine of analogy are the two fundamental reasons for this traditional opinion.

1) According to moderate realism, the universe exists fundamentally in things, and there is a foundation for this in them. Thus in Peter there is a virtual distinction between rationality, animality, and entity. In like manner, there is a virtual distinction between God's attributes.

2) Being is analogous, and is not a genus, for the differences of being would be outside being, and what is outside being is a nonentity. Nor is being equivocal, for this would mean the abolition of all true resemblance between beings. God would be absolutely unknowable, and it could be said of Him, as Nicholas of Autrecourt contended, "God is" and "God is not." [47] In fact, if being were equivocal, the principle of contradiction would be false.[48]

Therefore the divine attributes apply to God analogically, and are present in Him formally and eminently; but between the attributes and between each of them and the divine essence there is only a virtual distinction. Expressed more briefly: the attributes are formally in God, but they are not formally distinct.

[46] *Summa theol.*, Ia, q.28, a.2.
[47] Denz., no. 555.
[48] *Summa theol.*, Ia, q.13, a.5.

The Simplicity of God

Prologue

CONCERNING God we must consider what He is and how He is, or rather how He is not, for in this life we cannot know His essence, since this would be to see the Deity.[1] Hence we inquire how God is not, by removing from Him what does not apply to Him, such as composition and motion. Thus we must treat of God's simplicity, perfection, infinity, immutability, and unity. But we shall afterward see how God is known and named by us.

This question of God's simplicity starts out by excluding from Him what is known as physical composition, or of really distinct parts. In the first four articles it is established: (1) that God is not a body; (2) that He is not composed of matter and form; (3) nor of nature and suppositum; (4) nor of essence and existence. Then what is known as metaphysical composition, which consists of genus and *differentia*, is excluded in the fifth article.

Finally, it is shown that there is no accident in God (a. 6), that God is altogether simple (a. 7), and that He does not enter into the composition of other things, either as form or matter, since He is the extrinsic cause, which means that He is the efficient and final cause of all things (a. 8). In these last three articles we have the refutation of pantheism, and they are the result of the conclusions of what was established in the fourth article, namely, that only God is the self-subsisting Being. This fourth article contains the dominating principle of this question, that is, it is the terminus in the ascending order by way of investigation, and the beginning in the descending order by way of judgment, since wisdom judges of all things by the highest of reasons.

FIRST ARTICLE

WHETHER GOD IS A BODY

State of the question. A body is defined as a substance that is extended according to three dimensions. But Holy Scripture speaks

---

1 Wayfarers, as regards the Deity, since they have not the adequate concept of this, but know it only in name, are like men who would have seen the seven colors and never have seen whiteness; this latter they would know only in name, and they would understand that by this name is implied the origin of colors. Thus for wayfarers the Deity is the root of all divine perfections that are naturally participable and knowable. The Deity is participable only by grace, and the participation is physical, formal, and analogous.

metaphorically of God's arm, right hand . . . , as pointed out in the beginning of this article, and we must carefully distinguish between the metaphorical and literal senses in Holy Scripture. Tertullian did not sufficiently observe this distinction. But among philosophers Spinoza, as a pantheist, maintains that extension is an attribute of God, and he admits that it is infinite.

The reply, which is *de fide,* is as follows: God is a spirit and therefore is not a body. Jesus said to the Samaritan woman: "God is a spirit, and they that adore Him, must adore Him in spirit and truth." [2] Similarly St. Paul says: "The invisible things of Him from the creation of the world are clearly seen, being understood by the things that are made." [3] Preaching to the Athenians, he said: "We must not suppose the divinity to be like unto gold or silver or stone, the graving of art and device of man." [4] The Vatican Council says: "The Holy Catholic Church believes that there is one true and living God . . . absolutely simple and immutable spiritual substance." [5]

Three proofs from reason are given, that God is not a body. The first proof discusses the body as a physical entity; in the second proof the quantitative aspect is considered; in the third proof the metaphysical element is stressed.

First proof. No body is in motion unless it is put in motion; but God is the first unmoved Mover (first way); therefore God is not a body. Against the major there is the difficulty of attraction, since the magnet attracts other bodies to itself, although it is not itself set in motion. In reply to this we say that, although the magnet has this property of attraction, its action is not its own, its power to act is not its action; for this it would have to be its own being, because operation follows being, and the mode of operation the mode of being. Therefore the magnet is moved invisibly by the first Mover, at least as a qualitative motion. Moreover, as Cajetan observes, the magnet can also be moved locally, and every moving body is moved at least as in potentiality for this, since it is by nature apt to be moved, and this suffices to distinguish it from the absolutely immobile first mover (this immobility not being that of inertia but of perfection), which is the terminus of the first way in proving God's existence. Hence the major can be construed as meaning: every body is mobile. But God is the first immobile Mover. Therefore He is not a body.

Second proof. It considers rather the quantitative aspect in bodies,

2 John 4: 24.
3 Rom. 1: 20.
4 Acts 17: 29.
5 Denz., no. 1782.

inasmuch as the parts are continuous. Every body is in potentiality, at least because the continuous is divisible to infinity. But God is pure act and there is absolutely no potentiality in Him. Therefore God is not a body.[6]

The minor is proved as follows: actuality is, absolutely speaking, prior to potentiality, for whatever is in potentiality can be reduced into actuality only by some being in actuality; but God is the first Being, as established in the fourth way of proving God's existence; therefore God is pure Act.[7] Every potentiality presupposes actuality, for every being that is in potentiality expresses a relation to actuality and cannot be reduced into actuality except by a being that is in act. Therefore the supreme Being is in no way in potentiality.

Third proof. It considers the metaphysical aspect in bodies. The noblest of all beings cannot be a body; but God is the noblest of all beings, as established in the fourth way of proving God's existence; therefore God is not a body.

The major is proved by showing that corporeity is something inferior. For a body is either living or non-living, and a living body is nobler than a non-living body; thus the ant is, absolutely speaking, nobler than a heavenly body. Moreover, the principle of life in a living body is nobler than the body as such. To put it more briefly, life is something nobler than corporeity, otherwise every body would be a living body. Vegetative life and sensitive life come from the specific form in the living body; this form, however, is not a body, but vivifies the body.[8] From this third argument, as also from the other two, it is proved, indeed, that God is not a body; but this does not as yet prove that God is not the form of a body, so that He might be the soul of the world. This is proved, however, in the following articles, especially in the eighth article.

In the reply to the objections, St. Thomas explains the metaphors of Holy Scripture, when it speaks of the height or the depth of God and of His knowledge.

SECOND ARTICLE

WHETHER GOD IS COMPOSED OF MATTER AND FORM

State of the question. According to St. Thomas, everything composed of matter and form is a body, as he affirms in the counter-

[6] The major is explained by St. Thomas in his commentary on Aristotle's *Physics*, Bk. VI, chaps. 1 f., where he discusses especially the question of the continuous.

[7] This had already been clearly proved by Aristotle in his *Metaphysics*, Bk. XII, chap. 7.

[8] *Summa theol.*, Ia, q.75, a.1.

argument. But in Avicebron's opinion there is a composite of matter and form that is not a body, because this philosopher said that even spiritual substances are composed of spiritual matter and form. Perhaps he said this so as to explain their individuation, and thus there could be several angels of the same species. Contrary to this, St. Thomas is of the opinion that the only composition in created spiritual substances is that of essence and existence, and of substance and accident. Each of them is a subsistent and immaterial form; and hence there cannot be two angels of the same species.

The conclusion of the article states the impossibility of matter existing in God. The proofs for this are given by considering: (1) matter in itself; (2) matter in its relation to its participated form; (3) matter in its relation to the action of the first agent.

First proof. Matter is in potentiality. But God is pure act, as stated in the preceding article, because He is the first being, the maximum in being (fourth way). Therefore God is immaterial. This article is expressed according to Aristotle's terminology.

Second proof. Here Plato's terminology concerning participation is more in evidence. Everything composed of matter and form is a participated good, or a participated form in matter; but God, inasmuch as He is the greatest good, is the essential good (fourth way); therefore God is not composed of matter and form.

Third proof. It starts from the principle that God is primarily and essentially an agent. Since the agent acts by its form, the manner in which it has its form is the manner in which it is an agent. But God, since He is the first agent (second way), is primarily and essentially a form, but not composed of matter and form.

The major is evident from the fact that the agent acts by its form, that is, the form is the reason of its acting; for to act is to determine, to actuate, and it is only by reason of its own determination that any being can determine. Thus fire heats and water cools. Hence it is said that the agent acts inasmuch as it is in act, and it is in act by means of its form, primarily by its substantial form from which the natural qualities originate.

Minor. God, being the first agent, is primarily and essentially an agent, which means that He is not moved by some higher power, but is of Himself essentially and immediately operative, just as the triangle of itself and immediately (or essentially and primarily) has three angles equal to two right angles. But this is a necessary property of the triangle, whereas God, as we shall see farther on,[9] is free in His external operations.

There arises a difficulty from this third argument. It seems that

9 *Ibid.,* q.19, a.3.

we can conclude only that God has essentially and primarily a form that is the reason of His action, but not that He is essentially and primarily a form. There is considerable difference between the verb "to be" and the verb "to have." Thus fire essentially and primarily generates heat, because it has essentially and primarily heat, but it is not heat.

In reply to this we say with Cajetan: It can truly be concluded that God is primarily and essentially a form, because He is primarily and essentially an agent, and not dependent upon any other being. For if God were an agent who, by reason of His form, constituted a part of a composite, He would not be primarily and essentially an agent; for action in this sense could be attributed to all that participate in such a form. Thus fire is not, strictly speaking, essentially and primarily generative of heat, because it is not heat, but participates in heat. If fire were unreceived heat, then, just as in the case of unreceived or subsistent heat, it would be unique of its kind. Hence St. Thomas' argument holds good. From the fact that God is primarily and essentially an agent, it follows that He is primarily and essentially a form not received in matter. This is also evident, as was said, from the fact that God is pure act and essential good. Thus God is pure spirit.

In the replies to the objections St. Thomas explains the metaphorical use of terms in Holy Scripture, when discussing the questions of a soul and of anger in God. It is said in the reply to the third objection: "The form which cannot be received in matter, is individualized precisely because it cannot be received in a subject."

Hence God is an unreceived and unreceptive form. We shall see in the fourth article that God is also the unreceived and unreceptive being, and in the sixth article that He is the unreceived being because He cannot be the recipient of accidents. Thus what is meant by participation and unparticipated being is made increasingly clear, and we already find this vaguely presented to us in the writings of Plato.

THIRD ARTICLE

WHETHER GOD IS THE SAME AS HIS ESSENCE OR NATURE

State of the question. It is asked whether there is composition of suppositum and nature in God. In the order of created things the suppositum is the complete subsisting being, of which the nature is the essential part. Thus the suppositum is really distinct from the nature, as the whole is from its principal part. Thus man is not his humanity (as stated in the second objection), but has humanity. The question is therefore, whether God is His Deity or has Deity.

Thus it becomes increasingly evident that there is a difference between the verb "to be" and the verb "to have." By this name "God" in the concrete sense, St. Thomas understands that which is, namely, suppositum or the Godhead as it connotes the individual, whether this word is previously taken to mean that He consists of three Persons or is one of the three Persons. This point is at present undetermined.

Reply. God is the same as His essence or nature. In other words, God is His Godhead and not only has the Godhead.

1) There is evidence of this on the authority of Holy Scripture, and it is a revealed truth, since Jesus said: "I am the way, and the truth, and the life." [10] He did not say: "I have truth and life," or merely: "I am true or truthful and living," but "I am the truth and the life." So that underlying the logical difference between subject and predicate, the verb "is" expresses real identity between them. Just as life, however, refers to the living being, so the Godhead refers to God. Hence God is His Godhead whereas, on the contrary, man is not His humanity, because the whole is not its part, but has its part, a point that will be more clearly explained in the body of the article.

In like manner, "God is charity," [11] and not only has charity. Contrary to this, the just, whether angels or men, have charity and are not charity. It must be observed that the Council of Reims defined against Gilbert de la Porrée, who denied that abstract terms can be predicated of God in the concrete: "We believe and confess that the simple nature of the Divinity is God, nor can it be denied in any Catholic sense that the Divinity is God and God is the Divinity." [12]

2) Proof from reason. In corporeal things nature differs from suppositum, just as the essential part differs from the whole, for besides the essential part there are the individualizing principles, for example, these bones and this flesh. But God is not corporeal, or composed of matter and form, but is a pure subsistent form (preceding article). And thus in God nature does not differ from suppositum. In other words, the suppositum is the subsistent form itself of the Godhead.

This proof rests upon the principle that, if affirmation is the cause of affirmation, negation is the cause of negation. But the affirmation that nature is a part of the suppositum, is the foundation for the aforesaid distinction. Therefore to deny that nature is a

10 John 14: 6.
11 I John 4: 8.
12 Denz., no. 389.

part of the suppositum, is to deny the aforesaid distinction. This argument is of validity provided it is properly understood.[13]

A difficulty, however, presents itself, since it seems to follow from this that, since the archangel Michael is a pure subsistent form apart from matter, he is his Michaelness. But this is false, for Michaelness is only an essential part of Michael, who in addition to this has existence and accidents.

In reply to this we say that, from the very fact that God is a pure form without matter, St. Thomas excludes from Him in this article individuating principles that are distinct from the common nature. In the angel, too, there are no individuating principles distinct from the nature.

But in the present article St. Thomas is not yet explicitly considering the fact that in God there is no composition of either essence and existence, or of substance and accident. This he will do in the fourth and sixth articles, in which it will be more clearly seen that God is His Godhead, because the Godhead in God is not solely an essential part, whereas, on the other hand, Michaelness is but an essential part in Michael, who is also a contingent being with the accidents of intellect and will. Hence Cajetan says in reference to this article: "Although this process of argumentation taken by itself can be criticized, yet when taken in conjunction with the doctrine of the subsequent articles it was found to be irreproachable, because the subsequent articles of this question exclude all composition." [14] Hence, to bring out more clearly the force of this argument, it may be expressed by the following syllogism: Where nature is not a part of the suppositum they do not differ; but in God nature is not a part of the suppositum; therefore in God nature and suppositum do not differ. The major is explicitly enunciated by St. Thomas in several places.[15]

Proof of minor. Since God is pure form, there are no individuating principles in addition to His nature. In fact, His existence is

---

[13] *Summa theol.*, IIIa, q.2, a.2; q.4, a.2.

[14] *Com. in Summam theol.*, IIIa, q.4, a.2.

[15] Thus St. Thomas says in his *Quodl.* II, a.4, "Whether suppositum and nature are identical in the angel": § 4, "To whatever being anything can accrue that does not belong to the concept of its nature, in that being suppositum and nature differ. . . . It is only in God that His essence excludes the presence of anything accidental, because His existence is His essence. Therefore suppositum and nature are absolutely the same in God. In the case of an angel, however, these are not absolutely the same, because there accrues to an angel something that does not belong to the species as such, for an angel's essence or nature does not include existence, and there are certain other accidental notes in an angel (contingent thoughts and volitions), and these do not belong to the nature but to the suppositum."

identical with His nature, nor is there such distinction as that between accidents and nature. Thus God and the Godhead are absolutely identical whereas, on the contrary, Peter is not his humanity, nor also, strictly speaking, is Michael his Michaelness.

But if God is His Godhead, then why the use of the concrete noun God and the abstract noun Godhead? The reply to the first objection solves this difficulty by saying: "We can speak of simple things only as though they were like the composite things from which we derive our knowledge." But the composite is the subsistent concrete thing, and its nature is spoken of in the abstract, as its essential part.

FOURTH ARTICLE

WHETHER ESSENCE AND EXISTENCE ARE THE SAME IN GOD

State of the question. This article, as we already pointed out, is the terminus in the ascending order by way of finding, of the five proofs for God's existence, and it is also the principle in the descending order by way of judgment, by which wisdom judges of all things by the highest of reasons and causes. We shall at once see that what St. Thomas says in this article is already a refutation of pantheism, since he gives us the reason why God is really and essentially distinct from every finite being.

But it must be well understood what is meant by existence, so as to distinguish the divine existence from existence as applied to various other things. The first objection of this article refers to this difficulty. The second objection, however, is as follows: We can know whether God exists, but we can cannot know what He is (at least know Him quidditatively). Therefore His essence is not existence.[16]

Reply. God and God alone is His existence, or in God alone are essence and existence identical.

There is at least a veiled reference to this in the Scripture, for we read: "God said to Moses: I am who am. . . . Thus shalt thou say to the children of Israel: He who is hath sent me to you."[17] This constitutes God's proper name. Creatures, however, have existence, and cannot be so named. Therefore from this it is intimated that God not only has existence but is existence, that He is His own existence.

Also truth and being are convertible terms. But Christ said: "I am the truth," and not merely: "I have truth." Therefore this sup-

---

[16] Concerning this article, cf. Norbert del Prado, O.P., *De veritate fundamentali philosophiae christianae*, p. 89; also pp. 20, 60.
[17] Ex. 3: 14.

poses that He is essential being. But being derives its name from existence, because being is that which exists or can exist, whose act is existence. Similarly, St. Hilary, who is quoted in the counter-argument, says: "In God existence is not an accidental quality, but subsisting truth." [18] This does not mean that existence is properly an accident of created substance, but that it is predicated contingently of the creature, though not so of God.

St. Thomas replies in the body of the article by advancing three proofs from reason for his conclusion. In the first he proves that God is the first efficient cause (first and second ways); in the second, that He is pure act (third and fourth ways); in the third, that He is the first being. Thus we can truly say that in this article we have the one end expressed to which the five proofs for God's existence by the ascending process of reasoning converge.

First proof. Essence and existence are the same in the first uncaused cause. But God is the first uncaused cause (second way). Therefore essence and existence are the same in God. The minor presents no difficulty, and it is the terminus of the second proof for God's existence.

The major is proved as follows: Whatever a thing has besides its essence must be caused either by the essential principles or by some exterior agent; but in the first uncaused cause, existence is not caused either by any other cause or by the essential principles of the thing, because "no thing is its own cause," since operation follows being; therefore existence is not something besides essence in the first uncaused cause, but is identical with it.

It cannot be said that God is cause of Himself, because to cause is to operate, and operation follows being. But it can be said that God's essence is the reason of His existence, inasmuch as He exists of Himself, is of Himself the reason for His existence. Thus this proposition, *God exists,* as stated above,[19] is self-evident in itself, but not to us.

Corollary. Father N. del Prado rightly infers against Suarez that in all other efficient causes existence differs from essence. He says: "It belongs therefore to the nature of the first efficient cause that its essence and existence is one and the same, since the first efficient cause must of necessity have its existence uncaused; and it is of the essence of uncaused existence in a being that this is identical with its nature, which exists without being caused. Therefore . . . it must be inferred that in all other efficient causes existence differs from essence. Otherwise there would be no secondary efficient causes, and before we could establish God's existence by means of

18 *De Trinitate,* Bk. VII, chap. 1.
19 *Summa theol.,* Ia, q.2, a.1.

efficient cause we should also have to find out what properly belongs to an uncaused cause, namely, identity of essence and existence." [20]

Thus this first argument serves a double purpose: (1) It points out the terminus of the first, second, and third proofs for God's existence, namely, of first unmoved Mover, of first uncaused Cause, and of the first necessary Being who is His own existence, or of the self-subsisting Being. (2) It assigns the ultimate reason for the distinction between caused or created being and the uncreated Being, as also between contingent being and the necessary Being. Contingent being is a potentiality to be or not to be, because it is not its own existence, but, if it exists, has existence. There is a vast difference between the verbs "to be" and "to have." Hence it is said that "the powers tremble" with reverential fear in seeing the self-subsisting Being, because the angels are not their own existence, but only have existence, and they could be annihilated by God's absolute power.

Second proof. It has its foundation in the principle that God is pure act, and is as follows: Existence is compared to essence, which is a distinct reality from it, as actuality to potentiality; but God is pure act, in whom there is no potentiality; therefore God's essence is not potentiality for existence, but is identical with existence. The major is the very definition of *esse* or existence. It is that which makes every form or nature actual. Thus humanity is not spoken of as actual except so far as it is spoken of as existing.

The minor was proved in the first article of this question. The reason given was that, absolutely speaking, actuality is prior to potentiality, since a being is said to be in potentiality with reference to its actuality, and is not reduced into actuality except by some being in actuality. But God is the first Being (fourth way). Therefore nothing of potentiality is in Him, but He is pure act. This is also evident from the fact that God is the first Mover, the first Cause, the first necessary Being. God must be His action, and hence His own existence, because operation follows existence, and the mode of operation the mode of existence. This argument points out the one end to which these three proofs for God's existence converge.

Corollary. Therefore in everything that is caused by God, essence is potentiality with reference to existence, and hence is really distinct from it, just as matter is from form. Before the consideration of our mind, matter is not form, but is potency that is made actual by its form, and hence is really distinct from it. In like manner, the essence of a caused thing is not its existence, previous to the

[20] Del Prado, *op. cit.*, p. 320.

mind's consideration of this. In other words, it is not identical with
its existence, but is distinct from it previous to the mind's consideration. Therefore this distinction, however slight it may appear,
is real. The angel, knowing its own essence directly, sees this to be
distinct from its existence. From this it is already apparent that
there can be only one essence that is existence itself, for multiplication presupposes participation. Thus participated existence is
manifold, as the existence of a stone, of a plant, of an animal, of
a man.

Third proof. It is derived from the principle that God is the first
Being (fourth way). That which is essential being is its own existence; but God is essential being, since He is the first being; therefore God is His own existence.

The minor presents no difficulty, for it is the terminus of the
fourth way in proving God's existence. The major is declared as
follows: "That which has existence, but is not existence, is a being
by participation," just as that which has fire, but is not itself fire,
as a coal fire, is on fire by participation. Therefore, "that a thing
be essential being, it must be its own existence."

We have in this argument a transcendent confirmation of the
principle of efficient causality. This principle, which is invoked in
proving God's existence, is thus formulated: Some other being is the
efficient cause of every contingent being. It is commonly held among
the Scholastics that an uncaused contingent being is a contradiction
in terms, that is, it is something not only unintelligible (which
Kant admits), but is also an absurdity and an absolute impossibility,
as for instance, that Lucifer originates from nothing, without any
efficient cause.

However, an "uncaused contingent being" is not so clearly repugnant to reason as a "caused non-contingent being"; to say that it is
uncaused is not a direct denial of the definition of contingent being,
but of its property. "The uncaused contingent being" would be
neither self-existent nor dependent on another for existence, and the
proposition, "the uncaused contingent being exists," would be the
affirmation of the positive agreement between two terms that in no
way agree. Hence what exists, but is not self-existent, depends on
another for its existence.

But now it is said that the contingent being has existence and
is not its existence. Therefore it is participated being, and hence it
depends on the essential Being. The idea of participated being,
however, is not completely intelligible apart from the correlative
idea of essential Being. Therefore it is better to use this term after
and not before the proofs for God's existence. Plato, indeed, practically started out with this notion of being but, on account of his

extreme realism, he thought he had a certain intuition of the supreme Good, or of God.

St. Thomas, in accordance with moderate realism, makes use of this notion of participated being preferably after the proofs of God's existence. Then the principle of causality receives its confirmation as from a transcendent source, since participated being is shown to be dependent on essential being, or being composed of potency and act on pure act.

Corollary. Father del Prado [21] concludes from this argument that the division of real being into essential being and participated being has its root in the distinction between the self-subsisting Being and that which is composed of essence and existence.

In this distinction we have the foundation for the refutation of pantheism. For if God is the self-subsisting Being, then nothing can be added to His being,[22] because He is ultimate actuality. Hence there can be no accident in God,[23] because the self-subsisting Being is not capable of further determination, but is the maximum in determination, although not limited, for limitation is on the part of matter that receives the form, or of essence that receives existence. From this we have the refutation of absolute evolutionism, according to which God is becoming in the world, and of Spinoza according to whom God is the recipient of finite modes that are, as it were, His accidents. Neoplatonic emanatism is likewise virtually refuted. This theory states that the soul is not made, not created out of nothing, but is "of God's substance," generated, as it were, from God. St. Thomas says in contradiction to this: "The soul is not its own existence, but is a being by participation. Therefore it is not a pure act like God." [24] Hence it is not the same as God's nature, and therefore is not generated from Him, is not of His substance, because generation is the origin of a living being from a living principle in the likeness of nature.[25] Thus man generates man, and as stated in revelation, God the Father generates the Son in the likeness of His nature, communicating to Him even the whole of His indivisible nature, which cannot be multiplied.

Thus we readily see from this that pantheism, by confusing God with the creature, must end either in the absorption of the world in God, as in the acosmism of Parmenides, or else in the absorption of

21 *Op. cit.,* p. 329.
22 *Summa theol.,* Ia, q.3, a.4 ad 1um.
23 *Ibid.,* a.6.
24 *Ibid.,* q.90, a.1 ad 2um.
25 *Ibid.,* q.27, a.2.

God in the world, as in the absolute evolutionism of Heraclitus and of several modern philosophers.

There are other corollaries to which Father del Prado alludes,[26] such as that the real distinction between created essence and existence is the foundation of the division of real created being according to the various grades of perfection, for the formal concept of existence does not denote either imperfection or limitations, and it is not susceptible to divers limitations in the stone, the plant, the animal, and man, unless it is received in some subject, namely, in some essence which is capable of existing, or in which there is a real capacity for existence, just as in matter there is a real capacity for its form, which is received in it and thus limited by it. Hence the various grades of being or of perfection are the result of the diversity of participation in being. Thus the fourth way of proving God's existence is illustrated from a transcendent source, namely, from the grades of being.

Finally, in accordance with this doctrine of a real distinction between created essence and existence, which Suarez rashly rejected, St. Thomas admits one existence for the composite of matter and form, although the essence is composite, that is, the parts of the essence (matter and form) have not partial existences. Thus the unity of the natural composite is much better safeguarded. There is one existence even in the human composite; and the soul, which is essentially subsistent and immortal, will again communicate its existence to the reassumed body on the resurrection day. Moreover, as St. Thomas teaches, there is one existence for the two natures in Christ, which is the divine existence.[27] All these things presuppose that created essence is really distinct from its existence. And this is the corollary of the conclusion of this article, namely, that only in God are essence and existence identical.

Hence this truth is rightly termed by Father del Prado [28] the fundamental truth of Christian philosophy, fundamental indeed, not by way of investigation (which starts from facts attested by experience and the first principles of reason), but by way of judgment, by which wisdom judges of all things from the highest reason and cause.

Father del Prado expressly says: "This is the primary fundamental truth of Christian philosophy, not by way of investigation by which the mind ascends from creatures to God . . . but by way of judgment, since we decide about those things and resolve the

26 *Loc. cit.*
27 *Summa theol.*, IIIa, q.17, a.2.
28 *Loc. cit.*

truth of our knowledge into its ultimate causes, and we seek for the ultimate reason why there must be only one unrelated absolute immutable being that is endowed with every perfection, and why all other beings except this one have received and must receive both what they have and desire to have, because of their absolute dependence on the first Being from whom, through whom, and in whom are all things." [29]

Thus it is apparent why the proper name of God is "Who is" or "I am who am," and why God said to St. Catherine of Siena: "I am who am; thou art who art not," because, as St. Augustine says, creatures in comparison to God are as if they did not exist. For after creation, although there are more beings, there is not more of being or more of perfection.

Hence with good reason Father del Prado says: "All those things that are set forth by St. Thomas in his first consideration of the one God are contained fundamentally, virtually, and as to their beginnings, in the third article of the second question, and the subsequent questions are but explanations of those five ways by which God's existence can be proved. And the golden key of entrance in the explanation of these proofs is presented by St. Thomas in the fourth article of the third question, where he gives many reasons why it is impossible for God's existence to differ from His essence. In this we have the secret for finding out not what constitutes but rather what does not constitute the nature of the one who is the mover, the causer, the necessary in being, the maximum in being and in intelligence. In this we have the scientific foundation of the whole treatise on the one God. This constitutes the cornerstone of all subsequent statements, namely, the identity of essence and existence in God," [30] and in God alone.

CONFIRMATION OF THE THESIS FROM THE SOLUTION OF THE OBJECTIONS

Reply to the first objection. The divine being is being to which nothing can be added, because being is the ultimate actuality of essence, and therefore divine being is neither received nor receivable, but is irreceptive, and is not in potentiality to further actuality; wherefore, as stated in the sixth article, there can be no superaddition of any accident in God. In fact, it is only in an improper sense that addition can be attributed to God in His external operations by way of causality and creation. For after creation, although there are more beings, there is not more of being, of perfection, because

29 *Ibid.*, p. 372.
30 *Ibid.*, p. 469.

God already possesses unlimited being and perfection. Contrary to this, universal being is that to which something can be added, as in the determination of the genus and the species, or in the modifications of being, and these are contained actually and implicitly in being.

Reply to the second objection. From the fact that we know a posteriori that God is, we do not, however, know that God's existence is His essence; but from the effects we know that this proposition is true, when we say: "God is." In creatures, "to be" concerns in itself only the question of the existence, not of the quiddity, of a being. In God, "to be" concerns also, and even in the strict sense, the question of His quiddity, for God alone is the self-subsisting Being, and what this self-subsisting Being is in Himself, this we shall see only in heaven, because, as stated farther on, in this life we know God only by means of His effects, from the concepts derived from creatures, and "every effect which is not an adequate result of the power of the efficient cause, receives the similitude of the agent not in its full degree, but in a measure that falls short." [31] This existence in creatures is a contingent, but in God an essential, predicate, which is not really distinct from God's essence that is unknown to us. Hence in this life we know God's essence not as it is in itself, but as it is the foundation for the truth of the proposition known from effects, namely, "God is."

Doubt. Has St. Thomas clearly deduced the corollary of this article, namely, that in every creature its essence differs from its existence? He explains this at length in another of his works (*Contra Gentes*), where he says: "Now being, as being, cannot be diverse, but it can be differentiated by something besides being: thus the being of a stone is other than the being of a man. Hence that which is subsistent being can be one only. Now it was shown above (Bk. I, chaps. 22, 42) that God is His own subsistent being: therefore nothing besides Him can be its own being. Therefore in every substance, besides Him, the substance itself must be distinct from its being." [32] Likewise in every creature, what is (or the suppositum) and existence are different.

Father del Prado [33] proposes this fundamental argument in the deduction of the above corollary as follows: Act is multiplied and limited by the really distinct potency in which it is received; but in creatures existence is multiplied and limited by the essences of different creatures; therefore in creatures essence is potency, or

---

[31] *Summa theol.*, Ia, q.13, a.5.

[32] *Contra Gentes*, Bk. II, chap. 52; see also *Summa theol.*, Ia, q.7, a.1; q.54, a.2; *De ente et essentia*, chap. 5.

[33] *Op. cit.*, p. 26.

real capacity, which is really distinct from existence, just as matter is real capacity for the form, and really distinct from the form. In other words, previous to the mind's consideration, essence and existence are not identical in creatures, just as matter is not form.

The major is explained by stating that the division of being into potency and act is absolutely necessary for the understanding of change and multiplicity, as Aristotle shows [34] in solving the arguments of Parmenides against change and multiplicity in beings, by appealing to the real distinction between potency and act. Being does not come from what is already being, just as a statue does not come from a statue, for it is already such. Nothing comes from nothing. But being comes from potential being, just as the statue can be sculptured from the wood, and just as the plant is developed from the seed.

In like manner, the act of existence cannot be multiplied or limited by itself, because in its formal concept it implies no limitation. Therefore it can be limited and multiplied only by the real capacity in which it is received, that is, by the essence which is capable of existing, for instance, by the essence of either stone, plant, animal, or man. Thus the form is limited and multiplied by the matter, which is the principle of individuation; thus intellection is limited and multiplied according to the various intellectual capacities of human beings, and so forth.

Thus by means of the distinction between potency and act we have not only the reconciliation of the principle of identity or of contradiction, a principle to which Parmenides always appealed, but also change and multiplicity, which Heraclitus defended. In other words, it is only in this way that the first principle of reason is reconciled with the most certain facts of experience. But because there is a certain lack of identity in change and multiplicity, in virtue of the principles of identity and causality our mind of necessity soars to the first Cause who is absolutely identical with Himself, who is to being as A is to A, and in whom there can be neither change nor composition, but who is absolutely simple. This point will be made still clearer in the subsequent articles.

FIFTH ARTICLE

WHETHER GOD IS CONTAINED IN A GENUS

State of the question. By genus, in the strict sense, is meant the logical genus. Thus, according to Aristotle, there are ten genera or categories, namely, substance, quantity, quality . . . and under the

[34] *Physics*, Bk. I.

supreme genus come the less universal genera ranging down to the
proximate genus, and this latter is expressed together with the
specific difference in a definition, for instance, by the words rational
animal, by which man is defined.

The principal difficulty is that God seems to come at least under
the genus of substance, because substance is a being that subsists
of itself, and we speak of the divine substance. But, on the other
hand, it is generally admitted that God transcends the genera and
species. But it may be asked whether God is at least reducible to
the genus of substance, as habitual grace is to the genus of quality,
or as the point is to the genus of quantity, as the terminus of the
line.

Conclusion. God is not in any genus either directly or as reducible to it.

It is proved in many ways that God does not come directly under
any genus, and this first of all in the counterargument from general
notions. For genus is prior in the mind to what it contains. But
nothing is prior to God either really (because He is the first Being),
or mentally, because He is the self-subsisting Being, and all formal
concepts, such as those of substance, quality, presuppose being
whose act is to exist. Yet for us there is something prior to God,
namely, being in general.

In the body of the article three proofs are given why God is not
directly in any genus. The first is founded on the notion of genus,
the second on the notion of being, and the third on the identity of
essence and existence in God.

1) On the notion of genus. Genus takes the place of potency,
whereas specific difference takes the place of act. But God is pure
act. Therefore God is not in a genus.

The minor has been proved. The major needs explanation.
Genus is not indeed matter; but it is to the specific difference as
matter is to form. For just as the matter is determined by the form,
so the genus is determined by the specific difference. Thus, for instance, the genus animality is determined by rationability; for
animality is derived from the material body endowed with sensitive life, and rationability is derived from the rational soul. Hence
no being is in a genus unless there is really something potential in
it, something susceptible of further determination. The genus is
in potentiality for the differences by which it is determined.

2) On the notion of being. Being cannot be a genus, but transcends the genera. But if God were in a genus, then being would
be His genus. Therefore God is not a genus.

The major is proved by Aristotle.[35] For the genus is diversified

35 *Met.*, Bk. III, chap. 3.

by the differences that are extrinsic to it, for instance, animality by
rationality. But being cannot be diversified by differences that are
extrinsic to it, for what is not being is nothing. Whereas rationality
is not animality, substantiality still is being, and the same is true
of vitality and other notes. Whereas the genus contains only virtually the differences extrinsic to it and is not contained in them,
being contains actually and implicitly the modes of being and is
contained in them. Therefore being is transcendent, or transcends
the genera or the categories of being, and hence is analogous. It
signifies in the different categories something that is proportionately alike, namely, that whose act is to exist. But the existence of
substance is existence not in another, whereas the existence of
accident is inexistence or existence in another. Hence being is
not a genus.

The minor. If God were in a genus, being would be His genus,
because God is essential being, since He is His existence. Manifestly,
if God were in a genus, His genus would have to be most universal
and unlimited being.

3) On the identity of essence and existence in God. Essence and
existence differ in all things that are in a genus. But essence does
not differ from existence in God. Therefore God is not in a genus.

Cajetan given us the following explanation of the major: "When
St. Thomas says that 'all in a genus differ in existence,' 'esse' is
taken both for specific existence (specific difference) and for actual
existence; and from the verification of one is inferred the verification of the other"; for those things that differ in species differ also
in existence, because specific (and individual) existences are the
proper recipients of the act of existence. Hence from the fact that
God is His existence, He is above all the genera. This proves that
God is not at least directly in a genus.

Corollary. God cannot be defined by genus and *differentia*.

In the last part of the body of the article it is proved that God
is not in any genus as reducible to it. For "a principle reducible
to any genus does not extend beyond that genus; as a point is the
principle only of continuous quantity; and unity, of discontinuous
quantity. But God is the principle of all being" and of all the
genera of being. Likewise habitual grace, which is reduced to the
genus of a quality, is not in the other genera. The solution of the objections confirms this.

Reply to the first objection. God is not in the genus of substance,
because the word "substance" does not signify the self-subsisting
Being, but an essence that has the property of existing in itself
and not in another. Now existence is predicated contingently of
every substance, for the substance of a stone, plant, animal, man,

or angel exists contingently. Spinoza refuses to give this consideration, defining substance as being that exists of itself, in this sense, that existence is not a contingent but an essential predicate of substance. It follows from this that there can be only one substance.

Reply to second objection. If God is said to be the measure of things, He is not the homogeneous measure, as unity is the principle of number, but He is the heterogeneous measure since everything has being only according as it resembles God, who is the maximum in being (fourth way).

Thus it is evident that God is not in a genus, and this is commonly admitted, even by Scotus, although he holds that being is univocal. We shall comment on this farther on.[36]

SIXTH ARTICLE

WHETHER IN GOD THERE ARE ANY ACCIDENTS

State of the question. Composition of substance and accident is excluded from the exposition of God's simplicity. We are here concerned with accident as a predicament, the existence of which is to exist in another, whether this accident is necessary as a property as, for instance, the intellective faculty in our soul, whether this accident is contingent, as this man who happens to know geometry. The difficulty here is because wisdom and virtue, which are accidents in us, are attributed to God.

Conclusion. There cannot be any accident in God.

For this conclusion three proofs are given, based on the fact that God is (1) pure act, (2) the self-subsisting Being, (3) the first Being.

1) A subject is compared to its accidents as potentiality to actuality by which it is perfected; but God is pure act;[37] therefore there cannot be any accident in God.

The major is evident; for the subject is determined and perfected by a positive accident, for instance, the soul by faculties and habits. But God is pure act and therefore is not in potentiality for any further actuality. He is not determinable but is supremely determined.

2) Being that is absolute and unreceived cannot have anything superadded to it; but God is the absolute and unreceived being; therefore God cannot have any accident superadded to Him.

Cajetan explains the major by pointing out that what is not received cannot have anything else superadded to it without re-

[36] *Summa theol.*, Ia, q.13, a.5.
[37] *Ibid.*, q.2, a.3.

ceiving. But absolute being cannot receive or be determined, because it is the ultimate actuality of a thing. Therefore unreceived being cannot have anything superadded to it, and so is at the same time incapable of receiving anything.

Contrary to this, therefore, it must be said that if, as we see in creatures, being has an accident superadded to it, for instance, operation, then this is not unreceived being, but is received in the essence, which is potency in relation to being; and this essence or substance is capable of further determination by the faculties and operations. Hence created essence can be determined in two ways, namely, by the act of existence and by the faculties and operations. On the other hand, God is the self-subsisting Being and is therefore incapable of further determination.

3) What is essential is prior to what is accidental, and accident is what comes after; but God is the absolute primal being, and in Him there cannot be anything that comes after, whether this be caused or derived; therefore nothing accidental can be in God.

In the reply to the first objection it is stated that virtue and wisdom, which are accidents in us, are not so in God, because they are predicated only analogically of Him.[38] Indeed, as we shall see, God is not in potentiality, either as to the act of understanding, or as to that of loving, but is self-subsisting intelligence and essential love. We already have some evidence of this inasmuch as God is pure act.[39]

Corollary. This article gives us a complete refutation of pantheism, for pantheism, willingly or unwillingly, must posit accidents in God. Thus Spinoza posited in God not only necessary attributes (which are, according to his theory, thought and infinite extension), but he also posited finite modes of thought and extension, these being successively produced in the world from eternity. But Spinoza never succeeded in deducing these finite modes from the divine substance, and he did not refute the doctrine of St. Thomas in the present article, in which it is shown that there can be no accident in God, since God is incapable of further determination. Likewise it follows from this that God cannot be "creative evolution," which is always capable of further determination and perfection. Creative evolution cannot be to being, as A is to A. Only the true God is the self-subsisting Being, and for this very reason He absolutely transcends the composite and changeable world.

Difficulty. We shall have the completion of this doctrine in a subsequent article,[40] in which it will be shown that God's free act of

38 *Ibid.*, q.13, a.5.
39 *Ibid.*, q.2, a.3.
40 *Ibid.*, q.19, a.3.

creation, although it would be possible for Him not to act, is not an accident. Free will in God is not as in us a faculty that must be perfected by act, but it is self-subsisting will, by which the divine good is necessarily loved, and creatable good not necessarily so. In other words, God's liberty is the dominating indifference, not of a faculty in need of perfection, but of pure act itself. Thus it is said of Him:

> "God, powerful sustainer of all things,
> Thou who dost remain permanently unmoved,
> Determining the course of time,
> By the successions of the light of day."

SEVENTH ARTICLE

WHETHER GOD IS ALTOGETHER SIMPLE

State of the question. This article is a recapitulation and synthesis, as it were, of the preceding articles.

The difficulty is that creatures are but images of God, and among created things the composite are better than the simple, as chemical compounds are better than simple elements, plants than stones, and animals than plants. The higher organisms are more complex. The same is to be said of sciences that have acquired their final development.

The reply is, however, that God is absolutely simple. It is of faith, and is thus enunciated by the Vatican Council: "God, as being one, sole, absolutely simple and immutable spiritual substance, is to be declared as really and essentially distinct from the world (which is composite and changeable)." [41]

In the body of the article many proofs from reason are given for this conclusion. They have their foundation in the doctrine of the preceding articles, which is here recapitulated, and in the truths that God is the first Being, the first Cause, pure Act, and the self-subsisting Being.

1) From the very start, composition of many kinds is excluded, such as that of quantitative parts, of matter and form, of suppositum and nature, of essence and existence, of genus and *differentia*, of substance and accident. This means the exclusion of all composition, both physical and metaphysical.

2) Every composite is posterior to its component parts, and is dependent on them; but God is the first Being; [42] therefore He is absolutely simple.

[41] Denz., no. 1782.
[42] *Summa theol.*, Ia, q.2, a.3.

To understand the major we must note that every composite is posterior to its component parts, at least by a posteriority of nature if not of time, for the composite results from the parts, and is dependent on them. Thus man results from matter and form, from body and soul. But God is the first Being according to priority not only of duration, but of nature and dignity, so that there is nothing in God that is caused or dependent, or that is resulting. Therefore He is absolutely simple.

3) Every composite has a cause; but God is the first uncaused cause; therefore in God there is no composition.

The major is explained by St. Thomas as follows: "Things in themselves different do not unite unless something causes them to unite"; or the uncaused union of different things is impossible. This principle is implicitly contained, as we have said, in the fourth way of proving God's existence, which starts in the ascending order from a consideration of diverse and imperfect composites to establish the existence of the maximum and uncaused in being. Expressed more briefly: things in themselves different, do not in themselves unite.

In another of his works, St. Thomas thus explains this principle: "A diversity of causes produces a diversity of effects." [43] In like manner he writes: "Whatever a thing may fittingly have, if it does not originate from its nature, accrues to it from an extrinsic cause; for what has no cause is first and immediate." [44] This means that what has no cause is to existence as A is to A; it not only has existence, but is identical with its existence, in virtue of the principle of identity: being is being, not-being is not-being. This principle is absolutely verified, without any lack of identity, only in the one who can say: "I am who am." [45] More briefly: the uncaused being has not existence, but is its existence.

4) In every composite there must be potentiality and actuality; but God is pure act; therefore God is in no way composite.

The major is evident, whether the reference is to essential and natural unity, or to accidental unity. If it is a question of essential unity, as in the human composite, then one part, matter, is in potentiality as regards the other. If it is a question of accidental unity, as in the proposition, the man is a musician, then the subject is to its accident as potentiality is to actuality.

5) In every composite there is something which is not it itself, or which is not predicated of it first. Thus the parts are distinguished from the whole. But since God is pure form, in fact the

---

[43] *De pot.*, q.3, a.5 (2a ratio).
[44] *Contra Gentes*, Bk. II, chap. 15, § 2.
[45] Ex. 3: 14.

self-subsisting Being, there is not anything that is not predicated of Him first, for this latter would be less perfect than the self-subsisting Being, and therefore cannot be in God.

In other words, whereas no part of man is man, whatever is in God is God. Likewise, whereas the parts of the air, although they are air, are not the whole air, whatever is in God is the whole of God and not a part of Him. This has its foundation in the principle that is inserted in the body of the article about the end of the fifth proof, and which is very briefly expressed as follows: "In the form itself (that is not received), there is nothing besides itself. Hence since God is absolute form, or rather absolute being, He can be in no way composite." Thus the fourth way of proving God's existence is illustrated from on high, by the very fact that we have reached the terminus of this proof. Thus when we are on the summit of a mountain we have a better knowledge of the way that leads to it.

Reply to the first objection. It declares that there is a real distinction between created essence and existence: "It is of the essence of a thing caused, to be in some sort composite, because at least its existence differs from its essence, as will be shown hereafter." [46]

Reply to the second objection. "With us composite things are better than simple things, because the perfection of created goodness cannot be found in one thing, but in many things." However, there is a certain likeness in creatures to God's higher simplicity, inasmuch as the soul is of a higher and simpler order than the body, the angel than the soul, and although a perfect science is more complex than one in its rudimentary stage, yet its tendency is toward a simplicity of a higher order, for it sees all things in a few principles. Thus we must distinguish between the lowest simplicity of pure potency, of matter, for instance, and the highest simplicity of the most pure Act. Thus this makes more complete the refutation of pantheism, namely, that God, being absolutely simple, is really and essentially distinct from the composite world.

A certain difficulty still presents itself, for according to revelation there are three distinct Persons in God. Does this mean then that God is composed of three Persons? St. Thomas considers this difficulty in one of his works, and says: "A plurality of Persons posits no composition in God. For we may consider the Persons from two points of view. First in their relation to their essence with which they are identified; and thus it is evident that there is no composition remaining. Secondly we may consider them in their mutual relations, and thus they are related to one another as distinct, and

---

[46] *Summa theol.*, Ia, q.4, a.3 ad 3um.

not as united. For this reason neither from this point of view can
there be composition: for all composition is union." [47] Elsewhere
he remarks: "All the divine relations are not greater than only one;
because the whole perfection of the divine nature exists in each
Person"; [48] otherwise any one of the Persons would not be God.

Therefore God is absolutely simple, and it will be stated farther
on that the three Persons have, in fact are, one existence, one intellect, one essential will.

EIGHTH ARTICLE

WHETHER GOD ENTERS INTO THE COMPOSITION
OF OTHER THINGS

State of the question. The purpose of this article is to complete
the refutation of pantheism, or to prove that God absolutely transcends the world and all finite beings.

In the title, as Cajetan observes, "enter into the composition of
other things" is said of form and matter that constitute a composite, and of substance and accident. Hence the meaning is
whether God can be joined to another in the entitative order, as
the informing act or as potency, as if He were either the matter
or soul of the world, or the common substance of the whole universe. This must be carefully considered, so as to distinguish the
composition in question here from the hypostatic union, which
according to revelation is possible and *de facto* exists. In the hypostatic union, the Word is united, indeed, in the entitative order
with the humanity of Christ, but not as the informing form, but
as the Person terminating the humanity and communicating to it
His existence. And thus the Word does not enter into composition with Christ, because the Word is not related to Christ as a
part, for the part is always less perfect than the whole.

To explain the doctrine of St. Thomas against pantheism, let
us see: (1) what forms of pantheism were known to St. Thomas,
which he wished to refute; (2) how he refuted them; (3) how, in accordance with the principles formulated by St. Thomas, modern
pantheism can be refuted; (4) how the doctrine of St. Thomas on
the divine causality preserves that portion of truth, which pantheism distorts.

1. THE FORMS OF PANTHEISM KNOWN TO ST. THOMAS

This question is not of minor importance, for many and also
modern philosophers tend toward pantheism. Moreover, several

[47] *De pot.*, q.7, a.1 ad 10um.
[48] *Summa theol.*, Ia, q.42, a.4 ad 3um.

modernists said that St. Thomas in his treatise on the one God did not professedly consider, and therefore did not refute, pantheism. So says Hébert.[49]

On the other hand, others said that Thomism exaggerates the divine universal causality, and that it tends toward occasionalism and pantheism, as if God alone existed and acted in every agent. Thus do those sometimes speak who reject physical premotion. Hence it must be carefully considered whether St. Thomas wished to refute various forms of pantheism. The present article already makes this point clear, for the body of the article distinguishes three forms of pantheism. The first form is of those who said that God is the soul of the world or at least of the highest heaven. It is the pantheism of the Stoics, who to some extent revived the evolutionism of Heraclitus, who taught that the principle of all things is the artificer, fire, which is endowed, as it were, with intelligence. St. Thomas mentions in this article the error spoken of by St. Augustine.[50]

This type of pantheism was to some extent retained by Spinoza, who said that God is the only substance, whose two principal attributes are thought and infinite extension, in which finite modes are distinguished, which from all eternity are successively produced in time.

The second type of pantheism to which St. Thomas alludes is of those who said: "God is the formal principle of all things," even of the lower order. So said Amalric of Chartres or of Bena, who died in 1209, and whose disciple was David of Dinant.

The third type is materialistic pantheism or rather the atheism of David of Dinant, who, as St. Thomas says, "most absurdly taught that God is prime matter." He says "most absurdly," because this teaching is quite opposed to wisdom, which judges of all things by the highest cause. David of Dinant judges of all things, even of the highest, by the lowest cause, and his is simply foolishness, which is contrary to wisdom. Thus St. Thomas, after the question on the gift of wisdom, professedly treats of folly.[51] For what is there more absurd than to say that the minds of St. John the Baptist and of St. Augustine, and their holiness, come from matter or are the result of material and blind necessity? This means that the greater comes from the less, the more perfect and the nobler from the least and the ignoble. It means a return to the doctrine of the first Ionian philosophers, to Thales, Anaximenes . . . who said that the

---

[49] Cf. "*La dernière idole*" (*Revue de Métaphysique et de Morale*, July, 1902).
[50] Cf. *De Civitate Dei*, Bk. VII, chap. 6, in which the doctrine of Varro is discussed.
[51] *Summa theol.*, IIa IIae, q.46.

principle of all things is a material element, either water, air, or fire.

It must be observed that the Fourth Lateran Council condemned the pantheism of Amalric in the following words: "We reject and condemn the most perverse teaching of the impious Amalric, whose mind was so blinded by the father of lies, that his doctrine is to be considered not so much heretical as insane." [52] In like manner, the Council of Sens condemned the following error of Abélard: "The Holy Spirit is the world-soul." [53]

What has just been said suffices to show, contrary to what certain modernists declared, that the error of pantheism was not unknown to St. Thomas. In fact, St. Thomas has elsewhere [54] explained more fully these types of pantheism, beginning with that of Parmenides. Moreover, St. Thomas refuted, as Aristotle did,[55] two ancient types of pantheism. These are: (1) the static monism of Parmenides, who reduces all things to one being, in fact, to the sole and motionless being, and this by denying change and multitude; [56] (2) the absolute evolutionism of Heraclitus, who denied the real validity of the principle of contradiction or of identity, because according to his view everything becomes, nothing is, and being and non-being are identified in the very becoming, which is its own reason for such. The first type is a sort of acosmism, the second is rather atheism.

St. Thomas, following Aristotle, solves the arguments of Parmenides by distinguishing between potency and act; and from this distinction the four kinds of causes are derived.[57] Thus becoming and multitude are explained, but as dependent on the sole supreme Cause, who is motionless and most simple. Against Heraclitus, however, St. Thomas defends the real validity of the principle of contradiction.[58] Thus St. Thomas not only knew the various

[52] *Denz.*, no. 433.

[53] *Ibid.*, no. 370.

[54] *Com. in II Sent.*, d.17, q.1, a.2.

[55] *Com. in Met.*, Bk. I, chap. 9; *in Phys.*, Bk. I, chap. 8.

[56] Parmenides said: It is only from being or from non-being that something could come. But being does not come from being, because it is already being; just as a statue does not come from a statue, because it is already a statue.

To this Aristotle replies: Being does not come from actual being, this I concede; but being does come from potential being, just as the plant comes from the seed, and the animal from the semen.

In like manner, Parmenides denied multiplicity in being, because being cannot be diversified by itself, but only by another, and what is not being is nothing. To this Aristotle replies that being is not univocal but analogous, and is predicated in various ways of different beings. Also act is multiplied by the potency in which it is received, just as the form of a lion or man is by matter.

[57] See *Physics*, Bk. I; *Met.*, Bks. IX, XII.

[58] See *Met.*, Bk. IV (almost *in toto*), but especially chaps. 3–5.

types of ancient and medieval pantheism, but he examined and refuted the sources of these errors.

Finally, throughout his life St. Thomas refuted Averroism, which is another type of pantheism, for the Averroists say that there is a single intellect for all men.[59]

Afer having explained the article we shall consider the principal types of modern pantheism condemned by the Vatican Council. It suffices at present to say, as noted in the schemata of the Vatican Council,[60] that for the modern pantheists either God becomes the world, or the world becomes God.

According to Spinoza and Schelling, God, actually existing from all eternity and prior to the world, becomes the world; thus in some way we have a revival of the teachings of Parmenides and the Neoplatonists, which is descendent evolution or emanation.

On the contrary, in absolute evolutionism, according to the ascendant process of evolution, the world becomes God. According to the modern pantheists, however, absolute evolutionism appeared under two forms. It was conceived either from the materialist (Haeckel), or the idealist point of view (Hegel). It is a quasi revival of the Heraclitean evolutionism.

There is always a return to the two ancient types of pantheism, those of Parmenides and Heraclitus. The former is a quasi absorption of the world in God, the latter is rather the absorption of God in the world. Thus it is clearly enough established from the history of pantheism that it cannot be defined unless it includes the tendency to deny either God or the world. From this we already see clearly the contradiction in identifying God with the world.

2. WHERE AND HOW ST. THOMAS REFUTED THE ABOVE-MENTIONED TYPES OF PANTHEISM

a) St. Thomas explains, indeed, in his commentaries on Aristotle's works [61] how this philosopher refuted Heraclitus and Parmenides by the division of being into potency and act, and also by the principle of causality: nothing is reduced from potency to act except by a being that is in act, and in the final analysis by the pure Act, who by reason of His immutability and absolute simplicity is

[59] See the opusculum of St. Thomas, De unitate Dei, against the Averroists; also Summa theol., Ia, q.76, a.1: "Whether there is one intellect for all men"; also Contra Gentes, Bk. II, chap. 23: "That God does not act by a necessity of His nature or by a necessity of knowledge"; also chaps. 26–29.

[60] Cf. Vacant, Etudes sue le Concile du Vatican, I, 200, 211 f., 230–44, 571, 581.

[61] Cf. Com. in Phys., Bk. I, chap. 8, lect. 14; in Met., Bk. I, chap. 9; Bk. IV, chap. 3 (end); Bks. XI, XII, De actu puro.

really and essentially distinct from the changeable and composite world. But Aristotle said nothing about the divine liberty in the production of things, and so he left unanswered the question whether God, who is distinct from the world, is the cause of it by a necessity of nature or of knowledge. These questions are solved by St. Thomas himself in his own works.

b) In the body of the article St. Thomas shows that God cannot enter into the composition of other things either as the formal principle or as the matter of the world. Three proofs are given for this in the present article, from the truth that God is (1) the first efficient Cause, (2) the first and essential Agent, (3) the first and unparticipated Being.

1) The agent and the form are not numerically identical, and the agent and matter are not so specifically; for the matter is potential, whereas the agent is actual; but God is the first efficient Cause; therefore He cannot be either the form or the matter of any composite.

This is a simple application of the distinction between potency and act, from which the four kinds of causes are derived. Of these, the efficient and final are the extrinsic causes, whereas the form and matter are the intrinsic causes. Thus it is evident that the efficient cause is not numerically identical with either the form or the matter, for nothing produces itself.

A difficulty arises concerning the proof. Perhaps God is the form of another composite, that is, of the one generating but not generated. To this Cajetan replies: "To be a composite implies being an effect (because every composite is made, as evident from the preceding article)"; but every effect depends on the first efficient cause; therefore the first efficient cause is neither the form nor the matter of any composite, because it would be the form or matter of its effect, which is impossible, since the agent is not numerically identical either with the form or matter of its effect, as was said.

2) No part of the composite is primarily and essentially the agent; but God is primarily and essentially the agent; therefore God is not a part of any composite.

The major is illustrated by the following example: "For the hand does not act, but the man by his hand." St. Thomas does not mean by this, as Cajetan observes, that the composite is primarily and essentially an agent. On the contrary, he said [62] that God is primarily and essentially an agent, therefore He is primarily and essentially a form, that is, a form separated from matter; in fact, He is the Being that is not received in another.

3) The major is evident, for matter is potency, and thus is pos-

terior to act and less perfect. But the form which is part of a compound is a participated form; and as that which participates is
posterior to that which is essential, so likewise is that which is
participated. Therefore no part of a compound can be absolutely
primal among beings.

These three proofs can be compendiously expressed as follows:
God is not the matter of the world, because matter which is potency
or capacity susceptible to further determination, can be determined
only by another, namely, by an agent, and in the final analysis by
the first agent, who is His activity and His being. (First, second,
and third proofs of God's existence.)

Moreover, God is not the form of the world, because thus He
would be something participated and less perfect than the composite of which He would be a part. In fact, everything composite
requires a cause.[63] Therefore God must be superior to everything
composite, as being the absolutely simple and unchangeable cause,
not capable of further determination.

N.B. In the hypostatic union, the Word is not a part, either as
matter or as informing act, but as terminating act, just as in some
way, in the order of being as in that of intelligence, the divine essence clearly seen terminates the intellect of the blessed. This is a
mystery, and the existence or even the possibility of this can be
neither proved nor disproved by reason. Apparent contradiction is
excluded, since the terminating perfection is not participated as
an informing form. Thus the statue of Moses seen by me, terminates my vision, but it is not something participated in me, as is
the case with the representative similitude which is received in the
visual faculty. Thus the confusion of the divine and human natures is avoided in the hypostatic union. They remain unconfused,
and the one is not to the other as matter is to form.

Even if God were to unite Himself hypostatically to all created
natures, this would not result in pantheism, for there could not
be a fusion of the assumed natures with the divine nature. We know
from revelation that God is hypostatically united only with Christ's
humanity, and if He were united with the humanity of other human beings, these would be impeccable as Christ is, which is
manifestly not so.

We shall find the completion of the refutation of pantheism in
two subsequent articles,[64] in which St. Thomas shows that God did
not produce the world either by a necessity of His nature, or by
a necessity of science, but with absolute freedom: (1) because God's
goodness, which He necessarily loves with utmost joy, is infinite

[63] *Ibid.,* a.7.
[64] *Ibid.,* q.19, a.3 f.

and can exist without other things, "inasmuch as no perfection can accrue to Him from them"; (2) because God acts not only freely but immediately by His intellect and will in things external to Himself, not by nature as man does in freely generating. For every natural agent by the very fact that it acts for an end must be directed by the supreme and intelligent agent (fifth way). Therefore already from the fifth way of proving God's existence it is to some extent clear that God acts by His intellect and will.[65]

Finally, emanatism is refuted when St. Thomas denies that the soul is of God's substance,[66] for God would be material if things were not produced from nothing, but from God's substance as their pre-existing subject. Thus God's substance would not be His existence, for He would be capable of further determination. In like manner, he shows that there cannot be one intellect for all men,[67] nor even one active intellect for all; [68] for the human soul, which is intellectual, is the form of the body and is multiplied with the body. The same man understands that he understands, and that he wills freely.

Summing up, we must therefore say that these refutations of pantheism proceed from the five proofs for God's existence, and they can be reduced to this one statement of the Vatican Council: "God is really and essentially distinct from the (mutable and composite) world," [69] for He is required as the absolutely immutable Cause (first, second, and third proofs), and is absolutely simple and perfect (fourth and fifth proofs).

3. HOW MODERN PANTHEISM CAN BE REFUTED BY INVOKING THE PRINCIPLES FORMULATED BY ST. THOMAS

The Vatican Council refers to the various types of modern pantheism. "If anyone shall say that the substance and essence of God and of all things is one and the same; let him be anathema." [70] Here we have pantheism in general. Then the Council condemns emanatism in the following terms: "If anyone shall say that finite things, both corporeal and spiritual, or at least spiritual, have emanated from the divine substance; let him be anathema." [71]

---

[65] Consult also on this point *Contra Gentes*, Bk. II, chaps. 23, 26–29, in which St. Thomas says against the Averroists that God does not act by a necessity of His nature or of His intellect.

[66] *Summa theol.*, Ia, q.90, a.1.

[67] *Ibid.*, q.76, a.2.

[68] *Ibid.*, q.79, a.5.

[69] Denz., no. 1782.

[70] *Ibid.*, no. 1803.

[71] *Ibid.*, no. 1804, § 1.

Here we have descendent emanatism in which God exists with all His perfections prior to the world, and He then becomes the world, since the world emanates from Him. Thus God would be capable of further determination, and thus He would not be the pure Act, at least He would have accidents. After this the pantheism of Schelling is condemned, in which God still becomes the world: "If anyone shall say that the divine essence by the manifestation and evolution of itself becomes all things; let him be anathema." [72]

Finally pantheism of universal being is condemned, and it is especially this type that was proposed by Hegel. It is evolution of the ascendant order; hence in this type it is rather the world that becomes God: "If any one shall say that God is universal or indefinite being, which by determining itself constitutes the universality of things, distinct according to genera, species, and individuals; let him be anathema." [73]

The various types of pantheism are refuted by one and the same principle already formulated by St. Thomas.[74] It is thus expressed by the Vatican Council: "God, as being one, sole, absolutely simple, and immutable spiritual substance, is to be declared as really and essentially distinct from the world . . . and ineffably exalted above all things." [75]

The reference is to a real distinction. God and creatures are not one being but many beings, although after creation there is not more being, namely, more perfection. The reference is not only to a real but to an essential distinction, since the divine nature infinitely transcends other natures.

The Vatican Council [76] confirms the condemnation of pantheism by its definition of the absolutely free creation of all things, both corporeal and spiritual, from nothing and not from God's substance. Pantheism is absolute determinism, which is a denial of both divine and human liberty, and hence of the distinction between moral good and moral evil, of merit and demerit. It excludes the moral life from man, just as it excludes true personality from him.

But previous to this, the Syllabus of Pius IX had clearly set forth the contradiction in pantheism, condemning the following formula propounded by it: God is one and the same thing with the world, and, therefore, spirit with matter, necessity with liberty, good with

---

[72] *Ibid.*, § 2.
[73] *Ibid.*, § 3. On this point see Vacant, *Etudes sur le Concile du Vatican*, I, 212 f., 581.
[74] *Summa theol.*, Ia, q.3, a.7, 8.
[75] Denz., no. 1782.
[76] *Ibid.*, no. 1805.

evil, justice with injustice." [77] It would follow from this, of course, that all things in the world, even the gravest errors and crimes, would be, with the destruction of contingency and liberty, neces sary moments of universal evolution, in which nothing could be absolutely and simply true; but there would be something that is relatively true and good in the present state of knowledge and of ethics, which would be followed by an opposite state or antithesis, which again would be succeeded by a superior synthesis, and so on in succession. There would be nothing stable, not even the prin ciple of contradiction or of identity, because the fundamental reality would be this universal becoming, which would be its own reason for such. Contrary to this, it must be said that the greater does not come from the less, and what is already in existence is greater than what is becoming. Hence there is an eternally self-existing Being, who is the self-subsisting Being, who said of Himself: "I am who am." [78]

It must be noted that certain theses of the ontologists savor some what of pantheism, and for this reason they were condemned. Such are the following propositions: "That being, which is in all things and without which nothing is understood by us, is the divine be ing. Universals considered in the concrete are not really distinct from God." [79] In this way universal being is confused with the divine being, and universal truth with the divine truth. . . . The same is to be said of certain propositions propounded by Antonio Rosmini.[80]

All these declarations are a confirmation for us that the funda mental truth of Christian philosophy is, that God alone is the self-subsisting Being, that essence and existence are identical only in God. The first truth by way of investigation is the principle of identity: being is being, not-being is not-being. The supreme truth by way of investigation and the first by way of judgment is: God alone is His existence, so that He is really and essentially distinct from any other being whatever.

4. DOES ST. THOMAS IN HIS DISCUSSION OF THE DIVINE CAUSALITY PRESERVE INTACT THE TRUTH THAT IS DISTORTED BY PANTHEISM?

In every error there is a distortion of some part of the truth. Yet it is there not as "the soul of truth," but rather as the servant of

---

[77] *Ibid.*, no. 1701.
[78] Ex. 3: 14.
[79] Denz., nos. 1660 f.
[80] *Ibid.*, nos. 1894–99.

error, because it serves to seduce or deceive the intellect. Thus in pantheism it is, as it were, the grain of truth that is distorted. This is most apparent in the natural order. (1) There is nothing that is not, as to the whole of its being, caused by God.[81] (2) There is nothing that is not preserved by God, for the being of things is the proper effect of God. Just as the becoming ceases when the cause of any becoming ceases to act, so when the cause of the being of things ceases to act, the being of things would cease to exist, just as the light in the air disappears when the sun ceases to give us its light, or just as there is no longer evidence in the conclusions when there is a cessation of evidence in the principles, or just as the means to the end lose their attraction for us when the end ceases to attract us.[82] (3) There is not any being in existence to which God is not intimately present, contacting it by His power and keeping it in existence.[83] Thus God is intimately present in all things, and is even more intimately present to our soul than it is to itself, for He moves it to acts that are more intimate and profound to which it could not move itself. (4) God operates in every agent, not to dispense the creature from acting, as the occasionalists think, but to apply it to action.[84] (5) God moves every intellect,[85] and immediately moves the created will,[86] but He does no violence to it, for He moves it interiorly in accordance with its inclination for universal good, and He moves it to a particular good which can be the object of its deliberate choice; or He permits sin, and then He is the cause only of the physical entity of the act of sin, but not of the sin itself as it is a defect, for which only a deficient cause is needed.

Thus there is nothing real and good external to God that is not related to Him as causally dependent on Him. Even the free determination of our will, inasmuch as it is something real and good, cannot be external to God so as not to be in a relation of dependence on Him. Thus the fruit of the tree comes all from the tree as from its secondary cause, and all from God as its first cause; so also my choice, inasmuch as it is real and good, is all from God as first cause and all from myself as secondary cause. Thus God is present in all things by a virtual contact, keeping them in being, and He operates in every agent applying it to its act.

It is this truth which pantheism distorts. This truth is strikingly affirmed by St. Thomas, although he absolutely rejects pantheism,

---

81 *Summa theol.*, Ia, q.45, a.5.
82 *Ibid.*, q.104, a.1, 2.
83 *Ibid.*, q.8, a.1.
84 *Ibid.*, q.105, a.5.
85 *Ibid.*, a.3.
86 *Ibid.*, a.4.

since God is neither the material cause nor the formal cause of the world, nor its necessary and efficient cause, but its absolutely transcendent and free efficient cause.

Then after our elevation to the order of grace, the intimacy of our union with God is increased, since habitual grace is a formal and physical, although analogical, participation in the Deity, or in God's intimate life, so that we are like to Him not only in being, life, and intelligence, but in the very Deity. Thus a soul in the state of grace is the temple in which the most Holy Trinity dwells, dwelling indeed in the blessed as clearly seen by them, but dwelling in us as obscurely known.

Finally, the union of the divine and human natures in Christ is the greatest that can be. The union is substantial and personal, so that there is only one person and one existence. However, there is not the least trace of pantheism in this, for there is an infinite distinction between the two natures and without any confusion of the natures. All these truths are strikingly affirmed by St. Thomas.

Moreover, in none of the teachings of Catholic theologians is the truth more clearly expressed than in Thomism, namely, that God is distinct from the world, and yet He is most intimately present to it by His efficacious influx. The doctrine of analogy as set forth by St. Thomas [87] brings out far more clearly, indeed, the distinction between God and the world than does univocation of being, which is admitted by Scotus, and which is retained to some extent by Suarez.[88] On the other hand, St. Thomas stresses the intimacy of divine motion in us more than Scotus does, and he stresses especially its efficacy more than Suarez and Molina do.[89]

Thus we terminate the question of God's simplicity. The principles enunciated here about being can easily be applied to cognition and volition, by treating of the most eminent simplicity of God's wisdom and love.[90] But this will be discussed in subsequent questions.[91]

[87] *Ibid.*, q.13, a.5.
[88] *Disp. Met.*, Disp. II, sect. 2, no. 34.
[89] Some have said that Thomism is pantheism in disguise. This could be said with greater truth about univocation of being, and the denial of a real distinction between created essence and existence. "A slight error in the beginning is great in the end."
[90] We have explained this in another work; see *Providence*, pp. 79–90.
[91] *Summa theol.*, Ia, q.14, 19 f.

CHAPTER IV

QUESTION 4

THE PERFECTION OF GOD

THIS question contains three articles: (1) whether God is perfect; (2) whether the perfections of all things are in God; (3) whether creatures can be said to be like God. The third article contains the fundamentals of the teaching of analogy between God and creatures, and under this aspect it concerns the present question, namely, whether God is so perfect that no creature can be like Him.

WHETHER GOD IS PERFECT

State of the question. The title, as Cajetan observes, does not mean: whether God has some perfection; for the various perfections are discussed subsequently. Nor does it mean: whether God possesses all perfections, since this point is discussed in the second article. The question is whether God is pre-eminently that which He is, for instance, pre-eminently the efficient cause.

Reply. God is most perfect. The conclusion is of faith, for Jesus says: "Be you therefore perfect, as also your heavenly Father is perfect." [1] The same is affirmed in very many texts of Holy Scripture. The Vatican Council affirms it in these words: "The holy Church believes that there is one God . . . infinite in all perfection . . . who, to manifest His perfection by the blessings which He bestows on creatures, with absolute freedom created them." [2]

Proof from reason. In the body of the article it is proved that God is most perfect for the reason that God is the first active principle, whereas, on the contrary, the ancient philosophers of Ionia thought that the first principle of all things is something material (water, air, or fire) and hence most imperfect, nay even absolute evolutionism, in which by an ascendant process of evolution the greater is produced from the less.

The argument of St. Thomas is reduced to this syllogism: The first active principle must needs be most actual and hence most

[1] Matt. 5: 48.
[2] Denz., no. 1782.

perfect; but God is the first active principle (second way); therefore God is most actual. The major is proved from the fact that
the agent, as such, is in actuality; for if any agent needs to be
premoved so as to act, inasmuch as it is moved it is mobile as regards a higher agent; but as an agent it is already in actuality, as
in the case of water which heats, not inasmuch as it becomes hot,
but inasmuch as it is already hot. From this we see that the supreme agent is most actual and motionless, and hence most perfect. For, as stated at the end of the body of this article: "We call
that perfect which lacks nothing of the mode of its perfection."

It must be observed that, according to the opinion of several
historians of philosophy, Aristotle [3] held that God is only the final
but not the efficient cause of the world, because, in explaining how
the first mover is immobile, he gives the example of the end, which,
although it is immobile, attracts other things to itself. But it does
not follow from this that Aristotle denied that God is the efficient
cause of the world, as if the immobile agent could not move others.
On the contrary, he said on several occasions that an agent, inasmuch as it is an agent, is in actuality; for nothing is reduced from
potentiality to actuality except by a being that is in actuality. Thus
the agent, as an agent, already is in actuality and so is perfect.
Hence the supreme agent is most in actuality and most perfect.

In the reply to the third objection it is remarked that the existence of anything is not only more perfect than matter, but also
more perfect than form, for it is its ultimate actuality. But God is
unreceived or subsisting existence; therefore He is most perfect.
St. Thomas, like an eagle that makes the same circular flight several
times high up in the air, always returns to the same supreme truth.
He makes it the object not only of direct contemplation (by ascending from one fact to be explained) and of oblique (in spiral form),
but also of circular.[4]

SECOND ARTICLE

WHETHER THE PERFECTIONS OF ALL THINGS ARE IN GOD

State of the question. It concerns all perfections, whether these
include no imperfection or admit an admixture of imperfection.
The difficulty is (1) that God is absolutely simple whereas the perfections of things are manifold; (2) that, in fact, there are several
perfections of things which are in opposition to one another, for
example, opposite *differentiae* in the same genus, and they cannot
be at the same time in the same subject; (3) that God's essence is

[3] *Metaph.*, Bk. XII, chap. 6.
[4] *Summa theol.*, IIa IIae, q.180, a.6.

His existence, but life and intelligence are more perfect than existence.

The conclusion, however, is: all created perfections are in God. This truth is affirmed in equivalent terms in many texts of Holy Scripture, and they are not difficult to find. Such are: "All things were made by Him, and without Him was made nothing that was made. In Him was life, and the life was the light of men." [5] "For of Him and by Him and in Him are all things." [6]

Two proofs from reason are given for the conclusion: (1) because God is the first effective cause of things; (2) because He is the self-subsisting Being.

1) Whatever perfection exists in an effect must pre-exist in the agent, and in a more eminent way in the supreme agent. But God is the supreme agent, the effective cause of all things. Therefore the perfections of all things pre-exist in God in a more eminent way.

Molina ought to have taken note of the major of this argument; for whatever perfection there is even in the free determination of our choice pre-exists in the supreme agent, and this free determination of ours cannot exist externally to God unless it is in a relation of dependent causality to Him.

If anyone objects that the plant reaches the perfection of its growth from an imperfect shoot, and that the animal is developed from the seed, we must reply that the seed is but the instrumental cause of the agent. It is not indeed the seed of the ox that generates the ox, but the fully developed ox by means of the seed generates an ox; in like manner the fully grown plant by means of the shoot generates a plant like itself in species; for it is only the fully developed that generate. Otherwise the greater would be produced from the less, and this more of being would have no reason for its existence. Therefore it is a common saying among theologians that after creation there are more beings but not more of being or perfection, because whatever perfection is in the effect pre-existed in a more eminent way in the first eternal cause. Thus the validity of the notion of efficient cause in its relation to the First Cause becomes increasingly clear.

2) The conclusion is proved also from the principle that God is the self-subsisting Being. The perfections of all created things are included in the perfection of being, for a thing is perfect in that it has being, for instance, in that there is in it either solely corporeity, or life, whether this is vegetative, sensitive, or intellectual; for being is the actuality of all these things; in fact, the existence

[5] John 1: 3 f.
[6] Rom. 11: 36; see also Ex. 33: 19; Ps. 93: 9.

of intellection is its actuality. But since God is the self-subsisting Existence, He has in Himself the whole perfection of being. Therefore God contains in Himself the perfection of all things.

If He did not have the whole perfection of being, then He would have only participated being, and would not be essentially the self-subsisting Being. Thus "if heat were self-subsisting, nothing of the virtue of heat would be wanting to it"; self-subsisting heat would have the whole perfection of heat.

Reply to first objection. All these perfections, because they are in God in a more eminent way, are in Him without detriment to His simplicity. Thus white light contains eminently whatever perfection there is in the seven colors of the rainbow; yet it contains them only virtually and eminently (in that it can produce them), whereas the Deity contains formally and eminently absolutely simple perfections, a point that will be more clearly brought out in subsequent articles.[7] Whereas white light is neither azure blue nor red, the Deity is formally and eminently real, one, true, good . . . ; and, moreover, it contains mixed perfections, such as rationality, virtually and eminently. Now, indeed, visual sensation contains in a unified form a great variety of sensible objects, and scientific synthesis contains many experiences, for what is divided in things of the lower order is found united in those of the higher order. Similarly our soul, although simple, is vegetative, sensitive, and intellective.[8]

Reply to third objection. Although participated being, as in a stone, is without life and intelligence, the self-subsisting Being, in that He is plenitude itself of being, contains life and intelligence. And therefore this can be what constitutes the divine nature according to our imperfect mode of conceiving it. "Nothing of the perfection of being can be wanting to Him who is subsisting being itself."

THIRD ARTICLE

WHETHER ANY CREATURE CAN BE LIKE GOD

State of the question. The meaning of the title is, as Cajetan remarks, whether God's perfection is so great that no creature can be like Him. It concerns likeness to Him as He is the first Being and the first Cause, and not as He is the triune God; nor is it concerned with this special likeness that is called image, for this is discussed elsewhere.[9] We are concerned here with the general likeness that is

[7] Summa theol., Ia, q. 13, a. 2–5.

[8] The rational soul is not only virtually, but also formally and eminently vegetative and sensitive, because it not only can produce the principle of the vegetative and sensitive lives, but is in us the radical principle of these lives.

[9] Summa theol., Ia, q. 93.

found in every created being. This article contains the fundamentals of the doctrine about the analogy between God and the creature as explained in a subsequent article.[10]

The difficulties that present themselves are the following: (1) that God and the creature are not contained even in a genus, therefore they are absolutely different; (2) that they do not communicate in any form, which is the foundation for similitude; (3) that, if the creature were said to be like God, then it could be said that God is like the creature, which seems to be inappropriate and contrary to Scripture.[11]

The conclusion, however, is: all created beings, so far as they are beings, are like God; moreover, in many this likeness is in life and intelligence. Not infrequently Holy Scripture speaks of this likeness, even of the likeness according to image, as when it says: "Let us make man to our image and likeness." [12]

About this question we should note what the Fourth Lateran Council says: "The similarity which we note between the Creator and the creature cannot be so great as to prevent us from detecting a greater dissimilarity." [13] Moreover, this statement is made about the similarity of grace, and in this sense the Scripture says: "Be you therefore perfect (by grace) as also your heavenly Father is perfect (by nature)." [14] In this text of the Fourth Lateran Council we have a quasi definition of analogy between God and creatures, and this text is more in conformity with the Thomist definition of analogy than it is with the Suarezian. According to St. Thomas and the Thomists: things that are analogous are those having a common name, but the idea signified by the name is simply different in each of them, and relatively or proportionately the same; thus being is predicated of essential being, of substantial being that is produced by another, and of accident. On the contrary, according to the principle of Suarez: "things that are analogous are those having a common name, but the idea signified by the name is simply the same in each of them, and relatively different.[15] To this the Thomists reply by asking why the Fourth Lateran Council there-

10 *Ibid.*, q.13, a.5.
11 Is. 40: 18.
12 Gen. 1: 26.
13 Denz., no. 432.
14 Matt. 5: 48.
15 Suarez indeed says (*Disp. Metaph.* 2, § 2, no. 34): "Now I merely assert that everything which has been said concerning the unity of the concept of being, appears to be clearer and more certain than that being is analogous. Therefore, in order to defend analogy, it is not right to deny the unity of the concept; but if one of the two is to be denied, it is analogy, which is uncertain, that is to be denied rather than unity of concept, which seems to be demonstrated by sound arguments.

fore had said: "The similarity which we note between the Creator and the creature cannot be so great as to prevent us from detecting a greater dissimilarity." Moreover, animality, which is predicated univocally of the lion and the worm, is simply the same and relatively different in them; analogical similarity, however, is less than univocal similarity.

Lastly, the Vatican Council says: "Reason enlightened by faith when it seeks earnestly, piously, and calmly, attains by a gift of God to some . . . understanding of mysteries; partly from the analogy of those things which it naturally knows, partly from the relations which the mysteries bear to one another. . . ." [16] Therefore the analogy that prevails between God and the creature is a certainty; in fact, its certainty is that of faith.

The conclusion is proved from reason in the body of the article by one argument which is founded on causality. But first of all, by way of introduction, St. Thomas distinguishes between three kinds of likeness.

Likeness is of three kinds: (1) of form which is of the same formality and of the same mode, as two things equally white, or two grown-up men; (2) of form which is of the same formality but not of the same mode, as something less white is like something more white, or as the boy is like the man; (3) of form but not according to the same formality, as between the effect and the non-univocal agent, or as prevails in things of a higher nature, as in the subordination of causes. [17] Thus, inasmuch as the intellective life arouses the action of the sensitive life, as when the intellect by a rational process arranges in an orderly manner the phantasms and words for the expression of some syllogism, then the verbal expression, which previously exists in the imagination, is indeed rationable, but by participation, being dependent on the reason as directing it. Thus the rationability of the verbal expression and the rationability of the conception or judgment are alike according to form but not according to the same formality; there is indeed unlikeness on the part of the one directing and of that which is directed. Thus rationability is primarily in prudence and secondarily by participation in the virtues of fortitude and temperance by which the sensitive appetite is directed by reason. In like manner and with greater reason, order is not according to the same formality in the supreme Ordainer of the universe and in the natural agents which are directed by Him to a certain end (fifth way).

16 Denz., no. 1796.

17 According to the physics of ancient times, heat in the sun differs in formality from that in other bodies. This is no longer admitted; but there are other examples.

Thus likeness is of three kinds: (1) univocal and according to the same mode; (2) univocal and not according to the same mode, as between the boy and the man; (3) non-univocal, which is not either according to species or according to genus, but is analogical.

With these preliminary observations, the conclusion is proved by one argument as follows: every agent reproduces itself, either specifically or generically or at least analogically; but God, who is not contained in a genus, is the efficient cause of creatures; therefore creatures are analogically like God.

For some the major, like the experimental laws, is evident only by induction, in so far as a man generates a man, an ox generates an ox, and a plant one like itself in species. Yet, in truth, this major is more than an experimental law; it is a principle that is directly known from the analysis of the terms; for to act is to determine or reduce from potentiality to actuality, from indetermination to determination; for actuality is the principle of determination. But a thing can determine only according to its own determination; hence the common saying: every agent acts inasmuch as it is in actuality, and it is in actuality by means of its form. Thus a man generates a man, and a body that is hot makes another hot. Hence St. Thomas says in this article: "Since every agent reproduces itself so far as it is an agent, and everything acts according to the manner of its form, the effect must resemble the form of the agent." This principle is self-evident from an analysis of the terms.

But this principle is applied in various ways in accordance with the previous remarks, namely: (1) If the agent is contained in the same species with the effect, there is likeness according to the same formality of the species; (2) if the agent is not contained in the same species, but in the same genus, then there is only generic likeness. The old example of the sun is here given. Nowadays we can say: There are various effects of heat, since it expands metals, produces the fusion of solids and the evaporation of liquids. In like manner, there are various effects of electricity and magnetism, and these effects are not specifically but generically like the cause. Thus electricity produces local motion, atmospheric changes, chemical combinations . . . ; (3) lastly, if the agent is not contained in any genus, "its effects will still more distantly reproduce the form of the agent," that is, not specifically or generically, but analogically.

The minor, however, was proved in a previous article,[18] in which it was shown that God, who is not in any genus, is the efficient cause of all creatures. Therefore creatures are analogically like God, at least inasmuch as they are beings. Many creatures, too, are like God

[18] *Summa theol.,* Ia, q.3, a.5.

in life (as plants), in intellect (as our soul), and the just are like God according to His intimate life or His Deity.

Being indeed is that which exists or can exist; in other words, it is that whose act is to exist. But it is not predicated according to absolutely the same formality of the self-subsisting Being, of the caused substantial being, and of its accidents. Of these three it is predicated proportionately or according to a similarity of proportions. Thus God is to His existence as the created substantial being is proportionately to its existence. Thus the likeness is true and not merely metaphorical (as when it is said that God is angry), but it is according to the proper meaning of the name "being."

However, as the Fourth Lateran Council said: "A greater dissimilarity is to be noted" in that God is the self-subsisting Being, whereas created substance is not its own existence, but has existence in itself, and accident has existence in another. When we shall see God face to face, then it will be clearly seen that creatures are as if they do not exist in comparison with God, as St. Augustine often says.

This means that the analogous perfection cannot be perfectly abstracted from the analogates [19] because it expresses a likeness of proportions, and this cannot be conceived by the mind without having actual and explicit concepts of the members of the proportionality. Being is that which exists either of itself, or in itself, though dependent on another, or in another that is dependent on some other.

Contrary to this, the genus (for instance, animality) can be perfectly abstracted from the species, because it is diversified by *differentiae* that are extrinsic to it. Thus animal signifies what is simply one and the same; the living body signifies the sensitive life, whereas being signifies what is proportionately one. The analogical concept can be represented by 8, and the universal concept by 0.[20] There is a certain intrinsic variety in the analogical concept; for every mode of being is still being, whereas the *differentia* of animality, for example, rationality, is not animality.

Objection. Being abstracts perfectly from the modes of being in that it is defined as that which exists independently of its modes (*id quod est independenter ab his modalitatibus*). In like manner, "knowledge" is the union of the one knowing with the thing known

---

[19] Cf. Cajetan, *De analogia nominum*, chap. 5.

[20] These signs are merely arbitrary. (See, *God, His Existence*, II, 205.) What the author seeks to show is that being, as predicated of various things, is proportionately the same, whereas the univocal concept is the same in those things of which it is predicated. Hence being is analogical in concept, whereas animal is univocal. Rationality is extrinsic to the notion of animal, but not to the notion of being. (Tr.)

or of subject and object without any reference to sensation and intellection. The same applies to "love" and "cause" in reference to first cause and second cause: for the efficient cause is that from which another being comes into existence.

Reply. This seems to be so if the words of the definition are considered only materially, but it is not so if they are taken in their formal sense; for these very words of the definition of being are analogous; namely, *id* is predicated analogically, as also are *quod* and *est*. The same must be said of other definitions, such as those of cause, knowledge, love. Cause is predicated analogically of the four causes, as it is also of the first efficient Cause and of the secondary cause. In like manner, although our cognitive faculties are univocal as faculties in the genus of quality, as they are cognitive, they are analogous. Thus knowledge can be attributed analogically to God, and the same applies to love.

It is already quite clear from St. Thomas' own words that being and existence are not predicated of God and creatures purely "according to the same formality," but proportionately, as stated at the end of the body of the article. And what is said here of existence applies to all absolutely simple perfections, and this will have to be discussed in a subsequent article (q. 13, a. 5). Thus it applies to the intellect that is specified by intelligible being, and to the will that is specified by good.

Reply to second objection. God is related to creatures as the principle of all genera.

Reply to third objection. Likeness of creatures to God is therefore "solely according to analogy, inasmuch as God is essential being, whereas other things are beings by participation."

Reply to fourth objection. Although the creature is like God, God is not like the creature, because there is no real relation of God to creatures, but only of creatures to God; for God does not depend on creatures, nor is He in the same order. Thus the image is said to be like Caesar, but Caesar is not said to be like his image: "When two extremes are not of one order, in one of the extremes the relation is a reality, and in the other it is an idea." [21] Thus knowledge refers to the knowable, but the knowable thing, as a thing, is outside the order of intelligibility, and does not refer to knowledge.[22] Thus all creatures are ordered to God, but God is not ordered to creatures.[23]

[21] *Ibid.*, a.7.

[22] Conversely, there is a real and mutual relation if the two extremes are of the same order, as between father and son, as also between two brothers who are sons of the same father; this is especially so if one extreme is dependent on the other, as the son on the father.

[23] *Summa theol.*, Ia, q.13, a.7.

CHAPTER V

QUESTION 5

OF GOODNESS IN GENERAL

THE attribute of goodness follows perfection, for, as will be said immediately, everything is good in so far as it is perfect. Therefore St. Thomas treats of God's goodness before treating of His truth and unity, although unity and truth are predicated before goodness of being and the divine nature. St. Thomas inserts here the question of the divine goodness as being a part of the divine perfection. And he treats first of goodness in general.

The question is concerned with transcendental good, which is a property of being, and is being viewed as perfect and appetible. It is called transcendental, because it transcends all the categories of being, and is common to all of them, such as good substance, good quantity, good quality. . . . However, in this question, goodness is also divided into the pleasant, the useful, and the virtuous, and from this division we get the idea of moral goodness, which is discussed by St. Thomas in the moral part of his theology,[1] where he shows that moral goodness is virtuous goodness in so far as it is governed by the rules of moral actions and especially by the eternal law. Moral goodness is conformity of the object and the action with the rules of moral actions. But we are at present concerned with transcendental good.

There are three points of investigation in this fifth question: (1) The relation of goodness to being (a. 1–3); (2) of goodness in itself, considered under the aspect of end and order in goodness (a. 2–5); (3) the way goodness is divided (a. 6). The explanation of these articles must be brief, for they pertain rather to metaphysics.

FIRST ARTICLE

WHETHER GOODNESS DIFFERS REALLY FROM BEING

Conclusion. Goodness and being are really the same, and differ only in idea. The first part is proved as follows: That which is included in the idea of being is not really distinct from being; but goodness is included in the idea of being, for it is being considered

---

[1] *Summa theol.*, Ia IIae, q. 18.

as perfect and desirable; therefore goodness is not really distinct from being.

The major is certain. Just as humanity, which contains in its connotation animality as genus, is not really distinct from animality, so that which in its connotation contains the idea of being is not really distinct from being. On the contrary, created essence, which in its connotation does not contain the idea of existence, is really distinct from it. Where we have two concepts irreducible to each other and to a third concept, there we have irreducibility of realities, in virtue of the objective validity of our intellect. But if two concepts are reduced to one concept, as animality and rationability are reduced to humanity, then there is no real distinction between them. Animality is included in the idea of humanity, although the latter includes something else, namely, rationality.

The minor. The idea of being is included in the idea of goodness. For goodness is that which is desirable; but it is desirable in so far as it is at least somehow perfect and perfective; therefore the idea of being is included in the idea of goodness, although it explicitly denotes something else.

Thus a fruit is good in so far as it is desirable. But for this it is necessary that the fruit be ripe, that in its species it be perfect and perfective, as a food that is preservative of life. And it would not be so unless it were actual being. Thus we speak proportionately of a good stone for the construction of a building, of a good horse for drawing a carriage, of a good sculptor or of a good painter. Hence it is clear that good is predicated of things by analogy of proportion, and is not really distinct from being.

The second part of the conclusion, namely, that goodness and being differ in idea, is easily proved; for "goodness presents the aspect of desirableness, which being does not present." In other words, being contains the notion of goodness actually and implicitly, but not actually and explicitly. Something explicitly is declared in the notion of goodness, which is only implicitly declared in the notion of being. Thus there is no addition of any extrinsic difference to being, but of an explicitly signified mode of being.

It must be remembered with Cajetan, however, that desirableness does not constitute the idea of goodness, but presupposes it, as a property its essence. However, if the desirable is viewed not formally but fundamentally, then goodness is intrinsically desirable in so far as it is the foundation for desirableness. Hence many Thomists say: The formal notion of goodness consists in perfection as being the foundation for desirableness. And this foundation is not really distinct from the desirableness, because it is a relation, not indeed real but logical as regards the appetite. On the contrary, there is a real relation of the appetite to the appetible on which it depends. Thus there is a real relation of knowledge to the thing knowable, but not of this latter to knowledge.

Hence for goodness to be fundamentally desirable, it must be perfect and perfective and therefore actual being. As John of St. Thomas says against Durandus and Vasquez: If goodness were to consist formally in desirableness, it would not be anything real, but a logical relation.

The reply to the first objection confirms this: Although goodness and being are not really distinct, for what is simply being (which a thing has through substantial being) is not simply goodness (which a thing has through some superadded perfection). Thus a barren tree is simply a being in so far as it has substantial being, but it is not something simply good in its species, because it is barren. The same applies to an unripe or overripe fruit, as also to a young or old carriage horse.

Hence what is simply being is good relatively, for example, a young horse not yet fully grown is, however, truly a horse and not a mule. Thus it has relative goodness of its species, although it has not as yet attained its due perfection. The same may be said of wine that has not much body to it, which, however, is truly wine and not vinegar.

Conversely, that by reason of which something is good simply, is being relatively, since it is an accidental perfection superadded to substance, as ripeness in fruit.

It must be observed that according to Scotus [2] the properties of being, such as goodness, are distinct from being by a distinction that is formal and actual on the part of the thing. In reply to this we say that such distinction posits an impossible intermediary between the real distinction and the logical distinction that has its foundation in the object; for a distinction exists either before or not before the mind's consideration; if before, it is real; if not, it is logical. In the present case, however, there can be no real distinction, because then goodness would be outside being; it would not be being, and thus would be nothing. Being is included in all its modes, which are still being.

Consequently there is only a virtual distinction between being and goodness; in fact, a virtual minor distinction, since being includes goodness actually and implicitly, but not explicitly. In other words, the mode of goodness is not an extrinsic difference with reference to being, as rationability is with reference to animality.

[2] I Sent., d.3, q.3.

WHETHER GOODNESS IS PRIOR IN IDEA TO BEING

State of the question. The Platonists taught that goodness is prior to being. For Plato the supreme reality is the separate Idea of Good.[3] Likewise, Plotinus held that the supreme hypostasis is the One-Good, the super-Intelligence.[4] According to this tendency some, such as Scotus, said that the will, which is specified by good, is simply superior to the intellect, which is specified by being.

St. Thomas, by way of a difficulty he puts to himself in the beginning of the article, refers to the opinion of the Platonists in the words of Dionysius who, among other names, assigned the first place to good rather than to being. Likewise, in the counterargument the Neoplatonist Proclus is quoted, the author of the book *De causis.*

Plato and Plotinus placed good above being and essence, because every essence is intelligible, and the intelligible is the correlative of intellect, and is distinct from it. Hence above the duality of intellect and intelligible, there must be a higher and ineffable, a most perfect unity, from which all things proceed, namely, the One-Good.[5] But the divine causality is explained by the Platonists independently of the divine liberty, in that good is essentially diffusive of itself. We already find this principle admitted by Plato, who does not sufficiently distinguish between final causality and efficient causality. It is also admitted by Plotinus, who held that the supreme Good is essentially, or by a necessity of nature, diffusive of itself, and not because of a most free creative act.

Contrary to this, St. Thomas, following Aristotle, correctly distinguishes between the final cause and the efficient cause, and he maintains that good is diffusive of itself as the end which attracts the agent to act.[6] St. Thomas adds that in accordance with the dogma of creation the supreme agent is absolutely free since He already contains within Himself infinite goodness, and is not in

---

[3] See Plato's *Republic*, Bk. VII, 517, D; "In the world of knowledge the idea of good appears last of all, and is seen only with an effort; and when seen is also inferred to be the universal author of all things beautiful and good, and the immediate source of reason and truth in the intellectual world."

[4] Cf. *Enneades*, Bk. III, ii, 12; V, i, 6; ii: 1; VI, viii, 9, 11.

[5] The Neoplatonists speak of the One-Good, which transcends being, somewhat as subsequently Catholic theologians say that the Deity in some way transcends all absolutely simple perfections, which are contained in it eminently. But for the theologians, the Deity contains formally being, the one, the good; whereas, contrary to this, the One of the Platonists virtually contained the inferior notes, which necessarily proceeded from it.

[6] *Summa theol.*, Ia, q.5, a.4; Ia IIae, q.1, a.4 ad 1; IIIa, q.1, a.1; *Contra Gentes*, Bk. IV, chap. 11.

need of created goods, which cannot increase His perfection and happiness.[7] The conclusion of St. Thomas is: In idea being is prior to goodness.

This had been already proved by him,[8] in that the idea of being is included, as presupposed, in the idea of goodness, which is perfect and desirable being. In this article, however, the same argument is proposed as follows: That is prior in idea which is first conceived by the intellect; but the first thing conceived by the intellect is being; therefore in idea being is prior to goodness.

The major is not concerned with the order of time and investigation, according to which we first have a knowledge of sensible things; it concerns, however, the order of nature and of formal concepts or notions. But the notion of being is the first of all notions. Why is this? It is because everything is intelligible inasmuch as it is actual. Thus the proper object of the intellect, as such, and not as it is human, is intelligible being,[9] just as color is the first thing visible, and sound the first thing audible. Hence every formal concept or notion, for it to be intelligible, presupposes the concept or notion of being.[10]

As Bannez remarks, St. Thomas is speaking of goodness in general. From this it follows that, both in God and in created beings, being is prior in idea to goodness. Being is included implicitly in goodness, and it implicitly includes goodness, as its transcendent mode.

St. Thomas deduces from this the following corollary: "If therefore the intellect and will are considered with regard to themselves, then the intellect is the higher power. And this is clear if we compare their respective objects. For the object of the intellect (namely, intelligible being) is simpler and more absolute than the object of the will (which is goodness). Now the simpler and the more abstract (and more universal) a thing is, the nobler and higher it is in itself (at least as an object). . . . Thus the intellect is absolutely higher and nobler than the will."[11] Therefore it directs the will, knowing the very concept of good in the good willed.

7 *Summa theol.*, Ia, q.19, a.3.

8 I *Sent.*, d.8, q.1, a.3.

9 The proper object of the human intellect as such is the nature of sensible things, or intelligible being of sensible things in the mirror of sensible things.

10 Thus the notion of being is not in generation and time prior to that of goodness, but it is prior simply, in the order of nature, just as essence is prior to its properties. The reason for this priority is the principle already admitted by Plato and Plotinus, that "the simpler and the more abstract a thing is, the nobler and higher it is in itself" (*Summa theol.*, Ia, q.82, a.3).

Thus the idea of being, while it is included in the idea of goodness, is somehow already limited and contracted, because it can be found also in the ideas of truth and unity.

11 *Summa theol.*, Ia, q.82, a.3.

Second conclusion. We discover this in the reply to the first objection, which states that goodness is relatively prior to being, that is, as a cause, as the end is prior to the form. This is goodness considered not in itself, but with respect to something else.

To the Platonists and Neoplatonists, and particularly to Dionysius, St. Thomas makes the concession that, "among the names signifying the divine causality, goodness precedes being." The reason is that, in the order of causality, goodness conveys the idea of end; but the end is the first in the order of causes, since it attracts the agent to act, and by the agent the matter is prepared to receive the form. Thus in this order of causality God is called the supreme Good, or the good God.

Yet, absolutely speaking, it is still true to say that in idea being is prior to goodness. By *simpliciter* is meant, if the essence of the thing in question is discussed; but by *secundum quid* is meant, if something secondary in this thing is considered. Thus a wise man is *simpliciter* better than unwise Hercules; but as regards physical strength, Hercules is better *secundum quid. Simpliciter loquendo* means about the same as "absolutely speaking" or "in its primary aspect," whereas *secundum quid* means "in some secondary aspect."

Thus being, "relatively" considered with respect to the four causes, and not in itself, corresponds to the formal cause; for being is predicated of a thing in so far as it is in actuality by reason of its form, as in stone, wood, animal, or man. But the form, in the order of causes, is posterior to the end and the agent, because it is produced by the agent operating in view of the end. Thus it must be conceded to the Platonists that the supreme Good is prior to created being, which is produced in manifestation of divine goodness. Likewise the supreme Good is prior to finite intelligence, the object of which is finite good, in which God is known as in a mirror.

It may be asked whether St. Thomas gives us a correct statement of Plato's doctrine. It must be said that Plato, in calling God (or the supreme reality) the supreme Good, considered God with reference to inferior realities, which He produces by a diffusion of Himself, to be the sun from which emanate light and heat. Hence Plato said: Since God is good, He produced the world. Yet Plato and Plotinus seem to hold also that good is absolutely prior to being.[12]

---

[12] Plato and Plotinus seem to admit that the One is indivisible, whereas being is divided; and they identify the One with the Good. Thus they solve the arguments of Parmenides by positing "the One-Good" above being, and explaining causality, which Parmenides denied, in that good is essentially diffusive of itself.

On the contrary, St. Thomas and Aristotle solve the arguments of Parmenides against multiplicity in being and motion by distinguishing between potentiality and actuality. They also hold that unity, by the very fact that it is convertible with being, is divided, like being, into potentiality and actuality.

If such is the case, then St. Thomas on this point separates from them. Hence we conclude that in idea being is prior to goodness absolutely, but posterior to it relatively, namely, in causation.

Corollary to the second conclusion. The will is relatively prior to the intellect (namely, in moving to the exercise of the act). Thus the intellect in the exercise of its act, or attention to its object, is moved by the will. Thus at the end of deliberation it is the will that causes the final judgment to be final. Likewise, as stated by St. Thomas,[13] in this life "the love of God is better than the knowledge of God," because, whereas the intellect draws God to itself, to its imperfect conception of Him, the will is drawn to God, since goodness is in things and not in the mind. So also, though seeing is absolutely nobler than hearing, yet the hearing of a beautiful symphony is nobler than the seeing of something mediocre.

It must be observed that St. Thomas, at the end of the reply to the first objection, gives us a good explanation why the Platonists held that goodness applies to more things than being does. The reason is that in their opinion being does not apply to matter, which they thought to be a privation and non-being. Yet they said: Matter manifests its appetency for good.

On the contrary, St. Thomas and Aristotle, distinguishing matter from privation or non-being, declare it to be, indeed, a real potency or a real capacity for receiving a form, and thus matter is being in potentiality, for example, it is in potentiality to receive the form of either air, wood, or animal. Hence being is just as extensive in application as goodness; in fact, it is more universal than goodness, for not every being is perfect and appetible.[14]

The following objection may be raised against the first conclusion: Goodness is absolutely more perfect than being because it includes being and its perfection.

Reply. It is true to say this of the suppositum or subject, about which good is predicated; but it is not true to say this of the formal concept of goodness. This means that the suppositum, which is said to be absolutely good, such as wine of the best vintage, is more perfect than the suppositum which is only being, such as wine not of the best vintage. But the formal concept of goodness is by nature posterior to the formal concept of being, which is simpler, more abstract and more universal, and thus more perfect as an object.

But I insist. Although animality is simpler than humanity, yet it is more imperfect.

---

13 *Summa theol.,* Ia, q.82, a.3.
14 *Ibid.,* q.5, a.2 ad 2um et 3um.

Reply. It is simpler logically, since it is the genus of humanity; but it is not so really, because it is derived from matter, which has not the unity, simplicity, and perfection of a form, especially of man's form, which is the intellectual soul.

This article, however, is concerned with being and goodness, not only in their logical aspect, but as they are realities. It must be conceded that only the concrete suppositum which is good, is a more perfect suppositum than if it were not good. But St. Thomas is not speaking in this article of the good as suppositum, but of the idea of goodness, which is viewed, however, ontologically and not merely logically. Being, which is prior to goodness, derives its name from existence, namely, from its ultimate actuality. This must be our reply to the Neoplatonists and also to Scotus.

Thus the intellect truly is absolutely nobler than the will, because it is specified by being (that is, the faculty is specified by the object, and not by the suppositum), so that the will is specified by this object that is good, viewed as such, but it is not specified by the good as suppositum.

THIRD ARTICLE

WHETHER EVERY BEING IS GOOD

State of the question. It seems that not every being is good, for good adds perfection and desirableness to being. Matter, however, is being, but it has not the aspect of desirableness. Likewise Aristotle says: "In mathematics goodness does not exist." [15]

The conclusion, however, is: Every being, as being, is good.

This doctrine is of faith against the Manichaeans, who said that some beings are good, and some are evil, in accordance with their error of a twofold principle. The Scripture says: "And God saw all the things that He had made, and they were very good." [16]

The conclusion is proved from reason as follows:

Perfect presents the aspect of what is desirable and good; [17] but every being, inasmuch as it is being, is actual and in some way perfect; therefore every being, inasmuch as it is being, is good.

This means to say, as remarked above,[18] that every being is such simply and good relatively, in that it has at least its essence and existence, even though it is not good simply. Thus every wine, pro-

---

[15] *Metaph.*, Bk. III, ii, 4.
[16] Gen., 1: 31.
[17] See *supra*, a.1.
[18] *Ibid.*, ad 1um.

vided it still is wine and not vinegar, can be said to be good, or not corrupt, although it is not the best of wine.

Reply to first objection. Good does not contract being to any of the predicamental modes, that is, it does not limit being to any category, such as substance, quantity . . . ; however, goodness is a transcendental mode of being that is not so universal as being itself. For being applies also to unity and truth.

Reply to second objection. Evil is the privation of any good that is due to any subject.

Reply to third objection. Prime matter is being in potentiality and good in potentiality. Moreover, it implies goodness for the composite to have its matter, which cannot exist without it.

Reply to fourth objection. "In mathematics goodness does not exist," because it abstracts from motion and end. Wherefore Spinoza, who sought to proceed geometrically in metaphysics, excluded the efficient and final causes from the subject matter of metaphysics. He wanted to deduce everything from God, just as the properties of a triangle are deduced from its nature.

Thus the foregoing consideration sufficiently explains goodness with reference to being, which does not differ really but logically from being, and which is absolutely posterior to being. Every being is good at least relatively, although it frequently is lacking in that perfection by which it could be said to be good absolutely. In the two following articles goodness is considered, not in its relation to being, but as it is in itself.

FOURTH ARTICLE

WHETHER GOODNESS HAS THE ASPECT OF A FINAL CAUSE

State of the question. The difficulty is that Dionysius often says that goodness is self-diffusive.[19] But to be diffusive implies the aspect of an efficient cause. Also St. Augustine says: "We exist, because God is good." [20]

The conclusion, however, is: Goodness has the aspect of a final cause.

1) It is proved on the authority of Aristotle, for he thus defines the end and the good as "that for the sake of which something is done." [21]

2) It is proved by reason as follows: The desirable has the aspect of an end; but goodness is desirable; therefore goodness has the aspect of an end, at least as regards the act of the one desiring; and

19 *De nom. div.*, chap. 4.
20 *De doctr. christ.*, chap. 31.
21 *Physics*, Bk. II.

it can be desirable either because it is pleasant (as a fruit), or because it is useful (as a bitter medicine), or because it is virtuous.[22]

There is furthermore another conclusion in the body of the article, which may be enunciated as follows: Goodness is the first in causation and the last in being, because the end is the first in causation, in the order of intention, since it attracts the agent to act; and the end is the last in being, or in the order of execution. Thus the generator tends to reproduce its form, for instance, fire tends to reproduce the form of fire, the ox the form of an ox, and the form of the thing generated terminates the passive generation, and afterward what is generated is made perfect. Thus when the animal acquires its complete development, then it is perfectly like the one generating.

Reply to first objection. Goodness and beauty differ logically, for goodness relates to the appetite, whereas beauty relates to the cognitive faculty; for things are said to be beautiful that please the eye.[23] Thus beauty is the splendor of form in material things, as in the rose or the lily; but if it is a case of intellectual beauty, then it is the splendor of truth or the irradiation of some principle in the many conclusions deduced from it. In like manner the splendor manifesting itself in a life of heroic moral acts constitutes moral beauty; transcending all, we have the sublime, when there is the greatest of diversity in the closest of unity, as in Holy Communion: O wonderful thing, he that is poor, and a servant, and lowly, eateth the Lord.

Beauty seems to be a transcendental property of being, for everything produced by the divine artist is beautiful; but every being is produced by the divine artist as the author of nature; therefore every being is beautiful, at least according to its nature or essence, for it conveys to us some idea of God. But integral beauty, as seen in God, in Christ, in the Blessed Virgin Mary, is splendor of being according to unity, truth, and goodness, that is, splendor and harmony of all the properties of being.

Reply to second objection. There is a brief solution of the difficulty arising from the Platonist conception, that goodness is self-diffusive: and this pertains to the efficient cause. St. Thomas replies: "Goodness is described as self-diffusive, as being the end," namely, in that it attracts the agent to act, and the appetite to desire. But as remarked farther on,[24] by way of a logical sequence, goodness is an active diffusion inasmuch as the agent operates effectively be-

[22] *Summa theol.,* Ia, q.5, a.6.
[23] *Ibid.,* q.39, a.8, where it is stated that three conditions are required for the pleasing effect of beauty, namely, integrity, due proportion, and clarity.
[24] *Ibid.,* Ia, q.19, a.2.

cause of the end intended, and this either by a necessity of nature, as the ox generates an ox, or else freely, as when man communicates his knowledge to others or exhorts them to good.

Hence St. Thomas says: "It belongs to the essence of goodness to communicate itself to others. Hence it belongs to the essence of the highest good to communicate itself in the highest manner to the creature, and this is brought about chiefly by . . . (the incarnation of the Word)." [25] Thus self-diffusion primarily belongs to the end as attracting, and afterward to the agent. But God is not necessitated, however, in His external operations, but is absolutely free, for He is in no need of finite goods,[26] and He operates to manifest His goodness, as will be stated farther on.

Therefore, when the Neoplatonists said: "Goodness is essentially self-diffusive," they did not sufficiently distinguish between the agent and the end, and so they unwarrantably asserted that God operates externally by a necessity of His nature, as the sun diffuses heat and light in the air. The consequence of this was pantheistic emanatism, which is contrary to the dogma of an absolutely free creation.

Reply to third objection. The saying of St. Augustine, "We exist, because God is good," refers to the final cause. This means that we exist because God willed to manifest His goodness in loving and creating us; thus we receive a certain participation of the divine goodness. Therefore goodness has the aspects of an end.

FIFTH ARTICLE

WHETHER THE ESSENCE OF GOODNESS CONSISTS IN MODE, SPECIES, AND ORDER

State of the question. It is concerned with causated good, as Cajetan says, and this is manifest from the counterargument, which quotes the following definition of goodness given by St. Augustine, as consisting "in everything which God has made."

The reply in the affirmative is thus presented: "For a thing to be perfect and good it must have a form together with all that precedes and follows upon that form," for everything is what it is by its form. But the form is itself signified by the species, that which is prerequired for it by the mode, and that which follows upon it by the order. Thus the form of a fruit constitutes it in a certain species; but this presupposes the mode of commensuration of the material and efficient principles, for instance, of the

25 *Ibid.*, IIIa, q.1, a.1.
26 *Ibid.*, Ia, q.19, a.3.

earth and the sun, so that the fruit may attain its ripeness. Finally, in the fruit there is order toward an end, for instance, the preservation of life in man. Likewise these three conditions are required so that one may be a good painter, a good sculptor, or a good musician. The mode is required for the acquisition of the art, and its order for the end. Thus goodness demands the congruent concurrence of the four causes, because the end is last in the order of execution. Thus the reason is assigned for this descriptive definition given by St. Augustine.

SIXTH ARTICLE

WHETHER GOODNESS IS RIGHTLY DIVIDED INTO THE VIRTUOUS, THE USEFUL, AND THE PLEASANT

State of the question. This question is concerned with transcendental goodness, but in the formal and not in the material sense of the term. Good in the material sense, subjectively considered, is divided into the ten categories. Thus we speak of a good substance, a good quantity, a good quality. . . . Goodness in the formal sense, however, is divided according to the idea of goodness, namely as it is something perfect and desirable. But this division is the foundation for the notion of moral goodness, which is virtuous goodness that is in conformity with the rules of moral action, that is, with the eternal law and right reason.[27]

Certain difficulties are raised against this division. (1) It seems better to divide transcendental goodness by the ten categories in which it is found. (2) This division is not made by members that are opposites to one another, for some thing, for instance, a virtue, is both objectively good and pleasant. (3) There is the aspect of end in goodness, but there is no such aspect in the useful.

The conclusion, however, is affirmative.

1) It is proved on the authority of St. Ambrose,[28] who gives the aforesaid division, which he found in Cicero's works. It was already given by Aristotle.[29] Thus Aristotle distinguishes between three kinds of friendship, in so far as it is the foundation for goodness that is either useful, or pleasant, or virtuous. This last kind is friendship among the virtuous. This classical division is found in the writings of St. Augustine and Dionysius. The Master of the Sentences divided the subject matter of theology, according as some parts are useful, but as other parts are virtuous and capable of being enjoyed by us.

27 *Ibid.*, Ia IIae, q.18.
28 *De officiis*, Bk. I, chap. 9.
29 *Ethics*, Bk. I, chap. 5.

This classical division, however, is not retained by the Epicureans who, like all materialists and sensualists, belittle virtuous good, and consider that goodness consists only in what is useful and pleasant. Thus they recommend a virtuous life only as a means of avoiding the inconveniences of vices that are in opposition to one another, and not because the object of virtue demands our love.

2) The genuineness of this classical division is proved from reason, for it applies, as St. Thomas says, not only to human goodness, but to goodness as such. A good division has its foundation in the formal aspect of the whole that is to be divided, and so it is with this division. For goodness, inasmuch as it is desirable, terminates the movement of the appetite. But this terminus is either the means (and thus it is called the useful), or it is the ultimate end, as the thing desired for its own sake (and thus it is called the virtuous), or else it is the ultimate end in the form of rest in the thing (and thus it is called the pleasant). This division properly has its foundation in the formal aspect of the whole that is to be divided, and it is effected by parts that are opposites to one another. Thus the division is not accidental, but essential and adequate.

We must particularly insist on the definition of virtuous good. It is that good which is desired for its own sake, as stated in the body of this article, and the reply to the second objection says that "the virtuous is predicated of such as are desirable in themselves," that is, regardless of any pleasure or usefulness resulting from it, as in the case of telling the truth even though death or martyrdom may be the result of this. As St. Thomas says elsewhere,[30] honest means the same as worthy of honor, and is indeed the object of virtue, and the source of spiritual elegance and beauty. It is also called rational or moral goodness, in so far as it is in conformity with right reason, as the object of the upright will.

Reply to first objection. This division is derived formally in accordance with the formal aspect of goodness, and not materially according as the subject serves as the foundation for this.

Reply to second objection. "This division is not by opposite things but by opposite aspects." Therefore the same thing, such as a virtue, can be both virtuous and pleasant, and even useful as regards the ultimate end.

However, those things are properly called pleasant that are only pleasant, being sometimes hurtful and contrary to virtue. Likewise those things are properly called useful that are only useful, as money and bitter medicine. St. Thomas shows elsewhere [31] that the virtuous is desired for its own sake by the rational appetite; that

---

[30] *Summa theol.*, IIa IIae, q. 145, a. 1, 2; Ia IIae, q. 39, a. 2.
[31] *Ibid.*, IIa IIae, q. 145, a. 3.

the pleasant is desired for its own sake by the sensitive appetite, and that nothing repugnant to virtuous good is absolutely and truly useful, but relatively so.

Reply to third objection. Goodness is not divided into these three as something univocal, but as something analogical; and it is predicated chiefly of the virtuous, secondly of the pleasant, and lastly of the useful.

First corollary. In this division we have the principle for the refutation of hedonism and utilitarianism, namely, of the false ethics that has its foundation in the pleasant and the useful, but not in the virtuous good. But the sensualists cannot truly preserve in their system the idea of virtuous good, which is good as such, regardless of the pleasure and usefulness resulting from it, as in the case of suffering martyrdom for the love of divine truth.

Second corollary. The first principle of ethics is: "We must do good and avoid evil." The reference here is to virtuous good toward which our rational nature is inclined by its Author.[32] Hence when a person comes fully to the use of reason, such person must love efficaciously the virtuous good for its own sake, and this more than himself. But this implies that confusedly or implicitly, though efficaciously, God, the author of nature and the supreme good, is loved more than oneself. But since this efficacious love, in the state of fallen nature, is impossible without a healing grace, which is also elevating,[33] St. Thomas, speaking of the age of reason, concludes: "If he (the child) then directs himself to the due end, he will by means of grace receive the remission of original sin," [34] namely, by baptism of desire. This remark alone suffices now, so as to show clearly how virtuous good transcends the pleasant and useful.

Doubt. It may be asked whether the brute beast tends at least materially toward the virtuous good that is proportionate to its natural inclination, although it has no knowledge of the end or of the virtuous as such.

We reply in the affirmative with St. Thomas, who says: "Everything (whatsoever creature) naturally loves God more than itself . . . since each part (in the universe of created things) naturally loves the whole more than itself. And each individual naturally loves the good of the species more than its own individual good." [35] Thus the malice of onanism is clearly seen, for it is against the good of the species and of its preservation. In like manner St. Thomas in commenting on these words of Christ, "How often

---

[32] *Ibid.*, Ia IIae, q.94, a.2.
[33] *Ibid.*, q.109, a.3.
[34] *Ibid.*, q.89, a.6.
[35] *Ibid.*, Ia, q.60, a.5 ad 1um; see also Ia, q.6, a.1 ad 2um; IIa IIae, q.26, a.3.

would I have gathered thy children together as the hen gathers her young under her wings, but thou wouldst not!" has this to say: "The hen, feeling concerned about her young, defends them, and gathers them under her wings. So also Christ takes pity on us, and truly bore our infirmities." [36] From this we clearly see how sublime is virtuous good, which is already materially present in the nobler actions of animals, so that Christ speaking of generosity could appeal to this example of the lower order, an example that is known to all.

And so with this we bring to a close the question of goodness in general.

This question gives us the nominal definition of goodness (that which all things desire), its real definition (perfect and desirable being), its relation to being and to causality, and also its division into the virtuous, the pleasant, and the useful.

[36] *In Matt.*, 23: 37.

CHAPTER VI

QUESTION 6

THE GOODNESS OF GOD

IN this question there are four points of inquiry. It treats first of God as He is in Himself, and then in His relation to creatures. The first two articles consider the question of God's goodness: whether God is good, and whether He is the supreme good. After this there is a discussion of the mode in which goodness belongs to God, namely, whether He alone is essential goodness. Lastly, the question is discussed, whether all things are good by the divine goodness, at least in so far as all things proceed from the divine goodness and tend toward it.

Therefore it treats of ontological goodness, by which God is good and desirable in Himself, and according to which He is the end of all things and the supreme agent communicating to creatures all good things they receive.

But this ontological goodness is the foundation of benevolence or of the love of benevolence, and it is also the foundation of justice and mercy, these being discussed by St. Thomas after his question about the divine will, since justice and mercy are, so to speak, virtues of the divine will.[1] We must draw special attention to this, for many already expect that the discussion of God's goodness means a discussion of His love of benevolence.

In this question it will be seen that St. Thomas proceeds by the way of affirmation and excellence, since goodness is a positive attribute. The middle term of the demonstration in these articles is the first efficient Cause (second proof of God's existence). For the first efficient Cause is the source of all good, and hence it is thus a posteriori evident that this Cause is the essential Good.

FIRST ARTICLE

WHETHER GOD IS GOOD

State of the question. Among philosophers, Plato had said that the supreme reality is the subsistent good. Aristotle, too, says that God is pure Act and, as the end or the supreme good, attracts or

[1] *Summa theol.,* Ia, q. 19-21.

draws all things to Himself. Several historians maintain that God, according to Aristotle, is only the end of all things, but not the efficient cause. Certainly Aristotle did not get so far as to admit the idea of a free creation from nothing; but he did not deny that God is in some way the efficient cause of the change in things, and of things themselves. In this question St. Thomas shows that God would not manifest Himself to us as the supreme good and the ultimate end of all things, unless He were the supreme efficient cause. But with this admission, there must be an application of the following principles, namely, that every agent acts with an end in view, and the order of agents must correspond to the order of ends, and the supreme agent to the ultimate end.

The reply of the article is this: Since God is the first effective cause of all things, evidently the aspect of good and of desirableness belong to Him.

1) This truth is revealed in countless passages of Holy Scripture, and is, so to speak, more than of the faith; for if God's goodness is denied there would be nothing left of Christian faith; this denial would be, in a certain sense, something more than heresy, for the heretic denies something and retains something; but with the denial of God's goodness there would be nothing left of the Christian mysteries.

From the Holy Scripture the following text is quoted: "The Lord is good to them that hope in Him, to the soul that seeketh Him." [2] In like manner Christ says: "Why askest thou Me concerning good? One is good, God." [3]

Manichaeism is condemned, which denies that the supreme Good is the sole principle and source of all goodness.[4] Against this heresy the Council of Florence defined that "God is the creator of all things visible and invisible, who when He willed, of His goodness created all creatures, both spiritual and corporeal; the good, indeed, because they were made by the supreme Good; but they are changeable, because they were made from nothing; and it (the Church) asserts that no nature is evil, because every nature as such, is good." [5] In like manner, the Vatican Council says: "God of His goodness . . . to manifest His perfection which He bestows on creatures . . . created them out of nothing.[6]

2) The reply is proved from reason as follows: The effective cause is desirable and good as regards its effects (thus the father is so as

[2] Lam. 3: 25.
[3] Matt. 19: 17.
[4] Denz., nos. 234 f., 367, 707, 710.
[5] *Ibid.*, no. 706.
[6] *Ibid.*, no. 1783.

regards his children); but God is the first effective cause of all things (2nd, 3d, 4th, and 5th proofs of God's existence); therefore God is good as regards all creatures.

The major is proved as follows: The proper perfection of the effect is its likeness to the agent, for every agent makes its like; but everything seeks its own perfection; therefore everything seeks to be like its efficient cause. But if the likeness of the efficient cause is desirable, then a fortiori the effective cause itself is desirable.

Some object that this argument is very involved for the affirmation of this most simple truth: God is good.

We reply by saying that this rather involved argument is expressed more simply by the Christian mind when it is said that God, inasmuch as He is the source of all good things, is in the highest degree good.[7]

But this argument brings out more clearly this great law of progressive development in all created things, namely, that the perfection of anything whatever is for it to be like its cause. Thus the perfection of the boy is that he becomes a man, just as his father is who begot him. In like manner the perfection of the disciple is for him to become like his master. Hence it is natural for the son to love his father, just as it is natural for the father to love his son; but the father's love is stronger because it is the love of one who is the cause.[8]

Hence because God is the first effective cause of all things, evidently He is good. Thus men and especially apostolic men, must manifest His goodness, by laboring effectively as true causes for the salvation of souls. They must have the goodness of a true intermediate cause which is intimately united with the supreme Cause of salvation. Thus the apostles are the salt of the earth and the light of the world, provided they receive the power to live an interior life not from inferiors but from God, who is the source of life. If the apostolic man is thus the true intermediate cause of salvation, he will certainly be desirable and desired, and all will say, as was said of the saints, whose effective influence was an evident manifestation of their goodness, how good he is. This applies far more so to God Himself. This is the profound meaning of this article, which at first sight seems very abstract and metaphysical, and yet there is in it some reference to the intimate life of a spiritual and apostolic man. In fact, the doctrine of this article is above sentimentalism, and is truly Christian realism.

This will be made much clearer to us in a subsequent article in which it is stated that "the love of God infuses and creates good-

---

[7] *Summa theol.*, Ia, q.2, a.3: fourth proof of God's existence.
[8] See reply to second objection in this article.

ness in things," [9] for His love does not presuppose lovableness in creatures, but posits or creates, preserves and increases, this in them. Thus goodness is appropriated to the Holy Spirit, who proceeds by way of love as personal love.

Reply to first objection. Mode, species, and order, which give us the descriptive definition of goodness, are in God as in the One who is the cause of order.

Reply to second objection. That which all creatures either knowingly or unknowingly love is a certain participated similitude of the divine goodness; thus when the hen gathers her chickens under her wings, she is loving the good or conservation of her species.[10]

SECOND ARTICLE

WHETHER GOD IS THE SUPREME GOOD

State of the question. It is still a question whether there is such goodness in God. Certainly it is of faith that God is supremely, in fact, infinitely, good.

The same middle term is employed in proving this from reason as in proving the conclusion of the preceding article. It is as follows: In the univocal cause the likeness of an effect is found uniformly, but in the higher and non-univocal, cause it is found eminently; but goodness belongs to God as the supreme effective cause of all things, which is non-univocal, yet transcending every genus; therefore goodness belongs to God in a most excellent way. For "all desired perfections flow from Him as from the first cause." However, the objections of this article are of minor importance, but they are formulated, such as they are, in accordance with the scholastic method of the thirteenth century.

THIRD ARTICLE

WHETHER TO BE ESSENTIALLY GOOD BELONGS
TO GOD ALONE

State of the question. Essential goodness is set in opposition to participated goodness. This article is the explanation of our Lord's words when He said: "None is good but God alone." [11]

The reply is in the affirmative; and its proof is the synthesis of what St. Thomas already wrote in another of his works,[12] and is

[9] *Summa theol.*, Ia, q.20, a.2.
[10] See Plato's *Phedrus* (on beauty) and his *Symposium* (banquet on love, toward the end).
[11] Luke 18: 19.
[12] *De veritate*, q.21, a.5.

reduced to this syllogism: A thing is good in so far as it is perfect, (1) according to its being, (2) as to its operative principles, (3) according as it attains its end; but this threefold perfection belongs to God essentially, because He alone is His own existence, His own action, and His own end; therefore essential goodness belongs properly to God, and all else is goodness by participation.

The difficulty is that St. Thomas, in virtue of the minor, concludes rather that only God is essentially good, whereas he intended to conclude that only God is the Good essentially, not by participation, that is, He does not participate in goodness. These two conclusions are not however universally the same; for Socrates is by reason of his essence a man, and yet he is not man *per essentiam,* but by participation. For it is only the "separate man," of which Plato speaks, who would be man *per essentiam* or the archetype of man.

In reply to this it must be said that in God, though nowhere else, these two modes of predication coincide, or, as Cajetan says, coincide "because of their matter." This means that not only does it follow from the argument of St. Thomas that God is essentially good, but also that He is the Good *per essentiam;* for God not only has goodness, but He *is* the very plenitude of being, or He is the supreme perfection, hence supremely desirable, or, in other words, He is *bonum per essentiam.*

On the contrary, although Socrates is by reason of his essence a man, yet he is not his humanity; for humanity is an essential part in him, and Socrates has this; but he is not his humanity.[13]

Reply to first and third objections. Anything whatever is one or undivided by reason of its essence, but it is not absolutely good by reason of its essence, but because of a superadded perfection.

Reply to second objection. "The essence of a created thing is not its existence," [14] and this is true before the mind considers it. Thus, in the teaching of St. Thomas, created essence and existence, which are not included in one and the same concept, are really distinct. We can find any number of similar expressions in his works.

FOURTH ARTICLE

WHETHER ALL THINGS ARE GOOD BY THE DIVINE GOODNESS

State of the question. This article was written to refute Plato's error, who held that the species of things are separate entities from individual things; in like manner, he held that the goodness of things is a separate entity from them, so that things are called

13 *Summa theol.,* Ia, q.3, a.3; IIIa, q.2, a.2.
14 *Ibid.,* Ia, q.3, a.4.

good by extrinsic denomination and by a certain participation, the nature of which is a secret of Platonism.

This teaching is the result of absolute realism, which maintains that the universal exists not only fundamentally but formally, apart from the thing in which it is found, or that it exists extramentally. Thus universal being is confused with the divine being, universal good with the divine good. In other words, the universal in predication is confused with the universal in being and causation. The pupils of Gilbert de la Porrée revived this extreme realism in the Middle Ages.

St. Thomas already examined this question in another of his works.[15] He now briefly recalls to mind Plato's opinion and concludes: Everything is called good from its own goodness formally and intrinsically as such, and it is called good from the divine goodness as from the effective and exemplary principle of all goodness.

The proof of the first part of this conclusion, which is against absolute realism, is that the species of things are not separated from them, any more than entity, unity, and goodness of things are separated from them. Everything is called formally good by intrinsic denomination, or by reason of its own goodness, which in an individual thing is its individual goodness. Thus the universal does not exist formally outside the mind, but fundamentally inasmuch as in individual things the similarity is either specific, generic, or analogical.

The proof of the second part of the conclusion is clearly deduced from the fourth proof of God's existence, since more and less are predicated of different things according as they resemble in their different ways something which is the maximum; for multitude does not explain the idea of unity of similarity to be found in them, and everything that is a compound (of receptive capacity and received perfection) needs a cause.

Hence Plato unwarrantably posited a separate or essential man, because man cannot exist apart from matter, and bones and flesh cannot exist unless they are the bones and flesh of this particular person. But he had a good reason for contending that there is a separate and essential Good. Yet he did not sufficiently distinguish this from universal good; and so we must say that in Platonism there is a pantheistic trend, which is more accentuated in the necessary emanatism of the Neoplatonists, which is radically in opposition to the dogmatic teaching of an absolutely free creation.

St. Thomas does not explicitly refute Manichaeism in this

15 *De veritate,* q.21, a.4.

sixth question, because he does this later on when discussing the problem of evil.[16] But this heresy is virtually refuted, since the supreme principle of all things, as stated, is the essential Good.

16 *Summa theol.*, Ia, q.47–49.

Summa theol., Ia, q.19, a.9.

CHAPTER VII

QUESTION 7

THE INFINITY OF GOD

AFTER a consideration of the divine perfection, the question of God's infinity is discussed, because infinity is a mode of perfection of the divine nature and of every divine attribute. This question considers infinity in the divine nature, and is not concerned with the mode of this infinity in this or that particular divine attribute, such as wisdom or power.

First we consider God's infinity, then we discuss whether anything except God can be essentially infinite, or at least infinite in magnitude or multitude.

FIRST ARTICLE

WHETHER GOD IS INFINITE

State of the question. It concerns infinity of perfection or infinite perfection. The difficulty is: (1) that infinity is attributed also to matter, since there is in matter an infinite capacity for receiving all kinds of forms; (2) that it is attributed likewise to quantity, which can always be increased, as a series of days can; (3) that the coexistence of the finite and the infinite seems an impossibility, for, if the infinite in magnitude exists, no place is left for the finite.

The reply is in the affirmative, however, and it is of faith that God is infinite, or infinitely perfect.

1) Several texts in Holy Scripture assert this. Thus we read: "Great is the Lord and greatly to be praised; and of His greatness there is no end." [1] The Vatican Council declared: "God is incomprehensible and infinite in all perfection." [2]

2) The reply is proved from reason by the following fundamental argument, which St. Thomas considers a simple corollary of the assertion that God is the self-subsisting Being. [3]

Whereas matter is called infinite by an infinity of imperfection,

[1] Ps., 144: 3; also Bar. 3: 25.
[2] Denz., no. 1782.
[3] *Summa theol.*, Ia, q.3, a.4.

the unreceived form is infinite by an infinity of perfection, at least relatively so. Thus if whiteness were not received in anything, it would have the total perfection of whiteness without any limit. But being is the most formal of all things, as it is the actuality of forms themselves. Therefore being that is not received in anything —and this being is God—is infinite by an infinity of perfection, and not merely relatively as included in some genus as would be the case with whiteness that is not received in anything, but is so absolutely, transcending every genus.

The major is explained in the beginning of the body of this article. The ancient philosophers of the Ionian school, such as Thales, Anaximenes, Anaximander, Heraclitus, attributed infinitude to the first principle because it is the source of an infinity of things. But they erred about the nature of the first principle, considering it to be something material, such as water, air, or fire. Hence they erred about its infinity, which they thought was something material and quantitative as consisting in an infinitely extended body. But infinity of matter is infinity of imperfection or something privative in that matter, which is pure potentiality and lacking in all determination, since it is made finite by the form, is perfected or determined by it.

On the contrary, the form is limited by the matter in which it is received, and the form considered in itself, or as not received in anything, has an infinity of perfection, since it is unlimited and is infinitely capable of being participated in, as in the case of whiteness. Hence if whiteness were not received in anything, it would have the total perfection of whiteness without any limit and would be infinitely perfect in a restricted sense, that is, in the genus of whiteness, though not of heat. Hence the common assertion: Matter is determined by the form, and the form is limited by the matter in which it is received. Thus determination is perfection or action; whereas limitation is imperfection.[4] It is a question of the form as such, which is thus infinitely perfect in a relative sense, if it is not received in anything. But such a form (for instance, that of an ox) is perfected together with matter, without which it cannot exist.

The minor, however, is evident, namely, that being is the most formal of all things, since it is the actuality of the forms themselves.[5] Therefore being that is not received in anything, which is God, is infinite with an infinity of perfection, and absolutely so.

---

[4] Not understanding this distinction between determination and limitation, Spinoza said: "Every determination is a negation." In truth, God is in the highest degree determined or perfect, but He is unlimited.

[5] *Summa theol.*, Ia, q.4, a.1.

Thus St. Thomas makes the transition from the relative infinity—for instance, of whiteness, that cannot be limited by matter; or of Michaelness, that is not indeed limited by matter—to the absolute infinity of the self-subsisting and unreceived Being, who is not limited by an essence which is distinct from Himself and in which He would be received.

Reply to the first and second objections. The infinity which is attributed to quantity has reference to matter and therefore does not apply to God.

Reply to third objection. Pure Act or being that is not received in any other is really and essentially distinct from every finite being; for every finite being is a compound of limiting essence and of limited or participated existence. Thus is solved the difficulty of the coexistence of the finite and the infinite. The existence of the infinite does not prevent the existence of the finite, which is distinct from it. Even if it were to prevent the existence of the finite, this would be because the infinite could not produce anything external to itself; and thus this being would not be infinite, because the power of causing, or infinite power, would be denied this being. The infinite being can indeed not create, because He was most free in creating; but He must of necessity have the power to create.[6]

Objection of Suarez. Suarez, who came after Scotus, says that the aforesaid argument presented by St. Thomas presupposes something not admitted by all theologians, namely, the real distinction between created essence and existence. In fact, Suarez denies this distinction and says: "Being is not finite, because it is received in some other; and it is not infinite, because it is not received in any other."[7]

In reply to this, we say with John of St. Thomas [8] that, even apart from the direct consideration of the real distinction between essence and existence, the reason given by St. Thomas is still cogent. Indeed, before we consider that the existence of the creature is received subjectively in the created essence and is really distinct from it, we see that it is received objectively and by participation, since it is produced contingently by God and contingently belongs to the subject, which does not have to exist. On the contrary, self-subsisting Being is not received in any other objectively and by participation, because it is not produced, and is not a contingent but a necessary predicate of the subject.

But from this it follows that God alone is His own existence,

---

6 *Ibid.*, q.45, a.5.
7 *De attributis Dei*, Bk. III, chap. 1.
8 *In Iam*, q.7, a.1.

and that contrary to this the creature,[9] before any consideration on our part, is not its existence, but has existence, just as matter is not form, but receives it. Thus it remains true, as St. Thomas says, that there is a real distinction between created essence and existence, and this for three reasons: (1) because actuality (which of itself is unlimited), is *de facto* limited only by the real capacity in which it is received; (2) because created essence and existence cannot be reduced to the same concept (as animality and rationality are reduced to the concept of humanity); (3) because existence is a contingent predicate for every creature, and is not included in the adequate concept of its essence.

But how does Suarez prove God's infinity? He proves that God is infinite because no being can be thought of greater than God; whereas it is possible to think of something greater than any finite being whatever.[10]

As John of St. Thomas remarks,[11] even St. Thomas proposed this argument;[12] but it does not bring out clearly what is the very foundation and reason for God's essential infinity, since it does not take as its starting point the very lack of terms limiting His existence.

On the contrary, when it is said that God is the self-subsisting and unreceived Being, the reason is given for His infinite perfection, just as, if whiteness were of itself subsistent and unreceived, it would have all the perfection of whiteness without limitation. The self-subsisting and unreceived Being has, without limitation, all the plenitude of being.

St. Thomas shows farther on[13] that there cannot be two angels of the same species, because the angel's nature is a subsistent form, which is not received in matter and is not capable of being participated in by matter. Thus, by the very fact that Michaelness is not received in any other, it is relatively infinite; the Deity, however, is absolutely infinite. Briefly stated: God is supremely determined or perfect, and therefore unlimited. The reference is to intensive infinite perfection.

But from the infinity of God's being is derived the infinite perfection of His operation, namely, of His intellection, love, and power: for operation follows being, and the mode of operation follows the mode of being.[14]

---

9 *Summa theol.,* Ia, q.3, a.4.
10 *De attributis Dei, loc. cit.*
11 *In Iam,* q.7, a.1, no. 19.
12 *Contra Gentes,* Bk. I, chap. 43, §§ 7 f.
13 *Summa theol.,* Ia, q.50, a.4.
14 *Ibid.,* q.25, a.2.

SECOND ARTICLE

WHETHER ANYTHING BUT GOD CAN BE ESSENTIALLY INFINITE

State of the question. This article is written for the purpose of distinguishing more clearly between absolute infinity and relative infinity. It begins by proposing three difficulties. (1) Why cannot God produce anything infinite, since His power is infinite? (2) The human intellect, for the very reason that it has knowledge of the universal, has infinite power in knowing all the singulars contained in the universal. (3) Prime matter itself is said to be infinite.

Conclusion. Things other than God can be relatively infinite, but not absolutely infinite.

This conclusion is of faith. Only God is infinitely perfect, "ineffably exalted above all things besides Himself which exist or are conceivable" [15] as the Vatican Council says.

The reason is that absolute infinity is the infinity of the being that is not received in any other, and there can be only one such infinity, just as, if whiteness were not received in any other, there would be but one whiteness.

However, immaterial forms, such as Michaelness, are relatively infinite with an infinity of perfection. Thus Michael has all the perfection that belongs to his species. [16] Infinity that is said to be *secundum quid* is also relative, or as referring to some genus of infinity, whereas infinity that is said to be so *simpliciter,* is absolute infinity. But matter is relatively infinite, with an infinity of imperfection, since it has a real capacity for receiving all natural forms. [17]

It must be noted that the end of the argumentative part of this article again affirms clearly the real distinction between created essence and existence in the following words: "Because a created subsisting form (as Michaelness) has being, yet is not its own being, it follows that its being is received and contracted to a determinate nature. Hence it cannot be absolutely infinite."

Likewise, in the **reply to the first objection** we read: "It is against the nature of a made thing for its essence to be its existence; because subsisting being is not a created being." Thus God, although He is omnipotent, cannot make something that is absolutely infinite, because this is really an impossibility.

Reply to second objection. Our intellect, since it transcends matter, naturally tends to extend itself in a way to know an infinity

---

[15] Denz., nos. 1782, 1804.
[16] *Summa theol.,* Ia, q.50, a.4.
[17] *Ibid.,* ad 3um.

of things; yet it knows them in a finite way. Thus farther on [18] it will be stated that our intellect elevated by the light of glory can directly see God's essence, but in a finite way, not comprehensively as it is seen by God Himself.

THIRD ARTICLE

WHETHER AN ACTUALLY INFINITE MAGNITUDE CAN EXIST

State of the question. It is asked, for instance, whether it is possible for air to be infinite in extent, and yet for it to be finite according to the essence of air. The purpose of this article and the following one is to distinguish between actual or categorematic infinity, and potential or syncategorematic infinity, which is the finite that is always perfectible, or which is always capable of having something added to it, as in the case of magnitude or a series of numbers. This distinction was already made by Aristotle,[19] who showed that everything which is continuous is, indeed, infinitely divisible, but is never infinitely divided; for it consists, indeed, of parts that can always be divided and of terminating points. In like manner, the sides of a polygon inscribed in a circle can always be subdivided, and yet the polygon will never be equal to the circumference. It must be observed that Spinoza, not sufficiently distinguishing between infinity of perfection and infinity of imperfection—a distinction which St. Thomas had made in the first article of this question—said that actually infinite extension is one of God's attributes.

The conclusion of St. Thomas is: "No natural body, in fact, no mathematical body can be actually infinite."

A physical body is an existing subject of three dimensions; in it are matter, form, and sensible qualities. A mathematical body is merely quantity according to three dimensions. This distinction was not sufficiently upheld by Descartes.

The first part of the conclusion, concerning natural bodies, is proved in two ways; metaphysically and physically.

The metaphysical proof may be thus enunciated: Determinate accidents, and hence determinate quantity, follow upon a determinate form. But every natural body, for instance, air or water, has a determinate specific form; so also has every created being. Therefore every natural body has a determinate quantity.

The major has its foundation in the principle that accidents inhere in substance, and, as it were, flow from it or are derived or emanate from it. Therefore an infinite accident is not derived from

18 *Ibid.,* q. 12, a. 7.
19 *Physics,* Bk. III, chaps. 1 f.

a finite substantial form; otherwise this finite form would be infinite in power.

It may be objected, however, that infinite air or infinite water would not constitute one individual body, but would be an aggregation of molecules of either water or air. In reply we say that then this would be another question, which is solved in the subsequent article about infinite multitude.

The physical proof is thus formulated:

Every natural body has some natural movement, either direct or circular. Thus the direct tendency of a stone is downward, but the movement of the planets is circular (or elliptical). But an infinite body could not be so moved; not indeed by a direct movement, because it would already occupy every place; nor could it be so moved by a circular movement because the lines, the farther they are drawn from the center of such a body as this toward the circumference (which would be in no place), would be infinitely distant from one another, and thus one of these lines could never reach the place occupied by another; but such a condition is required for the circular movement of any body revolving in the same place by a rotatory motion. There would be neither periphery nor circular motion in this periphery. Thus Paschal speaks of some sphere whose center would be everywhere and its circumference nowhere.

This physical argument presupposes the doctrine of natural motion as opposed to violent motion and as terminating at some natural place, as in the motion of a stone downward to the center of the earth. But after Galileo's experiments dealing with the falling of any body in a vacuum, this doctrine of the natural motion of bodies cannot now be admitted, at least without some modifications. However, modern physics has retained something of this teaching in the law of the diminution of energy. In accordance with this law, the heat required for the production of local motion cannot be fully restored by the conversion of this local motion into heat, and thus the whole world tends by a natural motion toward a certain state of equilibrium.

The proposed argument seems a sound one, if it is conceded that every natural body has a natural motion, at least in the same place. But some may say that this infinite body cannot be moved all at once as a compact mass, but perhaps the parts of this body can be moved.

In reply to this we say that then we are concerned with another question, namely, that of the actually infinite multitude of distinct parts, which is discussed in the following article.

But can one imagine an actually existing mathematical body that

would be infinite in magnitude? St. Thomas replies in the negative at the end of the argumentative part of this article. His reason
is that this body could not be actual without some form or figure.
But every figure is finite. Therefore it is impossible to imagine an
actually existing body that would be infinite in magnitude.

Nevertheless St. Thomas himself, commenting on this last proof,
says: "It is not conclusive but only probable, because whoever
would assert the existence of an infinite body would not concede
that it is of the essence of a body to be bounded by a surface, unless
perhaps potentially, although this view is probable and much
argued." [20] Furthermore it must be said that a mathematical body
cannot naturally exist without a subject that is a composite of
matter and form, and thus the previous arguments remain in force.

Reply to first objection. In geometry by the expression "infinite"
is meant an actually finite line that can always be extended.

Reply to second objection. Infinite is not against the nature of
magnitude in general, but it is against the nature of any of its
species, because any species whatever of magnitude has a finite
figure. "Now what is not possible in any species cannot exist in the
genus." This last proposition confirms the probable argument about
a mathematical body, given at the end of the argumentative part
of this article.

Reply to third objection. "The infinite is not in the addition of
magnitude, but only in division." The first part of this statement is
true of a natural body, because it increases until it reaches a determinate size that is proportionate to its specific form. Moreover,
even if a body were capable of infinite increase, it would never
be actually or categorematically infinite, but only potentially or
syncategorematically.

Reply to fourth objection. It is conceded that infinite is not
against the nature of time and movement, because time and movement differ from magnitude inasmuch as they are not in actuality
as to the whole of their being, but only successively. Hence there
seems to be no repugnance in the idea that the movement of the
heavenly bodies and time should be from eternity, as Aristotle
thought, and then there would be neither a first revolution of the
sun nor a first day.

FOURTH ARTICLE

WHETHER AN INFINITE MULTITUDE CAN EXIST

State of the question. This question, is a very difficult one, this
being the decision of St. Thomas, as will at once be seen, especially

[20] *Com. on Physics,* Bk. III, chap. 5, lect. 8, no. 4.

from what he wrote on this subject in another of his works in which he stated: "Whoever would assert that any multitude is infinite, would not mean that it is a number, or that it belongs to the species of number. For number adds to multitude the idea of measurement. Number is, indeed, multitude measured by one." [21] Hence it is certain that an infinite number is a contradiction in terms, because every number bears a fixed relation to unity, and is the result of addition beginning from one, which is the principle of number. But the question is, whether an actually infinite and innumerable multitude, such as of grains of sand, is an impossibility. We have already discussed this question elsewhere.[22]

It is difficult for the peripatetic philosopher to give a negative reply to this question, because for him, as also for St. Thomas, there does not seem to be any repugnance in the idea that the world may have been created from eternity.[23] In this case there would have been no commencement of motion, for instance, of the sun; there would have been no first revolution of the sun, no first day, and there would be no difference between creation and preservation of things in existence. We find it difficult to imagine this, yet there does not seem to be any repugnance in it according to St. Thomas. It would be like a footprint made in the sand from eternity by an eternal foot, which would have a priority not of time but of causality as regards its imprint.

But if it were so, already the series of days antecedently would be actually infinite, just as the series of acts of immortal souls subsequently will be infinite. It is indeed true that past days, since they no longer exist, do not constitute an actually infinite multitude of actually existing parts. But in this hypothesis, there is nothing repugnant in the idea of God creating from eternity on any day whatever a grain of sand or an angel, and forever conserving these effects in being. In this case there would already be antecedently an actual infinite multitude of grains of sand, or of angels, although there could always be made an addition to these subsequently.

But these difficulties were not unknown to St. Thomas; in fact, he hints at them in the beginning of this article by remarking: (1) Number can be multiplied to infinity; nor is it impossible for a potentiality to be made actual; (2) the species of figures are infinite; thus the sides of a polygon can be multiplied to infinity; (3) if we suppose a multitude of things to exist, for instance, grains of sand, there can still be infinitely many others added to these.

21 *Ibid.*, lect. 8.
22 *God, His Existence and His Nature*, I, 77–80.
23 *Summa theol.*, Ia, q.46, a.2 ad 7um.

This third difficulty finds its confirmation in the consideration of the non-repugnance of the world having been created freely from eternity, without a first day; for as was said, if on any day whatever, God had eternally created one grain of sand, and had afterward conserved all these grains in being, then the multitude of these grains would be actually infinite antecedently, and the multitude of these grains would be innumerable in a regressive series starting from the last created and going back to the earlier creations, because in this hypothesis there would not have been a first grain created, just as there would not have been a first day. But the days and years would have been from eternity, just as forever without end the intellectual and volitional acts of immortal souls are multiplied.

We shall see that it can be denied that St. Thomas took a definite stand in this difficult problem. Nevertheless the Thomists and many other Scholastics commonly deny the possibility of an actually infinite multitude of actually coexisting things. Many of them, however, grant that a multitude of past days could be actually infinite antecedently and innumerable, just as a multitude of intellectual acts of an immortal soul will be infinite subsequently, but these acts do not all exist at the same time.

Contrary to this among those who maintain the possibility of an actually infinite multitude of even coexisting things, must be named Scotus, and the nominalists Gregory of Arimini, Ockham, Gabriel Biel, as also Vasquez. The Jesuits of Coimbra University considered it to be a probable opinion that there is no repugnance in the idea of an actual infinite. Cardinal Toletus was of the same opinion.[24] Of modern philosophers, Descartes and Leibnitz admit the actual infinite. Likewise Spinoza admits in a pantheistic sense the infinity of all things, in existence, magnitude, and multitude. In more recent times this point has been the subject of great controversy, for instance, in France. Charles Renouvier keenly defended finiteness, and Milhaud defended the opposite thesis.[25]

We must first of all exclude arguments that have no probative force, before we consider the more cogent reasons advanced by St. Thomas.

It is quite astonishing that several authors did not even see the difficulty of the problem and said: Every multitude is divisible into two parts. But any part of it is finite. Therefore the whole multitude is finite. Those who assume that multitude is actually infinite antecedently, would reply: Certainly multitude can be divided into

24 In Iam, q.7, a.4.
25 Essai sur les conditions de la certitude logique, 177 f.

two parts, one of them being finite both antecedently and subsequently, and the other being infinite antecedently. Others wish to prove the impossibility of an actually infinite multitude, because something could be added to and subtracted from it whereas nothing can be added to or subtracted from the infinite. It is easy to reply to this objection by saying that an actually infinite multitude requires merely that it have antecedently no beginning, and then something can be added to or subtracted from it subsequently, just as this could be done to the succession of days, if it were from eternity.

Finally, some unwarrantably assert that of two actually infinite multitudes, one cannot be greater than the other. But it would be so if the series of days were from eternity, because the series of hours would still be much greater.

We reply by distinguishing the antecedent: of two actually infinite multitudes one cannot be greater than the other, in their infinite aspect, this I concede; in their finite aspect, this I deny. Thus the series of hours would be greater in their finite aspect, so that there could be a series of days greater in their finite aspect by the addition of new days.

St. Thomas begins the argumentative part of this article by referring to the opinion of Avicenna and Algazel and then refuting it. He denies the possibility of an actually infinite multitude of coexisting things, and admits the possibility of a potentially infinite multitude.

The opinion of Avicenna and Algazel is this: An actually infinite multitude of things not essentially but accidentally subordinated, is possible. Examples of this are, if the generation of man actually depended on the man generating, and on the sun and on other agents actually exerting their influence in an infinite series; or if we take the case of a hammer moved by the hand, and by the will, and so on in an infinite series. In such cases there would be no supreme efficient cause, and hence no secondary causes which in their causation are dependent solely on the supreme cause.[26]

But according to Avicenna and Algazel, it is not repugnant to reason that there should be an infinite series of accidentally subordinated causes. This would be the case if the artificer were to make something with an infinite multitude of hammers, inasmuch as one after the other may be broken. This is accidental multitude, for it happens by accident, inasmuch as one hammer or mallet is broken and another is used.

It must be observed that St. Thomas admits this saying: "It is not impossible to proceed to accidental infinity as regards efficient

[26] *Summa theol.*, Ia, q.2, a.3.

causes . . . as an artificer acts by means of many hammers accidentally, because one after the other may be broken." [27]

But St. Thomas denies that any particular consequence follows from this general assertion: namely, that now there would be an actually infinite multitude of coexisting things, for instance, of broken hammers or of immortal souls, granted that the series of generations is eternal. St. Thomas seems to see no repugnance in an actually infinite multitude of past things or of past days, which are no longer in existence, of generations of animals, for instance, which are now not in existence; but he denies this for the generation of men, because there would now be an actually infinite multitude (antecedently) of immortal souls.[28] He excludes the particular reason given by Avicenna, with the following remark: "One might say that the world was eternal, or at least some creature, as an angel, but not man. But we are considering the question in general, whether any creature can exist from eternity." [29] In like manner, in the reply to the first objection he says: "A day is reduced to act successively, and not all at once," so also a series of days.

The conclusion of St. Thomas is this: An actually infinite multitude of coexisting things, even accidentally connected, is an impossibility.

Reasonable proofs are given which, however, according to the judgment of St. Thomas, do not appear to be incontestable.[30]

The counterargument is taken from the Scripture: "Thou hast ordained all things in measure, and number, and weight." [31] But this is said of those things that have been made, so that it leaves undecided the question of those things that can come into existence. The body of the article has two arguments; the first is derived from the determinate species of multitude, the other from the fixed intention of the Creator. The first argument is reduced to the following syllogism: Every kind of multitude must belong to some species of multitude. But no species of multitude is infinite; for the species of multitude are to be reckoned according to the species of numbers and any number whatever is finite, being multitude measured by one. Therefore no kind of multitude is infinite.

Doubt. Is this an incontestable argument? In answer we should note what St. Thomas wrote, following the statement of this proof as given by Aristotle. St. Thomas says: "It must be observed that

[27] *Ibid.*, q.46, a.2 ad 7um.
[28] *Ibid.*, ad 8um.
[29] *Ibid.*
[30] *Com. on Physics*, Bk. III, chap. 5, lect. 8; also *De aeternitate mundi*, and *Quodl.* 12, q.2, a work which he wrote near the end of his life.
[31] Wis. 11: 21.

these arguments are probable, expressing the commonly accepted view; they are not, however, rigorously conclusive: because . . . if anyone were to assert that any multitude is infinite, this would not mean that it is a number or that it belongs to the species of number: for by number a multitude becomes measurable, as is stated in the tenth book of the *Metaphysics,* and thèrefore number is said to be a species of discrete quantity; but this is not the case with multitude which is of the nature of a transcendental." [32] Thus it is that things of the same species are numbered, and the multitude of angels, who are not of the same species, is not a number. However, it must be observed that St. Thomas wrote his commentary on the *Physics* in 1264, and the first part of the *Theological Summa* in 1265. In fact, in 1264 he wrote in another work: "It has not yet been proved that God cannot bring it about that there be actually infinite beings," [33] for instance, the creation from eternity on any day whatever (without there being a first day) a grain of sand, and the conservation in being of all these grains. Then this multitude would be antecedently infinite and innumerable.

Likewise St. Thomas wrote later on (1274) as follows: "To make something actually infinite, or to bring it about that infinites should exist actually and simultaneously, is not contrary to the absolute power of God, because it implies no contradiction; but if we consider the way God acts, it is not possible. For God acts through the intellect, and through the word, which assigns to all things their forms, and hence it must be that all things are formally made (that is, determined) by Him." [34]

This last consideration belongs to the discussion of the second argument. But on first inspection it does not appear to be incontestable. An adversary could say that a multitude of things accidentally connected (as grains of sand) is not necessarily in any determinate species, and in this it differs, for instance, from a plant or animal. Every plant must be in a certain genus and species, and the same is to be said of every animal, because its parts unite to form one natural and determinate whole. But it is not so evident that such is the case with a multitude of accidentally connected things; for it would have to be proved that an innumerable and actually infinite multitude of things antecedently and simultaneously existing is an impossibility. It is indeed evident that an infinite number is a contradiction in terms; but it is not so clear that such is the case with an actually infinite multitude, because, as St. Thomas says, "by number a multitude becomes measurable; for

---

[32] *Com. on Physics,* Bk. III, chap. 5, lect. 8.
[33] *De aeternitate mundi* (the end).
[34] *Quodl., loc. cit.*

number is multitude measured by one." [35] Moreover, there is an infinite multitude of possible things.

St. Thomas says that "God can make something else better than each individual thing." [36] Why then could not God from eternity (that is, without any first day) have created every day an angel and always more perfect angels, and preserve them in being? Then the multitude of these would not be a certain number or measurable by number, but would be infinite antecedently. Hence the first argument does not appear to be incontestable; to consider it as absolutely certain would seem to be exaggerated realism. Moderate realism can indeed prove that every body, for instance, a mineral or a living being, which is essentially one as a natural whole, is in some species under some genus; but it does not conclusively prove anything like this of a multitude of simultaneously existing things that are accidentally connected.

The second argument is derived from the clear intention of the Creator, and is reduced to the following syllogism: Everything created is comprehended under some clear intention of the Creator; but multitude in nature is created; therefore it is finite.

St. Thomas seems to propose this as a certain argument, for he wrote: "If we consider the way God acts, it is not possible. For God acts through the intellect and through the word, which assigns to all things their forms." [37]

What force has this argument? The work just quoted gives us the answer in these words: "To make something actually infinite is not contrary to the absolute power of God, because it implies no contradiction. But if we consider the way (assigning the forms) God acts, it is not possible." [38]

This is the same as saying that it is not intrinsically impossible according to God's merely absolute power, but that it is so if we consider God's power of ordaining all things in accordance with His divine wisdom, whether this power is ordinary or extraordinary. Thus it is shown farther on [39] that God could by His absolute power annihilate all creatures, immortal souls, the Blessed Virgin Mary, and the humanity of Christ, but this is not possible in accordance with God's power in ordaining all things (whether it is ordinary or extraordinary), for there can be no purpose or end in view in such annihilation, "since the power of God is conspicuously shown in His preserving all things in existence." [40] But it is not

[35] *Com. on Physics, loc. cit.*
[36] *Summa theol.,* Ia, q.25, a.6 ad 1um.
[37] *Quodl., loc. cit.*
[38] *Ibid.*
[39] *Summa theol.,* Ia, q.104, a.3 f.
[40] *Ibid.,* a.4 ad 1um.

so clear that this argument applies as to the impossibility of an actually infinite multitude.

Is this argument as thus set forth incontestable? It is not quite certain that St. Thomas himself considered it an incontestable argument, for farther on he proposes the following objection: "Everything that works by intellect works from some starting point; but God acts by intellect; therefore His work has a starting point. The world, therefore, which is His effect, did not always exist." [41] He replies to this objection as follows: "This is the argument of Anaxagoras (*Physics*, Bk. III, chap. 4, no. 5, lect. 6 of St. Thomas). But it does not lead to a necessary conclusion, except as to that intellect which deliberates in order to find out what should be done, which is like motion. Such is the human intellect, but not the divine intellect." [42]

Moreover, this argument would have more force if it referred to any created thing whatever taken by itself, the parts of which unite to form one natural whole; for instance, if it referred to every plant or animal. But it has less force if it refers to a multitude of accidentally connected things; for if, every day from eternity, God had created the souls of men, any one of these would be determinate, and yet the multitude of these souls would be infinite antecedently. Nor it is easy to prove that God cannot so bring them into being and preserve them in being.

Finally, it must be observed that no serious consequence arises if we say with St. Thomas [43] that these arguments are not incontestable; for no truth of great importance has its foundation in them. On the contrary, a very serious consequence would arise if the proofs of God's existence depended on this conclusion. We have already seen [44] that the proofs of God's existence have not their foundation in the principle that it is impossible to proceed to infinity in a series of accidentally subordinated past causes, but in the principle that it is impossible to proceed to infinity in a series of essentially subordinated and actually existing causes. And this last process is impossible, not because an actually infinite multitude is impossible, but because secondary causes do not act unless they are premoved to act by the supreme Cause. If therefore the supreme Cause does not exist, or does not move others to act, then there are no secondary causes actually in motion and no effects. Therefore no serious consequence arises, if the aforesaid arguments of this article are not incontestable.

[41] *Ibid.*, q.46, a.2, obj. 3.
[42] *Ibid.*, ad 3um.
[43] *Com. on Physics*, Bk. III, lect. 8.
[44] *Summa theol.*, Ia, q.2, a.2.

From the very fact that the arguments are not considered by St. Thomas to be incontestable,[45] this brings out more clearly the demonstrative validity required by him in a truly apodictic argument, in such arguments, for instance, as the proofs of God's existence.

Cajetan in his commentary is moderate in his statements. He writes: "It is sufficiently in agreement with the art of logic, so that it can be enunciated as a universal proposition, that every species of multitude is according to some species of number." [46] But when it is a question of an apodictic argument, he says more than "it is sufficiently in agreement with the art of logic."

At the end of the argumentative part of this article, St. Thomas says without any hesitation: "A potentially infinite multitude is possible," whether this be the continuous divisible to infinity, or the multitude to which something can always be added. From the replies to the objections evidently St. Thomas understands an actually infinite multitude as consisting of things simultaneously existing, so that it does not seem to be contrary to reason for a series of past days to be infinite antecedently.[47]

RECAPITULATION

Thus the question of the divine infinity comes to an end. There is infinity of perfection, so that God is both in the highest degree determined, as pure Act, and unlimited, since He is the unreceived and self-subsistent Being, possessing in Himself all plenitude or perfection of being, just as whiteness that is not received in any other would have all the perfection of whiteness. Only God, who is not a body, is infinitely perfect. Hence also, if besides God there existed an infinite body or an actually infinite multitude either of angels or of bodies, none of these would be confused with God. It was therefore a great mistake for Spinoza to say that an actually infinite multitude is one of God's attributes. This would mean that God is a body, just as man is. But this has already been refuted.[48] It would follow, of course, from this that God is a composite of spirit and body; but every composite demands a cause, and in the final analysis a most simple cause, which is to being as A is to A, the self-subsisting Being without limitation of essence. "Things in themselves different (as spirit and body) cannot unite unless some-

[45] *Ibid.* See also *De veritate*, q.2, a.10, in which St. Thomas leaves the question undecided. He speaks more forcibly in *Quodl., loc. cit.*

[46] See a.4, no. 6.

[47] *Summa theol.*, Ia, q.46, a.2.

[48] *Ibid.*, q.3, a.1.

thing causes them to unite," says St. Thomas,[49] in treating of God's absolute simplicity, which would be destroyed in saying with Spinoza that infinite and divisible quantity is one of God's attributes. Thus not everything that is in God would be God, but a part of God.

All these things are contrary to reason if it is properly understood that God is the self-subsisting Being, who is (without any limitation of essence) not received in any other, incapable of this, and to whom there can be no superaddition of any accident, as are the finite modes of Spinoza, which would be successively produced from eternity.

From all that has been said we are assured that the supreme truth of the treatise on the one God is this: in God alone are essence and existence identical.[50] It follows from this, as we have said, that God is absolutely simple and unchangeable and hence He is really and essentially distinct from the composite and changeable world. The infinity of God's intelligence, of His love, justice, mercy, power, follows from the infinity of the divine nature, because infinity is a mode of any of the divine attributes.

[49] *Ibid.*, a.7.
[50] *Ibid.*, a.4.

CHAPTER VIII

QUESTION 8

THE EXISTENCE OF GOD IN THINGS

IN this chapter we consider how God is immanent to the world, although at the same time transcending it. We shall also clearly distinguish between this immanence and pantheism, inasmuch as immanence belongs to God not as the formal or material cause of the world, but as its efficient or extrinsic cause, which is intimately connected, however, with the effect that immediately proceeds from it.

This question is placed right after that of God's infinity, because God's immensity and omnipresence are discussed in it, and these are in some way related to God's infinity.

First of all, we must note that immensity and omnipresence have not absolutely the same meaning. Immensity, or impossibility of being circumscribed by real space, is commonly defined as the aptitude or capacity to exist in all things and places. But omnipresence is the actual presence of God in all places. Hence immensity is an attribute that is an indispensable accompaniment of the divine nature. Even if God had not created, He would have been immense; on the contrary, omnipresence is a relative attribute since it refers to actually existing creatures.

There are four points of inquiry in this question. (1) Whether God is in all things. The question considers His actual presence, but the mode of His presence is likewise touched upon in this article. (2) Whether God is everywhere, or in all things in so far as these are in place. (3) How God is everywhere: whether by essence, power, and presence. (4) Whether to be everywhere belongs to God alone. The first article is of great importance, and from this article it is evident that there is a considerable difference between the doctrine of St. Thomas and that proposed later on by Scotus, as we shall at once see.

FIRST ARTICLE

WHETHER GOD IS IN ALL THINGS

State of the question. Several difficulties are proposed: (1) that, since God is above all, He is not in all things; (2) that God rather contains things than is contained by things; (3) that God is the most powerful of agents and therefore He can, like the sun, act at a distance, and all the more so inasmuch as He is the more powerful agent; (4) that God does not seem to be in the demons, and therefore He is not in all things that exist.

It must be observed that because of these and similar difficulties several persons denied that God is in all things. Thus the Manichaeans said that only spiritual things are subject to the divine power, but that corporeal things are subject to the power of the contrary principle. Some denied God's existence in things by His general presence, inasmuch as they said that divine providence does not extend to the lower grades of being. Moreover, certain Jews confined God to the temple of Jerusalem.[1] Lastly, the Socinians and certain Calvinists said that God is everywhere by His power and action, making His presence felt as the sun does on things here below, but that He is substantially present only in heaven.

Reply. God is in all things, and intimately so.

1) In evidence of this we may quote the following texts from Holy Scripture: "Whither shall I go from Thy spirit? Or whither shall I flee from Thy face? If I ascend into heaven, Thou art there; if I descend into hell, Thou art present." [2] "Do not I fill heaven and earth, saith the Lord?" [3] "He is not far from every one of us, for in Him we live and move and are." [4] "In Him are all things." [5] "One God and Father of all, who is above all and through all, and in us all." [6] Moreover, Isaias says: "Lord, Thou hast wrought all our works for us." [7]

But we must seek for the reason why God, who is pure spirit, and ineffably exalted above all things, is in all things, even those that are corporeal. St. Thomas gives us the reason for this in the body of this article, when he says: "God is in all things, neither as part of their essence (matter or form) nor as an accident, but as an agent is present to that upon which it works." It is proved as follows:

Every agent must be joined to that wherein it acts immediately, by virtual contact if not by quantitative contact, which does not belong to an incorporeal agent; but God is the proper and immediate cause of the production and conservation of all things in being; therefore God is in all things as agent, not by quantitative

1 Cf. St. Jerome, *Com. on Isaias,* chap. 66.
2 Ps. 138: 7 f.
3 Jer. 23: 24.
4 Acts 17: 27.
5 Rom. 11: 36.
6 Eph. 4: 6.
7 Is. 26: 12.

contact, since God is incorporeal, but by His virtual contact, which is really not distinct from His essence.

Then St. Thomas proves that God, as agent, is innermost in all things, because He conserves in them that which is more inherent, namely, "being which is formal in respect of everything found in a thing," Just as, in anything whatever, form is more inherent than matter, because it contains and determines the matter (for instance, in us the soul remains just the same, whereas the body undergoes a change), so being is more inherent in anything whatever than the form, because it is related to the form as its ultimate actuality. All that is contained in anything is actuated by being, either by substantial being or by accidental being.

In this article St. Thomas declares but does not prove, that God is the conservative and immediate cause of being in all things. This he proves farther on, saying: "As the becoming of a thing cannot continue when that action of the agent ceases which causes the becoming of the effect (as when the building of the house ceases, the house ceases to be built), so neither can the being of a thing continue after that action of the agent has ceased which is the cause of the effect not only in becoming but also in being." [8]

Thus when color ceases to affect the sense of sight, sense perception of color ceases; likewise, when the end, such as health, ceases to attract, then the desire ceases for the means, such as medicine, to attain the end; also when the principles of a demonstration cease to have any force, then there is no more evidence in the conclusion. When the sun ceases to illumine, there is no longer light in the air. If therefore God is the proper cause of created being, which is distinct from the becoming of things, then the being of things cannot continue in existence without God's preservative action.

In the body of the article, however, it is proved in a few words that "created being is the proper effect of God, just as to ignite is the proper effect of fire." The reason is that God is essentially being. Thus He is the cause of participated being. For the proper effect is that which necessarily and immediately depends on its proper cause.[9] The proper effect is like a property manifested *ad extra,* for it is related to its proper cause, as a property is related to its essence; but it is external to its cause. Thus the killer kills (for there can be no one killed without a killer); so also the builder builds, the painter paints, the singer sings. Thus God brings things into existence and preserves them in being. Indeed, as St. Thomas

[8] *Summa theol.,* Ia, q.104, a.1.

[9] St. Thomas, *Com. on Posterior Analytics,* Bk. I, lect. 10: "the fourth mode of direct predication."

says more explicitly, "the more universal effects must be reduced to the more universal and prior causes. But among all effects the most universal is being itself. Hence it must be the proper effect of the first and most universal cause, and that is God." [10]

Thus my free choice, as it is my own personal choice, is the proper effect of my will; but as it is a being, it is the proper effect of God. Thus God is in all things by a virtual act, preserving them in being.

However, there is still a difficulty in this demonstration. We have yet to show that God immediately preserves things in being, and not through the intermediary of some other being.

It is only in one of his subsequent articles that St. Thomas explicitly proves this for us, when he shows that there can be no instrumental cause in God's creative act: "Now the proper effect of God creating is what is presupposed to all other effects, and that is absolute being. Hence nothing else can act dispositively and instrumentally to this effect, since creation is not from any presupposed (subject), which can be disposed by the action of the instrumental agent." [11] There would be no effect produced by the instrument, and, moreover, the instrumental action would be an accident in God, and it would have to terminate in something that is acted upon, that is, in a pre-existing subject, and there is nothing such in creation.

In like manner, St. Thomas shows farther on that God preserves the being of things directly, and indirectly the less universal effects, for he says: "An effect is preserved by its proper cause on which it depends. Now just as no effect can be its own cause, but can only produce another effect, so no effect can be endowed with the power of self-preservation, but only with the power of preserving another." [12] Thus the sun is the conservator of light in the air inasmuch as it is light, but not inasmuch as it is being, because the sun is just as much a created being as light is. Hence just as God does not create by means of an instrument, neither does He preserve things in being, inasmuch as they are being, by means of an instrument, but does so immediately, as stated in this article.

Thus the major of this article is explained; namely, "Every agent must be joined to that wherein it acts immediately, and be in virtual contact with it." But if the agent is corporeal, there are two ways in which it comes immediately in contact with its effect, namely, by its quantitative matter and by its power. But if the agent is incorporeal, it does not come immediately in contact with its effect

10 *Summa theol.*, Ia, q.45, a.5.
11 *Ibid.*
12 *Ibid.*, q.104, a.2 ad 2um.

by quantitative matter, but by its power.[13] In this case there is immediate contact both of power and suppositum.

There is immediate contact of power because the divine power does not produce its effect through some intermediary power; for it does not operate by the power of a higher agent, but immediately of itself.

There is also immediate contact of suppositum, that is, there is no intermediate suppositum between God preserving and the being of the thing preserved; for there is no instrumental cause in the creative act and in the immediate preservation of things in being. Nor is the divine power something distinct from God, for it is the very essence of God, since God is His own action and His own being. Thus St. Thomas proves that God is in all things by His preservative action.

This conclusion is confirmed by the solution of the objections.

Reply to first objection. God, who transcends all things, not locally but by the excellence of His nature, is in all things, not as a part of their essence but as the agent who is the cause of being in all things.

Reply to second objection. God, being pure spirit, is in things as containing things, in a way, as the soul contains the body. However, God contains things, not as a form determining matter, but as a cause conserving the effect.

Reply to third objection. No agent acts upon any distant thing except through some medium. Thus the sun illumines and imparts heat to bodies on this earth through the medium of the air and ether, for the power of the agent can be only in a subject; but if it is not in the subject to which it properly belongs, then it is in an intermediate subject, as in an instrument.[14] But, as stated, God cannot make use of an instrument in creating and preserving things in being, inasmuch as they are being. Therefore He preserves them immediately. As St. Thomas in this article says: "But it belongs to the great power of God that He acts immediately in all things," [15] because He alone is the proper Cause of being as such in things.

Hence to the objection, "The more powerful an agent is, the more extended is its action," we must reply with the following distinction: that it is so when there is some medium, this I concede;

[13] *Contra Gentes*, Bk. III, chap. 68.

[14] In fact, creative action cannot be an accident, because as an accident it would be received and would terminate in a subject. But there is no presupposed subject in creation. Hence creative action is not really distinct from God's essence. See Ia, q.45, a.3 ad 1um. Conservative action, however, is continued creative action.

[15] Cf. ad 3um.

when there is no medium, then I deny it. Thus while the sun preserves light as such, God preserves the same as being; just as He preserves the sun as being. Moreover, matter, the human soul, and angels can be produced only by God's creative act, and their preservation in being depends on God alone.[16]

Reply to fourth objection. God is in the demons, not as preserving the deformity of sin in them, which is not from Him, but as preserving them in their nature.

In order to bring out more clearly the meaning and validity of St. Thomas' doctrine, these objections may be presented in syllogistic form. Thus the syllogism serves as a means of direct perception.

1) What is above all things is not in all things; but God is above all things; therefore God is not in all things.

Reply. I distinguish the major; what is above all things because of the dignity of its nature is not in all things as an essential part, this I concede; that it is not in all things as their cause, this I deny. I concede the minor, and distinguish the conclusion in the same way as the major.

2) But neither is God in all things as cause. Therefore the difficulty remains. The proof: The supreme cause produces inferior things only through the mediation of secondary causes; but God is not the sole, but the supreme cause; therefore God is not in all things as cause, at least not in inferior things.

Reply. I distinguish the major: that the supreme cause does not produce particular being, luminous being, for instance, this I concede; that it does not produce absolute being, or being as such, this I deny. I concede the minor, and distinguish the conclusion in the same way as the major.

3) But neither God as cause of being as such is in all things. Proof: The more powerful an agent is, the more it can act at a distance; but God is the most powerful of agents; therefore God can produce the being of things at a distance.

Reply. I distinguish the major: that the agent can act at a dis-

16 As Goudin says, and rightly so (*Metaph.*, disp. II, q.3, a.2), God not only premoves secondary causes, but, by a simultaneous concurrence that is properly explained, He produces the being of their effects.

Whereas the divine motion ceases when the causality of the created agent ceases, the divine concurrence preserves the effect produced as long as the effect continues in being. Thus absolute being in all things is the immediate result of the divine concurrence. Therefore God, by producing and preserving the being, for instance, of the ox generated, after the generating action of the ox has ceased, comes in immediate contact with this effect not only by His power, but also by His suppositum.

However, creation does not enter into the operations of nature, for the ox generated is not produced from nothing, but from a presupposed subject.

tance without an intermediary, this I deny; through an intermediary, again I distinguish; that it can so act by producing such or such being, this I concede, by producing being as such, this I deny.

4) It seems that God can create and maintain things in being by means of an instrumental cause, that is, by not acting immediately. For God, indeed, creates every day the souls of children, while the parents give to the matter the final disposition requisite for the human form.

Reply. The parents are not, strictly speaking, the instruments in the creation of the soul, because the spiritual soul is not educed from the potentiality of matter. But the matter is duly disposed so that it can be informed by the soul, which is created from nothing. On the contrary, there is an instrument (namely a sacrament) in the production of grace, which is educed from the obediential potentiality of the soul, on which it depends as its accident.

5) Nevertheless the action of the creature can extend to being as such, at least instrumentally. For my freedom indeed is the proper cause of my choice, as it is my choice, and it is the instrumental cause of the same choice as it is being. Then being as such is not immediately produced by God.

Reply. This is not a case of creation from nothing, but under the divine motion our will elicits its act. Nevertheless the being as such of my choice depends of itself and immediately as such on God as its proper effect, and God produces it immediately not only by the direct contact of His power but also of His suppositum. In a broad sense we can speak of the will as an instrument with reference to the being as such of our choice. Nevertheless God, who maintains immediately our soul in being, is intimately present in it and in its operations.[17]

6) How is it, then, that creation does not apply to operations of the natural order, if God is the proper cause, for instance, of the being as such of the ox that is generated?

Reply. Although the being as such of the generated ox depends of itself and immediately as such on God as His proper effect, yet it is not produced by way of creation, namely, from no presupposed subject. Hence in this case the total entity of the ox is not produced, because the matter, which is immediately preserved in being by God, was already in existence.[18]

OBJECTIONS OF SCOTUS AND THE SCOTISTS

Scotus and the Scotists attacked this doctrine of St. Thomas.[19]

[17] See Cajetan, *Com. on Summa*, Ia, q.45, a.5, nos. 5–11.
[18] *Ibid.*, no. 10.
[19] *In I Sent.*, d.37, q. unica.

They deny that God's virtually transitive operation is precisely the reason for His existence in things, just as material quantity is precisely the reason why a body occupies a place. Scotus attacks the major of St. Thomas, namely, "an agent must be joined to that wherein it acts immediately." He holds this proposition to be true only as regards corporeal and limited agents, which must be in quantitative contact with the subject to which they are joined, before they can act upon it.

Reply. This major of St. Thomas is true of every agent as such, and does not apply merely to a corporeal agent, which first occupies a place before it acts. Although indeed the agent may be a pure spirit and likewise the effect be merely spiritual, as the angel maintained in being by God, the agent must be joined to its effect at least by a virtual contact, and this for two reasons. (1) Because the perfecter and the perfectible that is immediately actuated by the perfecter must be joined together; for the effect seeks immediate contact with the active power from which it dynamically (though not always spatially) proceeds. There is no other way possible of conceiving this. (2) If it were not so, then there is no reason why this causative power would produce that particular effect rather than a certain other. The divine power is not something distinct from God, but is the very Deity, a formally immanent action, which is said to be virtually transitive in that it produces an effect external to itself.

1) Objection. It may be said that this is something merely philosophical, which has not at all been revealed, not even virtually.

Reply. There is at least a veiled reference to this proposition in the following familiar words of St. Paul: "He is not far from every one of us. For in Him we live and move and are." [20] Here the Apostle clearly shows from God's operation in us that He is present in us, even in those who do not know Him. The reference is to God's general presence or to His immensity, and not to His special presence in the souls of the just, in whom He dwells as knowable by them by a quasi-experimental knowledge, and by whom He is loved.[21] Moreover, St. Augustine says: "Since we are something other than God Himself, it is not because of something else that we are in Him, but because this latter is the result of His operation." [22]

2) Objection. The Scotists say that it is not repugnant for God to operate in things by a power that goes forth from Him, and to

---

20 Acts 17: 27.
21 *Summa theol.*, Ia, q.43, a.3.
22 *De Gen. ad lit.*, chap. 12, no. 23.

make use of creatures as instruments. Therefore the difficulty remains.

Reply. I distinguish the antecedent. It is not repugnant for God to operate by a power that goes forth from Him and is created, so as to produce such or such being, for instance, luminous being, this I concede; to produce being as such or absolutely, this I deny. There can be no instrument, indeed, in the act of creation, no presupposed subject being required for this.

3) **Objection.** Just as operation follows being, so operation in a place follows the presence of a being in a place, and not vice versa. Therefore a being must be there where it operates.

Reply. I distinguish the antecedent. I concede that operation in a place follows the presence of a being in a place, as regards a corporeal agent, which essentially occupies a place by reason of its quantity; I deny that this applies to a spiritual agent. For the spiritual agent occupies a place only in so far as it operates in a place; and yet in the order of being, not of location, its operation follows upon its being.

4) **Objection.** However, God's operation does not appear to be the reason for His presence where He operates. For, what is not distant is present. But, if by an impossibility, God did not act in any thing, He would not, however, be distant from it, because God is not absolutely assigned to a place. Therefore He would be present.

Reply. I distinguish the major. What is not locally distant is present, always positively present, this I deny; always negatively present, or not distant, this I concede. That God would be negatively present, which means not locally distant, this I concede; that He would be positively present, this I deny.

5) **Objection.** But a necessary attribute of God cannot be dependent on His free action. But ubiquity is one of God's necessary attributes. Therefore it cannot be dependent on His free action.

Reply. I distinguish the minor. That this is true of ubiquity in the broad sense of the term, or of immensity, this I concede; of ubiquity in the strict sense, this I deny. For immensity is only the aptness to exist in all things and places. But ubiquity is the actual existence in all things.

Final objection. Just as God by His eternity is immediately co-existent in all time, so by His immensity He is immediately present in every place.

Reply. The difference between the two is that eternity is the actual and simultaneously whole duration of the immutable God, whereas immensity is not the actual existence in things, but only the aptness to exist in them. The reason is that God is by His very nature absolutely and actually immutable and His life is simultaneously whole and interminable without any successive duration, and He would be so if there were no created beings. On the contrary, it is not in accordance with God's nature to occupy a place, because He is a pure spirit. And before creation He was nowhere, transcending the spatial order.[23]

This last reply shows that the teaching of St. Thomas on this subject follows as a logical conclusion from the principle that God is incorporeal, a pure spirit. Those, on the contrary, who seek to explain God's presence in all things apart from His divine action in them, willingly or unwillingly posit a certain virtual extension in God prior to His action, and thus they do not sufficiently distinguish between immensity and ubiquity. Thus Suarez, who follows Scotus to some extent in this thesis as in several others, maintains that God actually exists in imaginary spaces, beyond the limits of the universe.

To this the Thomists reply that God is virtually present in imaginary spaces, in that He can create some body in them; but He is not actually and positively present in them, for these imaginary spaces are not actual realities, but only possible receptacles of bodies. This question, however, belongs rather to the following article.

SECOND ARTICLE

WHETHER GOD IS EVERYWHERE

State of the question. The subject of inquiry in this article is whether God is not only in all things, but also in all places, inasmuch as they are places. The liquid is formally in the dish inasmuch as it is a place, whereas the picture is in the painted dish, inasmuch as it is a thing, and not formally inasmuch as it is a place. Can it be said that God is in a place, and in all places?

It seems this cannot be said of God, because incorporeal things are not in a place. Moreover, if God could be in a place, then He could not be everywhere, because He is indivisible and unextended, and because, if He were in a place, He would be there totally, and therefore He would not be everywhere.

Reply. God is in all places not absolutely but relatively, inasmuch as they are formally places. The reason is that God is in a place, not as a body is by filling the place to the exclusion of an-

---

[23] St. Augustine says in his commentary on psalm 122: "Where was God before He made heaven and earth? He was in Himself, with Himself." Without Him nothing was; therefore He was not in another.

other body, but because He gives being to all things placed, and also to the real place itself, or to the surface of the encompassing body. Hence God does not exclude other things from being there, but He causes things placed to be there.

Reply to first objection. Incorporeal things are in place by virtual contact.

Reply to second objection. God is indivisible, though not like a point which is the term of the continuous, for He is outside the whole genus of the continuous. Thus, unlike the point, He can be everywhere, and for this it suffices that He maintain all bodies in being by His divine power.

Reply to third objection. God, inasmuch as He preserves things in being, is whole in all and in each of them, somewhat as the soul is whole in the entire body and whole (by a totality of essence) in each and every part of it. Even whiteness is whole, by a totality of essence in each and every part of the wall, but it is not whole by a totality of extension.

Descartes, who is referred to, and rightly so, as an extreme spiritualist, since he denies that the soul is the form of the body, did not properly understand the indivisibility of the soul; he viewed it in a sort of material way as if it were a point, saying that the soul can contact the body only in one point, namely, the pineal gland. Likewise Leibnitz calls the monads metaphysical points. They failed to see that the substantial form is indivisible, not as a point is, but inasmuch as it is outside the whole genus of the continuous, as St. Thomas says in this article; [24] and so it can be whole in each and every part of the body. With far greater reason it must be said that God, not as form, but as agent, maintains things in being.

THIRD ARTICLE

WHETHER GOD IS EVERYWHERE BY ESSENCE, PRESENCE,
AND POWER

State of the question. The purpose of this article is to explain the classical statement of St. Gregory quoted in the counter-argument, that "God by a common mode is in all things by His presence, power, and substance; still He is said to be present more familiarly in some by grace." [25]

In the body of the article St. Thomas distinguishes between God's general presence by way of agent in all things and His special presence in the just inasmuch as He is present in them as

[24] Cf. ad 2um.
[25] *Com. on Cant. Cantic.*, 5: 17.

the object of quasi-experimental knowledge in the knower,[26] and as the beloved is in the lover, and especially so in the blessed, being in them as clearly seen.[27]

This article mentions the three ways by which God, after the manner of an agent, is in all things: (1) by His power, inasmuch as all things are subject to His power, as the King of the universe; (2) by His presence, inasmuch as all things are bare and open to His eyes, since all things, even the smallest, are the immediate object of divine providence; [28] (3) by His essence, inasmuch as God's essence, which is not really distinct from His omnipotence and preservative action, is present to all things as the cause of their being.[29]

The error of the Manichaeans was in denying God's universal presence by His power, maintaining that corporeal things were not subject to His power. Others, such as Plato and Aristotle, denied that individual things are the immediate concern of God's providence. If Aristotle admitted a certain general providence, as the Averroists did later on, he did not acknowledge its extension to each particular thing.

Also, since he never had a clear idea of creation, he could not conceive of God's existence in all things. We see that great advance has been made on this point from the time of Aristotle to that of St. Thomas. This has been accomplished by the light of revelation, which is truly like a guiding star for the Christian philosopher, and it is, moreover, the proper light of theology, whose *objectum formale quo* is virtual revelation.[30]

In the body of the article St. Thomas notes that there were certain philosophers who, although they said all things are subject to God's providence, still maintained that all things are not immediately created by God, but that He immediately created the first creatures, and these created the others. So thought certain Neoplatonists. If such were the case, God would not be present by His essence in inferior things, because He would not have immediately created them and would not immediately preserve them in being.

On the other hand, according to revelation it is certain that "God, with absolute freedom of counsel, created out of nothing, from the beginning of time, both the spiritual and the corporeal creature, namely, the angelic and the mundane; and afterward the

---

[26] So it is with faith that is illumined by the gift of wisdom. Thus God is, as it were, experimentally knowable, and sometimes He is actually known.

[27] *Summa theol.*, Ia, q.43, a.3, 5 f.

[28] *Ibid.*, q.22, a.3.

[29] See q.8, a.1.

[30] See p. 57, no. 37.

human creature, as partaking, in a sense, of both, consisting of spirit and of body." [31]

Certainly it is only by creation from nothing that the angels, the soul, and matter can be produced, for these are not educed from any presupposed subject; it is equally certain that they can be immediately maintained in being only by God. In this there is a vast difference between our Catholic faith and the teaching of Aristotle, which says nothing either about God's liberty, or about His absolute freedom in creating all things. Aristotle wrote very well the elements of metaphysics, as Euclid did those of geometry, but he never soared to the sublime in metaphysics, except in a very imperfect way, when he spoke of the pure Act as "the self-contemplative thought" or the self-subsistent intellection. [32]

In reply to the fourth objection we should note the following: "No other perfection except grace, added to substance, renders God present in anything as the object known and loved; therefore only grace constitutes a special mode of God's existence in things. There is, however, another special mode of God's existence in man by the (hypostatic) union."

This is explained in a subsequent article. [33] There we see that the philosophical knowledge of God, which can be acquired without grace, does not suffice for His special presence; for God is known only in an abstract way, as something distant, not as something really present. On the contrary, by habitual grace and living faith enlightened by the gift of wisdom, a quasi-experimental knowledge of God can be acquired and sometimes He is known as the principle of our interior life, prompting us to intimate acts of filial love, as St. Paul assures us in the following passage: "The Spirit Himself giveth testimony to our spirit that we are the sons of God." [34] St. Thomas, explaining this text in his commentary on this epistle, says that the Spirit gives testimony by means of the filial love which He arouses in us, as when the disciples going to Emmaus said: "Was not our heart burning within us whilst He spoke in the way?" [35]

From this it cannot be argued against what was said in the first article of this question, that there is another way by which God can be present in all things than by His preservative action; for this special presence presupposes the general presence, that is, God gives being to the just; in fact, He causes and effectively preserves

[31] Denz., nos. 428, 1784.
[32] *Metaph.*, Bk. XII.
[33] *Summa theol.*, Ia, q.43, a.3.
[34] Rom. 8: 16.
[35] Luke 24: 32.

charity in them. Thus He preserves the humanity of Christ, which is hypostatically united to the Word.

FOURTH ARTICLE

WHETHER TO BE EVERYWHERE BELONGS TO GOD ALONE

State of the question. The purpose of this article is to determine more accurately the mode of the divine omnipresence, and to distinguish it from the mode of omnipresence of universal being, prime matter, the universe, and the human soul that sees even remote stars. As Augustine says: "The soul feels where it sees, and lives where it feels, and is where it lives." [36]

Reply. To be everywhere primarily and absolutely, belongs properly to God alone.

1) Proof from authority. St. Ambrose says: "Who dares to call the Holy Ghost a creature, who in all things and everywhere and always is, which assuredly belongs to the Divinity alone." [37]

2) Proof from reason. That is everywhere absolutely and primarily, which is everywhere not accidentally but necessarily, and immediately in its whole self, and not according to its parts in different places. But God alone, after creation, is necessarily and immediately in His whole self in all things and places, for He maintains all things in being. Therefore, to be everywhere belongs primarily and absolutely to God alone.

In opposition to what is stated in the major and in explanation of it, it may be said that a grain of sand would be accidentally everywhere, on the supposition that no other body existed. But God, after creation, is necessarily everywhere, no matter what may be the number of things and places, even though the number of places should be infinite.[38]

Moreover, contrary to this, the whole world is everywhere, not primarily or immediately, namely in its whole self, but according to its different parts.[39]

Reply to first objection. Abstract being and prime matter are indeed everywhere, but not according to the same mode of existence. This view is moderate realism. Contrary to this, extreme realism confuses abstract being with the divine being, inasmuch as it maintains that the universal (in predication) exists formally and not only fundamentally in the objective world, that is, extramentally. If it were so, pantheism would be true, and abstract being

---

[36] *Epist. 3a ad Volusianum.*
[37] *De Spiritu Sancto*, Bk. I, chap. 7.
[38] Cf. ad 5um.
[39] Cf. ad 3um.

would be everywhere according to the same mode of existence. God would not only preserve immediately the being of all things, but He would be the very being of all things.

Prime matter is everywhere, but not according to the same mode of existence, for it receives its existence from the form, and under the different quantitative dimensions of the universe the form is not the same, and consequently neither is the matter the same according to existence. However, prime matter is negatively one, inasmuch as there are not two prime matters.

Reply to sixth objection. How are we to understand St. Augustine when he says: "Where the soul sees and feels, there it lives and is"? He must be understood as meaning that the soul, seeing the heavens, reaches the heavens as object; but subjectively it lives only in itself, because to live is an immanent act. Hence it does not follow that the soul is everywhere. Seeing is an immanent act, but the thing seen is not immanent, whatever the idealists may say. In fact, there can be no true seeing (as distinct from hallucination) without a thing seen, or a true sensation without an object of sense perception, or a true sensation of resistance without a resistant object. "Bodily vision (as distinct from imaginary apparition) is that whereby the object seen exists outside the person beholding it and can accordingly be seen by all. Now by such vision only a body can be seen." [40] Hence the soul, although it is not everywhere, can see even remote bodies; it is, of course, in the very act of seeing, in transcendental relation to these bodies.

With this we conclude the question of God's existence in things, a question in which immensity must be carefully distinguished from omnipresence, namely, aptitude to exist in all things from actual existence in them. Before creation, God was immense, but He was not everywhere, because there were not things and places in which God was; but He was with Himself, in Himself, for as the Gospel says, "In the beginning was the Word, and the Word was with God, and the Word was God." [41]

40 *Ibid.*, Ia, q.51, a.2.
41 John 1: 1.

CHAPTER IX

QUESTION 9

THE IMMUTABILITY OF GOD

FROM the truth that God is the self-subsisting Being, we have thus far deduced that He is absolutely simple, perfect and good, infinite and immense, and everywhere present inasmuch as He maintains all things in being. From the very fact that God is the self-subsisting Being, it likewise follows that He is absolutely immutable, with an immutability not of inertia but of supreme perfection, which belongs to God alone.

We shall see that, although this immutability is expressed in negative terms (inasmuch as our knowledge is first of mutable things), yet in itself it is something absolutely positive; and it can be expressed by the word "stability," whereas the mutability of things in the world is their instability.

Evolutionist philosophy does its utmost to eliminate the word "stability," for it maintains that all immutability is imperfect, being like the immobility of an inert, lifeless thing. On the contrary, supreme life is absolutely immutable or supremely stable. The refutation of pantheism is completed in this question, inasmuch as the self-subsisting Being, since He is absolutely identical with Himself and stable, is really and essentially distinct from the changeable world and from the soul that is always capable of further perfection in knowledge and love. There are now two points of inquiry: (1) Is God altogether immutable? (2) Does it belong to God alone to be altogether immutable?

FIRST ARTICLE

WHETHER GOD IS ALTOGETHER IMMUTABLE

State of the question. The difficulty here is that St. Augustine says: "The Creator Spirit moves Himself neither by time nor by place."[1] In like manner wisdom is said to be more mobile than all active things.[2] We also read in the Scripture: "Draw nigh to God, and

[1] *De Gen. ad lit.*, Bk. VIII, chap. 20.
[2] Wis. 7: 24.

He will draw nigh to you." [3] In all these utterances we must distinguish between the metaphorical and the literal sense. The analysis of concepts contained in revelation is of great importance in speculative theology, and this is prior to the deduction of the theological conclusion. This point is brought out clearly in the present article, in which the reply is not a theological conclusion but an explanatory proposition of the faith.

Reply. God is altogether immutable. This must be stated most emphatically against absolute and pantheistic evolutionism.

This truth is expressed in Holy Scripture by the following texts: "I am the Lord and I change not." [4] "God is not a man, that He should lie; nor as the son of man, that He should be changed." [5] "The heavens shall perish, but Thou remainest; and all of them shall grow old like a garment. And as a vesture Thou shalt change them, and they shall be changed, but Thou art always the self-same, and Thy years shall not fail." [6] "For she is the brightness of eternal light. . . . And being but one, she can do all things; and remaining in herself the same, she reneweth all things, and through nations conveyeth herself into holy souls." [7] "Every best gift and every perfect gift is from above, coming down from the Father of lights, with whom there is no change, nor shadow of alteration." [8] "And they changed the glory of the incorruptible God into the likeness of the image of a corruptible man." [9]

The councils on several occasions also affirmed God's immutability. Thus the Council of Nicaea anathematizes those who say that the Son of God is "changeable." [10] The Fourth Lateran Council says: "We firmly believe and absolutely confess that the one and only God is eternal, immense, and unchangeable." [11] In like manner, the Vatican Council declares: "God, as being one, sole, absolutely simple and immutable spiritual substance, is to be declared as really, and essentially distinct from the world." [12]

Three proofs are given from reason that God is absolutely immutable: (1) inasmuch as He is pure Act; (2) inasmuch as He is absolutely simple; (3) inasmuch as He is not perfectible.

1) Everything that is changeable must be in potentiality, as re-

[3] James 4: 8.
[4] Mal. 3: 6.
[5] Num. 23: 19.
[6] Ps. 101: 27.
[7] Wis. 7: 26 f.
[8] James 1: 17.
[9] Rom. 1: 23. See also Eccles. 42: 16; Prov. 19: 21.
[10] Denz., no. 54.
[11] *Ibid.*, no. 428.
[12] *Ibid.*, no. 1782.

ceiving determination; but God is pure Act without the admixture of any potentiality, because He is the first Being (fourth proof), and act is absolutely prior to potentiality; therefore God is absolutely immutable.[13]

It is, indeed, quite clear that potentiality is spoken of with reference to its act, and, in the order of dignity and nature, it presupposes this act. If, then, there were potentiality in God, He would not be really the first Being, and there could be imperfection in Him; a certain part in Him would not be God. He would thus be no longer the self-subsisting Being. But if He were not the self-subsisting Being, then existence would be predicated contingently of Him. Thus God would be participated being; He would be like the highest angel in whom there is an admixture of potentiality, namely, essence subordinate to existence, and an operative faculty that is subordinate to operation. There is here a recapitulation of what was said on this subject, but without repetition, which is somewhat like circular contemplation.[14]

God's immutability is proved from His absolute simplicity. Indeed, everything that is mutable is in some way composite; for it partly remains as it was, and partly passes away, or at least can do so. This means that it is variable. In other words, every mutation presupposes a subject that is susceptible to variation. Thus in everything that is moved, there is some kind of composition to be found; but there cannot be any composition in God.

God's immutability is proved from the fact that He is not susceptible to further perfection. For indeed everything that is moved acquires something. But God, since He is the very plenitude of being, cannot acquire anything; nor can He lose anything, for He is the necessary Being, the self-subsisting Being.

This must be said in refutation of absolute evolutionism, whether of the idealist type as proposed by Hegel or of the empirical type as proposed by Henry Bergson. Hence universal being, which according to Hegel's opinion is the principle of all things, cannot be the true God; for, if it were, it would be the self-subsisting Being, absolutely immutable or stable, incapable of any evolution. Absolute evolutionism must say that the principle of all things is "the creative evolution of itself." It then admits that something becomes universal which is its own reason for this. Such an admission means the denial of the real or ontological validity of the principle of identity or of contradiction (being and non-being are identified in this becoming, which is its own reason for such); it likewise means the denial of

---

[13] Aristotle affirmed this in his *Metaphysics,* Bk. XII, chaps. 7, 9.
[14] *Summa theol.,* IIa IIae, q.100, a.6.

the real validity of the principle of efficient causality and of finality; for the evolution of anything to something more perfect would always tend to this without any efficient cause and without being directed to any end. Thus the greater would always be produced from the less, the more perfect from the less perfect; for there is more in what exists than in what is becoming and does not as yet exist; there is more in the adult and developed man than in the embryo and the child.

Corollary. Hence the immobility of inertia, which is inferior to motion and our activity, must not be confused with the immobility of perfection, which is the supreme stability of Him who is self-subsisting Being, Intelligence, and Love. These two immutabilities are distinct, just as the infinity of matter, which is always capable of further determination and perfection, is distinct from the infinity of perfection, as was stated above.[15] Thus equally so, supreme and permanent contemplation is distinct from the ever changeable aberrations of error, as also the supreme love of the supreme good is distinct from the human emotions.[16]

Reply to first objection. Augustine says that "God moves Himself neither by time nor by place," meaning that God's mode of operation, namely, by understanding, willing, and loving, transcends time. The expression is metaphorical, and it owes its origin to the fact that there is no intellection in us without movement or transition from ignorance to knowledge. Hence what must be carefully considered in analogy, is the analogical concept, which is attributed formally and analogically to God (such as life, intellection, love), and the imperfect and created mode (movement), which is not attributed properly but only metaphorically to God.

Reply to second objection. Wisdom [17] is called mobile by way of similitude, or metaphorically, not formally but causally, according as it diffuses its likeness even to the outermost of things. This means that it is mobile, not in itself, but according as it produces all mutations of things. We find this stated in the canonical hour of none as follows:

> God, powerful sustainer of all things,
> Thou who dost remain permanently unmoved,
> Determining the course of time
> By the successions of the light of day.

15 *Summa theol.*, Ia, q.7, a.1.

16 See what St. Thomas says farther on (Ia, q.18, a.3), in the article entitled: "Whether life is attributed to God," which discusses God's absolutely immobile and most perfectly stable life, a life that is without variation and succession, and that is measured by eternity, as stated in q.10, a.2.

17 Wis. 7: 24.

Thus also metaphorically and causally God is said to be angry, inasmuch as, like an angry man, He punishes sinners.

Reply to third objection. In like manner, it is in a metaphorical sense that God is said to approach to us inasmuch as we receive the influx of His goodness.

SECOND ARTICLE

WHETHER TO BE IMMUTABLE BELONGS TO GOD ALONE

State of the question. The purpose of this article is to distinguish between God's absolute immutability and that of the angel and the human soul, their substances being incorruptible. It is also the purpose of this article to distinguish between God's absolute immutability and that of the blessed, who are in possession of eternal life.

Conclusion. God alone is altogether immutable.

Thus St. Augustine says: "God alone is immutable; and whatever things He has made, being from nothing, are mutable." [18]

It is proved from reason by distinguishing between incorruptible and corruptible creatures.

1) All created things, even the incorruptible, are, as regards substantial being, mutable by an extrinsic power that is in God. For God, indeed, by a most free act of His power brought creatures into existence, and He freely preserves them in the same. He can, therefore, by His absolute power, annihilate all things, although He would never do so by His well-ordered power (whether ordinary or extraordinary).[19]

2) All created and corruptible things are mutable, as regards their substantial being by an intrinsic power that is in them; for these are composed of matter that can lose its present form and receive another.[20]

3) All creatures, as regards their accidental being, are mutable by an intrinsic power. Even in the angels there is mutability as regards their choice of either good or evil. All were created good and in grace, and some freely merited their eternal happiness, whereas others sinned. In fact, the blessed are capable of receiving

---

[18] *De natura boni,* chap. 1.

[19] *Summa theol.,* Ia, q. 104, a. 3 f.

[20] St. Thomas, along with the ancient physicists, thought that the heavenly bodies are incorruptible, since there were no signs of corruptibility to be seen in them. This was explained inasmuch as the form of ether (quintessence) perfectly completed the capacity of matter.

But nowadays spectral analysis has shown that the same chemical combinations are to be found in the stars and in terrestrial bodies. Heavenly bodies are therefore corruptible.

new accidental illuminations and of acquiring accidental glory. Finally, there is mutability in the angels by way of virtual contact, inasmuch as they can act in this place or that, and do not always act in the same place.

On the contrary, God is absolutely immutable as regards substantial being, which is absolutely necessary and not contingent, nor is there any accident in God. Moreover He always preserves in being all existing things by His virtual contact. Hence it is only in those things external to God that there can be mutability, as when the blessed begin to see Him. God's free act is a difficulty which must be later examined.[21]

It must be noted that God can annihilate all created things by His absolute power, but not by His well-ordered power (whether ordinary or extraordinary), for no end can be assigned as reason why God should annihilate the angels, the blessed, and Christ's humanity. Yet it remains true to say that all created things can be annihilated by an extrinsic power.

On this point Cajetan remarks that the potentiality of created things does not refer primarily to non-existence, because potentiality refers essentially to actuality, and not to its opposite. Real potentiality by its very nature is directed to actuality, although it cannot directly reduce itself to actuality; hence a thing is said to be in potentiality to exist in a particular way and not to exist in a certain other, just as active potency of itself means that a thing is capable of acting and not acting. In other words, potentiality is really ordained for actuality, and is not really but logically ordained for its opposite.

Hence in created things there can be no real potency for non-existence except in a secondary sense, inasmuch as in anything there is a potency to exist in another way that is incompatible with the existence that it actually has. Thus in composites of matter and form there is a real potency to exist in another way, inasmuch as the matter can receive another form, which can give it a different existence. Hence for anything to have a real potency and not merely a logical potency for non-existence, it must have matter that is capable of receiving another form.

Therefore in the essence of the angel and of the soul there is a

---

[21] *Summa theol.,* Ia, q.19, a.3. We must say that God's free act is not an accident, for it is not the actuation of divine liberty that was prior to this simple potency. There is only one act of love in God, by which He necessarily loves His own goodness, and not necessarily creatable and created goodness. Thus the possibility of a free act in God does not posit mutability in Him. Moreover, this act is eternal and irrevocable.

On this point consult what St. Thomas says about the incorruptibility of the angels (Ia, q.50, a.5), and of the soul (Ia, q.75, a.6).

real potency for existence, and only a logical potency for non-existence; corresponding to this there is the real power of God, who can annihilate all things created and freely maintained in being by Him. For just as the power of creating presupposes only a logical potency or a possibility on the part of the thing creatable, so the power to annihilate presupposes only the possibility of annihilation. In incorruptible things there is therefore no real potency for non-existence.

Corollary. Therefore the instability in any being arises solely from the possibility of its desiring some other reality which it does not have, for nothingness is not desired by anyone. Hence instability comes from the imperfection of that which is possessed, inasmuch as this does not fully satisfy the capacity for desiring.

Therefore the more we approach to God, the more stability takes the place of instability. This is the immutability of perfect sanctity that exists in heaven.[22] The saints in heaven adhere immutably to God, so that sin is no longer possible.[23] This immutability is of a higher order and is by participation.

On the other hand, there is an inferior kind of immutability that proceeds not from the illimitation of being, but from the limitation of its capacity or desire, which is found in those, as St. Paul so vividly expresses it, who are already filled and have no higher aspirations. For he says: "You are now full, you are now become rich." [24] This is an inferior kind of immutability, a sort of inert egotism, fanaticism, or sectarianism, since such persons do not sufficiently aspire to the higher truth and goodness.

Intermediate between this inferior kind of immutability of those who are now filled and the higher immutability of the blessed, is the praiseworthy mutability of the holy wayfarer who is, like Daniel, "a man of desires" [25] and who always aspires to something higher. This praiseworthy mutability, which tends toward the higher immutability, differs entirely from the instability of the dilettante, who regards no truth as immutable, who does not tend toward God, but who is always of a fickle disposition.

Reply to second objection. The good angels have a participated immutability of the will for good.

And so this terminates the question of God's immutability compared with that of any created being whatever. This question perfects the teaching proposed by St. Augustine since it brings out

22 *Ibid.,* IIa IIae, q.81, a.8.
23 *Ibid.,* Ia IIae, q.5, a.4.
24 I Cor. 4: 8.
25 Dan. 9: 23.

clearly the distinction between mutability that is the result of intrinsic power, and mutability that is the result of extrinsic power. In this we have a wonderful application of the Aristotelian distinction between real potentiality and actuality.

CHAPTER X

QUESTION 10

THE ETERNITY OF GOD

WE now come to consider eternity, because, as will at once be seen, eternity follows from immutability, since it is the duration of the absolutely immobile being. There are two things which St. Thomas considers in this question: (1) eternity as such is considered in the first three questions, namely: what is eternity, whether God is eternal, whether to be eternal belongs to God alone; (2) in the remaining articles eternity is compared with created durations, that is, with reference to our continuous time, to the discrete time of the angels which is measured by their successive thoughts, and to aeviternity, or the duration of the angelic substance and the separated soul, which as substances are immutable, though they had a beginning.

In these last three articles the comparison is made from on high, namely, from eternity as it has already been defined. In the first three articles, however, there is already a similar comparison made, but it starts as it were from below, and by way of investigation finally formulates the definition of eternity.

FIRST ARTICLE

WHETHER THIS IS A GOOD DEFINITION OF ETERNITY: "THE SIMULTANEOUSLY-WHOLE AND PERFECT POSSESSION OF INTERMINABLE LIFE"

State of the question. The definition of Boethius is the subject of inquiry.[1] It must be observed that this definition is implied in what Holy Scripture says about God's immobility, as we shall state in the second article. Among the philosophers, Plato likewise says that time is the mobile image of immobile eternity.[2] Aristotle says equivalently, "God is the everlasting and noblest living being. In God there is both life and duration that is continual and eternal." [3] In like manner, farther on,[4] he shows that God is subsistent

---

[1] *De Consolatione,* Bk. III, pros. 2.
[2] *Timaeus,* 37, d.
[3] *Metaph.,* Bk. XII, chap. 7 (end).
[4] *Ibid.,* chap. 9.

intellection who continually understands Himself, transcending succession of time. Moreover, Aristotle defined time as "movement that is estimated according to its before and after." [5] Thus the motion of the sun is measured in time, inasmuch as one revolution is called a day, and this day consists of distinctly different hours according to a before and after. Thus we have already at least a confused notion and a nominal definition of eternity.

Plotinus [6] explains eternity in the same way, speaking not only of the immobility of eternity but also of its indivisibility, whereas time is divided into years, days, and hours. Hence Plotinus says that, if one were to say that eternity is life interminable and totally present to itself, none of it pertaining to the past or to the future, such a one is not far from its true definition.

St. Augustine says the same,[7] speaking of the indivisible and ever constant now of eternity, whereas time is fleeting. Thus gradually the transition is effected from the nominal and confused definition to the real and distinct definition. Then Boethius (†524) gave us the same concept of eternity in the aforesaid classical definition, saying that it is "the simultaneously-whole and perfect possession of interminable life."

St. Thomas shows here that this definition is a good one, since it is in accordance with the laws governing the search for a definition, inasmuch as by these laws there is a methodical transition from a confused to a distinct notion.[8] But St. Thomas first of all sets forth the difficulties, the two principal ones being these: (1) a whole is what has parts. But this does not apply to eternity, which is simple; (2) further, if a thing is said to be whole, perfect is a superfluous addition; nor does it seem that possession implies duration.

Yet the reply is that this definition is a good one, since it properly expresses eternity as the interminable duration, which is without succession, and so it is spoken of as "being simultaneously whole."

This is not, strictly speaking, demonstrated in the body of the article, for, as it is pointed out elsewhere,[9] it is not the definition of a thing but its property that is, strictly speaking, demonstrated. The definition is sought by a certain investigation, says Aristotle,[10] by a division of its genus or quasi-genus (in the present instance, the notion of duration) and then comparing the thing to be de-

[5] *Physics*, Bk. IV, chap. 11, lect. 20.
[6] *Enneades*, IIIa, Bk. VII, chap. 4.
[7] *De vera religione*, chap. 2, no. 97.
[8] *Post. Anal.*, Bk. II.
[9] *Ibid.*
[10] *Ibid.*

fined with things similar and dissimilar (in the present instance, by comparing the confused notion of eternity, according to its nominal definition, with time). Yet in the body of the article there is a sort of demonstration, inasmuch as eternity is deduced from God's absolute immobility. This will be made clearer in the second article.

The argument of the article by the way of investigation may be summed up as follows: We must come to the knowledge of eternity by means of time. But time is but the numbering of movement by before and after. Contrary to this, in the duration of that which is without movement, there is absolute uniformity, without any before and after. Moreover, what is absolutely immutable is interminable, without beginning and end, whereas those things that are measured by time have a beginning and an end. Thus, therefore, eternity has two characteristics: (1) uniformity without succession, and so it is truly spoken of as "being simultaneously whole"; (2) interminableness, so that it can be truly said to be "the simultaneously-whole and perfect possession of interminable life."

It must be observed that the first characteristic is the principal one, and so also if the movement of the heavenly bodies and time were eternal, as Aristotle thought, that is without beginning and end, time would still be distinct from eternity; for in time there is always a succession of centuries and years, although there would never have been a first or last day. Hence the principal difference between eternity and time is that the former is without before and after or that it is "being simultaneously whole."

Contrary to this, our life is not simultaneously whole, for it consists of the distinct periods of infancy, youth, adult age, prime of life, and old age. Our life is also divided into periods of labor, prayer, sleep, and the like, so that there is a great variety and instability in this succession. Hence the *now of time* is the *current now* between the past and the future, so that past and future do not actually exist but exist only in the mind, whereas the *now of eternity* is a standing now, which is absolutely permanent and immobile, and we find this already equivalently expressed, although less distinctly, in the writings of Plato, Aristotle, and Plotinus.

Thus the definition of Boethius is a good one, since it complies with the rules to be observed in the search for a definition.[11] The transition is effected methodically from a confused to a distinct notion, and this by a correct division of duration, and by a com-

11 *Ibid.*

parison of one's already confused notion of eternity with that of time.

This hunt or search presupposes the true definition of time as given by Aristotle, who says that it is movement estimated by its before and after, for example, the movement of the sun is estimated by its successive revolutions and portions of one revolution. It seems that this definition [12] is a good explanation of what is obscurely implied in the popular or common notion of time and its parts, namely, century, year, day, hour. This is the realistic notion of time. On the contrary, Kant proposed an idealist notion of time, which in his opinion is an a priori subjective form of our sensibility, in which things appear to us as a succession of phenomena.

But Kant unjustifiably denied the reality of time, giving as his reason the false antinomies that would result from this. In his opinion, it is equally demonstrated that the world had and did not have a beginning in time. But, as St. Thomas points out: "By faith alone do we hold, and by no demonstration can it be proved, that the world did not always exist." [13] God, who created with absolute freedom, could have eternally created, so that there never would have been a first day; just as the imprint of a foot in the sand would be eternal, if the foot were eternal. And even if the movement of the sun and time had been eternal creations, as we remarked, there would still be a complete distinction between time and eternity, only this latter being simultaneously whole.

The proof given in the argumentative part of the article may be presented in the following syllogistic form: What is absolutely immutable is simultaneously-whole and interminable; but eternity is attributed to a thing that is absolutely immutable, just as time is attributed to things that are mobile; therefore eternity must be simultaneously-whole and interminable duration.

The solution of the difficulties confirms this conclusion.

Reply to first objection. Eternity is conceived by us as being negatively interminable, because our knowledge is first of things that come to an end.

Reply to second objection. "Interminable life" is predicated of eternity rather than "interminable being," because what is truly eternal is not only being, but also life, in fact, self-subsistent life. But life extends to operation, and not to being. Hence it is clear that both God's being and His operation are measured by eternity,

---

12 See St. Thomas' commentary on Aristotle's *Physics*, Bk. IV, chap. 11, lect. 20.
13 *Summa theol.*, Ia, q.46, a.2.

whereas · the angel's immutable essence and operations are not measured the same way.[14]

Reply to third objection. Eternity is called whole, not because it has parts, but inasmuch as it is wanting in nothing. In this we see the imperfection of our knowledge.

Reply to fourth objection. Sacred Scripture speaks metaphorically of the "days of eternity." [15]

Reply to fifth objection. The word *perfect* is not a superfluous addition, for *simultaneously whole* excludes past and future, and *perfect* excludes the *passing now,* which is imperfect.

Reply to sixth objection. Lastly eternity is said to be perfect possession rather than duration, to designate the indeficiency of eternity; for what is possessed, is held firmly and quietly. On the contrary, a boy does not yet possess the maturity of old age, nor does the old man possess the complete vitality of youth. So also in the interior life, the beginner does not yet possess the perfection of the unitive life.

Therefore the above definition of eternity is a very fine one, especially as regards the words "being simultaneously whole." This last expression must be the object not only of speculation, but also of acquired contemplation resulting from sacred theology, and of infused contemplation which is the result of living faith that is illumined by the gifts of intellect and wisdom.

As a complement to this investigation into the true notion of eternity, it must be observed that great geniuses have a certain experimental knowledge of a life which by remote comparison can be called "simultaneously whole." For the most sublime manifestations of art (for instance, of music) are a certain remote participation of this kind of perfection. Thus it is said of Mozart that he heard all together a whole melody that he was composing, in that he was hearing it or previously heard it in the thought that gave it birth; whereas others heard it only successively. Thus great mathematicians by one intellectual act perceive the many elements of a very complex problem. In like manner great philosophers and theologians toward the end of their life have a sort of *simultaneously whole* knowledge of their science, inasmuch as they see it from on high as an irradiation of its principles. So also the contemplative experiences the joy of infused contemplation, and it remains with him during the day as a sort of latent reserve force, possessing this throughout the day as it were from on high; for when the time of prayer comes to an end, there is not a complete cessation of prayer, for it continues as it

[14] *Ibid.,* q. 10, a. 5.
[15] Mich. 5: 2.

were during the time of study or even of recreation. Thus the inferiority inherent in multiplicity gradually resolves itself into the superiority of unity, and this finds its realization in the unitive life of the saints. Hence St. Augustine [16] exhorts us to a loving union with God and His eternity, peacefully awaiting the events of time, which are, as it were, beneath us, beneath the summit of the soul that is united with God.

But if Mozart heard all at once the various parts of a melody which he was composing, so we can conclude that God possesses His life all at once and sees simultaneously from on high the entire sequence of centuries. Thus eternity is like the apex of a cone, the base of which represents time. All the successive points of this base correspond to the one point of the apex.

But many difficulties, especially about the problem of evil, result from the fact that we do not see from on high the succession of time, but only successively. Thus we do not know that it is for the greater good of the world and of the Church that God permits this or that very great evil actually to happen. But if this succession of time were seen from on high by one glance, then evil would appear as a certain particularization that is a condition of the higher good, as in a picture we have the harmonious blending of light and shade, especially so in the "light transcending obscurity." In the above examples, as in that of the musical composition which is quoted by H. Bergson, there is a certain experimental knowledge of a life that bears a certain analogical resemblance to eternity. Thus the investigation is completed in a less abstract and more concrete way.

Solution of certain difficulties. As Cajetan remarks, Aureolus raised several objections against this article of St. Thomas. In the first place, he says that uniformity, because it does not differ from immutability, is not the chief characteristic of eternity.

In reply we must say with Cajetan that uniformity differs from immutability as a property differs from its essence. Immutability is the denial of the possibility of change. Uniformity adds to immutability the idea of unity of form, and this can be attributed also to motion; for we speak of uniform motion, the velocity of which is always the same, and thus it differs from variation in motion. In fact, we speak of a uniformly accelerated motion, such as the fall of a stone, or of the uniformly retarded motion of a stone thrown in the air. And just as there is uniformity in motion or succession, so also there is the same in immobility or permanence. Immutability is opposed to motion, whereas, on the other hand, uniformity is not, for there can be uniformity in motion. Consequently it is false to

[16] *Com. on Ps.* 91.

say that there is no distinction between uniformity and immutability. Hence eternity is correctly and more briefly defined as the uniformity of an absolutely immutable thing.

But again Aureolus objects, saying that time is not the variation of motion, and therefore uniformity is not the uniformity of the immobile.

We reply to this by distinguishing the antecedent. That time is not solely the variation of motion, this I concede; that it is not variation of motion according to before and after, this I deny. Therefore the uniformity of the immobile, in which there is no before and after, suffices for the constitution of eternity. This point will be made clearer in the following article.

SECOND ARTICLE

WHETHER GOD IS ETERNAL

State of the question. The purpose of this article is to show in what particular sense God is eternal and is His eternity, and also to explain how eternity can be called the measure of God, although He is not measured; whereas even the sun's motion is measured, inasmuch as its revolutions are numbered.

Reply. God is not only eternal, but He is His eternity.

1) It is of faith that God is eternal and is so essentially. This truth is clearly stated in many texts of Holy Scripture. Thus we read: "Abraham . . . called upon the name of the Lord God eternal." [17] "For He is the living and eternal God." [18] God is often called eternal.[19]

The Athanasian Creed says: "The Father is eternal, the Son is eternal, the Holy Spirit is eternal." The Fourth Council of the Lateran declares: "We firmly believe that there is only one true God, who is eternal." [20]

According to Vacant,[21] it is of faith that God has neither beginning nor end. That there is no succession in God is a certain truth and is proximate to the faith. Vacant [22] thinks, however, that this does not as yet appear to be a dogma of the faith.

2) In the body of the article God's eternity is deduced from His immutability, and may be expressed by the following syllogism: Eternity follows immutability, as time follows movement; but God

---

17 Gen. 21: 33.
18 Dan. 6: 26.
19 Ps. 101: 12–26; John 8: 58; 12: 34.
20 Denz., no. 428; also no. 1782 (Vatican Council).
21 *Etudes sur le Concile du Vatican*, I, 183 f.
22 *Ibid.*, p. 188.

is supremely immutable; therefore it supremely belongs to Him to be eternal. It is also stated that God is His own eternity. For God and God alone is His own existence and essence; consequently God is His own duration.

This is the same as saying that everything survives inasmuch as it retains its existence; but God alone is His existence. Therefore He alone is His own uniform duration. Thus St. Thomas holds that eternity is God's duration. Wherefore the notion of duration is far more universal than that of time. Duration is predicated analogically of eternity, of our continuous time, of the discrete time of the angels, and of aevum or aeviternity, as will be stated farther on.

In the reply to the first objection the words of Boethius are explained, namely: "The now that flows away makes time, the now that stands still makes eternity." This latter *now* is said to make eternity according to our apprehension. This means that the apprehension of eternity is caused in us inasmuch as we apprehend the *now* standing still. Eternity has complete existence extramentally, whereas, on the other hand, time has complete existence only in the mind, inasmuch as past and future exist only in the mind.

What is real in time is the now that flows away, and it is said to flow away like movement, which is the act of a being in potentiality inasmuch as it is such, the act of a further perfectible and to be perfected being, the successive transition from potentiality to perfect actuality. Contrary to this, the now of eternity is spoken of as standing still, and corresponding to it are all the successive moments of time, just as all the points in the base of a cone correspond to its apex. Thus there is but one instant in the immobility of eternity.

In this reply to the first objection there is an explanation of St. Augustine's words: "God is the author of eternity," which are to be understood of participated eternity consisting in the eternal life of the saints. Their beatific vision begins but will not end, and there is no succession or variation in this vision at least as regards the primary object, which is God's essence clearly seen. Thus, strictly speaking, their life is not only said to be a future life with reference to ours, but it is eternal life, because it is measured by participated eternity.

It must be observed that just as a beginning is not repugnant to the idea of participated eternity, so also the end is not absolutely repugnant to this idea, provided there is no succession in this participated eternity. Therefore if St. Paul had on this earth the beatific vision as a transient act, this vision could have been measured by participated eternity, transcending our continuous time and the discrete time of the angels in which their successive thoughts are measured.

Reply to second objection. When the Scripture says that "the Lord shall reign forever and ever," [23] this means always. Others change the phrase to "forever and always," thus making it in a way redundant. St. Thomas points out that eternity transcends time, and this would be the case even if time were unlimited as regards the future.

Reply to third objection. It is pointed out that eternity is said to be the measure of God "according to the apprehension of our mind alone." In several other passages St. Thomas says that eternity is the measure of divine life. This must be understood of intrinsic measurement, inasmuch as God is His eternity. Thus God is not measured. Contrary to this the motion of the heavenly bodies is measured by a recurrent succession of revolutions or of days, and all the more so is the motion of other bodies, which is measured extrinsically according to solar time. There was formerly a dispute of minor importance on this subject, as can be readily seen by consulting Billuart.

Reply to fourth objection. "Eternity includes all times" or "comprises all time," which means that it virtually contains all inferior durations, just as the apex of a cone virtually contains all the points of its base, or the center of a circle all the radii and points of its circumference.

Doubt. How are created things said to be present in eternity?

The Thomists hold, as will be stated farther on, that creatures are physically present in eternity, coming under God's direct vision. John of St. Thomas says: "Eternity does not immediately measure created things on the supposition that they have already undergone a passive change and been passively produced, but it measures them precisely for the reason that they are contained in the divine action, which contacts and regards created things as its terminus.[24] Indeed, not only God's intellection and volition are eternal, but even His external action is eternal, and yet it has its effect in time. "From the eternal (free) action of God an eternal effect did not follow; but such an effect as God willed, namely, that which has being after not being." [25]

Thus created things are really present in eternity, and are not merely either possible or future. They are contained in the divine essence not as merely having the power or will to produce them, but as actually producing them. Thus God's knowledge of these things is intuitive, although they may not as yet have been passively produced. It is evident that this presence of things in eternity or in God's

23 Ex. 15: 18.
24 *Com. in Iam*, disp. IX, a.3. Billuart (*De Deo*, diss. VI, a.3), Gonet, and many other Thomists say the same.
25 *Summa theol.*, Ia, q.46, a.1 ad 10 um.

eternal action presupposes God's free decree, for the action spoken about here is a free one. Thus St. Paul's conversion was eternally present to God's intution only because He eternally willed it; otherwise this conversion would not be a contingent but a necessary act.

THIRD ARTICLE

WHETHER TO BE ETERNAL BELONGS TO GOD ALONE

There are two conclusions in this article: (1) Eternity truly and properly so called is in God alone, because eternity follows on absolute immutability, which is in God alone; (2) creatures share in God's eternity, just as they do in His immutability. Thus it is said by participation that "the earth standeth forever." [26] Thus, because of the length of their duration, the mountains are said to be eternal and their peaks to be covered with perpetual snow. Incorruptible spiritual substances share more fully and in a nobler manner in the nature of eternity. This is especially so of the blessed, who are said to have eternal life, inasmuch as the beatific vision, whose primary object is always the same, is measured by participated eternity. It is, indeed, an absolutely immutable operation.

Several Thomists remark that, just as the different motions of the earth are measured by solar time, or according to the measure of the sun's motion, so also the beatific vision is measured according to God's eternity, inasmuch as, by reason of the object or of God who is clearly seen, there is a participated eternity in this vision.[27]

Reply to second objection. The punishment in hell is eternal inasmuch as it never ends. However, "in hell true eternity does not exist, but rather time" in accordance with a certain change in sensible pain.

Reply to third objection. The principles of demonstration are called eternal truths but in a negative sense, in that they abstract from time and place and are absolutely necessary. Moreover, they are positively eternal inasmuch as they are positively in the intellect of God, who alone is positively eternal.

FOURTH ARTICLE

WHETHER ETERNITY DIFFERS FROM TIME

State of the question. It is not, strictly speaking, a question here as to whether there is a difference, but it is asked what is the reason for this difference. Thus eternity and time are compared from on high, whereas in the first article the ascent of the mind was made by

---

[26] Eccles. 1: 4.
[27] Consult the commentaries of Bannez and John of St. Thomas.

the way of investigation, from time to the definition of eternity. Now by the way of sapiential judgment, time is judged from the highest of causes, or from eternity as already defined. There are three difficulties: (1) It seems that eternity does not differ from time, because they occur together. Hence it seems that time is a part of eternity, just as an hour, which occurs along with a day, is a part of a day. In other words, the finite cannot coexist with the infinite, unless it is a part of the infinite, as several pantheists say. (2) According to Aristotle,[28] the now of time remains the same in the whole of time. Therefore it does not differ from the now of eternity. (3) Eternity, which comprises all time, seems to be the measure of all things inasmuch as they proceed from God, and so it does not differ from time.

Yet the reply is that time and eternity are not the same, because eternity is simultaneously whole, whereas time has a before and an after.

In the body of the article, St. Thomas shows that, even if time had neither beginning nor end, it would differ from eternity, inasmuch as it would consist of a succession of years and centuries, namely, of a before and an after; whereas only eternity is simultaneously whole. He even says that the difference, which is founded on the fact that time has a beginning and will have no end, is an accidental one, which means that it could as well not be so. Therefore the reason for the difference lies essentially in the fact that eternity is the measure of permanent being, whereas time is the measure of movement. The solution of the difficulties confirms this.

Reply to first objection. Eternity and time can coexist and yet time is not a part of eternity, because they are not of the same genus, but only analogically agree in point of duration. So the finite being and the infinite being can coexist, and yet the finite is not a part of the infinite, because they are not of the same genus; but they are alike in this, that being is predicated analogically of each. Infinite being is self-existing being, whereas finite being is participated being, and is not its own being. There is never any variation from this in the refutation of pantheism.

Reply to second objection. What sort of identity is there between the now of time and the whole of time as this differs from the identity between the now of eternity and eternity? The now of time is the same as regards its subject in the whole course of time, just as movement is measured by time; but it differs in aspect, for what is movable is first here and then there. On the contrary, the permanent now of eternity is absolutely the same as regards both its subject and its aspect.

St. Thomas says with profundity of thought in this article: "The

[28] *Physics*, Bk. IV, chap. 11.

flow of the now as alternating in aspect, is time," just as the progressive passive actualization of the movable is movement. When he says that the now differs in aspect in the whole course of time, he does not mean that alternation is merely according to aspect and is not anything real. He is speaking, as he does in one of his commentaries,[29] in which he says that terminative transitive action and passion are the same as movement, but differ in aspect, inasmuch as action is movement as coming from an agent, and passion is movement as found in the movable. This means to say that they are the same as regards their subject, but that they differ according to their constitutive aspects, and so, according to the Thomists, there is a modal distinction between terminative action and passion. In like manner, St. Thomas says: "Man and white are the same in subject, and different in idea; for the idea of man is one thing, and that of whiteness is another." [30] He does not mean that whiteness, which is an accident, is not really distinct from the substance of man; but it can be said that this man is white, so that in this proposition as in every affirmative proposition, "the predicate and the subject signify the same thing in reality." [31]

There is a most manifest difference, at least in the abstract sense, between the passing now of time and the permanent now of eternity. The passing now of time comes within our experience, but the permanent now of eternity does not. Hence eternity is less intelligible to us than time, but it is more intelligible in itself. For in itself the now of time is scarcely intelligible, because it is almost nothing, is among the inferior limitations of being, is always changing, and when it is said that the present moment *is*, it already is not. On the contrary, the now of eternity is always permanent, always is; in fact, it is the self-subsisting Being, inasmuch as God is His eternity.

Reply to third objection. The being of corruptible things, because it is changeable, is not measured by eternity, but by time. However, as we remarked above, since created things are not passively produced in themselves, but are present in God as the terminus of His eternal action, they are measured by eternity. Thus eternity is the measure of all measures and includes all times.

FIFTH ARTICLE

THE DIFFERENCE BETWEEN AEVITERNITY AND TIME

State of the question. The purpose of this question is to inquire into the proper meaning of *aevum* (age). This word, which is still

[29] *Ibid.*, Bk. III, lect. 5.
[30] *Summa theol.*, Ia, q. 13, a. 12.
[31] *Ibid.*

one in common use, as when we speak of the Middle Ages (*medium aevum*), means, among Latin authors, either a certain age of the human race or that of some man—thus the first age corresponds to the period of youth, whereas full age corresponds to maturity—or perpetual duration (Varro). Aeviternal means also perpetual.

The Scholastics say that aeviternity is "the measure of spiritual substances." Previous to this, St. Augustine [32] had said that we must admit a certain intermediate duration between eternity and time. This intermediate duration is difficult to conceive. It is, indeed, not so intelligible in itself as eternity, and not so intelligible to us as time, because it does not come within our experience. The principal difficulty that confronts us in distinguishing between aeviternity and time is that, if aeviternity is not eternity, then it is not simultaneously whole. Therefore it has a before and an after, and hence it does not seem to differ from time.

Yet the reply is that aeviternity differs from time and from eternity, as the mean between them.

The proper reason for this difference is not given by some, whose conception of eternity is more material than formal. They said that eternity has neither beginning nor end; that aeviternity has a beginning but no end (inasmuch as the angels were not created from eternity); that a time has both beginning and end. But this difference is accidental, because even if aeviternal things had always been, aeviternity would be distinct from eternity.

Others said that aeviternity differs from eternity, in that it has a before and an after; and that it differs from time, because it has neither youth nor age. But this involves a contradiction; for if aeviternity has a before and an after, it also has youth and age. It would have youth when the after part appears, and age in the receding of the first part. In like manner, if the aeviternal thing were not subject to youth and age, this would be because it is immutable, and hence it would have neither before nor after.

But the true difference consists in this, that aeviternity is the mean between eternity and time, because it is unchangeable, though it has changeableness annexed to it. It is proved as follows: In so far as anything recedes from permanence of being, it recedes from eternity. But mutation, whose measure is time, recedes more from eternity, than does immutation, to which, however, mutation is annexed, whose measure is aeviternity. Therefore aeviternity is the mean between eternity and time

St. Thomas explains this in his reply to the first objection, in which he says: "Spiritual creatures, as regards successive affections and intelligences, are measured by time (not by continuous time, however,

---

[32] *Book of 83 questions*, q.72.

such as solar time, but by discrete time). . . . But as regards their nature, they are measured by aeviternity, and as regards the vision of glory, they have a share of eternity."

Thus aeviternity is the measure of an immutable thing, which in its operations, however, is connected with change. Hence aeviternity has not in itself either before or after, as stated in the second opinion; but before and after are compatible with it.[33]

Scotus objects to this, remarking that at least several angelic operations are not successive but permanent. Hence they are measured, he says, not by discrete time but by aeviternity.

Bannez replies by saying that there are three kinds of angelic operations. (1) There are those angelic operations that are connatural to the angel and unceasing. These are measured by aeviternity, as St. Thomas himself says.[34] Thus the angel's natural knowledge of himself, of God as the Author of nature; and his natural love of himself and of God are of this first kind. (2) Then there are those immanent angelic operations that are not permanent but successive. These are measured by angelic discrete time. This time refers to the number of angelic thoughts, as St. Thomas states farther on as follows: "If the time of the angel's motion is not continuous, but a kind of succession of nows, it will have no proportion to the time which measures the motion of corporeal things, which is continuous, since it is not of the same nature."[35] Thus one angelic thought constitutes one angelic moment, and it can last for several years of our continuous solar time. Thus with those saints who are still wayfarers, when they are in ecstasy, there is a sort of immobile and loving contemplation that takes place in the summit of their soul, and sometimes this lasts for several hours of our continuous time. (3) There is finally, the virtually transitive operation of the angel by which he locally moves bodies. It is measured terminatively by our continuous time, in that the movement of this body is measured by solar time and it lasts, for instance, half an hour.

Doubt. How can aeviternity be simultaneously whole, although before and after are compatible with it, as St. Thomas says in his reply to the second objection?

The difficulty is that if aeviternity is simultaneously whole, it contains time eminently, just as eternity does. Such being the case, the angels would have a natural knowledge of future contingent things, and they would not have to wait for their realization.

St. Thomas replies to this by saying that aeviternity is simultaneously whole inasmuch as the angel's substantial being is im-

[33] Cf. ad 2um.
[34] *Quodl.*, q.5, a.7.
[35] *Summa theol.*, Ia, q.53, a.3 ad 1um.

mutable, and is not the subject of succession.[36] However, aeviternity does not contain time eminently as eternity does, because angelic being does not contain eminently the being of mutable things, as the first cause in its action contains all things that are. Moreover, as it has been remarked, the angelic knowledge of particular things is not measured by aeviternity but by discrete time. Thus angels cannot have a natural but only a conjectural knowledge of future contingent things. Hence aeviternity coexists with our continuous time somewhat as an immovable stone placed in a river, coexists with the various parts of the flowing water. But eternity is like a mountain peak from which the whole river is seen by one glance. And so this proves that aeviternity is the mean between eternity and time.

SIXTH ARTICLE

WHETHER THERE IS ONLY ONE AEVITERNITY

State of the question. The purpose of this article is to compare the unity of aeviternity of all aeviternal things, namely, of angels and of disembodied spirits, with the unity of time of all sensible movements.

The reply of St. Thomas is that, according to the truer opinion, there is one aeviternity for all subordinate aeviternal things, just as there is one time for all subordinate sensible movements in the universe. For it is evident that to form an idea of the unity of duration of spiritual beings, we must first consider the unity of duration of sensible things. But the unity of duration of sensible things or the unity of continuous time depends on the fact that the movement of the first movable (we are speaking of the sun in our solar system) is supposed to be uniform. Thus solar time is the intrinsic measure of solar movement and the extrinsic measure of other subordinate movements. Thus time is one and continuous. By analogy, therefore, there is one aeviternity, inasmuch as there is subordination among the angels, and thus the being of all subordinate aeviternal beings is measured extrinsically, as it were, according to the intrinsic measure of the first aeviternal being, or of the highest angel. This opinion presupposes that the angels are not equal, but are subordinated, or that they proceed from God in a certain degree and order.[37]

It must be observed that unity of continuous time presupposes, but does not apodictically prove as many think, that the apparent movement of the sun is uniform, or that the real movement of the earth around the sun is uniform, that is, always of the same velocity.

[36] *Quodl.*, q. 10, a. 4; also reply to third objection of this article.
[37] *Summa theol.*, Ia, q. 47, a. 2.

But this, as many think, is not apodictically true, for there would have to be first a fixed unity of time which is reckoned according to a presupposed uniformity of movement. Nevertheless the hypothesis of the uniformity of the sun's apparent movement is confirmed by the harmony that prevails between the various ways we have of measuring time, for instance, in the clocks we use.[38] Moreover, this hypothesis, which was already explicitly formulated by Aristotle,[39] is more in conformity with the simplicity of the laws of nature than is the hypothesis of some non-uniform but accelerated or retarded movement, or of one that is sometimes accelerated and sometimes retarded with compensation, whose velocity is not always the same. Therefore the truer opinion is that there is one time and one aeviternity.

Yet the fourth objection in this article states that things not dependent on one other, do not seem to have one measure of duration. But aeviternal things do not depend on one another, for one angel is not the cause of another angel. Consequently there is not only one aeviternity.

St. Thomas replies by saying: "For things to be measured by one, it is not necessary that the one should be the cause of all, but that it be simpler than the rest." Thus arithmetical unity is the principle of number, and the letter is the principle of unity for the syllable.

Recapitulation. And so we bring to an end this beautiful question of eternity, which is compared with other durations. From the foregoing we clearly see that the principle characteristic of eternity is not to be without beginning and end, but to be simultaneously whole, without succession and variation, according to a most perfect uniformity. Hence there is but one and permanent now of eternity. On the contrary, the now of continuous time alternates between the past and the future. Aeviternity is the mean between time and eternity, and so it is "simultaneously whole, but before and after are compatible with it," [40] according to a succession of thoughts in the angels. Finally, in the discrete time by which these successive thoughts of the angels are measured, there are several standing, successive nows; so that one angelic thought or contemplation is present in the same moment of time, and a subsequent thought in another, without any continuous time intervening; whereas in our time two moments are always separated from the one time that is infinitely divisible. Thus also, while the angels move bodies locally, as stated farther on, "the time of an angel's motion can be non-continuous; so an angel can

---

[38] Cf. Lechalas, *Espace et temps*, p. 84.
[39] *Physics*, Bk. VIII, chap. 14; *Metaph.*, Bk. X, chap. 1.
[40] *Summa theol.*, Ia, q. 10, a.5 ad 2um.

be in one place in one instant, and in another place in the next instant without any time intervening." [41]

Wherefore "the standing now" of eternity is like the apex of a cone, the base of which would represent the successive parts of time. But between the apex and the base is aeviternity to which change is annexed, and discrete time consisting of several successive standing nows. Thus a more profound knowledge is acquired of the definition of eternity as formulated by Boethius, who says it is "the simultaneously-whole and perfect possession of interminable life." [42] The unitive life of the saints, already here below, approaches this eternity, and especially so does the beatific vision of which participated eternity is the measure.

[41] *Ibid.*, q.53, a.3 ad 3um.
[42] *De consolatione*, Bk. III, pros. 2.

CHAPTER XI

QUESTION 11

THE UNITY OF GOD

WHY does St. Thomas now treat of God's unity? It seems that he should have discussed it before God's goodness, because unity is the first property of being considered in itself, and it precedes truth and goodness. Moreover, it seems that St. Thomas had already discussed God's unity in the third question in connection with God's simplicity, because unity is the undividedness of being, and it was already shown in that question that God is the absolutely undivided and indivisible being, because He is not composed of matter and form, of essence and existence, of substance and accident, or of other parts.

In reply to this it must be said that in this eleventh question, as appears particularly from the third article, in which St. Thomas inquires whether there are one or several gods, he is concerned especially with God's unicity; but God's unicity has its foundation in the absolute indivisibility of the divine nature,[1] that is, in the unity and absolute simplicity of the divine nature. Therefore, in order properly to discuss God's unicity, St. Thomas speaks also of His indivisibility or of unity in the strict sense.

St. Thomas first treated of the divine nature, having considered it quasi-metaphysically as it is in itself.[2] He now inquires whether this divine nature can be in several gods, just as one would ask whether Michaelness can be in several angels, as humanity is found in several numerically distinct human beings. It is therefore more a discussion of God's unicity, as is evident from the third article of this question; but the two preceding articles treat of unity in general, in that it is along with simplicity the foundation of unicity.

Thus there are four articles. (1) Whether one adds anything to being. (2) Whether one and many are opposed to each other (this article confirming, as it were from on high, the fourth proof for God's existence). (3) Whether there is only one God. (4) Whether God is supremely one.

---

[1] *Summa theol.,* Ia, q. 11, a. 3 (first proof).
[2] Cajetan's commentary may be consulted concerning this difficulty about the arrangement of the subject matter of this part of the *Summa.*

To some this seems a repetition of the preceding; yet it is not, properly speaking, a repetition, but rather a case of circular contemplation,[3] which always returns to the same supreme truth (God is the self-subsisting Being), to behold the new rays emanating from it.

FIRST ARTICLE

WHETHER ONE ADDS ANYTHING TO BEING

State of the question. The discussion is not about numerical unity, which is the principle of number and which belongs to the category of quantity, but it concerns transcendental unity, which is a property of being and which is found in every category of being, inasmuch as we speak of the unity of substance, of the unity and simplicity of quality, of the unity of action, and similarly of the other predicaments. This distinction is implied in the first objection of this article.

It must be noted that in ancient times Parmenides and Heraclitus seriously disputed this point. Parmenides affirmed the unity and unicity of being, even denying the multiplicity of beings. He proceeded along the lines of absolute realism, conceiving the universal as existing formally in the concrete, and thus he confused universal being with the divine being and said: Being cannot be diversified by itself (because being is being and nothing else); nor can it be diversified by something other than itself (because what would be other than being would be non-being, and non-being is nothing). Hence he concluded: "Being is being, non-being is non-being, and it is impossible to think of anything else." In other words, multiplicity of beings is absolutely impossible. This argument was revived by Spinoza to prove the unicity of being.[4]

St. Thomas, following the lead of Aristotle, examined this argument of Parmenides, and says of it: "In this Parmenides and his disciples were deceived, since they always referred to being as if it had one meaning and one nature, as is the case with any genus (which is diversified by extrinsic differences). But this is impossible. For being is not a genus, but is predicated (analogically) of various things and in many different senses." [5] For the modes of being are not extrinsic to being, but being is included in them. Thus quantity still is being.

But on the other hand, of ancient philosophers it was Heraclitus who denied the unity or indivisibility and identity of being; for he said that experience tells us that everything is becoming, and noth-

[3] *Summa theol.*, IIa IIae, q.180, a.6.
[4] *Ethica*, def. III, axioma 7, prop. 7.
[5] *Com. on Metaph.*, Bk. I, chap. 5, lect. 9.

ing is, and so to some extent Heraclitus identified being and non-being with becoming, which thus would be its own reason for such, as the absolute realists maintain. Thus, contrary to Parmenides, he ends in denying the real validity of the principle of contradiction or of identity, namely, "being is being, non-being is non-being," or "being is not non-being."

Thereupon Plato sought to solve the problem of unity and multiplicity by admitting the intelligible order of ideas, the highest of which is the Idea of Good, which is one, indivisible, and immutable, and also admitting the sensible order in which all things undergo a change. This was a sort of juxtaposition of the doctrines of Parmenides and Heraclitus.[6]

Finally, Aristotle with greater penetration investigated the problem of unity and multiplicity, showing that unity is a transcendental property of being, and is found in every category of being.[7] In like manner, what makes Aristotle famous is his affirmation of the indivisibility and unicity of God, of the pure Act. But he did not explain how multiplicity of beings proceeds from the one God. For his reasoning did not lead him to admit the idea of a most free creation. The Neoplatonists, however, sought to explain by necessary emanation how plurality of beings proceeds from the One-Good, inasmuch as good is essentially self-diffusive. But in doing so they denied the revealed doctrine of an absolutely free creation, and contradicted themselves, because God in operating from a necessity of His nature could not produce anything finite or limited.[8] Now St. Thomas proceeds, however, in accordance with Aristotle's doctrine, very much improving upon it.

Conclusion. One does not add any reality to being, but is only a negation of division.

This conclusion is proved from the analysis alone of the terms, for "one means undivided being." This is evident from inductive reasoning, by considering the various categories of being: unity of substance is undivided substance, unity of quantity is undivided quantity, and the same applies to unity of quality, action, passion, relation, place, time, position. Nevertheless, one or undivided being is capable of being divided. Thus substance, which is composed of matter and form, man, who is a composite of soul and body, likewise the continuous (magnitude, movement, time), each is undivided, but indefinitely divisible.

Hence from the analysis of the terms it is clear that unity is

---

6 *Dialogues*, Parmenides (on unity), *Sophista* (on being).

7 St. Thomas' *Com. on Metaph.*, Bk. V, chap. 6, lect. 7 f.; also Bk. X for a fuller discussion.

8 *Summa theol.*, Ia, q. 19, a. 4.

nothing but undivided being, as Aristotle had already shown.[9] Hence unity does not add any reality to being, but is only a nega-tion of division.

From this we get the following corollary: one is convertible with being. Indeed what is convertible with another is that which is predicated absolutely first of it, or necessarily and immediately, whether as specific difference, or as an inseparable property. But every being is one, because it is either simple or composite. But what is simple is perfectly one, because it is undivided and indivisi-ble. But what is composite has not being while its parts are divided. Hence every being is one.

That everything guards its unity as it guards its entity, is a sign in confirmation of this truth. Thus in every living being, whether rational or irrational, in every nation whose country is in danger of being attacked, we find this instinct for self-preservation. Thus the Church guards her unity of faith, government, and worship, just as she guards her being.

From this it is clear that one does not add any reality to being, but is only a negation of division. Thus there is only a distinction of the mind between them. And contrary to the teaching of Par-menides, just as being is predicated not univocally but analogically of the different categories of being and of different beings, so also is one. Thus unity can be merely either analogical, or generic, or specific, or numerical. The solution of the objections confirms this doctrine.

Reply to first objection. Transcendental unity, which is found in all the categories of being, differs from unity that is the principle of number, this belonging solely to the category of quantity. Py-thagoras, and Plato to some extent, as also Bannez among modern philosophers, erred in not distinguishing between these unities. Yet there is clearly a distinction between them. Thus we say of a doctrine lacking in coherence that it is one among many others, but that it lacks unity.

Does unity that is the principle of number add any reality to being? It does not add anything really distinct from being, because what is not being is nothingness; but it adds a special and limited mode of being, which is actually and implicitly contained in being, so that quantity still is being and not other than being.

It is in this sense that St. Thomas says at the end of his reply to the first objection: "The one which is convertible with being does not add a reality to being; but the one which is the principle of number does add a reality to being, which belongs to the genus of quantity." In other words, although quantity is not an extrinsic

9 *Metaph.*, Bk. V, chap. 6; also Bk. X.

differentia to being, as rationality is an extrinsic *differentia* to the genus of animality, yet quantity *connotes* a special nature which the notion of being does not connote, and which does not apply to every being. On the contrary, one which is convertible with being does not connote any other nature than being, but the transcendental mode of this nature.

Reply to second objection. In this reply several arguments are presented that serve to elucidate the fourth way of proving God's existence.

1) What is one or undivided absolutely may be divided accidentally. Thus what is one in essence and subject may have many accidents. Likewise the continuous is one absolutely or is actually undivided, but it can be divided indefinitely into still smaller parts. Thus it is one absolutely and many accidentally.

2) On the other hand, those things that are absolutely divided and many, are one accidentally. Thus those things that are many in number are one in species or in principle. Thus many men are absolutely many.

3) Therefore, since being is one absolutely, "being is divided by one absolutely and by many accidentally." This means that one and many do not refer on equal terms to being; they are not coordinated but subordinated. "For multitude itself would not be contained under being, unless it were in some way contained under one." Thus Dionysius says that "there is no kind of multitude that is not in a way one. But what are many in their parts, are one in their whole; and what are many in accidents, are one in subject; and what are many in number, are one in species; and what are many in species, are one in genus; and what are many in processions, are one in principle." [10] Similarly, what are many in genera, are one in analogous being.

4) The elucidation of the fourth way [11] follows from this, namely, that multitude, which is subordinate to one, cannot be the reason for the unity found by participation in it, the unity of similarity, for instance, either specific, generic, or analogical. Therefore, as St. Thomas says, "if one of some kind is found as a common note in several objects, this must be because some one cause has brought it about in them; for it cannot be that the common note of itself belongs to each thing, since each thing is by its very nature distinct from the other, and a diversity of causes produces a diversity of effects. Since, therefore, being is found as a common note in all things, which, in all that they are, differ from one another, it must of necessity be that being is attributed to them not

[10] *De nom. div.,* last chapter.
[11] *Summa theol.,* Ia, q.2, a.3.

of themselves but from some one cause. And this seems to have been Plato's idea, whose wish was that, prior to any multitude, there should be some unity, not only in numbers, but also in the natures of things." [12] For this reason, too, it was stated in a previous article that "every composite has a cause, for things in themselves different cannot unite unless something causes them to unite." [13] Thus the unity of being is preserved, which was the wish of Parmenides; yet it is neither univocal unity nor unicity of being that is preserved, but analogous unity of beings, which are dependent on the supreme Being.

Reply to third objection. "It is not nugatory to say being is one, because one adds an idea to being." Likewise it is not nugatory or tautological to say every being is one and the same with its phenomena; for this is the principle of identity so determined that it can be called the principle of substance. Nor is it nugatory to say being is being, non-being is non-being, because by such statements it is affirmed that being is not non-being. Likewise if we say: Flesh is flesh, spirit is spirit; good is good, evil is evil. As our Lord says: "Let your speech be yea, yea: no, no." [14] This means that being is necessarily by its nature opposed to non-being, as good is to evil, as spirit to flesh. By this the identity of being is affirmed against the contentions of absolute evolutionism.

Therefore one is undivided being. Hence one and being differ only in idea, and because our first concept is of being, one is related to being as a property to the essence from which it is derived, as, for instance, incorruptibility is related to a spiritual substance.

SECOND ARTICLE

WHETHER ONE AND MANY ARE OPPOSED TO EACH OTHER

State of the question. This article completes the idea of unity, inasmuch as it is compared with its opposite. The principal difficulty is enunciated in the fourth objection of this article, namely, that a vicious circle must be avoided in definitions, and there seems to be a vicious circle here; for if one is undivided being, it is opposed to the previously accepted notion of the divided, or to multitude. Thus multitude would come before and not after one, which is contrary to what was stated in the previous article,[15] and this would nullify the fourth way of proving God's existence.

---

12 *De potentia*, q.3, a.5. See also *Summa theol.*, Ia, q.44, a.1.
13 *Summa theol.*, Ia, q.3, a.7.
14 Matt. 5: 37.
15 Cf. ad 2um.

Reply. One is opposed to many, but in various ways, inasmuch as one is considered the principle of number, or as it is convertible with being. For the one which is the principle of number, is opposed to multitude which is number, as the measure is to the thing measured; for number is multitude measured by one, as Aristotle says.[16] But the one which is convertible with being, is opposed to multitude by way of privation, as the undivided is to the thing divided. Thus we speak of a united kingdom as being against a kingdom that is divided.

The first kind of opposition referred to here is of the relative order, as between father and son; the other is privative. Aristotle mentions two other kinds of opposition;[17] namely, contradictory (as between a thing and its negation, between being and non-being, one and not one), and contrary (as between two opposite habits, for instance, between virtue and vice). Among these four kinds of opposition, the kind that is verified between transcendental unity and multitude is privative opposition.

Objection. But how is the principal difficulty to be answered? It is contended that if one is opposed to multitude, then it would follow that one comes after multitude, and is defined by it, as privation is by the want of form or perfection, as blindness is defined by privation of sight. But if unity is defined by privation of multitude, there is a vicious circle in definitions, for one is posited in the definition of multitude. Thus some define humility by its opposite, which is pride, as if it were a privation of pride; also pride is defined by humility, as if it were a privation of humility.

St. Thomas, in his reply to the fourth objection, concedes that "division is prior to unity, not absolutely in itself, but according to our way of apprehension. For we apprehend simple things by compound things; and hence we define a point to be what has no part, or the beginning of a line." Hence unity is defined by us as the privation of division, but not of multitude. Thus we conclude that one is prior to multitude, and is conceived as prior to multitude. In fact, as stated in this reply: what first comes to the mind is being; secondly, that this being is not that being, and thus we apprehend division; thirdly, comes the notion of one; fourthly, the notion of multitude. Hence we conclude that one is prior to multitude, although according to our way of apprehension it comes after division; for "we do not understand divided things to convey the idea of multitude except by the fact that we attribute unity to every part." Hence there is no circle in definitions. Moreover, as Cajetan observes, division is negation, which is logical being. Hence

---

[16] *Metaph.*, Bk. X, chap. 1.
[17] *Ibid.*, Bk. V, chap. 10 (lect. 12 of St. Thomas' commentary).

division is absolutely prior to unity in the intelligible order, but not in the natural order.

In the reply to the first objection, it is pointed out that multitude is the privation of unity and has its foundation in unity, because privation neither takes away entirely the existence or being of a thing, nor unity which is converted with being. For privation is the want of some perfection in a subject. Thus privation of being and of unity has its foundation in being and in unity. But this does not happen in the privation of special forms. Thus the privation of whiteness is not founded on whiteness, nor is the privation of sight on sight, but on the subject apt for sight.

It remains true, however, that opposition between one and many, inasmuch as, although many is one relatively and has its foundation in one, yet it is not one absolutely. What is many absolutely is one relatively, namely, according to either specific, generic, or analogical similarity. Also what is one absolutely, as man, is many relatively, by reason of its parts and accidents.

Reply to second objection. The other difficulty is solved, namely, that multitude is constituted by one, and therefore it is not opposed to multitude. In the reply it is stated that unities constitute multitude in so far as they have being, but not in so far as they are opposed to multitude. Thus the parts of a house make up the house by the fact that they are beings, not by the fact that they are "not houses," namely "not the whole." Every distinct part has a unity that is distinct from the unity of the whole.

The particular conclusions to be drawn from these first two articles are that unity is a property of being, inasmuch as one is undivided being, and that multitude by way of privation is opposed to this transcendental unity, but presupposes it, and this for two reasons: (1) because multitude is a plurality of unities; (2) because multitude results from the division of a being that is one either by unity of genus or of species or of quantity or of subject.

THIRD ARTICLE

WHETHER GOD IS ONE

State of the question. The discussion is not about the absence of division in God, for we have already seen, when treating of God's simplicity,[18] that He is absolutely indivisible since there is no kind of composition in Him, either physical, metaphysical, or logical. But the discussion concerns God's unicity. A being, how-

---

[18] *Summa theol.*, Ia, q.3.

ever, is said to be unique, when there cannot be or at least are not other beings of the same species or genus. Therefore God is unique, if there cannot be many Gods. But, as we shall at once see, unicity has its foundation in unity, and God's unicity in the absolute indivisibility of the Deity.

It must be noted that all polytheists denied God's unity, and likewise many heretics who admitted two principles, one of good and the other of evil, such as the Gnostics, the Marcionites, the Valentinians of the second century. Along with these we must include the Manichaeans of the third century, and finally the Albigensians of the thirteenth century. In the sixteenth century, too, the Tritheists, not having a proper conception of the real distinction between the three divine Persons, spoke as if there were three Gods.

Finally, the pantheists implicitly deny God's unity, inasmuch as they admit a necessity of emanation of the divine nature in its external communication, just as the sun's rays of necessity proceed from it. St. Thomas gives three reasons for idolatry or polytheism: (1) an excessive love for certain men, who were the objects of veneration; (2) ignorance of the true God; (3) demoniacal inspiration.

Reply. There is of necessity but one God.

1. This conclusion is of faith, as clearly seen from very many texts of Holy Scripture; e.g., "Hear, O Israel, the Lord our God is one Lord." [19] There is scarcely a page of the Old or New Testament in which there is not a reference to monotheism. Likewise the first words of the Nicene Creed are: "I believe in one God." The Fourth Lateran Council says: "We firmly believe that there is only one true God . . . the one principle of all things." [20] This same truth is equivalently expressed in the Vatican Council.[21]

2. Three proofs from reason are given of God's unicity. It is proved: (1) from God's simplicity; (2) from His infinity; (3) from the unity and order in the world. It is proved from God's simplicity as follows: It is impossible to communicate to many that by which any singular thing is this particular thing, for instance, that by which Socrates is this particular man as distinct from others. But because Socrates is not humanity, there can be many men. Since God, however, is His Deity, for the same reason He is both God and this God. Therefore it is impossible that there should be many Gods.

[19] Deut. 6: 4.
[20] Denz., no. 428.
[21] Ibid., nos. 1782, 1801.

This reasoning is clear, and is made clearer by contrasting it with its opposite, when it is said: "If Socrates were a man by what makes him to be this particular man, as there cannot be many Socrates, so there could not be many men." Hence, because in the same way God is God and this God, there cannot be many Gods.

For the understanding of the major, it must be noted that this whereby any singular thing is this particular thing cannot be communicated to many, whether we are speaking of individuality resulting from matter which is the foundation of quantity, or whether we are speaking of subsistence or of personality. Indeed, matter which is the foundation of quantity cannot be communicated to inferior things, that is, it cannot be participated by another subject, since matter is the ultimate subject and pure potency, capable of receiving but not of being received. But if we consider subsistence or personality, then that by which this particular thing cannot be communicated is that by which the nature is made incommunicable to another suppositum or person. Therefore in these two acceptations of the term "singularity" we have the verification of the major.

The minor, however, has its foundation in the truth that God is His own Godhead,[22] which means that there is no distinction between either the Godhead and this Godhead (because Godhead is not a form received in matter), or between this Godhead and this God (because God is absolutely simple, and He does not constitute a whole of which the Godhead would be only an essential part).

On the other hand, although there is not any distinction between Michaelness and this Michaelness, Michael is not his Michaelness, because Michael represents the whole, of which Michaelness is the essential part, and besides this there is in Michael contingent existence and accidents.

Moreover, in contradistinction to the Godhead, the angelic nature taken generically can be communicated to many, inasmuch as there can be many subordinated angelic species according to the perfections of their intellectual power. But this plurality does not apply to the Godhead, for this is not only separated from matter, but transcends every species and genus.[23] From this first proof it is clear that God's unicity is deduced from His unity, and from His simplicity or indivisibility.

The second proof is derived from God's infinity.

There cannot be two or many infinitely perfect beings. But God

[22] *Summa theol.,* Ia, q.3, a.3.
[23] *Ibid.,* q.3, a.5.

is the infinitely perfect being as stated above.[24] Consequently, there cannot be many Gods.

Proof of major. If there were two infinitely perfect beings, there would have to be a difference between them, and this difference would have to be a perfection and not an imperfection. Hence a certain "perfection would be wanting to one of them." This means that each of them would have to be the self-subsisting Being, and then there would be no way of distinguishing between them, either on our part or in themselves. In other words, there is only one unreceived subsisting Being, just as there would necessarily be but one whiteness, if this were not received in anything. On the other hand, there is a real distinction between God and creatures, inasmuch as these are not their existence, and this, being an imperfection, cannot be in the infinitely perfect Being.

From this proof given by St. Thomas many Thomists deduce that the subsistent relations in the divine Persons, according as they denote regard to another (*esse ad*), are not absolutely simple perfections, for since filiation is not in the Father, He would be without some absolutely simple perfection and thus would not be God. For an absolutely simple perfection not only implies no imperfection, but it is better for one to have than not to have this. Hence the divine relations, according as they denote regard to another (*esse ad*), do not add a new perfection to the infinite perfection of the divine nature. The same is to be said of God's free act, for instance, the creative free act.

The third proof is derived from the unity of the universe, and thus the fifth way of proving God's existence is perfected from on high.[25]

Things that are diverse do not harmonize in the same order, unless they are ordered thereto by one, because one is essentially the cause of one. But there is ordination, either of subordination or of coordination, between all existing things in the universe. Therefore all these things are ordered by the one, which must be most perfect, so that all things may be ordered by it. And this one is God.

The major is evident from what we said about unity and multitude; for multitude does not convey the idea of unity that is found in it.[26] There must be an intelligent Ordainer, for He must perceive the reasons for the existence of things, and the means in the end. Moreover, He must be the self-subsisting Intellection, otherwise His intelligence would be ordered to intellection and

[24] *Ibid.*, q.4, a.3.
[25] *Ibid.*, q.2, a.3.
[26] See above, q.2, a.3, fifth way.

truth by a higher Ordainer. But there must be only one self-subsisting Intellection, just as there is only one self-subsisting Being.[27]

Reply to second objection. God is said to be one or undivided
by a privation of division. But this privation is only according to
our mode of apprehension, because with us the concept of the
composite is prior to that of the simple. Hence we define a point
to be "what has no part." [28]

FOURTH ARTICLE

WHETHER GOD IS SUPREMELY ONE

State of the question. We are concerned here with unity that is
the foundation for unicity. This follows as a corollary from what
was said about God's simplicity.[29] The difficulty that could be
raised from the mystery of the most Holy Trinity is solved when
we come to discuss this mystery. For the present, as regards the
Trinity, only St. Bernard's words are quoted: "Among all things
called one, the unity of the divine Trinity holds the first place"; [30]
that is, the unity is so sublime and intimate that it persists in the
very Trinity of Persons. From this most exalted point of view
God's unity is revealed. On the contrary, if this unity is not considered with reference to the Trinity, it constitutes the preamble
to the faith, and is proved by reason alone, as we have seen. In fact,
in this article it is proved by reason alone that God is supremely
one.

The proof. What is supremely being and supremely undivided
is supremely one; but God is supremely being (because He is the
self-subsisting Being) and supremely undivided (because He is
absolutely simple); [31] therefore God is supremely one. This means
that He is infinitely farther removed from composition than even
the highest angel, who is composed of essence and existence. In
fact, God alone is essential unity; for creatures have not unity as
an entity except by participation.

In the treatise on the Trinity, however, it is shown that the real
distinction between the Persons does not take away from God His
supreme unity, for this distinction has its foundation in the opposition of relation. This means that there is a real distinction between the Persons and not between these and the divine nature.[32]

27 *Ibid.*, q. 14, a. 4.
28 *Ibid.*, q. 11, a. 2 ad 4um.
29 *Ibid.*, q. 3.
30 *De consideratione*, chap. 5.
31 *Summa theol.*, Ia, q. 3, a. 7.
32 *Ibid.*, q. 39, a. 1.

Thus in the equilateral triangle the three equal angles are really distinct from one another and not really distinct from the superficies of the triangle, which is one and the same in these three angles. The closer is the unity effected by the real distinction, the nobler is this unity. This constitutes the very mystery of the Trinity.

Cajetan most correctly draws attention to this point so as to show that, although the divine nature is no way either really or formally distinct from paternity, yet this nature is communicable and is really communicated, whereas paternity is incommunicable. In like manner, although the first angle of a triangle is not really distinct from its superficies, and is not communicated to the other two angles, yet its superficies is really communicated. On this point Cajetan says: "As in the real order, so also in the formal order, or of formal aspects in themselves, and not as we speak of them, there is in God but one formal aspect, which is neither purely absolute nor purely relative, neither purely communicable nor purely incommunicable. But this aspect most eminently and formally contains whatever there is of absolute perfection and whatever the relativity in the Trinity demands. . . . But we are deceived when we proceed from the absolute and relative attributes in our approach to God, in that we imagine that the distinction between the absolute and the relative is, as it were, prior to the divine reality; and consequently we believe that this must be put under the other member. And yet there is totality of opposition, for the divine reality is prior to being and to all its differences; for it transcends being and one." [33]

This means that the divine reality, as it is in itself, contains formally and eminently all the most purely simple or absolute perfections, and also the divine relations, so that these real and subsistent relations are neither really nor formally (as realities) distinct from the nature. There is only a *rationis ratiocinatae* or virtual distinction between them and the divine nature.[34] Thus we see the sublimity of God's unity from revelation more clearly than from the most searching investigation of reason.

[33] *Com. in Iam*, q.39, a.1, no. 7.

[34] By the *rationis ratiocinatae* distinction is meant a distinction for which there is a foundation in the object distinguished. Thus there is a distinction *rationis ratiocinatae* between the spirituality and simplicity of the soul.

Rationis ratiocinatae means that the mind has reasoned out this distinction because of the object that is distinguished. (Tr.)

CHAPTER XII

QUESTION 12

THE KNOWABILITY OF GOD

AFTER speaking of "how God is not," St. Thomas now treats the question, "How God is known by us," as he had already announced.[1]

The importance of this question. It is of the greatest importance. Just as the second question, concerning God's existence, is of fundamental importance as regards those truths that belong to natural theology, so this twelfth question is of fundamental importance as regards those truths that are of the supernatural order. For this question concerns the possibility of the rational creature being elevated to the order of grace and glory, namely, to the supernatural end of the beatific vision. It is, strictly speaking, a discussion of the essentially supernatural nature of this vision, which far surpasses the supernatural nature of miracle. For a miracle is supernatural only as regards the manner of its production. Thus by the resurrection the natural life, both vegetative and sensitive, is supernaturally restored to one who is dead; whereas, contrary to this, as we shall at once see, the immediate vision of the divine essence is intrinsically and essentially supernatural, for it is essentially supernatural life. Several theologians of more recent times, wishing to prove conclusively from reason alone the possibility of the beatific vision, because of the natural desire for this, forgot to take into account this distinction between the essentially supernatural nature of eternal life and the supernatural nature of miracle, the existence and possibility of which latter can be known in a natural way. We shall see that reason alone cannot prove apodictically either the existence or the possibility of the beatific vision; for the knowability of what is essentially supernatural is itself supernatural, inasmuch as truth and being are convertible. We shall see, however, that the possibility of the beatific vision cannot be disproved, that it is defended against those who deny it, that reason alone persuades us of this by means of a most profound argument of its fittingness, and that it is firmly held by faith. This is the common opinion of the theologians, and it is only by inadvertence that this can be denied.

[1] See prologue to q.3.

Therefore in this question we already have the concept of the essentially supernatural life developed for us in its fundamental aspects, and completed in the treatises on happiness [2] and on grace, inasmuch as grace is the seed of glory.[3]

St. Thomas in his treatise on happiness says: "Neither man nor any (angelic) creature can attain final happiness by his natural powers," because "the vision of the divine essence (is of that) which infinitely surpasses all created substance," [4] which means that it surpasses the natural powers and exigencies of such. It is likewise shown farther on that "without grace man cannot merit everlasting life" because "everlasting life is an end exceeding the proportion of human nature," [5] and even of the angelic nature.[6]

The fundamental principles of all these truths are contained in this question, which is divided into three parts as follows: (1) God's knowability by direct vision is discussed in the first eleven articles; (2) God's knowability by the abstractive method of reasoning from natural effects is discussed in the twelfth article; (3) God's knowability by faith is the subject of the thirteenth article.

The first part of this question, which is the principal part, has four divisions: (1) the possibility of the beatific vision, or of our being elevated to the supernatural order of grace and glory (a. 1); (2) the intuitiveness of this vision; whether God is seen through some similitude or idea (a. 2); (3) the faculty and the light of glory by which the created intellect can see God (a. 3, 4, 5); (4) the remaining articles are concerned with the various modifying circumstances of this vision, inasmuch as there is difference of degree in this among the blessed, since it is not a comprehensive penetration of the divine essence, and inasmuch as these circumstances modify the state of blessedness.

FIRST ARTICLE

WHETHER ANY CREATED INTELLECT CAN SEE THE ESSENCE OF GOD

State of the question. It is a discussion not only of the human intellect, but of every created intellect, even that of the highest angel, and even of higher angels that could be created. The word *can* in the title is taken in the unrestricted sense, as referring either to the natural power of the created intellect or to the elevation of

---

[2] *Summa theol.*, Ia IIae, q.5, a.5.
[3] *Ibid.*, q. 109, a. 5; q. 110, a. 5; q. 112, a. 1, 5.
[4] *Ibid.*, q.5, a.5.
[5] *Ibid.*, q. 109, a.5.
[6] *Ibid.*, Ia, q.62, a.2.

this power by God. The question is whether the vision of God is possible (or non-repugnant) for the created intellect. But the existence of this vision is of faith, and it is purely a gift. Lastly, to see God's essence means to know God's essence, not partially but completely, although it is stated in the seventh article that this knowledge is not comprehensive. This is what the Scholastics say is not the abstractive but the quiddative knowledge of God.

The intellect has no difficulty in understanding this terminology. The abstractive knowledge of God is incomplete and imperfect; for by it we acquire a knowledge of God by predicating, indeed, attributes that are essential but only analogically common to Him and to creatures. Thus God is known as the first Cause, the first Being, the self-subsisting Being, the infinite Being. . . . On the contrary, the quiddative knowledge of God is complete and perfect, because by it we know God according to all His essential predicates, down to and including the ultimate difference, that is, to His Deity or intimate life. But the Deity as such contains formally, enimently, and explicitly all absolute perfections, which are intimately reconciled in His eminent Deity; in fact they are identified therein (without any real distinction between them), although without destroying one another. The Deity as such, however, is named by us wayfarers, but it is not known by its proper concept, because it is not naturally capable of being participated in by created natures from which by the abstractive method we get our ideas; these natures participate, indeed, in being, unity, truth, goodness, intelligence, and love, but not in the Deity, which can be participated in only by grace, which is strictly a participation of the divine nature, or of God's intimate life.

Hence there is a great difference between knowing God abstractively, or, as it were, externally, in some created image, and knowing Him quiddatively, in His intimate life. Thus there is a great difference between knowing some man, for instance, the supreme pontiff, only according to his external characteristics and knowing him in his intimate life. This terminology, however, has its immediate foundation in Holy Scripture. Thus St. Paul says: "Eye hath not seen nor ear heard, neither hath it entered into the heart of man, what things God hath prepared for them that love Him. But to us God hath revealed them, by His Spirit. For the Spirit searcheth all things, yea, the deep things of God [that is, the intimate life of God, or the Deity as such]. For what man knoweth the things of a man [intimately] but the spirit of a man that is in him? So the things also that are of God no man knoweth, but the Spirit of God." [7]

[7] I Cor. 2: 9–11.

St. Thomas has spoken in several other places of the distinction between the abstractive and intuitive or quiddative knowledge of God.[8] This question has been discussed at length by us in another work,[9] and therefore we shall mention here only the principal points.

Let us see: (1) what is defined to be of faith about the beatific vision; (2) the errors of those who deny either the possibility of the beatific vision, or its supernatural character; (3) what Sacred Scripture and tradition have to say about it; (4) how St. Thomas defends the possibility of this vision in this article and in other places; (5) the terminology of later theologians on this point; (6) the various opinions; (7) the common opinion among the Thomists.

WHAT IS DEFINED TO BE OF FAITH
ABOUT THE BEATIFIC VISION

We have the following definitions and declarations of the Church: [10] "Those who, having been baptized, die without any actual sin on their souls, go immediately to heaven, the state of grace being required for entrance therein; [11] heaven or beatitude is not a substantial transformation into God,[12] but man is raised to supernatural happiness,[13] and this cannot be found out by reason alone." [14] It is also declared that this supernatural happiness cannot

8 Cf. *Contra Gentes*, Bk. I, chap. 3; Bk. III, chaps. 49, 50.

9 Cf. *De revelatione*, I, 337–403.

10 Cf. Denz. (theological index, no. XIV, a), nos. 464, 530, 693, 3048.

11 *Ibid.*, nos. 800, 809, 842, 1011.

12 *Ibid.*, no. 510.

13 *Ibid.*, no. 1808.

14 *Ibid.*, no. 1669. This declaration is directed against the semirationalism of Froschammer, who is condemned for having held the following; "Man's supernatural end and all that pertains to this . . . come within the scope of human reason and philosophy, and reason can by its own natural strength and principles acquire the knowledge of these truths, provided they be proposed to it as its object" (Denz. 1669).

This declaration also states: "Therefore, according to this same author's opinion, it can and must most certainly be concluded that reason is able of itself, not now as accepted on the principle of divine authority, but by its own natural powers and principles, acquire knowledge or certainty not only of the most abstruse mysteries of God's wisdom and goodness but also of the free decrees of His will, although it is admitted that these have been revealed. No one with rudimentary or slight knowledge of Christian doctrine can fail to see and fully realize how false and erroneous is this teaching of the author."

Those who seek to establish from reason alone not only persuasive but also apodictic arguments in proof of the possibility of the beatific vision do not sufficiently take into consideration what Pius IX wrote on this subject against the semirationalism of James Froschammer. The whole Letter of Pius IX, *Gravissimas inter,* must be read, or at least those parts of it quoted in Denzinger's *Enchiridion,*

be had in this life,[15] but in the future,[16] and that it consists in seeing God immediately and intuitively face to face, and in the enjoyment of this vision.[17]

A special quotation must be given from the Constitution *Benedictus Deus* of Benedict XII, which states: "By apostolic authority we define that, according to God's common ordination, the souls of all the saints . . . immediately after death and the aforesaid purgation of those who are in need of this even before their souls are again united to their bodies and the general judgment . . . see the divine essence by direct intuition and face to face, in such wise that nothing created intervenes as an object of vision, but the divine essence presents itself to their immediate gaze, unveiled, clearly and openly, and that in this vision they enjoy the divine essence. . . . Also in this vision and enjoyment of the divine essence, they do not make acts of either faith or hope in the same . . . and this vision and fruition will continue . . . forever." [18]

In this constitution emphasis must be placed on the words "nothing created intervening as an object of vision." This does not mean, however, the condemnation of the opinion of those who maintain that there is a created impressed or expressed species in the beatific vision; for these do not say that such species intervenes as the object of vision, but only as that *by which* or in which the divine essence is seen, just as the angel sees his essence in some expressed intelligible species. In like manner the Council of Florence says: "The souls of the saints in heaven know by clear intuition the one and triune God as He is in Himself, yet one more perfectly than another according to the diversity of their merits." [19]

CONDEMNED ERRORS

As for the condemned errors on this subject, some recede from the true doctrine by denying the possibility of the beatific vision; others go to excess by saying that no absolutely gratuitous gift is required to make this vision possible.

Those who denied the possibility of the intuitive vision of God appealed to the arguments quoted by St. Thomas at the beginning of this article, namely, that there is no existing proportion between the created intellect and God, for there is an infinite distance be-

nos. 1669–73. These refutations received their final formulation in the Vatican Council; see Denz., nos. 1795, 1796, 1816.

[15] *Ibid.*, nos. 474 f.
[16] *Ibid.*, no. 287.
[17] *Ibid.*, nos. 530, 693, 1928 f., 3030.
[18] *Ibid.*, no. 530.
[19] *Ibid.*, no. 693.

tween them. In fact, the Deity in a certain way transcends being, but the object of the intellect is being. Moreover, God can be seen only in a finite manner, and then His essence is not immediately seen.[20] St. Gregory speaks of this error.[21] Amalric, who lived during the pontificate of Innocent III, erred likewise on this point. But particularly the fourteenth century Palamites denied the possibility of the beatific vision, maintaining that the divine nature, as it is in itself, cannot be even supernaturally seen by the created intellect. Therefore the Palamites admitted that a certain uncreated light emanates from God, which can be seen by the bodily eye, such, they say, as the apostles saw on Mount Thabor, and it is this light which constitutes the enjoyment and happiness of the saints in heaven. The Greeks in four pseudo-synods accepted and confirmed this doctrine.[22]

Among modern philosophers, Rosmini seems to have denied the possibility of the absolutely immediate vision of God even with the help of the light of glory. The following propositions of Rosmini were condemned: "God is the object of the beatific vision inasmuch as He is the author of *ad extra* works." "Since God cannot, even by the light of glory, entirely communicate Himself to finite beings, He could reveal and communicate His essence to the possessors only in that way which befits finite intelligences, namely, by manifesting Himself to them, inasmuch as He enters into relation with them as their creator, foreseer, redeemer, and sanctifier." [23] These propositions seem to deny the immediate vision of God's essence, even with the help of the light of glory.

In contradistinction to these, the fourth century heretics, Eunomius, Aëtius and the Anomoeans, attributed to the merely natural powers of the intellect not only the intuitive but also the comprehensive vision of God. They were most strenuously attacked by Chrysostom, Basil, Gregory of Nazianzus, Gregory of Nyssa, Ambrose, Epiphanius, and others

St. Thomas in the first objection of this article quotes a text from St. Chrysostom which suggests a difficulty, for he says: "Not only the prophets have not seen God, but neither have angels or

[20] There is a tendency in the Neoplatonism of Plotinus to deny the possibility of the beatific vision, because it maintains that the supreme hypostasis, the One-Good, transcends Intelligibility and Intelligence, which is the second hypostasis. Hence the One-Good cannot be seen, but is known only by a certain mystical and obscure contact. Moreover, this pantheistic doctrine, according to which all things proceed from God by a necessary emanation, denies the possibility of our free elevation to the order of grace.

[21] *Morals*, Bk. 18, chap. 28.

[22] Cf. *Dict théol.*, art. "Palamas."

[23] Denz., nos. 1928, 1930.

archangels." [24] A similar text is quoted from the works of Dionysius.[25] St. Thomas replies: "Both of these authorities speak of the
vision of comprehension," not of the merely intuitive vision. And
he proves this by quoting what Chrysostom says farther on in this
text about Dionysius; "He says this of the most certain vision of the
Father, which is such a perfect consideration and comprehension
as the Father has of the Son." Indeed the words of Chrysostom
here are directed against the Anomoeans, who said that they see
God as God sees Himself.[26]

In the fourteenth century, the Beguines and Beghards likewise
erred on this point, and were condemned in the ecumenical Council of Vienne. They asserted "that any intellectual nature whatever is naturally blessed in itself, and that the soul does not need
the light of glory, elevating it to see God and to enjoy seeing Him
in this blissful state." [27] This means that the beatific vision is not
only possible, but natural.

Later on Baius denied the gratuity of our elevation to the order
of grace and glory, admitting a natural and efficacious desire in us
for the beatific vision, as a gift due to our nature or as not being
one to which we have no claim, and which is not gratuitous. He
said: "The elevation and exaltation of human nature to a participation in the divine nature was due to it because of its original
state of integrity; hence it must be declared natural and not supernatural." [28] He likewise asserted that "the opinion of those is absurd, who say that in the beginning man was raised above his natural state by a certain supernatural and gratuitous gift, so that he
might worship God by the supernatural virtues of faith, hope,
and charity." [29]

He also said: "That distinction between the two kinds of love,
namely, the natural by which God is loved as the author of nature,
and the gratuitous by which God is loved as the beatifier, is vain
and false, its purpose being to ridicule Scripture and the very many
testimonies of ancient writers." [30] All these condemnations are of
the greatest importance, for they are a condemnation of the natural
and *efficacious* desire for the beatific vision. This desire is called
efficacious, not that the beatific vision would exceed the exigencies,
but only the powers, of our nature; for the beatific vision, like the
elevation and exaltation of human nature to a participation in the

[24] *Hom. XIV in Joan.* 1: 18.
[25] *Div. nom.*, I.
[26] Consult the commentary of Francis Silvius on this article.
[27] Denz., no. 475.
[28] *Ibid.*, no. 1021.
[29] *Ibid.*, no. 1023.
[30] *Ibid.*, no. 1034. See also nos. 1012, 1013, 1014.

divine nature, would be due to this nature and not gratuitous. This means the denial of the gratuity of grace itself.

It must be noticed that subsequently the ontologists expressed a preference for this error, as is evident from their condemned propositions, such as the following ones: "The immediate and at least habitual knowledge of God, is so essential to the human intellect that without it nothing can be known; it is indeed the very light of the intellect." "That being, which is in all things and without which nothing is perceived by the intellect, is the divine being." [31] If the beatific vision were such as just stated, then there would be no essential distinction between the formal object of this vision and that of natural knowledge; but the formal object of each would be the same, known confusedly at first and afterward distinctly, just as we say that the formal object of natural reason is specifically the same in the rustic and the great metaphysician, though known in a different way by each, since it is known vaguely by the former and clearly by the latter. This would do away with the essential distinction between the two orders of nature and grace.

Semirationalists, such as Frohschammer, said about the same.[32] Their doctrine was more explicitly condemned in the Vatican Council, which most clearly affirmed "that there is a twofold order of knowledge, distinct both in principle and in object." [33]

Finally Pius X, in his Encyclical *Pascendi,* says against several modern apologists who stressed excessively our natural aspirations and came near teaching the error of Baius: "We cannot refrain from once more and very strongly deploring the fact that there are Catholics who, while repudiating immanence as a doctrine, nevertheless employ it as a system of apologetics; they do so, we may say, with such a lack of discretion that they seem to admit in human nature not only a capacity and fittingness for the supernatural order, both of which Catholic apologists, with due reservations, have always demonstrated, but they assert that it truly and vigorously demands the same. As we may more truly say, however, this need of the Catholic religion is attacked by the modernists, who seek to be looked upon as more moderate in their views. For those whom we may call integralists want it to be taken for a demonstrated fact that there is this latent supernatural *germ* in the unbeliever, which was transmitted to mankind from the consciousness of Christ." [34]

[31] *Ibid.,* nos. 1659 f.
[32] *Ibid.,* nos. 1669, 1671, 1673.
[33] *Ibid.,* nos. 1795, 1816.
[34] *Ibid.,* no. 2103.

The second part of this encyclical rejects the opinion of those who wish to find in our nature (which for them is in a process of becoming) the germ of the Christian life, which thus would not be strictly supernatural. The first part rejects the natural desire that postulates the beatific vision, or proves effective of the same. This would be to revive the error of Baius, who said: "The exaltation of human nature to a participation in the divine nature, was due to it because of its original state of integrity; hence it must be declared natural and not supernatural." [35]

What we have said suffices concerning mutually conflicting errors, that is, those that are such either by defect or by excess. But from this we already have the beatific vision correctly explained, especially if these mutually conflicting errors are taken exactly into consideration. Similarly, in the question on grace, the doctrine that is of faith is already to a great extent explained by a careful consideration of the Pelagian and Semipelagian errors, and of Predestinationism, Protestantism, and Jansenism.

THE TESTIMONY OF SACRED SCRIPTURE AND TRADITION CONCERNING THE BEATIFIC VISION

The aforesaid definitions of the Church are more explicit propositions of the truth that is already contained in the deposit of revelation, namely, in Sacred Scripture and Tradition.

The principal texts of Sacred Scripture, as Tradition has interpreted them, must here be quoted. [36]

In St. Matthew's Gospel we read: "Blessed are the clean of heart, for they shall see God." [37] This text is explained by the following one: "See that you despise not one of these little ones; for I say to you, that their angels in heaven always see the face of My Father who is in heaven." [38] These words refer of course to the angels; but from this text and several other texts of the Gospel it is clear that our heavenly happiness, as regards the object seen, does not differ from that of the angels.

Moreover, St. John says: "In that day you shall know that I am in My Father, and you in Me and I in you." [39] "That they all may be

[35] Ibid., no. 1021.
[36] On this point consult Petavius, Dogmata theologica, Vol. I, Bk. VII, chaps. 5, 6, p. 593; Rouet de Journel, S.J., Enchiridion Patristicum (theological index, nos. 105, 607).
[37] Matt. 5: 8.
[38] Ibid., 18: 10.
[39] John 14: 20.

one, as Thou, Father, in Me and I in Thee; that they also may be one in us. . . . Father, I will that where I am, they also whom Thou hast given Me may be with Me; that they may see My glory which Thou hast given Me, because Thou hast loved Me before the creation of the world." [40] The words "I will that where I am" are explained elsewhere by the Evangelist in these words: "We testify what we have seen. . . . And no man hath ascended into heaven, but He that descended from heaven, the Son of Man who is in heaven.[41]

Similarly, in his first epistle St. John says: "Beloved, we are now the sons of God, and it hath not yet appeared what we shall be. We know that, when He shall appear, we shall be like to Him, because we shall see Him as He is." [42] However, if God's essence is not known by an intuitive vision, but by means of a created image, then this cannot be called "seeing Him as He is"; for a created image is something altogether imperfect with reference to God considered just as He is in Himself. This will be more fully explained in the following text.

Lastly St. Paul says: "We see now through a glass in a dark manner, but then face to face. Now I know in part; but then I shall know even as I am known." [43]

This means that we know God at present through a mirror, namely, the mirror of created things, even if it is a question of the knowledge acquired by faith which is a gift of God; for the mysteries of faith are expressed according to concepts, for instance, of nature and person, and these are obtained from created things. Likewise it is said that "we see in a dark manner" because of the obscurity in the mysteries of faith, which is not an immediate and clear knowledge of these just as they are in themselves, but a knowledge that rests solely on God's testimony confirmed by divine signs. "But then face to face," which means that God will be directly seen. And this is confirmed by the last words of the text, "as I am known." But God's knowledge of us is absolutely perfect, for the Scripture says: "All things are naked and open to His eyes." [44]

There is, however, some difficulty about the expression "face to face," for the Scripture says: "And the Lord spoke to Moses face to face as a man is wont to speak to his friend." [45] It also says:

[40] *Ibid.*, 17: 21–24. See also commentaries of St. Augustine and St. Thomas on St. John's Gospel.
[41] *Ibid.*, 3: 11, 13.
[42] I John 3: 2.
[43] I Cor. 13: 12. See commentary of St. Thomas.
[44] Heb. 4: 13.
[45] Ex. 33: 11.

"And there arose no more a prophet in Israel like unto Moses, whom the Lord knew face to face." [46] In fact, we also read that after Jacob had seen the angels and heard God's message, he said: "I have seen God face to face, and my soul has been saved." [47] This text does not refer, however, to the immediate vision of God's essence, because, as stated in this text, Jacob fought with the angel who appeared in a sensible form, and he received only God's blessing and had his name changed.

The reply to this difficulty is that the expression "face to face" in these passages from the Old Testament is materially the same as the text quoted from St. Paul's epistle,[48] but the words of this text are to be taken in a more sublime sense, as is evident from the context: "Then I shall know even as I am known."

St. Thomas explains these texts of the Old Testament farther on in this question. He says: "So when Jacob says, 'I have seen God face to face,' this does not mean the divine essence, but some figure representing God . . . , or that Jacob spoke thus to designate some exalted intellectual contemplation, above the ordinary state." [49]

It is no wonder, however, that this expression "face to face" is not used exactly in the same sense in the Old Testament and in the text just quoted from St. Paul's First Epistle to the Corinthians; for the expression is analogical and metaphorical. Therefore God's appearance in some sensible form first suggests itself to us in this utterance; but it is afterward understood in a nobler sense of God's immediate manifestation without any intervening sensible image. Finally it must be said that not all the Fathers declared that this text of St. Paul refers strictly to the beatific vision. Nevertheless this is commonly admitted, because the text concerns our knowledge as it will be in heaven, which transcends faith and all the charismata.[50] In the Old Testament there is veiled reference to the beatific vision, as in the following text: "I shall be satisfied when Thy glory shall appear." [51]

As early as the second century we find the Fathers speaking of the beatific vision. Among them is St. Irenaeus, who says: "(God) grants this to those who love Him, namely, to see Him, which the prophets also prophesied. . . . For man does not see God by his own powers. But when He pleases He is seen by men, by whom He

46 Deut. 34: 10.
47 Gen. 32: 30.
48 I Cor. 13: 12.
49 Cf. a.11 ad 1um.
50 Cf. Estius, *In omnes canonicas apostolorum epistolas*, Vol. I, *in ep. ad Cor.*, 13: 12.
51 Ps. 16: 15.

wills, and when He wills, and as He wills." [52] Likewise, too, St. Cyprian says: "What will be the glory and how great the joy, to be admitted to see God, to be honored with the companionship of Christ the Lord Thy God, and experience the joy of salvation and light eternal!" [53] Petavius [54] quotes the principal texts from the Fathers, and explains several passages in the works of St. Chrysostom and St. Basil, who seem at first sight to deny the immediate vision of God, whereas from the context it is clear that these Fathers are speaking against the Anomoeans, who said that the merely natural power of the intellect is sufficient not only for the intuitive but also for the comprehensive vision of God, as St. Thomas remarks. [55] Long before the scholastic period, even the Stoics knew that comprehension means complete perception; for Zeno distinguished between simple sensation and comprehensive perception, comparing the former to the unclenched hand, and the latter to the clenched hand, which grasps what it holds. Thus St. John Chrysostom defines the comprehensive vision as the adequate knowledge which the Father has of the Person of His Son. [56]

THE BEATIFIC VISION AND THE VIEWS
OF NON-CHRISTIAN PHILOSOPHERS

As for the ancient philosophers, it must be noted that Plato spoke of the future life especially in his *Phaedo*, and in a mythical manner about the contemplation of the supreme Good. But in another of his works [57] he says that the Idea of the Good is the source of all truth and intelligence, so that it appears to transcend intelligible essence and intellection.

For Plotinus [58] the supreme hypostasis, namely, the One-Good, transcends intelligence (the second hypostasis, which consists of a certain duality of subject and object), and therefore the supreme Good cannot be seen, but is known by a certain obscure and mystic contact. [59]

Among modern philosophers, Spinoza [60] had a pantheistic conception of the vision of God. He held that there is but one substance, which is endowed with two attributes, namely, thought and

[52] *Adv. haer.*, Bk. IV, 20, 5. Cf. Rouet de Journel, *op. cit.*, no. 236.
[53] Ep. 56, ad Thibarit. Cf. Rouet de Journel, *ibid.*, no. 579.
[54] *Dogmata theologica*, Bk. VII, chaps. 5, 6; Vol. I, p. 567.
[55] *Summa theol.*, a.1 ad 1um.
[56] Hom. XIV. Consult also St. Augustine, *De civit. Dei*, XXII, 29, 30; *Retractationes*, Bk. I, chap. 13; *De Trinitate*, Bk. IX, chap. 11; Bk. XV, chap. 9.
[57] *Republic*, Bk. VII, 517, D.
[58] *Ennead*, Bk. VII, nos. 34–36.
[59] *Ibid.*, Bk. IX, no. 12; also Bk. IV, no. 6.
[60] *Ethica*, II, § 47; V, § 36.

extension; and just as our bodies are finite modes of infinite extension, so our intellect is a finite mode of divine thought. Among
men, however, those are immortal who attain to the idea of God,
which is an eternal and not a transitory mode of God. Thus there
is a certain impersonal immortality, and beatitude consists in a
certain knowledge of God from which proceeds the intellectual love
of God. He says: "The intellectual love of the mind for God is the
very love of God by which He loves Himself, or the intellectual
love of the mind for God is a part of the infinite love by which
God loves Himself." [61]

All this results from the pantheistic definition of substance, in
which abstract being is confused with the divine being, from which
Spinoza seeks to deduce all things geometrically, according to the
principles of absolute determinism. Thus the denial of God's liberty results in the denial of the possibility of supernatural revelation and of miracles. In fact, this means the absolute denial of
everything supernatural even in God, because the divine naure is
identified with our nature. Human nature cannot be elevated to
the supernatural order, since there is now no real and essential
distinction between it and the divine nature. [62]

But it is quite clear that Spinoza was wrong, as stated above, [63]
in confusing abstract being with the divine being, by conceiving
infinite extension as one of God's attributes. He never did succeed
in deducing from God the finite modes of extension and thought,
for he considered the successive series of these as eternal.

Against this mental attitude toward God, it has already been
established that He is the self-subsisting, absolutely simple and immutable Being, and thus He is really and essentially distinct from
the changeable and composite world. There can be no finite modes
in God, which could be considered as His accidents, because the
self-subsisting Being is not capable of further determination. He is
pure Act without any admixture of potency.

HOW DOES ST. THOMAS DEFEND THE POSSIBILITY
OF THE BEATIFIC VISION IN THIS ARTICLE
AND IN PARALLEL PASSAGES?

This article consists of three parts: (1) the reason for doubting
this vision; (2) the opinion of those heretics who deny this truth;
(3) refutation of opinion because it is opposed to the faith and

---

[61] *Ibid.,* V, § 36.

[62] The same, too, must be said of pantheistic Brahmanism from which Buddhism
is derived.

[63] *Summa theol.,* Ia, q.3, a.1, 4.

because the denial of the possibility of the beatific vision is against reason.

In the first part it is proved that God is in Himself supremely knowable; because everything is knowable according as it is actual. But God is pure Act. Thus Aristotle said that the pure Act is both supreme intelligence and the supreme intelligible. But this in some measure is directed against Plotinus, who held that the first hypostasis, the One-Good, transcends intelligence (second hypostasis) and essence. Nevertheless Plotinus admitted a superintellection in the first hypostasis.

Furthermore St. Thomas remarks: "But what is supremely knowable in itself may not be knowable to a particular intellect on account of the excess of the intelligible object above the intellect; as, for example, the sun which is supremely visible cannot be seen by the bat on account of the excess of light." [64] Aristotle had alluded to this.[65] Hence there is reason for doubting this vision, since the created intellect, not as an intellect, but as it is created and weak or deficient, is like the owl in this respect.

The second part of this article reports the opinion of those who "held that no created intellect can see the essence of God." Thus several Neoplatonists, followers of Plotinus, said that finite intellects, even in a state of supreme ecstasy, cannot see God, or the first hypostasis, but are only in mystic and obscure contact with Him. Similarly, in the pontificate of Innocent III, as we remarked, the Amalricians denied the possibility of the immediate vision of God's essence.

The third part of this article proves the falsity of denying the possibility of the beatific vision, both because that denial is "opposed to the faith" and because it is "against reason."

It is said to be *"opposed to the faith,"* at least as an erroneous doctrine. In fact, St. Thomas says: "This point of view cannot be upheld, since it is *heretical.*" [66] Several definitions of the Church have made this increasingly clear, especially the definition of Benedict XI.[67]

St. Thomas shows that the opinion is opposed to faith, since it is of faith that our ultimate happiness is to be found in God. But, as Aristotle declares,[68] man's ultimate happiness consists in his highest operation, which is intellection. And any being whatever is perfect in so far as it attains to its principle, as even the Neoplatonists said.

[64] *Ibid.,* q. 12, a. 1.
[65] *Metaph.,* Bk. II, chap. 1.
[66] *De veritate,* q. 8, a. 1.
[67] Denz., no. 530.
[68] *Ethics,* Bk. X, chap. 9.

There is still a difficulty concerning the natural premise which is here posited, for it must be proved that ultimate happiness does not consist in the abstract knowledge of God, but in the intuitive and absolutely direct knowledge of Him. It may be said, as John of St. Thomas observes, that a thing is perfect by the fact that it is united to its principle according to its capacity.

In reply to this we say that this immediateness is sufficiently established by the Scripture passages quoted above and from the definitions of the Church, and especially, since the time of St. Thomas, from the definition of Benedict XI.

Finally it is shown that the denial of the possibility of the beatific vision is against reason. This means that reason cannot demonstrate the impossibility of this vision, or the possibility of this vision cannot be proved false; moreover, it is reasonably defended against those who deny it.

A natural desire cannot be to no purpose. But every man naturally desires to know the cause when he sees the effect. Therefore it is against reason to say that no created intellect can see God.

Much has been written by the commentators of St. Thomas about this argument.[69] We must first see how St. Thomas enunciates this argument in other parts of his works. Thus in one passage he says: "The object of the intellect is what a thing is, that is, the essence of a thing, according to *De anima*, Bk. III. Wherefore the intellect attains perfection in so far as it knows the essence of a thing. . . . Consequently, when man knows an effect, and knows that it has a cause, there naturally remains in man the desire to know about that cause, what it is. . . . Consequently, for perfect happiness the intellect needs to reach the very essence of the first Cause." [70] Elsewhere he says: "This natural and imperfect knowledge the angels have of God does not set their natural desire to rest, but rather urges it on to see the divine substance." [71]

From these and other places the argument is thus better construed as follows: A natural desire cannot be void or tend to something that is impossible.[72] But there is in man a natural desire to know not only whether there is a cause, but also what it is in itself. Therefore to know the essence of the first cause, as it is in itself, does not seem impossible to man, that is, there does not seem to be

[69] This has been more fully explained in another work. Cf. *De revelatione*, I, 376–403.

[70] *Summa theol.*, Ia IIae, q.3, a.8.

[71] *Contra Gentes*, Bk. III, chap. 50.

[72] It is the possibility of the beatific vision rather than the fact of this vision that is defended by St. Thomas in this article. For our elevation to the supernatural order, as our Catholic faith teaches, depends on God's free will; in fact, it is absolutely gratuitous since it is essentially supernatural.

any ineptitude in man for this possibility of being elevated; and therefore the denial of this possibility is "against reason."

A doubt arises concerning the meaning and force of this argument. Several have objected that it proves too much or not enough.

It proves, of course, too much, if it is a question of a natural and efficacious desire, or of an exigency for the beatific vision; for, in such a case, this vision would be due to our nature and not gratuitous, as Baius and later on Jansenius said, who appealed to St. Thomas' argument in defense of their opinion. Such an interpretation of this argument would evidently prove too much; for it would prove also the beatific vision itself and would lead to a confusion between the two orders of nature and grace.

It does not prove enough, however, if it is a question of a conditional and inefficacious natural desire, or of a velleity; for this velleity can be frustrated and be ineffective. In fact, perhaps it tends toward an impossibility, just as if anyone, thinking that the intuitive vision of God must be also comprehensive, were to desire conditionally and inefficaciously not only the intuitive but also the comprehensive vision of God, which latter is incommunicable. But to desire conditionally is to desire on condition that the thing desired be possible, as if, for instance, one were to desire to have wings on condition that such be possible.

Moreover, there is another difficulty, inasmuch as a perfect, abstractive knowledge of the essence of the first Cause is all that is required for the explanation of things in nature, because God is the cause of things not by reason of His essence, acting from a necessity of His nature, but by a most free intervention of His intellect and will. Therefore, to explain things in nature, it suffices for us to know that the first Cause is endowed with intellect and will. Contrary to this, for a perfect explanation of sanctifying grace, which is participation in the divine nature, we would have to see God's essence.

The Thomists, especially those after the time of Baius, generally reply to this difficulty by observing that St. Thomas is certainly not speaking of an unconditional and efficacious natural desire or one of exigence. Therefore he has in mind a conditional and inefficacious desire, by reason of which we defend not the existence but the probability of the beatific vision, and are intimately persuaded of the same, although it is not conclusively proved. We have evidence of this from the following observations.

1) St. Thomas certainly is not speaking of a natural efficacious desire but of an inefficacious one. For, in his opinion, there is no natural efficacious and necessitating desire except with reference to

good that is proportionate to and due to our nature. He says:
"Everlasting life is a good exceeding the proportion of created
nature; since it exceeds its knowledge and desire, according to
I Cor. 2: 9: Eye hath not seen nor ear heard, neither hath it entered
into the heart of man, what things God hath prepared for them that
love Him." [73] Likewise, on the necessity of grace for the angels, he
says: "To see God in His essence is beyond the nature of every
created intellect. Consequently no rational creature can have the
motion of the will directed toward such beatitude unless it is
moved thereto by a supernatural agent. This is what we call the
help of grace." [74] Similarly when defining predestination, he says:
"The end toward which created things are directed by God is twofold. One is that which exceeds all proportion and faculty of
created nature; and this end is life eternal, which consists in seeing
God, and this is above the nature of every creature, as shown above
(q. 12, a. 4). The other end, however, is proportionate to created
nature, to which end created being can attain according to the
power of its nature." [75] Elsewhere, too, he says: "Man's ultimate end
is twofold; one kind, the happiness to which philosophers refer, is
proportionate to human nature; the other is a good that exceeds
the proportion of human nature." [76]

It is therefore certain that St. Thomas has not in mind in this
article an unconditional and efficacious, or exigitive natural desire;
for he most certainly holds that grace and glory are gratuitous gifts,
which are in no way due either to our nature or to the angelic
nature.

2) But if the natural desire here in question is not unconditional
and efficacious, it must be conditional and inefficacious. This means
that to see God's essence would be supreme happiness, if God were
freely to raise me so as to make this immediate vision possible.

[73] *Summa theol.*, Ia IIae, q.114, a.2.

[74] *Ibid.*, Ia, q.62, a.2. In the reply to the first objection of this article, St.
Thomas says: "The angel naturally loves God, so far as God is the author of his
natural being. But we are speaking of turning to God, so far as God bestows
beatitude by the vision of His essence." It is this distinction which Francis Silvius
(Ferrariensis) stresses, and rightly so, in his commentary on the Third Book of
the *Contra Gentes*, the fifty-first chapter. And so we find very many Thomists
saying that there is in man not an innate, but a naturally elicited, conditional,
and inefficacious desire to see God's essence as He is the author of nature (but not
the triune God, as He is the author of grace; for in this most sublime aspect,
God is not known in a natural way). So say John of St. Thomas, Gonet, Salmanticenses, Gotti, Billuart, and others.

[75] *Ibid.*, Ia, q.23, a.1.

[76] *De verit.*, q.27, a.2. For this same doctrine, consult the treatises on grace:
Ia IIae, q.109, a.5, 6; q.112, a.3; q.114, a.5; on the necessity of the theological
virtues, Ia IIae, q.62, a.1 ad 1um et ad 3um; on the necessity of the gifts of the
Holy Ghost, Ia IIae, q.68, a.2.

One may raise the objection that the words "conditional" and "inefficacious," in use among the Thomists, especially after the time of Baius, do not occur in the works of St. Thomas. We reply that it is certain from the passages quoted from the works of St. Thomas that this natural desire is not efficacious, and is therefore inefficacious. But the inefficacious desire supposes a condition which, as a matter of fact, may not be realized.

A general explanation is given of this in the passage in which St. Thomas distinguishes between God's will to save all mankind, which is conditional and efficacious, and His efficacious will to save the elect. In this passage St. Thomas shows that "a thing, taken in its primary sense, may be good," [77] and desired (such as the salvation of all men), which, however, taking all things into consideration, is not absolutely or efficaciously but only conditionally willed. St. Thomas then goes on to say: "Nor do we will simply, what we will antecedently, but rather we will it in a qualified manner; for the will is directed to things as they are in themselves, and in themselves they exist under particular qualifications. Hence we will a thing simply inasmuch as we will it when all particular circumstances are considered; and this is what is meant by willing consequently. Thus it may be said that a just judge wills simply the hanging of a murderer but in a qualified manner he would will him to live, namely, inasmuch as he is a man. Such a qualified will may be called a willingness rather than an absolute will." [78]

Similarly, as regards ourselves, to see God's essence, on first consideration, is a good and one that is desired; but, taking all things into consideration, this vision does not appear to be naturally possible; it is made possible, however, only by a gratuitous elevation of our nature. Hence this desired good is not willed absolutely and efficaciously, but conditionally. Thus wings for flying would be good for us, if this were granted to us; and the same is to be said of even some better gift. To continue to live is a desirable good, but on condition that this privilege be granted by God as a preternatural gift.

Hence in this article St. Thomas, speaking of the natural desire of seeing God's essence, has in mind a desire that is not efficacious, but inefficacious; and it is inefficacious because it is conditional, since it presupposes our free elevation to this order. Otherwise this elevation to grace would be due to our nature, which is a heresy that destroys the very notion of grace, and there is not the slightest doubt that St. Thomas most certainly held this doctrine, even before the Church condemned the heresy of Baius.

[77] *Ibid.*, Ia, q. 19, a.6 ad 1um.
[78] *Ibid.*

On the accepted terminology
concerning the division of
the appetite or of love

The division as commonly accepted among theologians may be clearly presented by the following schema: [79]

$$
\text{Love}
\begin{cases}
\text{supernatural}
\begin{cases}
\text{of charity} \\
\text{of hope}
\end{cases} \\
\\
\text{natural}
\begin{cases}
\text{innate} \\
\text{elicited}
\begin{cases}
\text{necessary} \\
\text{free}
\begin{cases}
\text{efficacious} \\
\text{conditional and} \\
\text{inefficacious}
\end{cases}
\end{cases}
\end{cases}
\end{cases}
$$

Love is called natural when it proceeds from a natural principle, and not from grace. On the contrary, it is called supernatural when it proceeds from a supernatural principle, namely, from grace, or from charity, or hope, or even from actual grace that disposes one for habitual grace. Even "the pious impulse to believe," [80] required for unformed faith, is supernatural. The following proposition of Baius is condemned: "That distinction between the two kinds of love, namely, the natural by which God is loved as the author of nature, and the gratuitous by which God is loved as the beatifier, is vain and lying, and is devised in ridicule of Sacred Scripture and the very many testimonies of the ancients." [81] This distinction is frequently formulated by St. Thomas, as when he says: "The angel does naturally love God, so far as God is the author of his natural being. But here we are speaking of turning to God, so far as God bestows beatitude by the vision of His essence." [82]

Natural love is of two kinds, innate and elicited. The innate desire is, so to speak, a very tendency or natural inclination for good, before the good is apprehended. Thus the plant instinctively and of necessity seeks the light of the sun.[83] Similarly we speak of the sensitive appetite (concupiscible and irascible) and of the rational appetite, which are faculties of our soul. But all creatures,

---

[79] See Cajetan's *Com.* on Ia, q. 19, a. 1; also John of St. Thomas on Ia, q. 12, a. 1. Also commentaries of Salmanticenses and Gonet on q. 12, a. 1. Against Baius and the Jansenists, consult Billuart, *De gratia*, diss. III, a.4.

[80] Denz., no. 178.

[81] *Ibid.*, no. 1034.

[82] *Summa theol.*, Ia, q.62, a.2 ad 1um. Cf. Gardeil, O.P., *Dictionaire de théologie catholique*, art. "Appétit."

[83] *Ibid.*, Ia, q.19, a.1.

each in its way, thus naturally love God, the author and preserver of nature.[84] Thus in the physical order it is natural for the part to love the whole more than itself, and so the hand is naturally exposed to ward off a blow on the body, and especially on the head; otherwise this would mean the perversion of a natural inclination.[85]

The elicited love is that by which the knower, after apprehending the good, starts out in pursuit of it. And just as cognition, which directs this movement, is an act elicited by the cognitive faculty, so this is an act elicited by the appetitive faculty.

The elicited act is of two kinds. It is either necessary, or free and elective. The act is necessary when its object is universally good, so that all men necessarily (at least as regards the specification of the act) love happiness as such, or necessarily will to be happy, even when they do not as yet know in what true happiness consists in the concrete.[86] The free or elective love is concerned with an object that is not universally good, or that is proposed as an object of indifferent judgment.[87]

Lastly, love is said to be efficacious, or else it is conditional and inefficacious. The efficacious presupposes a judgment on the goodness and natural attainableness of the object desired. The conditional and inefficacious love presupposes a judgment on the goodness and natural unattainableness of the object desired.[88] Thus man would will not to die, and this would be good for him if such a preternatural gift were granted to him, as was granted to man in the state of innocence. This last mentioned appetite is a velleity. This good is most desirable, but it is naturally unattainable. I would wish it if God freely gave me the means for attaining it. What a happiness this would be! Lastly, this velleity is either explicit or implicit, according as the object desired and the presupposed condition are either clearly or confusedly known.

THE VARIOUS OPINIONS OF THE THEOLOGIANS

In the eighteenth century, the Augustinians Noris and Berti [89] were of the opinion that there is a natural and innate desire in us for the intuitive vision of God. In a way this desire is efficacious, though not as Baius meant. For the intuitive vision of God con-

[84] *Ibid.*, q.60, a.5.
[85] *Ibid.*, IIa IIae, q.26, a.1.
[86] *Ibid.*, Ia IIae, q.10, a.1, 2.
[87] *Ibid.*, a.2.
[88] Cf. Billuart, *De gratia*, diss. II, a.2, Solv. objectiones; also diss. III, a.4.
[89] *Berti opera*, Bk. V, diss. II, chap. 1, nos. 1, 8.

stitutes our natural end in the appetitive order, but it is our supernatural end as regards its attainment and the means for attaining it.

Criticism. This opinion scarcely differs from Baianism, since it
does not uphold the absolute distinction prevailing between the
natural and the supernatural orders. By way of retaining some
semblance of a distinction, it denies the principle of finality. For
God as the Author of nature would have given us an innate appetite (a sort of ponderousness of nature) for the end, toward which
as the Author of nature He could not direct us. Thus there would
be no relation between the efficient and final causes. This would
mean the violation of the corollary to the principle of finality, that
every agent acts for a proportionate end.

The view of Scotus [90] is that we have a desire for the intuitive
vision of God, which is both innate and natural, though inefficacious. The reason is that this most sublime happiness is the fitting
and final end of all human beings, and therefore the innate appetite
has its foundation therein. But it is not efficaciously desired, since
not all have a knowledge of this happiness.

Criticism. The only conclusion we can draw from the reason
given by Scotus is that we have a natural and innate appetite for
happiness as such, but not for the beatific vision; for this vision is
not so in agreement with our nature as to be proportionate to it.[91]

Moreover, the general view taken by the Thomists [92] is that the
desire of seeing God's essence cannot be innate, and if it were innate
then it would have to be efficacious. For the innate appetite, as
distinct from the elicited, implies in the object desired a natural
relation and positive fittingness, which have their foundation in
the very nature of the one desiring, even before there is any knowledge of this desired good. Now there is not in our nature any natural
relation and positive fittingness for an object that is essentially
supernatural, but only an obediential potency or possibility of being elevated to this order. Therefore our nature is not endowed
with an innate and natural appetite, which would be a sort of ponderousness of nature for the immediate vision of God. In fact, if
there were this appetite, it would be, for this very reason, efficacious;
for, inasmuch as the desire is the result of a conditional judgment,
it is inefficacious. Thus I would wish this naturally attainable good
if God were freely to elevate me to this order. The innate appetite,
however, is not the result of knowledge, but springs from nature
itself and corresponds to the forces or at least the exigencies of

---

90 Cf. *in Prol. Sent.*, q.1; *in IV Sent.*, d.49, q.10.
91 *De veritate*, q.22, a.7; q.14, a.2.
92 See John of St. Thomas, *Com. in Iam*, q.12, disp. XII, a.3, no. 8.

nature; hence it is not concerned with that to which nature is not entitled, but with that to which it is entitled.

Furthermore, it must be said that if Scotus' opinion were true, then God as the Author of nature would have given it an innate appetite, a ponderousness of nature, for an end to which He could not bring it as the Author of nature, as already stated against the Augustinians Berti and Noris. Thus there would be no relation between the efficient and final causes, as demanded by the principle of finality, which states that every agent acts for a proportionate end.

Lastly, this innate appetite which Scotus speaks of, would be both essentially natural as being a property of nature, and essentially supernatural inasmuch as its object of specification would be formally supernatural. Nor can it be said to be specified by an entitatively supernatural object, but by one that is naturally and, as it were, materially known; for this appetite, being innate, independently of any knowledge whatever would tend toward God as He is in Himself. Thus there would be a natural tendency in our nature toward something essentially supernatural, which is a contradiction in terms and which would end in the denial of the distinction between the two orders, as it would also mean the univocity of being, which, according to the doctrine of Scotus, is included in this opinion.

It must be observed that the Thomists consider this final criticism a valid argument in refutation of the theory of an active obediential potentiality admitted by Suarez in his search of a *via media* between the view of Scotus and that of St. Thomas. This active obediential potentiality, as the Thomists generally admit,[93] would be both essentially natural, since it is a property of the nature, and essentially supernatural, since it is specified by an essentially supernatural object. Suarez admitted only a natural desire that is elicited and inefficacious, however, as regards the beatific vision, and in this he differed from Scotus.

In opposition to the view of Suarez, according to the view held by St. Thomas and the Thomists, the obediential potentiality is passive, and, as its name implies, refers directly to an agent of a higher order whom it obeys and from whom it receives this supernatural elevation and relation or positive fitness for this essentially supernatural object.[94] Hence for the Thomists the obediential potentiality is nothing else, as John of St. Thomas shows,[95] but a

---

93 Cf. *ibid.*, q. 12, disp. XIV, a 2, no. 11; also Billuart, *De Deo*, diss. IV, a. 5, § 3.
94 *Summa theol.*, IIIa, q. 11, a. 1; q. 1, a. 3 ad 3um; *Quaest. Disp., de virtutibus in communi*, a. 10 ad 2um et 3um; *Compendium theologiae*, chap. 104.
95 *Com. in Iam*, q. 12, disp. XIV, a.2.

potentiality that denotes a possibility of being elevated to the order of grace and glory.

Cajetan's opinion. It differs radically from that held by Scotus. He says: "In convincing proof of what we have said, understand that the rational creature can be considered in two ways, either absolutely or as ordained to happiness. If the rational creature is considered absolutely, then the natural desire is for that which is within the scope of the natural faculty; and thus I concede that there is no natural desire of seeing God absolutely as He is in Himself. But if the rational creature is considered in the second sense, then it naturally desires to see God, because, as such, it has knowledge of certain effects, namely, those of grace and glory, God being the cause of these, considered as He is absolutely in Himself and not as universal agent. But when the effects are known, then it is natural for any intellect whatever to desire to know the cause of these." [96] And Cajetan adds that St. Thomas is here speaking as a theologian; hence it is a question of the natural desire of the creature ordained by God to eternal life. [97]

Criticism. Francis Silvester (Ferrariensis) and several other Thomists have attacked this opinion of Cajetan in their commentaries. After quoting Cajetan's opinion, Ferrariensis says: "But this does not seem to be the view of St. Thomas. . . . For the reason given by St. Thomas (Ia, q. 12, a. 1, and Contra Gentes, Bk. III, chap. 50) is not restricted to the knowledge of the effects of grace and glory, but is also concerned with knowledge of whatsoever effects and with knowledge of every cause. . . . (Moreover) it would then follow that only those who know the supernatural effects of grace and glory would have such a desire; but this conclusion is false, for, as St. Thomas says (Contra Gentes, Bk. III, chaps. 51, 57), every intellectual being has this desire." [98] Therefore it is not a question of a natural desire for eternal life. So writes Ferrariensis, and very many Thomists are of the same opinion, such as Bannez, John of St. Thomas, the Salmanticenses, Gonet, Billuart, Gotti, and others. [99]

It must furthermore be remarked that the desire which Cajetan speaks of, cannot be called natural, absolutely as such, but is natural only in a relative sense, or is connatural; and once the effects of grace are known, it is truly a supernatural and efficacious desire that proceeds either from infused hope or from charity. On the

---

[96] Cf. ibid., q. 12, a. 1.

[97] Consult also Cajetan's Opusc., III, tr. 7.

[98] Com. in Contra Gentes, Bk. III, chap. 51.

[99] Consult their commentaries on the Summa theol., Ia, q. 12, a. 1; also their treatises De gratia: Whether the state of pure nature was possible.

contrary, St. Thomas is referring to an absolutely natural desire that originates from a knowledge of natural effects, as is evident especially from a passage in which he discusses this desire arising in the angels from their natural knowledge of God as mirrored in their essence.[100]

In fact, we even find that this natural desire, which originates from a knowledge of natural effects, is truly and wonderfully described by Plato. For he teaches that, in accordance with the ascendant dialectic of love, we must first love beautiful bodies, sounds, colors, and then, in a loftier flight, proceed to love the beauty of the soul. But since the intrinsic worth of the soul consists in glorious actions which have their foundation in the best of precepts and maxims, we must love sublime teachings which are the rule of human actions. But the excellence of these teachings is derived from the extraordinary perfection of the supreme science, whose object is the self-subsisting Beauty and Goodness. Then he goes on to say: "This beauty, O Socrates, in the first place is eternal, neither coming into being nor perishing, never increasing or decreasing. . . . It is the absolute and eternal beauty, in which all other beauties participate, without inducing in it by their birth or destruction the least diminution or increase. But what a felicitous sight shall we not deem it to be, if one were to gaze upon the genuine, perfect, pure and simple beauty . . . beholding that divine unvarying beauty . . . ? Do you not think that (a man who attains to this contemplation of God) acquires no longer the semblance of virtues but real virtues . . . , since by this he will be the friend of God and by all means will be immortal?" [101]

Hence Plato rises from the consideration of natural effects to the knowledge of the existence of the supremely Good and Beautiful. Expressing this as a velleity, he says: "What an immense happiness this would be for man if he could directly see this supreme Good!" Of course traditional religious beliefs contributed to this view of Plato, as did also his exaggerated realism; but even excluding these, it is possible to attain this end by the way of ascendant dialectic.[102]

Lastly, we must say that even Cajetan seems in some measure to concede what Ferrariensis asserts, for, after repeating the reply quoted above from his commentary,[103] he says: "Yet in a special sense . . . it can be said that the human intellect, knowing of

---

[100] *Contra Gentes,* Bk. III, chaps. 50, 51.

[101] *Banquet,* chap. 29, p. 211.

[102] For this desire of Plato and the Platonists, consult St. Augustine's *De civitate Dei,* Bk. VIII, chap. 8.

[103] *Com. in Iam IIae,* q.3, a.8.

God's existence and of His general attributes, naturally desires to know what He is, inasmuch as He is included in the category of causes, and not absolutely as He is, except as a certain consequence of this previous knowledge. And this is true, because we are naturally inclined, on seeing the effect, to desire to know the cause whatever this may be. Hence take note, thou beginner, that to know God's essence is the same as to see it. This point is made clear, of course, in the proof of the last article of this question." [104]

THE MORE COMMON OPINION
AMONG THE THOMISTS

This question was very much disputed in the schools during the time of Baius and Jansenius; then the Thomists, so as to avoid all equivocation, by more explicit definitions restricted the application of the terms used. But previous to this, Ferrariensis and Bannez had helped to solve the problem by introducing the finest of distinctions.

Ferrariensis said: "We naturally desire to see God in so far as He is the first Cause, but not as He is the object of supernatural happiness. For it can be known by the natural power of the intellect that God is the cause of other things, but it cannot be known in this way that He is the object of supernatural happiness." [105] Thus the object of the aforesaid desire is clearly determined, but a certain difficulty remained about this desire subjectively considered.

However, Bannez offers the following explanation: "Man can have a natural appetite, that is, elicited by one's natural powers, which is a certain conditional and inefficacious desire of seeing God. . . . For, if . . . St. Thomas were referring to the ponderousness of nature (or to an innate desire), then man would be inclined thereto even without having seen the effect. . . . I have said *conditional*, because by his natural powers man cannot be certain that such a good is possible. Thus man can desire and wish never to die, if this be possible. And although such a condition is not explicitly conceived by the mind, yet it is implicitly contained in the object, which is represented as good, and not as possible." [106]

Later on, many Thomists admit that man's natural desire to see God's essence as He is the Author of nature, is not innate but elicited, conditional and inefficacious.[107] Furthermore, the Thomists

---

[104] Cf. q. 12, a. 1.

[105] *In Contra Gentes*, Bk. III, chap. 51.

[106] *Com. in Iam*, q. 12, a. 1.

[107] So say John of St. Thomas, Gonet, Salmanticenses, Gotti, Billuart, and others.

generally remark that this desire is also free, inasmuch as it is not a necessary act as regards the specification of the object.[108]

And so this desire is explained both objectively and subjectively. Objectively, a desire of seeing God's essence as He is the Author of nature, but not as He is the triune God and the Author of grace; for this cannot be known in a natural way. Subjectively considered, this desire is said to be elicited, conditional and inefficacious.

It follows from this desire, as so conceived, that there is a natural knowledge of God's natural effects and of His naturally knowable divine attributes. This natural knowledge, indeed, of God's attributes is imperfect, since the intimate reconciliations of several of these attributes is mysterious, for instance, the reconciliation of supreme immutability with supreme liberty, likewise of infinite and omnipotent goodness, with the permission of evil, or even of infinite mercy with infinite justice. Hence St. Thomas says: "Therefore this knowledge (so imperfect) does not set the natural desire to rest, but rather urges it on to see the divine substance," [109] which means that the divine essence as constituting the foundation for the naturally knowable attributes, or God's essence as He is the Author of nature, may clearly be known by the intellect. However, the essence is the same both in God as the Author of nature and in God as the Author of grace.[110] Thus, therefore, the object of this natural desire is not formally supernatural, but only materially so, for it is by the natural light of reason that this object is known to be desirable or, as the Salmanticenses say, "the thing desired is materially supernatural, but not the reason for desiring it. . . ; for it is desired under the aspect of a certain maximum good." [111]

Thus there is an immense abyss between this natural desire and infused hope or charity. This distinction, which Baius eliminated,[112] was long before expressed by St. Thomas when he wrote: "Charity loves God above all things in a higher way than nature does. For nature loves God above all things inasmuch as He is the beginning and the end of natural good; whereas charity loves Him, as He is

108 Cf Salmanticenses, *De Deo*, tr. II, disp. I, dub. IV, no. 3. It is somewhat in disagreement with Francis Silvester (Ferrariensis), Suarez, Vasquez, and Valentia that the above statement is made.

109 *Contra Gentes*, Bk. III, chap. 50.

110 As a matter of fact and rightly so, there can be no immediate vision of God as He is the Author of nature without seeing Him as He is the Author of grace; for the Deity is the immediate object of this vision, which actually and implicitly contains both the naturally knowable attributes, and the divine subsistent relations by which the three divine Persons are constituted.

111 *De Deo*, tr. II, disp. I, dub. V, nos. 75, 77. Likewise John of St. Thomas, *De gratia*, disp. XX, a. 1, Solv. obj., no. 5.

112 Denz., no. 1034.

the object of beatitude, and inasmuch as man has a spiritual fellowship with God." [113]

Doubt. Can the possibility of this beatific vision be strictly demonstrated by the natural light of reason? In these latter days some have contended that from Cajetan's time many of the great commentators of St. Thomas, including Bannez, John of St. Thomas, and the Salmanticenses, did not correctly interpret St. Thomas' doctrine about the natural desire to see God's essence, because they did not properly distinguish between the order of possibility and the order of existence or, as we say, between the metaphysical order of intention and the physical order of execution. [114] But having posited this distinction, we should have to say that from this natural desire, inasmuch as it arises from a knowledge of the natural effects of the first Cause, the possibility of the beatific vision can be strictly demonstrated by reason alone, and hence that there is an obediential capacity in our nature of being elevated to the order of grace. Yet this elevation and even the beatific vision must still be regarded as essentially supernatural, inasmuch as, in the order of existence, or in the physical order of execution, they are dependent on God's free and gratuitous good pleasure. And thus, as already stated, it is only in this latter order that this desire is conditional and inefficacious, although in the metaphysical order it is efficacious in demonstrating apodictically the possibility of the beatific vision. [115]

But is it true that from Cajetan's time many commentators of St. Thomas did not correctly interpret his teaching about the natural desire, and that they erred in not admitting the metaphysical demonstrability by reason alone of the possibility of the beatific vision?

We have discussed this question at sufficient length in a recent book, [116] but it seems fitting at this point to explain briefly the fundamental reason for the traditional stand taken by the theologians. This reason may be regarded as the pith or germinal idea of an earlier work, [117] though many of our readers are not sufficiently aware of this fact.

---

[113] *Summa theol.*, Ia IIae, q.109, a.3 ad 1um. See also IIa IIae, q.26, a.3; *De veritate*, q.14, a.2; *in I Cor.*, c.13, lect. 4.

[114] Cf. P. Mag. A. Fernandez, in the periodical *Divus Thomas*, nos. 1, 5, 6.

[115] This last acceptation of the word "efficacious" does not seem to preserve the natural meaning of the words, because the desire is said to be efficacious as regards the attainment of the desired object and not as regards the demonstration of the possibility of this object.

[116] *Le Sens du mystère et le clair-obscur intellectuel*, pp. 176–205.

[117] *De revelatione* (4th ed.).

The present problem resolves itself into this more general question, namely, whether the intrinsic possibility of essentially supernatural mysteries can be strictly demonstrated by reason alone.

1) The question is about their intrinsic possibility or their non-repugnance objectively considered. Thus we may ask whether the Trinity of divine Persons is really possible, extramentally, or really and *in itself* non-repugnant, and not merely so *for us*. What is for *us* non-repugnant, is something whose non-repugnance is urged and defended against those denying it, although it is not positively and apodictically demonstrated.

2) We are concerned here with essentially supernatural mysteries, those that are intrinsically supernatural and entitatively so as regards their substance or essence. Such are the Trinity, the Incarnation, grace and glory. We are not concerned with those that are supernatural only in the mode of their production, such as the resurrection of the dead in whom natural life is supernaturally restored.

3) The reference here is to a metaphysical or apodictic demonstration, and not merely to a very probable argument. The reference is also to a demonstration that is obtained solely by reasoning, or from the natural light alone of reason, which means that it is not dependent on revealed premises either explicitly or even implicitly presupposed. I say, even "implicitly" presupposed.

Moreover, it must be observed that very probable arguments, those proposed by the great doctors of the Church concerning divine truths, may be most profound or most sublime, without being apodictic. And the intellect, either human or angelic, can always continue to see more clearly the force of these arguments, which, however, may not be convincing. These great arguments of congruence compared with those that give us evidence and absolute certainty, are like polygons inscribed in a circle. The number of sides may be increased indefinitely, yet they will never be equal to and be identified with the circumference of the circle.

Such are the most profound arguments of congruence which, taken from the traditional teaching of the doctors of the Church, are advanced in defense of the possibility of the Trinity, the Incarnation, and other mysteries. In heaven we shall see how much truth there is in these arguments of congruence, which even the highest of the angels by his natural powers could always penetrate more deeply, and yet never acquire conviction of evidence in this state.

I. To the question as thus stated we reply according to the traditional teaching of the theologians as follows:

What is supernatural not only as to the mode of its production but also as to its essence, or entitatively, is likewise supernatural as to its knowableness, because truth and being are convertible. This major is a fundamental principle throughout theology, and its denial means the denial of truth and of the supernatural. But the intrinsic possibility of the aforesaid mysteries is the intrinsic possibility of the essentially supernatural. Therefore this possibility is supernatural as to its knowableness, and hence it cannot be apodictically demonstrated by the natural powers alone of any created intellect, either human or angelic, or even any creatable intellect.

The major is evident, for it concerns the essentially supernatural, that which is "far removed from our knowledge" not only in its contingent aspect, like future contingent things of the natural order which depend on God's most free good pleasure (for instance, the hour when this material world will come to an end), or even future miracles (such as the resurrection of the dead), but also in its aspect of intrinsic supernaturalness. There is no doubt that truth and being are convertible. As St. Thomas says: "The true that is in things is convertible with being as to substance (anything is knowable inasmuch as it has being); while the true that is in the intellect is convertible with being, as the manifestation with the manifested." [118] There must be, or course, a proportion between the manifestation and the manifested. Hence what is essentially supernatural can be known formally as such only in a supernatural way (clearly by the beatific vision, obscurely by infused faith, and as virtually revealed by sacred theology). [119]

In other words, what is essentially supernatural cannot be known in a natural way, because there is no necessary and evident connection between it and things of the natural order. If it were so related, then it would become a philosophical truth, as is the case with natural truths about God as the Author of nature. The supernatural mysteries about God properly belong to the order of naturally unknowable truths, for there is no necessary and evident connection between them and things of the natural order. We must include among these not only the Trinity and the Incarnation, but also the mystery of God's eternal life, which is essentially supernatural, since it is a formal participation of His intimate life.

It is indeed true that supernatural mysteries can be known materially by a natural and certain knowledge derived from the signs of divine revelation. In this way the mysteries are known by an acquired faith, which is the way the devil knows them. [120] But

---

[118] *Summa theol.*, Ia, q.16, a.3 ad 1um.
[119] See a.4 of this question; also IIa IIae, q.6, a.1.
[120] *Ibid.*, IIa IIae, q.5, a.2.

apart from revelation and its signs, the mysteries are materially known only as probable, for there is no necessary and evident connection between them and natural things that are naturally knowable.[121]

Neither can it be strictly demonstrated that anything essentially supernatural (such as the beatific vision) is really possible, abstracting from its supernatural formality. In a word, such an object is not necessarily and evidently connected with things of the natural order.[122]

The minor is equally certain, for intrinsic possibility is evidently of the same order as the thing itself that is said to be possible. It is its non-repugnance to existence, not only considered as such by us, but as it is really so in itself.

Therefore the conclusion is that this intrinsic possibility or real non-repugnance, cannot be naturally known, and that it cannot be apodictically proved solely by the natural light of the human intellect or even of the angelic intellect. But, after this truth has been revealed, we are persuaded of this intrinsic possibility, or real non-repugnance, by congruent and even most profound arguments, which can always penetrate more deeply into the mystery; yet the arguments are not such as to become convincing.

Thus Billuart expresses the common opinion among theologians when he says: "That a positive and evident proof can be given that no contradiction is implied in this mystery (of the Trinity), this I deny; that a negative and probable argument can be given, this I concede. This suffices, indeed, so that this mystery cannot be declared impossible, yet not so as to be known as evidently possible." [123] In like manner St. Thomas had said: "We can make use of philosophy in sacred doctrine . . . by defending the faith against those who attack it, either by showing that their statements are false or that they are not convincing." [124] For theology shows that the objections proposed against the possibility of the Trinity, the Incarnation, life eternal, and other mysteries, are not convincing. Thus this possibility is neither disproved nor positively and apodictically proved, but we are reasonably persuaded of the same. This

---

[121] It can indeed be demonstrated by reason alone that there is an order of supernatural truths in God; but then these truths are known only negatively, as naturally unknowable truths. But to prove that the beatific vision is possible (a positive predication), it would have to be positively known and demonstrated that the Deity or the intimate life of God can be directly seen by the created intellect. The subject of this proposition, however, is not positively known by reason alone.

[122] See synopsis at the end of this doubt.

[123] *Cursus theol., De Trinitate,* diss. prooem., a. 4.

[124] *In Boetium, De Trinitate,* q.2, a.3.

possibility is defended against those who deny it, and it is firmly held by faith.

II. This fundamental reason is without difficulty elucidated by examples, if we may be permitted further comment on this disputed point.

1) If the intrinsic possibility of the Trinity were demonstrated by reason alone, then its existence would be apodictically demonstrated, for the Trinity is not a contingent but a necessary truth, and in necessary things from their real possibility the existence of the same is legitimately inferred. This would mean the revival of the error of the semirationalists and of Rosmini, who said: "Provided the mystery of the Trinity has been revealed, its existence can be demonstrated by merely speculative arguments, though they are negative and indirect, so that by such arguments this truth is classed among the philosophical subjects and, like the rest of them, becomes a scientific proposition. If it were denied, the theosophical doctrine of *pure reason* would remain not only incomplete, but also abounding in every respect with absurdities, which would mean its utter extinction." [125]

2) If the real and intrinsic possibility of the Incarnation were demonstrated apodictically by reason alone, then it would be only because of its contingency that the Incarnation would transcend our natural knowledge, as being a future contingent of the natural order that is dependent on God's most free good pleasure, such as is the hour when this material world will come to an end, or even when it came into existence. The Incarnation would no longer be an essentially supernatural mystery; at most it would be a miracle supernatural as to its mode of production, as the resurrection from the dead is, the possibility of which can indeed be strictly demonstrated, inasmuch as God is evidently the Author and Lord of nature, and hence of natural life, which He can miraculously restore. But the Incarnation is concerned not only with the miraculous restitution of natural life, but also with the essentially supernatural life of the Word and the hypostatic union of the same with the human nature.

3) Likewise, if the real possibility of the mystery of eternal life or of the light of glory and of the beatific vision were apodictically demonstrated solely by the light of reason, then the beatific vision and the light of glory required for this would no longer be substantially supernatural, for that which is substantially or essentially supernatural is by this very fact supernaturally knowable inasmuch as truth and being are convertible. These principles are

[125] Denz., no. 1915.

absolutely necessary and absolutely fundamental, and they are not even examined by several of the more modern theologians, who seek to depart from the traditional stand.

If the real possibility of the beatific vision were apodictically proved by the sole light of reason, then this vision and the light of glory would transcend our natural knowledge solely by reason of their contingency, inasmuch as they depend on God's most free good pleasure, like contingent futures of the natural order (such as the last day of the material world); and at most they would be reduced to what is supernatural as to its mode of production, like the resurrection from the dead or the glorification of the body.

Even if, leaving the light of glory out of consideration, the real and intrinsic possibility of the beatific vision were apodictically demonstrated by reason alone, then it would follow necessarily from this that we could deduce the real and intrinsic possibility of the supernatural gifts required for this vision, namely, of those gifts now called by us habitual grace and the light of glory. But the intrinsic possibility of habitual grace cannot be proved by reason alone; for then grace would no longer be essentially supernatural, but only as to the mode of its production, as when the natural life is supernaturally restored to the corpse by the resurrection. That a participation in God's intimate life is possible or that it is communicable by way of participation, cannot be proved by reason alone. The possibility of grace is beyond the scope of demonstration.

Therefore the arguments deduced from reason alone concerning the intrinsic possibility of the beatific vision are indeed very probable, and as such most profound. They can always be more deeply penetrated by the intellect, whether human or angelic, yet they are not convincing, and compared with those arguments that give us evidence and certainty of conviction, they are like the polygon inscribed in a circle, since the number of its sides can always be increased. In fact, if these arguments of congruence were proposed as apodictic, then they would lose their force, since they do not come within the scope of demonstrability, but transcend it. What we are here discussing is indemonstrable because of the excess and not because of the deficiency of its light.

Hence the great commentators of St. Thomas, those who came after Cajetan (such as Bannez, John of St. Thomas, the Salmanticenses), did not have a false conception of St. Thomas' argument, which is founded on the natural desire to see God's essence. It is still true to say that the possibility of the mystery of eternal life is neither disproved nor apodictically proved, but we are reasonably persuaded of the same. It is defended against those who deny it, and it is firmly held by faith.[126]

BRIEF SUMMARY OF THIS REPLY

1) In God, that is said to be essentially supernatural which cannot be known through creatures, because there is no evident and necessary connection between creatures and this object. In God this is "that which is known to Himself and revealed to others." [127] God is not here considered under the aspect of being, but in what intimately and most properly belongs to the notion of the Deity. And St. Thomas shows that the Trinity pertains to this order because "the creative power of God is common to the whole Trinity." [128]

2) In those things extrinsic to God, the essentially supernatural is defined as that which is a formal participation of the Deity or of God's intimate life (such as grace, the infused virtues, the gifts, the light of glory), and there is no evident and necessary connection between creatures and this object. Hence this object cannot be formally known by the natural power of the intellect, but only materially and this in various ways, as is evident from the following synopsis.

[126] Some object that from the natural desire of seeing God, the possibility of the beatific vision is at least indirectly and extrinsically but apodictically proved; for this desire is in transcendental relation to the beatific vision.

Reply. This desire would be in transcendental relation to the beatific vision, if it were a desire resulting either from infused hope or from charity. In created things only the essentially supernatural is transcendentally related to God's intimate life. It is the very definition of the created substantially supernatural. If any natural entity were to be actually in such positive relation to God's intimate life, then grace would not be absolutely necessary, but only required for the easier performance of supernatural acts, as the Pelagians said.

Indeed, this natural desire of seeing God does not terminate formally but only materially in what is objectively supernatural, as was stated above. Otherwise it would be both essentially natural (as originating from nature) and essentially supernatural (as specified by a supernatural object).

That this would mean that the possibility of the beatific vision would be apodictically demonstrated, if the desire were efficacious, let this pass without comment; but the desire (unless the doctrine of Baius be admitted) is conditional and inefficacious. It presupposes two conditions that have not yet been proved, namely, if the elevation be possible and if God will to grant it to us. Therefore this desire, since it presupposes the uncertainty of the possibility of this vision, does not enable us to give an apodictic proof of the same, but it serves as the basis for a probable argument of greater cogency, to be sure, though it has not the force of a demonstration. Reason alone can penetrate the essentially supernatural only by means of probable arguments, for it is beyond the scope of demonstration.

[127] *Summa theol.*, Ia, q.1, a.6; also Vatican Council, Denz., no. 1816.

[128] *Ibid.*, Ia, q.32, a.1.

The essentially supernatural is known
- formally as supernatural
  - perfectly as to its quiddity
    - comprehensively by God alone
    - not comprehensively by the blessed
  - imperfectly
    - by infused faith and the gifts
    - by sacred theology under the guidance of virtual revelation
- materially in a less formal aspect
  - from the signs of revelation, and it is thus known by the devil with the certainty of acquired faith
  - not from revelation
    - *negatively,* and thus is proved the existence of naturally unknowable truths in God
    - *positively,* and thus we are persuaded of the possibility of the beatific vision from the natural desire to see God, the Author of nature

What has been said suffices for the solution of this problem.[129]

SECOND ARTICLE

WHETHER THE ESSENCE OF GOD IS SEEN BY THE
CREATED INTELLECT THROUGH AN IMAGE

State of the question. That the beatific vision is enjoyed by the blessed is now known to be a revealed fact, and we have defended the possibility of this truth. In this question an inquiry must be made into those things that of necessity concur or do not concur in this vision, on the part both of the object seen and of the seer. In other words, on the part of the object seen, is it necessary or at least possible to have a species or similitude of God's essence, and then on the part of the seer, must there be an infused light that fortifies the created intellect?

As regards the similitude on the part of the object seen, St. Thomas, in stating the question at issue, recalls the following text from St. Augustine: "When we know God, some likeness of God is made in us." [130] And he also says that the intellect, like the sensitive faculty, in the act of knowing is informed with the like-

---

[129] This has been fully explained by us elsewhere. Cf. *Revue Thomiste,* March–April, 1936, "La possibilité de la grace est-elle rigoureusement démonstrable?" pp. 194–218. See also *Revue Thomiste,* 1933, pp. 669–88, and *Angelicum,* April, 1936, pp. 241–48.

[130] *De Trinitate,* Bk. IX, chap. 11.

ness of the thing to be known. Thus Aristotle says that in sensible things the object of sense perception is potentially intelligible, then, through the light brought to bear upon it by the active intellect, it becomes actually intelligible in the impressed intelligible species, and finally it is actually understood in the expressed species, or in the word, which is the *medium in which* the nature of the thing understood is understood, such as the nature of a stone or of a plant.

Therefore the question is whether in the beatific vision there is an infused intelligible species in the intellect, and also an expressed species or a mental word.

This was not a question of minor importance for St. Thomas. We read in his life that, when his confrater Aegidius Romanus, after dying, appeared to him by God's permission, St. Thomas asked him the following question: "Do you see God directly?" He received this answer: "As we have heard, so do we see in the city of the Lord of hosts." [131] St. Thomas looked upon this answer as confirming what he considered to be the true interpretation of scriptural texts on this subject, and there is reference to this in the counterargument of this article.

It reads as follows: "On the contrary, Augustine says (*De Trin.*, Bk. XV, chap. 9) that when the Apostle says, 'We see now through a glass, in a dark manner,' by the terms 'glass' and 'in a dark manner' certain similitudes are signified by him, which are accommodated to the vision of God. But to see the essence of God," as St. Thomas adds, "is not an enigmatic or speculative vision, but is, on the contrary, of an opposite kind. Therefore the divine essence is not seen through a similitude."

St. Thomas' conclusion is: God's essence cannot be seen by any created similitude representing the divine essence itself as it really is.

All the disciples of St. Thomas unhesitatingly accept this conclusion, saying that there can be no question either of an impressed or expressed species in the clear vision of God. Or else they say that, according to the imperfect way we conceive it and speak of it, the divine essence takes the place of both the impressed and the expressed species. This terminology is interpreted in a benign sense by the Thomists, but it is faulty; for the impressed and expressed species take, so to speak, the place of the object, as representing it. And therefore to say that the divine essence takes the place of the species, is to say that it acts as substitute for the same. However, this terminology is permissible according to our imperfect mode

131 Ps. 47: 8. The above words are but a slight variation of this text in the Book of Psalms.

of conceiving it, just as we say that God enters into logical relations with creatures.

But St. Thomas' conclusion is not admitted by all theologians. Several, such as Aureolus, Suarez, Vasquez and Valentia, are of the opinion that there is nothing derogatory in admitting the presence of an impressed species in the beatific vision, although such is not actually the case. In fact, Suarez affirms the impossibility of the beatific vision without the utterance of the mental word or the expressed species. A comparison of these opinions with that held by St. Thomas most clearly shows what an exalted notion the Angelic Doctor had of this mystery.

Although St. Thomas' opinion is not *de fide,* it appears to be more in harmony with the definition given by Benedict XII, who declared: "The blessed . . . see the divine essence by direct intuition and face to face, in such wise that nothing created intervenes as an object of vision, but the divine essence presents itself to their immediate gaze, unveiled, clearly, and openly." [132]

This definition does not exclude a created species, because a created species does not function as *an object of vision,* but is the medium *by which* or *in which* the thing seen is reflected. Nevertheless, the concluding words of this definition emphasize the immediateness of this vision.

The question is freely disputed, and it can be solved only in a speculative way. First of all, it must be said that intuitive vision in general does not exclude either an impressed or an expressed species. Thus the sense perception of color is obtained through the impressed species (although St. Thomas differs from Suarez in that he does not admit such through the expressed species). But St. Thomas maintains that the intuitive vision which the angel has of his own essence is obtained through the expressed species or the mental word. This is clearly enough affirmed by him in the following passage: "(The angel) knows itself by itself. Yet the life of angels does not reach the highest degree of perfection because, though the intelligible species is altogether within them, it is not their very substance, because in them to understand and to be are not the same thing." [133] This means to say that the angel's essence is indeed of itself *intelligible,* not merely potentially (like the essence of a stone), but actually, and so it is understood without an impressed species. However, it is not actually understood, because the angel's essence is not its act of understanding, and hence not itself understood. On the contrary, God's essence is His existence, and Himself understood, and is of Himself actually understood. Hence, to know

132 Denz., no. 530.
133 *Contra Gentes,* Bk. IV, chap. 11, § 1.

Himself, as will be stated farther on,[134] God is not in need, like the angel, of the accidental mental word. But from revelation it is known for certain that God the Father, not as denoting indigence, but by reason of His infinite fecundity, generates the *Word that is not accidental, but substantial.*

This substantial Word is not only "God understood" but "true God" of true God, "because the natural being of God is not distinct from His act of understanding (and its being understood). Hence it is said (John 1: 1): *The Word was God.* . . . (Thus) this shows that the divine Word is not merely an intelligible species, as our word is, but that it is, indeed, a real and subsistent being. On the contrary, man's word (concept of himself) cannot be called a man simply, but only with a qualification; namely, a man understood. Hence this statement is false: The word is a man; whereas this is true: The Word was God," [135] as St. Thomas very well explains in this passage.

Thus the state of the question clearly is this: by divine revelation we know indeed that the beatific vision terminates in the substantial Word, who is "the brightness of His glory and the figure of His substance." [136] But the question is whether there is or can be an accidental word in this vision.

It must be observed that the accidental word is not excluded from the intuitive vision, inasmuch as it is intuitive; for the angel's knowledge of himself is not abstractive but intuitive, and yet it is acquired by means of the accidental word, which is immediately received from the presence of the thing known. Neither is the impressed species excluded from intuitive vision, inasmuch as it is intuitive; for I intuitively see the flower, through the impressed species; but intuitive knowledge postulates that the species is immediately received from the presence of the thing known.

On the contrary, in the case of abstractive knowledge the species is not immediately received from the thing known, but from something resulting from it. Thus we have abstractive knowledge of God as reflected in creatures, and also of the essences of sensible things from the likeness of sensible qualities. Thus we have descriptive knowledge of the essence of the lion, the rose, or the lily, but we do not directly see the specific difference of the lion through the species that would be immediately received in the intellect from the very essence of the lion. The state of the question being thus precisely determined, let us see what St. Thomas says in the argumentative part of the article.

---

[134] *Summa theol.,* Ia, q.14, a.4.

[135] *Contra Gentes,* Bk. IV, chap. 11, § 4.

[136] Heb. 1: 3. Thus the general saying among theologians that the blessed see all things *in the Word.*

It consists of three parts: (1) it determines what is required both for sensible and for intellectual vision; (2) it establishes that a similitude is required on the part of the visual faculty for the vision of God, namely, a reinforcing light; (3) it is proved that God's essence cannot be seen by any created similitude on the part of the object seen.

1) Two things are required for sensible and for intellectual vision, namely, power of sight and union of the thing seen with the sight. Thus the similitude of the stone is in the eye, whereby the vision is made actual. But, as will be stated farther on,[137] the angel sees himself through his essence, without an impressed species.

2) To see God there must be some similitude of God on the part of the visual faculty. Now indeed, the intellective power is a certain intelligible light that is derived from God, the first intellect; but in addition to this, an infused light is required that reinforces the intellect, and this is called the light of glory, as will be more clearly explained in the fifth article. Mention of this is made here to explain St. John's statement quoted in the first difficulty: "We know that, when He shall appear, we shall be like to Him, because we shall see Him as He is." [138] As it is said in the reply to this first objection, "that authority speaks of the similitude which is caused by participation of the light of glory." The light of glory is analogically called a light inasmuch as it serves to show the reinforced light given to the intellect.

3) On the part of the object seen, God's essence cannot be seen by any created similitude. Three proofs are given for this principal conclusion: (1) in that God is of a higher order of immateriality; (2) in that God both entitatively and intellectually is His own existence; (3) in that the Deity is uncircumscribed.

First reason. It is reduced to this: The difference between the created and the uncreated is greater than that between the divers orders of created things. But the reality of a higher order, for example, the angelic nature, is not seen as it is in itself by a similitude of a lower order, for example, by a sensible species, nor even by an intelligible species abstracted from sensible things. Therefore much less can God's essence be seen by any created species whatever.[139]

It must be observed that in the minor there is no mention of an inferior species, but of a species of an inferior order; for the lower

---

137 *Summa theol.,* Ia, q. 56, a. 1.

138 I John 3: 2.

139 This is unhesitatingly affirmed by St. Thomas, whereas, on the contrary, several theologians of later times, as we shall see, say that the created species is possible in the beatific vision, though it is superfluous. In fact, the wish of Suarez is that there actually be such a species. St. Thomas clearly excludes it.

angel is able to see the higher angel by an inferior species of the same order. Yet in this case his knowledge of the higher is incomplete.

The second reason is that God's essence is His own very existence.[140] But no created form can be its own existence. Therefore no created form can be the similitude representing God's essence, as it is in itself. As will at once be stated in the solution of the objections, the major is to be understood as meaning that God alone is His existence both entitatively and intellectually. In other words, God alone is pure act in every respect; hence He alone is His intellection. On the contrary, the representative created species, however perfect it may be, cannot be its own subsistent intellection, because it is intelligible by participation.[141]

The third reason is that the Deity is uncircumscribed, containing supereminently in itself whatever can be signified or understood by the created intellect, namely, all absolutely simple perfections. But every created form (or idea) is determined according to some aspect of wisdom or of power or of being itself. Therefore God cannot be seen as He really is by any created species.

This third reason shows pre-eminently that the Deity in a certain way transcends being, unity, truth . . . , in that it contains formally and eminently all absolutely simple perfections, which are naturally participable. But the Deity as such, or God's intimate life, is not naturally participable, nor is it naturally knowable; for it is participated in only by grace, which is properly defined as the participation of the divine nature according to the following text: "He hath given us most great and precious promises, that by these you may be made partakers of the divine nature." [142]

In the reply to the third objection it is said that "the divine essence is existence itself . . . and is united to the created intellect (not only as the object actually intelligible, but as) actually understood, making (our) intellect in act by and of itself." This is practically what the Thomists mean when they state that the divine essence takes the place of the impressed and expressed species. But, as we have observed, this statement is to be accepted in accordance with our imperfect mode of understanding and speech; for the species substitutes for the object, and the Deity, strictly speaking, does not function as its substitute. It is, however, truer to say that the vicarious similitude of the object is neither necessary nor even possible when the object is present not only as actually intelligible,

140 *Summa theol.*, Ia, q.3, a.4.
141 *Ibid.*, Ia, q.3, a.4 ad 3um.
142 II Pet. 1: 4.

but as actually understood. Thus God is clearly seen, inasmuch as He Himself alone is His intellection and Himself as understood.

SOLUTION OF OBJECTIONS

Aureolus objected to the aforesaid reasons, and said that all are at fault since they do not distinguish between the species as an entity and the species as a representation. But, although the species as an entity is but a finite accident, why as a representation could it not intentionally manifest God's essence as it really is? In fact, the species of the stone, although it is an accident, represents the substance of the stone; likewise the species of the angel represents the substance of the angel.

In reply to this we say with Cajetan that it is a question of the species formally as such, namely, according to its intentional or representative existence, but not materially, according to its entitative existence. It is for this reason that St. Thomas calls it a similitude. Therefore it is correctly affirmed in the first reason that a thing of the higher order (for example, the angelic nature) cannot be seen as it really is by a species or similitude of a lower order (for example, by an idea abstracted from sensible things). Hence the infused created species, which is not of the same degree of immateriality or of actuality in intelligible being as the Deity itself, cannot be represented as it really is by such species.

The affirmation in the second reason is likewise correct, when it is stated that the divine essence is its existence, not only in the entitative order but also in the intelligible order, for it is only God who is His intellection and Himself as understood. But no created similitude, however perfect it may be, is its own intellection; but every similitude is intelligible by limited participation. Only God is His own subsistent intellection, an eternally existing, so to speak, intellectual flash. Therefore no infused created similitude can be God either entitatively or intelligibly. By the beatific vision, however, the intellect of the blessed in a certain way, namely, intentionally, becomes God, as Cajetan says, and it cannot become so by any created species.

This means to say that there is no distinction between the real and the ideal order in the Deity. Only in God are these two orders identical, since He alone is pure act both entitatively and intellectually. But the purpose of Hegel's idealism was to identify these two orders, inasmuch as he said that "everything intelligible is real," which is panlogism. In truth, this identification is to be found only in God, not in possible things that are known only as possible in God without actually existing as realities, and not in existing creatures, which truly are actually existing realities, though they are not their own intellection, nor themselves understood. Thus the essence of a stone or of wood is only potentially intelligible in itself, and the essence of the angel is indeed actually intelligible in itself, yet it is not of itself actually understood; it alone is its substantial intellection and itself understood.

Wherefore St. Thomas rejects St. Anselm's argument, saying: "God is His own existence. Now because we do not know the essence of God, the proposition is not self-evident to us, but needs to be demonstrated by things that are more known to us though less known in their nature, namely, by effects." [143] On the contrary, the blessed, in knowing God's essence, see that God necessarily and actively exists. We see a priori only this, namely, that, if God exists, He is self-existent; but the blessed see that God necessarily exists, and that the denial of His actual existence would be the denial of the Deity itself. Hence the proposition "God is," is self-evident to them since the transition from ideal being to real being is unwarranted.

Therefore the aforesaid Thomistic refutation of St. Anselm's argument is worthless if we admit the presence of a created species in the beatific vision. For St. Thomas holds that if one were to admit the presence of this created species, God would, indeed, be known as in fact actually existing, just as the archangel Michael clearly seen would be known as actually existing, but by this species it would not be known that God necessarily and actually exists. St. Thomas holds that, for this proposition to be self-evident to us, our intellect must have immediate knowledge of the Deity without the intervention of a created species. In other words, all that the created species would represent to us would be either that God is self-existent if He exists, or that God in fact exists, but not that God is actually self-existent.

As Cajetan remarks,[144] the expressed species is excluded for the same reason. For just as the impressed species acts as the *means by which*, namely, as the principle determining the intellect to elicit the act of understanding some particular object, so the expressed species or the mental word is *that in which* we understand the nature of the thing understood. Because of the reasons just given, no created species can thus represent the self-subsisting Intellection as it really is; for every created species is intelligible by participation, and the difference between it and the self-subsistent intellection is far greater than that between the sun and its ray; and just

143 *Summa theol.*, Ia, q.2, a.1.
144 *Com. in Iam*, q.2, a.1, no. 13.

as he who would see only the sun's ray would not see the sun itself, so he who would see only that which is expressed in the
highest infused species, would not in the strict sense see God.

Corollary. Wherefore it is commonly held that the extraordinary
intellectual visions of the most Holy Trinity still pertain to the
order of faith; for they do not give intrinsic evidence of the mystery
of the Trinity, and it is not sufficiently clear that God would cease
to be such if He were not the triune God. On the contrary, this
would be made manifest if one were to receive the beatific vision
by way of a transient act, which St. Augustine and St. Thomas believed that St. Paul received when rapt in ecstasy.

All that is expressed by these above-mentioned intellectual visions
of the most Holy Trinity is the idea of the fittingness of this mystery, inasmuch as, for instance, good is essentially diffusive of
itself; and the higher the nature, the more intimate and more
complete is this self-diffusiveness, so that the Father communicates
to the Son and to the Holy Spirit the whole of His nature without
any division or multiplication of the same.

Suarez proposes another objection. It is his opinion that, just as
there can be a similitude on the part of the seer, namely, the light
of glory, reinforcing the intellect, so also there can be a similitude
on the part of the object seen, consisting in the expressed word.

We reply with John of St. Thomas that the light reinforcing the
intellect of the seer is a similitude by way of a tendency, and that
which tends is not actually that toward which it tends; whereas,
contrary to this, the objective species must actually have the form
of the thing represented; in fact, it must be in its representative
existence, the object itself. Therefore, to represent the object as
this really is, it must be of the same order of immateriality and of
the same actuality in the intelligible order. For this reason, as
already stated, the species abstracted from sensible things cannot
manifest the angel as he really is, nor can the created species represent the Deity as it really is. Thus the negative conclusion is established, namely, that there can be neither an impressed nor an
expressed species in the beatific vision, because the created species,
however perfect it may be, cannot represent God or the self-subsisting Intellection as He really is.

First doubt. Does the divine essence take the place of the impressed and expressed species in the divine essence?

The Thomists reply in the affirmative, although this is but an
imperfect way of expressing it, and is not strictly applicable. For,
if we take care to note that the species substitutes for the object,
then the Deity cannot properly be said to take the place of this
substitute. But the theologians speak in this way according to the

imperfect manner of our intellectual perception, just as we speak of God's relation to creatures, which is not a real but a logical relation.

This commonly held opinion among the Thomists is equivalently expressed in many passages of St. Thomas' works. Thus, in this question he says: "When any created intellect sees the essence of God, the essence of God itself becomes the intelligible form of the intellect." [145] Similarly he says: "The divine essence must be united to the created intellect as an intelligible species," [146] so, then, instead of the impressed species. In this article, however, he says: "The divine essence is united to the created intellect, as the object actually understood, making the intellect in act by and of itself." [147] This means instead of the expressed species. The reasons for this assertion are those given in the body of the article to show that God cannot be seen as He really is by a created species.

Moreover, it must be noted that several doctors, who see no repugnance in admitting a created species for the beatific vision, yet maintain that *de facto* it is not present, because it is superfluous. And it is thus proved to be superfluous for both the impressed and the expressed species.

1) The impressed species is required either when the object is absent, or when it is not directly present to the intellect or is not sufficiently intelligible because of its immateriality. But the object of the beatific vision, namely, God, essentially exists, is already intimately present to any created intellect whatever, as preserving it in being, and is the maximum in intelligibility, because it is the maximum in immateriality. Therefore at least the impressed species is superfluous. It suffices that the created intellect be elevated and strengthened by the light of glory to see God's essence, which is already intimately present to it as preserving it in being. Just as the bat cannot see the sun, so in our present state we cannot see God because of His dazzling brilliance. We have a confirmation of this in the angel, who intuitively sees his own essence without an impressed species, for the reason that his essence exists, is in him, and is of itself actually intelligible.

2) The expressed species is required so that the object may be actually understood and be present in the intellect in its representative form. But the divine essence is most pure act in the intelligible order, i.e., it is not only actually intelligible, but actually understood, and, as St. Thomas says, "is united to the created intellect, as the object actually understood making the intellect in

---

[145] Cf. a.5.
[146] *Contra Gentes*, Bk. III, chap. 53.
[147] Cf. ad 3um.

act by and of itself." [148] It is also intimately present in it. Therefore the expressed species is at least superfluous. Thus there will
be an immediate and complete transforming union; and so it is
apparent that the inchoate union of which the mystics speak, accompanied by the ardent desire for the beatific vision, is the normal way that leads to eternal life.

But Suarez objects that there must be a created species, because
there must be a terminus assigned to the vision produced by it.

In reply to this the Thomists say that the concept of an immanent
act does not include that it should produce its effect, although this
may often be the case. But the beatific vision is an immanent act.
Therefore it is not of the essence of the beatific vision that it
should produce its effect. This reply has its foundation in the distinction between immanent and transitive actions. The transitive
action, indeed, which properly belongs to the category of action,
of which passion is the counterpart, is for the perfection of the
patient, and thus it necessarily produces the terminus as its effect.
Contrary to this, the immanent action is for the perfection of the
agent in which it remains, and it formally belongs to the category
of quality, not of action.

Therefore, when we contemplate the nature of anything already
expressed in the word, this is purely intellection and is no longer
a case of the utterance or production of the word. Similarly, in the
Trinity the three Persons understand by one and the same essential
intellection; only the Father utters, or generates the Word. Hence
the created accidental word is at least superfluous in the beatific
vision. The beatific vision terminates in the uncreated substantial
Word, and thus the blessed are said to see all things in the Word.

Not only is the created accidental word superfluous, but, as we
have stated, it is also repugnant. For, if there can be no impressed
species of such perfection and immateriality as to represent God as
He really is, then a fortiori there can be no created expressed
species, since this must be more perfect than the impressed species,
for in the expressed species the object must be present not only
as actually intelligible, but as actually understood.

Second doubt. How can the divine essence, without denoting
imperfection, take the place of the impressed and expressed species?

The difficulty is that this seems to imply imperfection, and for
two reasons. (1) For the created intellect must be informed by the
impressed species so as to enable it to elicit the determinate act
of seeing such object. But the divine essence cannot be the informing form, since thus the divine essence would form a compound
with the other, as being a part; and the part is less perfect than the

---

[148] Cf. *ibid.*

whole. (2) Because if the divine essence were to contribute to this act of seeing as the impressed species, then it would be subordinated to the created intellective faculty, from which this very act derives its being and vitality. Moreover, if the divine essence were to take the place of the impressed species, it would be of the nature of a *first act,* which is less perfect than the second act.

In reply to this first difficulty we say with Cajetan and John of St. Thomas that the species, taken not in its material sense as an inhering accident, but formally as a species, or as a similitude of the object, does not inform the intellect by inhering in it, does not inform the intellective faculty by constituting with it some third entity in the physical order; but this species informs the faculty objectively, so that the faculty becomes intentionally the object itself in first actuality. For as Aristotle says: "The soul is in a sense all things," [149] which means that the knower is in a sense the thing known, or what is other than itself. Hence Averroes was right in furthermore remarking that "a greater unity is effected between the knower and the known than between matter and form"; for matter is not form, but receives this as its own, and constitutes with it a third entity, namely, a composite, which is more perfect than its essential parts. On the other hand, the knower is intentionally the thing known, or is the form of the thing known, for it does not receive this form as its own but as the form of the other, as will be stated farther on. [150] Therefore the divine essence can function as the impressed species. To do so it does not have to inform the created intellect entitatively, constituting with it a third entity or a composite. All that is needed is for it to draw the created intellect into a participation of its intelligible being, and thus its function is not to inform but to terminate, somewhat as in the substantial order the incarnate Word terminates the human nature of Christ, which it does not inform. For just as in the incarnation the Word does not constitute with the human nature a third entity or a more perfect compound; that is, just as the Word is not a part of any composite and hence something less perfect, so the clear vision of God's essence does not constitute a third entity or compound with the created intellect, but only terminates it and by so doing gives it the greatest of perfection without being itself perfected. Just as the human nature in Christ is drawn into a close union with the divine being, so in the beatific vision the created intellect is attracted to the divine object.

We detect another remote analogy to this union inasmuch as number is terminated by the last unit, or inasmuch as two lines

---

[149] *De anima,* Bk. III, chap. 8.
[150] *Summa theol.,* Ia, q. 14, a. 1.

mutually terminate in the apex of the triangle. Cajetan remarks: "We must preserve intact the principle that God is by nature prior to the intellect when it sees God, and yet it is not that the intellect knows God intentionally and afterward sees Him." [151] What he means is this: The intellect must of necessity be God intentionally but not indeed entitatively, just as the knower is the thing known in first actuality, before it is known in second actuality. Such is the common opinion among the Thomists. This is the complete transforming union.[152]

Francis Silvester (Ferrariensis), as Billuart observes,[153] does not admit that the intellect is God intentionally in the order of intelligible being; his contention is that the union of the object with the intellect results in a third entity distinct from each. But this opinion of Francis Silvester seems to be not so profound a view, and to be less in agreement with the teaching of Aristotle and St. Thomas. Moreover, it does not appear to be a sufficient answer to the objection.

Cajetan seems to give a more profound explanation of the intimate union of the created intellect with God clearly seen in the intelligible order, without any pantheistic confusion resulting therefrom, since he appeals to the infinite distinction between the two in the entitative order. In fact, this infinite distinction persists between the two natures that are most intimately united in the one Person of Christ.

Nevertheless, as we stated in the commentary on the first article, as reason cannot prove conclusively the possibility of the Incarnation, so it cannot prove the possibility of the beatific vision. This means that it cannot be conclusively proved by reason that no imperfection is implied for the divine essence to perfect the created intellect by actually terminating it. We are indeed most profoundly persuaded of this, but it cannot be conclusively proved. For the supernatural mysteries are neither proved nor disproved, but they are defended; and there are solid grounds persuading us of their fitness, and either their existence or their possibility is firmly held by faith, which is essentially supernatural. What is essentially supernatural is supernaturally knowable, because truth and being are convertible. This point was not so clearly presented in the first article of this question.

[151] *Com. in Iam*, q.12, a.2, no. 15.

[152] Thus we have absolute confirmation of the thesis that the spiritual marriage or the inchoated transforming union is in this life the culmination of the normal way leading to eternal life, and that it likewise includes an ardent desire of seeing God's essence. Evidently this ardent desire is a prerequisite for this vision, either here on earth or in purgatory.

[153] Art. VII, Solv. obj.

As to this second difficulty, however, it must be said that the impressed species concurs with the faculty in the eliciting of the act, but it is not subordinated to the faculty, because it is not related to the faculty as an inferior instrument to the principal cause, but the purpose of this species is to give greater perfection to the faculty and determine it to elicit its act; hence it is truer to say that the species subordinates the faculty to itself. Thus the divine essence can take the place of the impressed species.

Finally, in this process the divine essence is not of the nature of a first actuality, which is less perfect than the second actuality, for it concurs as the principle by means of which the vision is effected, to the exclusion of all imperfections, as Cajetan observes. It constitutes, indeed, the created intellect in first actuality, but it is not itself of the nature of a first actuality. In other words, the pure act supplies the formality of the impressed species, but not its potentiality, because it supplies to the exclusion of all imperfections. Hence it is not subordinated either to the created intellect or to the created intellection.

Contrary to this, the divine essence can in no way take the place of the light of glory, because this latter functions on the part of the intellective faculty, informing it and constituting with it a third entity, or a composite that is more perfect than its parts. Unjustifiable, therefore, was the assertion of some, such as Master Francis of Good Hope and John of Ripa, who said that the blessed see God by His uncreated vision that is communicated to them. This cannot be, because the beatific vision is a vital act, and every vital act comes essentially from an intrinsic principle of the living being.

Thus we have sufficiently explained why there can be no created species in the beatific vision, and why the divine essence takes the place of both the impressed and the expressed species.

THIRD ARTICLE

WHETHER THE ESSENCE OF GOD CAN BE SEEN
WITH BODILY EYES

State of the question. The purpose of this article is to explain certain metaphorical expressions of Holy Scripture, such as: "In my flesh I shall see . . . God." [154] It was formerly said by some Catholics that God can be seen not by the bodily eye, but by the spiritualized

---

[154] Job 19: 26.

eye in its glorified state. So said Master Francis of Good Hope. Valentia considered this a probable opinion.

St. Thomas replies to this as follows: "It is impossible for God to be seen by the sense of sight or by any other faculty of the sensitive power." This opinion thus formulated by St. Thomas is the common one.

Although this conclusion is not explicitly defined to be of faith, yet it is a most certain truth; for its contradictory implies an error that is repugnant to the faith since it means that God is corporeal. There is foundation for this in several passages of Holy Scripture. Thus we read that "God inhabiteth light inaccessible, whom no man hath seen nor can see." [155] Thus God is declared to be "invisible." [156] Also we have: "No man hath seen God at any time." [157]

The argument from reason is as follows: The act of any sensitive faculty, since it is the act of a corporeal organ, cannot go beyond corporeal things; but God is incorporeal; therefore He cannot be seen by the sense or the imagination, but only by the intellect. Hence when Holy Scripture says that God is seen, this means that He is seen by the eye of the mind, but not of the body.[158]

Reply to second objection. If it is stated that we see the life of another living person, this is because life is accidentally sensible, and the object of sense perception is apprehended by the intellect immediately on its being presented. Hence St. Thomas says at the end of this reply: "But that the divine presence is known by the intellect immediately on the sight of corporeal things and through them, happens from two causes, namely, from the perspicacity of the intellect, and from the refulgence of the divine glory infused into the body after its renovation."

Reply to third objection. "The essence of God is not seen in a vision of the imagination; but the imagination receives some form representing God according to some mode of similitude."

In fact, it is impossible for the sensitive faculty to be elevated to see God, for it is impossible for any faculty to be referred to what is beyond the scope or extent of its adequate object. But God, since He is a pure spirit, is not included within the scope and extent of the adequate object of the sensitive faculty, for this object is something corporeal and sensible, such as color, sound, smell.

To deny this is to confound the sensitive faculty with the intellective. If the created intellect can be elevated to see God, this is

[155] I Tim. 6: 16.
[156] *Ibid.*, 1: 17.
[157] John 1: 18.
[158] Cf. ad 1um.

because God, although He transcends its proportionate object
(which for our intellect is the essence of material things), does not
transcend its adequate object, which is *being* according to all that
is implied by the term. The Deity is eminently and formally being,
and being in all its purity exists only in the Deity, and cannot be
seen without the Deity itself being seen.

From this it is clear that there is a vast difference between intellect and sense. And thus it is evident that the more material a
faculty is the more restricted is its range, because it is limited by
matter. It is only the intellect, at least as such if not as human,
which by reason of its absolute immateriality can be directed to
intelligible being of any kind. We are at least persuaded of this,
and it cannot be disproved.

Objection. Natural water in baptism, spiritually elevated as it is,
produces grace. Therefore the sense of sight can in like manner be
raised to see God.

Reply. There is no comparison. For water is merely the efficient
instrument, which acts through the power transmitted to it by the
principal agent, who is God. On the contrary, sight is the vital
and principal cause of seeing, and the faculty elicits the act of seeing by its own power. Hence its act cannot go beyond the scope
of its adequate object.

Nor can the bodily eye see God by a spiritual vision that is imparted to it, because seeing, since it is a vital act, must of necessity
come from an intrinsic principle. But spiritual sight is intellection,
and this cannot proceed from the eye as from an intrinsic principle.
Hence this intellectual sight would be a sort of extrinsic addition,
and the eye itself would not see by it; for the corporeal eye can
no more understand than can a stone or a piece of wood.

Final objection. There is a greater difference between the angel
and God than between the corporeal eye and the angel. But the
angel can see God supernaturally. Therefore the corporeal eye can
see the pure spirit supernaturally.

Reply. I distinguish the major. That there is a greater difference
entitatively between the angel and God than between the corporeal
eye and the angel, this I concede; that the difference is greater objectively, this I deny; or, in the order of being, I concede the major;
in the cognitive order, I deny the major; for, since God is true
and intelligible being, He is included in the adequate object of
both the angelic and the human intellects. But the angel, being
immaterial, cannot be included in the object of sense perception.[159]

[159] Cf. ad 1um et ad 3um.

WHETHER ANY CREATED INTELLECT BY ITS NATURAL POWERS CAN SEE THE DIVINE ESSENCE

State of the question. In the title "by its natural powers" denotes the sufficient cause. But nature is the radical and essential principle of operation. Therefore the question concerns the possibility of the created intellect's seeing God by its real and natural power, without being supernaturally elevated for this end. It is supposed from the first article that the created intellect can be raised to see the divine essence.

The principal difficulty is declared in the beginning of the article in the third objection, which is as follows: corporeal sense cannot be raised up to understand incorporeal substance, because such understanding is above its nature. Therefore, if to see the essence of God is above the nature of every created intellect, it follows that no created intellect can be elevated for this vision.

The answer is: It is impossible for any created intellect to see the essence of God, unless the intellect is supernaturally elevated for the vision.

1) This conclusion is *de fide,* and is defined as such in the Council of Vienne, in which the following proposition of the Beghards was condemned: "The soul does not need the light of glory elevating it to see God and enjoy Him in this blessed state." [160] This was, indeed, already implicitly defined against the Pelagians and Semipelagians, against whom the Church on several occasions asserted than man cannot by his natural powers merit eternal life, which is supernatural.[161]

The same was declared against Baius.[162] Likewise the Vatican Council declared: "If anyone shall say that man cannot be raised by divine power to a higher than natural knowledge and perfection, but can and should, by a continuous progress, attain at length of himself to the possession of all that is true and good; let him be anathema." [163] The Council also says: "There is a twofold order of knowledge, distinct both in principle and in object . . . ; in object because, besides those things to which natural reason can attain, there are proposed to our belief mysteries hidden in God, which, unless divinely revealed, cannot be known. . . . For the

---

[160] Denz., no. 475.
[161] *Ibid.,* nos. 176–200.
[162] *Ibid.,* no. 1021.
[163] *Ibid.,* no. 1808.

divine mysteries by their own nature so far transcend the created intelligence that, even when delivered by revelation and received by faith, they remain covered with a veil of faith itself, and shrouded in a certain degree of darkness, so long as we are pilgrims in this mortal life, not yet with God." [164]

From this definition it is clear that the supernatural mysteries transcend the created intellect, not only because of God's free decree, but by their very nature; that is, they are *essentially* supernatural, and not only *de facto* supernatural. But the contrary would be the case if God could give the light of glory to the created intellect as a natural property.

The following condemned proposition of Rosmini must also be noted: "God is the object of the beatific vision inasmuch as He is the author of *ad extra* works." [165] The ontologists likewise were condemned, because they did not sufficiently maintain the distinction between the two orders, for they said: "The immediate and at least habitual knowledge of God is so essential to the human intellect, that without it nothing can be known." [166]

This truth of the faith is equivalently expressed, although not so clearly, in several texts of Holy Scripture. Thus we read: "No one knoweth the Son but the Father; neither doth anyone know the Father but the Son, and he to whom it shall please the Son to reveal Him." [167] But if the created intellect by its natural powers could see God's essence, it could also see His paternity and filiation, which are not really distinct from it. St. Paul also says: "Eye hath not seen, nor ear heard, neither hath it entered into the heart of man, what things God hath prepared for them that love Him." [168] In like manner he says: "The grace of God, life everlasting." [169] But eternal life is the vision itself of God in accordance with the following text: "This is eternal life: that they may know Thee, the only true God." [170] The Greek and Latin Fathers, commenting on the aforesaid texts of Holy Scripture, on several occasions affirmed the impossibility of any creature's seeing God by its natural powers.[171]

2) Proof from reason. A careful reading of the argumentative part of this article of St. Thomas enables us to distinguish with Cajetan five consequences. But his argument can be expressed more

[164] *Ibid.*, nos. 1795 f.
[165] *Ibid.*, no. 1928.
[166] *Ibid.*, no. 1659.
[167] Matt. 11: 27.
[168] I Cor. 2: 9.
[169] Rom. 6: 23.
[170] John 17: 3.
[171] Cf. Rouet de Journel, *Enchiridion patristicum*, no. 105; also nos. 236, 451 f., 747, 913, 986, 1075, 1106, 1123, 1126, 1161, 2150.

simply by the following syllogism: Since the norm for knowledge is that it be according as the thing known is in the knower, according to the mode of immateriality of the nature of the knower, then the object whose mode of immateriality exceeds the mode of immateriality of the nature of the created intellect cannot be naturally known as it really is by this intellect; but God is such an object; therefore God cannot be naturally known as He really is by the created intellect, but only as it is elevated by grace.

The major has its foundation in the principle that knowledge is according as the thing known is present immaterially in the knower, according to the nature of the knower. But the more immaterial a cognitive faculty is the more universal is its knowledge.[172] This is evident by inductive reasoning in the cases of sensation and intellection. Whereas plants, because of their materiality, do not know, color is known by the sense of sight inasmuch as the similitude of color is in some way immaterially present in the sense of sight; [173] for, as Aristotle says, the sense is cognitive because it is capable of receiving species separated from matter.[174] But the intellect is all the more cognitive, because it is more separated from matter. Thus it knows not only sensible qualities, but the nature of sensible things. Hence the object, whose mode of immateriality exceeds the immaterial mode of the nature of the knower, cannot be known as this really is by it. Thus it is natural for our intellect, united as it is with the body, to see intelligible things only in the mirror of sensible things.

The minor is proved, because God is not only absolutely immaterial, but is His own existence, that is, He is pure act both in the existential and in the intellectual orders, is the self-subsisting Being. This will be more clearly explained in a subsequent article.[175] On the other hand, our intellect, although immaterial, is directly united to the body, because it is the lowest type of intellect, whose proportionate object is the least in the intelligible order, namely, the intelligible being of sensible things, and for this knowledge it has need of the senses. Thus, as will be more clearly stated farther on,[176] it is because of its debility that our intellect needs the aid of the senses.

But it is the merely immaterial essence of the angel, which is not his existence, that constitutes the proportionate object of the angelic

---

172 Cf. *Summa theol.*, Ia, q. 14, a. 1.

173 However, the soul of the irrational animal and its sensitive faculties, although they are not its body, intrinsically depend on the body, and the visual faculty depends on its organ of sight.

174 Cf. *De anima*, Bk. II, chap. 12; Bk. III, chaps. 4, 8.

175 *Summa theol.*, Ia, q. 14, a. 1.

176 *Ibid.*, q. 76, a. 5.

intellect. Therefore the mode of immateriality of the created and creatable intellect is a mode of essence that is not its own existence or its own intellection. Only God is in the highest degree of immateriality, and He thus absolutely transcends the mode of immateriality of any created intellect whatever. Hence God cannot be naturally known by the intellect as He really is.

The doctrine of this article may be expressed as follows: the object of the intellect is being, and the intellect is predicated analogically of the created intellect and of the uncreated intellect, just as being is so predicated of created being and of the uncreated being. Thus we may write:

$$\text{Intellect} \begin{cases} \text{divine;} & \text{its proper object:} & \text{divine essence} \\ \text{angelic;} & \text{its proper object:} & \text{angelic essence} \\ \text{human;} & \text{its proper object:} & \text{essence of material things} \end{cases} \Bigg\} \text{ being}$$

This means that the proper object of our intellect is the essence of material things. Thus it knows spiritual things in the mirror of sensible things. However, its correspondingly adequate object, not as it is strictly a human intellect, but as it is an intellect, is *being* in the widest sense of the term. This point will become increasingly evident from the explanation of the reply to the third objection.

Objection. Absolute immateriality does not admit of different degrees; but every intellect, even the human intellect, is as such absolutely immaterial; therefore there is no foundation for the above assertion.

Reply. That the exclusion of matter does not admit of different degrees, this I concede; that there are not different degrees of immateriality with reference to pure act, this I deny. Thus all the degrees of certitude exclude the fear of error, and yet there is certainly a distinction between these degrees as regards the firmness of assent, according as they are immediately referred back to first principles, that is, according as they are either without or with the intermediary of the senses and the testimony of men. Thus there is a distinction between metaphysical, physical, and moral certitudes.

Reply to first objection. The angel has a natural knowledge of God as mirrored in his essence; but he has not immediate knowledge of God as He really is.

Reply to second objection. Thus the angel, although he is a pure spirit, is most defective compared with God, because he is not his own existence.

THE ADEQUATE OBJECT OF OUR INTELLECT

The reply to the third objection solves the principal difficulty already presented in the beginning of the article, for it states: "The sense of sight, as being altogether material (being intrinsically dependent on the organism), cannot be raised up to immateriality. But our intellect, or the angelic intellect, inasmuch as it is elevated above matter (since it is not intrinsically dependent on a corporeal organism), can be raised up above its own nature to a higher level by grace." This means that it can be elevated to know any intelligible being whatever, even the highest. At least this cannot be disproved. In fact, there is proof of the possibility of this elevation, and this proof confirms what was said in the first article concerning the natural and inefficacious desire of seeing the essence of God.

St. Thomas says in this same reply: "The proof is, that the created intellect, although it naturally knows the concrete in any nature, still is able to separate that existence by its intellect, since it knows that the thing itself is one thing, and its existence is another. . . . (This proves) that it can by grace be raised up to know separate subsisting substance (as this really is)."

In other words, our intellect not only knows the nature of sensible things, and spiritual things in the mirror of sensible things, but it knows being itself as such. Therefore we can distinguish between its proper object, which is the essence of material things, and its adequate and extensive object, which is being in the widest sense of the term.

But God clearly seen comes under being in the widest sense of the term, because being in the most pure state of pure act is found only in the Deity, and cannot be seen in this most pure state, without the Deity itself being seen, in which it is found formally and eminently.

But it must be observed that sometimes the formulation of this adequate object of the human intellect is inexact; this object applies to it, not strictly as it is a human intellect, but as it is an intellect. This adequate object is not only *being as such*, which is the object of metaphysics; for metaphysics is still a human science, which knows its object in the mirror of sensible things. If the adequate object of our intellect were nothing else, then the possibility of metaphysics would be all that could be proved from this against positivism and Kantianism.

Indeed, the adequate object of our intellect is being in the widest sense of the term (a commonly accepted expression); so that nothing transcends it, which means that it includes the triune God as He really is, or as He is clearly seen. We cannot, of course, prove conclusively by reason alone that this is the adequate object of our intellect; but it cannot be disproved. In fact, we are persuaded that it is not repugnant for our intellect to be informed by any intelligible being, however perfect it may be, inasmuch as our intellect is absolutely immaterial, or is intrinsically independent of the organ of sight.[177] As St. Thomas says: "The soul is naturally capable of grace since, from its having been made to the likeness of God, it is fit to receive God by grace." [178] But the soul is made to God's image, inasmuch as it is made like to Him not only in existence and life, but also in intelligence. This means that it is absolutely immaterial or intrinsically independent of the body.[179] On the other hand, although the soul of the irrational animal has that measure of immateriality required for sensitive knowledge,[180] yet it is intrinsically dependent on the body and perishes with it; for it is then reduced to the potentiality of the matter in which it was first potentially. But the rational soul was not in the potentiality of matter, for it is created by God, and is intrinsically independent of the body in becoming, in being, and in operation. And the proof of this is that its intellect can be informed by any intelligible being whatever, even the most perfect.[181]

This means that the passive capacity of our intellect is greater than its active power; neither of itself is it limited to some order of intelligible beings; whereas, on the contrary, its active power extends only to what is knowable from sensible things. Indeed, every creature can receive from God more than it can effect; hence it is not surprising that there should be in our nature a passive capacity, and that there is nothing of repugnance for this nature to be raised to the knowledge of the most perfect intelligible being that transcends the mirror of creatures. This capacity for being elevated is called an obediential capacity.[182]

Hence it is only in a spiritual way, as transcending everything material, that the intelligible object, however perfect it may be,

[177] This has been more fully explained by us elsewhere. Cf. *De revelatione*, I, 380–84.

[178] *Summa theol.*, Ia IIae, q. 113, a. 10.

[179] *Ibid.*, Ia, q. 3, a. 2.

[180] *Ibid.*, q. 14, a. 1.

[181] See John of St. Thomas, *Com. in Iam*, q. 12, disp. XII, a. 2, nos. 9, 10, 12; also disp. XIV, a. 2, nos. 11, 21; a. 6, no. 6. Consult also his *Cursus phil., de anima*, q. X, a. 3.

[182] And as its name "obediential" indicates, its immediate reference is not to the essentially supernatural object to be known, but to the supreme agent whom it obeys, and from whom it gratuitously receives the *positive direction* both as to the eliciting of the supernatural act and as to the object of this act.

informs the intellective faculty. Consequently this does not appear to be beyond the elevatable or obediential capacity of our nature.

Thus we are persuaded of the existence of this obediential or elevatable capacity for the beatific vision. However, as the Thomists generally admit,[183] this argument is not conclusive, but only very probable and indeed most profound in this order. Neither can the possibility of the light of glory be proved solely by the powers of reasoning, because it is the possibility of what is essentially supernatural, and hence of what is supernaturally knowable, inasmuch as being and truth are convertible.

Therefore St. Thomas presents this argument only as a "sign," and he often distinguishes between the demonstrative argument and the sign.[184] The possibility of essentially supernatural mysteries is neither proved nor disproved, but is defended, urged upon us, and held firmly by faith.[185]

Doubt. Is it possible for God by His absolute power to create an intellect that by its own natural powers can see God as He really is? Further, can a supernatural substance be created, such that the light of glory would be connatural to it, as a property of its nature?

The theologians, especially the Thomists, generally answer in the negative to each. As Gonet says, these two negative conclusions are now commonly held "against Durandus, Molina, Ripalda, Arriaga . . . whose opinion Vasquez calls absurd, Nazarius looks upon as temerarious, and Bannez as extraordinary ignorance." [186]

Scotus and the Nominalists prior to Molina had defended a similar opinion, denying the absolute necessity of the light of glory so as to see God.[187]

Cajetan says that the condemnation of the Beghards in the Council of Vienne makes this view of Scotus no longer tenable. He writes: "Note well that this opinion of Scotus and his followers can no longer be maintained; for the encyclical of Pope Clement V, *Ad nostrum, de haereticis,* condemns as positively erroneous the assertion of those who say that the soul does not need the light of glory elevating it to see God. In this you perceive that the Church, accepting the teaching of St. Thomas, definitely decided not only as to the need of the light of glory, but as to the cause of this, since the soul needs to be elevated for such vision, as stated in the en-

---

[183] Cf. Salmanticenses, *Com. in Iam,* q.12, disp. I, dub. III, §§ 2 and 3, nos. 44–47.
[184] *Summa theol.,* IIIa, q.55, a.5; Ia, q.32, a.1 ad 2um.
[185] Consult St. Thomas' commentary on the *De Trinitate* of Boethius, q.2, a.3, in which it is shown that theology solves the objections against the mysteries, either as being evidently false, or as not necessary, or as not convincing.
[186] *Clypeus thomisticus,* tr. II, *De possibilitate visionis Dei,* disp. I, a.1, § 3.
[187] Cf. *in III Sent.,* d.14, q.1; *IV Sent.,* d.49, q.11; also *I Sent.,* d.3, q.3, nos. 24–25.

cyclical." [188] Gonet likewise contradicts Scotus on this point.[189]

According to the teaching of Scotus [190] and the Nominalists, the distinction between the natural order and the supernatural order of sanctifying grace is not one of necessity, as resulting from the very transcendence of God's essence over every created intellect; but the distinction is one of contingency, the result of God's free decree appointing angels and men in this state of wayfarers, such that they have not the immediate vision of His essence. This distinction of Scotus, however, is in harmony with his doctrine as formulated in two of his theses; for he says that being is predicated univocally of God and creatures, wherefore there is no essential and necessary distinction between the natural and supernatural orders. He states also that, since God's will is higher than His intellect, the distinction between the two orders is the result of God's free decree. This conclusion is also in accordance with the principles of Nominalism,[191] for the Nominalists maintain that the common name "humanity" designates a collection of men and not a necessary and immutable nature.

But it is difficult to see how this merely contingent distinction can be reconciled with the teaching of the Vatican Council, which says: "The Catholic Church with one consent has also ever held and does hold that there is a twofold order of knowledge, distinct both in principle and in object: in principle, because our knowledge in the one is by natural reason, and in the other by divine faith; in object because, besides those things to which natural reason can attain, there are proposed to our belief mysteries hidden in God, which, unless divinely revealed, cannot be known. . . . For the divine mysteries by their own nature [there is no mention of any free divine decree] so far transcend the created intelligence that, even when delivered by revelation and received by faith, they remain covered with the veil of faith itself . . . so long as we are pilgrims in this mortal life, not yet with God." [192] Hence this su-

---

[188] See his commentary on this article, no. 9.

[189] *Clypeus thomisticus, De gratia,* disp. II, a.3: Whether habitual grace is an essentially supernatural form. In this article he says: "The opinion of Scotus is commonly rejected, because he does not distinguish between the intrinsically supernatural, or as to its entity, and the extrinsically supernatural, or as to the mode (of its production). It is also against the common opinion of the theologians, who admit the existence of essentially supernatural beings; it is even against faith, which also emphasizes the same." Thus grace and the infused virtues are essentially supernatural, whereas it is the natural life that is supernaturally restored to a dead person.

[190] *In I Sent.,* d.3, q.3, nos. 24, 25.

[191] Cf. Zigliara, *Summa phil., Ontologia,* Bk. II, chap. 1, a.4: *Dotes essentiarum contra nominales.*

[192] Denz., nos. 1795–96.

periority has its foundation not in the divine liberty, but in the very transcendence of the divine nature. Thus, A. Vacant [193] and Scheeben [194] have not interpreted the above text from the Vatican Council in favor of Scotus' opinion.

OBJECTIONS OF SCOTUS [195]

First objection. From the fact that the thing known is in the knower according to the mode of the knower, it follows solely that the knower cannot know naturally an object of a higher order except in an inferior manner. But it does not follow that the knower is absolutely incapable of knowing this object in a natural way. Therefore a natural, confused, and finite knowledge of the Deity or of God's intimate life is perhaps possible.

Reply. I distinguish the antecedent: that the knower can naturally know an object of a higher order only in an inferior manner, that is, as it is related to the formal object of the lower order, namely, in some inferior image, this I concede; that it can naturally and immediately know this object according to the formal concept of the higher order, at least confusedly, this I deny. And I deny the consequent. We naturally know God in the mirror of creatures, according to the analogically common notions of being, goodness . . . , but not immediately according to the proper and intimate notion of the Deity. Otherwise our knowledge would be simultaneously according to two opposite modes of immateriality, namely, according to the human and the divine modes. This superior mode can be participated in only by the infusion of supernatural light, which is a certain participation of the divine nature. Indeed, to know God confusedly is to know God under the common notion of being, and not under the most proper and most eminent notion of the Deity. It was not in a formal but in a material sense that Scotus understood the proposition of St. Thomas, that "the thing known is in the knower according to the mode of the knower," that is, according to the mode of immateriality of the nature of this knower. This principle, however, has its foundation in the principle that the intelligent being differs from the nonintelligent being, since by reason of its immateriality it can become something other than itself.[196]

Second objection. There is no need of proportion between the

[193] Cf. *Etudes sur la philosophie de saint Thomas et sur celle de Duns Scot* (1891), p. 14.

[194] Cf. *Dogmatik, De Deo,* no. 278 f.

[195] Cf. *In IVam Sent.,* d.49, q.11; also *In Iam Sent.,* d.3, q.3, and Cajetan's replies *In Iam,* q.12, a.4.

[196] Cf. *Summa theol.,* Ia, q.14, a.1.

intellect and its proper object. St. Thomas maintains, to be sure, that for our intellect this object is of a lower order, as being the essence of things material. But if there is no need of proportion, then the proper object also of our intellect can be of a higher order.

Reply. There is no comparison, for our intellect by its natural power can elevate an inferior material object to its own mode of intelligibility; but it cannot in a natural way, or according to its mode of operation, be elevated to the higher mode of operation of the divine intellect.

Third objection. Then it follows that the angel of a lower order could not by its own power know the angel of a higher order, which is false.

Reply. Two angels are of the same order of immateriality; wherefore the lower by its own power knows the higher, but not so clearly as the higher knows itself.

FIFTH ARTICLE

WHETHER THE CREATED INTELLECT NEEDS ANY CREATED LIGHT IN ORDER
TO SEE THE ESSENCE OF GOD

State of the question. So far we know that the created intellect can be raised to see God's essence (a. 1) and that it cannot by its natural powers attain to this (a. 4). It is now a question of the necessity of the supernatural light of glory, which was already affirmed somewhat incidentally in the second article. The nature of this light must be determined. How does this necessity manifest itself and what is its proper effect?

What is of faith concerning this? The necessity of the light of glory is affirmed in the Council of Vienne, as is evident from the condemnation of the following proposition: "The soul does not need the light of glory elevating it to see God and enjoy Him in this blessed state." [197] Hence the Council affirms the light of glory in the blessed not only as being an actual fact, but also as necessary so that the soul may be raised to see God, and for this very reason it declares that this light is supernatural; otherwise the soul would not be raised to a higher order by this light. Yet even so, the Council does not determine the degree of this necessity. It is at least a necessity in accordance with God's ordinary power, although it may still be a disputed point whether this light is absolutely necessary, so that even by God's absolute and extraordinary power the created intellect could not see God unless it were elevated by means of this light. The Council, likewise, did not define that the

[197] Denz., no. 475. This error is expressly refuted by Clement V in the fifteenth ecumenical Council of Vienne.

light of glory is a quality, an infused habit; but we must say of it what was afterward declared by the Council of Trent [198] concerning habitual grace, namely, that it is something created, infused and inherent in the soul. St. Thomas says more, inasmuch as he declares more explicitly that the light of glory is an infused quality and an infused habit.

Billuart puts the following question to his readers: "You will ask whether it is of faith that sanctifying grace is, in the strictly philosophical sense, an infused quality and an infused habit? Not in the strict sense, we reply; yet that it is so must be held as certain doctrine." [199] The same must be said of consummated and inamissible sanctifying grace, which is in the essence of the soul, and which is the source of the light of glory for the intellect of the blessed, just as it is of the infused light of faith for the intellect of wayfarers. Thus theology, in the common acceptation of the term, explains still more precisely what is defined by the Church.

It must be observed that the Council of Vienne, in thus determining the necessity of the light of glory for the soul to be raised to this higher order, presents more clearly the doctrine already formulated against the Pelagians and Semipelagians in the Second Council of Orange [200] concerning the necessity of grace, which is the seed of glory.

THE VARIOUS OPINIONS OF THEOLOGIANS BEFORE AND AFTER THE COUNCIL OF VIENNE

Notice must be taken of two opinions proposed before the time of the Council, and conflicting with its decisions.

1) Opinion of Scotus. He understood the light of glory to be the beatific vision in its second actuality, inasmuch as it is communicated to us by God. This opinion is contrary to the teaching of the Council, which declares "that the soul needs the light of glory elevating it to see God." Therefore the light of glory, since it is necessary for the beatific vision, differs from this latter. Hence Cajetan [201] says that, since the time of the Council, this opinion of Scotus is no longer tenable, which is also what Gonet says.[202] John of St. Thomas says of Scotus' opinion: "Its affirmation cannot but be a very dangerous assertion." [203]

2) The opinion of Durandus. He, too, before the time of the

---

[198] Denz., nos. 799, 821.
[199] Cf. *De gratia*, diss. IV, a.3.
[200] Denz., nos. 176–200.
[201] Com. on this article, no. 9 f.
[202] Cf. *De gratia*, disp. II, a.3.
[203] See his commentary on this article.

Council, understood the light of glory to be the divine essence itself, inasmuch as it immediately manifests itself to the intellect and changes it in the order of intellection. This opinion, says John of St. Thomas, is not in accord with the spirit of the Council; for those condemned as heretics did not deny the necessity of the divine essence manifesting itself as the object of vision, but they denied the necessity of a light elevating the intellect so that it can be united with the object.

3) Vasquez, who lived after the time of the Council, thinks the light of glory, as a habit perfecting the intellect, to be superfluous. Similarly, Molina and Suarez are of the opinion that, by God's absolute power, all that is required is an actual help, but no infused habit elevating the soul. There is nothing surprising about this in the teaching of Suarez, for he admitted an actual obediential power, by which our nature would be positively and actively directed to the performance of supernatural acts, although it would need the divine assistance to pass into act. This active obediential power is somewhat like the innate natural appetite for the beatific vision admitted by Scotus, Suarez, and Molina, who conceive God elevating and our intellect more as two co-ordinated causes (like two men pulling a boat) than as two causes subordinated one to the other.[204]

4) The Thomists reject this actual obediential power, for they say it would be both essentially natural, as being a property of the nature, and essentially supernatural, as specified by a supernatural object. Therefore they say along with St. Thomas that the obediential power is passive, and that its immediate reference is not to the eliciting of a supernatural act, nor to the object of this act, but to the agent of a higher order, that is, to God the author of grace, whom it obeys, and from whom it receives the grace which has as its purpose the attainment of glory. However, the obediential power, which in itself is formally passive, also inheres in the active faculty, namely, in the will; but then it is only materially active because the will is its subject of inhesion.

This Thomist opinion agrees exactly with what St. Thomas teaches in his various works in which he discusses the obediential power, especially that which is required as a prerequisite for the beatific vision. There is also a vast difference between this latter and the obediential power required in bodies in which miracles are to be performed, or in the water that is instrumental in the

204 Thus Suarez holds that the beatific vision is a naturally vital act. This means that the essentially supernatural act of the beatific vision would consist of two parts, namely, the naturally vital act and the supernatural superadded mode, just as at times a thin coating of gold is superimposed on a common metal, and then we have a gilt object but not one of solid gold.

production of grace. But for St. Thomas every obediential power, since it refers to God as agent and elevator, is a passive power. The two following quotations suffice: "In the human soul, as in every creature, there is a double passive power: one in comparison with a natural agent; the other in comparison with the first agent, which can reduce any creature to a higher act than a natural agent can reduce it, and this is usually called the obediential power of a creature." [205] Also: "In every creature there is a certain obediential power, inasmuch as every creature obeys God so as to receive in itself whatever God may have willed." [206] But God's will and omnipotence are limited only by what is repugnant to existence; hence all that is required for the obediential power in a being, is that it be not repugnant for such being to be raised to a higher order. Thus there is an obediential power in our nature even for the hypostatic union, to which our nature is not positively ordained. Similarly there is an obediential power both in the disembodied spirits and in the angels of heaven for a greater degree of the light of glory, because the highest degree of this glory is inconceivable. The light of glory could always be intensively increased, and yet it would never attain to the comprehensive vision of God, for this can apply to God alone. [207] Therefore St. Thomas says that there is no limit to the obediential power, for it corresponds to divine omnipotence, which is always able to produce still greater effects. [208]

HOW ST. THOMAS PROVES THE NECESSITY OF THE LIGHT OF GLORY

In the body of the article he shows that the light of glory is necessary: (1) as a disposition preparing the intellect for union with the divine essence; (2) as a power strengthening the intellect to elicit this act of vision.

Proof of first requisite: Everything which is raised up to what exceeds its nature, needs to be supernaturally disposed for this; but the created intellect that sees God is so raised, and the divine essence takes the place of its intelligible species; [209] therefore the intellect needs to be disposed so as to see the divine essence.

Proof of second requisite: A power must be proportionate to the act that is to be elicited by it, so that it can elicit this act; but the natural power of the created intellect is intrinsically incapable, or

---

[205] *Summa theol.*, IIIa, q.11, a.1; see also IIIa, q.1, a.3 ad 3um; *Com. theol.*, c.104; *De potentia*, q.6, a.1 ad 18um.

[206] *Quaest. disp., de virt. in communi*, a.10 ad 13um.

[207] See a.7.

[208] *Summa theol.*, IIIa, q.7, a.12 ad 2um; q.10, a.4 ad 3um; *De veritate*, q.20, a.4 ad 2um et 3um.

[209] See a.2.

is not in proportion so as to elicit the supernatural act of seeing God; therefore the intellect needs the reinforcement of a supernatural light.

The following objection is raised against the first argument: if the major were true, then a disposition would be necessary for the reception of this infused disposition, and so on indefinitely.

In reply to this we say with Cajetan and John of St. Thomas, that the reception of a form or perfection necessitates some disposition, of course, in the subject; but the disposition itself necessitates no previous disposition. In other words, there is no such thing as a disposition for a disposition; otherwise there would never be a disposition in any order. Hence the major of St. Thomas must be understood in the sense that there must be a first actuality or proximate potentiality in everything which is raised up to that which exceeds its nature and by which it is disposed for this. Such is manifestly the case in material things, and it is verified in every order. Thus the necessary prerequisite for wood to begin to burn is that it acquire a certain degree of heat. Similarly, for the reception of a substantial form (e.g., the sensitive soul, as also the intellective soul), there must be a disposition for this as a necessary prerequisite.

In like manner, in the attainment of knowledge, the student needs to be disposed so as to be able to listen to and profit by the special lectures on metaphysics. It must be noted that the lack of this requisite disposition for a form results in a monstrosity both in the natural order and in the intellectual order. So it would be if, through lack of this previous disposition, one were to understand Thomism in the Calvinist sense.

Not only is the disposition required for the action of an agent, but also for the proper reception of some exalted perfection, such as the proper appreciation of one of Beethoven's symphonies, or the understanding of a difficult passage. So also the seven gifts of the Holy Ghost are required so as to dispose one to receive His inspirations.[210] Hence it is not surprising that a special infused disposition is required for receiving the divine essence as an intelligible form or impressed species.

For our intellectual faculty, which of itself is incapable either of making use of this essence as intelligible form so as to see God, or of receiving it without being elevated, must be proportioned to it. And this functioning of the light of glory by way of a disposition is closely connected with the second and principal function with which the second argument is concerned.

The probative force of the second argument is evident if we consider that the operative power, which of itself and intrinsically

---

[210] *Summa theol.,* Ia IIae, q.68, a.2.

is incapable of any act, needs to be intrinsically elevated, strengthened, and perfected by the reception of some habit that is either acquired or infused. It is this general principle that is invoked in showing the necessity of habits, and it is quite clear that there is no reference here to an acquired habit, because the object is of the supernatural order. Therefore an infused virtue is meant, which is commonly called the light of glory, since here we have a case of analogy of proportionality; for this light is to the created intellect as regards the beatific vision just as material light is to the eye as regards its object of vision.

Hence, as is more clearly seen in the answer to the first objection, the light of glory in the blessed is a permanent quality or a supernatural infused habit inhering in the intellect, elevating and perfecting it so as to see God. But this habit is always in second actuality, because the vision itself is permanent, and resides in the intellect as charity does in the will, and this light does away with the infused habit of faith. The principal function of this light is to elevate the faculty to elicit the act of vision, and its secondary function is to dispose the faculty to receive the divine essence as the intelligible form. Yet it is not of faith that the light of glory is a habit.

SOLUTION OF OBJECTIONS

The first series of objections denies the necessity of the light of glory.

First objection. What is of itself lucid needs no other light in order to be seen; but God is of Himself lucid, because He is light itself; therefore no other light is needed in order to see Him.

Reply. What is of itself lucid needs no other light on its own part in order to be seen, this I concede; on the part of the visual faculty, this I deny. I contradistinguish the minor in the same way.[211]

Second objection. A created light is not required even on the part of the visual faculty, for God takes the place of the impressed species; but the impressed species functions on the part of the visual faculty; therefore, in like manner, God can take the place of the light of glory.

Reply. I concede the major, but distinguish the minor. That the species functions as a perfection actuating the faculty by way of terminating it, this I concede; as informing form, this I deny. For it takes the place of the object. On the other hand, the light that strengthens the faculty belongs properly to the operative faculty,

211 Cf. ad 1um.

as informing form, and God cannot take the place of the informing form, which is essentially something participated and thus imperfect.

Third objection. But the divine concurrence suffices on the part of the subject so as to render the intellect capable of seeing God; therefore the intellect does not need to be strengthened by any created light so as to see God.

Reply. If the beatific vision transcended the faculty merely intensively in the natural order, then I concede the consequence. But this vision is essentially supernatural. Hence this faculty, which of itself is intrinsically incapable for such act, must be supernaturally elevated so as to be made intrinsically capable in first actuality for this vision.

SECOND SERIES OF OBJECTIONS, TO SHOW THAT THE LIGHT OF GLORY IS SOMETHING REPUGNANT

First objection. If God is seen by means of a light, then He is seen through a medium; but the beatific vision is absolutely direct; therefore the light of glory is incompatible with this vision

Reply. I distinguish the major. If God is seen by means of a light, then He is seen through an objective medium *quo* or *in quo*, this I deny; that He is seen through a subjective medium *sub quo,* or one that strengthens the faculty, this I concede. The minor I concede, and I distinguish the conclusion in the same way.[212]

Second objection. Even this subjective medium that strengthens the faculty is something repugnant. For what is finite cannot dispose one to see the infinite. But the light of glory is finite, since it is created. Therefore it cannot dispose one to see God, who is infinite.

Reply. I distinguish the major. What is finite in the entitative and natural order, this I concede; what is finite in the entitative and supernatural order cannot dispose one to see the infinite, this I subdistinguish: it cannot dispose one for an infinite or comprehensive knowledge of God, this I concede; that it cannot dispose one for a finite knowledge of God, this I deny.[213]

Third objection. The light of glory is incompatible even with a finite knowledge of God, for the power that perfects a vital faculty must itself be vital; but the light of glory is not vital, because it does not proceed from an intrinsic principle; therefore this light is repugnant to the faculty.

Reply. I distinguish the major. The power that perfects a vital

212 Cf. ad 2um.
213 Cf. *Contra Gentes,* Bk. III, chap. 54.

faculty must itself be vital, as being that by which the act is a vitally elicited act, this I concede; as being that which is vitally produced by the created intellect, this I deny. Although the light of glory is not vital as being what is produced by the intellective faculty, yet it is vital as being that by which the elicited act of vision is vital.

First doubt. How does the light of glory concur with the intellect in the beatific vision?

Reply. Each concurs actively, as two total and subordinated causes, but each under a different aspect. For the created intellect and the light of glory are not two partial and coordinated causes, such that the vitality of the beatific vision would be a natural vitality, as Suarez would have it in accordance with his conception of an active obediential power which, as we stated, almost dispenses with the necessity of an elevation or of an elevating grace.[214]

The created intellect and the light of glory are indeed two total and subordinated causes, such that the intellect is the total and radical principle, and the infused habit of the light of glory is the total and proximate principle by which the act of vision is elicited. Hence the vitality of the beatific vision is essentially supernatural, because it proceeds not from a purely natural faculty, but from an elevated faculty. Thus eternal life is truly a new life, the two aspects of life and vision being equally applicable in this sense; for it is essentially supernatural as being specified by an essentially supernatural object.[215] Thus the beatific vision differs entirely from the miraculous restoration of sight to a blind person, because this sight is essentially natural and is only supernaturally restored. In other words, it is only supernatural as regards the mode of its production.

It must be observed also that the created intellect is not the instrumental cause of intellectual vision, as baptismal water is of grace; but the beatific vision is its vital and connatural act, although it does not elicit this act independently of the infused habit. This habit, however, functions by way of a second nature of the higher order. So also the will of the blessed is not the instrumental cause of the act of charity elicited by it, but is its connatural act.

Second doubt. Can there be the creation of an intellect to which the light of glory would be connatural?

St. Thomas denies this in his reply to the third objection: "The light of glory cannot be natural to a creature unless the creature has

[214] See John of St. Thomas, *Com. in Iam,* q. 12, a. 2, no. 10 f.
[215] An essentially supernatural and simple act cannot be partly natural and partly supernatural.

a divine nature; which is impossible. But by this light the rational creature is made deiform, as is said in this article."

Scotus held the opposite view.[216] But from Scotus' opinion it follows that consummated grace, as a matter of fact, would be grace not essentially, but only contingently. This is contrary to the principle that powers, habits, and acts are specified by their formal object.[217] But the formal and proper object of the divine intellect evidently transcends the proper and natural object of any creatable intellect whatever; otherwise this intellect would be of the same nature as God, would be God created.

Third doubt. Why is a created and supernatural substance a contradiction in terms?

It is because the intellect of this substance would be of the same nature as the divine intellect, for it would be specified by the same formal object, and hence would be the divine nature created, which is a contradiction in terms, just as pantheism is.

Moreover, this substance would be supernatural; but it is intrinsically repugnant for a supernatural substance to be created. Indeed, nothing created can be essentially supernatural without its being essentially related to the Deity as such, to God's intimate life, and thus specified by it; for it is only God's essence that transcends every created nature. But no created substance can be essentially related to the Deity and specified by it, since substance is being in itself and for itself. This means that the reason for its specification is to be found in itself, and it cannot be defined because of its being referred to something else. On the contrary, an accident, such as a power or a habit, can be essentially related to something else. Thus grace, which is the seed of glory, is specified by God's essence, of which it is a participation, and by means of it we are ordained to see God in His essence.[218]

SIXTH ARTICLE

WHETHER, OF THOSE WHO SEE THE ESSENCE OF GOD, ONE SEES MORE PERFECTLY THAN ANOTHER

The answer is in the affirmative, and it is of faith against Jovinian, as also against Luther, who said that all men are equally blessed,

---

[216] *I Sent.*, d.3, q.3, nos. 24, 25.

[217] This principle, however, pervades the whole of psychology and theology as the searchlight in all that concerns the acquired virtues, the infused virtues, and the vices. Thus St. Thomas says: "The species of every habit depends on the formal aspect of the object, without which the species of the habit cannot remain" (IIa IIae, q.5, a.3).

[218] Cf. Gonet, *Clypeus thomisticus, De gratia*, disp. II, a.3; Billuart, *De Deo*, diss. IV, a.5, § 4.

in that they are justified not by their own justice, but by the justice of Christ which is imputed to them.

The Council of Florence defines it to be of faith in the following words: "The souls of the saints . . . clearly intuit the one and triune God, one seeing Him more perfectly than another, according to the diversity of their merits." [219] Likewise the Council of Trent condemns those who say that "men justified by good works do not merit an increase of glory." [220]

This doctrine of the faith is equivalently expressed in the following passages of Holy Scripture: "Star differeth from star in glory"; [221] and this is said of the blessed. Similarly we have: "In My Father's house there are many mansions"; [222] and these words must be understood as referring to the kingdom of heaven, because in this same chapter our Lord says: "I go to prepare a place for you . . . that where I am, you also may be." [223]

The Fathers, especially St. Augustine, frequently alluded to the doctrine of the various degrees of happiness in heaven that correspond to the varying degrees of merit among the blessed.[224] But Holy Scripture also discloses the reason for this inequality, which has its foundation in the merits acquired in this life. Such texts are: "Your reward is very great in heaven"; [225] "Who will render to every man according to his works." [226] But there is inequality of merit among wayfarers.

Theology, which explains more clearly the reason for this inequality, teaches that the more the intellect participates in the light of glory, the more perfectly it sees God. But the greater the charity, the greater is the participation in the light of glory; for desire actuated by charity in a certain degree makes the one desiring apt to receive the object desired.

First doubt. Does the inequality of vision result solely from the inequality of participation in the light of glory, or is it also because of the inequality of the natural power of the intellect?

Reply. The general answer to this, against the Scotists, Molina, and even partly against Cajetan, is that it is solely because of the inequality of participation in the light of glory. As St. Thomas says: "it [the inequality] will arise on the part of the diverse faculty of

[219] Denz., no. 693.
[220] *Ibid.*, no. 842.
[221] I Cor. 15: 41.
[222] John 14: 2.
[223] *Ibid.*, 14: 2, 3.
[224] Cf. Rouet de Journel, *Enchir. patristicum*, nos. 696, 710, 1383, 1502, 1831, 1931, 2308.
[225] Matt. 5: 12.
[226] Rom. 2: 6.

the intellect, not indeed the natural faculty, but the glorified faculty." [227] Why is this? It is because, as stated in the body of the article, "the faculty of seeing God does not belong to the created intellect naturally, but is given to it by the light of glory." Therefore the faculty of seeing God more perfectly does not belong to the created intellect according as it is by nature more perfect. Hence the penetrative vision of the divine essence is not greater in the angelic intellect than in the human intellect, if each receives an equal degree of the light of glory. The incongruity resulting from its denial confirms this view. For otherwise, granted equality of merit, one would see God more perfectly than the other, namely, the one whose intellect is endowed with greater penetration of vision; but this would be contrary to the notion of reward. There is another incongruity in that any degree of glory would not be according to the corresponding degree of grace, but would be according to one's natural powers, and thus man by his natural powers would claim something as his own in the spiritual order, which is contrary to what St. Paul says: "For who distinguisheth thee?" [228]

The opinion of the Scotists and Molina arises from the fact that they consider the intellect and the light of glory not so much as two total and subordinated causes, but rather as two partial and coordinated causes.

Second doubt. Do some of the blessed enjoy an equal degree of glory?

Reply. This we affirm, especially for baptized children who die before coming to the use of reason.

SEVENTH ARTICLE

WHETHER THOSE WHO SEE THE ESSENCE OF GOD COMPREHEND HIM

It is of faith that the blessed do not comprehend God, inasmuch as the Lateran Council declares that "God is incomprehensible." [229] It is commonly admitted among theologians that this incomprehensibility is to be understood as referring not only to the natural but also to the supernatural faculties; for there is a difference between invisibility and incomprehensibility. The blessed are called comprehensors, inasmuch as their immediate vision of God is construed as comprehension in the broad sense of the term. [230]

The theological proof given by St. Thomas is clear. To compre-

227 Cf. ad 3um.
228 I Cor. 4: 7.
229 Denz., no. 428.
230 Cf. ad 1um.

hend God is to know Him both intensively and extensively so far as He is knowable, that is, infinitely; but no created intellect, either by its own power or by means of the light of glory, can know God infinitely; therefore no created intellect can comprehend God.

The major has its foundation in the principle that the source of knowledge and of knowableness is immateriality. But God alone is absolutely immaterial as being most pure act both in the entitative and in the intellectual orders. Hence no created intellect can see God with the same clarity, distinction, and penetration, as God sees Himself, that is, intensively; nor even extensively, for the more profound one's knowledge of God is, the more profound one's knowledge is of what comes within the scope of omnipotence or divine causality.[231]

Objection. It is stated that the blessed see the indivisible God as a whole. Therefore it does not seem possible for their vision to remain imperfect.

Reply. In reply to the second objection it is pointed out that the blessed see the whole of God but not as He is infinitely knowable. Thus he who knows any demonstrable proposition by a probable reason, knows every part of the proposition, namely, the subject, the predicate, and the verb "is"; yet he does not know it as perfectly as it is capable of being known. So also in sense perception, when several persons see a mountain more or less perfectly, clearly, and distinctly, it is seen in all its details according as one has a keener vision than the other.

Similarily, it is pointed out in the reply to the third objection that the blessed see God as a whole, but not wholly, in the sense that the mode of the one knowing does not adequately correspond to the mode of the object known. This means that the blessed see God only in a finite way.

First doubt. Do the blessed see all the formal and necessary constituents of God, namely, the essence, the attributes, and the Persons.

Reply. That they do is commonly affirmed against the nominalists.[232] In fact, the common teaching against Scotus is that it is repugnant for the divine essence to be seen by the blessed apart from the attributes and the Persons, because there is no real distinction between the divine essence, the attributes, and the Persons,

---

[231] Cf. *Summa theol.*, Ia, q. 14, a. 1.

[232] Contrary to the nominalists, it must be said that omnipotence, which as its name implies denotes a reference to undefined creatures, can be known quidditatively provided the formal and primary object of its action be known, which is the idea of created being. It is not necessary that the material and secondary objects be known, which are all possible creatures. Thus the quiddative knowledge of matter does not necessitate the knowledge of all material things.

not even an actual formal distinction on the part of the object, as posited by Scotus; for there is no intermediary distinction. Either the distinction between objects is real and exists before the mind's consideration, or it is logical, and does not exist before the mind's consideration. Thus the divine reality, as it is in itself, actually and explicitly contains not only the divine essence, but also the attributes and the Persons. But if it is a question of the divine essence as conceived by us wayfarers, then the attributes and the Persons are contained actually and implicitly in it.

Second doubt. Do the blessed in seeing God see His free decrees?

Reply. They see them inasmuch as these are existing realities in God, but they do not see them inasmuch as these terminate defectibly in creatures, unless God wills to manifest this to them. Thus they do not know the day of judgment or the number of the elect. The reason is that future free things are contained in God's essence only by reason of His free decree, which is made known either by some effect or by God's special revelation. Having sufficiently discussed the primary object of the beatific vision, we now pass on to consider its secondary object.

EIGHTH ARTICLE

WHETHER THOSE WHO SEE THE ESSENCE OF GOD SEE ALL IN GOD

In the title the word "all" signifies everything outside God and everything that can exist.

Reply. It is denied that the blessed see all that God does or can do, for then they would have a comprehensive knowledge of God, which means that they would know all that God does or can do; for the more perfectly a cause is seen, the more of its effects can be seen, and all possible effects if it is seen comprehensively.

Doubt. What, therefore, do the blessed see in God?

It is generally admitted that the blessed see of past, present, and future things whatever pertains particularly and principally to them.[233] The proof is that the beatific vision must perfectly satisfy every lawful desire of the blessed. But the blessed lawfully desire to know what specially pertains to them. Therefore the blessed see all that specially pertains to them.

It is not easy to determine in detail what specially pertains to them. However, the theologians generally agree in saying that the blessed can be considered from three points of view: (1) inasmuch as they are elevated to the supernatural order; (2) inasmuch as they

233 *Summa theol.*, IIIa, q. 10, a. 2.

are a part of the universe in the natural order; (3) inasmuch as each is an individual person, either public, as the Pope, the king, or the founder of a religious order, or in a private capacity, as the father of a family.

But the blessed as raised to the supernatural order see the mysteries believed in this life, such as those of the incarnation, redemption, predestination, and grace. It is not necessary, however, that these be seen in all their circumstances of time and place, as is evident concerning the day of judgment, which not even the angels know. Nor is it necessary for them to see the fulfillment of these mysteries in all individual cases. The blessed as part of the universe see the genera and species, as St. Thomas teaches in this article.[234]

The blessed, inasmuch as each is an individual person, see all or at least the principal things that pertain to their state. Thus St. Peter and more likely the Pope, too, see all that pertains to the universal Church; so also does the king see all that pertains to his kingdom, and the father to his family. They likewise see all the prayers of the faithful who implore their intercession. Hence the knowledge of the Blessed Virgin Mary far surpasses that of any of the saints, especially as regards the prayers and thoughts of human beings; yet not, so it seems, all the thoughts of human beings. This privilege belongs to Christ, as judge of the human race, and thus He must know the acts of all those to be judged.[235]

Similarly, the blessed see God's free decrees in their fulfillment, those that specially pertain to them according to God's good pleasure.

NINTH ARTICLE

WHETHER WHAT IS SEEN IN GOD, BY THOSE WHO SEE THE DIVINE ESSENCE, IS SEEN THROUGH ANY SIMILITUDE

Reply. The answer is that the blessed see without the intermediary of a created species what they see in the divine essence or in the Word. In this case the divine essence is for them the medium previously known, in which creatures are known as in their efficient and exemplary cause. This vision of creatures in the Word is the beatific vision itself, which is one of simple intuition.[236]

This vision of creatures in the Word, which is called morning knowledge inasmuch as it is the vision of creatures as in their

---

234 Cf. ad 4um.
235 *Summa theol.*, IIIa, q.10, a.2.
236 *Ibid.*, Ia, q.58, a.7.

dawning, is a certain participation of the knowledge which God has of creatures in Himself. They are known not merely in a confused manner, but distinctly as possible participations of the divine perfections. Thus he who would have an intuitive knowledge of the intellective soul, would know the sensitive and vegetative souls. Hence the knowledge of things in the Word is without any created species.

But the blessed can also know creatures *outside the Word,* and this by created species.[237] This knowledge outside the Word is called evening knowledge, as though it were twilight knowledge, because it is of an inferior kind; for, as St. Augustine says: "The knowledge of created things contemplated by themselves is, so to speak, more colorless than when they are seen in the wisdom of God, as in the art by which they were made."[238]

From this it is evident that the vision of things in the Word is more or less perfect according to the degree of the beatific vision and hence of merits. On the contrary, in the vision of things outside the Word there is not this same correspondence to the degree of the beatific vision and merits. Thus it may happen that the knowledge of a Pope or a king, who enjoys a lower degree of the beatific vision, may be greater as regards those things that specially pertain to him, which the blessed of a higher order do not have, since they are unknown to the latter.

John of St. Thomas remarks that theologians who, out of love for God, take up the study of theology, see the object of theology more eminently in the Word, whereas those who take up the study of theology more from a natural desire of acquiring knowledge, see the theological conclusions outside the Word.

Objection. If the blessed see various created things in the Word, why can they not see God's free decrees even as to their fulfillment?

Reply. The reason is that God, just as He freely brings creatures into being, so He freely makes use of His essence as the intelligible species in representing these rather than the former. Hence the blessed see the free acts of the future that specially pertain to them, only if God expressly wills to make these known to them, and this manifestation is a certain revelation; but it is one that is effected in the Word, although it may also take place outside the Word.

The question may be asked whether the name "Word" imports relation to creatures. It certainly does, though not indeed essentially so, but only if there is a divine decree.

---

237 *Ibid.,* ad 2um.
238 *De civit. Dei,* Bk. XI, chap. 7.

TENTH ARTICLE

WHETHER THOSE WHO SEE THE ESSENCE OF GOD SEE ALL THEY SEE IN IT AT THE SAME TIME

The article is concerned with the knowledge of things in the Word. In the title "at the same time" means that things are not seen successively.

Simultaneity of vision is affirmed, because this vision of things formally in the Word, is a unique intuition that is effected by means of but one and absolutely invariable species both as a representation and as an entity. Hence all things at one and the same time are included in this vision.

Therefore the beatific vision is measured by participated eternity, and not by time, not even by the discrete time of the angels in which their successive thoughts are measured.[239] But participated eternity has indeed a beginning, but after its inception it is simultaneously whole, and it is not a fleeting but a permanent now. However, just as the beatific vision begins, so it could by God's absolute power come to an end; but as long as it endures, it is measured by participated eternity, by a single indivisible instant. This was so if St. Paul received it as a transient vision during his life here on earth.[240] Hence what the blessed see in the Word, they see at one and the same time and not successively. On the contrary, what they see outside the Word by their own different species, are not seen at one and the same time, but successively, and this for the opposite reason.

Corollary. Probably the blessed know outside the Word the prayers directed to them, because if they saw formally in the Word at one and the same time all the petitions of all those praying to them, they would already know the day of the last judgment.

ELEVENTH ARTICLE

WHETHER ANYONE IN THIS LIFE CAN SEE THE ESSENCE OF GOD

The answer is that no one in this life can see the essence of God. The Council of Vienne condemned the following proposition of the Beghards: "It is possible for man to acquire in this life the same degree of final happiness as he will have in heaven." [241] In like manner, the Scripture says: "Man shall not see Me and live." [242]

---

[239] *Summa theol.,* Ia, q. 10, a. 5 ad 1um.
[240] *Ibid.,* IIa IIae, q. 175, a. 3.
[241] Denz., no. 474.
[242] Ex. 33: 20.

"No man hath seen God at any time." [243] "While we are in the body we are absent from the Lord. For we walk by faith and not by sight." [244]

St. Thomas assigns as the reason for this that the soul, united as it is with the body and the senses, knows God in a natural way only as it is related to sensible things; that is, with reference to its proper object.

The same also applies to the soul in its supernatural belief, because it is by means of concepts naturally abstracted from sensible things that revelation is made possible, for example, concepts of nature, person. The proper object of the lowest in the scale of intellectual beings is the lowest in the degree of intelligibility.

However, as pointed out in the reply to the second objection, God could, by way of an exception, have given the beatific vision as something transitory to St. Paul, who was rapt in ecstasy so that he might be the teacher of the Gentiles. This is the opinion of St. Augustine, and of St. Thomas when he discusses the subject of rapture.[245]

TWELFTH ARTICLE

WHETHER GOD CAN BE KNOWN IN THIS LIFE BY NATURAL REASON

The answer is that we cannot see God by our natural power of reason, because our natural knowledge begins from sense, and sensible effects do not adequately express the power of the First Cause. However, we can by these effects know that God exists, and that He has perfections the lack of which would make it impossible for Him to be the First Cause.

Thus there are three ways of knowing God, namely, by causality, negation, and eminence.

THIRTEENTH ARTICLE

WHETHER BY GRACE A HIGHER KNOWLEDGE OF GOD CAN BE OBTAINED THAN BY NATURAL REASON

The answer is in the affirmative, and the superiority of this knowledge of God is considered from two points of view: (1) subjectively, inasmuch as our intellect is strengthened by the infusion of gratuitous light (light of faith, or also of prophecy); (2) objectively, inasmuch as it implies the presentation of an object that is not

[243] John 1: 18.
[244] II Cor. 5: 6–7.
[245] *Summa theol.*, IIa IIae, q.175, a.3.

naturally knowable; and this is effected either by the infusion of images or ideas, or by the divine arrangement of the acquired ideas to express a supernatural truth.

In the reply to the first objection it is remarked that "by the revelation of grace in this life we cannot know of God what He is," still we know Him more fully than by the power of natural reason, and thus we believe that there are three Persons in God. Hence, although the faithful do not know the Deity as it really is, yet they have an obscure knowledge of the same by means of God's revelation.

And so this terminates the question about the beatific vision both in itself as regards its proper object and its secondary object (created things seen in the Word), and also in its relation to other kinds of knowledge, which is knowledge outside the Word, these being faith, prophecy, and the natural knowledge of God. What St. Thomas made clear and particularly stressed is that the beatific vision is essentially supernatural. He is of the opinion that it absolutely demands the elevation of the intellect by the light of glory, such that this essentially supernatural light cannot be a natural property of any created or creatable intellect.

In like manner, St. Thomas shows convincingly that this vision is absolutely immediate, inasmuch as God's essence is united to our intellect as impressed and expressed species. For no created species, which is intelligible by participation, can represent God Himself as He really is, who is the self-existing Being and self-subsisting Intellection, in fact, His Deity, which in a certain sense transcends being and intellection, inasmuch as it contains these formally and eminently, which must at once be shown.

CHAPTER XIII

QUESTION 13

THE NAMES OF GOD

PROLOGUE

"AFTER the consideration of those things which belong to the divine knowledge we now proceed to the consideration of the divine names. For everything is named by us according to our knowledge of it." [1] For words are signs of ideas, and ideas express the nature of things, as explained by Aristotle. [2] Thus every science has its terminology, although we must not say with the nominalists, especially with Condillac: "The sciences are well-constructed languages." Science makes use of good terminology in expressing its ideas; but, since it consists especially in the well-ordered arrangement of ideas as expressive of the very nature of things, it transcends this terminology. In fact, science is a simple quality, a habit that is specified by its formal object, subordinating the ideas with reference to this formal object.

The importance of this question. This question is of great importance, as it treats of the analogy existing between God and creatures, and in this life God is known and named only analogically by us. We shall give here but a brief explanation of this analogy, not only because it has been already discussed in our refutation of agnosticism in the question concerning the demonstrability of God's existence, [3] in which we treated of analogy by way of investigation in the ascendant order, but also because we have written extensively on this subject in two other works. [4]

By all means the conclusions and reasons given by St. Thomas must be here presented, so that it may be clearly and distinctly seen how his theory avoids the two extremes, namely, of agnosticism and of a certain anthropomorphism. Agnosticism gets no farther than a certain symbolism in which there is no criterion so as to distinguish between what is predicated literally of God and what

[1] *Summa theol.*, Ia, q. 13, prologue.
[2] *Perihermenias*, Bk. I, chap. 1.
[3] *Summa theol.*, Ia, q. 2, a. 2.
[4] Cf. *God, His Existence and His Nature*, I, 206–41; II, 187–267, 397 f. See also *De revelatione*, I, 276–318.

is predicated metaphorically of Him; e.g., in determining why it can properly be said of God that He is just, but not that He is angry. Thus in the end we should have to say that God is absolutely unknowable and ineffable in a depreciatory sense.

On the other hand, there is a type of anthropomorphism which considers God, not indeed as a great man as the ancient anthropomorphists did, but which considers Him in too human a way, predicating the divine names univocally or quasi-univocally, as if they had absolutely the same meaning when predicated of God and of creatures, as when wisdom is predicated of God and of a wise man.

We shall see that St. Thomas maintains that divine names are not predicated either equivocally (this would be the symbolism of the agnostics) or univocally (this would be the tendency of anthropomorphism), but analogically; yet they are not predicated merely analogically in the metaphorical sense, as when God is said to be angry, but they are predicated analogically in the literal sense, as when it is said that God is just, and when absolutely simple perfections implying no imperfection in their formal signification are attributed to Him. Hence, as we shall state farther on, these analogical names that are predicated of God and creatures, do not in their concept signify what is absolutely the same, but what is proportionately so. Thus wisdom is the knowledge of things by their highest causes; but God's wisdom is the cause of things, whereas our wisdom is caused by things.

Having shown the importance of this question by the foregoing principles, we must point out that it is divided into three parts. The first part, which treats of the divine names in a general way and which includes the first seven articles, contains the following queries: whether God can be named by us, whether any names applied to God are predicated of Him substantially (or only causally); literally (or only metaphorically); whether any names applied to God are synonymous (so that it can be said that God punishes by His mercy, as He is said to punish by His justice); whether names are applied to God and creatures univocally, or equivocally, or else analogically; but if analogically, whether they are applied first to God or to creatures; finally, in the seventh article, whether some names are applied to God temporally, as Creator and Lord, and others eternally. The second part of the question, which includes four articles, is concerned with the meaning of this name "God" in the first three articles, and in the fourth with the meaning of this name, "*Who is,*" whether it is the supremely appropriate name of God. The third part is a sort of recapitulation and application of the preceding doctrine to the conclusion established in the last query, namely, whether affirmative propositions can be formed about God.[5]

WHETHER A NAME CAN BE GIVEN TO GOD

State of the question. Three difficulties present themselves: (1) because it is commonly held that God is ineffable; (2) because every name is either concrete (wise), or abstract (wisdom). But a concrete name does not belong to God, since He is simple; nor does an abstract name belong to God, because He is subsisting Being; (3) there are special difficulties for the names taken to signify substance with quality, because God is without quality; for demonstrative pronouns, because God is not pointed out; for verbs that have a temporal signification, since God transcends time.

Yet the answer is that God can be named by us from creatures, yet not so that the name signifying Him expresses the divine essence in itself or quidditatively.

1) It is proved from Sacred Scripture, in which God is referred to under various names, such as Lord, Omnipotent, Who is. On the other hand, it is likewise said in Sacred Scripture that God is ineffable. The Fourth Lateran Council also declares this in the following words: "We firmly believe . . . that there is only one true, eternal, immense, immutable, incomprehensible, omnipotent, and ineffable God, the Father and Son and Holy Ghost." [6] So also Dionysius calls God anonymous or ineffable; yet he says that God has several names.[7]

2) Proof from reason. We can give a name to anything inasmuch as we can understand it. But in this life we know God from creatures, as being their principle, and also by way of excellence and remotion; in this life, however, we cannot see the essence of God. Therefore God can be named from creatures, yet not so that the name expresses the divine essence in itself.

The major has its foundation in the following principle formu-

[5] Consult the commentary of St. Thomas on the work of the Pseudo-Dionysius, entitled, *De divinis nominibus*. There is evidence of considerable progress in the doctrine as presented in this commentary compared with that given in this article of the theological summa. As to what the predecessors of St. Thomas held on this subject, consult also Alexander of Hales, *Summa*, Ia, q.48–70, and St. Albert the Great, *Summa theol.*, Ia, tr. III, q.13, membr. 1; q.14, membr. 1; q.15, membr. 1; and q.50–59. As for the commentators of St. Thomas, consult Cajetan, John of St. Thomas, Xantes Mariales, and Gonet.

[6] Denz., no. 428.

[7] *De div. nom.*, chap. 1.

lated by Aristotle, which clarifies this entire question: "Words are signs of ideas (of concepts and judgments), and ideas are the similitudes of things." [8] Thus words relate to the meaning of things signified through the medium of the intellectual concept. This formula, transcending nominalism and subjective conceptualism, is realistic. For the nominalists maintain that ideas do not express the nature of things; for instance, the idea of humanity would not express the human nature, but rather an actually existing collection of men. Thus the purpose of ideas would be, not for acquiring a knowledge of the nature of things, but rather for action; this is pragmatism. Thus, according to the nominalists, the principle of contradiction is a grammatical law for avoiding contradiction in discourse, and is at most a law of discursive thought, but is not a fundamental law of extramental being. Thus they end in doctrinal nihilism.[9]

The minor is evident from what was said in previous articles.[10] God is known from creatures as their principle. But we cannot have a proper concept of the Deity, such as would define it, for we have not a quidditative knowledge of the Deity. On the contrary, our concept of man, which defines man, is a proper concept. As St. Thomas says: "Such names (those signifying the divine substance) do not signify what God is, as though defining His substance." [11]

This is what St. Thomas thinks that St. John Damascene means, whom he quotes in this objection. Hence, as will be more clearly seen farther on, by the name "Deity" we understand that eminence which contains formally and eminently all absolutely simple perfections and the divine relations; but with reference to the Deity we are in this life like men who would know the seven colors of the rainbow without ever having seen whiteness. They would understand that the name "whiteness" implies the eminent fount of all colors; but the difference between whiteness and the Deity is, that whiteness contains colors only virtually, whereas the Deity contains all absolutely simple perfections formally and eminently. As Cajetan remarks: "The Deity is conceived through the medium of another concept (of being, of wisdom), yet it is not a representative but an abstractive concept of the Deity; and this is a sufficient rea-

8 *Perihermenias*, Bk. I, chap. 1.
9 On this subject of the real validity of the principle of contradiction, as founded on the first notion of being and on the principle of its primary opposition to non-being, consult Aristotle's *Metaphysics*, Bk. IV.
10 *Summa theol.*, Ia, q.2, a.3; q.4, a.3; q.12, a.4.
11 *De potentia*, q.7, a.5 ad 1um.

son for distinguishing between the Deity thus known and what is
directly known by us." [12]

Hence the names attributed to God do not accurately express
Him as He is, inasmuch as we have but an inadequate knowledge
of Him from creatures, whether by way of causality (as when we
say that He is the first Mover, the first efficient Cause, the first Ordainer), or by way of excellence (by means of such common concepts as supreme Being, supreme Truth, supreme Goodness), or by
way of remotion (by means of such negative concepts as immaterial,
immobile), or by a combination of common and relative concepts,
as when we say that He is the First Being.[13]

The solution of the objections confirms this conclusion.

Reply to first objection. God is ineffable inasmuch as "His essence is above all that we understand about God and signify in
word." For we do not know it quidditatively. We cannot say what
formally constitutes the Deity in itself, just as a person who never
saw whiteness cannot say what whiteness is. On the other hand,
we know what man is, namely, a rational animal; although his
specific difference is known by us abstractively and not intuitively,
as the angels know it.

Reply to second objection. With reference to creatures, abstract
names, such as wisdom, signify a simple form, whereas concrete
names, such as wise, signify a composite subsisting being in which
such form is found. And as God is both simple and subsisting, we
attribute abstract names to Him to signify His simplicity, and concrete names to signify His subsistence. In addition to this we say
that God is His Godhead; [14] for God not only exists, but is His
existence, His goodness, and similarly for His other attributes.

Reply to third objection. "Verbs and participles signifying time
are applied to God because His eternity includes all time." Thus
it is said of God that He is, was, will be, no distinction being made
between present, past, and future. But the way we speak of God
shows that we have an imperfect conception of Him, and this is
because in this life we know Him only from creatures.

Corollary. The perfect name of God, that is, the adequate name,
cannot be a name uttered by the voice, or formed in the imagination, or the word of a created mind but is the uncreated Word, in
whom the Father adequately declares His essence.[15]

[12] *Com. in Iam*, q.1, a.7; q.86, a.1, no. 7.
[13] Cf. *ibid.*, q.1, a.7.
[14] *Ibid.*, q.3, a.3.
[15] *Summa theol.*, Ia, q.34.

SECOND ARTICLE

WHETHER ANY NAME CAN BE APPLIED TO GOD
SUBSTANTIALLY

State of the question. God can be named; but how?

The title says "any name." Yet the inquiry is not about every name, for there are relative names that do not properly express the substance of God, but His relation to creatures, as Creator, or even Father as regards the only begotten Son. Hence the question is whether any name is applied to God substantially to signify His substance (although not quidditatively), or whether all God's names refer to creatures. Is this name "essential Being," for instance, applied to God substantially?

The difficulty is that we know God only from creatures. But, on the other hand, it is sufficiently clear that there is a certain distinction between absolute names, such as "essential Being," and relative names, such as "supreme Cause." Moreover, St. Augustine, who is quoted in the counterargument, says: "The being of God is the being strong, or the being wise, or whatever else we may say of that simplicity whereby His substance is signified." [16]

Conclusion. Negative names and names referring to creatures do not signify the substance of God; but, of course, absolute and affirmative names do, although they do not fully represent Him.

Examples of negative names are "incorporeal," "immense"; of relative names, "Lord," "efficient," "end"; of absolute and affirmative names, "being," "living," "wise." The first part of the conclusion is evident, for negative names signify the elimination of some imperfection, and relative names signify God's relation to creatures, or rather the relation of creatures to Him. Hence the second part must be proved, which concerns absolute and affirmative names.

That his argument may be convincing, (1) St. Thomas presents two opinions, (2) he proves his point by refuting these opinions, (3) he proves the same directly.

1) Two opinions are presented. The first was proposed by Maimonides (Rabbi Moses). He was born in Cordova in 1135, and his purpose was to give the true conception of anthropomorphism by distinguishing in Sacred Scripture between what is predicated metaphorically of God and what is predicated properly of Him. He believes that, to preserve God's simplicity, we must say that affirmative names, too, have been brought into use to express the elimination of something from God, rather than to express anything that exists

---

[16] *De Trin.*, Bk. VI, chap. 4.

positively in Him. Hence to say "God is living" would mean "God is not non-living."

Others said that absolute and affirmative names also are not predicated substantially, but causally. Hence to say "God is good" would mean that "God is the cause of goodness in things." [17]

2) The conclusion is proved indirectly by refuting both opinions at the same time. (1) If these opinions were true, it could be said that God is a body, because this could have but one of two meanings, either that God is the cause of bodies, or else that He is not primary matter without any actuality.[18] (2) Hence not only metaphorical names, but all names applied to God, would be predicated of Him in a secondary sense, and primarily of creatures. Thus, being and goodness would apply primarily to creatures, and this not only as regards the name that is imposed (by the way of investigation), but also as regards what is signified by the name.[19] Then God could not be called the essential Being, the first Being; and creatures could not be called being by participation. Christ said: "No one is good, but God only." [20]

3) Names express what is conceived by the mind of those uttering them. But the above opinions are contrary to what is meant by those speaking of God. For when they say that God is good, they do not mean to say that God is the cause of goodness, but that God is good in Himself. It is especially to this that Christ referred.[21]

Moreover, it must be noted that St. Thomas says against Maimonides: "It would also follow from this that we could not say of God that He was wise or good before creatures were. . . . Moreover, a negation is always understood on the basis of an affirmation, for every negative proposition is proved by an affirmative. Hence, if the human intellect could not positively know anything about God, it could not deny anything about Him." [22]

4) The conclusion is proved directly. Absolute and affirmative names are predicated of God substantially, but imperfectly. For names express God so far as our intellect knows Him from creatures. But creatures are made like to God, the likeness being

---

[17] Concerning these opinions, consult St. Thomas' *De potentia*, q.7, a.5.

[18] The reference is here to the Aristotelian and scholastic theory of matter and form. Primary matter is the substratum, or that which underlies every existing material thing. It is never found apart from its actualizing form. It is, in relation to its form, a pure potentiality; yet it is something real, and not merely a logical entity. [Tr.]

[19] Cf. ad 2um and a.6.

[20] Mark 10: 18.

[21] Cf. *ibid.*

[22] *De potentia*, q.7, a.5.

imperfect, which is neither specific nor generic, but which is analogous. Therefore absolute and affirmative names are predicated of God substantially but imperfectly.[23]

The major is proved from the preceding article. The minor is evident from what was said in the third article of the fourth question, in which it was proved that creatures are like God inasmuch as every agent reproduces itself either specifically or generically or at least analogically.

Likewise, in the second article of the fourth question it was said: "Whatever perfection exists in an effect must be found in the effective cause: either in the same formality, if it is a univocal agent, or in a more eminent degree, if it is an equivocal agent (non-univocal). . . . Since therefore God is the first effective cause of things, the perfections of all things must pre-exist in God in a more eminent way," to the exclusion of imperfections.

But as St. Thomas points out in this article and in the following one, as also in another of his works,[24] we must carefully distinguish between absolutely simple and mixed perfections, in that the former imply no imperfection in their formal concepts. Such are being, truth, goodness, wisdom, and love, although the created mode of these perfections is imperfect. On the contrary, mixed perfections, such as rationability and discursive knowledge, denote imperfection in their formal concepts.

Hence, as St. Thomas says in this article, when we say God is good, the meaning is not that God is the cause of goodness, or that God is not evil; but the meaning is that whatever good we attribute to creatures pre-exists in God, and in a higher way. And also, "because He is good in Himself, He causes goodness in things." The solution of the objections confirms this.[25]

What Dionysius meant when he said[26] that such expressions as not-good, or super-good, not-wise . . . must be attributed to God, is explained elsewhere by St. Thomas.[27] His opinion is that these names are affirmed of God according to the thing signified, or according to what is meant by the name; but they may be denied because of the mode of their signification. For, according to the mode of their signification, abstract names, such as wisdom, signify a form apart from its subject, and concrete names, such as wise, signify a composite, consisting of a subject that has such a form. But God is pure self-subsisting form. To say that God is super-

---

[23] This adverb "imperfectly" will be more fully explained in the third and fifth articles of this question.

[24] *Contra Gentes*, Bk. I, chap. 30.

[25] Cf. ad 1um, ad 2um, ad 3um.

[26] *De div. nom.*, chaps. 1, 5.

[27] *De potentia*, q.7, a.5 ad 2um.

good is to say that the Deity or God's intimate life, contains all absolutely simple perfections in an eminent way, which was proved in the preceding article. In the next article it is proved that God contains these perfections not only eminently, but also formally and eminently, that is, more than virtually. But this is already suggested in the present article, in which it is said that absolute and affirmative names are predicated of God "not only causally but substantially, although imperfectly."

And so the danger of agnosticism is already avoided, which maintains that God is absolutely unknowable, inasmuch as He transcends the genera and the species.

THIRD ARTICLE

WHETHER ANY NAME CAN BE APPLIED TO GOD IN ITS LITERAL SENSE

State of the question. It is not "commonly" but "metaphorically" that is here contrasted with "literally." Thus we speak frequently of the literal meaning of words, meaning what is not metaphorical. In the interpretation of Sacred Scripture the distinction between the literal and the metaphorical senses must be very carefully noted. Thus it is often said that God is just, and sometimes He is said to be angry. He is said to be angry metaphorically, since anger is, strictly speaking, a passion, which has no place in the pure Spirit. But the question is whether the word "just" is to be applied to God in its literal sense, or is not to be so applied, because He is super-just. This difficulty arises from what Dionysius is quoted as saying in the second objection, who maintained that these names, "good," "wise," "just," are more truly withheld from God than predicated of Him.

The conclusion of St. Thomas is that, as regards the signified perfection, several names are predicated properly of God and more properly and primarily than they are of creatures. But as regards their mode of signification, they do not properly apply to God.

First the terms are explained; for instance, as regards the perfection signified by the name, "wisdom" signifies knowledge by the highest of causes. But as regards the mode of its signification, wisdom is an accident, that is, a quality of the mind either acquired or infused, or a habit of the created mind. Thus wisdom is in a certain genus and in a certain species of quality; hence under this aspect it cannot be properly attributed to God, who is not in any genus.

The terms being thus explained, the reason for the conclusion, which is stated more clearly in the reply to the first objection, is that the perfection signified by these names implies no imperfection, as in the case of wisdom; whereas the mode of their significations is imperfect and applies to creatures. On the contrary, other names which, in their formal signification, imply imperfection, such as "angry," are predicated of God only metaphorically.

The reply to the first objection finds fuller expression in another of St. Thomas' works.[28] According to what he states there, it may be said that God is not wise, but super-wise, if the imperfect mode is considered, inasmuch as wisdom is found in man as an acquired or infused habit.

It must be noted that the expression "properly as regards what is formally signified and not properly as regards the mode of signification" is somewhat the equivalent of "formally" and "eminently," that is, formally as regards the perfection signified, eminently and virtually as regards the mode of signification. However, this term "formally" must be understood as referring to predication not in the univocal sense but in the analogical, as will be stated in the fifth article.[29]

FOURTH ARTICLE

WHETHER NAMES APPLIED TO GOD ARE SYNONYMOUS

State of the question. Synonymous names are those that have absolutely the same meaning, so that to say that God is wise, good, merciful, just, would be the same in meaning. If this were so, then, as it is said that God punishes by His justice, it could likewise be said that He punishes by His mercy, for justice and mercy would have the same meaning. This would result in agnosticism, and any distinction between justice and mercy would be no longer tenable. Yet evidently they are distinct from the way Sacred Scripture uses these terms.

But the difficulty here is to show why such names are not synonymous. This question is the same as the problem about the distinction between God's attributes. As previously remarked by us, the nominalists admitted only a logical distinction between them, such as between Peter the subject and Peter the predicate in a proposition, as when we say: Peter is Peter; or they admitted a nominal distinction, such as that between Tullius and Cicero. Scotus Eriugena said about the same. Similarly, these two propositions of Master Eckhart were condemned: "Any distinction in God

---

[28] *Ibid.*
[29] See Cajetan's *Commentary on Summa*, q. 13, a. 5, no. 7.

is both impossible and inconceivable. Any kind of distinction does not apply to God." [30]

On the contrary, Gilbert de la Porrée said: "The divinity is not God, but the form by which He is," [31] because abstract names do not signify the subsisting subject. There is a certain anthropomorphism in this, since the imperfect mode of creatures is thus transferred to God.

Duns Scotus posited his actual-formal distinction between the divine attributes, considered as objects. There appears to be no possibility of a medium between the distinction that is not the result and that which is the result of the mind's consideration. But if this distinction of Scotus is more than a virtual distinction, as previously stated, then it is incompatible with God's absolute simplicity.

Very many theologians admit a minor virtual distinction between God's essence and His attributes, inasmuch as His essence, which is conceived by us actually and implicitly, but not explicitly, signifies the attributes that are derived from it. [32]

The exclusion of synonymous names is still the difficulty that confronts us; for, as stated in the objections, all divine names mean the same thing, namely, God's substance, which is most simple. If it is said that they signify the same thing, but differ in idea, there seems to be no purpose in different ideas that do not correspond to different things. Moreover, God is supremely one, not only in reality, but also in idea, which means that there is one proper and most eminent concept which expresses Him, this being the concept of the Deity.

Nevertheless the conclusion is that names attributed to God, although they signify the same reality, are not synonymous.

1) This conclusion is proved indirectly in the counterargument, for if these names are synonymous then their multiplication would be redundant or absolutely superfluous; because it would be affirming the same thing when we say that God is just and that God is merciful. In fact, if these names were synonymous, it could be said that God punishes by His mercy, and forgives by His justice. This would be agnosticism.

2) Direct proof. Names that signify the same thing but have different meanings are not synonymous. But such are the divine names: supreme being, wisdom, goodness, justice, mercy. . . . Therefore divine names are not synonymous.

The major has its foundation in the principle that names signify

[30] Denz., nos. 523 f.
[31] *Ibid.*, no. 389.
[32] See introduction to third question: the divine attributes.

the thing only through the medium of the intellectual conception.[33] The minor, however, is proved in the body of the article as follows: "But our intellect, since it knows God from creatures, forms conceptions proportional to the perfections flowing from God to creatures, which perfections pre-exist in God unitedly and simply, whereas in creatures they are received, divided, and multiplied."

This means that being, wisdom, goodness, belong indeed properly to God, as was stated in the third article, but they are identified in the eminence of the Deity; and they are so identified in the Deity as not to be destructive of one another, but are there in a most pure state. Thus the divine being is the self-subsisting Being, who is identical with His self-subsisting intellection; also the divine existence is identical with the self-subsisting will of God. But there is only a virtual distinction between God's subsistent intellection and His subsistent will. Thus what inferior beings have separately, superior beings have unitedly.[34]

So, analogically, the rational soul is eminently and formally both sensitive and vegetative. This means that there are not three subordinated souls in man, but only one, which is at one and the same time the principle of the intellective, sensitive, and vegetative lives. These three names are not synonymous, although they denote the same soul, because they denote it under different aspects. Nor need we have recourse to the actual-formal distinction on the part of the object, because this distinction is either previous to or the result of the mind's consideration. In the latter case the distinction is virtual; in the former case, the distinction is already real, which is repugnant to God's absolute simplicity.

Reply to second objection. "The many aspects of these names are not empty and vain, for there corresponds to all of them one simple reality represented by them in a manifold and imperfect manner." This means that the eminence of the Deity, which is most simple, is virtually multiple, since it is variously imitable. Similarly, in the natural order the same cause is virtually multiple, inasmuch as it produces different effects in different subjects. Thus fire expands iron, melts wax, burns flesh. . . . It is also evident a priori, as was shown above,[35] that multitude does not explain the reason for unity, and that it must proceed from the supremely One, who must hence be virtually multiple. In like manner, great artists,

---

[33] Cf. ad 1um.

[34] See Cajetan's commentary on a.5, no. 7. He shows most clearly that intellection and volition can be identified only in one formal concept of a higher order, namely, in the concept of the Deity; otherwise they would be destructive of each other, since volition would be completely changed into intellection, or vice versa. Thus the Deity is eminently and formally intellection and love.

[35] *Summa theol.*, Ia, q.2, a.3 (fourth way).

such as Leonardo da Vinci, in their portraits of persons seek to depict what is, so to speak, the predominant trait, which, though simple in itself, is virtually multiple. So also the fundamental principle of any doctrine is simple in itself and virtually multiple, such as the Aristotelian distinction between actuality and potentiality. In the reply to the difficulty proposed in the third objection, it is stated that God is supremely one, not only in reality but also in idea. In other words, there is not only one reality in God, but also only one most proper and most eminent concept of Him, namely, the concept of the Deity, which, according to revelation, is expressed in His only Word.

St. Thomas also says in his reply: "The perfect unity of God requires that what are manifold and divided in others should exist in Him simply and unitedly." This must be given careful consideration, since it is the foundation for the distinction between the most imperfect unity (for instance, of primary matter) and the supreme unity. This inferior kind of unity is potential, and is found in primary matter, which is quasi-negatively the same in all bodies; for this inferior kind of unity is found even in inferior elementary bodies and in the primitive cell from which the embryo originates, before the multiplicity or diversity of the parts of the organism appear in it. Contrary to this, the higher kind of unity is not potential but actual, and is then virtually multiple; such is the unity of the rational soul on which the divers parts of our exceedingly complex organism depend. But transcending all is the divine unity, which is the maximum in actuality, and of such virtual multiplicity that it contains an infinite multitude of possible things. At the end of this reply to the third objection the reason is given why "our intellect apprehends God in a manifold manner," because it apprehends Him "as things represent Him, which is in a manifold manner."

First Corollary. There is only one truth for the divine intellect concerning God, the one and only Word being the adequate expression of this truth. This truth not only expresses equality but also identity between the divine intellect and the divine reality.

Second Corollary. As for the created intellect, especially the human, there are many truths about God, and there are many names applied to Him that are not synonymous, which means that they do not have the same meaning. The reason for this is that truth exists formally in the mind and not in the thing; for it denotes conformity between the judgment formed by the mind and the thing judged conformable to it. Hence for us there are certain revealed truths about God, others that are deduced from revealed truths, and also others that are naturally knowable.

Third Corollary. To say that these two truths, "God is intelligent" and "God is free," have the same meaning and that therefore, if the first is revealed, by this very fact the second is revealed, is to say that divine names are synonymous. Then it could be said that God punishes by His mercy, and forgives by His justice.[36]

Fourth Corollary. The lower the degree of intellectuality of the created intellect, the more it apprehends God by a multiplicity of concepts.

FIFTH ARTICLE

WHETHER WHAT IS SAID OF GOD AND OF CREATURES
IS UNIVOCALLY PREDICATED OF THEM

State of the question. We know that many names applied to God, who is most simple, are predicated of Him substantially and in the literal sense, yet not so as to be synonymous. The question is whether they are predicated univocally or analogically. Now it is certain from what has been said that they are not predicated equivocally, because they are attributed to God in the literal sense. St. Thomas adopts Aristotle's terminology,[37] and this must be explained, as St. Thomas himself explains at the end of the argumentative part of this article.

A univocal term is one that is predicated of things simply in the same sense. Thus "man" is predicated univocally of various men, as "animal" is predicated of the horse, the wolf, and the lion. For by these names is meant either the species that is simply the same in individuals of the species, or else the genus which is likewise simply the same. Thus the name "animal" signifies a living body endowed with sensitive life, and this genus is diversified by *differentiae* that are extrinsic to it. Thus the univocal concept ad-

---

36 Father Marin Sola does not pay sufficient attention to this, for in his *Evolution homogène du dogme catholique* (Fr. tr., II, 333), he says: "Two propositions that have the same subject (God) differ or are identical in meaning according to their predicates. If, therefore, the predicates are really identical, the meaning of the propositions will be also." If the predicates are really identical in reality and idea, then the propositions will have the same meaning, this I concede; if the predicates are identical in reality and not in idea, then I deny this. It is quite clear that in God, inasmuch as He is a reality, there is no real distinction between intelligence and liberty. But divine intelligence and divine liberty are not the same in meaning, are not synonymous; they do, indeed, concern the same thing, as it is a reality, but not as it is an object, as Cajetan says in his commentary on Ia, q. 1, a. 3, no. 8. Otherwise, in wishing nothing else but to consider the point, under the pretext of avoiding nominalism, this nominalist thesis would be admitted by us, namely, that divine names are synonymous.

37 See *Categories,* chap. 1, no. 2; *Post. Anal.,* Bk. II, chaps. 13, 14; *Metaph.,* Bk. IV, chap. 1; Bk. X, chap. 1; Bk. XII, chap. 4; *Ethics,* Bk. 1, chap. 6.

396 THE ONE GOD

mits of complete logical separation from the different subjects to which it is attributed.

An equivocal term is one that is predicated of things in an entirely different sense. Thus "lion" is predicated equivocally of the quadruped and of one of the signs of the zodiac. Similarly "dog" is predicated of the animal and of a certain constellation.

An analogous term is one that is predicated of different things neither in simply the same sense nor in an entirely different sense, but according to a certain proportion or proportionality.[38] An example of analogy of proportion or of attribution is the following: health is predicated primarily of the animal; and then proportionately, as referring to the healthy animal, the urine is said to be healthy (as a sign of health), the air, the food (as being the causes of health), medicine. . . . There is a proportion among these analogates, and extrinsic denomination suffices for this, as health is intrinsically in the healthy animal, and only extrinsically in the air, the urine. . . . Hence this analogy is also called analogy of attribution, because extrinsic attribution suffices for such analogy.

An example of analogy of proportionality is the following: what the head is to the organic body, such is the general to his army, and the king to his kingdom. But this analogy of proportionality can be either metaphorical or proper. The king is metaphorically said to be the head of his kingdom. On the contrary, being is predicated in the proper sense of substance and of accident; for substance has existence in itself, and accident in another. Similarly, cognition is predicated properly and proportionately of sensation and intellection, because sensation is to the sensible what intellection is to the intelligible. Similarly love is predicated properly of sensitive love and of rational love. Nor does this demand a deter-

[38] Certain eclectics, refusing to decide which is the true general metaphysics, whether it be the Thomistic, the Scotist, or the Suarezian metaphysics, say: "Those things are analogous which have the same name, but what is signified by the name is partly the same, and partly different." This was, indeed, at one time the view of St. Thomas; but it is merely a nominal and as yet confused definition of analogy. For Scotus and Suarez, the analogical concept is simply the same and relatively different; on the other hand, for the Thomists such a concept is simply different and relatively (or proportionately) the same. (See the appendix to the seventh article of this question, in which these doctrines are compared.) St. Thomas knows quite well that the definition of analogy must declare in what the analogical concept (or perfection) simply consists: whether it has absolutely the same or has absolutely a different meaning in the things it represents. And he says at the end of the argumentative part of the article: "For in analogies the idea is not, as it is in univocals, one and the same, yet it is not totally diverse as in equivocals; but a term which is thus used in a multiple sense signifies various proportions to some one thing." The same applies to analogy of attribution, and it is proportionately the same idea that is signified by the term in the analogy of proportionality. See also Ia, q.4, a.2, 3; De veritate, q.2, a.11.

minate proportion among these analogates; in fact, there is an immense or immeasurable difference among them, since intellection pertains to the higher order, so that the internal senses would always be susceptible to further perfection in their order, and yet they would never attain to the dignity of the lowest grade of intellection.[39]

This division of analogy may be expressed by the following schema:

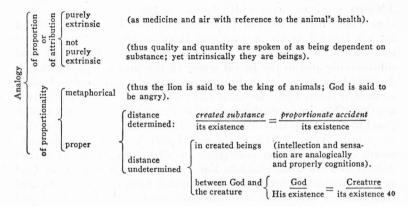

With these principles posited about the terminology, the chief difficulty about our knowledge of God is in the statement made immediately before the argumentative part of this article, namely, "God is more distant from creatures than any creatures are from each other." If, therefore, no corporeal being seems to be a sufficiently expressive image for our knowledge of the created pure spirit, far more so no creature whatever can be this for our knowledge of God.

Yet the reply is that names are predicated of God and creatures, neither univocally, nor equivocally, but analogically or proportionately. There are three parts to this reply.

First part. Not univocally: because the names are not predicated as having absolutely the same meaning. The reason for this is that "the effect which is not an adequate result of the power of the efficient cause, receives the similitude of the agent not in its full

[39] Read what St. Thomas says about this at the end of the argumentative part of this article. Although he does not clearly distinguish between analogy of proportion and analogy of proportionality in this article, yet he speaks about this latter in the body of this article, and in the replies to the first and second objections, in which he refers to the likeness of the creature to God. See also Ia, q.4, a.2, 3; q.13, a.2, 3; *De veritate*, q.2, a.11.

[40] For a fuller explanation of these matters consult what we wrote in *De revelatione*, I, 301–18.

degree, but in a measure that falls short." Thus wisdom in man is an accident that is distinct from his essence, his existence, his intellectual faculty, whereas in God wisdom is the same as the divine essence.

This terminology of St. Thomas must be carefully noted, for he says: "Hence it is evident that this term 'wise' is not applied in the same way to God and to man." St. Thomas says the same in several other passages.[41] Cajetan most faithfully preserves St. Thomas' teaching, with which Scotus disagrees.

2) These names are not predicated equivocally. This has been already refuted in the second and third articles of this question, in which it is shown that several names are predicated of God substantially and in the literal sense. In this article equivocation is disproved by reason of its inappropriateness, since "nothing could be known about God" which is contrary to Sacred Scripture testifying that "The invisible things of Him are clearly seen, being understood by the things that are made." [42] Moreover, it is quite clear that the words "being," "wise," do not signify in God and creatures totally different ideas or perfections, as when "dog" is predicated of animal and the constellation. For "being" signifies, both in God and in creatures, *that which is,* although God is self-existent and creatures are not. Similarly "wisdom" signifies, both in God and in man, knowledge by the highest of causes, although not applied in the same way to each.

3) These names are predicated analogically. The reason for this, which has already been given [43] and which is repeated in the body of this article and in the reply to the first objection, is that every agent reproduces itself, inasmuch as it determines according to its own determination, and therefore it produces something that is either specifically or generically or at least analogically like itself. Thus there is proportion or order, and proportionality between God and creatures. But St. Thomas speaks more of the analogy of proportion in this article. In other passages, however, he speaks explicitly of the analogy of proportionality.[44]

41 Cf. Ia, q.4, a.2: "Whatever perfection exists in an effect must be found in the effective cause: either in the same formality, if it is a univocal agent, as when man reproduces man, or in a more eminent degree, if it is an equivocal or non-univocal agent." Also in Ia, q.4, a.3, he says: "In a third way, some things are said to be alike which communicate in the same form (or perfection), but not according to the same formality, as we see in non-univocal agents." Likewise at the end of the argumentative part of the present article, he says: "For in analogies the idea is not, as it is in univocals, one and the same, yet it is not totally diverse as in equivocals."

42 Rom. 1: 20.

43 Cf. Ia, q.4, a.2, 3.

44 Cf. *De veritate,* q.2, a.11.

1) There is proportion, or preferably order of the creature toward God as to its principle and cause, so that the being of creatures depends on the divine Being. This is stated in the article.

2) There is proportionality, since there is a likeness between the being of creatures and the divine Being, between created wisdom and uncreated wisdom.

$$\frac{God}{His \ being} = \frac{creature}{its \ being} \qquad \frac{God}{to \ all \ things \ that \ must \ be \ known} = \frac{the \ wise \ person}{to \ all \ things \ that \ must \ be \ known}$$

This similitude is according to a formality that is neither absolutely the same nor totally different, but proportionally the same. The creature, like God, is intrinsically being, namely, that which exists, but it is not its existence. Man, like God, is intelligent, but he is not his intellection; created wisdom is knowledge of things by the highest of causes, but it is not the cause of things. In all these examples there is similarity of two proportions, namely, as being is predicated of the creature in relation to its existence, so being is predicated of God in relation to His existence; but God alone is His existence. And as the Lateran Council says: "Between God and the creature so great a similarity cannot be detected, as not to detect a greater dissimilarity between them." [45]

Therefore the analogous notion cannot be perfectly prescribed from its analogates, because it expresses what is proportionally alike in each (for example, being is that which exists); and that which is proportionally alike cannot be conceived without the very members of the proportionality being included confusedly in the concept.[46] Contrary to this, the univocal notion, such as humanity, animality, can be perfectly prescinded or abstracted from its various subjects. The univocal notion can be represented by the symbol o; the analogical notion, however, by the symbol 8.

The analogy of attribution can express the relation of one thing to another (as of the air to the health of the animal), or of several things to one object (as of the salubrious air and the healthful remedy to the health of the animal). And since extrinsic denomination suffices for this analogy of attribution in the secondary analogates (for the air is not intrinsically healthy), this analogy does not as yet clearly make known in what the analogates are intrinsically alike, when they are truly so alike. Hence, although this analogy is

---

[45] Denz., no. 432.

[46] Being is that which exists either of itself (God), or by reason of another (creature), or in itself (substance), or in another (accident). Thus there is truly an analogical concept in the analogy of proper proportionality, whereas there is a univocal concept (as of health) in the analogy of attribution, which is applied to others by extrinsic denomination.

perhaps prior in the way of investigation, yet if we wish to know in what the analogates, which have something intrinsically in common, are intrinsically alike among themselves, we must have recourse to the more profound analogy of proportionality. Thus from the relation of sense perception to the sensible object, we know analogically the relation of the intellect to the intelligible object, although it is of a higher order; also from the relation of the sensitive appetite to sensible good, we know analogically the higher relation of the will to rational or spiritual good. Likewise from the relation of created being to its existence, we know analogically of the conformity between the uncreated Being and His existence, who is, however, the self-subsisting Being. Similarly from the relation of human wisdom to things known by it we know analogically what divine wisdom is, although this latter is the cause of things, whereas our wisdom is caused by things.

It is of this proportionality that St. Thomas frequently speaks, as in the following passage: "Sometimes the attention is directed to conformity between two terms not proportionate to each other, but which are proportional, as between 6 and 4, for 6 is to 3, as 4 is to 2. . . . Thus seeing is predicated (analogically) of both corporeal and intellectual vision because, as sense perception is in the eye, so intellectual perception is in the mind." [47] This is the similarity that prevails between the created being and the uncreated Being, and they are both intrinsically beings (that which exists, that whose act is existence), but it is a different mode of existence in each. God alone is His existence, whereas the creature has existence, and has it dependent upon another. St. Thomas speaks of this analogical likeness (and indeed intrinsic) in the reply to the first objection of this article: "The universal agent (God), while it is not univocal, nevertheless is not altogether equivocal, otherwise it could not produce its own likeness, but rather it is to be called an analogical agent." [48] In the reply to the second objection, he says: "The creature's likeness to God is imperfect, for it does not represent one and the same generic thing." [49]

SOLUTION OF OBJECTIONS

1) **Objection of the agnostics.** There is no proportion between the finite and the infinite. But the aforesaid analogy would suppose this proportion.

Reply. That there is no quantitative or proper proportion, this

[47] *De veritate*, q.2, a.11.
[48] See also Ia, q.4, a.2, 3.
[49] Cf. q.4, a.3.

I concede; that there is no proportion in the sense of proportionality, this I deny. Thus a likeness that is dependent on the divine causality is sufficiently established.[50]

Instance. The difference between God and the creature is greater than that between the creature and nothingness. Hence the Scripture says: "My substance is as nothing before Thee." [51] But there is no analogy between the created being and nothingness. Therefore there is no analogy between God and the creature.

Reply. I distinguish the major. That the difference is greater as regards the mode of being, this I concede; greater according to the idea of being, this I deny.

Instance. The divine perfections, such as intellection and volition, cannot be identified without being destructive of one another. But, according to the aforesaid doctrine, they are identified in God. Therefore they are destructive of one another.

Reply. I distinguish the major. That they cannot be immediately identified so that intellection is the same as volition, or vice versa, this I concede; that they cannot be identified in the formal and more eminent notion of the Deity without being destructive of one another, this I deny.[52] Superior beings unite in themselves the various perfections of inferior beings. So eminent is the formal notion of the Deity that it is equivalent to intelligence, will, and other perfections, which are contained therein formally and eminently. The Deity truly furnishes the foundation for these different concepts.

And the aforesaid perfections cannot indeed be thus identified according to their created mode, but according to the uncreated mode. In fact, essence and existence, as well as operative power and operation, demand according to their proper exigencies that they be identified, since they are contained in the Deity without any potentiality. But intellection and volition are identified not under the aspect of being, but under the aspect of Deity. Therefore the intimate reconciliation of God's attributes remains a mystery for us, since we have not the proper concept of the Deity.

Objections of Scotus and the Scotists. Although they admit analogy of being, yet they seek to retain univocity of being between God and creatures. For Scotus, the formal notion of being is not only proportionately but also absolutely one in God and creatures.

First objection. The concept of being prescinds completely from God and creatures, since anyone can be certain, for instance, that charity is an entity and yet can doubt whether charity is either

[50] Cf. *De veritate,* q.2, a.1, 11; q.22, a.7 ad 9um.
[51] Ps. 38: 6.
[52] See Cajetan, *Com. in Iam,* q.13, a.5, no. 7.

God or something created. Therefore the concept is absolutely one.

Reply. Concerning this doubt, it suffices to say that the analogous concept does not clearly express the analogates, though it actually implies them, and not merely virtually, as the genus includes the various species. For being, indeed, is that which exists either of itself or by reason of another, and the various modes of being are still being, whereas rationality is not animality.

Instance. If God and creatures were actually implied in the concept of being, then God would be predicated of anything whatever about which being is predicated. But the consequent is absurd. Therefore the antecedent is also.

Reply. I distinguish the antecedent: If the concept of being actually and conjointly implies God and creatures, then I concede the antecedent; if the concept implies them separately, then I deny the antecedent. For being is that which exists, either of itself or by reason of another; or it is predicated separately but not conjointly of God and creatures.[53]

SIXTH ARTICLE

WHETHER NAMES PREDICATED OF GOD ARE PREDICATED
PRIMARILY OF CREATURES

State of the question. It seems that they are predicated primarily of creatures, for our first knowledge is of creatures. "We name God from creatures." [54]

St. Thomas replies to this with the following distinctions:

1) All names that are applied metaphorically to God are applied primarily to creatures, for they mean only similitudes to creatures. Thus God is metaphorically said to be angry, and anger is primarily predicated of the movement of the sensitive irascible appetite.

2) Names that are not applied to God metaphorically but properly, are applied to Him primarily as regards what the names signify, and primarily to creatures as regards the imposition of the names. The reason for the first part of this conclusion is that they are applied to God not as the cause only, but also substantially.[55] The reason for the second part is that, in the way of investigation, our first knowledge is of creatures.

[53] Consult Cajetan's commentary on this article, and his treatise *De analogia nominum,* chaps. 5, 10. See also the appendix to the seventh article of this question, in which the doctrine of St. Thomas is compared with that of Scotus and Suarez.
[54] Dionysius, *De nom. div.,* chap. 1.
[55] Cf. q. 13, a. 2.

And so this explains why Christ said: "None is good but one, that is God," [56] and why St. Paul wrote: "I bow my knees to the Father of our Lord Jesus Christ, of whom all paternity in heaven and earth is named." [57] This article, in thus explaining these revealed words, is of great importance in the refutation of agnosticism, just as the third article is, in which it is stated that these names are applied to God in the literal sense, and not metaphorically or symbolically.

SEVENTH ARTICLE

WHETHER NAMES WHICH IMPLY RELATION TO CREATURES
ARE APPLIED TO GOD TEMPORALLY

The question is whether such names as Creator, Lord, Savior, can be applied to God eternally. It seems to be so, because the creative action is the same as God's essence, so that it is eternal, although its effect takes place only in time. Moreover, if these names were applied to God temporally, it could be said that God became the Savior, and this would denote a certain change in God. At least it would posit a new relation in God toward creatures, and not only a logical but a real relation, because God is really the Creator and the Savior.

The reply is: The names which import relation to creatures are applied to God temporally, and not from eternity.

The reason for this is clearly given at the end of the argumentative part of this article. It is that these names are predicated not indeed because of any change in God, but because of some change in the creature; so that these names denote a real relation of dependence of the creature upon God, and only a logical relation of God toward the creature.

This is possible because "the two extremes are not of the same order." Thus there is a real relation of the visual faculty to the thing visible; but there is not a real relation of the visible object considered according to its physical entity to the visual faculty, for this physical order is distinct from the cognitive order. Likewise there is a real relation of knowledge to the thing knowable; but the thing knowable considered in itself is not in real relation to knowledge, because the thing in itself is of another order, namely, of the physical. Hence the thing is said to be known only by extrinsic denomination, according to a logical relation. But God completely transcends the order of created beings, and all created beings are ordered to Him, and not conversely.

[56] Mark 10: 18.
[57] Eph. 3: 14.

Thus these names (Creator, Savior, Lord) are applied to God temporally, not because of a change in God, but because of a change in creatures.

Reply to first objection. " 'Creator' and 'Savior' are applied temporally in their relation to creatures, but not as they signify the divine essence," since the creative action is the same as the divine essence.

This completes the first part of this question, which is a discussion of the divine names in general. The solution of the following doubt is appended to this part by way of recapitulation.

THE DOCTRINE OF ST. THOMAS COMPARED WITH THE TEACHINGS OF SCOTUS AND SUAREZ

THE EMINENCE OF THE DEITY

What is meant by the statement that the divine perfections are contained "formally and eminently" in God?

It is generally admitted that absolutely simple perfections are contained "formally and eminently" in God. What this means, according to the teaching of St. Thomas, must now be the subject of inquiry.

All theologians are aware of the necessity of defending this doctrine so as to avoid the nominalism of modern agnostics, who to some extent revive the opinion of Maimonides (Rabbi Moses), who said that the divine attributes are contained virtually and eminently in God, as mixed perfections are, rather than formally and eminently.

But theologians are not all agreed as to the meaning of this last expression, and so its exact signification is now sought. First of all we must recall very briefly what is commonly admitted on this subject, as recorded by St. Thomas in the various articles of this thirteenth question, and in the same order as presented by him.

I. What does the adverb "formally" signify in the above expression?

1) These absolutely simple perfections are said to be formally in God inasmuch as they are in Him substantially and in the literal sense.[58] Substantially, indeed, and not merely causally, as if "God is good" meant, as Maimonides contends, merely that "God is the cause of good things." [59] In the literal sense, too, and not merely metaphorically. Thus, in the literal sense, God is said to be just, and metaphorically He is said to be angry.[60]

---

[58] Cf. a.1, 2, 3.
[59] Cf. a.2.
[60] Cf. a.3.

The reason for this twofold assertion is that absolutely simple perfections, such as goodness, wisdom, love, imply no imperfection in their formal signification, since they differ from the finite mode of these perfections in creatures. And it is clear that the First Cause must possess eminently all created perfections that imply no imperfection.[61] There is not the least doubt about this part of the question.

2) The names that express the above-mentioned perfections are not synonymous. This is said in refutation of the nominalists who asserted that there is only a logical and verbal distinction between the divine attributes, such as between Tullius and Cicero. If this were so, then, just as it is purely optional for one to write Cicero instead of Tullius, so it would be purely optional for one to write divine justice instead of mercy, and thus it could be said that God punishes by His mercy, and forgives by His justice.[62] This second assertion is likewise most certain, and is commonly admitted by Thomists, Scotists, and Suarezians.

3) The aforesaid perfections are predicated of God neither univocally nor equivocally, but analogically. Hence in the expression "formally and eminently" the meaning is: formally and eminently, not univocally. For St. Thomas says: "Every effect which is not an adequate result of the power of the efficient cause, receives the similitude of the agent not in its full degree (which means, according to the context, not univocally), but in a measure that falls short, so that what is divided and multiplied in the effects resides in the agent simply, and in the same manner. . . . All perfections existing in creatures divided and multiplied, pre-exist in God unitedly and simply."[63]

These texts are of great importance. St. Thomas defines analogy for us in these texts, though not in the way Suarez does.[64] For those who accept the principles of Suarez, analogues are such as have a

---

[61] *Ibid.*, Ia, q.4, a.2, 3.

[62] Cf. a.4.

[63] Cf. a.5; also Ia, q.4, a.2, 3.

[64] Consult Suarez (*Disp. metaph.*, disp. 2, sect. 2, no. 34), who, in discussing the unity of the concept of being, says: "Now I merely assert that everything which has been said concerning the *unity* of the concept of being, appears to be clearer and more certain than that *being is analogous*. Therefore, in order to defend analogy, it is not right to deny the unity of the concept; but if one of the two must be denied, it is analogy, which is uncertain, that is to be denied rather than unity of concept, which seems to be demonstrated by sound arguments. See also *Disp. metaph.*, disp. 28, sect. 3, nos. 9, 11; disp. 32, sect. 2. See also Delmas, S.J., *Metaphysica*, p. 61; Frick, S.J., *Ontologia*, no. 23. For those who take the opposite view, consult A. Martin: "*Suarez métaphysicien et théologien*" (*Science catholique*, July, September, 1898); Norbert del Prado, O.P., *De veritate fundamentali*, pp. 196 f.: "*Suarez recedens a D. Thoma per viam Scoti graditur.*"

common name, but the meaning signified by the name is *relatively speaking different* and *absolutely speaking the same*. But the Thomists maintain that St. Thomas defined analogues as having a common name, but the meaning signified by the name is *absolutely speaking different in the analogates*, and *relatively speaking the same in them*, that is, they are alike according to some proportion, or proportionally the same.[65]

This Thomistic formula expresses adequately the teaching of St. Thomas in the text just quoted, in which he speaks *ex professo* on this subject, and says: "Every effect which is not an adequate result of the power of the efficient cause, receives the similitude of the agent not in its full degree (that is, not univocally, as is evident from the preceding paragraph in the context), but in a measure that falls short." [66] A little farther on in this same article, he says: "This term 'wise' is not applied in the same way to God and to man." The term is predicated, indeed, in proportionally the same sense, inasmuch as wisdom in general is knowledge by the highest of causes; but God's wisdom is the cause of things, whereas created wisdom is caused or measured by things.[67]

The way St. Thomas expresses himself here is completely in agreement with what is commonly admitted in logic, which establishes a distinction betwen analogues and univocals. Thus it is said that the generic and univocal name "animality" expresses absolutely the same notion or "a living body endowed with sensitive life," in both the higher and the lower forms of animal life, as in the lion and the worm.[68] But the meaning signified by the name "knowledge" is absolutely speaking different and only proportionally the same in sensation and intellection, since sensation is related to the sensible as intellection is to the intelligible. Likewise the meaning signified by the name "love" is only proportionally the same in sensitive love and in spiritual love. Therefore, while the univocal perfection can be perfectly abstracted from the inferior grades of being, as in predicating "animal" of the lion and the worm, by not

---

[65] Consult Cajetan, *De analogia nominum*, chap. 6; also *Com. in Iam*, q.13, a.5, no. 15; John of St. Thomas, *Cursus phil.*, *Logica*, q.13; Goudin, *Philosophia*, *Logica major*, Ia, dist. II, q.1, a.2; J. M. Ramirez, "De analogia secundum doctrinam Aristotelico-thomisticam" (*La Ciencia Tomista*, July, 1921, January, 1922).

[66] Cf. a.5.

[67] Cf. q.13, a.5 (end of argumentative part of the article); also Ia, q.4, a.2, 3, in which St. Thomas says the same.

[68] Thus in the genus animality we already find verified what Suarez considers to be the definition of analogy; for in this case the meaning signified by the name is, absolutely speaking, the same (a living body endowed with sensitive life) and, relatively speaking, different, inasmuch as animality applied to the higher forms of life implies the presence of all the internal and external senses, but it is not so of animality as applied to the lower forms of life.

considering the *differentiae* that are extrinsic to the genus, the analogous perfection cannot be perfectly abstracted from its analogates,[69] because the similarity of the proportions is not conceived without conceiving confusedly or actually and implicitly the members of the proportionality. Hence it is difficult to define knowledge in general, so that it can be applied in the strict sense to sensation, to created intellection, and to the divine intellection. In like manner it is difficult to define being, such that it applies equally to God. to created substance, and to accident.

But from this, that the analogous concept is only proportionally the same, it follows, as St. Thomas notes,[70] that there can be an infinite difference between two analogates. Now there is, indeed, a vast difference between sensitive knowledge and intellective knowledge; yet the term "knowledge" is applied to both analogically and properly, and not merely metaphorically.

Moreover, the terminology of St. Thomas, according to which the idea of an analogical perfection is not absolutely but only proportionally the same in God and in creatures, is completely in agreement with that of the Fourth Lateran Council, which says: "Between the Creator and the creature not so great a similarity can be detected, as not to detect a greater dissimilarity." [71] Therefore, when we say that perfections implying no imperfection are in God formally, the word "formally" must be understood not univocally but analogically; in the literal sense, however, and not metaphorically; just as in the created order knowledge is predicated of sensation and intellection analogically, but properly.[72] Having explained what is meant by "formally," we must now declare what is implied by "eminently."

II. What is meant by the adverb "eminently" in the above-mentioned expression?

1) From what has been said, it follows that the most eminent mode in which the divine attributes are contained in God is in itself mysterious, and is expressed only negatively and relatively, as when God's wisdom is spoken of as not finite, as supreme, highest.

Hence St. Thomas says: "This term 'wise' applied to man in some degree circumscribes and comprehends the thing signified (as distinct from the essence of man, his existence, power . . .); whereas this is not the case when it is applied to God; but it leaves the

---

[69] See Cajetan, *De analogia nominum,* chap. 5.

[70] *De veritate,* q.2, a.11.

[71] Denz., no. 432.

[72] Cf. John of St. Thomas, *Logica,* q.13, a.5. M. T. L. Penido, *La rôle de l'analogie en théologie dogmatique,* pp. 53–60, 136–45. There are not two unknowns in proportion. Objections of Father Descoqs; Is proportionality fictitious? Is it primary?

thing signified as incomprehended, and as exceeding the signification of the name." [73] In this we already have the explanation of the
adverb "eminently" in the expression "formally and eminently."
But this requires further explanation.

2) From what has been said it follows likewise, against Scotus,
that there is no actual-formal distinction between the aforesaid
divine perfections arising from the nature of these. For this distinction, according to Scotus, is more than virtual, inasmuch as it
is prior to the mind's consideration. But a distinction that is prior
to the mind's consideration is already real, however slight it may
be. A real distinction, however, between the divine attributes is incompatible with God's absolute simplicity. Therefore the Council
of Florence says: "In God all things are one and the same where
there is no relation of opposition." [74]

Therefore a virtual and indeed minor distinction is the only kind
that can be admitted between the divine attributes. It is a distinction by way of implicit and explicit connotations, inasmuch as
one attribute actually implies the others.

Yet it must be maintained, against the nominalists, that the divine names are not synonymous, that there is not only a distinction
of names, for instance, between mercy and justice, as between Tullius and Cicero.

3) Then the difficult question is posited of the identification of
the divine perfections in God, in such a manner that they are not
destructive of one another, but remain in God formally, or substantially and properly, and are not synonymous. The question here
concerns the difficulty of combining the two adverbs "formally"
and "eminently." At first sight it seems that, as regards their signification, the latter is destructive of the former. It is indeed not
difficult to see how the seven colors of the rainbow are contained
in white light; but it contains them only virtually and not formally,
for white light is formally neither blue nor red, whereas the Deity
is formally good, intelligent, merciful. . . . It is particularly this
difficulty that Scotus proposed, and he defended his actual-formal
distinction between the divine attributes arising from the nature
of these, because he deemed their formal identification an impossibility. As Scotus sees it, for the divine attributes to exist formally in
God, they must be in Him as distinct formalities and more than
virtually.

Is this identity an impossibility? Cajetan replies that there are
two ways of understanding this: "(1) If we suppose that the proper
formal concepts of wisdom and justice constitute one formal con-

[73] Cf. a.5.
[74] Denz., no. 703.

cept, such that this one concept is not another concept, but is only the proper concept of wisdom and justice. And this sort of identity is absolutely impossible, involving two contradictories. . . . (2) If we suppose that the concepts of wisdom and justice are eminently included and formally identified in one formal concept of a higher order. And this identity is not only possible, but is actually so with all perfections in God. For it must not be thought that the formal concept that belongs properly to wisdom is found in God; but, as stated in the article, the concept of wisdom in God is not the proper concept of wisdom, but is the proper concept of a higher order, namely, of the Deity, and it is a concept that is formally and eminently common to justice, goodness, power, and other attributes. For, just as in rational creatures the reality which is wisdom and the reality which is justice are elevated so as to constitute one reality of the higher order, which is the Deity, thereby constituting one reality in God, so the formal concepts of wisdom and justice are elevated so as to constitute one formal concept of a higher order, the proper concept, namely, of the Deity. They constitute numerically one formal concept, containing eminently what is implied in each concept: not only virtually, as the concept of light includes the concept of heat, but formally, as the concept of light includes the concept of calorific energy.[75] Whence St. Thomas, with that most keen penetration of his divine-like intellect, inferred from this that wisdom is not predicated of God and creatures in the same sense." [76] This means, as Cajetan says farther on: "There is not absolute unity of concept," [77] but a proportionate unity, as Cajetan had said in another treatise.[78]

This, then, is the meaning given by the Thomists to the expression "formally and eminently." By "formally" is meant that the perfections are in God substantially and not causally, literally and not metaphorically; nevertheless they are predicated analogically. The term "eminently" excludes an actual-formal distinction between God's attributes, and expresses their identification or rather identity in the most eminent formal concept of the Deity, whose proper mode is in itself unknown to us, and is known only negatively and relatively in this life.

This is practically what St. Thomas says, as in the following passages: "These perfections pre-exist in God unitedly and simply, whereas in creatures they are received, divided, and multiplied. . . .

---

[75] Nowadays we would say: As white light contains the seven colors not formally but virtually, having the power to produce these colors.

[76] *Com. in Iam*, q. 13, a. 5, no. 7.

[77] *Ibid.*, no. 15.

[78] *De analogia nominum*, chap. 6.

So also to the various and multiplied conceptions of our intellect there corresponds one altogether simple principle, according to these conceptions, imperfectly understood." [79] Also: "The many aspects of these names are not empty and vain, for there corresponds to all of them one simple reality represented by them in a manifold and imperfect manner." [80] Hence the divine attributes are so identified in the most eminently formal concept of the Deity as not to be destructive of one another. They are contained formally in the Deity, yet not as distinct formalities. In fact, the divine perfections are so identified without being destructive of one another in the eminence of the Deity, that they exist there in their most pure state without any admixture of imperfection. Thus God alone is essential Being, essential Goodness, and similarly for the other attributes.

4) It is easier to explain this identification for those perfections which are of the same order, and between which there is only an extrinsic virtual distinction, namely, one that has its foundation only in creatures. Thus intelligence, intellection, the divine truth always understood, are most evidently identified, inasmuch as God is the self-subsisting Being, who is identical with the maximum Truth that is of itself and always actually understood.

It is more difficult to explain the identification of those perfections that do not belong to the same order, such as intellection and love, mercy and justice. Nevertheless, from what has been said it is clear that they are identified in the eminence of the Deity, which is eminently and formally intellection and love, mercy and justice.

5) This same explanation holds good for saying that there is no actual-formal but only a virtual distinction between the divine nature and the subsistent relations which constitute the divine Persons, as, for instance, between the divine nature that is communicable *ad intra* and incommunicable paternity.

Hence Cajetan says: "In itself, not according to our manner of speaking, in God there is but one formal concept, which is not purely absolute or purely relative or purely communicable or purely incommunicable. But it is a concept which in a most eminent and formal way contains whatever there is of absolute perfection, and whatever is demanded by the Trinity in a relative sense. . . . For the divine reality is prior to being and all its differences. It is above being and above the one. . . ." [81] For the same reason, therefore, the divine reality transcends the absolute and the relative, which are contained in it formally and eminently.

[79] *Summa theol.*, Ia, q.13, a.4.
[80] *Ibid.*, ad 2um. See also a.5, c.
[81] *Com. in Iam*, q.39, a.1, no. 7.

This doctrine of the eminence of the Deity elucidates especially three questions which are of the greatest importance in dogmatic theology.

1) What stands out clearly from this doctrine is that reason alone can demonstrate the existence in God of a truth and life that are of the supernatural order, inasmuch as the Deity or God's intimate life transcends the proper object and powers of any created or creatable being. As St. Thomas says: "It is most evident that some divine intelligibles absolutely transcend the native power of human reason." [82]

2) It is likewise evident from this doctrine of the eminence of the Deity that sanctifying grace must be called a participation of the divine nature, since it is a physical, formal, and analogical participation of the Deity as this is in itself; and so this participation radically ordains us to see the Deity as it really is. Thus the question of whether grace is a participation of the divine infinity is clearly seen to be of less importance. Certainly there is no subjective participation of the divine infinity, for by this it would be limited. But grace ordains us to see the Deity, of which it is a true participation. Now, stones are like God according to being, plants according to life, human and angelic intellects according to intellection, but by grace alone we are like God according to the Deity.

3) Finally, in this doctrine of the eminence of the Deity we have a sublime explanation of why we cannot perceive in this life how God's universal will to save is intimately reconciled with the mystery of predestination. This would be to perceive how infinite mercy, justice, and supreme liberty are intimately reconciled in the eminence of the Deity, and why God mercifully elected this particular person rather than a certain other.

This theological contemplation of the eminence of the Deity, provided it is united with an ever-increasing charity, normally disposes one for infused contemplation, which, under the special inspiration of the Holy Ghost, proceeds from vivid faith illumined by the gifts of understanding and wisdom, and which, in a mystic darkness and in a more exalted way, attains to the Deity or to "that" light inaccessible whom, as St. Paul says, "no man hath seen nor can see," [83] except in Heaven.[84]

---

[82] *Contra Gentes*, Bk. I, chap. 3, § 3. See also Ia, q.12, a.4. This has been proved extensively by us in *De revelatione*, I, 337–70, where it is proved that there is a truth and life of the supernatural order in God, or of an order of supernatural mysteries.

[83] I Tim. 6: 16.

[84] On this point consult the discussion in *Acta Pont. Academiae romanae sancti Thomae Aq.*, in which several objections are answered.

EIGHTH ARTICLE

WHETHER THE NAME "GOD" IS A NAME OF THE NATURE

State of the question. Certain divine names in particular are now considered. The question is whether "God" (Θεός) is a name of the nature or of operation.

Reply. God is a name of operation as regards the imposition of this name, by the way of investigation; but it is a name of the nature as regards what is meant by this name.

The reason is that we have not immediate knowledge of the essences of things, and especially of God's essence; but we know them only by their operations. Thus the name "stone" designates the nature of the stone, but many hold that this name is derived from its act, since it hurts the foot.[85] But the divine operation from which this name "God" is imposed, seems to be that by which God knows and ordains all things, at least according to the etymology given by Dionysius.[86] Hence the name "Deity" expresses properly the divine nature.

At the end of the reply to the second objection there is again a reference to the three ways by which God is known, namely, by causality, by eminence, and by negation.

NINTH ARTICLE

WHETHER THE NAME "GOD" IS COMMUNICABLE

Reply. This name "God" is incommunicable in reality (in the literal sense), but communicable in opinion and metaphorically.

The reason for the first part is that the divine nature or the Deity is in itself incommunicable to creatures. There can be only one God.[87] Nevertheless from revelation we know that God the Father communicates the Deity to the Son and the Holy Ghost. Hence nothing outside God can properly be called God.

The reason for the second part is that men, adopting the erroneous opinion of polytheists, spoke of several gods. Moreover this name is predicated metaphorically of the just because of the grace or participation of the divine nature which they have. Thus the Scripture says: "I have said, you are gods." [88]

Hence while being, life, and intellection are naturally partici-

---

85 The reference is to the Latin name; for *lapis* implies *laedit pedem* ("it hurts the foot"). [Tr.]

86 *De div. nom.*, chap. 12.

87 *Summa theol.*, Ia, q.11, a.3.

88 Ps. 81: 6.

pable in stones, plants, and rational creatures, the Deity is not naturally but only supernaturally participable by grace, which is a formal participation of the Deity, or of the radical principle of the operations by which God sees and loves Himself.

TENTH ARTICLE

WHETHER THIS NAME "GOD" IS PREDICATED UNIVOCALLY OF THE TRUE GOD, OF IDOLS, AND OF THE JUST

Reply. This name is predicated of God alone, in fact uniquely so. Of idols it is predicated analogically in accordance with the false opinion of the polytheists; of the just it is predicated analogically by a certain participated likeness.

ELEVENTH ARTICLE

WHETHER THIS NAME "HE WHO IS" IS THE MOST PROPER NAME OF GOD

Reply. It is in the affirmative, and for three reasons: (1) because God alone is His existence, so that His existence is His essence; (2) because this name, "He who is," determines no mode of being, and therefore it denominates the infinite ocean of substance, and thus it comprehends all other names confusedly. "Therefore the less determinate the names are, and the more universal and absolute they are, the more properly they are applied to God"; [89] (3) because this name, "He who is," signifies present existence, and so it expresses God's eternity, which transcends past and future.

Reply to first objection. Nevertheless, "as regards the object intended by the name, this name 'God' is more proper, as it is imposed to signify the divine nature," namely, the Deity which eminently and formally contains being, life, and intellection. St. Thomas distinguishes between the Tetragrammaton and the name "He who is"; but nowadays all identify these two names. [90]

Reply to second objection. Supreme Good is God's principle name, as regards causality, inasmuch as He is the end of all things, and the end is the first of causes. But "What is" is His principal name absolutely. [91]

[89] See argumentative part of this article.

[90] Undoubtedly the Scholastics knew that the Hebrew name "Yahweh" is the Tetragrammaton or word of four letters; but they were ignorant of its true pronunciation. This pronunciation of hybrid form is of recent origin, not being heard before the sixteenth century. This ignorance probably explains why several Scholastics erred in distinguishing, though on insufficient grounds, between the Tetragrammaton and the divine name, "He who is." Cf. Prat, *Dict. de la Bible* (III, 1225), art. "Jehovah."

[91] *Summa theol.,* Ia, q.5, a.2 ad 1um.

WHETHER AFFIRMATIVE PROPOSITIONS CAN BE FORMED ABOUT GOD

State of the question. This article may be looked upon as a re-capitulation of the preceding articles, its purpose being the laying down of rules for the forming of affirmative judgments. That diffi-culties arise is owing to the fact that Dionysius says, in what is called his negative theology: "Negations about God are true, but affirmations are vague." [92] For God is ineffable, and we have no proper concept of the Deity, which for us pilgrims is like "a great darkness" or "an obscure night." Moreover, God is a simple form, in no way composite, whereas there is composition in affirmative judgments.

Reply. Nevertheless, true affirmative propositions can be formed about God. The first proof of this is the fact that there are several propositions about God that are of faith.

Another proof of this may be expressed by the following syl-logism: In every true affirmative proposition the predicate and the subject signify in some way the same thing in reality, and different things in idea. Thus in the proposition "Peter is white" ("Peter" and "white" are the same in subject). But God, considered in Him-self, is altogether one and simple; yet our intellect knows Him according to different conceptions. Therefore two affirmative propo-sitions can be formed about God.

Reply to first objection. "Dionysius says that the affirmations about God are vague inasmuch as no name can be applied to God according to its mode of signification." [93] Thus abstract names signify the form only, and concrete names signify the composite subject in which there is such a form, whereas God is pure subsisting form.[94]

Reply to third objection. "Any intellect which understands that the thing is otherwise than it is, is false. But this does not hold in the present case; because our intellect, when forming a proposition about God, does not affirm that He is composite." But there is imperfection in its manner of understanding.

And so this terminates the question about divine names, in which St. Thomas most correctly determines the just and transcendent mean between the two opposite errors, namely, of agnosticism and a certain anthropomorphism. Agnosticism is avoided, as it is af-

[92] *Coel. Hier.*, chap. 2.
[93] Cf. a.3.
[94] Cf. ad 2um.

firmed that absolutely simple perfections are substantially and properly in God, and are primarily in Him rather than in creatures. Anthropomorphism is avoided, as it is affirmed that these perfections are not predicated univocally of God and creatures, but analogically, according to a likeness of proportions. Just as there is an existence that belongs properly to the creature, so there is an existence that belongs properly to God, and He is His own existence. Just as there is a wisdom that belongs properly to man, so there is a wisdom that belongs properly to God, and He alone is His own intellection, as will be more clearly explained farther on. This method of analogy is applied to all questions about the one and triune God, which is most accurately determined in this thirteenth question. Analogy is necessary both for the natural knowledge of God and for the supernatural knowledge of revealed mysteries. Thus with the former there is evidence resulting from demonstration, with the latter there is obscurity of faith. For God, in the manifestation of the mysteries of His intimate life, made use of such analogical notions as those of nature, person, paternity, filiation, and these are in us as naturally acquired. Hence, as regards God the author of nature, the legitimate analogies can be known by reason alone; but it is not so if it is a question of God the author of grace, in His intimate life.

CHAPTER XIV

QUESTION 14

GOD'S KNOWLEDGE

"HAVING considered what belongs to the divine substance," says St. Thomas, "we have now to treat of God's operation." Those commentators who maintain that self-subsisting Being is what formally constitutes the divine nature, according to our imperfect mode of conceiving it, say that the divine intellection, according to St. Thomas, belongs to His operations. But those who hold that subsistent intellection is what formally constitutes the divine nature, declare that St. Thomas does not say that he has so far treated of the divine nature, but of those things that belong to God's substance; nor does he say now that he is considering only the divine operations, but those things that belong to God's operations. But nature belongs to them as their principle. Nevertheless this passage of St. Thomas favors rather the first opinion, and it seems that St. Thomas did not wait for this fourteenth question in order to treat of what formally constitutes the divine nature.[1]

First are considered merely immanent actions, such as intellection and volition, and then virtually transitive operations, in which God's power is discussed.

In the fourteenth question, which concerns God's knowledge, four principal points are considered: (1) Is there intellection in God, and what is its nature? (2) the primary object of God's knowledge (a. 2, 3, 4); (3) the secondary object (a. 5–13); (4) the way the divine knowledge operates; whether it is enunciative, variable, speculative, practical (a. 14,16).

FIRST ARTICLE

WHETHER THERE IS KNOWLEDGE IN GOD

State of the question. In the title, "knowledge" is taken in its broad sense as referring to certain and evident intellectual cognition. The article is not concerned with knowledge strictly so called, as distinct from wisdom; and so it is cognition acquired by proximate causes, and not by the highest of causes. In fact, in the reply

[1] Cf. *supra*, q.3.

to the second objection, it is stated that the divine intellection is eminently, without distinction of habits, intelligence, science, wisdom, prudence, and art.

The difficulties enunciated at the beginning of the article apply, however, to knowledge in the strict sense, inasmuch as it is a habit distinct from act, being concerned with conclusions and with universal abstract cognition. All these pertain to the created and imperfect mode of our knowledge.

Reply. God occupies the highest place in knowledge, because He is in the highest degree of immateriality.

1) This conclusion is a revealed truth, for there are many texts in Holy Scripture in which it is clearly stated that God is intelligent. It is a dogma of faith; in fact, the Vatican Council states that "God is infinite in intelligence." [2]

It is also demonstrated by the following syllogism: The immateriality of a thing is the reason why it is cognitive, and the mode of knowledge is according to the mode of immateriality. Therefore God occupies the highest place in knowledge, for He is in the highest degree of immateriality.

The minor has already been proved.[3] God is not a body, not composed of matter and form, but is pure subsisting form; in fact, He is the self-subsisting Being,[4] and besides is infinite.[5] He transcends all limitations of essence, and a fortiori of matter.

The first part of the major is as follows: The difference between the intelligent being and the non-intelligent being is that the intelligent being is naturally adapted to have also the form of some other, which is therefore because of the amplitude of its nature; but the contraction of the form comes from the matter,[6] which limits the amplitude of the form; therefore the immateriality of a thing is the reason why it is cognitive.

This argument gives the proof for the second part of the major. The mode of knowledge is according to the mode of immateriality; thus the intellect is more cognitive than sense. Therefore, since God is in the highest degree of immateriality, He occupies the highest place in knowledge.

The whole of this doctrine has its foundation in the principle that the intelligent being differs from the non-intelligent being, inasmuch as the former can in a sense become something other than itself. Thus Aristotle says: "The soul is in a sense all things." [7]

2 Denz., no. 1782.
3 *Summa theol.*, q.3, a.2.
4 *Ibid.*, a.4.
5 *Ibid.*, q.7, a.1.
6 *Ibid.*
7 *De anima*, Bk. III, chap. 8.

Whereas the plant, which at first was cold, under the influence of the sun's rays undergoes a change, becoming warm, the intelligent being, on seeing the sun, does not undergo a change, becoming warm, but in a sense becomes something else. This demands for such a being the possibility of its having in itself not only its own form but also the form of the other thing, namely, the representative species of the thing to be known.

But if the contraction or limitation of the form comes from the matter which receives the form, and which individualizes it, the immateriality of a thing is the reason why it is cognitive. Hence plants, because of their materiality, are not cognitive, whereas God is in the highest degree cognitive, because He is in the highest degree immaterial.

Both the materialists and the subjectivist idealists fail to perceive this profound reason why anything is cognitive. Materialism denies this immateriality of the principle of cognition, maintaining that it is only an epiphenomenon of not much importance, which transcends the physico-chemical phenomena.

On the other hand, subjectivist idealism does not admit that the knower truly knows something other than himself, but that he knows only his subjective modifications.

In these two extreme systems, which are fundamentally in opposition to each other, there is no conception of what is meant by this intentional change necessary for our knowledge, and transcending the physical or organic change already existing in the non-cognitive plant.

Whereas in physical or material reception there is appropriation of the form, which thus becomes the proper form of the subject, as when a plant is first cold and then becomes warm; on the other hand, in immaterial or intentional reception there is no appropriation of the form received, this remaining the form of the other thing. Hence Averroes was right in saying: "The knower and the known are more one than matter and form"; for matter does not become the form which it receives, whereas the knower, in a sense, namely, intentionally or representatively, becomes the object known, or becomes something other than itself.[8]

St. Thomas says: "Change is of two kinds, one natural, the other spiritual. Natural change takes place by the form of the changer being received, according to its natural existence, into the thing changed, as heat is received into the thing heated. Whereas spiritual change takes place by the form of the changer being received, according to a spiritual mode of existence, into the thing changed. . . . Now, for the operation of the senses, a spiritual change is re-

8 Consult the commentaries of Cajetan and John of St. Thomas on this article.

quired, whereby an intention of the sensible form is effected in the sensile organ."[9] Previous to this, he had written: "But feeling is evidently accompanied with some change in the body. . . , and thus every operation of the sensitive soul is an operation of the composite. . . . Understanding alone is performed without a corporeal organ."[10] Now indeed, the sensitive faculty is in some way elevated above material conditions, although it depends intrinsically on the organism. The intelligent being, of course, first becomes intentionally other than itself in first actuality by the impressed species of the thing known, and then in second actuality it becomes other than itself while actually knowing the extramental reality. It does not go out of itself in a literal sense, as a man goes out of his house, for knowing is an immanent act; but it becomes intentionally other than itself, inasmuch as the intentional species and the cognition are essentially related to the object of cognition.

From all that has been said, it is clearly enough established that knowledge has its foundation in the immateriality of the knower, and that the "mode of knowledge is according to the mode of immateriality." Since, therefore, God is in the highest degree of immateriality (inasmuch as He is not only a pure spirit but pure Act, the self-subsisting Being), it follows that He is in the highest degree knowing.

Cognition and intellection in their formal signification imply no imperfection, and thus they can be predicated of God analogically and properly, and not merely metaphorically.

Reply to first objection. Knowledge is said to be a habit that is not so perfect as act with regard to the created mode of its being, but not with regard to what is meant by the name. Moreover, there is not even a virtual distinction in God between wisdom and knowledge.

Reply to second objection. Likewise in man, knowledge, as regards its created mode, implies the imperfect process of formally discursive reasoning, and the transition from the unknown to the known. But there can be a most perfect knowledge, with only virtually discursive reasoning, and thus it differs neither from intelligence nor from wisdom.[11]

Reply to third objection. Universal knowledge does not exist in

[9] *Summa theol.*, Ia, q.78, a.3.

[10] *Ibid.*, q.75, a.3; cf. *De veritate*, q.2, a.1.

[11] Yet it is knowledge in the strict sense which God has, namely, knowledge of things through their causes; because virtual discursive reasoning suffices for knowledge, as is the case with the angels, who know things not successively but by one intuitive act. God, as will be stated farther on, does not proceed from the known to the unknown, does not know the effects from their causes, but immediately in their causes.

God as abstracted from singular things; but by this knowledge God also knows at once singular things, a point that will be made clear in a subsequent article.[12]

SOLUTION OF OBJECTIONS

First objection. The following objection is raised against the fundamental proof in the argumentative part of this article: There are many immaterial things that are not cognitive, such as the will and its habits. Therefore the reason given by St. Thomas is of no value.

Reply. I distinguish the antecedent. That there are many immaterial *supposita* that are not cognitive, this I deny; that there are many operative principles, such as the will and its habits, I subdistinguish; that they are not cognitive as elective acts, this I concede; that they are not of the cognitive order, acting in concert with the intellect, this I deny.

Second objection. The air and the mirror receive the intentional species without undergoing any change, and yet they are not cognitive. Therefore the reason given is of no value.

Reply. That these species are received in the air and the mirror, as in their subject of inhesion, in which these species materially inhere, this I concede; that the air and the mirror receive them formally as intentional or representative species, this I deny. As a matter of fact, what the air and the mirror receive is rather the power by which the impressed species is produced in the senses, or in the visual faculty, and in this alone, as in its proper habitat, it is formed.[13]

Third objection. All angels are equally immaterial, and yet they are not equally cognitive. Therefore the mode of cognition is not according to the mode of immateriality.

Reply. That all angels are equally immaterial in the negative sense, which means that they are without matter, this I concede; that they are so in actual fact, this I deny, for they do not equally participate in the intellectual life.

Fourth objection. It is not repugnant for God to create an immaterial substance that is not cognitive. Therefore cognition is not dependent on immateriality.

12 Cf. a.11.

13 It must be noted that St. Thomas says the souls of irrational animals and their senses are in some way (or in a certain sense) spiritual, since they are already in some way elevated above material conditions. Thus the soul of the irrational animal is not a body, and is a higher form than that of the plant; nevertheless the souls and senses of such animals are intrinsically dependent on their organisms, and so they are simply of the material order.

Reply. That there is no repugnance in the creation of an immaterial substance that is not proximately cognitive, this I concede; that is not radically cognitive, this either I deny, or I say, please prove it. An immaterial substance that in some extraordinary case would be deprived of its intellective faculty, would still be radically cognitive. Thus it remains true that the degree of cognition of a being corresponds to the degree of its immateriality, or of its elevation above material conditions. Hence God, who is in the highest degree immaterial, is in the highest degree cognitive.

SECOND ARTICLE

WHETHER GOD UNDERSTANDS HIMSELF

State of the question. The next three articles are concerned with the primary object of the divine intellection. This second article begins by presenting the difficulty that arises from the imperfect way in which we know our own soul; for it is a reflexive knowledge which presupposes a direct knowledge. Thus there is a multiplicity of acts which cannot be attributed to God. Moreover, it is by means of a certain assimilation of the knower with the thing known that we have intellection, and this is accompanied by a certain duality of subject and object, which cannot be in God, who is most simple. Therefore Plotinus said that the supreme hypostasis, which is the One-Good, transcends the second hypostasis, which is Intelligence, in which there is duality of subject and object. This objection was revived by many modern pantheists, who denied the possibility of a personal or intelligent and free God, for intellection presupposes duality of subject and object, and this cannot be attributed to the most simple Absolute.

Reply. God understands Himself through Himself.

1) It is of faith that God understands Himself, and there are very many texts in Sacred Scripture confirming this, such as the following: "The things also that are of God no man knoweth, but the Spirit of God." [14]

2) It is proved from reason that God knows Himself; and also from reason is proved the manner in which He knows Himself, which is immediately through Himself, without any duality or real distinction between the divine intellect and His essence understood by Him. This is demonstrated as follows:

The intelligible is not understood unless it is in the intellect understanding (at least by some representation), and there is no distinction between these two, except that each is in potentiality,

14 I Cor. 2: 11.

namely, except that the intellect understanding does not of itself actually understand, and that the intelligible is not of itself the intellect in act.

But God, who is actually understanding and whose essence is intelligible, is without any potentiality. Therefore God understands Himself through Himself, so that "His intellect and (the primary object) understood are altogether the same," that is, without the duality which Plotinus speaks of as being necessary for intellection.

The major is proved because intellection is an immanent act, its object being actually understood only in the intellect. Thus in the case of our intellect, when we understand the nature of a stone, this nature, which is in the stone itself, is only potentially intelligible, and is actually understood only in the intellect. And there is no distinction between our intellect and this intelligible object, except that each is in potentiality; for, prior to our act of understanding, it was possible for the intellect to understand, and for the stone to be understood. But when the object is actually understood, the intellect and the object understood are more one than matter and form, because, as it was stated, matter does not become form; whereas the intellect in the act of understanding in a certain sense becomes the object understood.

The minor is evident, because God is neither a body nor a composite of matter and form,[15] and because He is intellect in act and pure Act without any potentiality.

Hence His intellect is of itself and eternally always in act, and His essence is not potentially intelligible (as the essence of a stone), nor is it only actually intelligible (as the angel's essence), but it is, of itself and eternally, actually understood. Hence there is no distinction between it and His intellection. This means that so long as all potentiality or imperfection is eliminated from the cognitive intellect and the intelligible object, they are identical. Aristotle had already said this.[16]

On the contrary, in the case of the angel understanding himself, there is not absolute identity between his essence that is understood and his intellective faculty; for the angel's essence is only actually intelligible and is not actually understood, and his intellectual faculty is not his intellection. The completion of this doctrine is in the fourth article of this question, in which the identity between God's intellect and His essence is considered not only objectively but subjectively, as the subject of intellection.

Reply to second objection. Intellection is not, properly speaking, movement, for it is an act of the agent, whereas movement, properly

---

[15] Cf. *supra*, q.3, a.1, 2.
[16] *Metaph.*, Bk. XII, chap. 9.

speaking, is in the thing moveable by the agent. "Likewise, that the intellect is perfected by the intelligible object, or is assimilated to it, belongs to an intellect which is sometimes in potentiality. . . . But the divine intellect, which is in no way in potentiality, is not perfected by the intelligible object, nor is it assimilated thereto, but it is its own perfection and its own intelligible object." This is the best answer to the objection of the Neoplatonists and of others who said that any intellection whatever implies a duality of subject and object, and hence this cannot be formally or properly in God, who is most simple.

Reply to third objection. "God is pure act in the order of existence, as also in the order of intelligible objects; therefore He understands Himself through Himself, which means without any impressed or expressed accidental superadded species. On the other hand, the angel is in need of an accidental mental word to understand himself, because his essence is not actually understood, but only actually intelligible." [17]

THIRD ARTICLE

WHETHER GOD COMPREHENDS HIMSELF

State of the question. Does God know Himself as much as He is knowable, or, in other words, is it an adequate and most complete knowledge which He has of Himself, knowing whatever is in Himself and in His productive power, which means knowing all possible things?

Reply. The conclusion in the affirmative is revealed (1) by the following statement from Holy Scripture, and in similar passages: "The Spirit searcheth all things, yea, the deep things of God." [18] (2) It is proved from reason as follows: A thing is, strictly speaking, comprehended when it is known to the extent that it is knowable, or when it is known adequately and completely. But the cognitive power of God is as great as His actuality is knowable; for His intellect is in no way in potentiality, being pure Act in the intellective order, just as He is pure Act in the entitative order. And both are identical, as was stated in the preceding article.

Hence, whereas man remains a sort of mystery unto himself, inasmuch as "the heart (of man) is unsearchable" [19] (this being the reason why St. Paul says: "Neither do I judge my own self, but He that judgeth me is the Lord" [20]), God knows Himself most per-

---

[17] *Contra Gentes*, Bk. IV, chap. 11.
[18] I Cor. 2: 10.
[19] Jer. 17: 9.
[20] I Cor. 4: 3, 4.

fectly, being no mystery unto Himself; and He likewise knows His power, which means that He knows all possible things, the multitude of which is infinite.

It must be noted that this conclusion is most evident for us, although there are several other truths about the divine intellect that remain for us most obscure, such as God's infallible knowledge and permission of sin, the sinner being charged with the offense. But in this treatise on the one God there is frequently to be found a wondrous "light-transcending darkness," in which what is for us most clear is accompanied by an obscurity, which is not because of any absurdity or incoherence of thought in the revealed truth, but because the light is far too bright for our intellectual vision. It is most evident that God most perfectly knows or comprehends Himself, and it is the commonly accepted opinon among Christians that to deny this would be truly foolishness.

FOURTH ARTICLE

WHETHER THE ACT OF GOD'S INTELLECT IS HIS SUBSTANCE

State of the question. We have seen [21] that God's intellect is absolutely identical with His essence as the object known. Now the question is whether the act of God's intellect is identical with His substance as the subject of this intellection.

The difficulties proposed at the beginning of this article are of less importance.

Reply. The conclusion is in the affirmative. It is proved in two ways, indirectly and directly.

1) Indirectly. The act of understanding is the perfection and act of the one understanding. But if God's act of understanding were other than His substance, then His substance would be related to His act of understanding as potentiality is to act, which is impossible, since God is pure Act. Therefore God's act of understanding is identical with His substance. This indirect argument is apodictic.

2) Directly and ostensively.[22] To understand follows on the intelligible species and perfects it, just as existence follows on the form. But God's essence is His existence [23] and His intelligible

---

[21] Cf. a.2.

[22] By "ostensively" is meant a demonstration in which the conclusion is virtually contained in the premises. When some general principle contains the proposition to be proved, the demonstration is said to be direct and ostensive. [Tr.]

[23] Cf. q.3, a.4.

species.[24] Therefore God's act of understanding is His essence or substance and His existence. In other words, as stated in the reply to the second objection, God is His subsistent act of understanding, like an intellectual and eternally existing flash of itself.

The major of this proof has its foundation in the proportionality prevailing between the existential and intellectual orders. But God in virtue of His essence is not capable of further perfection, and thus He must be pure Act, unreceived and unreceptive both in the existential and intelligential orders. This means that, just as God's essence does not differ from His existence, so His intelligible essence does not differ from His act of understanding.

At the end of the argumentative part of this article, St. Thomas, by combining this conclusion with that of the second article, sums up and says: "Thus it follows from all the foregoing that in God the intellect understanding (subject) and the object understood and the intelligible species and His act of understanding are entirely one and the same. Hence, when God is said to be understanding, no kind of multiplicity is attached to His substance." Thus it was an unwarrantable assertion on the part of Plotinus, for him to say that every intellection supposed a duality of subject and object which cannot be predicated of the first hypostasis, who is most simple. Hence the famous contrary statement of Aristotle, that "God is absolute self-thought," [25] or God is self-subsisting intellection.

Reply to third objection. "The act of divine understanding which subsists in itself and belongs to its very self and is not another's is absolute self-thought." The reference is to the primary object of the divine intellect; but the secondary object is not excluded.

First doubt. Is there a virtual distinction between God's essence, His intelligence, and His intellection?

Many Thomists with good reason reply that there is no intrinsically virtual distinction between these three, because, if this distinction were admitted, then God's essence and His intelligence would be conceived as in potentiality to His intellection, the divine reality constituting the foundation for this distinction. But this cannot be conceived of God, who is most pure Act; for nothing in Him can be conceived as potential or as capable of further determination or perfection. Therefore in God there is no intrinsically virtual distinction between these three.

If, therefore, there is a virtual distinction between these three, it is merely extrinsic, which means that the foundation for this distinction is not in the divine reality but in creatures, inasmuch as subsistent intellection is equivalent, in an eminent way, to the radical and proximate principles of intellection and to intellection itself.

Hence there is an intrinsically virtual distinction in God only between those perfections which, as found in created things, are distinct according to their objective concepts, and which belong to different orders, such as intellect and will. But intellect and actual intellection belong to the same order, and are concerned with the same formal object.[26]

However, there is a virtual distinction in God between His knowledge or wisdom and His providence. In fact, it can be said that the formal object of the divine intelligence is the divine essence, as absolutely knowable in itself. The formal object of the divine knowledge is the divine essence as the cause of this; of prudence or providence it is the divine essence as the reason of things to be done; of divine art it is the divine essence as the reason of things to be made.

Second doubt. What is the formal and primary object of the divine knowledge?

Reply. The primary object is God or the Godhead, as containing actually and implicitly God's essence, His attributes and relations. The reason is that the formal and primary object of divine knowledge is that which primarily and of itself is attained by it. Now this object is neither created being, nor being as such, abstracting from created being and uncreated being, but is God Himself. But God as He really is, not as conceived by us, contains actually and implicitly what we call the divine essence, the attributes deduced from it, and the relations. There is only a minor virtual distinction between these, as already stated.[27] "In God all things are one and the same, where there is not a relation of opposition," [28] says the Council of Florence.

Durandus rashly maintained that the formal and primary object of the divine knowledge is being as such, as abstracted from created being and uncreated being, because, so he said, it is more universal than uncreated being. Rosmini said about the same. This opinion must be absolutely rejected, for nothing is or can be conceived prior to God. It is only according to our manner of speaking that abstract being is more universal than God, since we conceive being as having universality of content according to ontological reality.[29]

---

[26] See John of St. Thomas, commentary on this article.
[27] Cf. q.3.
[28] Denz., no. 709.
[29] Cf. Cajetan, *Com. in Iam*, q.39, a.1, no. 7.

God knows being as such, not abstractively and imperfectly (for in this way He would know only actually and implicitly the various modes of being), but He knows it, so to speak, in the concrete, inasmuch as it exists in the divine being, namely, in the primary object of His knowledge, and inasmuch as it is in creatures, as in the secondary object of His knowledge. We must now treat of this secondary object of divine knowledge.

State of the question. The secondary object of the divine knowledge is discussed in this and the following eight articles. This object is considered first in general from the fifth to the eighth articles inclusive. The inquiry is about the existence, nature, and medium of this divine knowledge of creatures. Is it a proper knowledge of things as they are distinct from one another? Is it discursive? Is it the cause of things, and how is it the cause of things?

These articles, in which the question is discussed in a general way, are of great importance for the understanding of the following articles which treat in a special manner of such things as God's knowledge of contingent futures and of evil. The last articles of this question, as also what is said in explanation of God's will, especially whether God's will is the cause of things,[30] are closely connected with the eighth article, namely, whether God's knowledge is the cause of things.

In this fifth article there are two points of inquiry: whether God knows things other than Himself, and how, or through what medium He knows them.

That God has such knowledge is a dogma of our faith, or rather a dogma of Providence which is expressed in almost every page of Holy Scripture. But through what medium God knows things other than Himself, is a disputed question among theologians.

At the beginning of this article St. Thomas proposes three difficulties: (1) How can God know things that are outside Himself? Augustine says that "God does not behold anything out of Himself." [31] (2) If God were to know other things than Himself, He would be perfected by something other than Himself, as the intellect is by its object. (3) The intellectual act is so much the nobler, as the object understood is nobler. Therefore only the divine essence can be the object of the divine intellect.

It must be noted that Aristotle gave these difficulties at least

---

[30] *Summa theol.*, Ia, q.19, a.4.
[31] *Book of 83 Questions*, q.46.

some consideration, and was unable to solve them. In discussing the intellection of the first intellect, he says: "Clearly, then, it thinks that which is most divine and estimable, and does not change; for the change would be for the worse. . . . Clearly, then, there must be something else which is more excellent than Mind, namely, the object of thought; for both thought and the act of thinking will belong even to the thinker of the worst thoughts; wherefore this must be avoided. For it is indeed better not to see some things, than to see them. This is not so if thinking is the supreme good. Therefore Mind thinks itself, if it is that which is best. And its thinking is a thinking of thinking." [32]

Several historians, such as Zeller and Ravaisson, said that in this text Aristotle denies knowledge of the world to God, inasmuch as it is more becoming for one not to see some things, as being of an inferior order. Contrary to this, St. Thomas observes that Aristotle appeals to this general axiom merely to show that the nobility of intellection depends on the nobility of its object, and therefore that the proper object of the divine intellect must be God Himself and not things of this world. As St. Thomas says: "Since, therefore, some act of understanding is to be avoided on account of the unworthiness of the intelligible species, it follows that the nobility of this act, which is to understand, depends on the nobility of the intelligible species. Therefore the thing understood is more excellent than the act of understanding it. . . . (Hence) it is that the (supreme Intellect) must understand Himself. . . . Evidently there is no perfecting of God's intellect by any other thing besides Himself that is understood by Him. Nevertheless it does not follow from this that all things other than Himself are unknown to Him; for by understanding Himself He understands all other things (inasmuch as God is the cause of things)." [33]

This text from Aristotle's *Metaphysics* is indeed obscure. But it must be noted against Zeller and Ravaisson that the Stagirite has spoken more clearly in another chapter,[34] in which he praised Anaxagoras for having said that there must be a supreme intelligence who has ordained all things in the world. Aristotle said in this chapter that Anaxagoras thus showed himself to be the wise one among the foolish. He said likewise in another passage: "But the world refuses to be governed badly. The rule of many is not good; let one be the ruler." [35]

He also argued against Empedocles, that "God would be most

[32] *Metaph.*, Bk. XII, chap. 9.
[33] *Com. in Metaph.*, Bk. XII, lect. 11.
[34] *Ibid.*, Bk. I, chap. 3.
[35] *Metaph.*, Bk. XII, chap. 10 (end).

ignorant if He did not know discord." [36] Finally, Averroes, accepting the teaching of Aristotle, admitted a general providence, by which God has a general knowledge of things in the world which He directs, if not as to each detail, at least in a general way.

It must be admitted, however, that Aristotle was always in doubt on this point, because he never succeeded in acquiring a clear concept of creation, especially of eternal creation. Therefore he was at a loss to explain how God can have any knowledge of this world without a certain passivity or dependence on things, which cannot be attributed to Him who is pure Act. But St. Thomas gives us an excellent solution of this difficulty.

Two truths are affirmed in this article: (1) God necessarily knows things other than Himself; (2) God knows things other than Himself, not immediately in themselves, but in Himself.

The first proposition is of faith, and is included in the dogmas of creation and providence. The words of St. Paul are quoted in proof of this: "All things are naked and open to His eyes." [37]

It is also proved by reason from what was said in the preceding articles: Anything is not perfectly known unless its power is perfectly known and unless it is known to what its power extends. But God knows Himself perfectly (otherwise His existence would not be perfect, since His existence is His act of understanding), and the divine power, which is the first efficient cause of all things, extends to things other than Himself. Therefore God necessarily knows things other than Himself.

In affirming that the divine knowledge of things is according to the knowledge of the divine power, St. Thomas already implicitly assigns the medium of this knowledge.

This proof is confirmed from the fact that the divine power contains things other than Himself, after the manner of an intelligible species. For a thing is in another according to the mode of the other in which it is. But in God, as first efficient cause, His existence is His act of understanding. Therefore whatever effects pre-exist in God as in the First Cause, are in Him His act of understanding and His intelligible species.

As Cajetan observes, this proposition, "God's existence is His act of understanding," is to be taken rather in its formal sense than as expressing merely identity. There is identity (by reason of the reality or subject of the proposition) between God's act of understanding and His act of willing, because there is no distinction between them. But something more is affirmed when it is said that

---

[36] *Ibid.*, Bk. III, chap. 4 (Com. of St. Thomas, lect. 12); see also Ia, q.14, a.11; also *De caelo*, Bk. I, chap. 4, and Bk. II, chap. 9.

[37] Heb. 4: 13.

"God's existence is His act of understanding," for in God, as the First Cause, His existence is, strictly speaking, His act of understanding, inasmuch as His act of understanding is the foundation for His active power of intellectual cause as such. This is the case with the artificer, and it applies analogically to God, as will be stated more clearly in the eighth article.

In the second part of this article it is shown that God knows things other than Himself, not immediately in themselves, but in Himself. It concerns the medium of this knowledge, and is proved as follows: For a thing to be seen in itself, means that it is seen by its proper and adequate species (as through the medium by which it is seen); whereas a thing is seen in another when it is seen through the image of that which contains it, which is what is seen first, as the image of the mirror is what is first seen, and then what is reflected in it. But God knows things other than Himself inasmuch as His essence contains the similitude of other things, and He does not know them through the proper species of each thing. Therefore God knows things other than Himself, not in themselves, but in Himself.

This means that God knows things other than Himself in Himself first known as what is known. On the contrary, we know external things not in ourselves, but in themselves; for our senses know sensible qualities through the proper species impressed upon them by these qualities, and our intellect knows the nature of external things through their proper intelligible species, which are abstracted from the things. Hence it is commonly said that, whereas our knowledge is measured by things, God's knowledge is the measure of things. But although God knows things other than Himself, His knowledge of things is intuitive, because it extends both to the existence of the thing and the mode of its own existence.[38]

SOLUTION OF OBJECTIONS

The solution of the objections of this article confirms this opinion.

Reply to first objection. When St. Augustine says that "God sees nothing outside Himself," this must be understood as meaning that God does not see what is outside Himself except in Himself.

Reply to second objection. "Hence it does not follow that there is any perfection in the divine intellect other than the divine essence." Thus is solved the difficulty which baffled Aristotle, because for him creation was an unknown concept. If God is the

[38] Cf. a.6.

Creator, then He is able to know the things of this world in Himself, in His causality, without His being in any way dependent on the things themselves.

Reply to third objection. "Hence it does not follow that the divine intellectual act is specified by anything else than the divine essence itself, because the intellectual act is not specified by what is understood in another, but by the principal object understood in which other things are understood."

This opinion held by St. Thomas concerning the medium in which God knows things other than Himself is not admitted by all theologians, and especially by the Molinists; for if God cannot know things other than Himself except in Himself as the cause, this means the end of the *scientia media* by which, as Molina will have it, God knows conditionally free acts of the future (futurables) independently of His decree, or of His causality.

Therefore many Molinists, particularly Vasquez, hold that God knows things other than Himself immediately in themselves, or at least both ways, namely, either immediately in Himself as the cause (thus He knows created things), or immediately in themselves (thus He would know futurables independently of the divine decree).

But the Thomists refute this opinion, arguing from the principles laid down in this article. For to have immediate knowledge of external things is to know them by their proper species. But there is only one species in God, which is His essence, and the divine essence is not immediately representative of created things as the medium by which He sees them, but is that which is seen by God, and that in which God's effects are known. But whatever is external to God, must be in a relation of dependent causality to Him, who is the cause of all beings and their real modes of being. Nor can it be said that God has immediate knowledge of things other than Himself without a species, for then His knowledge would not be determined more to one particular thing than to a certain other. The final result of this would be that the divine intellect is determined and perfected by something extrinsic. Thus God would not be pure Act, and the first determining Being, but would be determined by another, and this would make Him dependent on another. This is the grave defect in the theory of the *scientia media,* as will be stated in a subsequent article.

Nor can the divine essence be considered as the immediately representative medium by which He knows created things; for immediate representation is effected by the proper and adequate species. But the divine essence infinitely transcends every created being. Nor can it be said evidently that God, by reason of His essence, knows, as it were on equal terms, both Himself and creatures. There must be not co-ordination but subordination of either a possible or an actual effect in relation to its cause. Thus God knows all things other than Himself in His essence as the cause.[39]

Objection. Some say that God knows created truths in as many ways as they are knowable. But truths are also knowable immediately in themselves, and they are thus known by angels and by us. Therefore God knows them immediately in themselves.

Reply. That God knows created truths in as many ways as they are knowable on the part of the thing known, this I concede; on the part of the knower, I subdistinguish: in every way that does not imply imperfection, this I concede; otherwise I deny it.

Objection. Still some insist that to know a thing in itself is a more perfect way than to know it in another. Therefore this way must be attributed to God.

Reply. I distinguish the antecedent: if the thing to be known is not so clearly expressed in another as it is in itself, then I concede the antecedent; if it is more clearly expressed in another than it is in itself, then I deny the antecedent. Things are contained, however, more perfectly in God, as in the most eminent intellectual cause, than in themselves. Just as the production of a work of art pre-exists in more perfect form in the mind of a great painter or sculptor than on the canvas or in the marble, and as he cannot produce in matter whatever is vividly conceived by him, then far more so are things contained in God in a more eminent way than in themselves. By knowing them in Himself, God knows them as in their dawning; by what St. Augustine calls morning vision, which is measured by the unique instant of motionless eternity. On the contrary, whereas we know things in themselves, we know them as in their twilight, by what is called evening knowledge, in the obscurity of sensible and material things. Therefore it is the common opinion among theologians in discussing the knowledge of the blessed, that it is a more perfect way for one to know created things in the Word than outside the Word.[40]

Final difficulty. God is not the adequate cause of our vital acts, especially of our free ones. Therefore God cannot know them in His causality.

Reply. Although God is not the proximate cause of our acts, yet

---

[39] But if certain Molinists say that God knows futurables in His essence, they do not mean by this that He knows them in His essence as the cause, for they maintain that futurables are not dependent on the divine decrees, as will be stated in a subsequent article.

[40] *Summa theol.,* Ia, q.58, a.7.

whatever entity and perfection they have come from God and are contained eminently in Him.

WHETHER GOD KNOWS THINGS OTHER THAN HIMSELF BY PROPER KNOWLEDGE

State of the question. This article is concerned with proper knowledge, not on the part of the knower as acquired by various acts, but on the part of the thing known. In other words, does God by a single act know things in the world as they are distinct from one another and according to their proper natures, or has He merely a general knowledge of them? The difficulty is that other things are in God as in their common and universal cause, and, moreover, the proper ratio of the divine essence cannot be the proper ratio of many and diverse things.

Reply. The conclusion is in the affirmative and is of faith.

1) It is revealed in several passages of Holy Scripture, as when it speaks of God's knowledge of things as "reaching unto the division of the soul and the spirit, of the joints also and the marrow, and is a discerner of the thoughts and intents of the heart. Neither is there any creature invisible in His sight; but all things are naked and open to His eyes." [41] The concluding words of this passage are quoted by the Vatican Council, and it adds "even those which are yet to be by the free action of creatures." [42]

It must be noted that this article is especially directed against those who, like Averroes and Algazel, maintained that God has a general knowledge of things in the world, as regards the general laws of nature, but that He does not know them in particular. [43]

2) **Indirect proof.** To know creatures in a general way would be to have an imperfect or confused knowledge of them. Therefore both God's understanding and His being would be imperfect, which is an impossibility. For it is evident that such knowledge is imperfect on the part of the thing known, because it would not be perfectly known.

3) **Direct proof.** It specifies the mode of this proper knowledge. St. Thomas does this gradually, first by giving the examples brought forward by others in explanation of this mode, as, for instance, if the center knew itself, it would know all lines that proceed from

---

[41] Heb. 4: 12.

[42] Denz., no. 1784.

[43] Malebranche wanted even more or less to restrict divine providence to general laws, so as to explain the presence of evil in the world and of free will in man.

the center; or if light knew itself, it would know all colors. But these examples are not sufficiently convincing, says St. Thomas, because multitude and diversity are not caused by that one principle as regards that which is the reason for the distinction but only as regards that in which they communicate. Hence, if the center knew itself, it would know only that to which the lines converge. It must be shown that whatever perfection exists in any creature, even what belongs properly to it as such, pre-exists either eminently and formally or eminently and virtually in the cause of the total being of things.

St. Thomas gives a more convincing example as evidence of this, namely, the perfect act, which is posterior in the order of generation, and which contains all imperfect acts, which are prior to it in the order of generation. Thus animal and living are included in man, and the sensitive and vegetative souls are included in the intellective soul, because whatever perfection there is in the imperfect act, is found eminently in the perfect act. Thus he who knows a man knows an animal by proper knowledge.

This gradual preparation leads up to the following direct proof: The divine essence contains in itself whatever there is of reality in all creatures even to what ultimately differentiates them, of which His essence is the total cause, inasmuch as there is nothing in the creature that is not caused by God, not even matter, which is the principle of individuation in sensible things. But God has comprehensive knowledge of His essence, which is the self-subsisting Being. Therefore God by knowing Himself, knows all things by proper knowledge. In other words: "God knows all the ways in which His own perfection can be shared by others."

In addition to this it is said: "Neither could He know the very nature of being perfectly, unless He knew all modes of being." Averroes, denying this, failed to perceive that the self-subsisting Being contains all modes of being. He judged of being, the modes of which are also being, as of any genus, the *differentiae* of which are extrinsic to it. Thus rationality is an extrinsic *differentia* of animality. Hence, whoever perfectly knows an animal does not by reason of this know a rational being by proper knowledge. But whoever knows a rational being knows an animal.

Corollary. Only God, who has comprehensive knowledge of self-subsisting Being, has perfect knowledge of the very nature of being, either as an act or as an entity. Thus He alone knows all possible modes of being, or the infinite number of possibles. We know by abstraction those things that are actually and explicitly in being, but not all those that are actually and implicitly in being, that is, we do not know all modes of being. We know these successively by experience and by discursive knowledge.

The solution of the difficulties confirms this conclusion.

Reply to first objection. Although God knows things in this world, not immediately in themselves, but in Himself as they are in Himself, nevertheless He knows them in their own nature as they are in themselves. Thus by one cognitive act, which is self-subsisting intellection, He knows them distinctly, and "all the more perfectly, the more perfectly each one is in Him."

Reply to second objection. "The created essence is compared to the essence of God, as the imperfect act to the perfect act. Therefore the created essence cannot sufficiently lead us to the knowledge of the divine essence, but rather the converse."

Reply to third objection. "The divine essence (by reason of its eminence) can be taken as the proper ratio of each thing according to the diverse ways in which diverse creatures participate in and imitate it." Thus, dependent on God, stones participate in being, plants in life, animals in cognition, men and angels in intellective life, and the just in divine life strictly as such. It is only this last participation that is called a "participation of the divine nature," all others being imitations of the divine essence according to being, life, and intellection.

This eminence of the divine essence is for us mysterious or invisible, but in it is verified the principle, that "superior beings unite in themselves the various perfections of inferior beings." Thus one visual act of sense perception includes within its range all visible things of a vast region, which are seen in one glance. Likewise one thing perfectly known includes within itself all intelligible objects pertaining to it. Transcending all beings, God has comprehensive knowledge of the self-subsisting Being, that is, of Himself, and He has perfect knowledge of all possible and actual modes of being.

SEVENTH ARTICLE

WHETHER THE KNOWLEDGE OF GOD IS DISCURSIVE

The reply is in the negative, and it follows as a corollary from the preceding. Discursion is of two kinds; either it is according to succession only, inasmuch as in point of time the things understood follow one another, as the night the day; or else it is according to causality, as when through principles we arrive at the knowledge of conclusions.

But neither kind of discursion belongs to God, because He sees all things together, seeing them all in one thing, which is Himself. Moreover, since God does not proceed from the known to the unknown, He knows effects not from their cause, but immediately in their cause, as we do when the terminus of discursive reasoning is reached.

WHETHER GOD'S KNOWLEDGE IS THE CAUSE OF THINGS

State of the question. The question asked in this article really includes two questions: (1) Whether God's knowledge is at least the directive cause in the production of things, these being truly produced by God, so that God, the Creator and Ordainer, operates most wisely, and not in a blind or ignorant way; (2) whether God's knowledge is the effective cause of things, so that it in no way is caused by or is dependent on things (not even on our future free acts). But, if the first question is solved in the affirmative, then so is the second, on the supposition that there can be nothing real or future (either absolute or conditional) that is not dependent on God.

The answer to this first question, however, is in the affirmative and is of faith; for it is expressed in very many texts of Holy Scripture, such as in the following: "Thou hast made all things in wisdom"; [44] "who made the heavens in understanding." [45] Moreover, this is already evident to reason from the proof of God's existence because of the order prevailing in the world; for the supreme Ordainer of things acts not in a blind way but most wisely, since He operates by His intellect in all things effected by Him.

But as for the second question, namely, whether God's knowledge is the effective cause of things, so that it is in no way caused by things, St. Thomas in the first objection and in the counter-argument, notes a certain difference of opinion on this point between Origen and St. Augustine. For Origen, who is quoted in the first objection, when commenting on the words, "Whom He called, them He also justified," [46] says: "A thing will happen not because God knows it as future; but because it is future, it is on that account known by God before it exists." [47] Taken literally, these words seem to mean that God's knowledge is in some way dependent on future things.

Contrary to this, St. Augustine says: "Not because they are, does

[44] Ps. 103: 24.
[45] *Ibid.*, 135: 5.
[46] Rom. 8: 30.
[47] *Com.* on Rom. 8: 30.

God know all creatures spiritual and temporal, but because He knows them therefore they are." [48] This means that things are dependent on God's knowledge, and not God's knowledge on things.

St. Thomas quotes St. Augustine, following him as his authority. In his reply to the first objection, he charitably interprets Origen's words in a good sense. If these words were taken literally, it would follow that God knew things to be created because they were to come into being, and not that they were to come into being because God knew and freely willed them. But, as a matter of fact, in this passage Origen is referring especially to sin, which God is not the cause of, and Origen means that the divine foreknowledge does not do away with human liberty. Moreover, as St. Thomas says, "if things are in the future, it follows that God knows them; but not that the futurity of things is the cause of God's knowing them." [49]

For a better understanding of the importance of this question, we should note that the difficulty arising from the conflicting statements of Origen and St. Augustine, persisted among theologians as regards the divine foreknowledge. This is especially the case with Molina who, in his theory of the *scientia media,* maintains that God foresees conditionally free actions of the future or futurables before there is any determining divine decree concerning them. Thus the divine knowledge of futurables in its relation to these would not be determining, but rather determined by them and dependent on them. For Molina says: "It was not in God's power to know by this *scientia (media)* anything else than He actually knew. . . . (But) if the created free will were to do the opposite, as it truly can, He would have known even this by the same knowledge, but not that He actually knows it." [50] Thus Molina speaks rather the language of Origen than that of St. Augustine.

Therefore, as for the question asked in this article, Molina holds that God's knowledge is indeed the directive cause of things which are produced by Him; but he maintains that God's knowledge is not the effective cause of the determination of our free will, the act of which, in his opinion, is first foreseen by God as a conditionally free action of the future; e.g., if Peter were situated in certain circumstances he would choose this particular thing, and then, with the positing of the conditions, it is foreseen as a future act; i.e., Peter, actually situated in certain circumstances, will choose this particular thing. But St. Thomas settles both questions by one answer.

[48] *De Trin.,* Bk. XV, chap. 13.
[49] Cf. ad 1um.
[50] *Concordia,* q.14, a.13, disp. 52 (Paris ed., 1876, p. 318).

His answer is: The knowledge of God, in so far as His will is joined to it, is the cause of things, and is not caused by them.

1) There is foundation for this doctrine in Holy Scripture, as shown from the following texts: "The Lord by wisdom hath founded the earth, hath established the heavens by prudence"; [51] "and God said: Be light made. And light was made"; [52] "by the word of the Lord the heavens were established"; [53] "Who is a more artful worker than she (Wisdom) of those things that are?" [54] "All things were made by Him (the Word)"; [55] "upholding all things by the word of His power." [56] But these complex terms, "The Lord by wisdom hath founded, hath established, is an artful worker," convey the idea that God's knowledge is the cause of things.

2) Among the Church Fathers, who stated this truth more clearly, prominent is St. Augustine, a quotation from one of his works being given in the counterargument of this article.[57] He also says in another of his writings: "This world could not be known to us unless it existed, but it could not have existed unless it had been known to God." [58] St. Gregory the Great asserts: "For even whatsoever things are, in His eternity are not therefore seen because they are, but therefore they are because they are seen." [59]

3) The conclusion is proved by the following theological argument: The knowledge of God is to all creatures what the knowledge of the artificer is to the things made by his art. But the knowledge of the artificer is the cause of the things made by his art so far as his will is joined to it. Therefore the knowledge of God is the cause of all things, in so far as His will is joined to it.

The major enunciates an analogy drawn from the Holy Scripture in which God's wisdom is called the "artificer" of all things. Moreover, this is also evident to reason from the proof of God's existence as supreme Ordainer by reason of the order prevailing in the world. Hence, as stated in the body of the article, "It is manifest that God causes things by His intellect, since His being is His act of understanding," a truth previously established.[60] This is also clearly seen from the fact that to act by the intellect is a

51 Prov. 3: 19.
52 Gen. 1: 3.
53 Ps. 33: 6.
54 Wis. 8: 6.
55 John 1: 3.
56 Heb. 1: 3.
57 De Trin., Bk. XV, chap. 13.
58 De civit. Dei, Bk. XI, chap. 10.
59 Morals, Bk. XV, chap. 23.
60 Summa theol., Ia, q.14, a.4.

more perfect and more universal mode of action than to act by nature.[61]

Now in man, for instance, the intellective life is above the vegetative which operates from a necessity of its nature. Finally, to act by the intellect is to determine the form and end of its action, whereas, on the other hand, to act by nature is to be determined by the Author of nature. This answers the objections of the pantheists.[62] Therefore it can truly be said that knowledge is predicated analogically of God and the artificer.

The minor of this proof states, however, that the knowledge of the artificer is the cause of the things made by his art, in so far as his will is joined to it. For it is evident that the artificer acts by his intellect, and therefore by his practical knowledge or by his art, which is the perfection or form of his intellect. But besides this it is of necessity that there be conjunction of will and intellect; for just as the natural form, for instance, of a plant, is for action by reason of its natural appetite or inclination, so also the intelligible form, by reason of its rational appetite or will, is for the same end. "For since the intelligible form," says St. Thomas, "has a relation to opposite things, inasmuch as the same knowledge relates to opposites (thus ethics is concerned with the performance of good and the avoidance of evil), it would not produce a determinate effect unless it were determined to one thing by the appetite." [63] For the intelligible form or the idea has a relation to opposite things, namely, to being and to non-being. Thus the artificer can produce or not produce the work of art that is conceived by him, and God can produce or not produce the world, and of possible things these particular ones in preference to others. But God's knowledge joined to His will constitutes the divine determining decree, and is not only the directive but also the effective cause of things, just as command presupposes freedom of choice.

St. Thomas states this more clearly in various passages of his works. Thus he says: "Knowledge never produces its effect except through the intervention of the will, the concept of which implies a certain influx into things willed." [64] "Hence it does not necessarily follow that things come into being whenever there is knowledge, but only when the production of these is determined by the will." [65] "The (divine) idea is determined as regards those things that are,

---

[61] *Ibid.*, Ia, q.19, a.4; *Contra Gentes*, Bk. II, chap. 23.
[62] *Ibid.*, Ia, q.19, a.4.
[63] *Com. on Aristotle's Metaphysics*, Bk. IX, chap. 5, lect. 4.
[64] *De veritate*, q.2, a.14.
[65] *Ibid.*, ad 2um.

or were, or will be produced, by a decree of the divine will; but it is not so determined as regards those things that neither are, nor were, nor will be." [66] "God does not, therefore, act by a necessity of His nature, but determined effects proceed from His own infinite perfection according to the determination of His will and intellect." [67] "The form, as it is in the intellect only, is not determined to exist or not to exist in the effect, except by the will." [68]

This determination just mentioned is nothing else but the determining divine decree, for which, just as for a human decree, there is required: (1) a judgment of the intellect directing the free choice of the will; (2) the choice itself by the will. Then there is the command of the intellect directing one to make use of the means willed. The gradual development of this doctrine is to be found in St. Thomas' treatise on human acts.[69] It is there shown that there are two orders, one of intention and the other of execution. In the order of intention, the intellect apprehends the end and proposes it to the will; the will intends the end, and in virtue of this intention the intellect inquires into the means more suitable for the attainment of the end, and the intellect judges of them or distinguishes between them (this being a practical judgment); then the will freely chooses these means, and this terminates the order of intention, by a descendent process from the end intended down to the first and least of the means chosen. After this begins the order of execution through a command of the intellect, which means that the intellect commands the use of the means willed, beginning with the lowest and ascending to the higher until the end is attained, which is first in intention and last in execution. In virtue of this command the will applies the faculties to the performance of their acts, and this application is called the active use, which is followed by the passive use of these faculties, and after this comes the attainment of the end.[70]

This is analogically verified in God. The divine intellect apprehends the divine goodness manifested to it as its end, and the divine will intends this end. In virtue of this intention the intellect, so to speak, inquires into the means, proposing these to the divine will, which wills them, and this terminates the order of intention. In this process the divine knowledge is directive but not effective. But, posited the efficacious choice of the means, in virtue of this the intellect commands the employment of the means,

---

[66] *Ibid.*, q.3, a.6.
[67] *Summa theol.*, Ia, q.19, a.4.
[68] *Ibid.*, ad 4um.
[69] *Ibid.*, Ia IIae, q.12, 13, 14, 17.
[70] *Ibid.*, q.17, a.1.

and thus the divine knowledge is not only the directive but is also the effective cause of things in second actuality. In this setting, the divine knowledge, presupposing as it does election, was usually called "knowledge of approbation" or even "of vision," because by producing the effect it sees, and by seeing it produces the effect, which means that it extends to things either as actually present or as belonging entirely to the future, not precisely as it is knowledge of vision, but as the will is joined to it.

Hence the knowledge of simple intelligence, which is concerned with possible things before God's free choice of them, is only the directive cause of things, whereas the knowledge of approbation, which follows the efficacious choice, is the effective cause of things. This commanded act is efficacious, inasmuch as it presupposes a determining choice, and this latter is often called the purpose or efficacious decree of the divine will.

Thus we understand why St. Thomas said: "Determined effects proceed from His own infinite perfection according to the determination of His will and intellect." [71] By "the determination of the will" is meant here the election which follows the directive judgment and which precedes the command moving one to make use of the means.

Conclusion. Therefore God's knowledge is the effective cause of things, as being a command that presupposes the efficacious act of election on the part of the divine will. And it is concerned with all things without exception, for there can be no reality that is not causatively dependent on God's knowledge and will, not even the free determination of our choices.

SOLUTION OF OBJECTIONS

Reply to first objection. It solves the difficulty presented by the text quoted from Origen, who spoke inappropriately and in too human a way about God's knowledge. Truly, his purpose is to prove that God's knowledge is not harmful to human liberty, and he is especially concerned with sin, which God is not the cause of, because He only permits it. Moreover, it is still true to say in an illative sense, but not in a causal sense, that if anything will come into existence, this is known by God before it exists.

Reply to second objection. Although God's knowledge is eternal, it does not follow that creatures are eternal, because it was not in God's knowledge that things should be eternal, but only that they should come into being in a time that is determined by God's will.

[71] *Ibid.*, Ia, q.19, a.4.

Reply to third objection. The knowable is prior to created knowledge, but not to the uncreated knowledge. Whereas our knowledge is measured or caused by things, God's knowledge is the measure and cause of things.

Objection. Created liberty cannot exist with that knowledge which, in virtue of an absolute and antecedent decree, is the cause of future action. But such is God's knowledge, in accordance with the preceding thesis. Therefore God's knowledge is not the cause of future actions.

Reply. According to what St. Thomas says in a subsequent question,[72] I distinguish the antecedent as follows: If the decree of the divine will concerns only the substance of the future action, I concede it; if it concerns also the free mode of this action, then I deny it. Replying to one of his objections in this subsequent question, St. Thomas says: "From the very fact that nothing resists the divine will, it follows that not only those things happen that God wills to happen, but that they happen necessarily or contingently according to His will." [73]

Another objection. Then God could not know sin, because He is not the cause of sin. Therefore the difficulty remains.

Reply. In the tenth article of this question St. Thomas solves this difficulty by pointing out that God knows possible evil things by their opposite good things; also actual and future sins, inasmuch as He wills to permit them for a greater good.[74]

Doubt. How does St. Thomas distinguish between the knowledge of simple intelligence and that of vision?

Reply. St. Thomas explains this in different works of his.[75] In his opinion, the knowledge of simple intelligence and the knowledge of vision are not two kinds of knowledge, but are one and the same in God; their difference arises only from the diversity of their objects. In other words, the knowledge of simple intelligence has not the will joined to it, and is concerned with possible things, thus being a necessary knowledge. The knowledge of vision has the will joined to it, and is concerned with really existing things, either present, past, or future. The knowledge of vision is said to have the will joined to it inasmuch as it is accompanied by either a positive or permissive decree of the divine will. As will be stated farther on, the knowledge of conditionally free actions of the future or of futurables refers back to the knowledge of vision inasmuch as it pre-

---

[72] *Ibid.*, a.8.

[73] *Ibid.*, ad 2um.

[74] *Ibid.*, a.9 ad 3um, in which this divine permission is discussed.

[75] Cf. Ia, q.14, a.16; *De veritate*, q.3, a.8 ad 8um; *Contra Gentes*, Bk. I, chaps. 60, 69.

supposes a conditional decree of the divine will, without which these conditionally free actions of the future would be undetermined. Such as these are: What would Peter do if situated in certain circumstances? Or what would Paul have done, if he had been in Peter's place, in the circumstances of our Lord's Passion? Confronted by the two possibilities of faithfulness or unfaithfulness, which would he have chosen? If we say that God is able to know this infallibly before His decree, then such knowledge is not the cause of things but is caused by conditionally free actions of the future or is dependent on them; nevertheless, inasmuch as they are contingent, they are still undetermined. From this we already see how very important the present article is as regards the foreknowledge of future things.

In this article we have a legitimate application of the analogical method, to the exclusion of all anthropomorphism, because what is said of the artificer's knowledge, inasmuch as it is the cause of things made by his art, does not in its formal concept imply any imperfection. Thus knowledge is predicated analogically of God in the literal sense and not merely metaphorically, those imperfections being removed, of course, which are found in the created mode of the artificer's knowledge.

NINTH ARTICLE

WHETHER GOD HAS KNOWLEDGE OF THINGS THAT ARE NOT

State of the question. By "things that are not" is meant things that do not actually exist but that exist only potentially so, either in God or in a creature.

The answer is affirmative. (1) It is of faith, for the Scripture says: "Before I formed thee in the bowels of thy mother, I knew thee." [76] There are very many parallel texts in Holy Scripture concerning God's knowledge of things that are not, but which are either possible or which did exist or which will exist.

2) Proof from reason. Things that are not absolutely, namely, that are not actually, are in the power either of God or of creatures. But God knows those things that are either in His power or in the power of a creature, otherwise He would not have comprehensive knowledge of Himself. Therefore God knows things that are not absolutely.

There are two more conclusions:

1) By the knowledge of vision, God knows past or future things, because God's glance is measured by eternity, which is without

[76] Jer. 1: 5.

succession and which comprehends all time, just as the apex of a pyramid corresponds to all the points of its base.

2) By the knowledge of simple intelligence God knows merely possible things, those which never were nor are nor will be. God knows these in His essence as it is infinitely imitable.[77]

St. Thomas in this article is not speaking of conditionally free actions of the future, for he treats of this elsewhere when discussing prophecy of denunciation.[78] He is now speaking of merely possible things, which must not be confused with futurable; for the futurable means this: of two possible things (for instance, of remaining faithful or of being unfaithful), which would one choose if situated in certain cicumstances? Thus the futurable adds a new determination to the possible.

The purely possible is merely what is capable of existence, what is not repugnant to existence. Inasmuch as it is something really possible, it is called a real possible, which is a different entity from what is purely a figment of the mind or mental being, which is not capable of real but only of logical existence, like the universality of any predicate. It also differs from real and actual being, or actually existing being.

TENTH ARTICLE

WHETHER GOD KNOWS EVIL THINGS

State of the question. The most serious difficulty is that God knows things other than Himself inasmuch as they are in Himself as in their cause. But God is not the cause of evil. Therefore it seems that God does not know evil things.

Nevertheless the contrary is affirmed frequently in Holy Scripture, as in the following text: "Thou hast set our iniquities before Thy eyes." [79] It is of faith that God knows physical and moral evils and, if God did not know sins and the grievousness of these, He could not justly punish them.

The body of the article contains two conclusions: (1) God knows evil things; (2) God knows evil things by their opposite good things.

Proof of first conclusion. There are some good things that can be corrupted by the presence of evil; but all good things and what can be accidental to them are perfectly known by God; therefore evil things are known by God.

The major is evident both as regards natural good, such as health, the loss of which may be due to various causes, and as regards moral

---

[77] *De veritate*, q.2, a.8.
[78] *Summa theol.*, IIa IIae, q.171, a.6, ad 2um; q.174, a.1; Ia, q.19, a.7 ad 2um.
[79] Ps. 89: 8.

good, such as virtue, which can likewise be corrupted so as to beget vice. The minor is evident, it having been established that God has comprehensive knowledge of those things that are in Himself as in their cause.

Proof of second conclusion. A thing is knowable in the degree in which it is. But the essence of evil consists in the privation of good. Therefore God knows evil things by their opposite good things, just as darkness is known by light. Thus God knows injustice by justice, and from the fact that He has knowledge of all justice, He knows the gravity of injustice. But because we have not intuitive knowledge of all justice, our valuation of it is obtained from injustice and from the grief caused by grievous injustice. These two conclusions are concerned more with the nature of evils than with their existence.

Doubt. With regard to the existence of evils and with regard to the elucidation of the second objection, the following question is asked: How does God foresee evils, especially sins?

The answer is: God knows them in His permissive decree. St. Thomas speaks of this permissive decree in the preceding article, saying: "The knowledge of God joined to His will is the cause of things. Hence it is not necessary that whatever God knows, is, or was, or will be; but only is this necessary as regards what He wills to be, or permits to be." [80] St. Thomas' answer is the same in the following replies to objections proposed by him: "God does not will evil to be done, but wills to permit evil to be done; and this is a good." [81] "One who provides universally, allows some little defect to remain, lest the good of the whole should be hindered." [82] "Reprobation includes the will to permit a person to fall into sin, and to impose the punishment of damnation on account of that sin." [83] "Permission is of many kinds. There is permission: (1) of licit concession; (2) of dispensation . . . ; (3) of tolerance, as when a lesser evil is permitted for a greater good. Such was the permission given by Moses, when he allowed a bill of divorce . . . ; (4) of favorable concession, as when something is permitted, though its opposite is better; as when the apostles permitted second marriages (I Cor., chap. 7) . . . ; (5) of forbearance, as when God permits evils to happen, that through them He may effect some good." [84]

Before the permissive decree God knows sins as possible, but not as future. Moreover, God wills to concur in the act of sin, so that

[80] Cf. ad 3um.
[81] *Ibid.*, Ia, q.19, a.9 ad 3um.
[82] *Ibid.*, q.22, a.2 ad 2um.
[83] *Ibid.*, q.23, a.3; see also Ia IIae, q.79, a.4.
[84] *Com. in Matt.*, 5: 31.

whatever actuality there is in it depends on the First Cause.[85] Nor does it follow from this that God is the cause of sin, namely, of the deordination in sin. Since God is indefectible, He cannot be either the direct or the indirect cause (as it were through negligence) of this deordination, which is a defect.[86] Thus evil is explained on three grounds: (1) on the part of the formal cause (as being the privation of a good that is due); (2) on the part of the material and defective cause (the defectible creature); (3) on the part of God permitting it, who in no way is the cause of sin, His permission being the indispensable condition for sin, which He ordains for a greater good as the end in view.[87]

Clarity and obscurity are combined in this solution. What is most clear is this, that, just as God cannot produce what is not included in the notion of being, so He can in no way be either the direct or the indirect cause of the deordination in sin, which is excluded from the adequate object of divine omnipotence. Nothing is more exclusive in itself than the object of any faculty. Thus the intellect knows good only under the aspect of the true; for although there is no real distinction between the true and the good, yet the intellect does not attain to the good under the concept of good, this being the province of the will, but it attains to this under the proper concept of the true. Thus God wills, and causes sin only as it is an entity, but not as it is a sinful act. This is an absolute certainty. Yet there is obscurity as to the intimate mode in which God, by permitting sin, concurs in its entity and in no way concurs in its malice. This intimate mode is hidden from us; and no wonder, for the mode is strictly divine, and is only analogically known by us in an inferior mirror.[88]

ELEVENTH ARTICLE

WHETHER GOD KNOWS SINGULAR THINGS

The answer is in the affirmative and is of faith, being a part of the dogmatic truth known as Providence which, according to Holy Scripture, extends even to the least of singular things, as is evident from the following passage: "Are not two sparrows sold for a farthing? And not one of them shall fall on the ground without your Father. But the very hairs of your head are all numbered. ' [89] St.

---

[85] Summa theol., Ia IIae, q.79, a.2.
[86] Ibid., a.1.
[87] Ibid., IIIa, q.1, a.3 ad 3um.
[88] Ibid., Ia, q.19, a.6, 8, 9; q.22, a.2, 3, 4; q.23, a.3, 5.
[89] Matt. 10: 30.

Thomas quotes a text from the Old Testament: "All the ways of a man are open to His eyes." [90]

In the body of the article it is shown: (1) that God knows singular things; (2) how He knows them.

The truth of the first statement is established by the following argument: All perfections found in creatures, which in their formal signification imply no imperfection, pre-exist formally and eminently in God; but knowledge of singulars is of this nature; therefore such perfections pre-exist in God formally and eminently.

The major was proved in a previous article.[91] The minor is evident. For, although sense perception of singular things implies imperfection, such is not the case with intellectual knowledge of singular things, if this intellectual knowledge does not have to be in conjunction with sensitive knowledge.

St. Thomas appeals to the authority of Aristotle, who, in refuting Empedocles, says: "God would be most ignorant if He did not know discord." [92] Yet it is not quite clear that Aristotle has in mind not only discord in general, but also particular cases of it.

In the second statement the question is asked: How does God know singular things? The answer is, that it will not do to say that God knows singular things in that He knows all their universal causes; for the singular thing, in its singularity, is dependent on individual matter, and thus the singular would not be realized as such. Nor will it do to say that God applies universal causes to particular effects, for this application presupposes but does not constitute the singular as known. It must be said that God, as shown above,[93] knows things other than Himself by His essence as their cause. But the divine causality extends to singular things inasmuch as it produces not only the form of things, but also the matter by which things are individualized. Therefore God knows singular things by His essence as their cause.

The minor is evident, for matter, although it is pure potentiality, still is being, and is distinct from both actuality and nothingness. Therefore it is not independently of God, the first Being, that this matter is caused and preserved here and now in such individual. "Matter, in so far as it has being in this or that way, retains a certain likeness to the divine Being." [94]

Hence, whereas we know spiritual things in the mirror of sensible things, God knows material things in the most exalted mirror of

90 Prov. 16: 2.
91 Cf. q.4, a.2.
92 *De anima*, Bk. I, chap. 5; *Metaph.*, Bk. III, chap. 4.
93 *Summa theol.*, Ia, q.14, a.8.
94 *Ibid.*, a.11 ad 3um.

His essence, which is the cause of all things even as regards their singularity. For us the spiritual is something immaterial: for the pure spirit and especially for God, the material is something non-spiritual, not having the amplitude of spirituality, something limited or confined here and now by matter, the ultimate subject, which is almost nothing. Thus in a spiritual way God knows from on high, for instance, a symphony which we perceive by the sense of hearing.

TWELFTH ARTICLE

WHETHER GOD CAN KNOW INFINITE THINGS

State of the question. It seems that the infinite, such as an unending series of days, is something unknown and unknowable, because a thing is knowable inasmuch as it is in act, or determined. Also the essence of the infinite is that it is untraversable, for it has no end. Such, for instance, is the successive and endless series of intellectual and volitional acts. For that alone is traversable which has a beginning and an end.[95]

The answer is, however, in the affirmative, and it is of faith, a point that will be more clearly established in the next article, which affirms that God knows future contingent things, even the intellectual and volitional acts of immortal souls, for there will be an unending series of such acts. It is first proved that God knows infinite things both by the knowledge of simple intelligence and by that of vision. Then the reason is given for the possibility of this knowledge.

1) As regards the knowledge of simple intelligence. Those things that are possible to God and to creatures are infinite. But God knows not only actual things, but all those that are possible to Him and to creatures. Therefore He knows infinite things, namely, an actually infinite and innumerable multitude of possible things. For, as St. Thomas says, "number adds to multitude the idea of measure; for number is multitude measured by one." [96]

2) As regards the knowledge of vision. The thoughts and affections of immortal souls will be multiplied to infinity. But God knows all these actually and simultaneously, and not successively, as we know them. Therefore also by His knowledge of vision He knows infinite things. The multitude of these thoughts is successively infinite, and absolutely innumerable.

3) The reason is given for the possibility of this knowledge of infinite things. Knowledge is measured by the mode of the form,

[95] See St. Thomas' *Com. on Aristotle's Physics*, Bk. VI, lect. 9.
[96] *Ibid.*, Bk. III, lect. 8. Cf. *supra*, q.7, a.4.

which is the principle of knowledge. But the divine essence, where- by God knows, extends as cause to infinite things, even as these are distinct from one another.[97]

The major is evident by an inductive process. Sense perception is co-extensive with the sensible species, and includes all sensible things represented by this latter. Our intellect, however, is co- extensive with the abstracted intelligible species, and includes an infinity of particulars as these communicate in the specific nature so understood, but not as they are distinct from one another.

But the minor is proved from the sixth and the eleventh articles of this question, in which it is stated that whatever perfection exists in creatures, even their individuating notes, pre-exist in God as in their most eminent cause, which most perfectly knows its power and causality.

The solution of the objections confirms this conclusion.

Reply to first objection. To know the infinite successively, part after part, is an impossibility even for God, because there would never be an end of this addition. But God knows the infinite or infinite things, not successively, that is, not part after part; for He knows all things simultaneously, inasmuch as they are contained in His power and eternal causality, which, as being simultaneously whole, includes all time. Thus it is not repugnant for infinite things to be contained in a most perfect and pre-existing Infinite, namely, in the power, intellect and eternity of God; for they exist unitedly in God, and are not as parts outside parts, as measured properly by time, but they are measured by the unique instant of motionless eternity.

Reply to second objection. "The infinite cannot be traversed by the infinite," because transition imports a certain succession of parts (and is not the terminus of the infinite multitude of parts). But the infinite can be adequately comprehended by the Infinite, in the higher reason of the divine essence, whose power is infinite.

Reply to third objection. Thus God's knowledge is not the quan- titative measure of things, but is their measure inasmuch as things imitate God's knowledge, as the things made by art agree with the art.

THIRTEENTH ARTICLE

WHETHER GOD'S KNOWLEDGE IS OF FUTURE THINGS

State of the question. The divine omniscience must indeed extend to all things, but it seems to eliminate contingency from things, because God's knowledge, which is the cause of things, is not a

[97] Cf. a.6, 11.

contingent cause but a necessary one, from which, therefore, a necessary effect proceeds. Moreover, everything known by God must necessarily be, whereas no contingent thing must necessarily be.

Hence, that the Stoics might defend God's foreknowledge of future things, they denied free will; so also did the Hussites. On the contrary, since Cicero [98] could not reconcile God's foreknowledge of future things with our freedom, in order to defend the latter he denied the former. The same also applies to Marcion, and in later times the Socinians maintained that God has only a conjectural knowledge of future free acts.

It is of faith, however, that God has infallible knowledge of all absolute futures, both contingent and free, without detriment to their freedom.[99]

This is evident from several texts in Holy Scripture, such as the following: "He who hath made the hearts of every one of them, who understandeth all their works"; [100] "Thou hast understood my thoughts afar off . . . and Thou hast foreseen all my ways"; [101]

[98] *De divinatione,* Bk. II.

[99] It must be noted that the future is correctly defined as that which is determined in its causes to exist in course of time. Such is the common teaching of the Thomists.

It is not a question here of a cause having precisely the power to produce such effect, because this denotes merely what is possible; nor is it a question of a cause as actually producing such effect, because this denotes an existing thing. Therefore the definition concerns an absolute future.

Evidently the future must be constituted as such by that which eliminates it from the mass of possible things and distinguishes it from both possible and existing things. But there is only one way by which this is effected, and that is by the determination of that cause; and from all eternity the only cause was the First Cause.

Hence St. Thomas says: "That which now is, was future, before it was; because it was in its cause that it would be. Hence, if the cause were removed, that thing's coming to be was not future. But the First Cause is alone eternal. Hence it does not follow that it was always true that what now is, would be, except in so far as its future being was in the sempiternal cause; and God alone is such a cause" (Ia, q.16, a.7 ad 3um).

The future is either necessary or contingent. The necessary is that which of its nature seeks to exist some time, nor can this be prevented by natural causes; such a future is the rising of the sun tomorrow. The contingent, properly so called, is that which of its nature is indifferent as to whether it exists or does not exist; such are those things that depend on free will. The contingent in the broad sense of the term, of its nature seeks to exist, but it can be prevented by natural causes; such a contingent is a long life because of robust health. The future contingent, properly so called, is either absolute or conditional. The absolute is independent of any condition; the conditional is dependent on a condition, and is called a futurable, because it mediates between the absolute future and the possible.

[100] Ps. 32: 15.

[101] *Ibid.,* 138: 3.

"For I know that transgressing thou wilt transgress, and I have called thee a transgressor from the womb." [102] It is likewise said of Jesus: "For Jesus knew from the beginning who they were that did not believe, and who he was that would betray Him." [103] These texts refer to future and, in fact, free contingent acts. Nor is the reference here solely to conjectural knowledge, for such knowledge is not expressed by the words "understands," "I know," "knew from the beginning." Moreover, a conjecture is fallible and is something repugnant to the most perfect Being, to the first Truth, and to supreme Intelligence. Finally, there is no reason why God should know one rather than another of many future things, as will be clearly seen from the proofs that follow.

Several councils have affirmed that the decrees of divine providence are infallible, and that they are accompanied by the most certain foreknowledge of future things. As the Council of Valencia says: "We unhesitatingly maintain that God absolutely foreknew that the good will be so by His grace, and that by this same grace they will receive the reward of eternal life; He foreknew that the wicked will be so through their own malice." [104] The Vatican Council says: "All things are naked and open to His eyes, even those which are yet to be by the free action of creatures." [105]

Theological proof. This truth of the faith is proved from other truths which are likewise revealed, and which can be known by the natural powers of reason. Thus St. Thomas proves in the body of the article: (1) that God certainly knows future contingent things; and he declares (2) how God knows them, by assigning the proper reason for this knowledge both on the part of the thing known and on the part of the knower.

1) Arguing from common principles it is proved that God certainly knows future contingent things; for God knows all things, not only those that actually are, but even those that are possible to Him or to creatures. But of these some are for us future contingent things. Therefore God knows them, which means that He certainly knows them. This is the reason that is deduced from common principles.

2) How does God know them? The proper reason is assigned for this both on the part of the thing known and on the part of the knower.

The contingent cannot be infallibly known unless it is known as actual and present. It is not enough for it to be known in its

102 Is. 48: 8.
103 John 6: 65.
104 Denz., no. 321.
105 *Ibid.,* no. 1784; Heb. 4: 13.

proximate cause, for this is not determined to one thing. But God knows all contingents as they actually are and are present to Him. Therefore God knows them infallibly, and yet they do not cease to be contingent; just as when I most certainly see Socrates sitting, the contingency of this sitting is not thereby destroyed.

The minor is proved, and at the same time this knowledge is explained on the part of the knower.

Eternity, being simultaneously whole, comprises all time, so that futures are present in it; but the divine knowledge is measured by eternity; therefore the divine knowledge extends to future things, as actually present in this higher type of duration.

In other words, in the very now of eternity "God's glance is carried over all things as they are in their presentiality." [106] In the reply to the third objection it is said: "Things reduced to act in time, are known by us successively in time, but by God they are known in eternity, which is above time . . . ; just as he who goes along the road, does not see those who come after him; whereas he who sees the whole road from a height, sees at once all traveling by the way."

Thus the unique and permanent instant of eternity corresponds to all the passing instants of time, just as the peak of a pyramid corresponds to all the points of its base. This was explained in a previous question,[107] in which it was declared that eternity is "simultaneously whole," but that time is not. In this same question it was said: "The flow of the now as alternating in aspect, is time. But eternity remains the same to both subject and aspect." [108] Eternity is the proper measure of the permanent Being, of His intellection and of His love, just as time is the proper measure of movement, suggesting succession and alteration, which cannot apply to God.

There are four points to be considered concerning this article of St. Thomas: (1) the interpretation proposed by the Molinists; (2) how future things are present in eternity, according to the teaching of the Thomists; (3) the objections proposed against the Thomist solution; (4) what is to be thought of the theory devised by Molina and known as the *scientia media*.

1. MOLINIST INTERPRETATION

It is generally admitted among the Molinists that St. Thomas, in those passages where he speaks professedly of the divine knowledge,[109] does not mention the divine decree spoken of subsequently

106 *Summa theol.*, q.14, a.13, c.
107 *Ibid.*, q.10, a.2, 4.
108 *Ibid.*, a.4 ad 2um.
109 *Ibid.*, q.14, a.13; *I Sent.*, d.38, q.1, a.5.

by the Thomists, but he has recourse to the presence of future things in eternity, which comprises all time. Hence, according to St. Thomas, the medium of the divine knowledge of future things is not, as the Thomists would have it, the divine decree predetermining these future things. They say that the holy Doctor's opinion is, that the foreknowledge of future free acts does not presuppose an absolute decree of the divine will concerning this future determination of our free will. Therefore his teaching can be reconciled with the theory of the *scientia media,* by which God, before His decree, certainly knows from all eternity conditionally free actions of the future (for instance, what Peter's choice would be if he were situated in certain circumstances), and then God decreed to place this man in these circumstances, in which He foresaw what his choice would be.

Examination of this interpretation. The Thomists generally reply that this interpretation lacks foundation and contradicts many texts of St. Thomas; in fact, it is contrary to the very principles laid down in the preceding articles of this question.

For in the fifth article St. Thomas said: "Since therefore the divine power extends to other things by the very fact that it is the first effective cause of all things, God must necessarily (by the perfect knowledge He has of His power) know things other than Himself. . . . He sees other things not in themselves, but in Himself," as in their cause.

Moreover, in the eighth article he wrote: "The knowledge of God is the cause of things . . . in so far as His will is joined to it." This is the decree of the divine will concerning which is the following clearer statement. "Determined effects proceed from His own infinite perfection according to the determination of His will and intellect." [110] In fact, the determination of the will is mentioned in this text before that of the intellect, for, as stated in the eighth article of this question: "Since the intelligible form has a relation to opposite things, inasmuch as the same knowledge relates to opposites, it would not produce a determinate effect unless it were determined to one thing by the appetite, as the philosopher says (*Metaph.,* Bk. IX, chap. 5)." St. Thomas says similarly in another passage: "God's idea as regards the things that are, or will be, or were to be produced, is determined by the purpose of the divine will." [111]

There is no retractation, however, of the universal principles laid down by St. Thomas in this question; but he is giving the particular application of this doctrine to future things that are contingent, by

---

[110] *Ibid.,* Ia, q.19, a.4.
[111] *De veritate,* q.3, a.6.

showing how these, although they are contingent, can certainly be known as present. It is not here a question of reconciling the determination of God's most efficacious will with the contingency of the thing willed by Him. This will be discussed in its proper place when St. Thomas inquires whether God's will imposes necessity on the things willed, in which we shall see that he says: "Since, then, the divine will is perfectly efficacious, it follows not only that things are done which God wills to be done, but also that they are done in the way that He wills," [112] namely, either contingently or necessarily.

This point belongs properly to God's will, and there was no need of discussing it here along with God's knowledge. It is precisely this alone that St. Thomas proves in the present question, namely, that the knowledge of the future contingent thing, inasmuch as it is certain knowledge, does not take away contingency from the thing, if the contingent thing is known as present, just as when I certainly see Socrates who happens to be sitting.

There remains, however, this question: how is it that this future contingent thing, such as the creation of the world in the passive sense, or the conversion of St. Paul, is present in eternity rather than its opposite, namely, that the world was not created, or that St. Paul was not converted? Most certainly, if this future contingent thing were eternally present to God independently of the determination of the divine will, it would be something necessary and not contingent. Therefore from the principles already mentioned in this question (concerning God's knowledge, which is the cause of things, inasmuch as the will is joined to it), it is evident that the presence in eternity of this contingent future rather than its opposite presupposes the determination of the divine will, which will be more clearly explained in a subsequent question.[113]

Therefore in the second argument of this article, St. Thomas does not speak so explicitly of the medium of this foreknowledge as of the condition required for it to be intuitive. This condition is that the divine knowledge refers to the future thing, not as it is future, but as it is already present to this knowledge. Abstracted knowledge can refer to those things that are not present, but intuitive knowledge, and this alone is most perfect knowledge, refers to things that are present.[114]

112 *Summa theol.*, Ia, q.19, a.8.
113 *Ibid.*, a.4, 8.
114 St. Thomas already spoke of the medium of God's knowledge of creatures in the fifth article, in which he said: "God knows things other than Himself in Himself," as in their cause. In the eighth article he said: "The knowledge of God is the cause of things, in so far as the will is joined to it," which means in so

Hence in this article St. Thomas most certainly presupposes that there is and will be nothing outside God, no matter what its grade of being may be, that is not related by way of causality to God, or is not dependent on Him. In fact, in the beginning of the argumentative part of this article he says: "Since God knows all things, not only things actual but also things possible to Him and the creature, and since some of these are future contingent to us, it follows that God knows future contingent things." This is the proof that is derived from common principles.[115]

There are many other passages from St. Thomas' works that confirm this interpretation, such as the following: "God knows our mind's thoughts and our secret wills in their virtual causes, since He is the universal principle of being. . . . God so knows other things in knowing His essence, as effects are known through their cause being known. Therefore by knowing His essence God knows all things to which His causality extends. Now this extends to the works of the intellect and of the will. . . . So by knowing His act of intelligence and will, He knows every thought and will." [116]

He also says: "But since the act of free will is traced to God as a cause, it necessarily follows that everything happening from the exercise of free will must be subject to divine providence." [117] "Just as the will can decide otherwise, far more so can God do this." [118]

But if St. Thomas says in this article, "a contingent thing as it is in its cause . . . is not subject to any certain knowledge," he is speaking of the created cause considered as such, which as regards its effect is contingent and future. He has not in mind the divine cause, for which nothing is future, all things being present to it.

---

far as the determination of the divine will is joined to it. On this point see q.19, a.4, 8.

[115] In fact, in this article St. Thomas alludes to the divine decree when toward the end of the argumentative part he says: "Hence, all things that are in time are present to God from eternity, not only because He has the types of things present within Him, as some say"; but the practical types of things are ideas determined by the decree of the will.

He said the same in *I Sent.*, d.38, q.1, a.5: "God, from all eternity, saw not only His relation to that thing which by His power was to come into existence, but He also directly saw the very existence of this thing." This means that He not only sees future things in the decree of His will, but as they are present to Him. Nor would these things be present to Him rather than their opposites, except by a decree of His will.

[116] *Contra Gentes*, Bk. I, chap. 68.

[117] *Summa theol.*, Ia, q.22, a.2 ad 4um; see also Ia, q.103, a.8; q.105, a.4; Ia IIae, q.10, a.4 ad 3um.

[118] *De veritate*, q.22, a.8; cf. *ibid.*, a.9.

II. HOW FUTURE THINGS ARE PRESENT IN ETERNITY

THE THOMIST VIEW

According to the Thomists and many other theologians, including Fonseca, Tiphanius, and others, future things are eternally present in God not only objectively and intentionally, but physically and really. They give two proofs for this, one indirect and the other direct.

Indirect proof. If futures were not so present, then they would be for God absolute futures, for simple representation does not exclude the notion of futurity. Thus what is foretold in prophecy precedes its realization. If God had only objective knowledge of future things, He would thus begin again to see things as actually existing. Thus God would be perfected in His knowledge, and only then would it become intuitive.

Direct proof. Eternity is duration which, as such, is infinite, indivisible and simultaneously whole. But this duration contains eminently, in the same permanent now, all successive durations, past, present, and future, and it so contains them as not to cause a variation in it when something new occurs in the inferior kinds of duration. Thus St. Thomas says: "Newness of effect does not demonstrate newness of action in God, since His action is His essence." [119]

Objection. Some say that this merely proves that eternity is without intrinsic but not extrinsic succession, just as the tree on the bank of a river undergoes no change, though the constant flow of the stream results in only a part of this water being present to the tree, and not all the water is simultaneoutly present to the tree. Therefore future things are not physically and really present in eternity.

Reply. I deny the antecedent. A better illustration of eternity would be to compare it with a tree planted equidistant from the source and mouth of the river, and of such vast size as to extend to all parts of the river. Similarly, it might be more fittingly compared with the apex of a pyramid, which at one and the same time without succession is coexistent with all points of its base. Hence there is no increase in God's knowledge when things appear in course of time.

But they again object that it is unintelligible for something to exist in eternity which does not have individual existence. But futures do not now have individual existence. Therefore they do not exist in eternity.

[119] *Contra Gentes*, Bk. II, chap. 35.

Reply. I distinguish the major: it is unintelligible for something to exist in eternity which does not have individual existence according to its proper duration, this I deny; that it does not have individual existence in duration of a higher order, this I concede. I explain with John of St. Thomas [120] as follows: Eternity does not measure created things immediately in themselves and by supposing them already in themselves passively produced; but it measures them properly, as they are contained in the divine action, by which created things are attained and viewed as the terminus of this action. For not only God's intellection and volition are eternal, but also His creative and motive action is eternal, although it has its effect in time. This action is formally immanent and virtually transitive. Thus the creative action in the creation of this particular soul, from eternity regards this individual soul, and yet it is produced only in time.

Futures indeed do not actually have individual existence, either in time or from eternity as passively produced effects, but they exist from eternity as terms implying actual eternal action. And under this aspect, the created thing, although it is not as yet passively produced, is however not only possible, or not only future, but it is really present in eternity, for the divine essence contains it not only as having the power or will to produce it but as actually producing it. Thus the created thing is the object of direct knowledge, although it does not yet exist in its own duration.

Doubt. Is this presentiality the medium of the divine knowledge of future contingent things?

Reply. Presentiality is not the medium of this knowledge, but a mode affecting the object known and a condition for this knowledge to be intuitive. The medium of this divine knowledge, however, is the determination of the divine will as actually causing from eternity. For St. Thomas, to see future things as present in eternity is to see them in the divine will as actually causing them. This is most evident from what St. Thomas has already said in this question, namely, that God does not see created things immediately in themselves, but in Himself as their cause.[121] Farther on he declares that God is the cause of things by His will.[122]

III. THOMIST SOLUTION OF THE OBJECTIONS AGAINST THE CONCLUSION
OF THIS ARTICLE

First objection. It is at the beginning of this article, and is as follows: From a necessary cause proceeds a necessary effect; but the

---

[120] *Disp.*, IX, a.3.
[121] *Summa theol.*, Ia, q.14, a.5, 8.
[122] *Ibid.*, q.19, a.4.

knowledge of God is the necessary cause of things known by Him; therefore things known by Him are necessary.

Reply. I distinguish the major: that a necessary effect proceeds from a proximate necessary cause, this I concede; that from the supreme cause such an effect proceeds, this I subdistinguish: with a proximate necessary cause, this I concede; with a proximate contingent cause, this I deny. Thus, owing to the necessary influence of the sun's rays, the germination of the plant is contingent by reason of the proximate contingent cause.

It must be noted that God's knowledge cannot be called a necessary cause, except in an improper sense: (1) in that it is a necessary prerequisite; (2) in that it is infallibly efficacious; but as such it is a free cause, and as St. Thomas says, "God wills some things to be done necessarily, some contingently." [123] Hence, as will be explained farther on,[124] the divine causality transcends the necessity and contingency that proceed from it.

Second objection. Every conditional proposition of which the antecedent is necessary, must have a necessary consequent; but in this conditional proposition, "If God knew that this thing will be, it will be," the antecedent is necessary, in that it is eternal and immutable; therefore the consequent is also necessary.

Reply. I distinguish the major: if the antecedent is absolutely necessary in fact, then I concede it; if it is necessary as something contingently seen, which cannot at the same time not be seen, then I deny it. Thus, if I see Socrates sitting, he must be sitting, but it is contingent, nevertheless, that he sits.

Third objection. Everything known by God must necessarily be; but no future contingent thing must necessarily be; therefore no future contingent thing is known by God.

Reply. That everything known by God must necessarily be, by reason of a conditional necessity or one of consequence, this I concede; by reason of an absolute necessity or one of consequent in itself, this I deny. Thus, if I see Socrates sitting, he must of necessity be sitting; but it is contingent, as stated above, that he is sitting.

In other words, this proposition, "Everything known by God must necessarily be," if it concerns the thing is divided, and is false; for the meaning is: Everything which God knows is necessary. But the same proposition is true, if understood of the saying and in the composite sense, for then the meaning is: That which is known by God is necessary.[125]

Similarly, we say that what is foreseen by God must of necessity

123 *Ibid.,* a.8.
124 *Ibid.*
125 Cf. ad 3um.

happen; but it happens contingently. For the mode of the necessity affects not the thing and the mode of the thing in itself, but the statement declaring that some foreseen contingent event will infallibly come to pass, such as the conversion of St. Paul.

Expressed more briefly, as stated in the body of the article and in the replies to the second and third objections, the necessity does not affect the thing as it is in itself, but as it is subject to the divine knowledge, as in the case of Socrates who is seen to be sitting.

By this reply contradiction is avoided, but we have still to give the reason why the infallible efficacy of the determination on the part of the divine will does not destroy the freedom of the human will. The divine will does not destroy this freedom, because it actualizes the same and extends even to the free mode of our choice. For God wills some things to be done necessarily, some contingently; and this infallibly happens as God wills.[126]

Another objection. Effects cannot be known with certainty in their universal and remote cause, because the power of the universal cause can be modified and even prevented by a particular cause, just as the sun's rays can be because of a defective disposition in the plant, which prevents the ripening of the fruit. But the divine cause is the universal and remote cause. Therefore effects cannot be known with certainty in it.

Reply. I distinguish the major; in the universal cause, which is not the supreme cause, this I concede; in the supreme universal cause, on which every other cause depends, this I deny. For nothing prevents the First Cause from producing its effect, unless this is permitted by it. But God does not permit such deficiency in those things which He efficaciously wills, namely, in future contingent things efficaciously willed by Him; and it is of these that we are speaking.[127]

Final objection. If the decree of the divine will is of itself infallibly efficacious, then our acts are necessary, and therefore not free.

Reply. I distinguish the antecedent: if the decree extends only to the substance of the act, this I concede; if it extends also to the free mode of this act, this I deny. For God moves creatures in the way that is befitting to their natures. What is more absurd than to say that God wills efficaciously that this particular sinner be converted freely, as Bossuet says,[128] and then to conclude that he cannot be converted freely?[129]

---

[126] Cf. Ia, q. 19, a.8.
[127] Cf. *infra*, q. 19, a.6 ad 1um.
[128] Cf. *Traité du libre arbitre*, chap. 8.
[129] *Summa theol.*, Ia, q. 19, a.8.

IV. THE "SCIENTIA MEDIA"

What must be said of the theory proposed by Molina, and known as the *scientia media?*

Molina says: "We must distinguish between three kinds of knowledge in God, unless we want to expose ourselves to the danger of laboring under a hallucination in reconciling the freedom of our will and the contingency of things with the divine knowledge. One kind is merely natural, and hence it could on no account be other than it is in God, (for it is concerned with necessary and possible things). . . . The second kind is merely free, by which God, after a free act of His will, regardless of any hypothetical condition, knew absolutely . . . what things would come into existence. The third kind, finally, is the *scientia media,* by which God, from a most profound and inscrutable comprehension of every free will in His essence, has intuited what each, according to its innate liberty, would do if placed in this or that condition, or even in infinite conditions of things, although it could, if it wished, do exactly the opposite." [130]

Hence Molina maintains that God's merely natural knowledge is concerned with necessary and possible things; His free knowledge with absolute contingent futures; and the *scientia media* with conditional futures, which are called futurables, inasmuch as they mediate between the merely possible and the absolute future.

Immediately after the preceding extract, Molina adds: "Perhaps someone will ask whether this kind of *scientia media* is to be called free or natural. In reply to this it must first of all be said that on no account must this knowledge be called free, both because it precedes every free act of the divine will, and because it was not in God's power to know by this knowledge anything else than He actually knew. . . . (But) if the created free will were to do the opposite of what it did, as it truly can do, God would have known this very act by the same knowledge, but not that He actually knows it." [131] Here we have a point of greatest difficulty.

The text of Molina is of great importance. Therefrom it seems to follow that there is a dependence or passivity in God as regards futurables, for instance, this one: If Peter the apostle were placed in the circumstances of the Passion, he would deny the Lord, so that in this order of things God could not have preserved Him from sin. For Molina says: "It was not in God's power to know by this knowledge anything else than He actually knew. . . . (But) if the created free will were to do the opposite of what it did, as it

[130] *Concordia,* q.14, a.13, disp. 52, pp. 317 f.
[131] *Ibid.*

GOD'S KNOWLEDGE 461

truly can do, God would have known this very act by the same knowledge, but not that He actually knows it." [132]

This consequence appears to be absolutely necessary: for if God is not the first determining Cause as regards free conditionate futures, He is determined by them, and there is no other alternative. If all things are not dependent on God, then God Himself is dependent on another. Here is the main difficulty of the question.

The Thomists maintain, indeed, that God infallibly knows free conditionate futures, referred to in prophecies of commination, such as the destruction of Ninive, if the Ninivites are not converted.[133] But they add: God infallibly knows these contingent futurables in a decree that is objectively conditional and subjectively absolute. Such are, for instance, the destruction of Ninive or the conversion of the Tyrians and Sidonians, if Christ had preached to them.

This decree is required, so the Thomists say against the Molinists, because, even posited the condition, these conditionally free acts of the future (*futuribilia*), as being contingent and free acts, are undetermined. To make the gratuitous assertion that they are determined in themselves, is to end in determinism of circumstances and to posit passivity and dependence in God as regards these acts. For God either is the first determining Cause or is determined by another, or dependent on another at least in the foreknowledge of conditionally free acts of the future.

Therefore the theory of the *scientia media* essentially consists in this, namely, that God, before the actual decree that is objectively conditional, infallibly knows free conditioned futures, namely, what the created free will would do if placed in certain circumstances. Afterward God decreed to put the will *de facto* in these or other particular circumstances; and thus dependent on the *scientia media* He knows absolute contingent futures. Thus God foresees before any decree of His that Peter, if placed in certain circumstances, would make good use of the sufficient grace to be offered him, and then God wills to place Peter in such circumstances.[134]

132 *Ibid.*
133 *Summa theol.*, IIa IIae, q.171, a.6 ad 2um; q.174, a.1; Ia, q.19, a.7 ad 2um.
134 Some want to prove the existence of the *scientia media* by the following argument: The divine knowledge gets its name, too, from the object. But between the merely possible and the absolute future there is an object of intermediate knowledge, namely, the conditionally free act of the future (*futuribile*). Therefore, in like manner, between the knowledge of simple intelligence, which is concerned with possible things, and the knowledge of vision, which is concerned with future things, there is the *scientia media*, which is concerned with conditionally free acts of the future. In reply to this we say that this is conceded also by the Thomists, provided the *scientia "media"* presupposes some objectively conditional

Molina wants to explain the *scientia media* by the divine super-comprehension of the created free will. Suarez preserves intact the *scientia media* in his congruism, but he explains it by the divine knowledge of the formal or objective truth of futurables, as if contingent futurables were in themselves determined before whatsoever divine decree; as if, before any decree, of two contradictory propositions in a contingent matter of the future, such as, Peter placed in these particular circumstances would or would not deny the Lord, one were determinately true and the other false.[135]

CRITICISM OF THE THEORY OF THE SCIENTIA MEDIA

This theory is not in agreement with the doctrinal principles of St. Paul, St. Augustine, and St. Thomas.

1) St. Paul says: "For who distinguisheth thee? Or what hast thou that thou hast not received? And if thou hast received, why dost thou glory, as if thou hadst not received it?" [136] Christ, too, had said: "Without Me you can do nothing." [137] According to St. Paul's words just quoted, the singling out of one from another must finally be sought not in the human will, but in God who singles out one from another by His grace. But the *scientia media* supposes that one by his own will singles himself out from another,

---

divine decree, and then it differs from the *scientia media* admitted by Molina.

It must be noted with Father Diekamp (*Theologiae dogmaticae manuale* (1933), I, 204): "This doctrine is very often proposed in such a manner as if Molina had set forth this knowledge as occupying a middle ground between the knowledge of vision and that of simple intelligence, and in this sense it is attacked by the Thomists. But the case is not exactly so. Conditioned futures can indeed in some way be conceived as occupying a middle ground between merely possible and really existing things. For this reason we may divide the divine knowledge into three parts, inasmuch as it is knowledge of existing things, of conditioned futures and of merely possible things. But this knowledge of conditioned futures cannot be identified with the Molinist *scientia media*. For it is precisely this that Molina asks, namely, whether God, before any free decree of His will, knows conditioned futures, and whether this knowledge necessitates a special mode of cognition in God, namely, a knowledge that mediates between His necessary knowledge and His free knowledge. This the Molinists affirm, though the Thomists deny it.

Consult Father N. del Prado, *De gratia et libero arbitrio*, III, 117 f. Consult also among Jesuit authors, Father M. de la Taille's article entitled, "Sur les diverses classifications de la science divine" (*Recherches de la science religieuse*, 1923, pp. 7 f., 528 f.). But Father de la Taille separates from the Thomists inasmuch as, instead of a predetermining decree, he admits one that is concomitant, which the Thomists say is not sufficient for the foundation of infallible certainty required for the divine knowledge of futurables, as will be stated farther on.

[135] Cf. Suarez, *De scientia futurorum contingentium*, chap. 7.
[136] I Cor. 4: 7.
[137] John 15: 5.

for instance, Peter from Judas. Therefore the *scientia media* does not seek for this singling out in God.

Proof of the minor. Let us suppose that Peter and Judas situated in equal circumstances receive equal prevenient grace; then God sees Peter consenting to accept that grace, and hence singling himself out from Judas who does not consent, not on account of the grace, for an equal grace is indifferently offered to each. Therefore it is because the will decides to accept the grace. Thus do all Thomists argue against Molina, and they thus affirm as revealed the principle that can be called "the principle of predilection," namely, that no one would be better than another unless he were loved more and helped more by God. This principle is frequently enunciated by St. Paul, as in the following text: "For the Lord saith to Moses: I will have mercy on whom I will have mercy. And I will show mercy to whom I will show mercy. So then it is not of him that willeth, nor of him that runneth, but of God that showeth mercy." [138]

But this principle cannot be reconciled with the *scientia media*. For what two persons equally have is not a reason for singling out one from another. But in the same circumstance the grace is supposed equal in Peter consenting and in Judas not consenting. Therefore this grace does not single out one from another, but in the final analysis Peter singles himself out by that which of himself he adds to it, namely, by his consent to and use of the grace. Moreover, St. Paul says: "For it is God who worketh in you both to will and to accomplish, according to His good will." [139]

2) St. Augustine often quotes the aforesaid text of St. Paul against the Semipelagians: "For who distinguisheth thee? Or what hast thou that thou hast not received?" [140] He says: "It is grace that singles out the good from the bad, not a grace that is common to both good and bad." [141] "And so this grace that is secretly given by the divine liberality to human hearts, is spurned by no one hard of heart, because it is primarily given to overcome this hardness of heart." [142] "Of two infants equally bound by original sin, why the one is taken and the other left; and of two wicked men already mature in years, why one should be so called that he follows Him that calleth, while the other is not called at all, or is not called in such a manner; these are unsearchable judgments of God." [143]

---

[138] Rom. 9: 15; cf. *infra*, Ia, q.20, a.3, 4.
[139] Phil. 2: 13; consult Com. of St. Thomas on this text.
[140] I Cor. 4: 7.
[141] *De praedest. sanctorum*, chap. 5.
[142] *Ibid.*, chap. 8.
[143] *De dono perseverantiae*, chap. 9.

Contrary to this, according to the theory of the *scientia media,* it would have to be said that of two wicked men situated in equal circumstances, and receiving an equal prevenient grace, God sees one consenting to that grace and then singling himself out from the other.

The considerable opposition between the doctrine of St. Augustine and that of Molina is therefore evident in their definition of predestination. St. Augustine thus defines it: "The predestination of the saints is nothing else than the foreknowledge and preparation of the gifts whereby they who are delivered are most certainly delivered." [144] "By predestination God foreknew those things which He was going to do." [145]

On the contrary, Molina says: "To the foreknowledge which includes predestination on the part of the intellect, there is the condition attached of the use of free will without which there would have been no foreknowledge in God." [146] He also says: "Of two called and helped by an equal grace, one is converted and the other not." [147] Hence no wonder that Molina acknowledges his departure from the teaching of St. Augustine, as is evident from many passages in the work just quoted.[148]

3) The principles of St. Thomas equally exclude the *scientia media.*

a) St. Thomas admits only the knowledge of simple intelligence, which is concerned with possible things, and the knowledge of vision which, granted a decree, intuits future things. The knowledge of conditioned futures belongs by a reductive process to this latter.

b) In reconciling the freedom of the will with the divine decrees, St. Thomas never has recourse to the *scientia media,* which explores the field of human liberty concerning the consent or dissent of the will before there is a divine decree, but with St. Augustine he asserts: "Since the divine will is perfectly efficacious, it follows not only that things are done which God wills to be done, but also that they are done in the way that He wills. Now God wills some things to be done necessarily, some contingently (and freely)." [149]

c) For St. Thomas, before there is an actual decree on God's part, there is nothing that will be, as is evident from the following pas-

---

144 *Ibid.,* chap. 14.
145 *De praedest. sanctorum,* chap. 10.
146 *Concordia,* p. 516; see also pp. 426, 505, 513, 514.
147 *Ibid.,* pp. 51, 565.
148 *Ibid.,* q.23, a.4, 5, disp. 1, membr. ult., pp. 546–48.
149 *Summa theol.,* Ia, q.19, a.8.

sage: "That which now is was about to be before it actually was; because it was in its cause that it would be. Hence, if the cause were removed, that thing's coming to be was not future. But the first cause is alone eternal. Hence it does not follow that it was always true that what now is would be, except in so far as its future being was in the sempiternal cause; and God alone is such a cause." [150] Also this text: "Contingent futures are not knowable in themselves, because their truth is not determined." [151] It is not determined before God's decree, and if it were determined before, God would be determined by these contingent futures in His foreknowledge.

d) According to the teaching of St. Thomas, "God sees things other than Himself, not in themselves but in Himself" [152] as in their cause. But in the theory of the *scientia media* God is not the cause of the determination of conditionally free acts of the future. Therefore, according to the principles of St. Thomas, God cannot know this determination. Moreover, the Angelic Doctor admits the principles which we now give.

4) Finally, the *scientia media* conflicts with many principles commonly accepted by the theologians.

a) Before the divine decree, there is no object for the *scientia media*, because the conditionally free act of the future is not determined either in itself or in another, as was stated.

b) The medium of the *scientia media* does not precede the divine decree, because there is no cause in which this conditioned future is determined; for it is not determined in the divine cause or in human liberty or in the circumstances; and if it is said that God knows infallibly this conditioned future by exploring the circumstances, then this theory would end in determinism of circumstances. Thus the *scientia media*, which is devised to save created liberty, would destroy it.

c) God's knowledge cannot be determined by anything which is extrinsic to Him, and which would not be caused by Him. But such is the *scientia media*, which depends on the determination of the free conditioned future; for this determination does not come from God but from the human liberty, granted that it is placed in such particular circumstances; so that "it was not in God's power to know any other thing . . . , but if the created free will were to do the opposite, He would have known this other thing," as Molina says in the passage just quoted. [153] Thus God

---

[150] *Ibid.*, Ia, q.16, a.7 ad 3um.
[151] *Ibid.*, IIa IIae, q.171, a.3.
[152] *Ibid.*, Ia, q.14, a.5.
[153] *Concordia*, p. 318.

would be dependent on another, would be passive in His knowledge, and would be no longer pure Act. The dilemma is unsolvable: Either God is the first determining Being, or else He is determined by another; there is no other alternative. In other words, the *scientia media* involves an imperfection, which cannot exist in God. Hence there is a certain tinge of anthropomorphism in this theory.

All the aforesaid arguments bring us to this conclusion: there is no determination without a determining cause, and the supreme determining cause is God, otherwise He would be determined by another. But this is nothing else than the principle of causality.

d) With the positing of the *scientia media,* God is no longer the first and universal Mover, the First Cause, for any movement of the created free will to determine itself is not from God. Thus the demonstration of God's existence by the first way (from motion) loses very much in forcefulness.

e) Thus this theory takes away from God His supreme dominion over created free wills. In such circumstances, God could not convert the will, if it wills the opposite. For Molina says: "It was not in God's power to know any other thing, but He would have known this other thing if the created will were to do the opposite of what it did." [154] But this is contrary to what Holy Scripture says, as in the following texts. "As the divisions of waters, so the heart of the king is in the hand of the Lord; whithersoever He will He shall turn it." [155] "As the potter's clay is in his hand, to fashion and order it . . . , so man is in the hand of Him that made Him." [156] "For it is God who worketh in you both to will and to accomplish, according to His good will." [157] The theory of the *scientia media* limits the divine omnipotence. For if God, by means of the *scientia media,* foresees that our will under certain conditions will refuse to be moved to perform some good act, then He is already incapable of moving our will so that in these conditions it freely consent to be moved to perform this good act.[158]

f) God would no more be the author of good than of bad acts, at least as regards their intrinsic and free determination, because neither good nor bad acts would come from Him, at least as regards the performance of these acts. He would be the cause of the good determination only by proposing the desirable object. And this even men can do.

154 *Ibid.,* p. 318.
155 Prov. 21: 1.
156 Eccli. 33: 13, 14.
157 Phil. 2: 13.
158 So does Father Diekamp very wisely remark in his *Theol. dogm.,* I, 224.

g) The *scientia media* puts less emphasis on the need for prayer. For the Molinist, who would wish to have his theory remain unimpaired in prayer, could not ask God for the efficacious grace that makes him will, that takes away from him the stony heart, that compels the rebellious will to turn to God, as the Church prays. He cannot pray with the profundity of meaning as in the prayer of the Mass: "Make me adhere to Thy commandments and never permit me to be separated from Thee." [159] But according to the Molinist's theory, he asks God merely to place him in those circumstances in which He foresaw that he would consent to the grace offered.

h) This theory seems to savor somewhat of Semipelagianism, which holds that the beginning of salvation is from ourselves, and not from God's grace.[160] Molinism admits a prevenient interior grace, indeed, but maintains that it moves the will only objectively and not infallibly; in fact, according to Molina, "of two that are called and equally aided by grace, it can happen that one of them is converted, and the other not." [161] Thus the true beginning of salvation appears to be only in the one who is converted, which appears to be a free determination that is from God only in so far as He objectively urges this one to the free determination, just as He urges the other who is not converted.

Finally, the *scientia media* has been frequently condemned because of the novelty of this theory. In fact, Molina acknowledges that he is the discoverer of this theory.[162] Nevertheless the Semipelagians made use of this knowledge according as it served their purpose, saying that God foresees the good use of free will and for this reason gives the grace. He also foresees the good works that would have been performed by the baptized infants if they had not died.

The Molinists object, indeed, that Christ said: "Woe to thee, Corozain! Woe to thee, Bethsaida! For if in Tyre and Sidon had been wrought the miracles that have been wrought in you, they had long ago done penance in sackcloth and ashes." [163] But, as they say, this reproof would have been unjust if understood in the Thomist sense; for, according to the opinion of the Thomists, the Jews could have justly replied to this by saying: Lord, if Thou hadst efficaciously decreed our penance on the supposition of Christ's preaching, just as Thou didst decree the penance of the

---

[159] Prayer before priest's communion.
[160] Denz., no. 178.
[161] Cf. *Concordia*, pp. 51, 565, and the index under the word "Auxilium."
[162] *Ibid.*, pp. 546–48.
[163] Matt. 11: 21.

Tyrians on the same condition of Christ's preaching and miracles, we would have repented, just as they did.

To this the Thomists reply: (1) This was the very way St. Paul argued in the objection which he put to himself; for, after having said: "So, then, it is not of him that willeth, nor of him that runneth, but of God that showeth mercy, (who) hath mercy on whom He will, and whom He will, He hardeneth," [164] he at once follows this up with the counterobjection: "Thou wilt say therefore to me: Why does He then find fault? For who resisteth His will?" [165] The apostle does not solve the objection, however, by having recourse to God's foreseeing our consent, whether this is for what is good or for what is bad; but he says: "O man, who art thou that repliest against God? Shall the thing formed say to him that formed it: Why hast thou made me thus? Or hath not the potter power over the clay, of the same lump, to make one vessel unto honor, and another unto dishonor?" [166] The apostle does not settle the dispute by saying that all have sufficient grace, the efficacy of which depends on their consent foreseen by God. He replies that God is not bound to give the efficacious grace, for it is something freely given, as the name grace indicates.

A direct answer is given to this objection by saying that it was the Jews' fault that they were hardened, whereas the Tyrians were not; because they made it more difficult for themselves to receive the efficacious grace, which was offered in the sufficient grace. The Tyrians would not have resisted Christ's preaching and miracles, and thus they would not have been deprived of the efficacious grace. The Jews showed themselves more unworthy than the Tyrians, because of their greater blindness of intellect and ingratitude.

Instance. Man of his own free will can at least not resist sufficient grace, just as he can resist it. Therefore the difficulty remains.

Reply. I deny the antecedent, for there is a great difference between resisting and not resisting. To resist sufficient grace is an evil, and is solely of our own doing; not to resist it is a good which is not solely of our own doing, but which comes also from the source of all good, God's efficacious will, who eternally willed this act of non-resistance to be performed right at this moment in time. As St. Thomas says: "Whatever God simply wills takes place; although what He wills antecedently, may not take place." [167]

---

[164] Rom. 9: 16, 18.

[165] *Ibid.*, 9: 19.

[166] *Ibid.*, 9: 20 f.

[167] *Summa theol.*, Ia, q. 19, a.6 ad 1um. See also our commentary on this article.

Final objection. God infallibly knows future sins, and yet He is not the cause of them. Therefore it is false to say that God's infallible knowledge has its foundation in the divine causality or in the decrees of the divine will.

Reply. I distinguish the antecedent. God infallibly knows future sins in His permissive decree as to what there is of deordination or privation in sin; and He knows them in His positive decree, as to the physical entity of sin, with which He concurs. And I deny the consequent. Without a permissive decree, God would know these sins as possible, but not as future.

This reply has its foundation in this most certain principle, namely, that just as no good, however insignificant it may be, happens to belong *de facto* to this man rather than to a certain other, unless God eternally and efficaciously willed that it should thus happen, so no sin happens to be in this man rather than in a certain other, unless God permitted it. The sinner, to be sure, in the very moment of sinning, can avoid committing the sin, and God eternally willed that it be really possible for the sinner to avoid committing the sin, and this is known as God's antecedent will. But God did not efficaciously will that this sinner right at this moment should *de facto* avoid committing sin; and if God had efficaciously willed it, this sinner *de facto* not only really could avoid sin, but would avoid it. As St. Thomas says: "Whatever God simply wills, takes place; although what He wills antecedently, may not take place." [168] This is the ultimate reason for the distinction between sufficient grace and grace that is of itself efficacious. There is, indeed, a mystery in this, but we now disclose the element of clarity in this light-transcending obscurity. It cannot strictly be said, however, that Molina directly denies these commonly admitted principles just given; but by introducing the *scientia media*, which posits a passivity in God, he impairs their validity.

ON THE VARIOUS WAYS OF EXPLAINING THE SCIENTIA MEDIA

The Molinists say that the divine decree is not necessary for God's infallible knowledge of conditioned futures, for He certainly knows them (1) either in His ideas before the decree, or (2) by His supercomprehensive knowledge of the causes, or (3) in the formal or objective truth of contingent conditioned futures.

In reply to this we say: (1) God cannot, before a divine decree, infallibly know conditioned futures in His ideas, because, according to the divine ideas, the thing may either exist or not exist;

[168] *Ibid.*

there may be either consent or no consent, and they do not include the determination of our free will.[169]

2) Nor is the supercomprehensive knowledge of causes a sufficient explanation of God's infallible knowledge of conditioned futures, because free causes are indifferent, and the examination of the circumstances does not suffice, unless we admit determinism of circumstances.

3) Nor does it suffice with Suarez to have recourse to the formal or objective truth of contingent conditioned futures, saying that before the divine decree, of two contradictory propositions concerning the future, one will be true and the other false, and that this is known by God from all eternity.

In reply to this we say with Aristotle,[170] that of two contradictory propositions concerning the future in contingent matter, one will be true and the other false, but that neither is determinately true (before the divine decree); [171] otherwise the result of this would be the logical fatalism of the Stoics.

RECAPITULATION

From the foregoing it is clearly enough established that Molinism is not a scientifically elaborated system, one that proceeds from certain and universal principles. But it starts out by presenting some particular objection for solution. Then it proposes the solution of the same, and ends willingly or unwillingly in the denial of the principle of causality (the transition of the created free will from potentiality to actuality would in this case be without cause) and of higher principles which concern God. Such principles are the following: God is pure Act without any potentiality, passivity, or even dependence in His knowledge; God is the first Cause and most universal Mover of both corporeal and spiritual beings to their acts of understanding and their voluntary choices.

Therefore the theory of the *scientia media* seems to imply not only a mystery, but a contradiction. Although it is devised for the preservation of free will, it seems to end in the destruction of the same through determinism of circumstances.

On the contrary, Thomism is a scientifically elaborated doctrine, which starts from certain and universal principles, and reaches its conclusions by a legitimate process. Therefore, if in these conclusions there is obscurity, this is owing to God's incomprehensibility

---

[169] *De veritate,* q.3, a.6; also Ia, q.14, a.8.

[170] *Perihermenias,* Bk. I, chap. 9, lect. 14 of St. Thomas' commentary.

[171] Truth follows being, and the being of the free future, or even of the free conditioned future, is undetermined.

and His intimate action on our free will, but it is not owing to contradiction.

Molinism says that it places the mystery in God's knowledge, namely, in the *scientia media*. Thomism finds that it consists in the efficacy of the divine will, which is able infallibly to move our will to choose freely, inasmuch as the divine will extends even to the free mode of our choice, actualizing but not destroying our free will.[172]

HOW CONDITIONALLY FREE ACTS OF THE FUTURE ARE KNOWN BY GOD, ACCORDING TO THE PRINCIPLES OF THE THOMIST DOCTRINE

The prophecies of commination are concerned with free conditioned futures which, as stated, occupy a middle ground between the purely possible and the absolute future. Such are, when the destruction of Ninive is announced, if the Ninivites are not converted, and when Christ our Lord said that the Tyrians and Sidonians would have been converted, if the Gospel had been preached to them, and they had seen the miracles performed.

According to the principles of Thomism, how does God know infallibly from all eternity these free conditioned futures? The Thomists commonly reply that these are known in God's decree, which is objectively conditional and subjectively absolute; and without this decree, the aforesaid conditionally free acts of the future would remain, as stated, undetermined and therefore unknowable even to God Himself.

1) St. Thomas proves this inasmuch as he acknowledges in God an antecedent will to save all mankind,[173] and he says that this will is sincere and is one of good pleasure.[174] But, according to St. Thomas, this antecedent will is subjectively absolute and objectively conditional. For the holy Doctor says: "The antecedent will can be called a conditioned will, and yet the imperfection is not on the part of the divine will, but of the thing willed, which is not accepted with all the required circumstances for its right ordering to salvation." [175] This means that God would save all mankind, if this did not conflict with the manifestation of His attributes, one of these being His justice.[176]

2) Proof from reason. Without this divine decree contingent and secondary causes are undetermined as to whether or not they pro-

172 *Summa theol.*, Ia, q.19, a.8.
173 *Ibid.*, a.6 ad 1um.
174 *De veritate*, q.23, a.3.
175 *Com. in I Sent.*, d.46, q.1, a.1 ad 3um.
176 *Summa theol.*, Ia, q.23, a.5 ad 3um.

duce the effect. Hence without this decree conditioned futures
would still belong to the order of possible things. But there is
clearly a difference between the conditionally free act of the future
and the purely possible. Thus it is evident that there are two possibilities for Peter as regards the situation in which he finds himself during our Lord's Passion: he can either deny our Lord or not
deny Him. But the conditioned future has this determination attached to it, namely, which of these two possible things Peter
would choose if he were placed in these circumstances. Therefore
without the aforesaid conditioned decree the free conditioned future would not be knowable, even to God Himself. "Contingent
futures are not knowable in themselves, because their truth is not
determined." [177]

WHAT MUST BE SAID OF THE OTHER OPINIONS CONCERNING THE FOREKNOWLEDGE OF CONDITIONED FUTURES

1) Certain Scotists, as also some later theologians, said that God
knows free futures in a concomitant and non-determining decree.
But if this decree is only concomitant, then it will not be the cause
of future things, for the cause, at least in the order of nature, precedes its effect. Hence this concomitant decree cannot be the medium for knowing the future. Thus all the disadvantages of the
scientia media reappear.

2) Others teach that God knows future things in a decree, either
absolute or conditional, multiplying the number of graces until
the creature consents. This opinion resembles the congruism of
Suarez, inasmuch as the multiplication of graces is equivalent to a
congruent grace, but not to one that is of itself efficacious.

Nor can such a decree be the foundation for certainty of foreknowledge. There is no certainty in this multiplication of graces as
to which of them will conquer the will, and when it will do so.
God's foreknowledge is insufficiently explained by saying that He
makes a shrewd guess; absolute certainty is required. Therefore
these opinions, whether those defending them wish it or not, end
finally in the theory of the *scientia media*. There is no other alternative between the *scientia media* and the doctrine of the divine
predetermining decree. Either God infallibly knows contingent
futures, even conditioned futures, in His determining decree, which
extends even to the free mode of our choices, or else He does not
know them in this decree, that is, before this decree, which is
precisely the theory of the *scientia media*.

177 *Ibid.*, IIa IIae, q.171, a.3.

It must be noted finally that what has been said against the Molinists applies also to the Jansenists as regards the state of innocence; for these admit the *scientia media* and extrinsically efficacious grace in this state. If, after original sin, they admit the presence of intrinsically efficacious grace, they do so not because of the dependence of the created will on God, but because of its weakness, by reason of the consequences of original sin.[178]

FOURTEENTH ARTICLE

WHETHER GOD KNOWS ENUNCIABLE THINGS

The answer is in the affirmative, because God knows whatever is in our power to perform. Yet He knows these enunciable things, not after the manner of enunciable things, by way of composition and division, but by simple intelligence. For all things are represented in the divine essence unitedly and undividedly, not like our intelligible species which represent one thing in such a way as not to represent another. So, in like manner, God knows material things immaterially.

FIFTEENTH ARTICLE

WHETHER GOD'S KNOWLEDGE IS INVARIABLE

The answer is in the affirmative, because God's knowledge is self-subsistent intelligence, which is altogether invariable, just as the self-subsistent Being is.

Therefore God's knowledge is measured by eternity, and it absolutely transcends time, embracing all time. It is in this sense that we must understand the following text: With God "there is no change nor shadow of alteration." [179]

Reply to first objection. "Created things are in God in an invariable manner, while they exist variably in themselves."

Reply to third objection. There is, indeed, variation in enunciable things known by God (e.g., Christ will be born, Christ was born). But God does not know enunciable things as we do, after the manner of enunciable things, by way of composition and division, but by simple intelligence, as was stated.

[178] For the solution of the objections raised against Thomism by those who say that it does not preserve intact human liberty and the divine sanctity, and also that the helps are insufficient, consult q.19, a.8, in which St. Thomas shows that the divine will is most efficacious, and that it does not impose necessity on all things, nor does it interfere with but actuates human liberty.

[179] Jas. 1: 17.

SIXTEENTH ARTICLE

WHETHER GOD HAS A SPECULATIVE KNOWLEDGE OF THINGS

In answer to this it is stated that knowledge is said to be speculative in three ways: (1) on the part of the thing known, which is not operable by the knower; (2) as regards the manner of knowing, if the operable thing be considered also by defining it, resolving it into its universal principles, for instance, stating what a harp is; (3) as regards the end, if there be a consideration also of the operable thing only as it concerns knowledge, not action.[180]

But God has only speculative knowledge of Himself, because He is not operable. He has speculative knowledge of other things as regards the mode, since He knows not only how things are made, but what they are; He has practical knowledge of those things that can be made but never will be, and this as regards both the object and the mode, but not as regards the end on the part of the knower; He has simply and actually practical knowledge of those things that come to be in some period of time. But it must be noted that God's knowledge is eminently speculative and practical, being in itself undivided, and the only distinction in it is on the part of the things known.

Scotus held that God's knowledge of Himself is simply practical, because it is naturally prior to divine love by which He loves Himself. In reply to this it must be said that it does not suffice for practical knowledge that love of the object known follow it; the form of the work or the object of operation must be determined by it, so that it can be called the rule of operation.

Thus we terminate this question of God's knowledge, in which it has been our special purpose to show that God, by reason of His absolute immateriality, is in the highest degree cognitive; in fact, that He is the self-subsistent Intellection; that He knows things other than Himself, in Himself and not immediately in themselves; that He knows possible things, indeed, inasmuch as they have their foundation in the divine essence, as it is imitable *ad extra,* and He knows existing things in the decree of His will, without which His

---

180 It must be remarked with Cajetan that practical and speculative are here taken in the sense not only as they are conditions of knowledge in themselves, but also as they are on the part of the knower. Therefore it is said that the house-building art in one who does not intend to build a house is speculative as regards the end. This must be further explained by saying, as it concerns the end on the part of the knower, not of the knowledge, because knowledge that is practical as regards the thing known and the manner of knowing it, is also as such practical as regards the end, although it does not essentially extend even to the actual execution of the thing known; and thus it differs from prudence. Cf. Ia IIae, q. 57, a. 4.

knowledge would not be the cause of things; [181] that He knows contingent futures not only in His decree, but inasmuch as they are already eternally present to Him, this being the intrinsic terminus of the eternal creative or motive action, the effects of which are passively produced in time. In this way the perfection of God's knowledge, which is intuitive and absolutely invariable, is preserved intact. Its measure is eternity, which includes all time within its ambit.

[181] See a.8.

CHAPTER XV

QUESTION 15

OF IDEAS

THIS question determines what must be retained of the exemplarism of Plato, as St. Augustine understood it, in that the exemplary ideas of things are not outside God as Aristotle interpreted it,[1] but are in Him.[2]

St. Thomas shows in this question that Augustinian exemplarism cannot be admitted on God's part without rejecting the principles of Aristotelianism.

FIRST ARTICLE

WHETHER THERE ARE IDEAS

The answer is: "As then the world was not made by chance, but by God acting by His intellect, there must exist in the divine mind a form to the likeness of which the world was made. And in this the notion of an idea consists."[3]

Reply to first objection. "God does not understand things according to an idea existing outside Himself." In fact, the idea, for instance, of man or dog cannot exist outside God and individuals of these species, for their nature implies a common matter (bones and flesh), and these cannot exist apart from individualized matter (these bones, this flesh). But matter in common can be abstracted, or it can be conceived apart from individualized matter, but it cannot exist apart from such matter.[4]

[1] Aristotle, in his *Metaphysics*, Bk. XII, maintained that God has knowledge only of Himself. His reason for this was that the knowledge of other things was derogatory to God's perfection. The divine intellect, in knowing such things, would have to be determined by them, so said Aristotle, in that it would receive some sort of intelligible impression from them; and this would imply potentiality in God, whereas He is pure actuality. The falsity of this statement has already been proved by St. Thomas in the previous question concerning God's knowledge. His knowledge is the cause of things, His essence is the prototype of all things, and He is not dependent on things for His knowledge. [Tr.]

[2] Even at the present day it is a disputed point among authors of the History of Philosophy whether Plato held that exemplary ideas are outside God, or in Him.

[3] End of argumentative part of this article.

[4] *Summa theol.*, Ia, q.84, a.4, 5.

Reply to second objection. The divine essence, as being representative of creatable and created things, is of the nature of an idea or exemplar. Similarly, in accordance with the reply to the third objection, it must be said that the divine idea is identical with God's essence, as known, and as it is capable of participation and imitation in various ways *ad extra*.

SECOND ARTICLE

WHETHER THERE ARE MANY IDEAS IN GOD

There are many ideas in God, inasmuch as there can be no idea of the whole world unless there are proper ideas of those things which constitute the world. But this plurality of ideas is not repugnant to God's simplicity, because the divine ideas are identical with God's essence as known and capable of imitation in various ways *ad extra*.

"Now it is not repugnant to the simplicity of the divine mind that it understand many things; though it would be repugnant to its simplicity were His understanding to be formed by a plurality of images," or determined by these in understanding them, as St. Thomas says in this article.

It must be remarked that God, by understanding His essence, inasmuch as it is the principle of variously possible creatural imitation, and as it is the terminus of this relation of imitability, which declares a real relation of the creature to it, is in no real relation to creatures.

St. Thomas likewise says in another of his works: "And therefore the divine essence, which implies a knowledge of the various degrees in which things are related to it, is the idea of each particular thing. Hence, since there is a diversity in the degrees of relationship of things to it, there must be a plurality of ideas owing to the various degrees in which creatures are related to it." [5] He also says: "God understands the relation of things to His essence, and so these relations are in God as understood by Him." [6]

THIRD ARTICLE

WHETHER THERE ARE IDEAS OF ALL THINGS THAT GOD KNOWS

The difficulty is whether God has ideas of evil, primary matter, and not only of created natures, but also of singulars and accidents. These questions were already raised by Plato in the elaboration

[5] *De veritate*, q.3, a.2.
[6] *Ibid.*, ad 8um.

of his exemplarism, a system which was perfected by St. Augustine.

The answer is that the idea, as an exemplar, refers to every-thing made by God in any period of time, and the idea as the principle of knowledge refers to all possible things. Hence, as stated in the reply to the first objection, "there is no idea of evil in God, neither in so far as an idea is an exemplar (because God is not the cause of evil) nor as a type (because evil is known by God not through its own type, but through the type of good)."

The reply to the third objection posits another corollary: "Since we hold matter to be created by God, though not apart from form, matter has its idea in God; but not apart from the idea of the composite; for matter in itself can neither exist nor be known.

Reply to fourth objection. Accidents that are properties of some created nature do not have a special idea that is distinct from the idea of this nature. But accidents which supervene to the subject have their special idea. And providence extends to individuals, as will be shown later.[7]

Hence, as the Thomists say, God has actually practical ideas of those things which He does or will do, because they are determined for realization by a decree of His will.[8] But God has virtually prac-tical ideas of possible things, because they are not meant for realization by a decree of His will. St. Thomas stated this clearly in the following passage: "The (divine) idea is determined by a decree of the divine will as regards those things that either are or will be or were produced; but it is not so determined as regards those things that neither are nor were nor will be produced; and so the ideas of things of this kind (possible things) are to some ex-tent undetermined."[9]

The causality of the divine idea is an exemplary causality, or one of extrinsic form, just as the idea of a house is in the mind of the architect. Therefore the divine ideas are the exemplars of things, but they are produced only "according to the determina-tion of the divine will and intellect."[10]

In this we see what St. Thomas retains of Platonism. Exemplary ideas are not outside God but in God, and the divine ideas are the supreme causes of things, but in so far as the determination of the divine liberty is joined to them, which is not what Plato said. But as regards our intellectual knowledge, the divine ideas are not immediately known by our intellect, as the ontologists said,

---

[7] *De veritate*, q.22, a.3.

[8] *Summa theol.*, Ia, q.19, a.4.

[9] *De veritate*, q.3, a.6.

[10] *Summa theol.*, Ia, q.19, a.4; see also q.14, a.8, in which there is already a veiled reference to this exemplarism.

nor can they be immediately seen without our seeing God's essence; but they are known mediately in the mirror of sensible things, as being the supreme norms and eternal types of things.

On this point St. Thomas says: "One thing is said to be known in another in two ways. First, as in an object itself known; as one may see in a mirror the images of things reflected in it. Thus the soul, in the present state of life, cannot see all things in the eternal types; but it is in this way that the blessed know all things in the eternal types, for they see God and all things in Him.

"Secondly, one thing is said to be known in another as in a principle of knowledge: thus we might say that we see in the sun what we see by the sun. And thus we must say that the human soul knows all things in the eternal types, since by participation of these types we know all things. For the intellectual light itself which is in us is nothing else than a participated likeness of the uncreated light, in which are contained the eternal types." [11]

Thus the divine ideas are the eternal exemplary forms of beings and created intellection. This means that the created being and created intellection have the same ultimate foundation. In other words, if there is harmony between being and intellect, between the laws of the mind and the laws of being, it is because created intellect and created being proceed from the same supreme cause.

This constitutes the ultimate metaphysical foundation for the ontological validity of our knowledge which by way of investigation begins with facts of experience and first principles of reason and being, and ascends to God. As St. Thomas says: "By way of investigation we come through knowledge of temporal things to that of things eternal. . . . By way of judgment, from eternal things already known, we judge of temporal things, and according to laws of things eternal we dispose of temporal things." [12]

Thus the holy Doctor retains what must be retained of Plato's exemplarism as St. Augustine conceived it; yet he does not depart from the moderate realism of Aristotle, and he avoids all the excesses of idealism.

[11] *Ibid.,* Ia, q.84, a.5.
[12] *Ibid.,* q.79, a.9.

CHAPTER XVI

QUESTION 16

OF TRUTH

SUMMARY OF DOCTRINE

St. Thomas first treats of truth in general and then of divine truth. Concerning truth in general he considers it in its threefold relationship: (1) to the intellect by which it is known or manifested; (2) to being on which it is founded; (3) to good which follows as a property of being. These questions are treated at length in metaphysics, so that we shall not devote much time to them.

In the first article it is shown that truth resides formally and primarily in the intellect and secondarily in things as they relate to the intellect. But things are measured by the divine intellect and by the divine ideas, and they measure our intellect, which is said to be true in so far as it is in conformity with them. Thus "a stone is called true which possesses the nature proper to a stone, according to the preconception in the divine intellect." [1]

In the second article it is shown that the conformity or identity between our intellect and the thing can indeed already be present in the intellectual act of simple apprehension by way of a representation that expresses conformity with the thing. But a conformity as known and compared with the thing, is found only in the act of judgment, or in the intellect composing and dividing, because it is there that the conformity or non-conformity of the predicate with the subject is first clearly seen, inasmuch as it is true to say that a thing is what it is, and is not what it is not; and that it is false to say that a thing is what it is not, and is not what it is.

The third article determines the relation of truth to being. Truth as found in things is convertible with being, entitatively or according to substance, by adding relation to the intellect, such as true gold. But truth as found in the intellect is not convertible with being entitatively, but manifestatively, as the manifestator is with the thing manifested, or regulatively, as the regulator is with the thing regulated. Thus the intellect is true when judging of a thing or regulating what must be regulated.

[1] Cf. a. 1, c.

The fourth article concerns the relation of truth to goodness. It is stated that, although the true and the good are the same entitatively, yet in their formal aspects the true is prior to the good, because the true has its foundation in the being of the thing, according to its very essence; but the good has its foundation in the thing according as it is perfect and desirable. Similarly, the true refers to knowledge, which is prior to the appetite, to which good refers; for nothing is willed that is not foreknown.

The second part of the question is about divine truth, namely, how it exists in God; and from divine truth it is shown that truth is one, eternal, and immutable.

The fifth article shows that God is not only true, but is Truth itself, because His being is not only conformed to His intellect, but is the very subsistent act of His intellect. Moreover, God is the supreme truth, because His act of understanding is the cause of every other being and intellect. Thus God is the first truth in the ontological, logical, and moral orders, in that it is impossible for God to lie.

The sixth article explains that truth which is absolutely one, is found only in the divine intellect, which is the measure of all things; but in creatures there are as many ontological truths as there are entities, and as many formal truths as there are things known to be true.

The seventh article shows that the positively eternal truth is found only in the divine intellect, which alone is eternal; but negatively some things are said to be of eternal truth, because they abstract from circumstances of place and time. Such are the principles of contradiction, causality . . . , and all necessary propositions. But the formal or cognitive truth of these statements is eternal only in the divine intellect, in that God alone knows from eternity these necessary truths.

Therefore we must not overlook what St. Thomas says in another of his works: "From the fact that truths known by the intellect are eternal with regard to what is thus known, one cannot conclude that the soul is eternal, but that the truths known have their foundation in something eternal. They have their foundation in that first Truth which, as the universal cause, contains within itself all truth."[2]

This is the proof of God's existence founded on the eternal verities, and it is referred back to the fourth proof of St. Thomas,[3] in that it ascends from different degrees of truth until it reaches the maximum truth. For it is evident that an absolutely necessary

[2] *Contra Gentes*, Bk. II, chap. 84.

[3] *Summa theol.*, Ia, q.2, a.3.

principle, such as the principle of contradiction, by which all actual and possible beings and all our intelligences are necessarily regulated, must have its foundation in some necessary and supreme Being and in some supreme and eternal Intellect. For this absolutely necessary principle, such as the principle of contradiction, cannot have its foundation in some contingent existence, or in a multiplicity of such contingent existences, for all these come under the law of this principle; but this necessary and negatively eternal truth postulates as its ultimate foundation one that is necessarily and positively eternal.

Finally, the eighth article shows that the truth of the divine intellect is immutable, whereas our intellect changes from truth to falsity; and this happens in two ways: (1) when one gets a wrong opinion about something which in itself has not changed; or (2) when the thing is changed, but not the opinion.[4]

[4] St. Thomas says in the body of this article: "The truth of our intellect is mutable, not because it is itself the subject of change, but in so far as our intellect changes from truth to falsity." Thus necessary truths, especially first principles, do not change. It is likewise always true that a thing was such as it once was. But our intellect, even in its judgment of immutable truths, sometimes undergoes a change, and this is because of its debility, that is, because of its want of consideration or forgetfulness.

At the end of the argumentative part of the article he says: "The truth, however, of the divine intellect is that according to which natural things are said to be true, and this is altogether immutable." This statement affirms both the immutability of the divine intellect and the immutable nature of things, which correspond to the divine ideas. Thus, too, for us truths which strictly pertain to the very natures of things, such as "man is a rational animal," are immutable and negatively eternal, inasmuch as they abstract from circumstances of place and time.

CHAPTER XVII

QUESTION 17

OF FALSITY

As opposed to truth, St. Thomas treats of falsity in its relation to things, to sense, to intellect, and to truth itself.

The first article shows that natural things, in so far as they are compared with the divine intellect, are not false, because in so far they exist, inasmuch as they are from God, and are from His idea to which they conform. Yet it is possible for moral actions even to withdraw themselves from God's rule, and therefore sins are called lies. But in relation to the created intellect things can be called false, either because they are signified by what is false, or because of their resemblance to the truth, as brass is false gold.

In the second article it is decided that falsity, formally as such, is not formally in the senses as in one knowing falsity, because the senses do not compare one thing with another. Nevertheless there is an occasion of falsity or of false judgment from the senses apprehending the thing as being like what it truly is. As remarked in this article concerning proper sensibles (such as color, sound), the senses have no false knowledge, except accidentally, because of a defect in the organ; but of the common sensibles (such as extension, distance) and of the accidental sensibles (such as substance, life) the senses, even rightly disposed, can have a false knowledge, because of the abnormal way in which the object is proposed to the faculty; for the senses are not directly and immediately referred to these. Thus a stick half submerged in the water appears to be broken.

The third article concludes that the intellect cannot be false in the simple apprehension of a thing, but in composition and division, or in judgment, inasmuch as it attributes to a thing what does not belong to it. Thus there can accidentally be falsity in the first act of the intellect, which is apprehension, in so far as composition of the intellect is mixed up in it, for instance, if in a definition parts are united which are mutually exclusive, such as "a reasonable four-footed animal."

Finally, in the fourth article, St. Thomas teaches that truth and falsity, which are found in the intellect, are opposed as contraries and not merely as privations, because each consists in some act, or acceptance on the part of the intellect, which is truth, indeed, according to an adequate apprehension or conformity, and falsity according to an inadequate apprehension.

Thus the questions about truth and falsity are concluded as they concern God, which is the way they must be concluded in theology.

CHAPTER XVIII

QUESTION 18

THE LIFE OF GOD

SINCE to understand belongs to living beings, after consideration of the divine intellect comes the question of the divine life.

The first article concludes that the difference between living and lifeless things is, that living things move themselves to their actions. We already see that such is the case with plants, which nourish or renew, and reproduce themselves; whereas, on the other hand, lifeless things are merely moved by another, such as stones, which do not move themselves, but are moved and drawn by another.

The second article shows that life is not an accidental but a substantial predicate in living things, although it manifests itself to us by vital operations, and these are accidents. Thus the substance of a plant, an animal, a man, is life in first actuality, although it is only in their operations that they have life in second actuality.

The third article concludes that life in the highest degree and essentially so is in God, because He is subsistent Intellection, so that He is not determined or moved by another; for in so far as a thing is lower in the scale of beings, or is less endowed with life, just so is it in need of being moved or determined by another, so that it move itself. Thus there is no created living being that is so completely endowed with life as to be absolutely the principle of its own action, and not need to be moved by another. Even the higher creatures, those of the intellectual order, need to be moved efficiently by God, the supreme agent, and to be drawn to Him as their ultimate end.

God alone is essentially Life, just as He is Wisdom itself, and subsistent Intellection. Hence Christ affirmed His divinity when He said: "I am the way, the truth, and the life." [1] Creatures of the higher order have life, but they are not life itself.

In this article St. Thomas has depicted for us the beautiful gradation in being, from the plant life to essential life, showing that the nobler the life, the more it is immanent and immobile.

[1] John 14: 6.

Plants live by nutrition, increase, and reproduction; but the form by which they act and the end for which they act are determined for them by nature. Animals move themselves, moreover, to their objects apprehended through the senses. Man, however, prescribes for himself the end for which he acts, and yet he must be moved by a higher efficient Cause and be drawn to Him as his ultimate end. Only God, who is subsistent Intellection, is essential life that is absolutely immanent and immobile. But this immobility of supreme life is fundamentally the very opposite of the immobility of inertia or death. This latter means the absence of operation or privation of movement, whereas the operation of God's intellect and will is most perfect, and is always in act. His life is always in second actuality, and is not a transitive action, but an immanent and most perfect action.[2]

The fourth article shows that all things that proceed from God have their life in Him, according to the ideal being they have in His act of understanding, in His divine idea. Thus all things live in God, as Holy Scripture says in the following text: "Without Him was made nothing that was made. In Him was life." [3]

[2] Cf. ad 1um.
[3] John 1: 3, 4.

CHAPTER XIX

QUESTION 19

THE WILL OF GOD

AFTER considering the things that belong to the divine knowledge, we must consider what belongs to the divine will. We shall proceed in the following order: (1) About God's will itself (q. 19). (2) About what strictly belongs to His will, namely, divine love, which is the act of His divine will (q. 20), and justice and mercy, which may be regarded as virtues residing in the divine will, by way of analogy with the moral virtues that reside in our will (q. 21). (3) About what belongs to the intellect in relation to His will, namely, Providence as regards all things (q. 22), and predestination in respect of man as regards his salvation (q. 23).

Already from this division as set forth in the prologue, it is evident that Providence is named by way of analogy with our prudence, which presupposes a rightly ordered appetite, or a rightly ordered will.

Thus the discussion is about the divine moral acts, by way of analogy with the virtues of the rational soul, namely, of the will and intellect; for it is evident that the virtues of the sensitive soul, such as temperance, cannot be analogically and properly in God, who is a pure spirit. In other words, the inferior virtues cannot be in God, nor even the theological virtues, which in us refer to God as our superior. Nevertheless, God's love for Himself and for us, which is discussed in the twentieth question, corresponds analogically to our love of God and of our neighbor.

The nineteenth question, which concerns God's will, is divided into twelve articles, and these again are subdivided into three principal parts. The first part includes the questions as to the existence (a. 1) and nature of the divine will (a. 2). The second part is concerned with the ways in which God's will operates as regards His acts and objects, in that creatures are freely willed by Him (a. 3), in that His will is the cause of things (a. 4), in that His volition is uncaused (a. 5), that it is most efficacious and immutable, and does not impose necessity on things willed (a. 6–8), and finally that His will is impeccable, or that He cannot will sin (a. 9). The third part, which includes the last two articles, concerns the manifestation of God's will: whether the will of expression is to be distinguished in God, and whether there are five expressions of will assigned to the divine will.[1]

In this arrangement, what constitutes the very kernel of this question is more clearly seen, for the division is not immediately made by means of twelve members in opposition to one another, but by means of two, which must afterward be subdivided. And, in fact, the first two parts are reduced to one, namely, God's will in itself, which must be considered before its manifestation is discussed.

But the subdivisions show that St. Thomas considered everything that pertains to this question, both as to God Himself and ourselves, according to the various modes of God's liberty, and as to His efficacious causality and impeccability, which directly pertain more to His will than to His intellect.

The fourth article of this question, whether God's will is the cause of things, must be carefully considered in its connection with the question of God's knowledge,[2] in which it is stated that God's knowledge is the cause of things in so far as His will is joined to it. The eighth article of this question: whether the will of God imposes necessity on things willed, which throws light on the foreknowledge of contingent futures, must also be most diligently examined.

FIRST ARTICLE

WHETHER THERE IS WILL IN GOD

State of the question. The word "will" has two meanings, for it means either the act of willing, as when one says: it is my will that you do this; or else it refers to the faculty of willing. But in this article it matters not in which sense the word is used, for the other meaning is implied, especially in God, who is pure Act.

The difficulty is: (1) that the object of the will is the end; but we cannot assign any end to God; (2) that the will is an appetitive faculty which is for something not possessed; but this denotes imperfection, which is not in God; (3) that the will moves, and is moved in that it is moved by the intellect; but God is the first cause of movement, and He Himself is unmoved. It may be further remarked that Aristotle, who discussed God's intellect at sufficient length,[3] did not at least explicitly refer to God's will and liberty;

---

[1] It must be presumed that the author assigns the tenth article to the second part, including it in the third article of St. Thomas. [Tr.]

[2] See q.14, a.8.

[3] *Metaph.*, Bk. XII, chap. 1.

perhaps he thought they could not be reconciled with the supremely determined although unlimited pure Act; for God is not capable of further determination by His divine free act, as though something might be wanting to Him. Hence the difficulty.

The answer is in the affirmative. There must be will in God, since there is intellect in Him.

1) This answer is not a theological conclusion, but is of faith, although the existence of God's will can be proved from His intellect. That this conclusion is of faith is evident from very many texts of Holy Scripture, such as the following: "Whatsoever the Lord pleased, He hath done." [4] "For who resisteth His will?" [5] The Fathers understood these and similar texts not in a metaphysical sense, as when it is said that God is angry, but in a proper although analogical sense. The reason for this interpretation is that, whereas anger includes imperfection, what is formally signified by will implies no imperfection.

Finally, it is the common teaching of the councils. The following quotation from the Vatican Council suffices for our purpose: "The Holy . . . Church believes that there is one God . . . infinite in intelligence, in will, and in all perfection." [6]

It must be noted that in this truth of the faith, namely, that will belongs properly to God, more is affirmed than in the following assertion from Plato: "Why did God produce the world? Because He was good and not avaricious, but free from envy." [7] Similarly, toward the end of his treatise entitled *The Banquet,* he speaks not only of the supreme Good, but of His love for those things that proceed from Him.

But Plato's idea of God's goodness is not so much a goodness of benevolence, as a metaphysical goodness that is essentially diffusive of itself and fecund. Similarly Plotinus' supreme hypostasis is the One-Good, diffusive of itself, but actually diffusive of itself by a necessity of its nature, by way of emanation, and not by a free act of will creating all things other than itself from nothing.

So, therefore, in these conceptions of the Greek mind, the world appears as a necessary irradiation from God, just as the rays of the sun proceed from the sun; and so the world is a manifestation of His goodness and physical perfection. This paves the way for pantheism.

On the contrary, God's will, and indeed His free will, the principle of a most free creation, are revealed to us far more clearly in

---

[4] Ps. 134: 6.
[5] Rom. 9: 19.
[6] Denz., no. 1782.
[7] *Timaeus,* no. 29.

the Old and New Testaments. Consequently God is conceived not only as the supreme Good, expressed in the neuter form, τὸ ἀγαθόν (the good), but as He who is supremely good, full of benevolence, ὁ ἀγαθός (He who is good); He is conceived, indeed, as the supreme Person. This is already evident from the first chapter of Genesis, for we read: "Be light made. And light was made." [8] So this thought is constantly recurring: "He hath done all things, whatever He would." [9] This becomes increasingly evident in the New Testament, especially when Jesus says: "For God so loved the world as to give His only begotten Son." [10] Similarly, "He that loveth not, knoweth not God; for God is charity. By this hath the charity of God appeared toward us, because He hath first loved us and sent His Son to be a propitiation for our sins. My dearest, if God hath so loved us, we also ought to love one another." [11] And again: "But God commendeth His charity toward us, because when as yet we were sinners, Christ died for us." [12]

This mode of speech differs very much from that employed by Plato, Aristotle, or Plotinus. For these Greeks, the world appears to proceed from God according to a certain necessity of His nature, as the rays emanate from the sun. In this way God's metaphysical goodness, which is diffusive of itself, is made manifest rather than His benevolence, which is analogically conceived as the benevolence of a living person who has companionship with us.

There is a considerable difference on this point between the Christian teaching and that of modern philosophers. If some of them exaggerated the divine liberty and said, as Descartes did, that the truth of the principle of contradiction and the primary distinction between good and evil depend on God's free will, nevertheless very many did not sufficiently recognize God's free will. Spinoza and the pantheists of his school absolutely denied it, for pantheism is absolute determinism. Others, such as Leibnitz and Malebranche, exceedingly restricted God's free will, saying that God would be neither wise nor good if He had not created, and if He had not created the best of possible worlds. [13] This paves the way for pantheism, for if such be the case, then the world is already, as it were, a necessary irradiation from God, not indeed by a metaphysical or physical necessity, but by a moral necessity.

On the contrary, God's will is affirmed most emphatically in

[8] Gen. 1: 3.
[9] Ps. 113: 3.
[10] John 3: 16.
[11] I John 4: 8–11.
[12] Rom. 5: 8.
[13] Œuvres de Leibnitz (Erdmann ed.), II, 563, a.

revelation, and His absolute liberty is particularly described whenever it refers to God's good pleasure, as in the following texts:
"Remember us, O Lord, in the favor of Thy people." [14] And again:
"I confess to Thee, O Father, Lord of heaven and earth, because
Thou hast hid these things from the wise and prudent and hast revealed them to little ones. Yea, Father; for so hath it seemed good
in Thy sight." [15]

There is evidently nothing like this to be found in the writings of
Aristotle. Similarly, in the writings of Greek philosophers there is nowhere any reference to the purpose of the divine will, so often spoken
of by St. Paul, as in the following text: "He hath predestinated us . . .
according to the purpose of His will." [16] And in another of his epistles
we read: "that the purpose of God, according to election, might
stand" ($\tilde{i}\nu a \; \dot{\eta} \; \kappa a\tau' \; \dot{\epsilon}\kappa\lambda o\gamma\dot{\eta}\nu \; \pi\rho\dot{o}\theta\epsilon\sigma\iota\varsigma \; \tau o\tilde{v} \; \Theta\epsilon o\tilde{v} \; \mu\dot{\epsilon}\nu\eta$).[17] The purpose of the
divine will is the same as the decree of the divine will. It still per-
tains to the order of intention, which precedes the order of execution, just as our purpose must afterward be put into execution.

Thus in the very first article on God's will, by the light of divine
revelation His will is affirmed in the strict and full sense of the
term, so that there is nothing like this to be found in the writings
of Aristotle, or even in those of Plato and Plotinus; and far more
so does this apply to the writings of Spinoza and the modern
pantheists.

2) In the body of the article, St. Thomas proves a priori that
there is will in God, and moreover that His will is His existence
and His act of willing. Under this aspect these truths seem to be
theological conclusions, but they are already revealed; for among
the revealed truths, some are dependent on others, as the immortality of the soul depends on its spirituality.

But the existence of will in God is proved a priori, in that the
will properly has its root in the intellect, and is reduced to the
following syllogism: Will follows upon intellect; but there is intellect in God; therefore there is will in God.

The major is proved in virtue of the similarity of proportion
that prevails between the natural form and the intelligible form,
since we know spiritual things in the mirror of sensible things.
For just as a natural thing, for instance, a plant, is in actuality by
its specific form, so the intellect is actually intelligent by its intelligible form, which represents the object. But everything tends
toward its natural form when it has not this form, and is at rest

[14] Ps. 105: 4.
[15] Matt. 11: 25 f.
[16] Eph. 1: 5.
[17] Rom. 9: 11.

therein when it has it; thus matter tends toward its form, or, when the form is acquired, it rests therein and retains it. Similarly every natural thing tends to possess and retain its integral parts, as the plant, for instance, seeks to have and retain its normal size. For all these things the natural appetite suffices, which is the thing itself tending by its very nature toward its natural perfection. It is often called a natural inclination, as in the case of the stone, that tends toward the center of the earth.

Hence proportionately so, as stated in this article, "intellectual natures have a like aptitude to good as apprehended through its intelligible form; so as to rest therein when possessed, and when not possessed to seek to possess it, both of which pertain to the will. Hence in every intellectual being there is will, just as in every sensible being there is animal appetite," which is called sensitive. And thus there must be will in God, since there is intellect in Him.

Cajetan and John of St. Thomas draw attention to the difficulty that is, nevertheless, inherent in this proof. There is, indeed, a similarity of proportion between the natural thing, for instance, the plant, and the intellect; but from this it does not seem that, besides intellect, some appetite should be admitted as a distinct power and a distinct act. A natural appetite in the intellect appears to be sufficient, just as in the stone there is a natural appetite or inclination for the center of the earth, Thus Spinoza refuses to admit that intellect and will in us are two distinct faculties.

In fact, there is another difficulty, in that there appear to be four terms in the proof given by St. Thomas, because in the major he speaks of the intelligible form that is in the intellect, and in the conclusion, of the good apprehended outside the intellect. This second difficulty is of less importance, for the good referred to is that which is apprehended by means of the intelligible form.

In reply to the first difficulty, however, we say with Cajetan and John of St. Thomas that the natural appetite of the intellect does not suffice for this inclination, but that another faculty is also required, which is called the will or the rational appetite. This is evident for three reasons: (1) because the natural appetite, even in the intellect, follows its natural form, and not the apprehended form, or that of the thing known; (2) because the natural appetite is consequently determined to one thing, as the inclination of the stone is for the center of gravity, of a plant for a determined height, and of the intellect for knowledge in general. On the contrary, the appetite that follows the form of the thing known is not determined to one thing, but extends to various things, and is an act elicited by the will (or even by the sensitive appetite), just as cognition resulting therefrom is an act elicited by the cognitive faculty, either intellective or sensitive; (3) finally, the natural appetite of the intellect is concerned only with truth to be known, which is the good of the cognitive faculty; whereas, on the contrary, the rational appetite is concerned with the good of the subject *in toto*, or of man *in toto*, just as actually the animal or sensitive appetite is concerned with the good of the brute *in toto*. Hence man is not said to be simply good, unless he be a man of good will, which means that he wills the true good of the entire man.

There is this remarkable difference, which many intellectuals are not sufficiently aware of, since with them there is a sort of atrophy of the will along with a certain hypertrophy of the intellect, and they often do not advert to the fact that Christian contemplation must have its foundation not only in the love of knowledge, but also in the love of God Himself, as St. Thomas says.[18]

And therefore, just as in the brute animal the appetite that is called animal or sensitive is a special faculty distinct from the cognitive faculty of the sensible order; so also the rational appetite in man, the act of which follows intellectual cognition, is a special faculty that is called will and that is concerned not only with knowing, which is the good of the cognitive faculty, but also with the apprehended good of the entire man.[19] Thus it is established that the will follows upon intellect. But, since there is intellect in God, there is also will in Him.

Confirmation. In fact, as St. Thomas frequently says, the distinction between these two faculties is evident from the fact that "knowledge comes about in so far as the object known is without the knower; consequently the intellect extends itself to what is outside it."[20]

In other words, truth is formally in the intellect, being conformity of judgment with the thing judged; whereas good is outside the mind, being in the things themselves. They are two operations that take place in an inverted order, as experience proves; for by knowledge we mentally absorb things, whereas by volition and love we are attracted by the object loved. And, as experience proves, we will not only the knowledge of the true, but also the possession of the good. Thus we love not only the knowledge of God but God Himself. As the Scripture says: "Where thy treasure is, there is thy heart also."[21] There is a great difference, for instance, between lov-

---

[18] *Summa theol.*, IIa IIae, q.180, a.1.

[19] *Ibid.*, Ia, q.80, a.1: Whether the appetite is a special power of the soul; also Ia, q.59, a.2: Whether in the angels the will differs from the intellect.

[20] *Ibid.*, Ia, q.59, a.2.

[21] Matt. 6: 21.

ing to know humility, so as to speak about it, and loving humility itself.

The proof given by St. Thomas has not four terms: when he says "the intellect is actually intelligible by its intelligible form," he subinfers "which is apprehended as good." Thus it is legitimately concluded that "the intellectual nature as regards the apprehended good" tends toward it or rests therein by means of the will. Thus the above-mentioned proportionality is preserved with natural things. Thus the ascent is made by the mind from the lowest degree of natural inclination, such as that of the stone for its center of gravity, until the supreme will is reached, in which there is no longer to be found inclination or desire, but rest in the good that is eternally possessed. In this mental ascent the natural inclination of sensible things is first considered, because spiritual things are known only in the mirror of sensible things, and this leads us to know the supreme act of the will that delights in the divine good.

In the second part of the body of this article it is shown that God's will is His existence and His act of willing, because there is no difference as to the mode in which will and intellect are in God. But it was shown that God's intellect is His existence and His act of understanding, without any admixture of potentiality. Therefore, so is His will.

Corollary. God's will is self-subsisting volition without any intrinsic virtual distinction; otherwise there would be a foundation in the divine reality for conceiving the will of God as in potentiality with regard to its act. Hence there is only an extrinsic virtual distinction between them, one that has its foundation not in the divine reality but in creatures, since the self-subsisting volition is the equivalent of our faculty of willing and our willing. On the contrary, there is an intrinsic virtual distinction between God's intellect and His will, for which there is a foundation in the divine reality, because they belong to different orders. Similarly there is a virtual distinction between subsistent intellection and subsistent volition; yet it does not follow from this that there is a foundation in God for conceiving anything as in potentiality with respect to another thing.

In other words, this same corollary may be expressed as follows: God's will is not of the nature of a potentiality as regards His volition, which means that this notion of potentiality is not found in the divine will formally and eminently, but only virtually and eminently, as mixed perfections are, such as rationability or discursive knowledge. For this pertains to the created mode of the will, and this created mode implies imperfection, which is not included in what is formally signified by the name "will." This formal signification is found in God not only virtually and eminently, but also formally and eminently, or properly. The solution of the objections confirms this.

Reply to first objection. The difficulty was that the object of will is the end. But God is not directed to any end. Therefore there is not will in Him. The reply is: "Although nothing apart from God is His end, yet He Himself is the end with respect to all things," and thus, as will be stated farther on, God wills things apart from Himself for the manifestation of His goodness.

Hence, for the solution of this difficulty, it must be said: there is no assignment of an end to the act of God's will, let this pass without comment; of things willed by God, this I deny. It is said that this non-assignment should pass without comment, because the divine goodness, which is willed by God, is not truly and formally the end of the divine volition, because the end is distinct from what is directed to the end, as being its extrinsic cause; yet it may be said that the divine goodness to be loved and made manifest is the reason for the divine volition, just as it is said that the divine immutability is the reason for eternity, and divine immateriality for subsistent intellection. In this sense the divine goodness can be said to be virtually, although not formally, the final cause of the divine will. This is a better way of distinguishing between what is formally signified by the name "will" and the created mode of our will.

Reply to second objection. Our will not only seeks the good that it does not possess, but loves the good which it possesses, and finds its delight therein. In this respect will is said to be in God. God's will is primarily directed to the divine good, which it actually possesses. This brings out still more clearly the distinction between the formal signification of the word "will" and its created mode.

Reply to third objection. The relationship between the will and its object is one of moveable to mover, if it is a question of the created will, which is distinct from its objects; but it is not so with the divine will, which is identical with its object. Thus there is will in God, and this in the strict sense of the term, or formally and eminently, to the exclusion of all imperfections that pertain to its created mode. In its formal signification, will excludes imperfection.

Instance. Even in its formal signification will includes imperfection, since it denotes dependence on the divine intellect, from which it is virtually distinct. Therefore the difficulty remains.

In reply to this we say, first of all, that if such were true, then even indirectly the intellect would include imperfection, since it depends on truth and on the divine Being. We may reply directly to this objection by distinguishing the antecedent: if the will proceeded from the intellect as from its cause, then I concede the antecedent; if it proceeded as from a previously known principle, then I deny the antecedent. Thus in the Trinity there is no imperfection in the Son, because He proceeds from the Father, not as cause, but from Him only as the principle, just as the line proceeds from the point as principle.[22] Whatever imperfection there may be in this is due to our imperfect mode of conception, since we distinguish between the divine intellection and the divine volition, by a distinction known as *rationis ratiocinatae,* for which there is a foundation in the divine reality. But this distinction, as such, exists only in our mind, and so it is called a logical distinction (*rationis*). In actual fact, the divine intellection and the divine volition are identified (although not destructive of each other) in the eminence of the Deity in which they are formally and eminently.[23] Thus in God, conceived as being, the divine attributes that must be deduced from Him are contained only actually and implicitly; whereas in God conceived as the Deity, namely, as He is in Himself, they are contained actually and implicitly, without the necessity of any deduction.

Finally, we must not overlook the importance of this assertion, namely, that will is properly or formally in God. We see the importance of this if we consider the superiority of our will as regards our sensitive appetite. For our will, inasmuch as it is specified by universal good and not by sensible good, is of almost infinite profundity on the part of the object willed, in the sense that God alone clearly seen can invincibly draw it; other goods do not of necessity draw it, and the will loves these freely.[24] But if it is actually true to say that our will is of almost infinite profundity on the part of the thing willed, what must be said of God's will, which is specified not by universal good, but by the divine good, which is not really distinct from it but is absolutely identical with it? For it is infinite complacency in this good, divine rest therein; so that what is found by participation in the prayer of quiet is essentially in the divine will, to the exclusion of all imperfections.

22 If it is said that the divine will depends on the divine intellect, such dependence is according to our imperfect mode of conceiving this, arising from the virtual distinction between God's will and His intellect. This distinction is also called *rationis ratiocinatae,* because it is one formed by the mind, reasoned out by the reason, for which there is a foundation in the object. [Tr.]

But if it is a question of the divine reality itself, then all theologians exclude all causality and dependence from the divine persons, admitting only an order of origin between them. See Ia, q.27, a.1, 2, and Billuart's commentary on the same.

23 See Cajetan's *Com. in Iam,* q.39, a.1, no. 7.

24 Tauler speaks frequently about this *fundus* of our will.

From this it is already clear that the formal object of the divine will is the divine goodness, which of itself is not only lovable, but is actually and eternally loved; just as the divine truth is of itself not only actually understandable, but is actually and eternally understood.

SECOND ARTICLE

WHETHER GOD WILLS THINGS APART FROM HIMSELF

State of the question. Right now we consider the secondary object of the will. St. Thomas begins by stating most correctly the difficulties of this problem. Perhaps these are the difficulties that caused Aristotle not to affirm that God wills the world, and especially that He wills it freely. In fact, these difficulties were revived by Spinoza [25] in establishing his thesis that God does not act for an end, and that the world proceeds from the divine substance by a necessity of nature.

The principal difficulties are in the second, third, and fourth objections. In the second it is said that the willed moves the willer, as the appetible the appetite, which means that it entices, draws the appetite to itself. But God cannot be moved or enticed by another. Therefore He does not will any other thing than Himself. In the third objection it is stated that His own goodness suffices God and completely satisfies His will. Therefore God does not properly will anything apart from Himself. If this is affirmed, it is only by way of metaphor, as when God is said to be angry. The fourth objection presents the difficulty that, if God wills Himself and things apart from Himself, then there are two acts of the will in God, because the acts of the will are multiplied in proportion to the number of their objects, and this is contrary to God's simplicity. These difficulties are presented to purify the concept of will from all imperfections in its relation to creatures. Thus the foundation is laid for the solution of the objections that concern the free act of God's will,[26] and of God's love for creatures.[27]

The answer given by St. Thomas consists of two parts: (1) God wills not only Himself, but also other things apart from Himself (and this indeed by taking will in the literal sense, not metaphorically); (2) God wills Himself as the end, and other things as ordained to that end.

1) Both are very often affirmed in Holy Scripture, and they are of faith. St. Thomas quotes the following text: "This is the will of

[25] *Ethics*, Bk. I, chap. 33.
[26] See a.3.
[27] See q.20.

God, your sanctification." [28] For the second part, the following text is usually quoted: "The Lord hath made all things for Himself"; [29] and also: "He hath done all things, whatsoever He would." [30] The Vatican Council expresses this second part in equivalent words, by defining as follows: "If anyone shall deny that the world was made for the glory of God, let him be anathema." [31] Just previous to this, the canon defines that creation is a free act.

2) The first conclusion is proved from reason as follows: There is a similarity of proportion between the natural inclination and the rational inclination, which is the will; but natural things, in so far as they are perfect, are naturally inclined to communicate their good to others; therefore much more so does it pertain to the divine will, in so far as it is most perfect, to communicate by like-ness its own good to others. Thus God wills Himself and things apart from Himself.

The major is not so clearly stated in this article as in the pre-ceding. It necessarily prepares the ground for us, because we know spiritual things only in the mirror of sensible things, and we judge of the spiritual inclination because of a certain resemblance it bears toward the natural inclination of sensible things. This is the normal mode of procedure in the ascent of the mind to higher things.

The minor is proved by reason of the effects produced, or from experience, as Aristotle remarked. "We see that every agent, in so far as it is perfect and in act, produces its like." From this it is evident that there is a natural inclination in every perfect thing to impart its good to others. Thus the fully grown plant produces its like, and so does every grown-up animal.

From this general observation, the mind proceeds by the in-ductive process to enunciate this general principle: "It pertains to the nature of the will to communicate to others, as far as possible, the good possessed."

The Neoplatonists, especially Plotinus [32] and Dionysius, often enunciated this principle: "Good is essentially diffusive of itself." The way they showed the truth of this was by an inductive and gradual process of reasoning in the ascendant order, observing that the sun gives out life and heat, the fully grown plant produces its like, just as the fully grown or developed animal does; also the natural tendency of a man who is master of his art or who excels in knowledge or wisdom is to communicate this knowledge to

[28] I Thess. 4: 3.
[29] Prov. 16: 4.
[30] Ps. 113: 3.
[31] Denz. no. 1805.
[32] *Enneade*, Bk. V, chaps. 1, 6, 7.

others. Similarly the source of all gifts is perfect love, which explains the loving generosity of parents toward their children. Hence from all this it is evident that good is diffusive of itself; in fact, the nobler the nature, the more intimately and completely it is diffusive of itself. This doctrine of mental ascent is in substance retained by St. Thomas in the present article, and in another of his works,[33] to illustrate God's interior fecundity in the generation of the eternal divine Word, and so as to enunciate elsewhere [34] the fittingness of the Incarnation. But if this principle is true, then its application to God's will is manifest inasmuch as His will is most perfect.

As St. Thomas remarks,[35] good is described as self-diffusive primarily and immediately in the genus of final cause as regards the agent, and then mediately in the genus of efficient cause, inasmuch as the inclination of the perfect agent is to communicate actively to others the good possessed by it.

From this, however, Plotinus concludes not only that the supreme Good is diffusive of itself, but that it actually diffuses itself, according to a necessity of its nature, just as the sun emits its rays. Thus the world would seem to be a necessary irradiation of the divine goodness or of the divine perfection. Something like this is said by Leibnitz, who, according to his theory of absolute optimism, affirms, not the physical, but the moral, necessity of creation, and of the creation of the best among possible worlds. Otherwise, he says, God would not be infinitely wise and good.[36]

St. Thomas affirms in this article that "it appertains to the divine will to communicate by likeness its own good to others, as much as is possible." By these words he affirms the fittingness, but in no way the moral necessity, of this communication.

There are three difficulties regarding this first part of the argumentative part of this article.

First difficulty. If good is essentially diffusive of itself, then it seems that God, being the supreme Good, is essentially diffusive of Himself *ad extra;* hence creation is not a free act. But, it is of faith that creation is a free act, as will be stated in the next article.

Reply. When it is said that good is essentially diffusive of itself, we must distinguish between the capacity of communicating and the act of communicating. Certainly the capacity of communicating good to others is a necessary perfection in God. Moreover, the act of communicating good to others or of perfecting involves no im-

33 *Contra Gentes,* Bk. IV, chap. 11.

34 *Summa theol.,* IIIa, q. 1, a. 1.

35 *Ibid.,* Ia, q.5, a.4 ad 2um; Ia IIae, q.1, a.4 1um.

36 *Œuvres de Leibnitz* (Erdmann ed.), *Theodicée,* §§ 7-10, pp. 506, 563; see also *La Monadologie,* § 53, p. 171, Boutroux ed.; also Introd. pp. 77-116.

perfection, and can be applied to God. But this suffices. Good entices the agent, inclines it to act; but the agent can act either
according to a necessity of its nature, or freely. In the following
article it is shown that God wills things apart from Himself most
freely, because "the goodness of God is perfect, and can exist without other things inasmuch as no perfection can accrue to Him from
them."

Second difficulty. Is the act of communicating good to others a
special perfection?

The answer is, that it is not, because God is neither better nor
greater in having created the universe. This conclusion, fundamentally the opposite of what Leibnitz taught, will be better explained in the following article. Leibnitz said that, if God had not
created or if He had not created the best of possible worlds, then
He would be neither infinitely wise nor infinitely good. On the
contrary, according to St. Thomas' teaching which was admirably
expressed by Bossuet against Leibnitz, God is not better in having
created the universe, and He would have been none the less good
if He had not created it. This point will be more clearly explained
in the next article. The statement just made serves its present purpose, which is to indicate that the present article is concerned with
the fittingness of creation, so much so that it would be equally
fitting if God had not willed to create, as will be stated in the
following article.

On this point the Thomists generally do not adopt the language
of Cajetan, who, in his commentary on this article, writes: "It is
a perfection for the divine will, that it tend in the manner that
pertains to it, to communicate its good to others; but . . . this perfection is voluntary . . . and absolutely free. But there is no un-
fittingness in conceding that God's willing of things apart from
Himself is a voluntary and absolutely free perfection . . . for this
means that its opposite is no imperfection." [37]

The Thomists, however, commonly repudiate such language as
this, for they say that God cannot be conceived as acquiring some
new and free perfection superadded, as it were, to the infinite and
necessary perfection of pure Act, and virtually distinct from it. In
such a case there would be a foundation in the divine reality for
conceiving the divine will as in potentiality with regard to this new
and free perfection that is superadded; in this there is a certain
danger of pantheism, since in this way the validity of the following
principle is impaired: "The divine being is being that can have
nothing added to it." [38] Hence there can be no accident in God.

[37] Cf. no. 7.
[38] *Summa theol.,* Ia, q.3, a.4, 6.

Therefore the Thomists say what Cajetan, after more mature reflection, wrote: "To communicate oneself to others implies perfection not in the one communicating, but in the recipients of this communication. . . . And it is of the nature of good to communicate itself to others, not for the betterment of the one communicating, but for the sake of others to be made good by it." [39]

Godoy [40] correctly observes that the way Cajetan first expressed himself must be understood as referring to a free perfection, which God may not possess, not inasmuch as it is a perfection, but in the sense that the object willed is contingent. But to express this exactly, the Thomists say that the free act in God does not add a new perfection in Him, but presupposes the infinite perfection of pure Act, and is defectible only because of the object willed. [41]

The terminology commonly accepted in the schools expresses in somewhat different language what Cajetan meant. It is formulated, of course, as a modal proposition that refers to the saying rather than as a modal proposition that refers to the thing. It does not say that the act of creating is a free and befitting perfection in God, for then the word "befitting" would terminate in an apparently superadded perfection. But it says that it is befitting that God created the universe, although it would have been just as befitting if He had not created. Similarly it is befitting that God raised us to the supernatural order, and that He sent His Son into the world to save us, although it would have been just as befitting if He had not raised us to the supernatural order, or if He had not willed the Incarnation. These are, indeed, absolutely free acts.

In the example just given, it is evident that a modal proposition referring to the thing is not equivalent to a modal proposition referring to the saying, as St. Thomas observed. [42] For it is false to say that everything known by God is necessary. But it is true to say that everything known by God must needs be (by a necessity of consequence but not of consequent). Similarly it is true to say that it is necessary (by a necessity of consequence) for the predestined to wish the good of salvation and be saved. But it is false to say that the predestined necessarily wills the good of salvation and is saved. Hence the argument of St. Thomas holds good, namely: "It appertains to God's will that He communicate His good to others as much as possible."

Third difficulty. It arises from the concluding words ("as much as possible") of the sentence just quoted. This seems to suggest that

[39] *Com. in IIIam,* q.1, a.1, no. 6.
[40] *Com. in Iam,* q.19, d.48, §§ 4, 5, no. 85.
[41] *Summa theol.,* Ia, q.19, a.3.
[42] *Ibid.,* Ia, q.14, a.13 ad 3um.

if God creates the world, He ought to create the best of possible worlds, as Leibnitz asserts.

Reply. St. Thomas holds, as we shall find him stating in the next article, that the volition by which God most freely wills things apart from Himself, cannot be known by us a priori but only after the act, or by revelation. But now, after the creative act, it is shown to be fitting for God to create, although it would have been equally fitting if He had not created, as will be stated in the next article. Hence these words, "as much as possible," indicate only this aforesaid fittingness. Moreover, as will be stated farther on, the supreme limit in the possible or creatable is impossible of conception, because "the (infinite) God can make something else better than each thing made by Him." [43] Thus He can create better angels and of a higher order, because, between any created being and the infinite perfection of God, the distance is infinite.

Second conclusion. It states that God wills Himself as the end and other things as ordained to that end. This follows as a corollary from the first conclusion, because God cannot, except by not observing the order of subordination, will Himself and things apart from Himself. He cannot will equally, as it were, two things that are co-ordinated; for all co-ordination presupposes subordination. Order is the arrangement of things according to priority and posteriority with reference to some principle. Hence it is verified first in subordination and then in co-ordination. Thus two soldiers are not so much co-ordinated as subordinated to the same general of an army.

A difficulty arises concerning this second conclusion. If God wills all things for Himself, this seems to impair the ordinary conception we have of His goodness or liberality, and of the generosity of His love for us. In fact, God's love for us is not a love of concupiscence but of benevolence. But by the love of benevolence we love others not for our sake but for their sake. Therefore, that God's love for us should be truly a love of benevolence, He must love us for our sake and not for His sake. Kant, Hermes, Gunther, and more recently Laberthonnière, proposed this objection. [44]

Reply. Against Hermes and Gunther it was defined by the Vatican Council in one of its canons: "If anyone shall deny that the world was made for the glory of God, let Him be anathema." [45] This same point is explained by the Council in the chapter to which this canon is attached, for it says: "This one, only, true God, of His own goodness and almighty power, not for the increase of His

---

[43] *Ibid.*, Ia, q.25, a.6.
[44] Cf. *Revue Thomiste*, 1935, pp. 568–605.
[45] Denz., no. 1805.

own happiness,[46] nor to acquire but to manifest His perfection by the blessings which He bestows on creatures, with absolute freedom of counsel, created out of nothing, from the beginning of time, both the spiritual and the corporal creature, namely, the angelic and the mundane; and afterward the human creature, as partaking, in a sense, of both, consisting of spirit and of body." [47]

The Vatican Council explained the following text from Scripture: "The Lord hath made all things for Himself," [48] as meaning "for the manifestation of His goodness." If a man's actions are performed to show how good he is, not directing them to God, then this is vainglory; but if either man's acts or God's acts are performed to manifest the divine or supreme goodness, there is no vainglory but true glory in this; for this manifestation results in God's being clearly known and praised, which is true glory and due recognition of His supreme excellence.

It does not follow, therefore, that God loves us, not with love of benevolence, but of concupiscence. For the love of benevolence is that love by which the lover wills good to the one loved, and not only to himself. But God wills good to us, and not only to Himself. In fact, God wills to give Himself to us, and gave us His Son; but we are subjected to God as the supreme good. Therefore God loves us with the love of benevolence, but He subjects us to Himself. In other words, God loves us as that for which He wills good, but not as the end of creation.

Unless this were so, there would be an inversion of the established order, which would be a perversion, as when a miser prefers money to his own dignity as a rational being, and through love of money loses his soul. In fact, if God were to love the creature as the end of creation, He would no longer love the supreme good above all things. Thus God would repudiate Himself, which would be a mortal sin in God, the height of absurdity.

Hence this would result in a false definition of the love of benevolence, and it could not be attributed to God if it were said to be the love by which another is loved for his own sake and not for the sake of the lover. The love of benevolence must be defined as the love by which we wish good to another, so that the other is the one to whom we wish the good, and not necessarily the ultimate end of our love.[49] But when we love God with the love of benevo-

---

[46] This would imply love of concupiscence.

[47] Denz., no. 1783. See also Vacant, *Etudes théologiques sur le Concile du Vatican,* I, 268, against Hermes and Gunther.

[48] Prov. 16: 4.

[49] If it is sometimes said that it is of the nature of friendship that the friend be loved for his own sake, the meaning is that the friend is loved as the end for

lence and of charity, we wish God His good, namely, His glory, and we love Him, moreover, as the ultimate end. Thus the Scripture says: "Not to us, O Lord, not to us, but to Thy name give glory." [50]

Thus teachers truly delight in expounding sublime truths to their students, even to only one student, and more indeed from love of God and of truth than from love of the student to whom the truth is communicated.

Moreover, from the stand taken by Kant, Hermes, and Gunther, it would follow rather that the creature, instead of being happy, would be unhappy. For if the rational creature were the end of creation, the ultimate end of man would not be the supreme Good, who is to be loved above all things, but it would be the limited good that is contained in the dignity of the human nature. Thus the natural aspirations of man for the infinite good would be frustrated even in the natural order.

Finally, it is false to say that it amounts to "egoism" in God, if He made all things for Himself. Egoism is that inordinate love of self by which a man prefers himself to a higher good, such as family, country, and the like. But God cannot prefer Himself to a higher good, because He is identical with the supreme Good. God, in loving Himself above all things, prefers, as one must, the supreme Good to all things.[51]

Hence this doctrine, no matter what Kant, Hermes, Gunther, and Laberthonnière may have said, by no means impairs God's liberality and His love of benevolence or of charity for us; but it most clearly ilustrates that the divine goodness is capable of being loved in the highest degree, which is the only object that can be loved by God as the end. Created goodness or the creature is the one to whom God by the love of benevolence wills good as a manifestation of His goodness.

In fact, because the love of creatures, as will be stated in the next article, is most free, it being not at all necessary for God's happiness, for this very reason it is absolutely gratuitous and therefore most liberal, being the very opposite of egoism, since it manifests God's generosity or His magnanimity. Billuart, in his commentary

---

which, or the one to whom, we wish the benefits. It does not mean that the good qualities we perceive in the friend are the reason why we love him; in fact, the friendship is more generous when there is nothing lovable in the one that is loved.

[50] Ps. 113: 1.

[51] In this we see how egregiously those erred who spoke of God's "transcendental egoism." Egoism is not an absolutely simple perfection, but is a defect, since it is an inordinate love of self. It does not, therefore, exist in God, nor does the addition of "transcendental" suffice to make this defect an absolute perfection.

on this article remarks: "The more generous and the more perfect is the friendship, so much the more is another loved and showered with benefits, who is most destitute of anything that is lovable, God's love being solely a gratuitous act of His will. Thus it is solely by reason of His goodness that God loves creatures, and communicates His good gifts to them, not for His sake, but that it may well be for them a means of seeing Him as their supreme Good and ultimate end." Many texts in Scripture are to this effect, such as: "Give glory to the Lord, for He is good, for His mercy endureth forever." [52] "He hath filled the hungry with good things." [53] In the parable of the talents, in rewarding the good deeds performed, the Lord says: "Well done, good and faithful servant. . . . Enter thou into the joy of thy lord." [54] Here we have the perfect love of friendship, since God gives us His own happiness.

The conclusion of this article is confirmed by the solution of the objections.

First objection. It is of minor importance. It states that the divine will is the divine existence. But God is not other than Himself. Therefore He does not will things other than Himself.

Reply. That the divine will is God's existence objectively and not conceptually, this I concede; objectively and conceptually, this I deny. It is of the nature of volition that it relate to something.

Second objection. The thing willed moves the will, entices the will. If, therefore, God wills anything apart from Himself, His will is moved, enticed by another, which is impossible.

Reply. I distinguish the antecedent: that the thing willed moves the will for its own sake, this I concede; for the sake of something else, this I deny. Thus in the case of a person who takes a bitter medicine for the sake of health, it is health alone that moves the will. But God wills things apart from Himself only for the manifestation of His goodness, which is the reason for His loving creatures, and the reason for all God's works *ad extra*. Nor can it be said, strictly speaking, that the divine goodness moves, entices, the divine will, but it is the reason for His loving creatures.

Third objection. What is willed suffices the willer, and he seeks nothing beyond it; but His own infinite goodness suffices God, therefore God does not will anything apart from Himself.

Reply. I distinguish the major: that he seeks nothing beyond it, unless such is a reason for its being made manifest, this I concede; that he wills absolutely nothing beyond it, this I deny. Thus God

[52] Ps. 105: 1; 106: 1.
[53] Luke 1: 53.
[54] Matt. 25: 23.

wills nothing besides Himself, except by reason of His goodness, but He wills things apart from Himself for the manifestation of His goodness.

Fourth objection. Acts of the will are multiplied in proportion to the number of their objects. If, therefore, God wills Himself and things apart from Himself, it will follow that the act of His will is manifold.

Reply. "As the divine intellect is one, as seeing the many only in the one, in the same way the divine will is one and simple, as willing the many only through the one, that is, through its own greatness.

First doubt. Is the divine goodness alone the formal object, the motive and what terminates the divine will, so that creatures are only its material object?

It follows from the reply to the second objection of this article that the answer is in the affirmative. For the formal object of a faculty, its motive and what terminates it, is that which and by reason of which it is directly moved to act, and which directly and by reason of which it attains its object. But God wills all things for the manifestation of His goodness. Consequently the moving and hence the termination of the faculty find their complete explanation in the divine goodness, because the principle that attracts and the terminus of volition coincide; but it is called principle with reference to the intention, and terminus with reference to enjoyment of the good intended and possessed. Moreover, the will is specified by its formal object. But the divine will can be specified only by the divine goodness, for otherwise it would be dependent on some other goodness.

Second doubt. Is the divine goodness alone the adequate object of the divine will?

The Thomists reply in the affirmative, because the divine goodness in the order of good is coextensive with the divine will as faculty, for each is infinite. Hence the distinction that is made as regards the created intellect between the proper and the adequate objects, does not apply to God. The adequate object of the created intellect is being in all that pertains to being, whereas the adequate object of the divine intellect is the Deity, which, in a certain sense, transcends being and good, as it contains these formally and eminently.

Objection. Nevertheless God is moved on account of our merits to reward us, and on account of our miseries to come to our assistance, for the misery of others is the reason why one is merciful.[55] Thus God willed the Incarnation for our redemption. Therefore

[55] *Summa theol.*, IIa IIae, q.30, a.2.

the creature in some way moves the divine will as the motivated object.

Reply. The antecedent is denied: for God is moved toward these things solely by reason of His goodness considered under various aspects. For God is not moved toward these things as we are moved, on account of some particular good quality reflected in these objects. But the divine goodness, being the reason for doing good, specifies the divine liberality; being the reason for giving everyone his due, it specifies divine justice, which rewards or punishes according to one's deserts. Similarly divine goodness, being the reason for coming to the assistance of those in misery, moves and specifies divine mercy, because the divine virtues cannot be specified by created good. If, therefore, St. Thomas says that "the misery of others is the reason why one is merciful," [56] he is then speaking of created mercy; and, moreover, he says this as regards the material cause, for the perfecting of it, and not as regards the final cause, or the end for the sake of which the act is performed. Thus God is said to have willed the incarnation of His Son for our sake, inasmuch as the redemption of the human race was the subject for the sake of which or the end for which the Incarnation was of benefit.[57] Thus it remains true to say that the ultimate end of the Incarnation is the manifestation of divine goodness.

Instance. Yet God wills one creature for another, and all things for the sake of the elect. Therefore, at least the higher creatures are the motivated object of the divine will.

Reply. I distinguish the antecedent in this sense, that "God wills this to be as means to that; but He does not will this on account of that." [58] In other words, the conjunction *propter* ("on account of") affects the object, for God wills one creature to be on account of another; but the conjunction does not affect the divine volition, which is one only and uncreated, and is not dependent on creatures. Thus God wills all things for the sake of the elect; but the elect are not the cause of this divine volition ("volition" in the subjective sense). On the contrary, our will has at least two acts, namely, intention and choice, and on account of the end intended we will the means by a subsequent act of choice, which is the effect of the first act of intention. Therefore it remains true to say that God wills no created good by reason of itself, but by reason of the divine goodness to which all created things are ordained.

Corollary. When it is said that all God's operations *ad extra* have been for His external glory, this must not be construed as meaning

[56] *Ibid.*
[57] *Ibid.*, IIIa, q.1, a.3, c. et ad 3um.
[58] See q.19, a.5.

that they have been for the created and distinguished knowledge of Him with praise, because this created knowledge and praise are ordained to God; but it must be construed as meaning that all His works are for the manifestation of His uncreated goodness. This most admirably confirms the answer of St. Thomas, that God wills both Himself and other things, but Himself as the end, and other things as ordained to that end.

From what has been said it is also evident that the ultimate end of all God's works *ad extra,* even the incarnation of the Word, is the manifestation of divine goodness, although there may be a subordinated end, since the Incarnation is for our salvation, as being beneficial to us.

Another corollary. Hence, just as only the divine good can completely satisfy the will of the blessed, far more so is this the case with the divine will. We say a fortiori, because the divine will is specified by the divine good, whereas the created will is specified by universal good. If we were to say that the created will is specified by the divine good, it would already have the same specified object as infused charity, and then it could not be elevated to the higher order of grace.

THIRD ARTICLE

WHETHER WHATEVER GOD WILLS, HE WILLS NECESSARILY

State of the question. The question in this article is whether God freely wills things apart from Himself, or whether He wills them from a certain necessity either of nature or of knowledge, namely, because of a physical or moral necessity. According to the pantheists, such as Spinoza, God necessarily produces things apart from Himself, this necessity being metaphysical, or at least physical; and so nothing would be possible besides that which exists. Thus Spinoza could not have been born in any other city than the one in which he was born, as Leibnitz replied to him. Yet Leibnitz himself said that God wills things apart from Himself by a moral necessity, because it would be unbecoming, contrary to wisdom and goodness, for God not to will things apart from Himself, and not to will better things. This same doctrine is found in the writings of Malebranche, and later on in those of Gunther and Rosmini. If such were the case, then it would have been morally necessary for Leibnitz to be born only in that city and at that time in which he was born. Thus in the opinion of Leibnitz, all things that happen would be necessary, at least morally so.[59]

59 *Theodicée,* first part, §§ 7–10.

St. Thomas in the state of the question makes known the difficulty of this problem. He begins by positing six objections.[60] Two of these present special difficulty. There is first the difficulty as regards the exercise of the free act, which appears to be something contingent in God, because there is a possibility of its absence. This difficulty is touched upon in the fourth objection by the following remark: "The divine will would be contingent upon one or the other of two things, and so imperfect"; in fact, there would be a free volition that could as well not be. The fifth objection inquires into the cause of this contingent determination in God. This difficulty is thoroughly examined by the Thomists.

The other difficulty is concerned with the specification and the motive of the free act in willing the object, since nothing is willed unless it is foreknown as suitable and better. Thus it is better to create; it would be unbefitting not to create, and not to create better creatures. Hence it seems that God ought to will things apart from Himself, if not from necessity of His nature, at least because either His knowledge or wisdom or goodness dictates this.

In other words, if there is not a metaphysical and physical necessity, at least there is a moral necessity for this, otherwise there will be imperfection in God. Leibnitz, Gunther, and Rosmini make this objection the subject of special discussion. St. Thomas knew of this objection, and he touched upon it to some extent.[61]

Aristotle never affirmed God's liberty, because he found himself unable to reconcile it with His immutability. It seems that he admitted not only that the world was from eternity, but that it was a necessary production. This was the view of the Neoplatonists, as expressed in their doctrine of emanation.

In the Middle Ages it was Abelard who denied God's liberty, saying that "God can do only what He does." [62] Aureolus taught that liberty was attributed to God only metaphorically, for otherwise His free act would be contingent. In later times, Wyclif, Bucer, and Calvin seem to have denied true liberty in God. This question has been discussed at length by us elsewhere.[63]

The answer is that God wills things apart from Himself, not necessarily, but most freely.

1) It is of faith and is often declared in Holy Scripture, as in the

---

[60] *De veritate,* q.23, a.4; *De potentia,* q.3, a.15; *Contra Gentes,* Bk. I, chaps. 76, 81, 82; Bk. II, chaps. 23, 24, 26, 27 (against the Averroists).

[61] See the second and sixth objections of this article; also q.25, a.6: Whether God can do better than what He does; and *Contra Gentes,* Bk. II, chaps. 26, 27, against Averroist determinism.

[62] Denz., no. 374.

[63] See *God, His Existence and His Nature,* II, 95–108; 268–354.

following texts: "And God said: Be light made. And light was made." [64] "The God of revenge hath acted freely." [65] "And the Lord said to Moses . . . I will have mercy on whom I will; and I will be merciful to whom it shall please Me." [66] "Therefore He hath mercy on whom He will, and whom He will He hardeneth." [67] "Who worketh all things according to the counsel of His will." [68] There are many other passages that refer to God's will of good pleasure and to the gratuity of His love for the elect. The divine election is, in the strict sense, a free act.[69] In the parable of the laborers in the vineyard, the Lord says: "I will also give to this last even as to thee. Or, is it not lawful for me to do what I will?" [70]

In fact, even in the Old Testament we find God's liberty frequently affirmed, as in the following texts: "As the potter's clay is in his hands . . . so man is in the hand of Him that made him, and He will render to him according to His judgment." [71] "For if it shall please the Lord, He will fill him with the spirit of understanding." [72]

The Vatican Council, in attacking the moral necessity of creation as taught by Gunther and Leibnitz, defined as follows: "If anyone shall say that God created not by His will, free from all necessity, but by a necessity equal to the necessity whereby He loves Himself; let him be anathema." [73] In the corresponding chapter it states that God "with absolute freedom of counsel" [74] created.

Likewise the following proposition of Anthony Rosmini was condemned: "The love by which God loves Himself even in creatures, and which is the motive that determines Him to create, constitutes a moral necessity which in the most perfect being always brings forth the effect; for it is only in the many imperfect beings that necessity of this kind leaves liberty intact on either side." [75] If such were the case, then liberty would be a mixed perfection, just as discursive knowledge is. On the contrary, liberty is an absolutely simple perfection, and so it must of necessity be in God. Nevertheless, as we shall see, this free act, such as that of creating, is not an

[64] Gen. 1: 3.
[65] Ps. 93: 1.
[66] Ex. 33: 17, 19.
[67] Rom. 9: 18.
[68] Eph. 1: 11.
[69] Rom. 9: 11; 11: 5, 28.
[70] Matt. 20: 14 f.
[71] Ecclus. 33: 13 f.
[72] *Ibid.*, 39: 8. See also Jer. 18: 3.
[73] Denz., no. 1805.
[74] *Ibid.*, no. 1783. See Vacant, *Etudes sur le Concile du Vatican*, I, 269, 270.
[75] Denz., no. 1908.

absolutely simple perfection in God, as least in the strict sense, because it is not better for God to have this act than not to have it.

2) It is proved by reason that God necessarily wills His own goodness, and things apart from Himself freely.

The first part presents no difficulty: "For the divine will has a necessary relation to the divine goodness, since that is its proper object." Moreover, there is not and cannot be any idea of evil resulting from the divine goodness, but in it we see clearly all that pertains to good. And then God is of necessity actually willing and not merely potentially so. Therefore God necessarily wills His goodness, and the necessity is one of specification and of exercise.

St. Thomas proves the second part of this proposition from the fact that God is in no way dependent on creatures for the possession of His infinite goodness. This point is made clear by the following argument.

In willing the end we do not necessarily will those things that are conducive to the end, unless they are necessary for the attainment of the end. But God wills things apart from Himself as ordained to His goodness (for its manifestation), which, since it is perfect, can dispense with creatures, and no perfection accrues to Him from them. Therefore God does not necessarily will things apart from Himself. But supposing that He wills these, He is unable not to will them, because His will cannot change.

There is another way of expressing the minor, by saying that after creation there are more beings, but not more being, or more perfection or goodness, because prior to this there necessarily and from eternity pre-existed infinite goodness that is necessarily and actually loved and possessed by God.

This proof is apodictic and most clear. This is the element of clarity in this light-transcending obscurity. The obscurity will be in what formally constitutes God's free act.

THE SOLUTION OF THE OBJECTIONS CONFIRMS THIS PROOF

Reply to first objection. Everything that is eternal is necessary either absolutely or hypothetically. Hence from the fact that God wills from eternity whatever He wills, it does not follow that it is absolutely necessary for Him to will things apart from Himself. This is only hypothetically necessary, on the supposition that He wills these.

Reply to second objection. The divine goodness, which God necessarily wills, can exist without other things. Hence God most freely wills things apart from Himself, and with absolute generosity.

Reply to third objection. It is not natural to God to will things apart from Himself; yet it is not unnatural but voluntary and free, in fact most free.

Reply to fourth objection. Every contingent being is imperfect. But the divine will is contingent to one or the other of two things. Therefore it would be imperfect. This difficult objection is solved by conceding the major and denying the minor. That the divine will would be in itself indifferent to one or the other of two things, this I deny; in that it is not necessarily related to something willed, this I concede. The conclusion is distinguished in the same way, so that the imperfection is only in the contingent thing willed, but not in the divine will. This is well explained by St. Thomas in his reply. He says: "Sometimes a necessary cause has a non-necessary relation to an effect, owing to a deficiency in the effect and not in the cause. Even so, the sun's power has a non-necessary relation to some contingent effects on this earth, owing to a defect not in the solar power, but in the effect that proceeds not necessarily from the cause." Thus certain fruits never become ripe.

Reply to fifth objection. Nothing determinate results from that which is indifferent to one or the other of two things, unless it is determined by an extrinsic cause; but God cannot be determined by an extrinsic cause; therefore God is not indifferent to one or the other of two things. This objection is answered by distinguishing the major. What is indifferent potentially or passively, this I concede; that the indifference is actual and active, this I deny. I concede the minor, and distinguish the conclusion as follows: That God is not indifferent potentially or passively so, this I concede; that the indifference is actual and active, this I deny. St. Thomas says the equivalent of this in his reply: "A naturally contingent cause, such as human liberty, must be determined to act by some external power (thus it is attracted by the object and moved by God to choose this object freely); but the divine will, which by its nature is necessary, determines itself to will things to which it has no necessary relation."

For the explanation of this distinction, it must be observed that there is a dominating potential or passive indifference in our free will before it chooses anything. But once it is determined by reason of its choice, although it remains free, it retains a dominating indifference, not indeed one that is potential or passive, but one that is actual and active, inasmuch as man, in freely choosing some particular good, not universal good, is not invincibly attracted by it, but actually wills it at the same time retaining the real power of not willing, in fact, of actually not willing it. In God, however, who is pure Act, there is no potential and passive indifference, but only a dominating actual and active indifference of His self-subsisting act of willing, or of His self-subsisting love, which is in no necessary relation to creatures.

These last two objections of St. Thomas, as we shall at once see, are of great help in explaining the nature of God's free act and its indifference.

Reply to sixth objection. Whatever God knows, He knows necessarily, because His knowledge is His essence. Therefore it likewise follows that whatever God wills, He wills necessarily. This objection may be answered by distinguishing the antecedent: I concede this statement of His knowledge of simple intelligence; I deny it of His knowledge of vision, and I deny the consequent and consequence, because in this case the will is now joined to God's knowledge of vision.[76] Moreover, God's knowledge of things is as these are eternally present to His knowledge, whereas the will is related to things as they are in themselves (inasmuch as good, unlike truth, is not in the mind but in the things). Things in themselves, however, are contingent.

There are especially two objections among others that are proposed. As already stated, good is essentially diffusive of itself. But God is the supreme good. Therefore God is essentially (or necessarily) diffusive of Himself.

We reply to this by distinguishing the major: good is essentially diffusive of itself, that it may communicate itself, and first in the genus of final cause, this I concede; that *de facto* it necessarily communicate itself, this I subdistinguish: if it is a question of communicable natural good, such as the light given by the sun, this I concede; if it is a question of communicable good by a free act of the will, this I deny. Hence God essentially diffuses or communicates Himself; but it is only by a free act of His will that He actually communicates a participation of His goodness, because for the complete possession of this goodness He is in no need of creatures.

Finally, the following objection must be noted. God is absolutely immutable, or, in other words, He cannot be otherwise than He is. But God would be mutable if He could will or not will to create, or, in other words, He would be otherwise than He is if He were not the Creator. Therefore the difficulty remains.

From what has already been said, we answer this by distinguishing the major and denying the minor. For God is absolutely immutable, although it was in His power not to choose that which He freely chose from eternity. For this free choice is not even in the least degree a superadded accident in God, and it posits no

---

[76] *Summa theol.,* Ia, q.14, a.8.

new perfection in Him. Hence the change and variation is solely on the part of the things willed, as stated in the reply to the fourth objection. This gives rise to some doubts, however, which must be examined.

First doubt. What formally constitutes God's free act?

The difficulty is that God either could or could not have been without His free act, for instance, the creative act. If He could, then how is He immutable? He is at least from eternity, otherwise than He could have been. If He could not, then how is He free? [77]

This is what is obscure in this light-transcending darkness, whereas what is most clear in it is that God most freely created, as He in no way is in need of creatures for the most complete possession of His infinite goodness. For the solution of this difficulty two contradictory and improbable opinions are proposed.

The first of these opinions states that God's free act is constituted by some intrinsic and defectible reality in Him, which is superadded, so to speak, to His pure Act.

Reply. If this reality were identical with God, then He would be intrinsically defectible. If, on the other hand, this reality were really distinct from God's substance, then it would be an accident in God, and then He would be neither absolutely simple, nor pure Act, since He would be in potentiality for this new determination, which, indeed, He would have from all eternity, but which it was possible for Him not to have. Thus the self-subsisting Being would no longer be the "being to whom nothing can be added." [78] He would not be both the unreceived and unreceptive Being. This opinion would prepare the way for pantheism, which posits certain accidents in God, such as are the finite modes admitted by Spinoza, the series of which would be infinite both regressively and successively.

The second opinion, which is proposed by Aureolus, states that God's free act consists in some extrinsic denomination that is appropriated from creatures. Thus Aureolus says that the free act is not formally and properly in God, but only metaphorically, as anger is, which is a passion of the sensitive appetite.

Reply. God is from all eternity free, before anything was created by Him. In fact, the free creative act exists eternally in God as a formally immanent and virtually transitive vital act, although its effect *ad extra* is passively produced only in time. Therefore God's free act cannot be constituted by something purely extrinsic to Him and created, but it must be something intrinsic to Him.

[77] See John of St. Thomas, Salmanticenses, Gonet, and Billuart in their commentaries on this article.

[78] *Summa theol.,* Ia, q.3, a.4 ad 1um et ad 6um.

Likewise we must reject the opinion which differs but little from that of Aureolus. This opinion states that a logical relation to creatures is what constitutes God's free act. For logical being cannot be the cause of real being. But God's free act is the cause of the real being of all creatures. Moreover, God's free act exists before there can be any logical relation in Him, which has existence only in the created intellect. Therefore God's free act must be something real and intrinsic to Him. But there is still the difficulty as to how this act is defectible in God, or may as well not be.

The more common opinion among the Thomists mediates between the above-mentioned contradictory opinions and is superior to them. It is, as it were, a higher synthesis, combining what is best in each of the other opinions, for it states that the entity of God's free act is indeed intrinsic to Him, but only its defectibility is extrinsic to Him.

To be more explicit, this means that God's free act is nothing else but the necessary act by which He loves His goodness, in so far as this connotes a non-necessary relation to creatures, and so it is only extrinsically defectible by reason of the defectibility in the thing willed. There is foundation for this opinion in many texts from the writings of St. Thomas. Thus in the preceding article he says: "The divine will is one and simple, as willing the many only through the one, that is, through its own goodness." [79]

In this article he says: "That God does not necessarily will some of the things that He wills, does not result from defect in the divine will, but from a defect belonging to the nature of the thing willed." [80] More explicitly he writes: "God's will by one and the same act wills Himself and other things. Now His relation to Himself is necessary and natural; whereas His relation to other things is by way of a kind of fittingness, not indeed necessary and natural, or violent and unnatural, but free." [81]

Thus, from the teaching as set forth in this present article, this opinion is proved by the following syllogism: Divine liberty does not, like human liberty, consist in the indifference of a potency with regard to several acts, but it consists in the indifference of one most simple act with regard to different objects. But this act, simple in itself, is virtually multiple, and is necessary and free under different aspects; for it is necessary in so far as it terminates the divine goodness, and free in so far as it connotes a non-necessary relation to creatures. Therefore this act, permanently unmoved in itself, is in God something vital and intrinsic by reason of its en-

[79] Cf. ad 4um.
[80] Cf. ad 4um; see also ad 5um.
[81] *Contra Gentes*, Bk. I, chap. 82. See also Bk. I, chap. 76, no. 1.

tity, and is only extrinsically defectible because of the defectibility in the thing willed, namely, the creature; for the aforesaid termination would be lacking in the case of a creature that does not or will not exist. This likewise explains why the free act is called volition in so far as it terminates in the being of the creature, and is called nolition in so far as it terminates in the non-being of the creature.

Thus the absolute actuality as well as the simplicity and eminence of the divine act gives us the solution of the question. St. Thomas illustrates this by a comparison in another of his works: "For every power tends by one operation or act to its object and the formal aspect of that object: even as by one sight we see light and the color made visible by light.[82]

In fact, by one and the same act of seeing, we see light together with many colors and objects seen by means of color; yet some of these colors are absent, though the act of seeing remains the same. Far more so does God by one and the same act see His goodness and the manifestation of this in different things, though His relation to these is not a necessary one. Thus it is said of Him:

> God, powerful sustainer of all things,
> Thou who dost remain permanently unmoved,
> Determining the course of time
> By successions of day and night.

Thus the entity of the divine free act is intrinsic to God, whereas its defectibility is extrinsic to Him.

Objection. The relation of the necessary act to creatures is only a logical relation. Therefore it seems that God's free act consists only in this logical relation.

Reply. I concede the antecedent, and deny the consequent. There is, indeed, a logical relation as a result of this act; but God's free act is something real, vital, intrinsic to Him, which is God's love that connotes a non-necessary relation to creatures, this being the foundation for the logical relation, and this free act is virtually distinct from the necessary love of His goodness.

Another objection. The very termination of the immanent and eternal free act must be intrinsic to God, and hence intrinsically defectible. So the difficulty remains.

Reply. I concede the antecedent, and deny the consequence. That this termination of God's immanent and eternal act is intrinsic to Him as regards the entity of this immanent act, this I concede; as regards its defectibility, this I deny. It is only extrinsically defecti-

[82] *Ibid.*, Bk. I, chap. 76.

ble, by reason of the defectibility in the thing willed.[83] Hence, as stated above, the entity of the free act is, indeed, intrinsic to God, and only its defectibility is extrinsic.[84]

Hence in answer to the principal objection posited at the beginning of this article, the following must be said: that God's free act could as well not be, this I distinguish: that it could not be as regards creatures, this I concede; in itself, as it is the unique act of God's love, this I deny. To put it in other words, God, who is permanently unmoved, had it in His power not to create, and to bring other creatures into being, for the divine liberty is the dominating indifference not of a potency but of a pure act of subsistent love. Thus the peak of a pyramid, which in itself is fixed, is the terminus of new lines converging toward it. So also he who, remaining in some place, and having within his view a certain territory, sees all the objects that change their locality in this territory, though he remains in the same place. This is indeed a feeble comparison, but it shows that even in sense perception the higher beings unite within themselves those things that are found dividedly in lower beings. It is the application of general principles. Thus the absolute simplicity and immutability of the pure Act is safeguarded. Hence this whole question consists in a proper understanding of dominating indifference, an indifference that is not potential and passive, but actual and active, and which formally and eminently, or properly, and not merely metaphorically, applies to God.

Second doubt. Can God, without undergoing any change, begin to will what He did not will, and not will what He willed?

The answer is in the negative,[85] for once the relation is established toward things willed, it cannot be changed, unless we presuppose a change either in the knowledge or in the disposition of the willer. But neither of these changes can take place in God.

Suarez advances the objection that from the mere idea of liberty, without anyone undergoing any change either in disposition or in knowledge, he could begin to will what before he did not will.

Reply. There cannot be another free choice without another practical judgment that immediately regulates the choice. But there is no change of judgment in God, for His judgment of all things is from all eternity immutable. There is something similar to this in the angel, because of the perfection of his intellect, as "the angel's free will is flexible to either opposite before the choice but

[83] Cf. ad 4um of this article; also what St. Thomas says in the *De veritate*, q.23, a.4, c. and ad 4um.

[84] Consult Gonet, Goudin, and Billuart in their commentaries on this article.

[85] See a.7 of this question.

not after." [86] Thus all the blessed in heaven are unchangeable in their love of God.

Third doubt. Can there be a suspension of any act on the part of God's free will concerning a created object?

The Thomists generally deny this against Gonet. They hold that God cannot remain, as it were, in suspense and undecided as to whether He will create or not create. Concerning this there must be either a volition or a nolition, because this suspension of any free act would seem in a way to detract from the divine perfection. For God is of necessity free, and His liberty is not a potential but an actual dominating indifference. Therefore it seems that God ought to have one or the other of these acts: to will to create, or to refuse to create. The refusal to will differs from non-willing.

Fourth doubt. Is God's free creative act an absolutely simple perfection?

Reply. It is not an absolutely simple perfection, at least in the strict sense; for this is defined as a perfection which implies no imperfection, and which it is better for one to have than not to have. But it is not better for God to have the creative act than not to have it. Therefore this free creative act is not an absolutely simple perfection.

Yet it remains true to say that liberty in God is an absolutely simple perfection, in the strict sense, for it is better for God to have it than not to have it; in fact, God is of necessity free, although it is not necessary for Him to have this particular act rather than a certain other. [87]

FOURTH ARTICLE

WHETHER THE WILL OF GOD IS THE CAUSE OF THINGS

State of the question. So far we know that God freely wills things apart from Himself, or acts freely *ad extra*. We now inquire whether He acts by His will. On first consideration, this seems to be a useless question after what has been said in the preceding question; for if God freely wills creatures, then He causes them by His will. Yet it is really another question that is now asked, and

[86] *Summa theol.*, Ia, q.64, a.2.

[87] Some raised the following objection against divine liberty: The divine goodness is of necessity perfectly willed by God; but it cannot be perfectly willed by God, without His willing the manifestation of this goodness by creation; therefore creation is not a free act.

We reply to this by distinguishing the major: that the divine goodness is of necessity perfectly willed by God, intensively as a perfection, this I concede; extensively as such, this I deny; for God's goodness is complete in itself apart from His diffusion of this *ad extra*.

one that requires special examination. For man does, indeed, freely generate, yet he does not do so by his will, but because he is of a certain nature. Hence, if he generates, he can generate only one like himself in species. Therefore it is now a question not only whether God freely willed to create, but whether God is the cause of things by His will, or by His nature.

This is clearly made known to us from the difficulties presented at the beginning of this article. They state that it seems God is not the cause of things by His will, but by His nature: (1) because, as Dionysius says, "the divine good by its very essence pours the rays of its goodness upon everything that exists"; [88] (2) because God is the first agent, therefore He acts by His essence, just as He is essentially being; (3) because God is essentially good, and Augustine says: "Because God is good, we exist"; (4) because God is the cause of things by His knowledge, He is therefore not so by His will.

Yet the answer is that God's will is the cause of things, or that God acts by His will, and not by a necessity of His nature.

In this article we get a much clearer conception of what was meant when it was said in a previous question that "God's knowledge is the cause of things, in so far as His will is joined to it." [89] We are now concerned with this conjoined will, and the determination of this divine will. There is special reference to this latter in the second proof of the argumentative part of this article, which is afterward frequently called the decree of the divine will. At the same time, this article completes the refutation of pantheism, for the pantheists, like the Averroists of the Middle Ages, hold that God is the cause of things by a necessity of His nature. The beginning of this refutation of pantheism is in God's transcendence as the extrinsic cause of the world, and this point is made clear in the proof of God's existence,[90] and from the fact that God is most simple, there being no accidents in Him,[91] and absolutely immutable,[92] whereas the world is composite and continually subject to change.

The truth of this answer is established in various texts of Holy Scripture. We quote the following: "And how could anything endure, if Thou wouldst not?" [93] "And God said: Be light made. And light was made," [94] which means that God is the cause of things by

[88] *De div. nom.*, Bk. IV, chap. 1.
[89] *Summa theol.*, Ia, q.14, a.8.
[90] *Ibid.*, q.2, a.3.
[91] *Ibid.*, q.3, a.6, 7, 8.
[92] *Ibid.*, q.9, a.1.
[93] Wis. 11: 26.
[94] Gen. 1: 3.

a command of His intellect and will. And again: "Who worketh all things according to the counsel of His will." [95]

Three proofs are given in the body of the article: (1) from the very order of active causes; (2) from the disposition of a natural agent; (3) from the relation of effects to their causes. These proofs given in the article are clear, especially after the explanation of the proof for God's existence as supreme Ordainer from the order prevailing in the universe.

First proof. The first agent must act by intellect and will. But God is the first agent. Therefore He must act by intellect and will. The major is proved as follows: since both intellect and nature act for an end, the natural agent must have the end and the means predetermined for it by some higher intellect; thus the end and definite movement are predetermined for the arrow by the archer.

The ultimate reason for this is that the things which lack intelligence do not know the nature of an end as such, even though, as animals, they have a sensitive knowledge of the thing which constitutes their end, as in the case of the swallow collecting the wisps of straw for building its nest. They have no knowledge of the end as such, or of the raison d'être of the means, because they lack the faculty whose object is intelligible being and the raison d'être of things. Hence, as stated in the fifth proof for God's existence: "Those things that are without (intellectual) knowledge do not move toward an end, unless they are directed by some being that is endowed with knowledge and intelligence; as the arrow is shot to its mark by the archer." [96] Hence the supreme agent must act not by nature, but by intellect and will.

Second proof. A natural agent always produces the same effect, unless it be prevented. This is because the nature of the act is according to the nature of the agent. But God in His being and nature is infinite or unlimited. Therefore, if God were to act, not by His intellect and will, but by His nature, then He would produce an infinite effect in being, which is impossible. [97]

It must be observed that the major of this syllogism is an inductive principle, already invoked by Aristotle, namely, that the same natural cause in the same circumstances always produces the same effect; for in this article it is stated that "the nature of the act of the natural agent is according to the nature of the agent; and hence, as long as it has that nature, its act will be in accord-

[95] Eph. 1: 11.
[96] *Summa theol.*, Ia, q.2, a.3.
[97] *Ibid.*, q.7, a.2.

ance with that nature." [98] If, therefore, it is certain that heat once
or on several occasions expanded iron, then there is no need of
having recourse to the method of induction by exhausting the
number of particular cases; but we can affirm that if heat is truly
the natural cause of the expansion of metals, it will always be so
in the same circumstances, so long as heat remains the same in
nature. And so, no matter what historians in our times may say,
Aristotle and St. Thomas well knew on what the inductive principle of the laws of nature rests, namely, that the natural agent is
determined to one thing.

At the end of this second proof St. Thomas speaks explicitly of
the determination of the divine will, which is afterward frequently
called the decree of the divine will. He says: "(God) does not,
therefore, act by a necessity of His nature, but determined effects proceed from His own infinite perfection according to the determination of His will and intellect." Why did he put the will before the
intellect? The reason is found in what was previously stated by
him: "Since the intelligible form has a relation to opposite things
(for the thing to be or not to be), inasmuch as the same knowledge
relates to opposites, it would not produce a determinate effect unless it were determined to one thing by the appetite." [99] Thus both
in ourselves and in God, the will in choosing brings it about that
the last practical judgment is the final one (so that there is an end
of deliberation), and after the will has made its choice (which terminates the order of intention, and which is frequently called the
purpose of the will), then the intellect is urged to command the
act (which begins the order of execution). [100]

Finally, it must be remarked concerning this second proof that
the determination of the divine will is required not only in electing
that things come into being or not, but also for the non-necessary
determination of these things, such as that the movement of the
heavenly bodies should be, as at present, from east to west, instead
of contrariwise. This point is made much clearer in a subsequent
question, [101] in which it is stated that "(God) produced things into
being in order that His goodness might be communicated to creatures, and be represented by them; and because His goodness could
not be adequately represented by one creature alone." [102] Thus

[98] Otherwise a change in the effect, without a change in the cause or circumstances, would be without a reason for its existence.
[99] *Summa theol.*, Ia, q.14, a.8.
[100] On this point consult the reply to the fourth objection of this article.
[101] *Summa theol.*, Ia, q.47, a.1, 2.
[102] Cf. *ibid.*, a.1.

God's intellect and liberty are the explanation for the many and different creatures that proceed from the supreme Agent, who in Himself is most simple. Contrary to this, the Neoplatonists, in denying the absolute freedom of the creative act, advanced the theory of emanation, namely, the One-Good, as if indeed, in accordance with this theory, the first hypostasis, namely, the One-Good, generated by a necessity of his nature a second hypostasis inferior to himself, then a third and so on in succession. But then it is not explained why the second hypostasis is inferior to the first; for if the first acts from a necessity of his nature, as man generates, he ought to produce an effect like to himself in nature and therefore infinite, which is impossible, as stated in this second proof.[103]

Third proof. Effects proceed from the agent that causes them, in so far as they pre-exist in the agent. But God's being is His own intellect. Therefore effects pre-exist in God after the mode of intellect, and therefore they proceed from Him after the same mode. Consequently these effects proceed from Him after the mode of will.[104]

Reply to first objection. When Dionysius says that God communicates a participation of His goodness just as the sun illumines all things, he does not mean to exclude election from God absolutely, but he means that, just as the sun illumines all things, so God communicates a certain participation of His goodness to all things.

Reply to third objection. God's goodness is the reason for His willing all things, and in this sense Augustine said: "Because God is good, we exist."

From this it is evident that God not only created most freely, but by His will, and so He differs from man, who does indeed freely generate; but he does so, however, by his nature, inasmuch as he is of a certain nature, and hence he can generate only a being like himself in species. In fact, as Cajetan remarks, in commenting on this article: "A vigorous male generates a male, and the irascible

---

[103] Grecian philosophers, who never succeeded in acquiring the concept of a free creation from nothing, were incapable of explaining how a multiplicity of things proceeds from one supreme principle. Plato wrote much in his dialogues, especially in the *Parmenides* and the *Sophist,* to solve this problem. He failed finally to show the relation between the different exemplary ideas and the idea of the supreme Good. In explaining the multiplicity of individuals, he admitted the eternal existence of matter which does not proceed from ideas, for they bear no resemblance to them. He also added that matter is not-being, which in a certain way exists.

[104] See Cajetan's commentary, and St. Thomas' reply to the second objection; also *Contra Gentes,* Bk. II, chap. 23; *De potentia,* q. 1, a. 5; q. 3, a. 15.

one that is irascible, as Aristotle says in his *Ethics,* Bk. VII, chap. 6." [105]

WHETHER ANY CAUSE CAN BE ASSIGNED TO THE DIVINE WILL

State of the question. It seems that some cause is to be assigned to God's will. The reasons for this are the following: (1) otherwise He would act irrationally; (2) otherwise there would be but one answer to any question whatever, namely, God willed it so, and thus it would be useless to seek the causes of things, which would mean the abolition of science, since it is knowledge by causes; (3) finally, we would have to say that all things depend simply on the will of God, there being no reason prior to this. Thus we could not even discover reasons of fittingness for any of the divine operations, such as creation, incarnation. Thus, in the fourteenth century, Ockham said, too, that the distinction between moral good and moral evil, or the first principle of the practical reason, namely, that good must be done and evil must be avoided, depends simply on the will of God, that is, on the divine positive law, so that this would be to do away with the natural law. Descartes says, too, that the truth of the principle of contradiction depends on God's free will. Contrary to this, St. Thomas wrote: "To say that justice depends simply on the will, is to say that the divine will does not proceed according to the regulations of wisdom; and this is blasphemous." [106] Leibnitz said likewise against Ockham and Descartes: "It is dishonoring God to hold that He established the distinction between good and evil by a purely arbitrary decree. . . . Why, then, would it not be the Manichaean principle of evil as the orthodox principle of good?" [107] This would result in the mind finally accepting the theories of absolute contingency and libertism, which are the very opposite of absolute determinism, such as that taught by Spinoza. Thus the statement of the question is evidently concerned with grave enough problems.

The answer is: There is no efficient cause of the divine will, or God does not will this on account of that (which is first intended), but He wisely wills this to be as means to that.

The first part is proved on the authority of St. Augustine in the counterargument, and then the following proof is given: The will follows from the intellect; but the divine intellect by one intuitive

[105] *Com. in Iam,* q. 19, a.4, no. 8.
[106] *De veritate,* q.23, a.6.
[107] *Theodicée,* II, §§ 176, 177.

act knows both principles and conclusions; therefore the divine will by one act wills its own goodness in itself and as it is the reason for loving creatures. Hence in God intention or the willing of the end is not, as in us, the cause of another act, namely, the choosing of the means. And so it is said that He does not will this on account of that; for God, the end is not the motive of His willing on the part of His act of willing, but only on the part of the thing willed.

The second part is proved as follows: The wise person wills the means to be for the end, the lower for the higher; but God wills most wisely whatever He wills; therefore God wills the means to be for the end, and the lower for the higher. This is stated in the body of the article and in the reply to the first objection. These two parts of the answer are summed up briefly in the following accepted formula: God does not will this on account of that, but He wills this to be as means to that. Hence, when we speak of the motive of either the creation or the incarnation, this does not mean the motive on the part of the willer, but on the part of the thing willed. Thus there is an end to difficulties.

Reply to second objection. It is not, therefore, useless to seek for causes secondary to the divine will. In fact, there are absolutely necessary laws in things, such as metaphysical principles, or the laws of being, for instance, the principle of contradiction, the truth of which does not depend on the divine liberty, notwithstanding what Descartes said. Similarly, mathematical laws, which abstract from both efficient and final causes, are absolutely necessary, for it is impossible that the three angles of a triangle be not equal to two right angles. Moreover, there are hypothetically necessary natural laws in things. Thus, if there is fire, then its action is to burn and not to cool, although God may miraculously prevent its action. In fact, there are certain laws of nature that are absolutely contingent and especially dependent on the divine liberty, such as that the motion of the heavenly bodies is from east to west, rather than in the reverse order. Finally, there are certain laws in things dependent solely on the will of God. As St. Thomas says: "In the things of nature, since primary matter is altogether uniform, a reason can be assigned why one part of it was fashioned by God from the beginning under the form of fire, another under the form of earth, that there might be a diversity of species in things of nature. Yet why this particular part of matter is under this particular form, and that under another, depends upon the simple will of God; as from the simple will of the artificer it depends that this stone is in this part of the wall, and that in another; although the plan requires that some stones should be in this place, and some in that place." [108]

First corollary. Two errors must be avoided: (1) absolute contingency, which denies the absolute necessity of metaphysical and mathematical principles, and the hypothetical necessity of the laws of nature; (2) absolute determinism, which denies all contingency, as in Spinozism, or in a certain kind of mechanical materialism, in which, for instance, the law of conservation of energy is declared to be absolutely necessary, so that the influence exerted by our liberty on our organism and God's miraculous intervention are excluded; for, as they say, there would thus be an increase in the quantity of energy in the universe, which remains the same. It does, indeed, remain the same in this sense, that when one form of energy is produced, such as heat, this is equivalent to an antecedent form, namely, of local motion necessary for the generation of heat. But the law of conservation of energy, without a begging of the principle, cannot be enunciated as a law that is by all means or absolutely necessary, in this sense, that the whole universe would be a closed system that would be removed from all external influence, even the invisible influence of God the Creator, who conserves and keeps it in motion. For how could experimental knowledge exclude this invisible influence, which is beyond the scope of experience? On the contrary, the transformation of energy demands not only a secondary cause, such as local motion for the generation of heat, but it also demands the First Cause; for only the First Cause is its own action and being, and without it the other causes produce no effect. Hence both absolute contingency and absolute determinism must be avoided.

Second corollary. It is hinted at in the reply to the third objection: the first effects willed by God depend on His divine will, namely, that creatures exist rather than that they do not exist depends solely on the most free will of God. Thus, for example, we may say that God willed man to have hands to serve his intellect by their work; or we may say that God willed the incarnation of His Son for our redemption, as the end for which or the subject to whom the Incarnation is of benefit.

Third objection. Hence it would be false to say with the absolute nominalists, that we must not seek for reasons of fittingness for the creation or the Incarnation. But we must say that creation is so expedient for the manifestation of divine goodness that it would be inexpedient if God had not created, so that creation is a most free act. The same observations apply equally to the decree

[108] *Summa theol.*, Ia, q.23, a.5 ad 3um.

of the Incarnation. We must not seek for reasons of fittingness in those things that depend only on the simple will of God or solely and merely on His will of good pleasure, for example, "why this part of matter is under the form of fire, another under the form of earth." [109]

State of the question. It seems that the will of God is not always fulfilled. (1) For the Apostle says that God "will have all men to be saved," [110] and it does not happen so. We have also the following texts: "How often would I have gathered thy children together . . . and thou wouldest not." [111] "I called, and you refused." [112] "You always resist the Holy Ghost." [113] (2) It seems that, just as God knows all truth, He wills all good, and yet many good things do not become realities. (3) The effects of the First Cause may be hindered by a defect of a secondary cause. On the other hand, there are many texts in Holy Scripture that state the opposite, such as: "Whatsoever the Lord pleased, He hath done." [114]

The answer is: It is of faith that there is a certain will in God which is always fulfilled. This will of God is called the simple or consequent will, or the will that is absolute and efficacious.

1) Revelation proves this clearly, for we read: "The Lord of hosts hath decreed, and who can disannul it?" [115] "My counsel shall stand, and all My will shall be done." [116] "There is none that can resist Thy will." [117] "He will do all that pleaseth Him." [118] "For who resisteth His will?" [119] "I give them (My sheep) life everlasting, and they shall not perish forever, and no man shall pluck them out of My hand. That which My Father hath given Me is greater than all; and no one can snatch them out of the hand of My Father." [120]

The Church has particularly defined that God's will concerning the bringing of the elect to glory is always fulfilled.[121] In fact, con-

---

109 Cf. *ibid.*
110 I Tim. 2: 4.
111 Matt. 23: 37.
112 Prov. 1: 24.
113 Acts 7: 51.
114 Ps. 134: 6.
115 Is. 14: 27.
116 *Ibid.*, 46: 10.
117 Esth. 13: 9.
118 Eccles. 8: 3.
119 Rom. 9: 19.
120 John 10: 28 f.
121 Denz., nos. 300, 316, 321.

cerning the two divine wills, one of which is not always fulfilled, but the other infallibly so, the Council of Quierzy declares as follows: "Almighty God wills without exception all men to be saved, though not all are saved. That some are saved, however, is the gift of Him who saves; if some perish, it is the fault of them that perish." [122] This formula is taken from the writings of St. Prosper.[123]

The Fathers, in explaining the above-quoted texts from Holy Scripture, often affirmed the infallibility of God's consequent will, as St. Augustine did in the following words: "Nor is there any other reason why God is truly called omnipotent except that He can do whatever He wills to do; nor is the effect of God's omnipotent will prevented by the will of any creature." [124]

The argumentative part of the article gives the following theological proof for the conclusion: It is not possible for anything to fall outside the order of the most universal cause, under which all particular causes are included; but God's will (which is the will in the absolute sense) is the most universal cause, under which all particular causes are included; therefore it is not possible for anything to fall outside the order of this cause, and it is contradictory for this cause not to produce its effect.

The major is illustrated by a comparison between efficient and formal causes; for the agent acts in so far as it is in act, by means of its form. But in forms, although a thing may fall short of a particular form, such as humanity or life, it cannot fall short of the most universal form, which is being; for it is not possible for anything not to be being. Similarly, in efficient causes, something can fall outside the order of a particular cause, for instance, the sun; but it cannot fall outside the order of the most universal cause, under which all other causes are included.

The minor is evident from the fact that God's will is the cause of all things, as already shown.[125] It presupposes a certain distinction which is explicitly made in the reply to the first objection, namely, the distinction between the antecedent or conditional and the consequent or absolute wills in God. It is only this latter which is called will in the absolute sense, and which is always fulfilled, a point that will be at once more clearly seen in the explanation that follows.

Immediately at the end of the argumentative part of the article

122 *Ibid.*, no. 318.

123 *Responsio ad secundam objectionem Vincentianam.*

124 *Enchiridion*, chap. 96. On the omnipotence of the divine will, consult Rouet de Journel's *Enchiridion patristicum*, nos. 111, 171, 194, 266, 323, 325, 402, 542, 628, 815, 1366, 1711.

125 Cf. a.4.

the following corollary is deduced: "That which seems to depart from the divine will in one order, returns to it in another order; as does the sinner, who by sin falls away from the divine will as much as lies in him, yet falls back into the order of that will when by its justice he is punished." The reason for this is that God's will is the most universal of causes, and He permits evil only for the sake of a greater good which is efficaciously intended by Him, and which will infallibly be realized. This is also what is said in the reply to the third objection of this article. Similarly, in the reply to the second objection it is remarked that God does not will all possible good.

THE ANTECEDENT WILL OF GOD

Nevertheless there is still a difficulty about the universal will to save. The first objection in this article refers to this will, and it is formulated by the Apostle as follows: "God will have all men to be saved, and to come to the knowledge of the truth." [126] But this does not happen.

St. Thomas' reply to this first objection must now be examined, and this universal will to save will be more fully discussed in our appendix to this article. We shall there see that the consequent will and even the antecedent will refer to the will of good pleasure, which properly belongs to God.

Now there are several things of great importance to be remarked concerning this reply to the first objection. It must first of all be read.

1) It mentions St. Augustine's explanation of St. Paul's words, "God wishes all men to be saved." St. Augustine interprets these words as applying to God's efficacious will which is always fulfilled, and therefore he says: "God wills all men to be saved that are saved; or God wills some men of every class and condition to be saved, males and females, Jews and Gentiles, great and small." [127]

It must be observed that as regards adults who actually are not saved, St. Augustine said, as mentioned in the Council of Trent: "God commands not impossibilities, but, by commanding, both admonishes you to do what you are able, and to pray for what you are not able (to do)." [128] These words declare that there is a certain will attributed to God, by which He wills that His divine precepts be right at the moment really possible of fulfillment for all adults,

[126] I Tim. 2: 4.
[127] *De praed. sanct.*, chap. 8; *Enchiridion*, chap. 103.
[128] *De natura et gratia*, chap. 43, no. 50.

and according as these know that they are bound by such obliga-
tions. Thus according to God's will it is really possible for these
to be saved, which is denied by Luther, Calvin, and Jansenius.[129]

2) St. Thomas in his reply to this first objection refers to the
opinion of St. John Damascene, who held that the words of St.
Paul, "God will have all men to be saved," apply to God's antecedent
will, but not to His consequent or efficacious will. This means that
God of His goodness wills all men to be saved by His antecedent
will which does not take into consideration, of course, the foreseeing of sin. But God, having foreseen the final impenitence of
many, wills by His consequent will to inflict upon them the punishment due to their sins.[130]

But this solution of St. John Damascene considers the problem
only under its moral aspects, so as to reconcile God's infinite goodness with His damnation of many. More briefly, according to St.
John Damascene, God, of Himself and prior to any consideration,
wills the salvation of all; but many sin and remain in sin, and
therefore, as a consequence of this, God damns them, and so *de
facto* they are not saved. This is the commonly accepted answer
among Christians.

But there is still the difficulty about how the will of the omnipotent God is not fulfilled concerning those who are not saved. Is
it not in God's power to preserve them from falling into the sin
of final impenitence? But if He has the power, does He permit this
sin for a greater good, and what greater good is this? Moreover, are
those who are actually saved, loved more and helped more by Him?
Thus does St. Thomas posit the problem as it was formerly posited
by St. Augustine, not only in its moral aspect as it was considered
by St. John Damascene, but in its higher metaphysical and theological aspects, considering it under the light of this higher principle in the present article, namely, that the will of the omnipotent
is always fulfilled. Thus the question is approached from a higher
plane.

3) St. Thomas solves the question by three syllogisms which have
their foundations in the following principles.

A. Everything, in so far as it is good, is willed by God. But a
thing taken in its primary sense, and absolutely considered, may
be good, and yet when some additional circumstances are taken
into account, it may be changed into the contrary. Thus that a man
should live is good; but if a man is a murderer, that he live is an
evil. Thus a just judge antecedently wills all men to live, but con-

---

[129] Denz., no. 1092.
[130] *De fide orthodoxa*, Bk. II, chap. 29.

sequently (on second consideration) he wills the man to be hanged. Therefore, in like manner God antecedently wills all men to be saved, but consequently wills some to be damned, as His justice exacts.

In the first syllogism St. Thomas retains the doctrine of St. John Damascene on the antecedent will, and thus he gives a better explanation of St. Paul's text than St. Augustine gave in the passages just quoted. But there is still the difficulty that is not sufficiently considered by St. John Damascene, though properly so by St. Augustine, i.e., whether the omnipotent God is incapable of saving all men or of preserving them from falling into sin? St. Thomas solves this difficulty by means of two arguments which he deduces from the first.

B. What we will antecedently we do not will simply but in a qualified manner, because the will is directed to things as they are in themselves (for good is not in the mind, as truth is, but in things), and in themselves they exist under particular qualifications, that is, they are willed as they are at the moment of willing.

Thus the just judge wills only in a qualified manner that the murderer should live, namely, inasmuch as he is a man. Hence it is not surprising that this antecedent will is not fulfilled, God's omnipotence, however, remaining intact, as will be more clearly seen now in the final argument to be presented.

We will a thing simply inasmuch as we will it when all particular circumstances are considered, and this is what is meant by willing consequently. Thus a just judge wills simply the hanging of a murderer, but in a qualified manner he would will him to live, inasmuch as he is a man.[131] Therefore "whatever God simply wills takes place, although what He wills antecedently does not take place." Thus the conclusion of this article is preserved intact, namely, that God's will, which is the will in the absolute sense, is always fulfilled. The principle of St. Augustine concerning the will of the omnipotent God and the opinion of St. John Damascene are likewise safeguarded by the previous arguments. The opinion of St. John Damascene is now presented in a clearer light, and this not only as regards its moral aspect, but also as regards its metaphysical and theological aspects.

First corollary. It follows from this that the antecedent will is not only that will which precedes the foreseeing of sin, but it is also the divine will that is never fulfilled, as in the case of those fruits that never get ripe, of those sufficient graces that make it possible

---

131 Cf. *Summa theol.,* Ia IIae, q.6, a.6, concerning the merchant who, during a storm, wills simply to throw his cargo into the sea, although he would wish to keep it.

to keep God's commandments, but which remain ineffective because of the resistance of the created free will.

Second corollary. Similarly not only is the consequent will the
divine will of punishing after having foreseen one's demerits, or of
rewarding after having foreseen one's merits, but it also refers to
every act of the divine will which is directed toward good considered as it actually is with its accompanying circumstances, for
instance, the fruits that actually get ripe, and the effective com-
pliance with God's commands.

Third corollary. Thus the principle of the distinction between
sufficient grace and that grace which is of itself efficacious is ascribed to a higher source, as will be more clearly explained in a
subsequent article.[132]

We shall also see farther on, after explaining the eleventh and
twelfth articles of this question, that the antecedent will is also the
will of good pleasure, which is truly found in God, and which is
not merely the will of expression, not merely an external sign of
the divine will.[133]

The whole of this most celebrated reply to the first objection can
be summed up in the following syllogism: Everything, in so far
as it is good, is willed by God, and good exists only as it actually
is; but the antecedent will is directed toward good considered in
the absolute sense and not as it actually will be, whereas the consequent will is directed toward good as it actually will be; therefore "whatever God simply or consequently wills takes place,
although what He wills only antecedently may not take place." Thus
we come to the final conclusion as established by St. Thomas, by
writing in the major of this argument what is expressed in each of
the majors of the three preceding arguments.

If these arguments, however, are given careful consideration,
then this reply of St. Thomas to the first objection is seen in all
its beauty of structure. All its concepts are expressed with absolute
precision and simplicity of language, and are in perfect harmony,
so that God's omnipotence, as affirmed by St. Augustine, is reconciled with His universal will to save, as affirmed by St. John Damascene. There remains indeed for our consideration the mystery about
how infinite mercy, justice, and supreme liberty are intimately
reconciled in the eminence of the Deity or of God's intimate
life.[134]

[132] Cf. a.8.
[133] See the appendix to this article: The teaching of St. Thomas on the universal will to save.
[134] On this point consult farther on our commentary on predestination, q.23,
a.5, c. et ad 3um.

All this doctrine may be summed up in this most certain principle formulated in the Council of Thuzey (860), which put an end
to the discussions on predestination arising from the works of
Gottschalk: "Whatsoever the Lord pleased He hath done in heaven
and on earth (Ps. 134: 6). For nothing is done in heaven and on
earth except what He Himself is pleased to do, or justly permits to
be done." [135] It follows from this: (1) that no good thing positively
and actually happens to be found in this man rather than in a
certain other, unless God from all eternity efficaciously willed that
it should so come to pass; (2) that no evil thing positively and
actually happens to be found in this man rather than in a certain
other, unless God from all eternity permitted it. The sinner, indeed,
in the very act of sinning, can avoid committing the sin, and from
all eternity God willed that it be really possible for the sinner to
avoid committing the sin (which is God's antecedent will); but
God did not efficaciously will that this sinner right at this moment
positively should avoid committing the sin, and if God had efficaciously willed this, then this sinner not only positively could avoid
committing the sin, but truly would have avoided committing it.
These are most certain and commonly accepted principles which
have their foundation in revelation, and from them is derived the
distinction between sufficient grace, which gives the power to do
what is right, and grace that is of itself efficacious, which causes
us freely to do what is right.

TEACHING OF ST. THOMAS ON THE UNIVERSAL WILL TO SAVE

This question is bound up with another, namely, whether Christ
died for all men, and this evidently concerns the mystery of predestination. In fact, every error about God's will to save brings us
back to an error about the mystery of predestination, and vice
versa.

Thus the Semipelagians held that the beginning of salvation and
final perseverance come from us, and not from God.[136] Hence they
said that God wills equally the salvation of all men, and went so
far as to deny the gratuity of predestination on the part of the
elect. On the other hand, the predestinarians and subsequently
the first Protestants and the Jansenists so vitiated the notions of the
gratuitous predestination of the elect and of human liberty, as to

---

135 *PL*, CXXVI, 123. See also Denz., no. 816.

136 Cf. Denz., nos. 178, 183, for condemnation of Semipelagianism by the Second
Council of Orange.

deny God's universal will to save and the existence of grace that is truly sufficient for those not predestined. They likewise said that Christ did not die for all men.[137]

We must therefore investigate: (1) what is defined of faith and what is theologically certain on these points; (2) what is the disputed point among theologians, especially between Thomists and Molinists, as regards God's universal will to save; (3) what is the validity of the Thomist view as compared with the teachings of St. Augustine, St. Prosper, and St. John Damascene. (5) Then there will be a solution of the objections.

I. WHAT IS OF FAITH

1) It is of faith that God sincerely wills the salvation not only of the predestined, but of all the faithful. This is evidently so for two reasons. (1) The fifth proposition of Jansenius, asserting that "it is a Semipelagian heresy to say that Christ died for all men without exception," [138] was condemned as heretical, if this means that Christ died only for the salvation of the predestined. (2) Moreover, the Apostles' Creed is binding upon all the faithful, and it says of Christ: "Who for us men, and for our salvation came down from heaven."

2) It is certain and proximate to the faith that God sincerely wills the salvation of even all adult infidels, in so far as He makes it really possible for them here and now to observe His precepts whenever these are binding upon them. To say otherwise would mean that God commands what is impossible.[139]

3) It is the common opinion of theologians that God sincerely wills even the salvation of all infants who die before they can be baptized. But it is more difficult to explain how it is really possible for these to be saved. The faith of the Church on these points has its foundation in revelation as variously expressed in Scripture and tradition. Thus we read: "We hope in the living God, who is the Savior of all men, especially of the faithful." [140] Even concerning infidels, St. Paul says: "I desire first of all that prayers be made for all men. . . . This is good and acceptable in the sight of God our Savior, who will have all men to be saved and to come to the knowl-

---

137 Cf. *Ibid.*, nos. 804–6, 814–16, 826 f., 1092–96.
138 *Ibid.*, no. 1096.
139 *Ibid.*, no. 804.
140 I Tim. 4: 10.

edge of the truth." [141] This text refers to all human beings. St. Augustine, too, understood these texts in this manner.[142]

IN WHAT SENSE CHRIST DIED FOR ALL

The Church has declared that Christ died for all,[143] not only for the predestined [144] or only for the believers,[145] although not all receive the benefit of salvation.[146]

How do the majority of Thomists explain this truth? They understand it in the sense that "Christ so died for all men that He truly and sincerely willed to offer His death to the Father for the eternal salvation of the whole human race, antecedently indeed and sufficiently salutary for the reprobates, consequently and efficaciously so for the predestined." [147]

St. Paul says: "If one died for all, then all were dead; and Christ died for all." [148] Similarly he says: "Therefore as by the offense of one, unto all men to condemnation; so also by the justice of one, unto all men to justification of life." [149] According to this parallelism it must be said that each and all died because of Adam's sin; therefore Christ died for all. Thus St. Augustine declares in one of his works: "Just as infants died through Adam's sin, so also Christ died for them," [150] even for those not baptized.

But the contrary teaching of Jansenius frustrates one of the principal articles of faith. Hope, which is founded primarily on Christ's death offered for us, becomes languid, and charity, which finds its source of energy in the remembrance of Christ's love as the Savior of mankind, becomes cold.

II. THE DIFFERENT OPINIONS OF MODERN THEOLOGIANS CONCERNING GOD'S ANTECEDENT WILL FOR THE SALVATION OF ALL MEN

This question is discussed at length by the Thomist, Gonzalez de Albeda,[151] who wrote after Molina and Bannez. His special purpose

---

[141] *Ibid.*, 2: 1 f.
[142] Cf. *De catechizandis rudibus*, PL, XL, 345.
[143] Denz., nos. 319, 795, 1096, 3026.
[144] *Ibid.*, nos. 1096, 1380 f.
[145] *Ibid.*, no. 1294.
[146] *Ibid.*, Index, VIII, h.
[147] Cf. Billuart, *De Deo*, diss. VII, a.7, § 11.
[148] II Cor. 5: 14 f.
[149] Rom. 5: 18.
[150] *Contra Julianum*, Bk. VI, chap. 4.
[151] *Com. in Iam*, q. 19, a.6.

is to show that sufficient grace, which depends on the antecedent will of God, is, in its order, truly sufficient. There is much that is helpful in his writings, although not all that he wrote is to be approved, and was not approved by the other Thomists. It must first of all be noted that there are two general and mutually conflicting opinions. These are the Thomist and Molinist opinions.

For the Thomists, who follow the teaching of St. Thomas,[152] the antecedent will of God is always of itself inefficacious, because it is concerned with what is considered absolutely as such to be good, but not with what is considered here and now to be good. But it is only good in this latter sense that comes into being.

On this point all Thomists agree, but they differ in this, that formerly some held the antecedent will to be more probably the will of expression, which is not found properly and formally in God, but only metaphorically, because it is more an external expression of God's will. Such was the opinion of Cajetan, Bannez, Zumel, as also of several of the old theologians.[153]

Other Thomists who wrote after the time of Bannez (such as Lemos, Alvarez, Gonzalez, John of St. Thomas, the Salmanticenses, Gonet, Billuart) hold that the antecedent will is the will of good pleasure, which is properly and formally in God.

The Molinists, however, have a different conception of the antecedent will. They are of the opinion that this will is not of itself alone always inefficacious; [154] for they define it as that will which precedes the foreseeing of our consent that is known by means of the *scientia media*. And they define the consequent will as the will which follows this foreseen consent, and is thus the will by which God punishes or rewards. Molinists are agreed on this point, although there are certain minor differences among them, as will be stated farther on.

These opinions must be examined, and they may be expressed by the following schema:

---

152 *Summa theol.*, Ia, q.19, a.6 ad 1um.

153 Alexander of Hales (Ia, q.36, membr. 2), St. Bonaventure (I, d.46, a.1, q.1), and Scotus (II, d.46, a.1) are also quoted as in favor of this opinion. These ancient authors said that the will of good pleasure is always fulfilled; but in other parts of his works, St. Bonaventure said that the antecedent will is the will of good pleasure, which was what St. Thomas said.

154 Even in Molinism the antecedent will of God is not properly "of itself alone" sometimes efficacious, but by reason of our foreseen consent. Nevertheless it can be said that the will is "of itself alone sometimes efficacious," understood in the sense that it is not found along with God's consequent will. In this Molinism differs from Thomism. See Molina's *Concordia* (Paris ed., 1876), pp. 384-94.

Antecedent will of itself alone	is always inefficacious	and is more probably the will of expression: the view of Cajetan and Bannez.
		It is the will of good pleasure: the view of St. Thomas and of the Thomists generally.
	is not always inefficacious	the absolute gratuity of predestination to salvation is preserved intact: the opinion of St. Robert Bellarmine and of Suarez.
		so that predestination to salvation is after our foreseen merits, at least the conditionally free and meritorious acts of the future: the opinion of Molina, Valentia, and Vasquez.

1) **Cajetan and Bannez** think it more probable that the antecedent will as regards the salvation of all men is only the will of expression, but not the will of good pleasure. They understand this distinction as explained by St. Thomas,[155] namely, that the will of good pleasure is the very act of the divine will, and thus it is formally in God; whereas the will of expression is only metaphorically and causally attributed to God, for it is, strictly speaking, something external which, as we understand it, is a sign that God wills something. Thus a divine command externally given to men, even the most wicked, is called the divine will, inasmuch as it is a sign that God wills us to do what is commanded. Thus God wills (by His will of expression), so they say, that all men, even criminals, be saved. Moreover, God does not command what is impossible, and so He wills at least that the fulfillment of His precepts be here and now really possible for all adults who have knowledge of these commands.[156]

Cajetan and Bannez also say that the will of expression, which is a command, sometimes is identical with the will of good pleasure, and sometimes not. Thus when God commanded Abraham to kill his son, this did not coincide with His will of good pleasure, since indeed He afterward commanded the contrary.[157]

2) **The opinion of other Thomists**, such as Lemos, Alvarez, Gonzales, includes a criticism of the preceding. They reply that the antecedent will is not only the will of expression, but is also the will of good pleasure, as expressly stated by St. Thomas, for he says: "Will in the strict sense of the term is found in God, and so will is, strictly speaking, predicated of God, which is the will of good pleasure, and this is subdivided into consequent and antecedent wills." [158] This is

---

[155] *Summa theol.*, Ia, q.19, a.11; *De veritate*, q.23, a.3.

[156] Cf. *De veritate*, q.23, a.3 ad 2um.

[157] *Summa theol.*, Ia, q.19, a.11 ad 2um.

[158] *De veritate*, q.23, a.3; see also *I Sent.*, d.46, a.2; *Com.* in Ep. I ad Tim. 2: 4.

also quite clear from the examples given by St. Thomas in his reply to the first objection of the present article, in which he points out that a judge truly and in the strict sense wills that a man, inasmuch as he is a man, should live, although he condemns the murderer to death. Moreover, this opinion is proved both from Holy Scripture, and by a theological argument.

A. Scriptural proof. The words of Holy Scripture are to be taken in their literal sense, provided nothing derogatory to God or contrary to faith or morals results therefrom. But Holy Scripture in various texts asserts that God wills the salvation of all men coming into the world since Adam's fall, and if this is understood, indeed, as referring to His conditioned but proper and formal will of good pleasure, and not to His will metaphorically so called, nor merely to His will of expression, then there is nothing either derogatory to God or contrary to faith that follows therefrom. Hence the words of Holy Scripture asserting that God wills the salvation of all men are to be taken in their literal sense. By all means the following texts must be so interpreted: "Who will have all men to be saved, and to come to the knowledge of the truth . . . (for) Christ gave Himself a ransom for all." [159] "The Lord . . . not willing that any should perish, but that all should return to penance." [160] "Jerusalem, how often would I have gathered together thy children, . . . and thou wouldest not." [161] St. John Chrysostom understood these texts as referring to God's will which He truly possesses, for he says: "In a wonderful way God yearns for and vehemently desires our salvation." [162] The Greek Fathers all speak in like manner, as Jansenius concedes. Even St. Augustine seems to admit this will of good pleasure, for he writes: "It is most sincerely to be believed and professed that God wills men to be saved, since indeed the Apostle, who was of this opinion, earnestly commanded what is faithfully observed in all the Churches, that supplications be made to God for all men." [163]

B. The generally accepted opinion among Thomists is proved by the following argument: The will of good pleasure derives its name from the interior inclination and ordination of God, and not solely from what is a sign of this will. But God interiorly wills the salvation of all men and provides them with sufficient means for this although, considering the circumstances, and because of the higher ends involved by reason of the manifestation of His justice and His other attributes, the defectibility of the human will presupposed, He

[159] I Tim. 2: 4–6.
[160] II Pet. 3: 9.
[161] Matt. 23: 37.
[162] *Hom.* Ia in Ep. ad Eph.
[163] *De spiritu et littera*, chap. 33.

willed to permit that a considerable number fail to attain this end. Therefore His universal salvific or antecedent will is His will of good pleasure.

The minor of this argument is proved as follows: as the choice of efficacious means for salvation presupposes the efficacious interior intention to save, so also the choice of sufficient means for salvation presupposes the inefficacious interior intention to save. So say the majority of the Thomists.

This argument is confirmed by a consideration of God's salvific will. For indeed an object that is in itself good and that is not only possible, but that is a conditioned future, terminates the internal decree of the divine will which is subjectively absolute but objectively conditioned. But the salvation of all men who are still wayfarers is something that is in itself good and that is a conditioned future or a futurable, and not something that is merely possible. Therefore the salvation of all men who are still wayfarers is a conditioned future that terminates the internal decree of the divine will which is subjectively absolute but objectively conditioned.

The major is explained by pointing out that, if this good object were merely possible, it would not terminate the internal decree of the divine will; if it were a contingent absolute future, it would terminate God's efficacious decree; but as a conditioned future it terminates the internal conditioned decree of the divine will, namely, a decree similar to that presupposed in the prophecy of commination.[164]

Therefore the conclusion we come to is, that the antecedent will is not only the will of expression, but is also the will of good pleasure, although it is objectively conditioned, as will be more clearly seen from the solution of the objections.

3) **The opinion of Molina and the Molinists.** Molina and Valentia think that St. John Damascene and St. Thomas held different opinions on this subject, and they seek to depart from the teaching of St. Thomas and return to that of St. John Damascene. But among the Molinists, Vasquez maintains that St. Thomas interpreted aright the viewpoint of St. John Damascene, though he himself departs from the teaching of St. Thomas.

What is Molina's teaching about the antecedent will? This is clearly made known to us from his writings.[165] He is of the opinion that the antecedent will as regards the salvation of all men is a conditioned will in this sense: "provided we, too, will." Hence sometimes God's antecedent will is fulfilled, that is, when man wills to make God's help efficacious in its second actuality; and sometimes

---

[164] *Summa theol.*, Ia, q.19, a.7 ad 2um; IIa IIae, q.171, a.6 ad 2um; q.174, a.1.
[165] *Concordia*, p. 386.

this antecedent will of God is only a velleity, that is, when man does not will to make God's help efficacious in its second actuality. Hence for Molina the antecedent will is the will that is prior to the foreseeing of our consent.

Nevertheless, that Molina may escape the taint of Semipelagianism, which declares that God wills equally the salvation of all men, so that predestination is made to consist in the foreknowledge of the merits, he holds that God, by reason of His most free will of good pleasure, decreed to place this man, for instance, Peter, in those circumstances in which He had foreseen his good consent; whereas Judas is placed in other circumstances in which his infidelity to grace was foreseen. Thus Molina vitiates the above definition of the antecedent will. But, according to this definition, Molina must define the consequent will in the opposite sense, as being the will which follows the foreseeing of our consent, like the will of rewarding and punishing, of which St. John Damascene speaks.

It must be noted that Molina's conception of the antecedent will is such that the predestination of the elect to salvation is considered the result of foreseen merits, at least of conditioned merits, which is the teaching of Valentia and Vasquez. In fact, Valentia maintains that all good acts which are dependent on free will are willed by God's antecedent will and not by His consequent will. On the contrary, St. Robert Bellarmine and Suarez, although they retain from Molinism the theory of the *scientia media* and its corresponding conception of the antecedent will, nevertheless maintain with the Thomists, Augustinians, and Scotists, the absolute gratuity of predestination to salvation. Hence their conception of the antecedent and consequent wills is more in agreement with the opinion of St. Thomas. Thus, according to these theologians, sufficient graces are the result of God's antecedent will; and congruous graces, are the result of God's freely predestinating consequent will and are infallibly efficacious, not indeed of themselves, but because of the foreseeing of our consent by means of the *scientia media*.[166]

CRITICISM OF MOLINA'S OPINION

1) This opinion rests on the theory of the *scientia media*. But the *scientia media*, which is concerned with the conditionally free acts of the future before God's conditioned decree, is a knowledge without an object, because before God's decree the conditionally free act

---

[166] Cf. Bellarmine, *De gratia et libero arbitrio*, Bk. II, chaps. 9–15; Bk. IV, chap. 15. Suarez, *De auxiliis*, Bk. III, chaps. 16 f.; *De causa praedestinationis*, Bk. II, chap. 23; *De scientia futurorum contingentium*, chap. 7.

of the future is undetermined, since it is a contingent and free act.[167]
But if it is said that God, because of His super-comprehensive knowledge of our will and of the circumstances, foresees our consent if we
should be placed in such and such circumstances, then this theory,
which was devised to safeguard our liberty, leads to determinism of
circumstances, and moreover, since God would not be determining,
then He would be passively determined in His foreknowledge. There
is no solution of the dilemma: God is either determining or determined, there is no other alternative. The same is also to be said of
the modified theory of the *scientia media* proposed by Suarez.[168]

2) The Molinist definition of the antecedent will results in a definition of the consequent will as the will which follows the foreseeing of our consent. But this definition applies to a certain kind of
consequent will, namely, to that of rewarding or punishing, but not
to every kind of consequent will. For indeed the consequent will of
calling one efficaciously to faith and grace does not presuppose but
precedes our consent, since it is the cause of this. Similarly the predestination of the elect to glory or salvation denotes the consequent
will, and yet it does not presuppose the foreseeing of merits, as will
be stated farther on,[169] because the merits of the elect are the effects
of their predestination. St. Robert Bellarmine and Suarez admit this.
Even in Molinism, the will to place Peter in circumstances in which
his good consent is foreseen, rather than to place him in certain other
circumstances, is the consequent will, and yet it does not presuppose,
like the will of rewarding or punishing, the foreseeing of Peter's consent as a future act, but only as a conditionally future act.

Hence we come back to St. Thomas' opinion,[170] that the antecedent will is directed toward good, considered absolutely as such,
and not as it is under particular qualifications. Thus of itself alone
it is not efficacious, because only what is good under particular qualifications comes into being. On the other hand, the consequent will

[167] *Summa theol.*, IIa IIae, q.171, a.3: "Future contingent things, whose truth
is not determined, are not in themselves knowable."

[168] Consult what was said about the *scientia media* in our commentary on
q.14, a.13.

[169] *Summa theol.*, Ia, q.23, a.5.

[170] *Ibid.*, Ia, q.19, a.6 ad 1um. The phrase "ante praevisa merita" which, translated literally, means "before foreseen merits," may be misleading for many
readers. It does not mean that God first predestined and afterward foresaw our
future merits; this would be an imperfection in God, which is impossible. By
one and the same act God decrees and foresees. Nor does it mean that God predestined certain persons to glory by a purely arbitrary act of His will, and that
they would get to heaven without having merited this. It does mean, however,
that the foreseen future merits of the elect were not the motive for God's predestination of certain persons to glory. [Tr.]

is directed to good considered as such here and now, that is, when all the particular circumstances are considered. This is what is known as will simply as such, and it is always efficacious, because good is in things themselves, and these exist only under particular qualifications.

These definitions, which consider the will and good in their metaphysical aspects, can be applied universally. The first definition applies to every antecedent will, and the second to every consequent will, which means that it applies not only to the will of rewarding or punishing, but also to the efficacious will of calling one to the faith and predestinating one to salvation before foreseen merits.

III. THE VALIDITY OF THE THOMIST OPINION AND HOW IT COMPARES WITH THE TEACHINGS OF ST. AUGUSTINE, ST. PROSPER, AND THE VIEWPOINT OF ST. JOHN DAMASCENE

The Thomist opinion is in harmony with the teaching of St. Augustine, whose interpreter was St. Prosper, and that of St. John Damascene. It reconciles these teachings from the exalted notion it has of the "simple will" of the omnipotent God, which is always fulfilled, as shown in this sixth article. A careful examination of the principal texts of St. Augustine, St. Prosper, and St. John Damascene establish this point with sufficient clarity.

It must be noted first of all that St. John Chrysostom distinguishes two wills in God.[171] One is the will to save all men, even sinners; the other is the will to punish consequent to the foreseeing of the sin. Yet he maintains that the elect are more loved and helped by God, in accordance with the scriptural text: "What hast thou that thou hast not received?"[172] In his commentary on this epistle he says: "Therefore thou hast what thou hast received, neither this only nor that, but whatever thou hast; for these are not thy merits, but God's gifts."[173]

But as St. Augustine frequently remarked, the Fathers who wrote before the time of the Pelagian heresy spoke only incidentally of predestination. It is a mystery that is intimately connected with God's universal will to save.[174]

[171] *Com. in Eph.*, hom. 1, 2.
[172] I Cor. 4: 7.
[173] Hom. 12. See also St. Gregory Nazianzus, *Com. in Rom.*, hom. XIV, 7; hom. XIX, 7. Cf. also Tixeront's *History of Dogmas*, II, 145 f.
[174] On this subject consult St. Robert Bellarmine's *De gratia et libero arbitrio*, Bk. II, chap. 14; also Tixeront, *op. cit.*, II, 497–500, for St. Augustine's teaching on God's universal will to save. This point had already been discussed by Petau in his *De incarnatione*, Bk. XIII, chaps. 3 f.

1) St. Augustine, as we already said, frequently understood St. Paul's text, "Who will have all men to be saved," [175] as referring to God's efficacious will; so he at once interpreted it as meaning: "God wills all men to be saved that are saved, and He wills some men of every class and condition to be saved, males and females, Jews and Gentiles, great and small." [176] What St. Thomas says of God's consequent will, which is always fulfilled, is absolutely in agreement with these texts of St. Augustine.

2) St. Augustine spoke in another of his works in equivalent terms of God's antecedent will, which is not always fulfilled. Thus he wrote: "God commands not impossibilities, but, by commanding, both admonishes thee to do what thou art able and to pray for what thou art not able (to do)." [177] From this text, which is quoted by the Council of Trent,[178] it is evident that, according to St. Augustine, God wills to make the fulfillment of His precepts really possible for adults, here and now, in so far as these are not only known by adults, but also as they are of obligation for them; otherwise God would be commanding impossibilities, and then sin would be unavoidable, in which case He would be punishing them unjustly, especially with eternal punishments. The Thomist doctrine of the antecedent will, by which God gives sufficient graces which make it really possible for us here and now to fulfill God's precepts, is absolutely in agreement with this and similar texts of St. Augustine.

3) Afterward, in various places, St. Augustine spoke more explicitly of the universal will to save, as referring to God's antecedent will, although he does not use these words. It is more a question of what is implied than of words used. Thus he writes: "God wills all men to be saved and to come to the knowledge of the truth; yet not in such a way that He deprives them of free will, for the good or bad use of which they will be most justly judged." [179] As is evident from the context, St. Augustine means this proffered statement of his to be taken as a probable way of explaining the words of the Apostle: "God will have all men to be saved." [180]

In like manner St. Augustine says: "God, in His mercy, sent His only begotten Son, wishing to free men from this death that consists in eternal punishments, provided they are not their own enemies, and do not resist the mercy of their Creator." [181]

175 I Tim. 2: 4.
176 *De praed. sanct.*, chap. 8, and the *Enchiridion*, chap. 103, one of his earlier works.
177 *De natura et gratia*, chap. 43, no. 50.
178 Denz., no. 804.
179 *De spiritu et littera*, chap. 33, no. 58.
180 I Tim. 2: 4.
181 *De catechizandis rudibus*, chap. 26. See also *ibid.*, no. 52.

Moreover, St. Augustine clearly affirms that Christ died for all, which presupposes in God the will to save all. For the holy Doctor says: "One, says the Apostle (II Cor. 5: 15), died for all, therefore all died: showing by this that He could have died only for those who died. For by this he proved that all died, because one died for all. . . . See, as a consequence of this, that he wanted us to understand that all died, if he died for all." [182]

Finally, in one of his uncompleted works, St. Augustine likewise says: "One died for all, therefore all died. This conclusion of the Apostle remains unchallenged, and by reason of this, because He also died for infants, assuredly, too, infants died." [183] The holy Doctor says this against the Pelagians, who refuse to admit the existence of original sin; but from this it is evident that, in St. Augustine's opinion, Christ died for all without exception, even for infants who die without being baptized, and who de facto are not saved. This shows clearly that there is a will in God to save all, which of itself, since it is not found in connection with His efficacious will, is not actually fulfilled. Therefore these texts of St. Augustine are fully in agreement with the Thomist opinion concerning the antecedent will.

On this point, what was the teaching of St. Prosper, who was a disciple of St. Augustine? [184] St. Prosper was prompted to write by reason of the error of Cassian, who in his Collations showed a preference for Semipelagianism.[185] Cassian, indeed, and many of the monks of Marseilles had rejected the absolute gratuity of predestination taught by St. Augustine. St. Prosper and St. Hilary wrote to St. Augustine about this (429), so that he wanted to refute them.[186] These monks of Marseilles said that "God's grace accompanies but does not precede human merits," [187] and that "God wills indifferently all . . . to be saved and to come to the knowledge of the truth." [188] Thus the predestination of the elect was reduced to the simple foreknowledge of their merits, as in Semipelagianism, and hence the elect were not the objects of God's predilection, nor were they more helped by Him.[189]

St. Augustin replied to these epistles of St. Prosper and St. Hilary by writing two treatises [190] against the Semipelagians, in which, to

[182] Contra Julianum, Bk. VI, chaps. 4, 8.
[183] Contra Julianum, op. imp., Bk. II, chap. 163; cf. ibid., chaps. 63, 174, 175.
[184] Consult Tixeront, History of Dogmas, III, 272–82.
[185] Cf. Collationes, XII, nos. 7, 17, 18; XVII, no. 25.
[186] Among the letters of St. Augustine, letter 225 is the epistle of St. Prosper, and letter 226 is the epistle of St. Hilary.
[187] Cf. epist. 225, no. 5.
[188] Ibid., nos. 3, 4, 6.
[189] Ibid.
[190] Cf. De praedest. sanct.; de dono persever.

make it clear that predestination is gratuitous, he stresses certain texts from St. Paul's epistles.[191]

After the death of St. Augustine, St. Prosper, who was a layman but a most faithful disciple of St. Augustine, defended his master's doctrine about the beginning of faith and the intrinsic efficacy of divine grace by which we perform good acts; hence he denied that God wills "indifferently" that all men be saved.[192]

Nevertheless, St. Prosper wrote: "It must be most sincerely believed and professed that God wills all men to be saved." [193] But he adds that this will is efficacious only for the predestined, whose number is determined. Thus he is clearer than St. Augustine in teaching that damnation is after foreseen demerits; yet he retains the absolute gratuity of predestination, which is thus before foreseen merits.

Shortly after St. Prosper's death, between the years 434 and 460, some unknown person wrote a work [194] in which he set forth the teaching of St. Augustine, yet not in all its rigor. The author of this work seeks to reconcile God's universal salvific will, which he admits, with the fact that many are lost. Therefore he distinguishes between a general grace, which is offered to all, and a special grace which, by God's special mercy, is granted to many and which is the efficacious cause of their salvation.

In the fifth century, however, the priest Lucidus seems to have denied God's universal salvific will. Faustus of Riez replied in the Semipelagian sense.[195] Finally the African, St. Fulgentius, strictly defended St. Augustine's doctrine on the gratuity of predestination, though it does not seem that he stresses enough God's universal will to save.[196] Yet St. Fulgentius refused to deny this proposition of St. Augustine: "God commands not impossibilities, but, by commanding, both admonishes thee to do what thou art able, and earnestly to ask for what thou art not able (to do)." [197]

Finally, in the eighth century, St. John Damascene distinguished between God's antecedent and benevolent will, by which He wills the salvation of all men, and His consequent will, by which He wills to punish sinners either for a time or for eternity.[198]

Nevertheless he says: "Without God's help we can neither will nor

---

191 Cf. Rom., chaps. 8 f.; Eph., 1: 4–12; I Cor. 4: 7: "For who distinguisheth thee? Or what hast thou that thou hast not received?"

192 Cf. *Pro Augustino responsiones ad capitula objectionum gallorum calumniantium*, 4, 5.

193 *Responsiones ad capitula objectionum vincentianarum*, chap. 2.

194 *PL*, LI, 647.

195 Cf. Tixeront, *op. cit.*, III, 284 f.

196 Cf. *ibid.*, 287 f.

197 *De natura et gratia*, chap. 43, no. 50; Denz., no. 804.

198 *De fide orthodoxa*, *PG*, XCIV, 968 f.

do what is good, but we are free either to persevere in doing good or refrain from so doing." [199] From this text it is clear that those who persevere in doing good (the elect) are more helped by God than the others whom He permits to fall into sin. For God is the cause of the meritorious act, but not of sin. St. John Damascene clearly states this, although he makes no profound statement about the necessity and efficacy of actual grace in the life of the predestined.[200]

As I said above, St. John Damascene considered this question in its moral aspect as it refers to God's goodness and man's culpability, rather than in its theological and metaphysical aspects as it refers to God's omnipotent will, which is always fulfilled when it is a case of His absolute will and not of His qualified or conditioned will.

On the contrary, it was particularly this second aspect of God's will that was considered by St. Augustine. And St. Thomas reconciles both aspects, by explaining the antecedent will, which St. John Damascene speaks of, as referring to good considered absolutely as such, and not as it is here and now; whereas the consequent will, he observes, is directed to good considered as it is here and now. But since good, which is in the things themselves, comes into being here and now only, it follows that the antecedent will of itself alone, when not joined to the consequent will, remains inefficacious. Hence the division of God's will into these two wills is the ultimate foundation for the distinction between sufficient grace, and grace that is of itself efficacious. The former is the result of God's antecedent will, which makes it really possible for us here and now to do what He commands; the latter is the result of His consequent will, which moves us so that we actually do what He commands. But from the fact that man resists sufficient grace, by reason of his defectibility, he deserves to be deprived of efficacious grace.

Thus the teaching of St. Thomas preserves intact both St. Augustine's opinion and St. John Damascene's, thus safeguarding the omnipotence of God, whose absolute will is always fulfilled, and the goodness of God, who does not command impossibilities and who makes it really possible for all to do what He commands.[201] What-

[199] *Ibid.*, col. 972, 973.

[200] On this point consult also his Com. in I Cor. 4: 7: "What hast thou that thou hast not received?"; and in II Cor. 3: 4 f., in which he affirms that every good act, and hence our merits, are the result of God's grace. Cf. Tixeront, *op. cit.*, III, 478.

Some, too, in recent times have sought to interpret St. John Damascene's doctrine in a Molinist sense. But several of his texts can be understood in the opposite sense. In truth, it must be said that St. John Damascene had not as yet so explicitly considered this question.

[201] Consult St. Thomas' *Com. in I Sent.*, d.46, a.1; d.47, a.1; *De veritate*, q.23, a.2; in I Tim. 2: 1–6, which agrees with what he said in the reply to the first objection of this sixth article.

ever the adversaries may say, Thomism acknowledges that this question of the salvific will is a mystery, not only as it affects our liberty, but also on God's part. And in this we clearly see both the exalted nature and insufficiency of sacred theology, which disposes one for the knowledge of infused contemplation, in which there is peace of mind and rest; for this contemplation is the effect of grace, which is a formal participation of the Deity, in which justice, mercy and supreme liberty are identified.

IV. SOLUTION OF OBJECTIONS

First objection. One fails to see why the antecedent will is conditioned, unless it is said that God wills all men to be saved, if they themselves will to be saved. But this is precisely Molina's opinion. Therefore, unless Molina's opinion is accepted, one fails to see why the antecedent will be conditioned.

Reply. This opinion, as we have said, presupposes the theory of the *scientia media,* for which there is no foundation and by which God, in His foreknowledge of conditionally free acts of the future, would be in a passive state. This theory was not fully approved even by Molina himself, who, to avoid Semipelagianism and preserve intact the dogma of predestination, admitted that God of His own most free will of good pleasure places the elect in circumstances in which He foresaw their good consent. And it is the gratuity of predestination that is more affirmed both by St. Robert Bellarmine and by Suarez.

Hence it is for Molina himself to answer this question, namely, why God did not will to place all men in those circumstances in which He foresaw their good consent.

But he must answer this question as St. Thomas did, by quoting St. Paul's text: "What if God, willing to show His wrath (i.e., the splendor of His justice), and to make His power known, endured (i.e., permitted) with much patience vessels of wrath, fitted for destruction, that He might show the riches of His glory upon the vessels of mercy, which He hath prepared unto glory (where is the injustice?)" [202]

Hence it follows that the antecedent will is conditioned in this sense, that God would will the salvation of all men if He did not will to permit in many the sin of final impenitence to serve the higher ends of either manifesting the splendor of His justice, or His inalienable rights to be loved above all things. Thus He willed to manifest His goodness, sparing by His mercy and punishing by His justice.

[202] *Summa theol.,* Ia, q.23, a.5 ad 3um; Rom. 9: 22.

'This condition is retained even by Molina, otherwise he would be absolutely denying the mystery of predestination. It is, indeed, an inscrutable mystery, and its reconciliation with the universal salvific will is nothing but the intimate reconciliation of infinite mercy, justice, and supreme liberty in the Deity, which is hidden from us, and which can be seen only in the beatific vision. But a strictly syllogistic objection, and one that is incapable of solution, cannot be raised against the possibility of God's permitting the sin of final impenitence.

But I insist: Nevertheless, what was said by several of the post-Nicene Fathers, namely, those who wrote before the rise of Pelagianism, and after the rise of this heresy what St. John Damascene said, practically meant that God wills the salvation of all men if they themselves will to be saved. Therefore the condition on which God's antecedent will depends, finds its explanation in none of the higher motives, but merely in man's will.

The Thomists reply to this by distinguishing the antecedent: God wills the salvation of all men, if they themselves will to be saved, waiting for them so to will, this I deny; if such volition is the result of God's operation in them, this I concede, according to what St. Paul says: "For it is God who worketh in you, both to will and to accomplish, according to His good will." [203] I distinguish the consequent in like manner. It was not the intention of the post-Nicene Fathers or St. John Damascene to deny this text of St. Paul or the following: "For who distinguisheth thee? Or what hast thou that thou hast not received?" [204]

To say otherwise would not be to uphold the definition of the Council of Orange, which says against the Semipelagians: "If anyone maintains that God waits for us to will that we be cleansed from sin, but does not confess that even this act of willing to be cleansed from sin is the result of the inspiration and operation of the Holy Spirit in us, such a person resists the Holy Spirit . . . and the Apostle preaching for our spiritual benefit that: It is God who worketh in you, both to will and to accomplish, according to His good will." [205] St. Augustine wrote in like manner.[206] To say otherwise, as we already remarked, would be to deny the mystery itself of predestination. Wherefore, as we pointed out, even Molina somewhat restricted his definition of the antecedent will. On the other hand, all Catholics admit that God wills all men to be saved, if they themselves will to be saved, that is, presupposing their co-operation prompted by grace.

[203] Phil. 2: 13.
[204] I Cor. 4: 7.
[205] Denz., no. 177; Phil. 2: 13.
[206] Cf. ad Bonifacium, Bk. I, chap. 19.

St. Augustine himself says: "He who created you without your help, will not save you without your help." [207] Nor did anyone ever think of saying that God wills to save those who refuse and do not wish to be saved.

Second objection. What is conditioned is imperfect. But the antecedent will is conditioned, because, as stated above, it presupposes a greater good, namely, the manifestation of God's attributes. Therefore it implies an imperfection, and hence cannot be properly and formally in God, but only metaphorically and virtually, as being the will of expression and not of good pleasure. This objection expresses the very opposite of the preceding.

Reply. I distinguish the major. The conditioned is imperfect, on the part of that which is conditioned, this I concede; otherwise I deny it. I contradistinguish the minor: that the antecedent will is conditioned on the part of the thing willed, which is not accepted with all its accompanying circumstances because of a higher good, this I concede; that it is conditioned, as if God were incapable of saving all men, this I deny. So say St. Thomas [208] and the majority of the Thomists when discussing God's subjectively absolute and objectively conditioned decrees.[209] This means that God wills all men to be saved, if this does not conflict with the manifestation of His divine attributes, the ordering of all things by His providence, and the contingency and defectibility of human beings.

But I insist: The efficacious will as such is a perfection; hence the inefficacious will as such is an imperfection. Therefore this cannot be properly and formally in God.

Reply. I distinguish the consequent: that the inefficacious will, which is the result of the nullification of its power by an extrinsic impediment, is an imperfection, this I concede. Such is the will of the merchant who desires to save his merchandise at the moment of shipwreck. That the inefficacious will, which is the result of the willer's positively ordaining things to higher ends, is an imperfection, this I deny.

It is the antecedent will, as conceived by Molinists, that posits imperfection in God; for they say God wills all men to be saved, provided they themselves will to be saved. In this case the antecedent will would be conditioned, the condition depending on the consent

---

[207] *Confessions*, II, 7.

[208] St. Thomas says (I Sent., d.46, q.1, a.1 ad 2um): "The antecedent will may be called conditioned; yet its imperfection is not on the part of the divine will, but of the thing willed, which is not willed with all the circumstances that are required for being rightly ordered to salvation." St. Thomas says about the same in his reply to the first objection of this article.

[209] For a critical estimate of the *scientia media*, consult their commentaries, for instance, Billuart, *De Deo*, diss. VI, a.6, § 10.

or dissent of human beings, and not solely because of a higher good intended by Providence, this being the manifestation of God's attributes.

This solution is confirmed by the fact that Holy Scripture records many instances of conditioned futures. Thus God promised Abraham to spare Sodom, if ten just men were found in it. Similarly it was revealed that the Tyrians and Sidonians would have been converted if Christ had come to them. But these conditioned futures are infallibly knowable by God only in His subjectively absolute and objectively conditioned decrees, and this we say against those who favor the theory of the *scientia media*. Hence a subjectively absolute and objectively conditioned decree must likewise be admitted with regard to the conditioned salvation of all men.

Third objection. But the subjectively absolute and the objectively conditioned decree implies a contradiction, for by it God wills and does not will the same object. Thus God wills the conversion of the Tyrians, and, on the other hand, He does not will it, because He does not will that the gospel be preached to them. Therefore the same holds good of His decree.

Reply. It is false to say that by this decree God wills and does not will the same formal object, but only the same material object, and this in different ways; that is, God wills inefficaciously the salvation of all men, absolutely considered, and He does not will efficaciously the salvation of all, having taken into consideration all the circumstances and the higher ends in view. Similarly He wills inefficaciously the conversion of the Tyrians, provided the gospel should be preached to them, and He does not will it efficaciously because, on account of higher ends in view, He does not will the gospel to be preached to them. There is no contradiction in this.

Thus the merchant during a shipwreck truly, though inefficaciously, wills to save his merchandise, and he efficaciously wills to cast it into the sea. It would be a contradiction if God willed antecedently the salvation of those already damned, to whom He no longer gives graces sufficient for salvation.

Fourth objection. If this decree of the antecedent will does not involve a contradiction, it is at least useless and illusory, it being as if a wealthy person were to say to a poor person: I will give you a hundred pennies if you fly.

Reply. This decree is not useless, because, although it fails to attain its ultimate effect, yet it serves many other useful purposes. (1) It establishes the foundation for the foreknowledge of conditionally free acts of the future. (2) By this decree God provides for all wayfarers sufficient means whereby they may be saved, whereas, on the other hand, for the salvation of those who are already damned, His attitude at most can be merely one of passive complacency. (3) It serves as the foundation for God's promise to save us on certain conditions; for He could not sincerely and conditionally promise anything, unless He willed by such decree.

Moreover, this decree of the antecedent will is not illusory, because the condition is possible, not impossible, such as the example given above by the objector: "I will give you wealth, if you succeed in flying." For God does not command impossibilities. But in this there is the mystery of God's permission of the sin of final impenitence for higher ends, and it is not in our power to judge of these.

Finally, we can turn back the objection on our opponent by saying: What we consider contradictory is the conditioned decree as conceived by the Molinists, namely, "I will concur in your action if you have first freely determined yourself to act." This, in our opinion, implies a contradiction, because the divine concurrence is no less necessary for man's self-determination than light is for seeing, or existence for acting. Hence to say: "I will concur in your action, if you have first freely determined yourself to act," is tantamount to saying: "I will give you light, if you see this object," or "I will give you existence, if you do this." No wonder Molinism leads to such conclusions, for, if Thomism is true, then Molinism is absurd, or vice versa. For the principles of these two systems are contradictory, that is, before God's determining decree, either He can or cannot know conditionally free acts of the future with infallible certainty.

But I insist: Nevertheless this antecedent will is *de facto* merely inoperative and sterile, for by its own power nothing is accomplished, but only when it is joined to the consequent will, for it is only this will that is directed toward good considered with its accompanying circumstances.

Reply. It is, indeed, true that the antecedent will by its own power never accomplishes anything, because it is directed toward good absolutely considered, and good comes into being only with its accompanying circumstances.

But it does not follow that the antecedent will is merely idle and sterile, for by it God gives sufficient graces, which make the fulfillment of His precepts here and now really possible for adults, although it is not here and now effective.

Moreover, all Thomists are agreed that every grace which is called proximately sufficient as regards some perfect act, for example, that of contrition, is infallibly and of itself efficacious, in virtue of some absolute decree, as regards an imperfect act, for example, that of attrition. But because man, by reason of his own defectibility, resists the sufficient grace, in which the efficacious help was offered to him, God justly denies the efficacious grace that was previously offered to him. This denial on God's part is of the nature of a penalty, and thus it presupposes at least a first offense. Hence there is a distinction between it and the divine permission of this offense, which, as is evident, precedes the offense. In fact, God often moves us wayfarers to pray as in the prayer of the Mass before Communion: "Permit me not, O Lord, to be separated from Thee."

Hence God's antecedent will concerning the salvation of all wayfarers is not inoperative and sterile. This is more clearly seen by comparing it with God's will concerning the salvation of the damned. For God ceases to operate as regards their salvation, because they are incapable of being saved, as they have reached the end of their course and are confirmed in evil. Hence, as we said, God's attitude toward the salvation of the damned can be only one of merely passive complacency. But it is not so as regards the salvation of the wayfarer, no matter how great a sinner such a person may be, because as long as a person is in this world there is possibility of conversion and salvation.

But you insist: St. Thomas says: "The antecedent will may be called a willingness rather than an absolute will." [210]

Reply. What is denied by this statement is that the antecedent will is an absolute will, but not that it is a will; for it is called "a velleity" compared with the consequent will, which is the simple or absolute will.

Final objection. The antecedent will in God does not denote what He sincerely and positively wills. For indeed, he who has the power to do what he is said to will, and does not do so, does not positively and sincerely will it; such would be the case with a merchant who could save his merchandise and would not do so. But it is in God's efficacious power to save all men, and He does not do so. Therefore He does not positively and sincerely will all to be saved.

Reply. I distinguish the major: he who has the efficacious power to do what he is said to will, and does not do so, does not positively and sincerely will it by the consequent will, this I concede; by the antecedent will, this I deny. For it may happen that something, absolutely considered, is good, and not merely a possible but a conditioned future, namely, unless this conflict with higher ends. Such a good terminates God's conditioned decree of His positive and sincere will, which is distinct, for example, from His quasi-negative will of permitting sin. Hence the object of God's universal salvific will is in itself good, but as it stands in the way of a greater good, it is not good, and consequently is not willed. Hence, just as the merchant sincerely wills to save his merchandise, which, however, he throws overboard because there is danger of shipwreck, so also God sincerely

[210] *Summa theol.,* Ia, q. 19, a.6 ad 1um.

wills to save all men, though He does not save all, considering the higher ends in view.

But you insist: I deny the parity in the above illustration, for God, unlike the merchant, can efficaciously save all human beings.

Reply. It is not a case of absolute parity, but of analogy. It is indeed in God's efficacious power to save all, if we consider His omnipotence; but it is not so, if we consider the present ordering of His providence, by which He wills to manifest His infinite justice, as also His infinite mercy, governing and moving defectible creatures in accordance with their natures. Thus He does not efficaciously will all the fruits of the earth to become ripe. Hence, if all these and other conditions are considered, whether they are occult or manifest, it is not good, if in each case the particular circumstances are considered, that all should be saved. For it pertains to the universal Provider to permit various evils to happen so that the higher ends in view may not be frustrated.

Finally, you insist, arguing that if such were the case, then there would be no more hope for anyone, and the value of prayer would be very much impaired. Such is the case with the congruism of the Sorbonne, especially as Tournely presents it, by which salutary acts easy to perform, such as prayer, do not require a grace that is of itself and infallibly efficacious, this being required only for acts that are difficult to perform.

Reply. Even a salutary act easy of performance is the positing of an act that is actually as such a good. Therefore it presupposes the divine consequent will that is of itself efficacious, and grace that is of itself infallibly efficacious. Otherwise the previously enunciated principles are no longer exclusively and metaphysically certain.

But it does not follow that hope is either destroyed or diminished, because the formal motive of this theological virtue is not to be attributed to our endeavor, but to God's help; for the formal motive of this virtue postulates the uncreated, and so God Himself. But in Molinism and congruism the formal motive of theological hope would be partly created, because our endeavor would enter into it; for a part of man's hope would be by reason of his endeavor, and to some extent he would be singling himself out, contrary to what St. Paul says: "For who distinguisheth thee? Or what hast thou that thou hast not received?" [211] For the result would be that of two persons equally loved and helped by God, one would be better than another, at least because of the salutary act easy to perform. But this is impossible, as we shall see farther on, for St. Thomas says: "Since God's love is the cause of goodness in things, no one thing would be

[211] I Cor. 4: 7.

better than another if God did not will greater good for one than for another." [212]

Nor are the value and necessity of prayer impaired by this doctrine. In fact, they become more convincing, for, according to the teaching of St. Augustine and of St. Thomas, we have to pray even for the grace that is of itself efficacious for the performance of salutary acts, whether these are difficult or even easy to perform. On the other hand, if either Molinism or the congruism of the Sorbonne were true, then human beings would not, in their temptations, have to pray to obtain the grace that is of itself efficacious for the performance of salutary acts, at least those easy to perform; all they would have to do would be to strive to give the salutary consent which God expects of them.

This brings us back, therefore, to our original conclusion, namely, if we wish to consider this mystery, not only in its moral aspect, as it concerns the exhortation of men in the order of execution or fulfillment of God's commands, but also as it concerns God's attributes, His omnipotent will, and the order of intention proposed by His providence, that is, in its metaphysical and strictly theological aspects, then the doctrine of St. Thomas remains intact. It is in agreement with the teachings of St. Paul and St. Augustine, and it resolves itself into this dogma, which is thus expressed by St. Augustine: "God commands not impossibilities, but, by commanding, both admonishes thee to do what thou art able and to pray for what thou art not able (to do)." [213] If one did not resist the sufficient grace to pray, then the efficacious grace to pray, and subsequently other graces, would be given. Hence St. Prosper's formula of God's salvific will, quoted by the Council of Quierzy (853), which is in agreement with St. Augustine's teaching, is the best way of expressing this dogma. It reads as follows: "The omnipotent God wills absolutely all men to be saved, although not all are saved. That some are saved is the gift of Him who saves. That some perish is the fault of those who perish." [214] These are two most certain aspects of this mystery. We have considered this second aspect, namely, "the fault of those who perish"; the other aspect: "the gift of Him who saves," will be discussed in the treatise on predestination.[215]

But the intimate reconciliation of these two aspects is for us mysterious, for it is the intimate reconciliation of infinite mercy, justice, and supreme liberty in the eminence of the Deity or of God's intimate

[212] *Summa theol.*, Ia, q.20, a.3.
[213] *De natura et gratia*, chap. 43, no. 50; Denz., no. 804.
[214] Denz., no. 318.
[215] *Summa theol.*, Ia, q.23, a.2–5.

life; and it is only by the beatific vision that this can be clearly known, and as it actually is.

Doubt. Does God provide sufficient means for all to be saved?

The answer is that He does. He not only prepares for all, without distinction, those general helps that are sufficient for salvation, but He also offers, in fact, He bestows upon each and every adult, means that are sufficient for salvation.

First part. That God prepares for all, without distinction, those general helps that are sufficient, is admitted by all Catholics against Jansenius. This conclusion is deduced from God's universal will to save and the fact that Christ died for all. For God cannot will the end without willing the means that are sufficient for attaining the end. Otherwise God would command what is impossible.

The universal salvific will not only refers, as Arnauld contends, to the human nature considered in the abstract, or as it exists in the mind; but it also refers to the human nature objectively as such, which means all human beings without exception, inasmuch as they are all individuals of the same nature which God has destined for salvation, even after Adam's sin. Nor can it be said that sufficient grace is merely sufficient in the abstract, as Arnauld contends, but it makes the fulfillment of God's precepts really possible here and now in the concrete, although it is not the cause of the actual fulfillment of the precepts. Thus a man who is sleeping, although he does not actually see, yet he has at the very time the power to see, for he is not blind; and to say that sufficient grace does not give the power to perform a good act is to say that one who is asleep, is blind.

Second part. The answer to this, namely, "that God offers, even bestows upon each and every human being, sufficient helps for salvation," is not admitted by all Thomists. It is denied especially by Gonet, not indeed for the just, but for all hardened and blinded sinners. But several of the best Thomists teach this, such as the Salmanticenses, Billuart, Bancel, and Goudin, who quote Ferrariensis as being on their side.

It does not, indeed, follow from this that an equal degree of sufficient grace is given to all. This second part of the reply, however, is to be understood in the sense that God gives to each and every one (at least to those who have the use of reason),[216] where and when the fulfillment of a precept is of urgent necessity, helps that are proximately or at least remotely sufficient for salvation, according to each one's condition. Hence if they do not keep some of God's commandments, this is not because God denies them the sufficient help,

---

216 This is said because of the special difficulty concerning infants who die without baptism, which will be examined farther on.

but because men either reject the proffered sufficient grace, or else resist the sufficient grace already given.

According to this conclusion, he who does not resist the remotely sufficient grace, will receive the proximately sufficient grace. Thus the proximately sufficient help to begin to pray is remotely sufficient with regard to the more perfect salutary act. There is the mystery, inasmuch as to resist sufficient grace is an evil that comes solely from ourselves, whereas not to resist it is a good that comes from the source of all good.[217]

Holy Scripture furnishes us with the foundation for this conclusion in the many texts by which it affirms God's mercy toward all wayfarers. Thus we read: "I called, and you refused. I stretched out My hand, and there was none that regarded." [218] "Thou hast mercy upon all, because Thou canst do all things." [219] "Jerusalem . . . how often would I have gathered together thy children as the hen doth gather her chickens under her wings, and thou wouldest not?" [220] "What is there that I ought to do more to My vineyard, that I have not done to it?" [221] "I stand at the gate and knock. If any man shall hear My voice and open to Me the door, I will come in to him." [222] "The Lord is compassionate and merciful, long suffering and plenteous in mercy." [223]

The theological reason is that otherwise God would command what is impossible. Thus sin would be unavoidable, and to punish it would be an act more of cruelty than of justice. For God would command what is impossible if He denied man the sufficient and necessary help to keep His commandments. Hence the Council of Trent quotes against the Protestants the following words of St. Augustine: "God commands not impossibilities, but by commanding, both admonishes thee to do what thou art able and to pray for what thou art not able (to do)." [224]

---

[217] In fact, that one at the very moment does not resist a sufficient grace is a good efficaciously willed by God's consequent will, which alone, as we said, is directed toward good that is at the very moment to be performed.

The sufficient grace, inasmuch as it is sufficient, or as it refers to the possibility of complying with God's commands, depends on His antecedent will; but, inasmuch as it is a gift and a good bestowed at the very moment, it depends on His consequent will, and it truly produces in us the good thought and often the pious desire that inclines the will in its choice of the means for salvation.

[218] Prov. 1: 24.

[219] Wis. 11: 24.

[220] Matt. 23: 37.

[221] Is. 5: 4. In this text we read: "what I ought to do," not "what I could do"; for God can, moreover, give the efficacious grace.

[222] Apoc. 3: 20.

[223] Ps. 102: 8.

[224] Denz., no. 804; *De natura et gratia*, chap. 43.

These principles must be applied to infidels and hardened sinners, when the occasion arises that the fulfillment of a precept is of urgent necessity. If these do not resist the remotely sufficient grace, they will receive the proximately sufficient grace and subsequent graces, in virtue of the commonly accepted principle that "to the man who does what he can (with the help of actual grace), God does not refuse the (habitual) grace." [225] Expressed more briefly: salvation is possible* for any wayfarer; for this, however, sufficient grace is required. As Pius IX declared: "It is known to us and to you that those who labor under invincible ignorance concerning our most holy religion and who, diligently observing the natural law and its precepts that are engraved in the hearts of all by God, and being ready to obey Him, lead an honest and upright life, can, through the operative power of divine light and grace, attain eternal life." [226]

According to several theologians it is sufficient for such persons to believe that God (the author of salvation) exists and is the rewarder of the good, and that they love Him above all things. Several Thomists, the Salmanticenses included, hold that, although strictly speaking an explicit belief in the mystery of the Incarnation is necessary, since it is the necessary means by which salvation is obtained, yet it may be that it is not necessary for the one to whom the mystery was not preached, or to whom it was not sufficiently proposed. [227]

A special difficulty presents itself about infants who die without being baptized. On this point it must be said that, the condition of these infants being taken into consideration, God has sufficiently provided for them by instituting the sacrament of baptism, inasmuch as it was instituted for all and can be conferred on all, although various natural and free causes sometimes intervene to prevent its actual administration. Not infrequently, indeed, infants fail to receive the grace of baptism through the fault of their parents who neglect to pray and make use of the means for salvation. The principle in the solution of this difficulty is that God, on His part, provides for the salvation of all according to each one's capacity; but infants are not capable of being saved by any salutary acts but only by baptism, the actual administration of which, since it depends on both natural and free causes, can be prevented by these causes. Nor does

---

225 *Summa theol.,* Ia, q.49, a.2 ad 3um; Ia IIae, q.109, a.6; q.112, a.3; *De veritate,* q.14, a.11.

226 Denz., no. 1677.

227 Cf. Salmanticenses, *Com. in IIam IIae,* q.2, a.7. Suarez was more or less of this opinion. Just recently Capéran defended this opinion in his theological essay entitled: *Le problème du salut des infidèles.*

it pertain to God's general providence that He interrupt the course of secondary causes.[228]

Finally, infants who die without being baptized are not punished for actual sins, but only for original sin. Therefore they do not suffer interiorly the pain of sense, nor do they suffer as adults do, at being deprived of the beatific vision.[229] They enjoy a certain natural happiness which, even in the natural order, is not absolute but relative happiness; for their will, which is directly turned away from their ultimate supernatural end, is indirectly turned away from their ultimate natural end; for every sin that is directly against the supernatural law is indirectly against the natural law, which demands obedience to God in whatever He commands.[230] Hence the limbo of the children clearly shows that the supernatural life is gratuitous, and also that in the present economy of salvation the absence of the state of grace makes perfect natural happiness simply impossible. Man's present condition is not the state of pure nature, but he is ordained to the life of grace, and if he does not attain to it, it cannot be said that he is absolutely happy even in the natural order. This does not denote a lack of harmony in the disposition of Providence, but, on the contrary, it is consistent with the principles, posited that the whole human race is ordained to the supernatural life. Thus the doctrine of God's universal salvific will remains intact, which is not His consequent will or that which of itself is efficacious, but it is His antecedent will by which He gives sufficient graces to all according to each one's capacity. What always remains a mystery in this doctrine is the intimate reconciliation of the salvific will with the gratuitous predestination of the elect, that is, the mystery of the intimate reconciliation of infinite mercy, justice and, supreme liberty in the Deity.

SEVENTH ARTICLE

WHETHER THE WILL OF GOD IS CHANGEABLE

State of the question. What is asked in this article is whether God can begin to will what He did not will, and not will what He willed,

---

[228] Consult St. Thomas' *Com. in IV Sent.*, d.6, q.1, a.1, sol. 1, ad 1.

[229] See Supplement to St. Thomas' *Summa theologica*, q.69, a.6 ad 2um, in which there is the following quotation from St. Augustine's *Enchiridion*, chap. 93: "The punishment of children who die only with original sin is most lenient." See also *ibid.*, q.71, a.7; *De malo*, q.5, a.3.

[230] *Summa theol.*, Ia IIae, q.82, a.1 ad 1um; q.85, a.1; q.109, a.3. John of St. Thomas, *De gratia*, disp. XIX, a.4; Salmanticenses, *De gratia*, disp. II, dub. 3, nos. 102, 116. Billuart, *De gratia*, diss. II, a.3.

so that from not willing He becomes willing, and vice versa. As a general rule, indeed, God's will is said to be unchangeable, but the Lord Himself says: "It repenteth Me that I have made man." [231] Moreover, God does not always do the same thing, for at one time He ordered the law to be observed, and afterward forbade it. Finally, God is free; therefore He does not have to will continually and irrevocably what He first willed. In fact, just as it was possible for God not to will what He willed, without undergoing any intrinsic change, why could He not, without undergoing any intrinsic change, begin to will what He did not will?

Yet the answer is that God's will is entirely unchangeable, just as His substance and His knowledge are.

1) Holy Scripture shows that the conclusion is of faith, for we read: "God is not as the son of man, that He should be changed." [232] "I am the Lord and I change not." [233] Likewise, the Vatican Council declares that God "is one absolutely simple and immutable spiritual substance." [234] It is the constant teaching of tradition that the determinations of God's will are unchangeable, that His decrees, which are measured by eternity, in which there is no before and after, are unchangeable, as the following text asserts: "There are many thoughts in the heart of man; but the will of the Lord shall stand firm." [235]

Theological proof. There would be a change in God's will if He began to will what before He had not willed; but this is impossible; therefore a change in God's will is impossible.

Proof of minor. A change in God's will would presuppose either a change in His substance (and thus something would begin to be good for Him, which before was not), or else in His knowledge (as He would know for the first time that a thing is good for Him, which He did not know before). But it has already been shown [236] that God's substance and His knowledge are unchangeable, inasmuch as He is pure Act, and not in potentiality for further actuality both in the entitative and intellectual orders, and therefore not in the volitional order.

Corollary. God, by His same permanently unchangeable will, wills a change in some things; for it is one thing to change the will, and another thing to will a change in things. Thus change occurs only in time, but not in eternity, which admits of no variation; for it is "the

---

231 Gen. 6: 7. See also Jer. 18: 17.
232 Num. 23: 19.
233 Mal. 3: 6.
234 Denz., no. 1782.
235 Prov. 19: 21.
236 *Summa theol.*, Ia, q.9, a.1; q.14, a.15.

simultaneously whole and perfect possession of interminable life." [237]

Reply to first objection. The Lord spoke metaphorically when He said: "It repenteth Me that I have made man," [238] thereby making known that it was His will to punish men; for from all eternity God foresaw their sins, and He decreed that they must be punished for them.

Reply to second objection. The same must be said of prophecies of commination concerning conditioned futures that are not realized, because the condition is not fulfilled.[239] Thus we read in the Old Testament: "Yet forty days, and Ninive shall be destroyed"; [240] but because the Ninivites repented, the Lord changed His sentence of condemnation, but not His counsel or the eternal decree of His will.

Reply to fourth objection. "Although God's willing a thing is not by absolute necessity, yet it is necessary by supposition, on account of the unchangeableness of the divine will." According to the teaching of St. Thomas, there is something similar to this by way of participation in the angels, because of the vigor of their intellect, for he says: "The angel's free will is flexible to either opposite before the choice, but not after." [241] With us wayfarers, the free will is flexible to either opposite even after the choice, because we can always reconsider the thing, about which we already made the choice, under new aspects. Thus, because of the imperfection of our knowledge, which is acquired gradually, we can make a different choice. Contrary to this, God's will is entirely unchangeable.

EIGHTH ARTICLE

WHETHER THE WILL OF GOD IMPOSES NECESSITY ON THINGS WILLED

State of the question. The question asked in this most famous article is how to reconcile the efficacy of the determination of the divine will with the freedom of our actions. This problem belongs properly to this question of God's will, rather than to the question of God's knowledge, which states merely "that contingent things are infallibly known by God, inasmuch as they are subject to the divine sight in their presentiality (as God's knowledge is measured by eternity, which comprises all time); yet they are future contingent things in relation to their own causes." [242] This left unsolved the

---

[237] *Ibid.,* Ia, q. 10, a. 1.
[238] Gen. 6: 7.
[239] *Summa theol.,* IIa IIae, q. 171, a. 6 ad 2um; q. 174, a. 1.
[240] Jonas 3: 4.
[241] *Summa theol.,* Ia, q. 64, a. 2.
[242] *Ibid.,* q. 14, a. 13.

question why this contingent future, for example, the conversion of St. Paul, is eternally present to the divine sight rather than Paul's resistance. It is certain and of faith that Paul's conversion would not have taken place in time, or have been eternally present to the divine sight, if God had not willed it; for if this conversion had been in this way present independently of God's free will, then it would have been of itself necessary, and not something contingent. Therefore it is now a question whether God's efficacious will, which is always fulfilled, imposes necessity on all things, even on our choices. This same question is discussed by St. Thomas when he treats of God's providence.[243] Hence this article is concerned strictly with the question of the transcendent efficacy of the determinations or decrees of the divine will with reference to our free acts. In other words, is this predetermination necessitating or non-necessitating?

The article begins by presenting three difficulties, and these constitute the state of the question. They are: (1) It seems that the will of God imposes necessity on all things, because St. Augustine says (*Enchir.*, chap. 103): "It must necessarily be, if God wills (anything)." (2) "God's will cannot be hindered. Therefore the will of God imposes necessity on the things willed." This objection is afterward revived by the Molinists against the Thomists. (3) Lastly, "this true conditional statement is necessary: If God wills a thing, it comes to pass." Now it is quite clear that the first and third difficulties are easily solved by means of the distinction between absolute necessity (or of consequent) and conditional necessity (or of consequence), as when I see Socrates sitting, he must be sitting, the necessity being one of consequence; but that he sits is contingent.[244] The second objection presents the principal difficulty, namely, that God's will cannot be hindered; and this is solved in the body of the article.

The answer is that God's will does not impose necessity on all things, but that some things happen contingently, because God wills that they should happen contingently. To say otherwise would be to do away with free will, merits, laws, counsels, rewards, guilt, and punishment, all of which must be acknowledged as pertaining to the faith, as stated in the counterargument.

This conclusion was subsequently expressed in equivalent terms by the Council of Trent in the following canon: "If anyone says that man's free will moved and aroused by God, by consenting to God's call and action, in no way co-operates toward disposing and preparing itself to obtain the grace of justification; that it cannot refuse its consent if it wishes, but that, as something inanimate, it does

---

243 *Ibid.*, q.22, a.4; Ia IIae, q.10, a.4, the title of which is: Whether the human will is moved of necessity by God. Also *De veritate*, q.23, a.5.

244 *Ibid.*, Ia, q.14, a.13 ad 3um.

nothing whatever and is merely passive; let him be anathema." [245]

The following Jansenist proposition was condemned: "For meriting and demeriting in the state of fallen nature, freedom from internal compulsion is not required; it is sufficient to be free from external restraint." [246] It was not defined, however, whether the divine decree concerning our future salutary acts is intrinsically efficacious, or extrinsically so, namely, because of our foreseen consent (by means of the *scientia media*), as the Molinists and congruists contend.

But all Thomists, as also Scotists and Augustinians, hold that the decrees of the divine will concerning our future salutary acts are intrinsically or of themselves infallibly efficacious, that is, because God wills, and not because man wills. They assert that such is the teaching of St. Thomas in this article and wherever he discusses this subject. In fact, they hold that this doctrine is connected with the principles of the faith, and is proximately definable.[247] Let us see what Holy Scripture, the councils, St. Augustine, and St. Thomas himself have to say on this subject.

According to Holy Scripture, even God's efficacious will does not impose necessity on all things. We find it frequently mentioned in the Old Testament that God's will is efficacious, and that we are free to choose. Thus we read: "As the divisions of waters, so the heart of the king is in the hand of the Lord; whithersoever He will, He shall turn it"; [248] and yet the king freely wills what he decides upon doing. Similarly, Queen Esther prays as follows: "O Lord, King of gods and of all power, . . . turn his heart to the hatred of our enemy"; [249] and farther on we read: "And God changed the king's spirit into mildness" (toward the Jews).[250] Again we have: "As the potter's clay is in his hand . . . , so man is in the hand of Him that made him." [251] "The Lord of hosts hath decreed, and who can disannul it? And His hand is stretched out, and who shall turn it away?" [252] Yet our freedom remains intact, as is clearly stated in the following text: "And I will give you a new heart and put a new

[245] Denz., no. 814.

[246] *Ibid.*, no. 1094.

[247] To know this truth with certainty there is no need of an objectively illative process of reasoning, but an explanatory discursive process suffices. It is sufficient, for example, that the following revealed words be explained: "It is God who worketh in you, both to will and to accomplish, according to His good will" (Phil. 2: 13). See *supra*, pp. 49 f.

[248] Prov. 21: 1.

[249] Esther 14: 13.

[250] *Ibid.*, 15: 11.

[251] Ecclus. 33: 13.

[252] Is. 14: 27.

spirit within you, . . . and I will cause you to walk in My commandments and to keep My judgments and do them." [253] Likewise in the
New Testament we have: "It is God who worketh in you, both to
will and to accomplish, according to His good will." [254] "No one can
snatch them (My sheep) out of the hand of My Father." [255] Especially
to the point is the following text: "I will have mercy on whom I will
have mercy; and I will show mercy to whom I will show mercy. So
then it is not of him that willeth nor of him that runneth, but of God
that showeth mercy." [256]

The Second Council of Orange likewise declares against the
Semipelagians "God does many good things in man, which man does
not accomplish; but there is no good work done by man which God
does not assist him to do." [257] The same council declares: "No man
can claim as his own anything except lying and sin. If a man hath
anything of truth and righteousness, it is from that foundation which
it behoves us to thirst after in this desert that being, so to speak, re-
freshed with some of its drops we may not faint by the way." [258] This
means that every salutary work is performed by means of at least
actual grace, and that every ethically good act is performed by God's
natural concurrence, which is due to the human nature, but not to
this individual here and now rather than to another whom God
permits to fall into sin.

Teaching of the Fathers. Those who wrote before the rise of
Pelagianism and against Manichaeism and its denial of free will,
sometimes did not speak quite so correctly on this point, as St.
Augustine often remarks. Yet they always said with St. Paul: "For
who distinguisheth thee? Or what hast thou that thou hast not received? And if thou hast received, why dost thou glory as if thou
hadst not received it?" [259] Hence St. Cyprian says: "We must not
boast of anything, since there is nothing that is ours." [260] St. Basil
likewise says: "Nothing is left to you, O man, of which you may boast;
for in all things we live by the grace and gift of God." [261] But if the
free determination of the salutary choice were in man's power and

[253] Ezech. 36: 26 f.; also *ibid.*, 11: 19.
[254] Phil. 2: 13.
[255] John 10: 29. See also Matt. 24: 24; John 7: 30; 13: 1; 15: 5; 17: 1; Acts 2: 23;
10: 41; 13: 48; 17: 26; 22: 14; Rom. 8: 28; 9: 11–18, 23, 37; 11: 1–7; I Cor. 4: 7;
Eph. 1: 5–7, 12.
[256] Rom. 9: 15.
[257] Denz., no. 193.
[258] *Ibid.*, no. 195.
[259] I Cor. 4: 7.
[260] *Ad Quirin.*, Bk. III, chap. 4.
[261] Hom. XXII, *De humilitate.*

not from God, then he would have something that would single him out from another equally loved and helped by God, and what is better in the created order would not come from God.[262]

It is particularly St. Augustine who, against the Pelagians and Semipelagians, explains the infallible efficacy of the divine will and grace, not because of our foreseen consent, but by reason of God's omnipotence. Commenting on the words of St. Paul, "It is God who worketh in you both to will and to accomplish," [263] he says: "Certainly we will, when we will; but He causes us to will what is good. . . . Certainly it is we who act when we act; but He causes us to act by enabling the will to act efficaciously. . . . When He says: I will cause you to act, what else does He say but: I will take away the stony heart out of your flesh and will give you a heart of flesh?" [264] Similarly he says: "God has power over the heart, moving it from within . . . ; and the wills of men are more in His power than in their own; who else causes it that chastisement is wholesome and that the heart being contrite there should be amendment of life?" [265] Similarly he says: "Secretly this grace is bestowed by the divine liberality upon human hearts, and it is spurned by no one that is hard of heart; for this very purpose it is bestowed, that the hardness of heart may first be taken away." [266] It is sufficiently clear that the text of St. Paul just quoted concerns grace that is of itself efficacious, because God wills it to be, and not because we will it to be so by reason of our consent.[267]

---

[262] Rouet de Journel (*Enchiridion patristicum, index theologicus*, no. 335), after having correctly said that "grace does not destroy free will," and having quoted the testimony of many of the Fathers on this point, then adds: "Hence also with an equal grace, one can consent, the other can dissent," which seems to be meant in the Molinist sense, namely, that one actually consents, the other actually dissents. But there are two quotations from the writings of St. Irenaeus (no. 247) and of St. Augustine (no. 1753), and these in no way prove that he is in favor of Molina's opinion. In fact, St. Augustine a little farther on in this passage just cited (*De civitate Dei*, Bk. XII, chap. 9), says: "If both the good and bad (angels) were created equally good, then, whereas the latter fell by their evil will, the former were more abundantly assisted, and reached that state of complete happiness which made them absolutely certain of never losing it." This is the simple application of the principle: "For who distinguisheth thee? Or what hast thou that thou hast not received?" (I Cor. 4: 7.) The angels who turned to God and received their reward, the others having fallen from grace, in this respect were better, and this same was the result of God's grace, as having been more helped, the freedom of the will, however, remaining intact.

[263] Phil. 2: 13.

[264] *De gratia et libero arbitrio*, chap. 16; Ezech. 36: 26.

[265] *De correptione et gratia*, chap. 14.

[266] *De praedest. sanct.*, chap. 8.

[267] See also, *De libero arbitrio*, Bk. III, chap. 3, no. 8.

In this article St. Thomas first of all mentions the opinion of some who maintain that the divine will imposes necessity on all things, because what God produces by necessary causes is necessary, but what He produces by contingent causes is contingent. Thus the distinction between contingent and necessary things would be the result only of secondary causes. This seems to be the opinion of the Averroists, that contingency would be the result only of secondary causes.

It is rejected by St. Thomas for two reasons. (1) The effect of a universal cause, such as the sun, is contingent on account of the secondary cause, from the fact that the effect of the first cause is hindered because of a defect in the secondary cause, as the sun's power is hindered by a defect in the plant, so that the fruit does not become ripe. But no defect of a secondary cause can hinder God's will from producing its effect; for God can remove this defect, otherwise He would not be omnipotent. (2) If the distinction between the necessary and the contingent is to be referred only to secondary causes, this must be independent of the divine intention and will; which is inadmissible. For everything external to God must of necessity be in a relation of causality or dependence with respect to God's will. Thus, as our immediate declaration will have to be, not even the free determination of our salutary choices can be made independently of God's will, who "worketh in you both to will and to accomplish." [268]

Then St. Thomas shows what is the ultimate reason for the distinction between the contingent and the necessary, and he proves his conclusion, namely, "God does not impose necessity on all things," by appealing to the absolute efficacy of the divine will.

He builds up his argument as follows: When a cause is efficacious to act, the effect follows upon the cause, not only as to the thing done, but also as to its manner of being done or of being. Thus the one generated is generated even in accidental points. Since then the divine will is perfectly efficacious, it follows not only that things are done which God wills to be done, but also that they are done in the way that He wills. But God wills some things to be done necessarily, some contingently, to the right ordering of things, for the building up of the universe.

Therefore to some effects God has attached necessary causes, which cannot fail, from which effects necessarily proceed (just as day and night follow in regular succession); but to other effects He has attached defectible and contingent causes from which arise contingent effects (such as the ripening of fruits and the acts of our free will). Hence it is not because the proximate causes are contingent that the effects willed by God happen contingently, but because God

[268] Phil. 2: 13.

has prepared contingent causes for them, it being His will that they should happen contingently.[269]

This whole argument has its foundation in the following principle: "When a cause is efficacious to act, the effect follows from the cause, not only as to the thing done, but also as to its manner of being done or of being."

There is first of all inductive evidence of this principle; for, because of the debility in the generative power, it happens that a child is born unlike its father in accidental points, which pertain to its mode of being. On the contrary, if the father is very vigorous, the child is born like him even in accidental points, for example, in the general expression of the face, as we observe in different families whose facial expression conforms persistently through several generations to a certain type. Similarly many soldiers die in war; but there is a heroic way of dying, and not many die heroically.

In like manner great generals not only lead their soldiers on to victory, but they lead them in that characteristic and genial way by which the latter obey willingly. This special manner is quasi-characteristic of this general. Likewise great writers, great poets, have their special manner of expressing themselves, also great musicians, but far more so God, whose will is perfectly efficacious.

The aforesaid principle is not only inductively evident, but its truth is clearly seen from the very analysis of the concepts of its constituent parts. For when a cause is efficacious to act, its influence extends not only to the thing done, but also to the manner in which it is done; because the whole effect depends on and is determined by its cause.

Lastly, this principle is not only found out by reason, but is also equivalently expressed in revelation, which speaks of the absolute efficacy of the divine will, as in the above quoted texts that follow the

[269] There is a considerable difference between this opinion which St. Thomas gives and the one he rejects at the beginning of his argument. For according to this discarded opinion, which seems to be that of the Averroists, God's providence would not at least be concerned particularly with the freedom of human acts, but He would be the prime mover, moving all things in the same way, without any free decree. Thus all things would happen of necessity, with the exception of some contingent things, their contingency being the result of defectible causes. This would explain why all the fruits of the earth do not become ripe.

On the contrary, according to St. Thomas' opinion, God in His providence first willed for the order of the universe that there be some necessary things, such as the movements of the heavenly bodies, and some contingent and even free things, such as free human acts. Therefore He prepared for necessary effects necessary causes or those that of their nature are determined to one thing; and for free effects He prepared causes that are not of themselves determined to one thing.

state of the question in this article. Thus we have: "As the divisions of waters, so the heart of the king is in the hand of the Lord; whithersoever He will He shall turn it," [270] and yet the king freely wills what God moves him to do. Similarly, "As the potter's clay is in his hand . . . , so man is in the hand of Him that made him." [271] "It is God who worketh in you, both to will and to accomplish, according to His good will." [272]

Are the Thomists justified in concluding from this article their doctrine of the intrinsic and infallible efficacy of God's decrees and of grace with respect to our free salutary acts?

The answer is in the affirmative. For St. Thomas already said as much, when he declared: "God's knowledge is the cause of things . . . in so far as His will is joined to it." [273] And again: "The will of God is the cause of things. . . . Determined effects proceed from His own infinite perfection according to the determination of His will and intellect." [274] This determination of God's will is often called His purpose.[275] We now take up the question of the absolute efficacy or decree of the divine will.[276]

But if it is admitted that God's decrees and His grace are only extrinsically efficacious, that is, because of our foreseen consent through the *scientia media,* then God's will is no longer perfectly efficacious, nor does it extend even to the contingent and free mode of our salutary choices. In fact, the free determination of these choices is then, as regards the performance of these acts, solely from us, not being referred to God as dependent on His will, which is impossible, since this is contrary to the universal causality of the supreme Cause. For nothing can exist that is external to God unless it is in a relation of causality toward Him or of dependence on Him; to say otherwise means the nullification of the proofs for God's existence, these having their foundation in this necessary dependence. Finally, in this way the mind would revert to the opinion refuted by St. Thomas in the beginning of the body of this article, namely, that the distinction

270 Prov. 21: 1.

271 Ecclus. 33: 13.

272 Phil. 2: 13.

273 *Summa theol.,* Ia, q.14, a.8.

274 *Ibid.,* q.19, a.4.

275 Rom. 9: 11; 4: 5; 8: 28; Eph. 1: 5, 11; II Tim. 1: 9; see also Commentary of St. Thomas on these texts.

276 Scotus uses the expression "decree of the divine will," and so do the Scotists; but it by no means follows that the Thomist doctrine on the divine decrees originated from Scotism and not from St. Thomas. St. Thomas himself, who uses an equivalent expression, speaking of "the determination of the divine will," and of the pre-ordainings of providence and predestination, which presuppose election on the part of the divine will. See Ia, q.22, a.1, 3; q.23, a.1, 4, 5, 6.

between the contingent and the necessary would arise from secondary causes, and would not be included in God's intention.

Moreover, St. Thomas spoke the same way in his other works and in other parts of his *Theological Summa,* as in the following passage: "We must remember that, properly speaking, necessary and contingent are consequent upon being as such. Hence the mode both of necessity and of contingency falls under the foresight of God, who provides universally for all being; not under the foresight of causes that provide only for some particular order of things." [277]

And again he says: "The divine will must be understood as existing outside the order of beings, as a certain cause that penetrates the whole of being and its differences; but the possible and the necessary are differences of being, and therefore necessity and contingency in things originate from the divine will." [278] On the contrary, the evil of sin is not included in the adequate object of divine omnipotence; [279] and even if, though this is an impossibility, God were to will to be the cause of the evil of sin, He could not be so, just as the eye cannot see sounds. Similarly, in another passage he says: "God moves all things in accordance with their conditions, so that from necessary causes, through the divine motion, effects follow of necessity; but from contingent causes, effects follow contingently. Since, therefore, the will is an active principle, not determinate to one thing, but having an indifferent relation to many things, God so moves it that He does not determine it of necessity to one thing, but its movement remains contingent and not necessary, except in those things to which it is moved naturally." [280] He says the same in the following reply: "If God moves the will to anything, it is incompossible with this supposition that the will be not moved thereto. But it is not impossible simply. Consequently it does not follow that the will is moved by God necessarily," [281] but it freely chooses and acts under the influence of the divine motion. Similarly, in one of his replies, he says: "God moves the will immutably on account of the efficacy of the moving power which cannot fail; but on account of the nature of the will that is moved, which is indifferently disposed to various things, the will is not necessitated but remains free." [282]

In these various passages St. Thomas says: "God moves all things in accordance with their conditions," that is, God adapts His move-

---

[277] *Summa theol.,* q.22, a.4 ad 3um.
[278] *Com. in Periherm.,* Bk. I, lect. 14; St. Thomas also speaks in like manner in his Com. on Aristotle's *Metaphysics,* Bk. VI, lect. 3.
[279] *Summa theol.,* Ia IIae, q.79, a.1.
[280] *Ibid.,* q.10, a.4.
[281] *Ibid.,* ad 3um. See also Ia IIae, q.112, a.3; IIa IIae, q.24, a.11.
[282] *De malo,* q.6, a.1 ad 3um; also *Quodlibet,* q.12, a.3.

ment to creatures according as He moves either natural agents or our free wills. Thus secondary causes do not actively modify God's motion, but only objectively and materially, inasmuch as God operates in our will according to its natural inclination which He gave it and preserves in it. He is more intimate to it than it is to itself.

Hence, according to St. Thomas, God moves our will not only by proposing to it the object that attracts it, but also by applying it to make the choice. "It belongs to God to move the will, but especially by an interior inclination of the will." [283]

First confirmation. God is with greater reason the cause of our free consent than angel and man are. But the angel guardian and man concur in our free consent by moral suasions. Therefore these moral suasions do not suffice on God's part.

Moreover, if an angel, or a human being very much loved by us, causes us to will what he wills, by proposing to us the object which attracts us, far more so can God do this by an interior movement of our will, moving it according to its natural inclination which He preserves intact in us, as the cause that is intimately present to all its effects.

Second confirmation. To say otherwise would be to deny that God is the truly efficient cause of our free consent. It is not enough to have recourse to moral suasion. For moral suasion does not belong to the order of efficient causalty, but of final and objective causality. Moreover, even Pelagius admitted that God moves us by moral suasion to good; yet St. Augustine rejects these movements as insufficient.[284]

Nor does it suffice to have recourse to simultaneous concurrence as advocated by Molina, which is offered indifferently, as to whether we consent or dissent; for such indifference of this simultaneous concurrence does not determine the will to consent rather than to dissent. The simultaneous concurrence and the human will are like two co-ordinated causes, like two horses pulling a boat; and one of these causes does not influence the other to act, but both of them influence only the effect. Hence what is better in the created order, namely, the free determination of our salutary choice, would not be from God, and, contrary to what St. Paul says,[285] man would be singling himself out, because of two men equally helped by God and situated in the same circumstances, one would become better than another, which is contrary to what St. Thomas says.[286]

Third confirmation. If God does not determine, then He is determined, that is, He assumes a passive role in this foreseeing by means

283 *Summa theol.*, Ia, q. 105, a. 4.
284 *De gratia Christi,* chaps. 7, 10, 11.
285 I Cor. 4: 7.
286 *Summa theol.*, Ia, q. 20, a. 3, 4.

of the *scientia media,* which is antecedent to the decree of the divine will. For, according to this theory, God, by concurring indifferently and by moral suasion, must wait for and ascertain our consent, or inquire by examining our will as to what it would choose if placed in such and such circumstances. The result of this would be passivity or dependence in God's knowledge; but there can be no passivity in Him who is pure Act. He is in the highest degree in actuality, and is nowise in potentiality.

Molina says: "It was not in God's power to know by this (middle) knowledge anything else than He actually knew. Then again it must not be called natural even in this sense, as if it were so innate in God that He could not know the contrary of what He knows by it. For if the created free will were to do the opposite of what it did, as it truly can do, God would have known this very act by the same knowledge, by which He really knows it, but not that He actually knows it." [287] Therefore passivity or dependence is thus posited in God's knowledge with regard to our free conditional future choices, which actually will be, if God decreed to place our will in these circumstances. The independence of God's knowledge is thus destroyed, and the conception of the divine knowledge becomes tinged with anthropomorphism.

Lastly, it is not possible in this way for God to know infallibly our conditionally free acts of the future, and then our future choices, because the determination of these choices cannot be seen by the supercomprehension of the human will, which in itself is undetermined, otherwise the will would not be free; nor is it possible for God to have this knowledge by foreseeing the circumstances, otherwise we would have to admit determinism of circumstances, and this would mean the end of freedom. This we have more fully explained in another work.[288]

Therefore the doctrine of St. Thomas is vindicated, which was subsequently expressed so brilliantly by Bossuet in the following passages: "To reconcile the decree and the omnipotent action of God with our free will, we have no need to give it a concurrence which is ready for all things indifferently, and which becomes what we please; still less do we have to make it wait for what our will is inclined to do, for it to formulate afterward with no risk its decrees about our resolutions. For without this poor circumspection which gives us a confused notion of the First Cause, it suffices for us to bear

---

287 *Concordia,* q. 14, a. 13, p. 318.
288 See *Predestination* (Eng. tr.), pp. 81 f., 300–309, 371–76. Consult also (*ibid.*) principle of predilection: "One thing would not be better than another if God did not will greater good for one than for another," pp. 16, 38, 75–80, 129, 149, 173–75, 195 f., 329, 344, 349.

in mind that the divine will, whose infinite power reaches everything, not only the essence, but also the modes of being, is of itself accountable for the complete effect, in which it puts everything which we conceive in it, ordaining that it will be accompanied by all the properties that are befitting it. . . .

"God wills from eternity, all the acts that will be performed by the free will of human beings, all the good and reality there is in them. What is more absurd than to say, that it is not because God wills, that a thing exists? Must we not say, on the contrary, that a thing exists, because God wills it? And just as it happens that we are free in virtue of the decree that wills us to be free, so it happens that we act freely in this or that act, in virtue of the decree which includes all this in detail?" [289]

SOLUTION OF THE OBJECTIONS IN THIS ARTICLE

Reply to first objection. When St. Augustine says, "Man must inevitably be saved, if God has willed it," [290] the reference is to conditional necessity or to that of consequence, but not to absolute necessity or to that of consequent. Thus, when it is said, "I see Peter running," Peter must at that very moment inevitably be running, by a necessity of consequence but his running is a contingent and free act, for he has the power not to run. Similarly, in the reply to the third objection it is said: "Things effected by the divine will have that kind of necessity that God wills them to have, either absolute or conditional."

Reply to second objection. It answers the principal difficulty revived by Molinists, namely, that every cause that cannot be hindered, produces its effect necessarily. But the will of God cannot be hindered, according to the following statement: "Who resisteth His will?" [291] It is not a question here of the antecedent will of God, on which sufficient grace depends, which a man often resists; but it refers to the consequent will of God, from which efficacious grace proceeds, which a man does not resist, but to which he consents. St. Thomas replies to this objection: "From the very fact that nothing resists the divine will, it follows that not only those things happen that God wills to happen, but that they happen necessarily or contingently according to His will." Hence St. Thomas does not have recourse to the foreseeing of our consent by God, as Molina did afterward in his theory of the *scientia media;* but again he affirms the absolute efficacy of

[289] *Traité du libre arbitre,* chap, 8.
[290] *Enchir.,* chap. 103.
[291] Rom. 9: 19.

the divine will, this absolute efficacy extending even to the free mode of our choices. Therefore we reply to the objection by distinguishing the major: every cause that cannot be hindered, produces its effect necessarily, if it is incapable of producing the contingent and free mode in its effect, this I concede; otherwise, I deny it.[292] Hence the absolute efficacy of the divine will not only does not interfere with the freedom of our choice, but causes this, as declared by St. Thomas in the following passage: "Just as by moving natural causes He does not prevent their acts being natural, so by moving voluntary causes He does not deprive their actions of being voluntary; but rather is He the cause of this very thing in them; for He operates in each thing according to its own nature." [293] The free mode of our choices is a mode of being, and it is thus included in the adequate object of divine omnipotence, since it is only the evil of sin that is excluded from it.

Doubt. To what is contingency ultimately to be ascribed? To the freedom of the divine will, or to its absolute efficacy?

The Thomists answer with Cajetan: "It is of importance to know that, after the divinelike Thomas had written these things, there arose a new opinion about the ultimate foundation of contingency, advanced by Scotus.[294] For he believes that the condition of the divine will truly constitutes the ultimate foundation of contingency, and on this point he is in agreement with us; but we say that the absolute efficacy of the divine will is that condition; but he says that it is its contingency. Concerning this theory of his, by contingency in the divine will he means its liberty: so that he imagines that because God wills and causes freely, for this reason there is contingency in the universe." [295] To this Cajetan replies: "If the contingency arises from the manner of God's willing, then it is not chosen, but is the consequence of the manner of choosing. Therefore, according to this proposed theory, the effect is not produced by God as the agent. And thus there is contingency in the universe over and above what is intended by God, inasmuch as it is the consequence of His manner of willing, but not of His willing." [296]

Moreover, God also wills freely that some things happen necessarily in the world, such as that the sun gives out light and heat. Therefore contingency is not the result of the free mode of the divine will, but is due to the fact that God efficaciously wills some things

292 *Summa theol.*, Ia, q.19, a.8 ad 3um.
293 *Ibid.*, q.83, a.1 ad 3um.
294 *Com. in I Sent.*, d.2, q.1; d.8, q.5; d.39, q.1.
295 *Com. in Iam*, q.19, a.8, no. 11.
296 *Ibid.*, nos. 13 f.

to happen contingently in the universe and some necessarily. And God can produce these divers modes of being, because He is the author of being.

SOLUTION OF THE OBJECTIONS OF OPPONENTS

The opponents, that is, the Molinists and the congruists, who admit the *scientia media* and deny the intrinsic efficacy of God's decrees and grace, object to this doctrine, basing their objections (1) on scriptural grounds, (2) on the impairment of free will, (3) on the insufficiency of the help, (4) on the contention that by such teaching God would become the cause of sin. These objections are examined at length by such Thomists as the Salmanticenses, John of St. Thomas, Gonet, and Billuart. We give only the principal objections. The replies taken together are like an ancient and exquisitely harmonious canticle. They are, so to speak, the leitmotif of ancient theology. They can be explained frequently, just as a symphony of Beethoven is heard many times. Our purpose is to show the intimate harmony that prevails in the whole Thomist system.

Objections from Holy Scripture. These are taken from texts that speak of man's resistance with reference to God's grace. Thus we read: "What is there," said the Lord, "that I ought to do more to My vineyard, that I have not done to it? Was it that I looked that it should bring forth grapes, and it hath brought forth wild grapes?" [297] "I called, and you refused. I stretched out My hand, and there was none that regarded." [298] "You always resist the Holy Ghost." [299]

Reply. These texts do not concern the consequent will of God by which He grants the efficacious grace; but they refer to His antecedent will by which He gives the sufficient grace, by reason of which the fulfillment of His precepts is made really possible, though not as yet effective. In fact, these texts refer to His will of expression, which is made known to us by His commands, which men do not always obey.

Therefore the first text just quoted does not say: "What is there that I could do more to My vineyard," but "What is there that I ought to do more to My vineyard, that I have not done to it?" This means that God gave the Jews many sufficient graces, which had made it possible for them to be converted; but He did not give them the efficacious graces, which God had indeed been able to give them, but was not bound to give them, because the order observed in His

297 Is. 5: 4.
298 Prov. 1: 24.
299 Acts 7: 51.

providence did not demand this. If God were bound to give His efficacious grace always and to all persons, sin would never happen, which, however, He can permit for a greater good. Hence in the aforesaid text the Jews are reproved, because of their own accord they refused to obey God's commands and make use of the sufficient grace, and thus they deserved to be deprived of the efficacious grace.

The other texts are explained in like manner, namely; "I called, and you refused"; "You always resist the Holy Ghost." Man often *de facto* resists sufficient grace by not obeying God's precepts; but he does not *de facto* resist efficacious grace, although he can resist it *in sensu diviso,* that is, inasmuch as he has the power to do the opposite; just as Peter cannot at the same time sit and stand, but when he stands, he has really the power to sit down. Likewise a man asleep has really the power to see, and, although he does not actually see, yet he has really the power to see, for he is not blind.

Hence these texts of Holy Scripture nowise render less convincing others which refer to God's consequent and efficacious grace. Thus we read: "As the divisions of waters, so the heart of the king is in the hand of the Lord. Whithersoever He will He shall turn it." [300] "As the potter's clay is in his hand . . . so man is in the hand of Him that made him." [301]

But I insist. Nevertheless we read: "Woe to thee, Corozain! Woe to thee, Bethsaida! For if in Tyre and Sidon had been wrought the miracles that have been wrought in you, they had long ago done penance in sackcloth and ashes." [302]

The Thomists in general reply to this by appealing to the same principles. They say this text means that the inhabitants of Corozain and Bethsaida showed themselves more unworthy than those of Tyre, because of their greater blindness of intellect, hardness of heart, and ingratitude. For man of his own accord resists God's grace, but there is a greater degree of resistance in some, for they resist even the greatest sufficient graces, as was the case with the preaching of Christ which was confirmed by miracles. The Jews of Corozain and Bethsaida placed a greater obstacle to the efficacious grace offered in the sufficient grace, just as the fruit is contained in the flower. Thus they were deprived of the efficacious grace.

Still I insist. According to the teaching of the Thomists, the Jews needed an efficacious grace so that they might not resist the sufficient grace and thus place an obstacle to the reception of the efficacious grace. Therefore, if Thomism is true, it was possible for these Jews to reply that they resisted the sufficient grace because they simply

---

[300] Prov. 21: 1.
[301] Ecclus. 33: 13 f.
[302] Matt. 11: 21.

did not have the efficacious grace required for not resisting the sufficient grace.

Reply. The cause of this resistance is not the lack of efficacious grace, but man's own defectibility. Resistance to sufficient grace is indeed an evil, or a deficiency, which comes from a defectible cause. An evil will, which is the first deficient principle, suffices for this. Hence it is false to say that our will resists the sufficient grace because it lacks the efficacious grace. But it must be said that our will lacks the efficacious grace because it resists the sufficient grace. The deficiency of a secondary cause is due to the fact that this cause is defectible. St. Thomas makes this clear by the following statement: "The first cause of the defect of grace is on our part; but the first cause of the bestowal of grace is on God's part, according to Osee 12: 9: "Destruction is thy own, O Israel; thy help is only in Me." [303]

To state the case more briefly: resistance to sufficient grace is an evil, and is therefore due solely to a defectible and defective cause. On the other hand, the non-resistance to sufficient grace is a good, and is therefore not to be attributed solely to the secondary cause, but also and primarily to the First Cause, the source of all good.

Hence the Jews of Corozain and Bethsaida, after Christ's preaching confirmed by miracles, had no reasonable excuse for their resistance, and they were deservedly deprived of the efficacious grace, which the Tyrians, by God's mercy, would have received in similar circumstances, because they would not have resisted with such hardness of heart and ingratitude.

It is because Thomism teaches that this divine bestowal of grace, which is of itself efficacious, is the cause of the salutary act, that this final objection seeks to infer that therefore the non-bestowal of the efficacious grace is the cause of the sin of omission and of the resistance.

But this does not follow; for, when two causes concur, one of which is indefectible and the other defectible, the deficiency comes from the defectible cause and not from the divine indefectible cause. Similarly, everything being in proportion, in that the clear explanation given by the teacher, arousing the attention of the pupil, is the cause of the pupil's knowledge, it does not follow that the cause of the pupil's error is because the teacher failed to give a clear explanation. This error can come from the defectibility in the pupil, from insufficient attention on his part.

More briefly: deficiency comes not from the indefectible cause but from the defectible cause. Thus we read: "Destruction is thy own, O Israel; thy help is only in Me." [304] Similarly the Council of Quierzy

---

[303] *Summa theol.*, Ia IIae, q. 112, a. 3 ad 2um.
[304] Osee 13: 9.

says: "That some are saved, is the gift of Him who saves; if some perish, it is the fault of them that perish." [305] This text is taken from the writings of St. Prosper, being his reply to the second Vincentian objection.

Therefore it remains true to say that the Jews of Corozain and Bethsaida were deservedly rebuked, compared with those of Tyre, because they placed a greater obstacle to the efficacious grace that was offered in the sufficient grace. The Tyrians would not have placed so great an obstacle to grace, and God in His mercy would have given them the efficacious grace of conversion.

This answer is clearly established from what our Lord says: "Without Me you can do nothing" [306] for salvation; also from what St. Paul says: "For who distinguisheth thee? Or what hast thou that thou hast not received? And if thou hast received, why dost thou glory as if thou hadst not received it?" [307] These words imply that every good thing comes from God, that is, to be able to keep His commandments, not to resist them, and actually to keep them. All these good things come from God, and if anyone not only can keep, but actually does keep, God's commandments, this is a new good that certainly comes from God, the source of all good. But if a man could by his own power make God's grace efficacious, then this would single him out from another equally loved and helped by God, and thus the words of St. Paul would be untrue: "For who distinguisheth thee? Or what hast thou, that thou hast not received?"

EFFICACIOUS GRACE IN ITS RELATION TO HUMAN LIBERTY

SOLUTION OF OBJECTIONS

The principal objection from this point of view is already solved by St. Thomas in this article, for he says: "From the very fact that nothing resists the divine will (consequent or efficacious), it follows that not only those things happen that God wills to happen, but that they happen either contingently (i.e., also freely) or necessarily according to His will." [308] In other words: the determination effected by God's consequent will, which is perfectly efficacious, does not interfere with the freedom of our will, because it extends even to the free mode of our choice, producing this in us and with us. For this mode is a modification of being and action, and hence is included in the adequate object of the power of Him who is the Au-

305 Denz., no. 318.
306 John 15: 5.
307 I Cor. 4: 7.
308 Cf. ad 2um.

thor of the being of all things and actions. Thus God by His primary contact does not interfere with, does not destroy, the freedom of our will, but actuates it.

The opponents bring forward another objection. They declare that the Council of Trent says: "If anyone says that man's free will, moved and aroused by God . . . cannot refuse its consent if it wishes . . . let him be anathema." [309] But this refers to grace that is in some manner efficacious, with which man *de facto* co-operates, and to which he assents. Therefore, under the influence of this grace, man cannot refuse his consent, if he would, and hence this grace is efficacious, not of itself, but because our consent was foreseen by God. So say Lessius, Molina, Vasquez.

Reply. I distinguish the major: that the free will of man, moved and aroused by God, can refuse its consent, this I concede; that it can refuse its consent in *sensu composito,* that is, unite actual resistance with efficacious grace, this I deny; for this grace would no longer be efficacious. Similarly, Socrates cannot stand and sit at the same time, but, while he sits, he can stand, that is, he has the power to stand at the same time that he actually sits. Thus a man asleep, although he does not actually see, yet he can see, for the fact that he is asleep does not mean that he is blind. That the minor, indeed, refers to efficacious grace, this I concede. The conclusion is distinguished in the same manner as the major: that a man under the influence of efficacious grace can refuse his consent if he so wills, *in sensu diviso,* this I concede; *in sensu composito,* this I deny. That is, under the influence of efficacious grace, a man can refuse his consent, if he so wills; but, under the influence of this grace a man never *de facto* so wills. Thus St. Thomas says: "If God moves the will to anything it is incompossible with this supposition that the will be not moved thereto. But it is not impossible simply," [310] because the will really has the power to do the opposite.

In fact, many Fathers of the Council of Trent, who were either Augustinians or Thomists, understood the aforesaid canon as referring to grace that is of itself intrinsically efficacious, which they admitted; and against the Protestants they held that grace of itself efficacious does not take away the freedom of the will. But if such is the interpretation of this text of the Council of Trent, then it is more against the Molinists who, along with the Protestants, admit that grace of itself efficacious takes away the freedom of the will.

The earlier Protestants said, just as the Jansenists did in later times, that grace of itself efficacious takes away the freedom of the will. But after original sin, for the performance of a salutary good

[309] Denz., no. 814.

[310] *Summa theol.,* Ia IIae, q. 10, a. 4 ad 3um.

act, grace of itself efficacious is required. Therefore, after original sin, free will is an empty title.

The Molinists reply to this by conceding the major and denying the minor. The ancient theologians, especially the Thomists, replied by denying the major and conceding the minor.

Hence from this text of the Council of Trent, in the formulation of which many Thomists and Augustinians collaborated, nothing can be concluded against Thomism.[311]

Moreover, from the complete text of this quoted canon it is clear that the doctrine condemned differs entirely from that of St. Thomas; for it says: "If anyone says that man's free will moved and aroused by God, by assenting to God's call and action, in no way co-operates toward disposing and preparing itself to obtain the grace of justification; that it cannot refuse its consent if it wishes, but that, as something inanimate, it does nothing whatever and is merely passive; let him be anathema." [312]

Yet I insist. But even Calvin admitted this distinction between the *sensus divisus* and the *sensus compositus;* yet he was condemned. Therefore this distinction does not suffice.

Reply. Calvin admitted this distinction, but not in the Thomist sense. The Thomists say that under the influence of grace that is of itself efficacious we can refuse our consent *in sensu diviso,* because our will really has the power to do the opposite. On the contrary, according to Calvin, under the influence of this efficacious grace, man has not the power to do the opposite; but when no longer influenced by efficacious grace, then the power to do the opposite reasserts itself, that is, as a consequence of original sin free will is extinguished, is an empty title.[313] He admitted only a certain contingency for the will, as in the case of the fruits of the earth, all of which do not ripen because of some impediment. Thus he reduced human liberty to spontaneity or to freedom from external restraint. The same was said by Jansenius, whose third proposition reads: "For meriting and demeriting in the state of fallen nature, freedom from internal compulsion is not required; it is sufficient to be free from external constraint." [314]

Second objection. A supposed condition that precedes and infallibly causes our choice, necessitates the will and takes away its freedom; but such is the Thomist opinion about predetermining decrees; therefore these decrees necessitate our choice.

Reply. I distinguish the major. That a supposed condition pre-

---

[311] Cf. Reginald, O.P., *De mente Concilii Tridentini,* on this canon.
[312] Denz., no. 814.
[313] *Ibid.,* nos. 793, 815.
[314] *Ibid.,* no. 1094.

ceding and infallibly causing our choice necessitates the will as regards the substance of the choice, this I concede; that it also does so as regards the free mode of this choice, this I deny. I contradistinguish the minor, and deny the consequent and consequence.[315]

But I insist. For our choice to be a free act, what it depends on and what it is infallibly connected with must be within our power; but the divine predetermining decree, on which our act depends and with which it is infallibly connected, is not within our power; therefore our choice is not a free act.

Reply. I distinguish the major: if the principle pertains to the order of secondary causes, as our ultimate practical judgment that regulates our choice, then I concede it must be in our power; if this principle pertains to the order of first cause, I subdistinguish: that this principle must be in our power in the originative sense, as it pertains to the order of first cause, this I deny; in the terminative sense, or as regards the execution of the act, this I concede; and so it is, because, while our will freely elicits the act of choice, it retains the power to choose the opposite.

Hence a distinction must be made before we can admit the Molinist definition of free will, namely, "that it is a faculty which, granted all the prerequisites for the will to act, can either act or not act." We must distinguish as follows: granted all the prerequisites for the will to act when the time comes for the performing of the act, the will is free to act or not to act even *in sensu composito;* but if we presuppose only all the natural prerequisites, such as are the divine efficacious motion and the ultimate practical judgment, the will is indeed still free not to act *in sensu diviso,* inasmuch as it retains the power to do the opposite, but not so *in sensu composito;* for the non-positing of the act cannot coexist with efficacious grace.[316] Thus, when Socrates is standing, he can sit down; but he cannot at the same time stand and sit down. The above-mentioned Molinist definition of free will implies a begging of the question, for it presupposes before it is proved, that the divine decrees and grace are not of themselves efficacious.

Moreover, this definition is contrary to the principle that "faculties, habits, and acts are specified by their formal object"; and to define these it suffices for us to declare their essential relation to this object. Thus free will is defined as the dominating indifference of the will (either divine, angelic, or human) with respect to an object that is not good in every respect, which can be judged as good under one aspect and as not good under another. Thus St. Thomas says: "If the will is offered an object which is good universally and from

[315] *Summa theol.,* Ia, q. 19, a. 8 ad 2um.
[316] *Ibid.,* Ia IIae, q. 10, a. 4 ad 3um.

every point of view, the will tends to it of necessity, if it wills anything at all; since it cannot will the opposite. (Thus it cannot but will God who is clearly seen.) If, on the other hand, the will is offered an object that is not good from every point of view, it will not tend to this of necessity." [317] This is the true definition of free will as obtained from its specified object, and without any begging of the question.

Moreover, this indifference of judgment remaining intact with respect to an object that is not in every respect good, God, by interiorly moving our will as regards the performance of the act, cannot necessitate it, because He cannot change the nature of this act that is thus specified by this object thus proposed to it; but the divine action really causes the free mode of our choice by actuating this dominating indifference, which before this was potential. In the very act of choosing there is an actual dominating indifference of the will with respect to particular good that is actually chosen and does not infallibly attract the will. On the other hand, the will of the blessed is infallibly attracted by God clearly seen, so that there is no longer indifference of judgment in this respect.

WHETHER SUFFICIENT GRACE IS AN INSUFFICIENT HELP

SOLUTION OF OBJECTIONS

First objection. That help is insufficient which, for us to act, requires another which is not in our power. But in addition to the help that is called sufficient, according to the Thomist opinion there is required another help that is of itself efficacious, which is not in our power. Therefore the first help is truly insufficient for the actual observance of God's commandments. Thus we must go back to the theory of the *scientia media*. This objection can be answered either indirectly or directly.

1) Indirectly. This objection is in substance the same as that which St. Paul put to himself.[318] Just previous to this, St. Paul, speaking of the divine election, had said: "It is not of him that willeth nor of him that runneth, but of God that showeth mercy. . . . Therefore He hath mercy on whom He will; and whom He will, He hardeneth." [319] He at once remarks: "Thou wilt say therefore to me: Why doth He then find fault? For who resisteth His will?" [320] But to this objection St. Paul replies: "O man, who art thou that repliest against

---

317 *Ibid.*, a.2.
318 Rom. 9: 19.
319 *Ibid.*, 9: 16, 18.
320 *Ibid.*, 9: 19.

God? Shall the thing formed say to him that formed it: Why hast thou made me thus? . . . What if God, willing to show His wrath (avenging justice) and to make His power known, endured with much patience vessels of wrath, fitted for destruction, that He might show the riches of His glory on the vessels of mercy, which He hath prepared unto glory (is there in this any injustice in God?)" [321] But St. Paul, in thus replying to the objection, does not have recourse to God's foreseeing our consent; for then man would single himself out, which is contrary to what he says in the following words: "For who distinguisheth thee? Or what hast thou that thou hast not received?" [322]

Therefore St. Paul's reply comes to this: on the one hand, God does not command impossibilities; on the other hand, no one would be better than another, unless loved and helped more by God; "for what hast thou that thou hast not received?" [323] These two principles taken separately are most certain; but how are they intimately reconciled? This cannot be known by us in this life. This would be to see how infinite mercy, justice, and absolute liberty are intimately reconciled in the Deity, or in the intimate life of God. But it is only in heaven that the Deity can be seen as it really is. Therefore St. Paul says farther on: "O the depth of the riches of the wisdom and of the knowledge of God! How incomprehensible are His judgments and how unsearchable His ways!" [324] It is in this way that the element of the mysterious must be safeguarded in this reply, so that the mystery be kept on its high plane, and that a human theory for which there is no foundation in the divine reality be not substituted for it. This would savor of anthropomorphism.

2) **A direct reply** in scholastic form must be given to this objection, so as to avoid an evident contradiction. That the help which requires another help is not absolutely sufficient and in every respect, let this pass without comment; that it is not sufficient in its own order, this I deny; for it confers a real power, in fact, the proximate power to act so that nothing is wanting on the part of the faculty or first actuality. Thus the visual faculty is sufficient for seeing, and the man who is asleep really has this faculty, although he does not actually see. Therefore, to say that sufficient grace as conceived by the Thomists is not truly sufficient and does not really give one the proximate power to act, is to say that a man when asleep is blind. Aristotle [325]

---

[321] *Ibid.,* 9: 20–23. This is the answer to his previous objection: "Is there injustice in God?" (*Ibid.,* 9: 14.)

[322] I Cor. 4: 7.

[323] *Ibid.*

[324] Rom. 11: 33.

[325] *Metaph.,* Bk. IX, chap. 3.

had already said this against the Megarics, namely, that a thing can be really in potency without functioning. Thus the art of building in the builder who is asleep and is not actually building, remains in him as an acquired art.

Moreover, to the first part of the distinction I said only *transeat* ("let it pass without comment"), and not "I concede." Why this? It is because the efficacious grace is offered in the sufficient grace, as the fruit is offered in the flower; but because man, through his own defectibility, resists the sufficient grace, he is deservedly deprived of the efficacious grace, by which he not only could have kept God's commandments, but actually would have done so. Thus the sin of resistance falls upon the sufficient grace, as the hail falls upon the trees in blossom which gave promise of the fruit, and so the fruit did not materialize.

Lastly, all Thomists admit that every actual efficacious grace for the performance of the imperfect salutary act, such as the act of attrition, is sufficient for the perfect act, such as the act of contrition. Yet, when the sin of resistance intervenes, the efficacious grace of contrition is not given, which was truly offered in the preceding grace, as the fruit is contained in the blossom, as the act is contained in the potency.[326]

To resist grace is an evil, which is to be attributed solely to our deficiencies; not to resist is a good which comes from God, the source of all good. And there is again in this a mystery, but not a contradiction.

But I insist. If affirmation is the cause of affirmation, then negation is the cause of negation. Thus the sun illuminating is the cause of day, and its absence is the cause of night. But the bestowal of grace that is of itself efficacious is the cause of the salutary act. Therefore the non-bestowal of grace that is of itself efficacious is the cause of the omission of this act, or of our resistance to grace.

Reply. I distinguish the major: if it is a case of one cause, which is, indeed, posited and then taken away, such as the rising of the sun, then I concede the major; if it is a case of two causes, one of which is supreme and indefectible, and which would not be bound to prevent the defect of the other, whereas the other is defectible, then I deny it; for then the defect is to be attributed solely to the defectible cause, and not to the indefectible cause. Thus the Scripture says: "Destruction is thy own, O Israel; thy help is only in Me." [327] Such is the teaching of St. Thomas.[328]

[326] Cf. Alvarez, *De auxiliis,* Bk. III, disp. 80; Gonet, *Clypeus, De voluntate Dei,* disp. 4, no. 147; N. del Prado, *De gratia et libero arbitrio,* III, 423.

[327] Osee 11: 9.

[328] *Com. in I Sent.,* d.40, q.4, a.2 ad 3um.

It must be observed that according to certain Thomists, such as Gonzalez, Bancel, Massoulié, and, among later Thomists, Guillermin,[329] the actual sufficient grace is virtually efficacious, in this sense, that it not only would give the power, but even would give one the impulse to act, although not infallibly, because it would not remove all the obstacles. Therefore, even according to these authors (who, like other Thomists, reject the *scientia media*), even the salutary act easy to perform is not posited and persisted in *de facto* here and now, unless God from all eternity willed this by His consequent and infallibly efficacious will, and unless God grants at the moment the grace that is of itself efficacious to overcome the obstacles to the performance of this salutary act here and now to be posited or persisted in.

All Thomists maintain that to resist grace is an evil that comes solely from a defectible cause, but not from God; whereas, on the contrary, here and now not to resist sufficient grace is a good here and now posited, which presupposes, therefore, a decree that is of itself and infallibly efficacious of God's consequent will, as explained by St. Thomas in the following statement: "Whatever God simply wills takes place; although what He wills antecedently may not take place." [330] But the distinction between God's antecedent and consequent wills is the ultimate foundation for the distinction between sufficient and efficacious graces.[331]

WHETHER THE INTRINSIC EFFICACY OF THE DIVINE DECREES AND GRACE BEARS ANY RESEMBLANCE TO CALVINISM

SOLUTION OF OBJECTIONS

Objection. It was defined in the Council of Trent that God in no way is the cause of sin: "If anyone says that it is not in man's power to make his ways evil, but that the works that are evil God worketh as well as those that are good, not permissibly only, but properly and of Himself, in such wise that the treason of Judas is no less His own proper work than the vocation of Paul; let him be anathema." [332] But, according to the Thomists, God is the cause of the

---

[329] See *Revue Thomiste*, 1903, pp. 23 f. We have examined this opinion in *Predestination* (Eng. tr.), pp. 345 f.

[330] *Summa theol.*, Ia, q. 19, a. 6 ad 1um.

[331] Cf. Billuart, *De Deo uno*, diss. VI, a. 6, *de scientia media*, § 9. This question has been treated more fully in *Predestination* (Eng. tr.), pp. 328, 333–35, 345–51; also *Revue Thomiste*, May–June, 1937: "Le fondement suprême de la distinction des deux graces suffisante et efficace."

[332] Denz., no. 816.

act of sin by physical premotion, which presupposes a divine predetermining decree that concurs in the physical entity of sin. Therefore it seems that God is the cause of sin itself, as He is according to
the tenets of Calvinism.

Reply. God is truly the author of the physical entity of sin; yet He
is neither directly nor indirectly the cause of the deordination that
there is in sin, as St. Thomas shows.[333] For God to be the direct cause
of sin, this means that He influences His or another's will to commit
sin. But God draws all things to Himself, as to their end, and He
cannot turn His will away from Himself. Therefore God is not the
cause of sin.

He cannot be the indirect cause of sin, because to be the indirect
cause of sin means not to prevent it. But God's wisdom and prudence
do not require that He should prevent sins, which He permits. He
can permit them, however, for a greater good, for the greater manifestation of His mercy and justice. Thus there would be no patience
of the martyrs without the persecution of tyrants, as St. Thomas
points out.[334] Hence St. Augustine gives the solution of the problem
of evil, when he says: "Since God is absolutely good, He by no means
would permit evil in His works, unless He were good enough and
powerful enough to bring good out of evil." [335]

Moreover, the evident conclusion we must come to from this is
that even if, by an impossibility, God willed to be the cause of sin,
He could not be, for the evil of sin is excluded from the adequate
object of divine and indefectible omnipotence, just as sound is excluded from the object of sight.[336]

Yet it is insisted that he who premoves efficaciously and determinately to the act of sin, is the cause of sin itself. But, according to
Thomism, God premoves efficaciously and determinately to the act
of sin. Therefore God is the cause of sin itself.

Reply. I distinguish the major: he who premoves, not prescinding
from the malice of sin, this I concede; otherwise, I deny the major.
I contradistinguish the minor. Similarly the motive power causes
whatever motion there is in lameness, though prescinding from the
defect of lameness.

Again it is insisted that God cannot prescind from the malice of
sin, for He moves the will to the act precisely as coming from the will;
but in the act of sin, as it comes from the will, malice is not excluded;
therefore God moves the will to the malice of sin.

Reply. I distinguish the major. God moves one to the act of sin, as

[333] *Summa theol.,* Ia IIae, q.79, a.1.
[334] *Ibid.,* Ia, q.22, a.2 ad 2um.
[335] *Enchiridion,* chap. 11.
[336] *Predestination,* pp. 208-12, 324-35.

it proceeds effectively from the will, this I concede; as it proceeds defectively, this I deny.

Still it is insisted that if two things are inseparably connected, the cause of the one is the cause of the other; but the act of sin and its malice are inseparably connected; therefore God is the cause of the malice in sin.

Reply. I distinguish the major: if the connected effect is included in the adequate object of this cause, let it pass without comment; otherwise, I deny the major. But malice is not included in the adequate object of divine omnipotence; for there is nothing that is more precise than the causality of a faculty that is specified by its object, even though something else is intimately connected with it. Thus it is only the color of the apple that is seen by the visual faculty, and not the smell; and just as smell is not included in the object of sight, so the evil of sin is not included in the adequate object of indefectible omnipotence.

Finally, it is insisted that the cause of anything is the cause of that which is essentially combined with it; but certain physical acts are essentially and morally evil, such as the hatred of God; therefore God in moving one to these acts, cannot prescind from their malice.

Reply. I distinguish the major: that the cause of anything in the physical order is the cause of that which is essentially combined with it in the same order, this I concede; when what is essentially combined with it is in the moral order, then I deny the major.

Hence God causes whatever there is of a positive nature in sin, as it is an effectible entity, but not as it is a defectible entity, because the evil of sin is not included in the adequate object of indefectible omnipotence. Even if, by an impossibility, God willed to cause it, He could not do so. This constitutes what is most clear in this chiaroscuro.

On the contrary, the objective motion to the act of sin, by reason of the object proposed to the will, does not prescind from its malice. Thus he who advises or commands the sinful act, is guilty of sin. But God does not move the will to the object of sin, but only to the performance of the act, and He does not determine it to the material element in sin, before it has in some manner determined itself to what formally constitutes sin, through the will deliberately refusing to consider at the very moment the fulfillment of the obligation imposed upon it. This deliberate refusal on the part of the will to consider the obligation imposed upon it is the beginning of sin, which coexists with sufficient grace, or the proximate power for the required consideration. And prior to this deliberate refusal of consideration, all that is required on God's part is the permission of sin, which is not the cause of sin, but its indispensable condition.

Moreover, we must carefully distinguish between the divine permission that is prior to the first offense, and which therefore is not a punishment, and the refusal of divine efficacious grace, which is already a punishment, and which therefore presupposes at least a first offense. To confuse these two, between which the Thomists take care to distinguish, as being that which is prior to the first offense, and that which follows it, would result, indeed, in Calvinism.[337]

Moreover, there is a vast difference between Calvinism and Thomism, inasmuch as Calvinism maintains the extinction of free will after original sin, it being an empty title. Thus there is an end of all merit, of all merit in obedience. The mystery of predestination is contaminated at its source by reason of the denial of God's universal will to save, which means the overthrow of the whole Christian religion. There is, besides, a more complete solution of this question in the following article.

Finally, it must be noted that this assertion maintained by the Thomists namely, "the divine decrees and grace are of themselves efficacious with reference to salutary acts," is connected with the principles of faith and proximately definable. In this almost all the schools, with the exception of the Molinist, agree with the Thomists.[338]

This assertion must not, therefore, be confused with the two following statements: "grace of itself efficacious must be explained by physical predetermination"; "predetermination must be applied to natural acts and to the material element in sin." These last two assertions may be looked upon as philosophical and logical deductions from the previous affirmation about grace that is of itself efficacious.

But the opponents strive to confuse these two questions, so that from the first assertion concerning the intrinsic efficacy of grace they may conclude that God becomes the cause of sin. Let them but remain faithful to the teaching of St. Thomas as set forth in this eighth article, and to his higher principles.[339]

---

[337] *Ibid.*, pp. 208-12.

[338] Cf. Billuart, *De Deo uno,* diss. VIII, a.5 (the end).

[339] It must be noted that there is no possible medium between these two propositions: God infallibly knows free conditioned futures either before He issues a decree about these (as stated in the theory of the *scientia media*), or else after He has issued a decree (as all those admit who reject the *scientia media*). But of late several theologians have sought to find a medium between these two contradictory propositions, confusing the conditioned future with the purely possible, as an anonymous author did in a recent brochure entitled: *Essai sur la determination exemplaire des futurs libres* (Paris, Mignard, 1937). But there is no excuse for this confusing of the issue: all indeed know that if Peter were placed in certain circumstances, either he would or would not betray his Master;

WHETHER GOD WILLS EVILS

State of the question. The difficulty consists in this: on the one
hand, God, who is infinitely good, cannot will evil; on the other hand,
He wills everything that appertains to the perfection and beauty of
the universe. But the evil, for example, of persecution, without which
there would not be the patience of the martyrs, pertains to the perfection of the universe. Moreover, if God in no way willed evils,
these would not happen, because nothing happens unless God wills
it. That is, as stated in the third objection of this article, "God does
not will that evil should not exist." Therefore it seems that God
wills evils.

It must be noted that evil is of three kinds.[340] For there is (1) the
evil of nature, which is the privation of good, even in irrational
things; then there is (2) in voluntary things the evil of sin, which is
the privation of moral rectitude; and there is (3) the evil of punishment, which is the privation of some good on account of sin.

There are two parts to the reply. The first part refers to the evil of
sin, and the second to the evils of nature and of penalty.

1) God does not at all will or cause the evil of sin, even accidentally, but only permits it. He cannot in any sense be called the
author of sin.

This conclusion is of faith according to Holy Scripture, which
says: "Thou art not a God that willest iniquity. . . . Thou hatest
all the workers of iniquity. Thou wilt destroy all that speak a lie." [341]

It was defined in the Council of Trent against Luther and Calvin:
"If anyone says that it is not in man's power to make his ways evil,
but that the works that are evil God worketh as well as those that are
good, not permissibly only, but properly and of Himself, in such wise
that the treason of Judas is no less His own proper work than the
vocation of Paul; let him be anathema." [342]

The reason for this first part of the answer is explained at length
by St. Thomas elsewhere,[343] by showing that God can be neither the
direct cause of sin (by inclining the will to sin), nor the indirect cause
(by not giving the required help, or giving it insufficiently), and
that He can permit sin on account of a greater good. Thus the evil

these are two possible events; but the conditioned future implies also a new
determination, that is, which of these two possibilities Peter would choose.

[340] Cf. *Summa theol.,* Ia, q.48, a.5.
[341] Ps. 5: 5; cf. Rom. 3: 5; 9: 14; James, 1: 13; I John 1: 5; 3: 9.
[342] Denz., no. 816.
[343] *Summa theol.,* Ia IIae, q.79, a.1.

of sin is a defect coming from a defective cause, not from God.

But in this article St. Thomas gives the general reason, which is: Since the aspect of good is the aspect of desirability, and since evil is opposed to good, it is impossible that any evil, as such, should be sought directly and essentially, though it can be sought indirectly and accidentally, inasmuch as it accompanies a good that is more desirable than the good of which it is a privation. Thus a lion kills a stag for the purpose of obtaining food.

But God wills no good more than He wills His own goodness. Hence God in no way, either essentially or accidentally, wills the evil of sin, which is the privation of the order toward divine good. But, as stated,[344] He only permits it.

Therefore, as we said previously,[345] God knows future sins in His permissive decree. It can now be said more explicitly that God knows future sins in a twofold decree, namely, permissive and effective; for there is a positive element in sin, that is, the act of effect, which can be produced only with the concurrence of the First Cause; and there is the privative element, and this comes, however, solely from a defectible and deficient cause.

The other part of the answer, that which refers to the evils of nature and of punishment, is worded as follows: God wills the evils of nature and of punishment, not indeed essentially but accidentally, by reason of the good that is connected with them.

What has been said makes this clear. (1) It is, indeed, impossible than an evil, as such, should be sought essentially and directly, for the aspect of good is the aspect of desirability. (2) God wills accidentally the evils of nature and of punishment, because He wills more the good to which this twofold evil is annexed, than the good of which the evil is the privation. Thus, by willing the preservation of the natural order, He wills accidentally or indirectly, as a quasi-consequence, the corruption of certain natural things. So, by willing of itself the life of the lion. He wills accidentally the death of the stag; so also in the moral order, by willing of itself justice, He wills punishment indirectly and accidentally.

Reply to first objection. This reply is against Hugo of St. Victor,[346] who taught that God willed that evils should be done, because it is a good thing, inasmuch as evils are directed to some good end. St. Thomas replies: "This, however, is not correct, since evil is not of itself ordered to good, but accidentally . . . ; as it was beside the intention of tyrants that the patience of the martyrs should shine forth from all their persecutions." That which of itself is ordered to

---

[344] Cf. ad 3um.
[345] Cf. *in Iam*, q.14, a.10.
[346] *De sacramentis*, Bk. IV, chap. 13.

good is not the evil itself which God permits, but God's holy permission. The reply to the second objection is to the same effect.

Reply to third objection. "God neither wills evil to be done, nor wills it not to be done, but wills to permit evil to be done; and this (willing to permit it) is a good."

Thus we must distinguish, as stated at the end of our commentary to the preceding article, between the permission of sin (especially the first sin), which is not a punishment, and the divine refusal of efficacious grace, which is already a punishment, and which presupposes, therefore, at least a first sin.[347]

TENTH ARTICLE

WHETHER GOD HAS FREE WILL

It has already been made clear to us in the third article that God does not necessarily will things other than Himself; for His goodness is infinite, and He is in complete possession of it apart from other things. But this article shows that free will is to be attributed to God, because what it formally signifies implies no imperfection.

There are two conclusions. (1) There is free will in God, because there is election in Him, inasmuch as He does not necessarily will things apart from Himself. This is of faith. (2) God is absolutely free, although it is not possible for Him to sin, this belonging to the imperfection of creatures. As St. Thomas says: "Since the evil of sin consists in turning away from the divine goodness, by which God wills all things, it is manifestly impossible for Him to will the evil of sin; yet He can make choice of one of two opposites, inasmuch as He wills a thing to be, or not to be." [348] This means that God enjoys absolute liberty, sin being for Him an impossibility, just as supreme wisdom excludes the possibility of error. This applies, though in a modified manner, to the most holy soul of Christ, which is both free and absolutely impeccable, for its liberty is the most pure image of the divine liberty, which is both absolute and impeccable.

ELEVENTH ARTICLE

WHETHER THE WILL OF EXPRESSION IS TO BE DISTINGUISHED IN GOD

State of the question. The purpose of St. Thomas in this article is to explain the commonly accepted distinction between God's will

---

[347] Cf. *Summa theol.*, Ia IIae, q.79, a.3 f. See also end of commentary to q.19, a.8: solution of the objections because of the supposed resemblance between Thomism and Calvinism.
[348] Cf. ad 2um.

of good pleasure, and His will of expression. The former has already been discussed in this question.[349]

That God's commands, which are not always observed, are called God's will, seems to be the foundation for this distinction. Thus we read: "Thy will be done on earth as it is in heaven." [350] Then the will of God is not the same in meaning as His consequent and efficacious will of good pleasure, which is always fulfilled, and this latter is not absolutely the same as His antecedent will of good pleasure, which is of itself never efficacious.[351] In what sense, therefore, is God's command called His will?

To understand this distinction, St. Thomas makes the following observations in this article: "What is usually with us an expression of will, is sometimes metaphorically called will in God, just as when anyone lays down a precept, it is a sign that he wishes this precept obeyed. Hence a divine precept is sometimes called by metaphor the will of God, as in the words: Thy will be done on earth, as it is in heaven." [352]

St. Thomas concludes: "Therefore in God there are distinguished will in its proper sense, and will as attributed to Him by metaphor. 'Will' in its proper sense is called the will of good pleasure (which is, as above stated, either consequent or antecedent); 'will' metaphorically taken is the will of expression, inasmuch as the sign itself of will is called will."

It must be observed that sometimes God's command does not coincide with His will of good pleasure, as is evidently the case when God commanded Abraham to kill his son Isaac, since indeed He afterward commanded the contrary. But this command was a sign that God wished the patriarch to will the slaying of his son and make the necessary preparations.

TWELFTH ARTICLE

WHETHER FIVE EXPRESSIONS OF WILL ARE RIGHTLY ASSIGNED TO THE DIVINE WILL

State of the question. There are five expressions of will that are generally assigned in various passages of Holy Scripture to the divine will. These are: precept, counsel, prohibition, permission, and operation.

The reason St. Thomas gives for this enumeration is that in these five ways we are accustomed to signify that we will something. For

[349] See *supra*, pp. 534 f.
[350] Matt. 6: 10.
[351] See q.19, a.6 ad 1um.
[352] Matt. 6: 10.

when we do anything it is a clear sign that we will it. When we command or advise something to another, it is a sign that we will it to be done (or not done, if it is something we forbid). Finally, when we permit someone over whom we have authority to do something, it is a sign that we do not will to prevent it. Hence St. Augustine says: "Nothing is done, unless the Almighty wills it to be done, either by permitting it, or by actually doing it." [353]

Doubt. How is the will of expression related to the will of good pleasure?

St. Thomas replies [354] by showing that there is sometimes, but not always, agreement between these two wills. He says more explicitly in another of his works: "It is necessary for us to know that there are three ways in which the will of expression is related to the will of good pleasure. For there is a will of expression which never coincides with the will of good pleasure, such as when God permits the perpetration of evil, since He never wills this; [355] but there is a will of expression that always coincides with the will of good pleasure, as in the case of operation; and sometimes, indeed, they coincide, and sometimes not, as in the case of command, prohibition, and counsel.[356] Thus when God commanded Abraham to kill his son Isaac, this did not coincide with His will of good pleasure, for He afterward commanded the contrary. Thus when a command is not fulfilled as it ought to be, it does not coincide with God's efficacious or consequent will of good pleasure, but with His antecedent will.

Objection. If the will of expression does not always coincide with the will of good pleasure, then it is incorrect to call it the will of expression; for a sign that is not in conformity with the thing signified is a false sign.

St. Thomas replies: "Although God does not will everything He commands or permits, yet He wills something concerning this; for He wills all to be under obligation to do what He commands, and that it be in our power to do what He permits, command and permission being an expression of this divine will." [357]

Finally it must be noted what is often said by spiritual authors, such as Bossuet: "Christian indifference being out of the question where the expressed will [358] of God is concerned, we must restrict it, as St. Francis de Sales does, to certain events controlled by His will of good pleasure, whose sovereign commands determine the daily

---

[353] *Enchiridion,* chap. 95.
[354] Cf. ad 2um.
[355] God wills only to permit the evil of sin.
[356] *De veritate,* q.23, a.3 ad 6um.
[357] *Ibid.,* ad 2um. See also Ia, q.19, a.11 ad 2um.
[358] What is said here is against Quietism.

occurrences in the course of life." [359] Dom Vital Lehodey says: "The good pleasure of God is the domain of abandonment; His expressed will, of obedience." [360] We have explained at length elsewhere [361] in what sense it is true to say that the divine will of expression made known by various commands is the domain of obedience, whereas the will of good pleasure not as yet made known is the domain of holy indifference and abandonment into God's hands. But we must now treat of God's love for Himself and for us, or of the act of His will of good pleasure.

APPENDIX

ON GOD'S PERSONALITY IN OPPOSITION TO PANTHEISM

The pantheists and monists either completely or partly identify the world with its principle, and therefore they deny the distinction between God and the world, and His real personality. For they teach that a personal God does not exist, since the notion of person implies limitation. For these, person or the ego presupposes another certain independent being, as a non-ego in opposition to the ego. Thus the notion of person implies limitation.

This error is refuted from the principles already established. We must bear in mind that a person is an intelligent and free subject.

But the teaching authority of the Church enunciates in the Vatican Council what is the foundation for this refutation, by attributing to God what formally constitutes person, namely, subsistence, intelligence, free will, and also a real and essential distinction from the world; and the reason assigned for this is that, whereas the world is essentially composite and mobile, it requires God as the supreme, absolutely simple, and unchangeable cause.

The Vatican Council says: "The Holy Catholic . . . Church believes and confesses that there is one true and living God, Creator and Lord of heaven and earth, almighty, eternal, immense, incomprehensible, infinite in intelligence, in will and in all perfection, who, as being one, sole, absolutely simple and immutable spiritual sub-

---

[359] *Etats d'oraison*, Bk. VIII, chap. 9.

[360] *Holy Abandonment*, p. 123. St. Francis de Sales explains this more fully in his *Love of God*, Bk. VIII, chap. 5: "Of the conformity of our will with that will of God which is made known to us by His commandments and his counsels"; also chap. 14: "A short method for knowing God's will"; similarly, Bk. IX, chaps. 1–5: "Of the union of our will with that divine will which is called the will of good pleasure, especially in afflictions, and of holy indifference."

[361] *Providence* (Eng. tr.), pp. 215–67, in which this doctrine is explained that, "in obeying as best we can God's will as made known to us, we must abandon ourselves for the rest with full confidence to His will of good pleasure." See *ibid.*, p. 218.

stance, is to be declared as really and essentially distinct from the world (which is composite and changeable), of supreme beatitude in and of Himself, and ineffably exalted above all things besides Himself which exist or are conceivable." [362]

From what has been said in previous questions, it is evident that this doctrine has its foundation in Holy Scripture; moreover, the reason is given for the distinction between the absolutely simple and unchangeable God and the composite and changeable world, and the reason why the term "person" is predicated of God, since He is the intelligent, free, and subsistent Being who is independent of any other being.

Although revelation declares that there are three Persons in God, yet God, speaking of His nature and creative power, which are common to the Trinity,[363] says to Moses: "I am who am. . . . Thus shalt thou say to the children of Israel: The Lord God of your fathers, the God of Abraham, the God of Isaac, and the God of Jacob hath sent me to you. This is My name forever." [364] And again we read: "I am the Lord and I change not." [365] "I am, I am the Lord; and there is no savior besides Me. I have declared and have saved." [366] God is always referred to in Holy Scripture as endowed with knowledge, volition, action, spiritually creating and exercising dominion over all things, and He often expresses that He is the personal Being, by using the pronoun "I" in speaking of Himself. Moreover, in accordance with revelation, God must be invoked as Father,[367] which is a personal name.[368] Therefore, whatever belongs to the notion of person (subsistence, intelligence, liberty) is found formally and eminently in God, without any imperfection.

Objection. But the subsisting ego is named in opposition to the non-ego, which is likewise independent. If, therefore, God were a person, this would presuppose something else independent of Himself, and thus He would not be the principle of all things.

Reply. I distinguish the antecedent: the subsisting ego, inasmuch as this is a created and limited person, is named in opposition to the non-ego that is likewise independent and existing, this I concede; that this pertains to what is formally signified by the name "person,"

362 Denz., no. 1782.
363 *Summa theol.*, Ia, q.32, a.1.
364 Ex. 3: 14.
365 Mal. 3: 6.
366 Is. 43: 11. See also Jer. 7: 11; 32: 27.
367 Matt. 6: 9.
368 St. Thomas remarks (Ia, q.33, a.3): "This name Father in the divine persons is predicated first personally, and afterward essentially (as common to the whole Trinity) with reference to creatures, especially rational creatures that by grace become the adopted sons of God."

inasmuch as it is distinct from its created mode, this I deny. And I deny the consequent and consequence.

For indeed, as stated, what is formally signified by "person" implies only subsistent, intelligent, and free being, which can be called ego. Thus in God, ego is what is formally signified by person, and with reference to God, non-ego signifies possible things, and after creation those things which, inferior to God, either are, will be, or were created by Him.

Thus the name "person" is not predicated univocally of God and created rational beings, but analogically, and this not only metaphorically but properly, so that what is formally signified by "person" is in God formally and eminently as absolutely independent subsistence, intellection, and free will.

Another objection. Every person must be endowed with self-consciousness. But all self-consciousness necessarily implies limitation, inasmuch as consciousness distinguishes the ego from the non-ego. Therefore God is not a person.

Reply. I distinguish the major: that a person must have the created mode of consciousness, this I deny; that a person can be without such mode, this I concede. I distinguish the minor: that the created mode of consciousness denotes limitation, this I concede; that what is formally signified by consciousness denotes limitation, this I deny.

Evidently a created person as such is self-conscious, inasmuch as it is this that makes such a person distinct from God and other created persons. But nothing prevents God from being most perfectly conscious of Himself, inasmuch as He is the self-subsisting Being, and by this He is distinct from possible beings and, after creation, from created beings.

THE SANCTITY OF GOD

From what has been said about God's will, it is evident that God enjoys the highest degree of sanctity, because He is infinitely perfect both in intellect and in will, and, as we shall see in the following question, God infinitely and immutably loves His most perfect goodness for its own sake and as the measure of any moral good. Hence God's will, which is impeccable,[369] is most holy; in fact, it is essential sanctity.

Holy Scripture repeatedly asserts this, as in the following texts: "The Lord is just in all His ways, and holy in all His works." [370] "Who is like to Thee, glorious in holiness?" [371] "Holy, Holy,

---

[369] Cf. q. 19, a. 9.
[370] Ps. 144: 17.
[371] Ex. 15: 11.

Holy," [372] the seraphim proclaim Him to be. God is often called 'The Holy One of Israel." This sanctity is the exemplar of our sanctity: "Be you therefore perfect as also your heavenly Father is perfect." [373]

This sanctity of God, inasmuch as it is communicative, is called benignity. This is declared many times in Holy Scripture: "When Thou openest Thy hand, they shall all be filled with good." [374] "O how good and sweet is Thy spirit, O Lord, in all things." [375] "Every best gift and every perfect gift is from above, coming down from the Father of lights." [376] Moreover, God in calling Himself Father, expresses His readiness to be beneficent. In fact, "God so loved the world as to give His only begotten Son." [377] As St. Thomas says: "It pertains to the divine will to communicate by likeness its own good to others as much as is possible." [378] Moreover, this benignity of God is especially evident in His love and mercy toward creatures, which we must now discuss.

Finally, from what has been said it is clear that there is infinite beauty in God, in fact, essential beauty not only of the ontological but also of the intellectual and moral orders.

For as St. Thomas says: "Beautiful things are those which please when seen; hence beauty consists in due proportion," [379] which means that this requires unity in diversity or harmony, and splendor of this unity as well as of truth and goodness.

But God most perfectly and essentially possesses the infinite plenitude of being, intelligence, and goodness, of all perfections in the highest unity of His Deity, so that it is said of His wisdom: "For she is more beautiful than the sun, and above all the order of the stars: being compared with the light, she is found before it." [380] "She is the brightness of eternal light." [381]

Hence God by reason of His beauty is to Himself the fount of infinite delight and beatitude,[382] and the vision of God produces in intellectual creatures ineffable complacency and supreme joy. Thus God is the first beauty, and the exemplar of all ontological, intellectual, and moral beauty.

---

[372] Is. 6: 3.
[373] Matt. 5: 48.
[374] Ps. 103: 28.
[375] Wis. 12: 1.
[376] James 1: 17.
[377] John 3: 16.
[378] *Summa theol.*, q.19, a.2.
[379] *Ibid.*, Ia, q.5, a.4 ad 1um.
[380] Wis. 7: 29.
[381] *Ibid.*, 7: 26.
[382] See *infra*, q.26.

CHAPTER XX

QUESTION 20

GOD'S LOVE

THIS question treats of God's love as being the principal act of His will: (1) its existence (a. 1); (2) its object (a. 2); (3) the mode of this love (a. 4, 5): Whether God loves all things equally, or whether He loves the better things more.

FIRST ARTICLE

WHETHER LOVE EXISTS IN GOD

State of the question. The point of inquiry in this article is whether love is formally and not merely virtually in God. It seems that love is not formally in God, for love is a passion, and there are no passions in God. Moreover, love is of the same order as anger and sorrow, and these are not in God. Lastly, love is a uniting force, the connecting link between lovers. Hence this does not seem to exist in God, who is most simple.

Yet the answer is: We must assert that in God there is love in the strict sense, not merely metaphorically.

1) This conclusion is of faith and is expressed many times in Holy Scripture. Thus we read: "God is charity." [1]

2) It is also proved by reason as follows: Love is the first act of the will; but will is formally in God; therefore love is formally in Him.

The major is evident from the fact that the will is specified by lovable good, and its love of good is prior to its avoidance of evil, and its love of good simply as such is prior to its sadness or its joy by reason of the absence or presence of good. To love means nothing else but to will good. Love is nothing else but the inclination to good, or, if one is already in possession of good, as God is, then it is complacency in the same. But this perfection includes no imperfection. Therefore love not only exists in God, but exists in Him formally and eminently. [2] It is not a question here of love as a pas-

[1] I John 4: 16.
[2] Cf. ad 2um.

sion, or as an act of the sensitive appetite, but as it is an act of the intellectual appetite.[3]

Corollary. Joy is likewise formally in God, because it is satisfaction in the good possessed. The reason is that there is no imperfection in the formal concept of joy, as there is none in the concept of love. On the contrary, anger and sadness imply imperfection, and can exist in God only virtually or metaphorically. Sadness is affliction of mind because of present evil, and this sadness at having been offended gives rise to anger, which is the appetite for revenge. Hence when Holy Scripture says that God repents or is angry, this repentance and anger must be understood in a metaphorical sense. Thus anger signifies justice that inflicts the deserved punishment.

First doubt. Of what kind is the love by which God loves Himself?

The answer. From what has been said it is clear that God infinitely and necessarily loves Himself.[4] But this most eminent love is not, in the strict sense either the love of concupiscence or of friendship, but is something higher.[5] For the love of concupiscence is that by which we will something as being good especially for ourselves; and the love of friendship is that by which we love another, wishing good for the other as we wish it for ourselves. But God is absolutely identified with His love for Himself. Hence this love transcends both the love of concupiscence and the love of friendship.

Objection. There is between the divine persons, for example, between the Father and the Son, a mutual and amicable love that is accompanied by a supreme communication of good things. Therefore the love of friendship exists formally in the divine persons.

Reply. I deny the antecedent; for this mutual love between the divine persons is not formally such on the part of the act itself of love, but only on the part of the Persons loving, who by one sole act love Themselves. Hence it is not simply friendship, but something more than this, that is, it is not unifying love, but unity of love and identity of good things.

Second doubt. Can zeal be properly attributed to God? It can, because zeal is intense love that vigorously repels all that is contrary to it; and there can be no imperfection in it, such as that of envy or suspicion. Thus God is said to be zealous.[6]

Third doubt. Is hatred properly attributed to God?

Reply. The evil of enmity by which we will evil as such to another is only metaphorically in God; for God does not will evil as such to the sinner, but as it is a just punishment. Now, to be sure, the just

---

[3] Cf. ad 1um.

[4] *Summa theol.*, Ia, q. 19, a. 2, 3.

[5] See John of St. Thomas' commentary on this article.

[6] Ex. 34: 14.

judge condemning the murderer to death, does not do this because of hatred for him, but from love of justice. Far more so, does God do this, of whom it is said: "Neither hath He pleasure in the destruction of the living," [7] but loves justice. Thus the devil is strictly so, the enemy of God; but God is not, strictly so, the enemy of the devil.

But as for the hatred of abomination by which the just person detests sin as an evil, it is disputed whether this is attributed properly or only metaphorically to God. Suarez, Vasquez, and several modern theologians affirm that it applies properly to God, because Holy Scripture says that God hates iniquity, and that sin is displeasing to Him. Hence they say that He formally detests it as simply evil, although He permits it, and afterward punishes it.

On the contrary, St. Thomas says: "Hence (because God cannot will evil) it appears that hatred of a thing cannot be ascribed (properly) to God. Just as love is related to good, so is hatred to evil; for we will good to those we love, but evil to those we hate. Therefore if God's will cannot be inclined to evil, as was said above,[8] it is impossible for Him to hate anything." [9] Hence several Thomists, such as John of St. Thomas and Gonet, hold that hatred of iniquity is only metaphorically or virtually in God, as a consequence of His love of justice. They say that no act of the divine will refers strictly to what is evil, either as to be pursued or as to be avoided, and that it is directly in conflict with it. No act of God can be formally avoidance of evil; for avoidance of evil belongs properly only to the created will, since it is imperfect, and it may find itself opposed by ₁evil, and be prevented from attaining its good. But God's will is most perfect; no evil can oppose it and prevent it from attaining its good. Therefore hatred of iniquity is not formally but virtually in God, inasmuch as it is virtually contained in His love of justice, and inasmuch as sin is directly opposed to His created virtue, that is, to charity or justice. Similarly, reasoning is virtually contained in the divine intellect. This seems at least to be the more probable opinion.

Fourth doubt. Do hope and desire properly belong to God?

The answer is in the negative. The reason is that hope refers to future good, which is something arduous or difficult of attainment, and this cannot be said of God. But desire refers to absent good, which is neither formally nor eminently possessed by the one who desires it. But God possesses all things eminently.

[7] Wis. 1: 14.

[8] *Contra Gentes*, Bk. I, chap. 95.

[9] *Ibid.*, chap. 96. See also the commentary of Francis Silvester (Ferrariensis) on this chapter.

SECOND ARTICLE

WHETHER GOD LOVES ALL THINGS

State of the question. It seems that God does not properly, but only metaphorically, love things apart from Himself, for Dionysius says: "Love places the lover outside himself," [10] and this, so it seems, would be an imperfection for God. Moreover, God's love is eternal and He alone is eternal; hence it seems that God loves only Himself and not things apart from Himself.

Aristotle seems to admit this, even Plato, as also the Neoplatonists, and among modern philosophers Spinoza, who maintains that the world proceeds of necessity from God, but is not loved by Him.

But the answer is: God loves all existing things, and indeed in the strict sense of the term.

1) This conclusion is of faith, for the Scripture says: "Thou lovest all things that are, and hatest none of those things which Thou hast made." [11] And in the New Testament we read: "God so loved the world as to give His only begotten Son." [12] Nor is there any reason, as will immediately be stated, for restricting these words to a metaphorical sense.

2) The proof from reason is as follows: To love anything is to will good to that thing; but God wills good to all things that are, were, or will be, that is, He wills at least their existence, which depends on His divine will; therefore God properly loves all existing things.

Moreover, "the love of God infuses and creates goodness (in things)," [13] whereas, on the contrary, our will is not the cause of the goodness of things, but is moved by it as by its object, and thus it calls forth our love, whereby we will the preservation and increase of goodness in another.

Therefore God's love with reference to creatures is in no way passive, but active; in fact, it creates, conserves, and vivifies this love in them. It does not presuppose lovableness in the object, but posits this in it. Thus grace that makes one pleasing to God is the effect of His love elevating us to a participation of His intimate life.[14] Thus the treatise on grace is connected with the treatise on God.

There is no imperfection in what is formally denoted by this concept. However, God's love of creatures is not said to be an ab-

---

[10] *De div. nom.*, Bk. IV, chap. 1.
[11] Wis. 11: 25.
[12] John 3: 16.
[13] See end of argumentative part of this article.
[14] *Summa theol.*, Ia IIae, q. 110, a. 1.

solutely simple perfection in the strict sense, because this love is a free act, as stated above,[15] and therefore it is not better for God to have this love than not to have it.

Reply to first objection. The expression, "love places the lover outside himself," is improperly used to signify that the lover wills good to the beloved; and in this latter, there is no imperfection.

Reply to second objection. As God knows future things eternally, He loved them eternally. In fact, the creative action is eternal, although its effect takes place in time. It is a formally immanent action, and is only virtually transitive inasmuch as it produces an external effect. Thus the effect is new, but not the action.

Reply to third objection. God loves rational creatures with the love of friendship, inasmuch as He wills them good, especially the good of eternal life. God, strictly speaking, does not love irrational creatures with the love of friendship (because they are incapable of returning this love and sharing in His life), but with the love of quasi-concupiscence, inasmuch as He orders them to rational creatures, and thus indirectly to Himself.

Reply to fourth objection. God loves sinners in so far as they belong to a certain kind of nature, and He preserves them in existence; but He does not love them in so far as they are sinners, or as they are deficient in good.

First doubt. Does God love possible things? He does not indeed in the sense that He wills to give them existence, and this constitutes the distinction between possible and future things. But God loves His essence as it is infinitely capable of being participated in *ad extra;* and as the number of possible things is infinite, so He loves His omnipotence.

Second doubt. Does God love *futuribilia,* conditioned futures that will not come into existence?

Reply. He loves these conditionally. We discussed this point when treating of [16] God's antecedent will, which is conditional.

THIRD ARTICLE

WHETHER GOD LOVES ALL THINGS EQUALLY

State of the question. The difficulty presents itself because we read in Holy Scripture that "He hath equally care of all." [17] Moreover, God's love, inasmuch as it is the unique uncreated act, does not

---

15 *Ibid.,* Ia, q.19, a.3.
16 *Ibid.,* a.6 ad 1um.
17 Wis. 6: 8.

admit of degree. Lastly, God is not said to know some things more than others. Therefore He does not love some things more than others.

On the other hand, St. Augustine says: "God loves all things which He has made, and among them rational creatures more, and of these especially those who are members of His only begotten Son; and, much more than all, His only-begotten Son Himself." [18]

The answer is that God loves all things equally on the part of the very act of the will, because by one and the same act He loves all things. But He does not love all things equally on the part of the good willed, but He loves the better things more.

The first part requires no special proof, for there are not several acts in God differing in intensity. Hence the saying, "God has equally care of all," [19] because He administers all things with a like wisdom and goodness.[20]

The second part of the proof presents no difficulty. On the part of the good willed, we are said to love that one more than another, for whom we will a greater good, although we do not will with greater intensity. But God wills a greater good for some creatures than for others; for some He wills only existence, for others life, for others intelligence, for others the life of grace, for others the life of glory, and for Christ the hypostatic union. Therefore God does not love all things equally on the part of the good willed.

Corollary. This is expressed at the end of the argumentative part of this article as follows: "Since God's love is the cause of goodness in things (a. 2), no one thing would be better than another, if God did not will greater good for one than for another." This can be called the "principle of predilection," and it is most universal. It holds good for whatever being is better than another: for the plant with reference to the stone, for the animal with reference to the plant, for man with reference to the animal, for the just person with reference to the wicked one, for the elect with reference to others.

The doctrine of gratuitous predestination is virtually contained in this principle. There is a better explanation of this doctrine in the following article, in which we see that it is both a naturally knowable and a revealed truth.

[18] *Tract. in Joan.*, 110.

[19] Cf. ad 1um.

[20] On the contrary it is proper for us to love God more intensively than creatures. For the observance of the precept, indeed, it suffices that we love God *appraisively* above all things; but the saints in heaven also love God *intensively* above all things, which is what we must strive to do.

FOURTH ARTICLE

WHETHER GOD ALWAYS LOVES THE BETTER THINGS MORE

State of the question. The difficulty arises from the following considerations. (1) Although Christ is better than the whole human race, yet "God delivered Him up for us all." [21] Therefore it seems that He loves the human race more than He loves Christ. (2) An angel is better than a man, and yet God showed that He loved men more by sending them His Son. (3) Peter was better than John, since he loved Christ more, as our Lord's question shows: "Simon, son of John, lovest thou Me more than these?" [22] Yet Jesus loved John more, who was called the disciple whom Jesus loved. (4) The innocent man is better than the repentant, and yet it is said: "There shall be joy in heaven upon one sinner that doth penance, more than upon ninety-nine just who need not penance." [23] (5) The just man who is foreknown (not predestined) is better than the predestined sinner, and yet God loves the predestined sinner more.

Nevertheless the answer is: "The reason why some things are better than others, is that God wills for them a greater good. Hence it follows that He loves the better things more.

1) This truth is expressed clearly in revelation, as stated in various texts of Holy Scripture. Thus we read: "How could anything endure (in good), if Thou wouldst not? [24] And our Lord said: "Without Me you can do nothing," [25] in the order of salvation. "For He saith to Moses: I will have mercy on whom I will have mercy; and I will show mercy to whom I will show mercy. So then it is not of him that willeth nor of him that runneth, but of God that showeth mercy." [26] Thus of the two thieves who died on Calvary, one of them by God's special mercy was saved. This is the principle of predilection, namely, that no one would be better than another unless loved more by God. This principle virtually contains, as we said, the whole doctrine of predestination, according to which some attain to eternal life and are called the elect, because they were loved and helped more by God.[27]

2) For this answer the proof from reason is more than a theological conclusion since it is a truth revealed in Holy Scripture. It is as

---

[21] Rom. 8: 32.
[22] John 21: 15.
[23] Luke 15: 7.
[24] Wis. 11: 26.
[25] John 15: 5.
[26] Rom. 9: 15; Ex. 33: 19.
[27] *Summa theol.*, Ia, q.23, a.4, 5.

follows: God's will is the cause of goodness in things; [28] but God's love for anything is greater in so far as He wills a greater good for it; therefore the reason why some things are better than others, is that God wills a greater good for them.

This conclusion follows as a corollary from the principle of causality, and may be fully expressed as follows: Every contingent being requires a cause, and in the final analysis the first cause, which is God. Thus God is the cause of the entity and goodness of things. Hence no being would be better than another unless God willed a greater good for this being than for another, as it was already stated in the preceding article.

It must be observed that this principle, as thus expressed, concerns God's consequent will, on which depends any good whatever that here and now happens, whereas what really can happen depends on His antecedent will, such as that His commandments can really be observed, even when they are not actually observed. [29]

Moreover, this principle is most universal and admits of no exception, that is, it applies to all created beings, and especially to men and angels, in this sense that no one would be better than another (by an act easy or difficult to perform, natural or supernatural, first or final), unless he were loved more by God.

This principle is declared by St. Augustine when he says of the good and bad angels: "If both the good and bad (angels) were created equally good, then, whereas the latter fell by their evil will, the former were more abundantly assisted, and reached that state of complete happiness which made them absolutely certain of never losing it." [30] This means that, as men are predestined, so the good angels were previously loved, chosen, and predestined.

The solution of the objections confirms this conclusion.

Reply to first objection. "God loves Christ more than He loves the entire created universe because He willed for Him the greater good in giving Him a name that is above all names, in so far as He was true God. Nor did anything of His excellence diminish when God delivered Him up to death for the salvation of the human race; rather did He become thereby a glorious conqueror," since he became the conqueror of sin, the devil, and death. Farther on we find St. Thomas saying: "Had sin not existed, the incarnation would not have been"; [31] but he adds: "There is no reason, however, why human nature should not have been raised to something greater after sin. For God allows evils to happen in order to bring a greater good

[28] *Ibid.*, q.19, a.4.
[29] Cf. *ibid.*, a.6 ad 1um.
[30] *De civitate Dei*, Bk. XII, chap. 9.
[31] *Summa theol.*, IIIa, q.1, a.3.

therefrom. Hence it is written (Rom. 5: 20): "Where sin abounded, grace did more abound." Hence, too, in the blessing of the paschal candle, we say: "O happy fault that merited such and so great a Redeemer." This means that, had sin not existed, the incarnation would not have been; but, on the other hand, God permitted Adam's sin and original sin only for a greater good, and after the Fall this greater good is known to be the redemptive incarnation, which is the source of all our graces. Hence the doctrine of this article is confirmed, namely, that no one thing would be better than another unless it were loved more by God, and Christ was and is loved by God more than the entire created universe.

Reply to second objection. "God loves the human nature assumed by the Word of God in the person of Christ more than He loves all the angels; for that nature is better, especially on the ground of union with the Godhead. . . . God therefore did not assume human nature because He loved man, absolutely speaking, more; but because the needs of man were greater; just as the master of a house may give to a sick servant some more costly delicacy, which he does not give to his own son in sound health."

But the fallen angels were incapable of redemption because, as stated farther on, "the angel's free will is flexible to either opposite before the choice but not after," [32] so that their choice is a participation in the immutability of the divine choice.

Reply to third objection. As to whether Christ loved Peter more than John, St. Thomas remarks at the end of his reply, that "it may seem presumptuous to pass judgment" on which of the two, either Peter or John, Christ loved more with the love of charity. It is also presumptuous to say which of the two God loved more, absolutely speaking, and ordained to a greater degree of eternal glory. For, as the Scripture says: "The Lord is the weigher of spirits," [33] and there is no other. Moreover, there is no certain statement about this in revelation.

Reply to fourth objection: "Whether innocent or penitent, those are the better and the better loved who have more grace. Other things being equal, innocence is the nobler thing and the more beloved. God is said to rejoice more over the penitent than over the innocent, because often penitents rise from sin more cautious, humble, and fervent." From this something of great importance follows concerning predestination. It is that, if one of two sinners rises from sin, this is solely because of God's special mercy, who converts one rather than another. But if anyone keeps baptismal innocence until death,

[32] *Ibid.,* Ia, q.64, a.2.
[33] Prov. 16: 2.

this is a sign of God's greater grace, who thus preserved such a person in the performance of good works.

Reply to fifth objection. The non-predestined just person is better than the predestined sinner, although according to some other time he is worse.

Corollary. The validity and importance of the principle of predilection.

Hence the principle enunciated in the preceding article remains intact, namely, that, other things being equal, no one thing would be better than another unless it were loved more by God, or unless God willed it a greater good. Hence God loves the better things more. The whole doctrine of gratuitous predestination, which is explained farther on,[34] is virtually contained in this most exalted and most universal principle.

Moreover, this most exalted principle precludes from either priority or posteriority, which are expressed in the formulas: "before the foreseeing of merits" and "after the foreseeing of merits," and in some measure it transcends the distinction between the orders of intention and execution. But, as we have already clearly seen, it contains virtually, as it were from on high, what is called predestination before the "foreseeing of merits." In a manner more sublime it abstracts from the less important principles on which perhaps too much stress is laid at times, whereas it does not present clearly enough this principle of predilection.

This exalted principle presupposes with reference to our salutary acts, whether easy or difficult to perform, that God's consequent will is of itself efficacious, and that consequently grace is of itself efficacious, and not because our consent was foreseen by God.

Therefore Molina indirectly denies this principle of predilection when he says that grace is not of itself efficacious, by asserting that "of two that are called and equally aided by grace, it can happen that one of them is converted and the other not. In fact, it is possible for one who has received a less grace to rise again, when another who has received a greater grace does not rise again, and remains obdurate."[35]

This principle is likewise indirectly denied for salutary acts easy to perform, by the congruism of the Sorbonne. Thus Tournely held that grace of itself efficacious is required only for salutary acts difficult to perform, but not for easy ones, as if greater and less differentiated the species. Then if this principle admitted of exceptions, it would no longer be metaphysically certain.

[34] *Summa theol.*, Ia, q.23, a.1-5.
[35] *Concordia*, pp. 51, 565 (Paris ed.). Consult also the index of this work under the word "Auxilium."

It is likewise indirectly denied by the Augustinians, such as Berthi and Noris, who in the time of Jansenism wrote and admitted that grace of itself efficacious is required only as a consequence of original sin, because of the moral weakness of human nature, but not because of man's dependence on God. Hence they indirectly denied the principle of predilection for the state of innocence and for the angels, as if Molinism truly applied to the angels. But a metaphysical principle that admits of exceptions is no longer metaphysical, and is, moreover, of no value. On the contrary, the sublimity and absolute universality of this exalted principle so beautifully illustrates all questions concerning grace and predestination, either for men in any state of life, or for the angels.

CHAPTER XXI

QUESTION 21

THE JUSTICE AND MERCY OF GOD

AFTER considering the divine love, we must treat of God's justice and mercy. For they are virtues that reside in the will, the principal act of which is love. Then providence will be discussed, which is a virtue of the practical intellect, inasmuch as it analogically corresponds to our prudence and especially to that part which provides for future things.[1]

There are no other virtues in God, because the rest imply imperfection. For it is evident that faith, which is obscure, cannot be in God; nor can there be hope, which concerns future good that is difficult of attainment. But charity corresponds to the uncreated act of love, which was discussed in the previous question. Nor can there be any moral virtues in God by which He is referred to another either as His superior or equal, such as religion and piety; nor are there in Him those virtues that regulate the passions, such as temperance and fortitude, which in us reside in the sensitive appetite as directed by reason, although fortitude bears a certain resemblance to omnipotence, which is discussed in a subsequent question.[2]

But this twenty-first question decides: (1) whether there is justice in God and of what kind; (2) whether justice is identical with truth of which Holy Scripture speaks, associating it with mercy: (3) whether mercy is in God, and how it can be analogically and properly attributed to Him without denoting imperfection; (4) whether mercy and justice are to be found in every work of God.

FIRST ARTICLE

WHETHER THERE IS JUSTICE IN GOD

State of the question. The principal difficulty is that the act of justice is to pay what is due, or what is peculiarly one's own. Therefore justice is not attributed properly to God, not even analogically, but only metaphorically.

[1] Cf. *Summa theol.,* Ia, q.21, a.1 ad 1um.
[2] Cf. q.25.

Yet the answer is: Justice belongs properly to God, and there are very many texts in Holy Scripture that show this to be of faith. Thus we read: "The Lord is just and hath loved justice." [3]

In these texts God's justice is clearly seen as His constant will of giving to all what is due to them, in accordance with their nature and condition, and in view of their merits as ordained and promised by God.

It must be noted that Luther implicitly denied God's justice, asserting that the just person, even though he was a murderer and unchaste, can never be punished by the supreme Judge. Likewise, in our times, those impious persons who deny punishments in the future life, also contradict God's justice.

There is only the difficulty as to what kind of justice is properly attributed to God. Now justice, as explained in the treatise on this virtue, is divided into general and particular, which is again subdivided into commutative and distributive.

General justice, however, is of two kinds. There is legal justice, that refers to the common good in accordance with law, and equity or epikeia, which regards the spirit of the law more than its letter, which, if it were applied in certain cases, would be more severe, according to the saying: "extreme law, extreme injustice." But since this twofold general justice is, as St. Thomas says,[4] by way of a mastercraft in the king who commands, and administratively in his subjects, it is evident that this exists formally in God, who is the King of kings and the Lord of lords. Thus God takes care of all things, providing for the common good of all things in the universe, as befitting the manifestation of divine goodness.

Therefore this leaves only the difficulty concerning distributive and commutative justice to be considered. St. Thomas examines this difficulty in the body of this article.[5]

Reply. Commutative justice does not belong properly and formally to God, because the obligation of commutative justice arises from this, that another gave us something belonging to himself over which we had no dominion. But man and angel can give God nothing that is not already His and under His dominion. Even our free action is under God's dominion, just as all created beings are. Hence St. Paul says: "Who hath first given to Him, and recompense shall be made him?" [6] Therefore commutative justice does not exist properly and formally in God.

---

[3] Ps. 10: 8. See also Deut. 10: 17; 32: 4; Prov. 8: 18; Jer. 23: 6; Dan. 9: 14; Zach. 9: 9; Acts 10: 34; Eph. 6: 9; Col. 3: 25; II Tim. 4: 8; I Pet. 1: 17; I John 1: 9; Apoc. 16: 5.

[4] *Summa theol.*, IIa IIae, q.58, a.6.

[5] See also *Contra Gentes*, Bk. I, chap. 93.

[6] Rom. 11: 35.

Objection. One who is under obligation by reason of a pact or promise to reward another, if a certain work is performed, is bound by commutative justice. But God put Himself under such an obligation, for He says of Himself: "Call the laborers and pay them their hire." [7] In fact, St. Thomas says: "This form of the divine judgment is in accordance with the conditions of commutative justice, in so far as rewards are apportioned to merits, and punishments to sins." [8]

Reply. I distinguish the major: That one who is thus under obligation by reason of a pact or promise to reward another, is bound by commutative justice, if what is given is not already belonging to the other by right, this I concede; otherwise, I deny the major. I contradistinguish the minor in like manner. Hence, on God's part, the obligation is one of fidelity, but not of commutative justice. But if it is said that the kingdom of heaven is obtained by good works, then this is said metaphorically.

As for the difficulty arising from the text quoted by St. Thomas, it must be said that God in rewarding adheres to the *mode* of commutative justice, because He gives so much for so much; but this divine act is not properly and formally an act of commutative justice, for the reason already given. Similarly vindictive justice, in so far as it exists in God, pertains to commutative justice only as regards the mode of retribution; but as regards the debt incurred, it seems to belong more to legal or distributive justice. [9]

Distributive justice, however, is found formally in God. It is that justice whereby a ruler or a steward gives to each what his rank deserves. But this is perfection that excludes all imperfection, and it most fittingly applies to God as the supreme lord and ruler of the universe. Therefore distributive justice is found formally in God. Experience clearly shows that God distributes to all creatures what is necessary so that they can attain their end, although all do not actually do so.

Objection. Distributive justice implies the payment of what is due. But God is debtor to nobody. Therefore distributive justice does not properly and formally belong to God.

In accordance with the reply to the third objection of this article, we may say: I distinguish the major: I concede that distributive justice implies the payment of what is due, sometimes as dependent on the proper ordering of the one who distributes, as in the distribution of one's own as reward; I deny that the payment of what is due is always independent of this ordering. I contradistinguish the minor: that God is debtor to nobody, independently of His ordering, this I

---

[7] Matt. 20: 8.

[8] *Summa theol.,* IIa IIae, q.61, a.4 ad 1um.

[9] See below after the second article, corollaries concerning vindictive justice.

concede; as dependent on it, this I deny. Hence it is said that God is a debtor to Himself to give to all creatures what is necessary so that they can attain their end. Wherefore it is stated in the reply to the third objection: "It is due to God that there should be fulfilled in creatures what His will and wisdom require, and what manifests His goodness. In this respect God's justice regards what befits Him inasmuch as He renders to Himself what is due to Himself." Similarly, St. Thomas says: "Since our action has the character of merit only on the supposition of the divine ordination, it does not follow that God is made our debtor simply, but His own, inasmuch as it is right that His will should be carried out." [10]

But I insist. In distributive justice he who disposes of anything abdicates his right over the thing disposed of and transfers it to another. But God cannot abdicate His right over created things. Therefore distributive justice does not belong formally to God.

Reply. I distinguish the major: that sometimes he who disposes of something abdicates his right over the thing disposed of, this I concede; that he does so always, this I deny. Thus the sovereign preserves intact distributive justice by bestowing goods in common use by way of emphyteusis, though retaining direct dominion over them. Thus God, though retaining His supreme dominion over all created things, grants us dominion inferior and subordinate to His.[11]

SECOND ARTICLE

WHETHER THE JUSTICE OF GOD IS TRUTH

State of the question. The purpose of this article is to explain these words: "Mercy and truth have met each other; justice and peace have kissed," [12] in which, according to the context and tradition, truth stands for justice.

The difficulty is, however, that truth resides in the intellect, whereas justice is in the will. If there is a virtue that is called truth or rather veracity, it is a virtue that is annexed to justice, but is not, however, justice itself.

But the answer is: God's justice is fittingly called truth. The reason is that, since the divine intellect is the rule and measure of things, the truth of these things consists in their conformity with the divine intellect. Similarly, our works are called just according as they are in conformity with the divine law. But God's justice establishes things in the order conformable to the rule of His wisdom, which is

---

[10] *Summa theol.*, Ia IIae, q. 114, a. 1 ad 3um.
[11] Consult John of St. Thomas on this article.
[12] Ps. 84: 11.

the law of His justice. Therefore God's justice is fittingly called truth.

Reply to first objection. Justice, as to the law that governs, resides in the intellect; but God's knowledge is the cause of things in so far as His will is joined to it, and command is an act in which the intellect and will concur.

Reply to second objection. The truth of justice is thus distinct from God's veracity, but they are interrelated.

COROLLARIES

THE PRINCIPAL ACTS OF DIVINE JUSTICE

There are three acts: (1) to give everyone his due in accordance with his nature and condition; (2) to inflict the punishment that is due to sins; (3) to assign the reward that is due to one's merits. This second aspect of justice is called vindictive, and the third remunerative.

1) Divine justice is the just distribution of natural goods and supernatural helps, without which it is impossible for any creature to attain its end. St. Thomas says on this point: "As then the proper order displayed in ruling a family or any kind of multitude evinces justice of this kind in the ruler, so the order of the universe, which is seen both in things of nature and in things of the will, shows forth the justice of God." [13]

This is affirmed by Christ our Lord in His Sermon on the Mount: "Do not be solicitous for your life, what you shall eat; nor for your body, what you shall put on. Is not the life more than the meat, and the body more than the raiment? Behold the birds of the air, for they neither sow nor reap nor gather into barns; and your heavenly Father feedeth them. Are not you of much more value than they? . . . For your Father knoweth that you have need of all these things. Seek ye therefore first the kingdom of God and His justice, and all these things shall be added unto you." [14] If there is a just distribution of material goods, far more so must there be a just distribution of spiritual goods: "Is not the life more than the meat?"

Nevertheless, without injustice on God's part, there is great inequality of both natural and supernatural conditions. The inequality of natural conditions in the human race already existed in the state of original justice, for, as St. Thomas says: "Man is naturally a social being, and so in the state of innocence he would have led a social life. Now a social life cannot exist among a number of people unless under the presidency of one to look after the common good; for many,

---

[13] *Summa theol.*, Ia, q.21, a.1, c. See also ad 3um.
[14] Matt. 6: 25 f. Consult St. Thomas' *Commentary on St. Matthew.*

as such, seek many things, whereas one attends only to one. . . . The natural order of things requires this; and thus did God make man." [15] Similarly, there are hierarchies among the angels, for some dominate others. In fact, inequality among creatures, which is necessary so as to make them specifically different, is required for the fitting manifestation of divine goodness, and this cannot be sufficiently made manifest by one creature or by several that are absolutely equal. Thus no one collects a thousand copies of Virgil of the same edition and binding for his library. St. Thomas shows farther on [16] that the universe would not be perfect if only one grade of goodness were found in things. Similarly, the plant would not be perfect if all its parts consisted of flowers, nor would the human body be perfect if all its parts were equal in dignity to the eye. Thus God has established inequality among creatures, and also inequality of conditions in the human race.

But after original sin, as also by reason of the concupiscence of the flesh, the eyes, and the pride of life, this inequality of natural conditions has been very much increased and accentuated, so that some are extremely wealthy and others are in dire need and distress. Hence Christ said: "But woe to you that are rich, for you have your consolation; woe to you that are filled, for you shall hunger; woe to you that now laugh, for you shall mourn and weep." [17] These words are a condemnation of the inordinate love of riches. The Gospel also records what our Lord said about the wicked rich man and the good beggar Lazarus.[18]

Wherefore, among the signs of His Messianic office, Jesus declares that "the poor have the gospel preached to them"; [19] and in the beginning of His Sermon on the Mount, in proclaiming the evangelical beatitudes, He shows that inequality of natural conditions is not infrequently compensated by inequality of graces inasmuch as "God resisteth the proud, and giveth grace to the humble." [20] Thus He says: "Blessed are the poor in spirit, for theirs is the kingdom of heaven. Blessed are the meek, for they shall possess the land. Blessed are they that mourn, for they shall be comforted. Blessed are the merciful, for they shall obtain mercy. . . . Blessed are they that suffer persecution for justice' sake, for theirs is the kingdom of heaven." [21]

In this we see clearly that the highest degree of distributive justice is joined indeed to mercy, and this justice is also expressed in the

[15] *Summa theol.*, Ia, q.96, a.4.
[16] *Ibid.*, q.47, a.2.
[17] Luke 6: 24 f.
[18] *Ibid.*, 16: 25.
[19] Matt. 11: 5.
[20] Jas. 4: 6.
[21] Matt. 5: 3 f.

Magnificat in these words: "He hath put down the mighty from their seat and hath exalted the humble. He hath filled the hungry with good things, and the rich He hath sent empty away." [22]

This distributive justice as regards the distribution of graces is clearly seen in this, that, as St. Augustine says, "God commands not impossibilities, but, by commanding both admonishes thee to do what thou art able, and to ask for what thou art not able (to do)." [23] Thus the common saying: To one who does what he can (with the help of actual grace) God does not refuse to give (habitual) grace. Thus God gives sufficient grace to all adults, by which the fulfillment of an actually pressing obligation is made really possible. The efficacious grace is offered to us in the sufficient grace, just as the fruit is contained in the flower; but if man resists this sufficient grace, he deserves to be deprived of the efficacious grace by which *de facto* he could have effectively observed God's commandments.

Hence God's distributive justice is preserved intact even as regards infidels, as Pius IX declared in the following statement: "It is known to us and to you that those who labor under invincible ignorance concerning our most holy religion and who, diligently observing the natural law and its precepts that are engraved in the hearts of all by God, and being ready to obey Him, lead an honest and upright life, can, through the operative power of divine light and grace, attain eternal life, since God, who clearly intuits, scrutinizes, and knows the minds, impulses, thoughts, and habits of all, because of His supreme goodness and clemency, by no means will allow anyone to be punished eternally who was not guilty of any willful offense." [24] Similarly, St. Thomas had said: "If anyone, brought up as a savage, were guided by the light of natural reason in seeking good and avoiding evil, it must be held as most certain that God would make known to such a person either by an interior revelation what must be believed, or else He would direct someone to preach the faith to such a person, just as He sent Peter to Cornelius." [25]

All these things pertain to distributive justice whereby God distributes to all creatures what is necessary so that they can attain their end. Thus God sees to it that the adult is not without the necessary help to escape damnation and, if such a person is lost, it is his own fault.

Not all indeed received five talents, for some received only one; but if they did not resist this divine grace, they would receive many

[22] Luke 1: 52.
[23] *PL*, XLIV, 271; cf. Denz., no. 804.
[24] Denz., no. 1677. See also no. 1648.
[25] *De veritate*, q.14, a.11 ad 1um; cf. Acts, chap. 10.

others. Not infrequently, as we said, it is by inequality of graces that there is compensation on God's part for this inequality of natural conditions, especially so in the case of poverty. Hence in these cases not only does distributive justice remain unimpaired, but it is often wonderfully made manifest.

2) Another act of distributive justice is to inflict the punishment that is due to sin. Thus the Gospel records the following words as being addressed to the wicked rich man after his death: "Son, remember that thou didst receive good things in thy lifetime, and likewise Lazarus evil things; but now he is comforted; and thou art tormented." [26] As St. Thomas clearly explains: "Whatever rises up against an order to which it belongs, is put down by that order or by the principle thereof. . . . (But) whoever sins, . . . acts against reason, and against human divine law. Wherefore he incurs a threefold punishment; one, inflicted by himself, namely, remorse of conscience; another, inflicted by man; and a third, inflicted by God,[27] as the just judge who, without any passion, inflicts the punishment through love of His justice and infinite goodness that must be loved above all things. Thus vindictive justice belongs properly or formally to God.[28]

In this there is most just retribution, which is according to the proportion between the punishment and the sin. Thus venial sin is punished by temporal punishment, and mortal sin that is not forgiven in this life, but that has become irreparable through the sin of final impenitence, is justly punished by eternal punishment, for as St. Thomas says: "Sin incurs a debt of punishment through disturbing an order. But the effect remains so long as the cause remains. Therefore so long as the disturbance of the order remains, the debt of punishment must remain also. . . . Consequently, if a sin destroys the principle of the order whereby man's will is subject to God, there will be a deordination such as to be considered in itself irreparable, although it is possible to repair this by the power of God. Now the principle of this order is the last end to which man

26 Luke 16: 25.
27 *Summa theol.*, Ia IIae, q.87, a.1.
28 It is quite clear that eternal punishments, of which there is evidence in Holy Scripture (Matt. 25: 41, 46), because of their eternity can be only vindictive; for they are not inflicted either to correct the damned or to deter them from evil, although the punishments are medicinal for others.

From what has been said it is also apparent that vindictive justice follows as a result of God's sanctity. For the moral order, which is the image of God's sanctity that is freely willed by Him, cannot be maintained unless there can be a recourse to punishments for sins, and punishments that are vindictive and not merely corrective of a will confirmed in malice and refusing any correction.

adheres by charity. Therefore whatever sins turn man away from God, so as to destroy charity, considered in itself, they incur a debt of eternal punishment." [29]

If therefore these sins are not forgiven before death, final impenitence, supervening upon this irreparable perversion of the order, is made permanent, and it is then *de facto* punished by eternal punishment. Proportionate contrition and satisfaction are required in strictest justice for a deliberate sin, and when these are wanting punishment is inflicted so that the order may be preserved.[30]

It is a manifestation of mercy, however, that sinners who have many times fallen into mortal sin, frequently and repeatedly turn again to God; but they must fear lest, falling again into mortal sin, it may never be forgiven, because they did not know the time of God's visitation.[31] This concerns the question of the inscrutable mystery of predestination. Nevertheless we must always hope in God's mercy.

3) Finally, there is another act of divine justice, which consists in the admirable assignment of rewards, and these in just proportion.

Thus we read: "Blessed are the poor in spirit, for theirs is the kingdom of heaven. Blessed are the meek, blessed are they that mourn,

---

[29] *Summa theol.*, Ia IIae, q.87, a.3.

[30] As St. Thomas says (*ibid.*, ad 3um): "God does not delight in punishments for their own sake; but He does delight in the order of His justice, which requires them." He wills the manifestation of His justice by proclaiming the inalienable right of His infinite goodness to be loved above all things. The act of supreme legal justice consists in this, that it must compensate for the imperfections of human justice which does not always punish as it ought or assign the fitting reward; for great crimes committed here below sometimes go unpunished, and heroic virtues, since they remain hidden, are unrewarded. But on Judgment Day all these things will be revealed, and then the splendor of divine justice will be made manifest.

It is not derogatory to God's goodness and mercy to impose eternal punishment upon one for mortal sin that is not forgiven or for final impenitence. In inflicting this punishment God freely and rightly wills to manifest His most holy love for justice, and consequently His hatred of iniquity, having set aside the manifestation of His mercy. In fact, those who are unworthy of this mercy who depart this life in a state of final impenitence, not asking for forgiveness. Nevertheless, as stated farther on (q.21. a.4 ad 1um), "even in the damnation of the reprobates mercy is seen, since God punishes them short of their deserts."

Hermes, although he did not deny eternal punishments, asserted that vindictive justice is derogatory to the ultimate end of God's operation *ad extra*, because he considered that this end was the happiness of creatures rather than the manifestation of God's goodness and perfections. It must be observed, however, that God is most free in the exercise of His vindictive justice, so that He can pardon the repentant sinner, without inflicting any punishment. For it is the privilege of the supreme legislator and supreme judge that he can grant pardon outright for an offense. (Cf. *infra*, q.21, a.3 ad 2um).

[31] Cf. Luke 19: 44.

blessed are they that hunger and thirst after justice, blessed are the merciful, blessed are the clean of heart, blessed are the peacemakers, blessed are they that suffer persecution for justice' sake, for theirs is the kingdom of heaven." [32] But there must be purity of intention and a certain proportion between merit and reward. Therefore our Lord says: "Take heed that you do not your justice before men, to be seen by them; otherwise you shall not have a reward of your Father who is in heaven." [33] In these words our Lord admonishes us to strive for the simplicity of a pure intention. Hence He says of the hypocrites who give alms so as to be honored by men, that "they have received their reward," [34] namely, human praise. On the contrary, "that thy alms may be in secret; and thy Father who seeth in secret, will repay thee." [35]

God's mercy and justice both intervene here in accordance with the following text from St. Paul: "I have fought a good fight, I have finished my course, I have kept the faith. As to the rest, there is laid up for me a crown of justice, which the Lord, the just judge, will render to me in that day; and not only to me, but to them also that love His coming." [36] And the degree of the light of glory will correspond to the degree of charity in each of the blessed.

THIRD ARTICLE

WHETHER MERCY CAN BE ATTRIBUTED TO GOD

State of the question. The difficulty is that mercy seems to be a kind of sorrow. But there is no sorrow in God. Moreover, it seems that mercy is a relaxation of justice. But God cannot remit what appertains to His justice; for He cannot deny Himself. Hence it seems that mercy is only metaphorically in God, just as anger is.

Yet the answer is: Mercy belongs properly or formally to God.

1) It is of faith, as attested by many texts in Holy Scripture and by the common interpretation of the Church, although there is no special and solemn definition on this point that is already most certain.

The following are some of the texts from Holy Scripture: "The Lord is compassionate and merciful, longsuffering and plenteous in mercy." [37] "The mercies of the Lord I will sing forever." [38] "Show

[32] Matt. 5: 3 f. See also Luke 6: 23.
[33] *Ibid.*, 6: 1.
[34] *Ibid.*, 6: 2.
[35] *Ibid.*, 6: 4.
[36] II Tim. 4: 8.
[37] Ps. 102: 8; see also Ps. 110: 4; 144: 8.
[38] *Ibid.*, 88: 1.

forth Thy wonderful mercies; Thou who savest them that trust in Thee." [39] "From the morning watch even until night, let Israel hope in the Lord. Because with the Lord there is mercy, and with Him plentiful redemption." [40] In the psalms and the prophetical books often the same three ideas are found inseparable, namely, man in his *misery* invoking God's *mercy* that the *glory of God* may be made manifest. Thus we read: "Help us, O God, our Savior; and for the glory of Thy name, O Lord, deliver us and forgive us our sins for Thy name's sake." [41] "We have sinned . . . and trespassed in all things . . . ; but deal with us according to Thy meekness and according to the multitude of Thy mercies. And deliver us according to Thy wonderful works, and give glory to Thy name, O Lord." [42] Thus the prophets see that God's mercy in its effect is the highest manifestation of His goodness and omnipotence. In fact, they say: "The earth, O Lord, is full of Thy mercy." [43] The ideal of this revelation is reached in the following text of the New Testament: "For God so loved the world as to give His only begotten Son, that whosoever believeth in Him may not perish, but may have life everlasting." [44] Thus mercy was the motive of the incarnation.[45] St. Paul often speaks of the riches of God's mercy and grace, as in the following text: "God, who is rich in mercy, for His exceeding charity wherewith He loved us, even when we were dead in sins, hath quickened us together in Christ." [46] God's mercy toward the children of Israel is described at length in the Old Testament,[47] and the mercy of Christ, the good Shepherd, is taught in all the parables, as in the parable of the prodigal son, and throughout the Gospel.

But it must be shown by a theological argument that what is formally meant by mercy implies no imperfection, and, as St. Thomas says, "is especially to be attributed to God." This is clearly shown in the argumentative part of the article.

The holy doctor distinguishes in human mercy toward those who are in misery between being affected with sorrow at the misery of another and dispelling the misery of this other. But this sorrow, by reason of the subject of this sorrow, constitutes the material part of mercy; whereas, on the other hand, by reason of the object of this

39 *Ibid.*, 16: 7.
40 *Ibid.*, 129: 6 f.
41 *Ibid.*, 78: 9.
42 Dan. 3: 29.
43 Ps. 118: 64.
44 John 3: 16.
45 *Summa theol.*, IIIa, q. 1, a. 3.
46 Eph. 2: 4 f.
47 Wis. chaps. 11, 12.

sorrow, the inclination of the will to alleviate the misery of another constitutes the formal element in sorrow.

But, although sorrow over the misery of another does not belong to God, to dispel the misery of another implies no imperfection, and belongs especially to God. For defects are not removed except by the perfection of some kind of goodness. But the primary source of goodness is God, who is essential goodness. Therefore mercy, according to its formal signification, belongs properly and not merely metaphorically to God.

Mercy in this sense is a most beautiful example of the analogy of proper proportionality. There is a relation of proportion between God's merciful attitude toward sinners imploring His pardon and that of man toward those who are in misery, all imperfections being removed, such as sorrow or a feeling of compassion.

In like manner, St. Thomas says in discussing the virtue of mercy: "A virtue may take precedence of other virtues in two ways: first, in itself; secondly, in comparison with its subject. In itself, mercy takes precedence of other virtues, for it belongs to mercy to be bountiful to others, and, what is more, to succor others in their wants, which pertains chiefly to one who stands above. Hence mercy is accounted as being proper to God, and therein His omnipotence and goodness are declared to be chiefly manifested.

On the other hand, with regard to its subject, mercy is not the greatest virtue, unless that subject is greater than all others, surpassed by none and excelling all, since for him that has anyone above him it is better to be united to that which is above than to supply the defect of that which is beneath." [48] Hence in us the most sublime of all virtues is charity, which unites us with God, but "of all the virtues which relate to our neighbor, mercy is the greatest." [49]

St. Thomas most correctly distinguishes between the virtue of mercy and the emotion of commiseration, which is a praiseworthy inclination of the sensitive appetite, and is not a virtue.[50] So also there is a distinction between the virtue of chastity and a sense of shame; but chastity implies imperfection, whereas the virtue of mercy does not. In fact, as St. Thomas remarks,[51] if the weak and timid are especially inclined to feeling compassion for others, on account of the possibility of suffering, in like manner the virtue of mercy pertains especially to the perfect, who so excel in goodness and fortitude that they can dispel the misery of others. Thus mercy be-

48 *Summa theol.*, IIa IIae, q.30, a.4.
49 *Ibid.*
50 *Ibid.*
51 *Ibid.*, a.2.

longs especially to God. "God takes pity on us through love alone, inasmuch as He loves us as belonging to Him." [52] Consequently, there is neither anthropomorphism nor sentimentality in this, but purely revealed truth that has been theologically explained. The motive of divine mercy is not properly the misery of the creature (this being the matter about which it is concerned), but it is God's goodness to be made manifest in the alleviation of a person's misery.

First doubt. What is the difference between God's mercy, goodness, justice, and liberality?

Reply. As stated in the body of the article, "to bestow perfections appertains not only to God's goodness, but also to His justice, liberality, and mercy; yet under different aspects. The communicating of perfections, absolutely considered, appertains to goodness. But, in so far as perfections are given to things in proportion, the bestowal of them belongs to justice. In so far as God does not bestow them for His own use, but only on account of His goodness, it belongs to liberality. In so far as perfection given to things by God expels defects, it belongs to mercy." What is here said explains the doctrine of the following article.

Second doubt. How is it that mercy which forgives sin that has been committed, is not a relaxation of vindictive justice that must inflict the punishment for sin?

The reply to the second objection answers this as follows: "God acts mercifully, not indeed by going against His justice, but by doing something more than justice. Thus a man who pays another person two hundred pieces of money, though owing him only one hundred, does nothing against justice, but acts liberally or mercifully. The case is the same with one who pardons an offense committed against him, for in remitting it he may be said to bestow a gift. Hence the Apostle calls remission a forgiving. "Forgiving one another even as God hath forgiven you in Christ." [53] Hence it is clear that mercy does not destroy justice, but in a sense is the fullness thereof. And thus it is said: "Mercy exalteth itself above judgment." [54]

I insist. But the human judge is in justice bound to inflict the penalty for the crime, and he cannot show mercy by remitting it. Therefore neither can God do so, if justice belongs formally and properly to Him.

Reply. I distinguish the antecedent: [55] The subordinate judge cannot, of course, without violating justice, let the offense go unpunished; but the supreme legislator can do so, and this right is a

---

[52] *Ibid.,* ad 1um.
[53] Eph. 4: 32.
[54] Jas. 2: 13.
[55] Cf. *Summa theol.,* Ia, q.25, a.3 ad 3um.

privilege that belongs either to the king of a country, or to the president of a republic, that he can pardon criminals imploring his mercy. Thus the goodness of either the king or the president is strikingly made manifest, and the common good is preserved intact as well as the king's honor. St. Thomas explains this very well: "Even this justice (which exacts reparation for sin) depends on the divine will, requiring satisfaction for sin from the human race. But if He had willed to free man from sin without any satisfaction, He would not have acted against justice. For a judge, while preserving justice, cannot pardon the offense without imposing a penalty, for he must punish the offense committed against another, for instance, against another man, or against the state, or any prince in higher authority. But God has no one higher than Himself, for He is the sovereign and common good of the whole universe. Consequently, if He forgives sin, which has the formality of fault in that it is committed against Himself, He wrongs no one; just as anyone else, overlooking a personal trespass, without demanding satisfaction, acts mercifully and not unjustly. And so David exclaimed when he sought mercy: "To Thee only have I sinned" (Ps. 50: 6), as if to say: "Thou canst pardon me without injustice." [56] This means that the exercise of God's justice and mercy depends on His free will. Therefore St. Augustine says: "Why He draws this (sinner) and not another, seek not to judge, if thou dost not wish to err." [57] On this point St. Thomas says: "The reason for the predestination of some, and the reprobation of others, must be sought for in the goodness of God." [58] This remains for us a mystery, namely, how infinite justice, mercy, and supreme liberty are intimately reconciled in the eminence of the Deity. Now in this article it is shown that God's mercy in sparing sinners is not a relaxation of His vindictive justice, but transcends it, for, as the Apostle says, "mercy exalteth itself above judgment." [59] But how some divine perfection can in a certain way excel another, will be discussed in the following article and in the corollaries on divine mercy.

FOURTH ARTICLE

WHETHER IN EVERY WORK OF GOD THERE ARE MERCY AND JUSTICE

State of the question. The purpose of this article is to explain the scriptural text: "All the ways of the Lord are mercy and truth." [60]

[56] *Ibid.*, Ia IIae, q.46, a.2 ad 3um.
[57] *Hom. 26 in Joan.*
[58] *Summa theol.*, Ia, q.23, a.5 ad 3um.
[59] Jas. 2: 13.
[60] Ps. 24: 10.

This difficulty arises chiefly for the following reasons: (1) Some works of God are attributed to mercy, as the justification of the ungodly; and others are attributed to justice, as the damnation of the wicked. (2) Many just persons are afflicted in this world, and this does not appear to be just. (3) The works of justice and mercy presuppose creation, which does not manifest these divine perfections.

Yet the answer is: "All the ways of the Lord are mercy and truth." [61] It must be observed that this assertion is verified, if mercy is taken in the broad sense as meaning the removal of any kind of defect, but not if it refers to mercy only in the strict sense of the term, as stated in the body of this article and in the reply to the fourth objection.

The reason is that the work of divine justice always presupposes the work of mercy, and has its foundation in this latter. For nothing is due to creatures (for instance, either help or reward or punishment) except on account of something pre-existing in them. In the final analysis, it must be because of something that depends solely on the goodness of the divine will that has gratuitously created and ordained us to a supernatural end. Thus we see that mercy (at least in the broad sense) is the primary source of all God's works.

First corollary. It is stated in the body of the article that "the power of this primary source of all God's works remains in all that follows therefrom, and operates indeed with greater force, just as the influence of the first cause is more intense than that of second causes." Thus all God's works have their foundation in His love for creatures, and it is manifested first by mercy, either in the broad or in the strict sense of the term, rather than by justice, which may be considered the branch in this tree of God's love; whereas mercy is, as it were, the principal part of the tree, its trunk, so to speak, which comes directly from the root. Nor is it to be wondered at that a certain order prevails between the infinite perfections of God; for, as the divine will is logically preceded by the divine intellect, so also mercy and justice presuppose God's goodness and love. But mercy is the first manifestation of love, whereas justice is, so to speak, its second manifestation. In mercy it is God's goodness as self-diffusive that is manifested, whereas it is especially in vindictive justice that the inalienable right of supreme goodness to be loved above all things is made manifest. Thus mercy is the primary source of God's works. St. Thomas says: "It is more proper to God to have mercy and to spare, than to punish." [62]

Second corollary. In the argumentative part of this article occurs

61 *Ibid.*
62 *Summa theol.*, IIa IIae, q.21, a.2.

the following statement: "For this reason God out of the abundance of His goodness bestows upon creatures what is due to them more bountifully than is proportionate to their deserts: since less would suffice for preserving the order of justice than what the divine goodness confers; because between creatures and God's goodness there can be no proportion." Thus the psalmist says: "The earth is full of the mercy of the Lord." [63] God gives generally to all creatures more than is strictly necessary for the attainment of their end; for He gives in the majority of cases what is befitting for their well-being, in the material, moral, and spiritual orders. Thus in all God's works mercy is the result of His superabundant good; but justice results from His operation, since He gives what is proportionately due to each.

Reply to first objection. In the damnation of the reprobate it is justice, indeed, that is more in evidence; nevertheless mercy is made manifest in it, as somewhat alleviating the punishment, because the reprobates are punished short of what is deserved.[64]

Reply to third objection. Prior to the works of mercy and justice taken in their strict sense, the ideas of these perfections are in some manner preserved in creation, inasmuch as beings are, as it were, mercifully changed from non-existence to existence, and justice is seen in the production of these beings in a manner that accords with the divine goodness and wisdom, particularly in sparing and having mercy.[65] Therefore the psalmist says: "Help us, O God, our Savior, and for the glory of Thy name, O Lord, deliver us; and forgive us our sins for Thy name's sake." [66] Thus in this prayer, the sinner in his profound misery invokes God's most sublime attribute of mercy, not only that his misery may be alleviated, but also that God may be glorified, and that His goodness and omnipotence may be made manifest. Likewise, the Scripture says: "We have sinned and committed iniquity . . . but deal with us according to the multitude of Thy mercies, O Lord." [67] Anyone who prays in this manner with humility, piety, and perseverance, is always heard.[68] The abyss of misery invokes the abyss of mercy, and God's goodness and omnipotence are made manifest.

2) In so far as God in His mercy bestows upon creatures more than is strictly necessary, punishes short of what is deserved, and rewards

---

[63] Ps. 32: 5.

[64] *Summa theol.*, Ia IIae, q.99; see also *Tabula aurea*, under the word "mercy," no. 26.

[65] Cf. *ibid.*, Ia, q.25, a.3 ad 3um.

[66] Ps. 78: 9.

[67] Dan. 3: 29, 42 f.

[68] Cf. *Summa theol.*, IIa IIae, q.83, a.15 ad 2um; also a.16.

beyond what is deserved, in these three acts His mercy in a certain manner transcends His justice.[69]

A. God in the majority of cases bestows upon creatures more than is strictly necessary. Thus He could have created us merely in the natural order; yet *de facto* He raised us to the supernatural order. After Adam's sin, God could have left us in the state of fallen nature, or He could have afforded us some relief by simply forgiving the sin on certain conditions, this being announced to us through some prophet. As a matter of fact, "God so loved the world as to give His only begotten Son." [70] "Mercy and truth have met each other." [71] "Mercy exalteth itself above judgment." [72] Christ manifested His love for us even by dying on the Cross. Moreover, of His superabundant mercy He gave us baptismal grace or the grace of regeneration, and actual graces to persevere, and also the Holy Eucharist and other sacraments. In all this it is quite clear that God in His mercy bestows upon creatures more than is strictly required by rigorous justice.

B. In like manner, as stated in this article, God punishes short of what is deserved. For He often reinstates sinners who throughout their lives have repeatedly fallen into sin. He raises up souls to make reparation for them, and as St. Thomas observes: "It is a remarkable sign of God's mercy when He punishes sinners in this life, in accordance with the saying of St. Augustine: Burn, cut here, provided Thou spare in eternity." [73] Even the damned, as stated in this article, are punished short of what they deserve.[74]

C. God also rewards beyond what justice demands, and of His fullness we have received graces beyond our merits. Certainly the first grace of justification, which is the principle of merit, is not the object of merit; and this also applies to the grace of final perseverance, which means to die in the state of grace.[75] The same is to be said of sacramental graces. Especially so is the nourishing grace which we receive in Holy Communion which is not the object of merit, for it is given without being merited by us; and, according to God's dispensation, every Communion, by increasing charity in us, if there is no venial sin of negligence on our part, ought to dispose us for a more substantially fervent Communion the following day.

God's mercy is especially made manifest toward the laborers in the Lord's vineyard who came to work at the last hour, shortly before

---

69 Consult the *Tabula aurea* of St. Thomas' works, under the word "mercy," no. 26.

70 John 3: 16.

71 Ps. 84: 11.

72 Jas. 2: 13.

73 *Com. in Ep. ad Hebraeos*, chap. 3, lect. 2 (at the end).

74 Cf. ad 1um.

75 Cf. Ia IIae, q. 114, a. 9.

their death,[76] and toward those in whom are found verified these words of Scripture: "Whosoever shall give to drink to one of these little ones a cup of cold water only in the name of a disciple, amen I say to you, he shall not lose his reward." [77]

But the splendor of mercy will be made manifest in behalf of those to whom the Lord will say: "Come, ye blessed of My Father, possess you the kingdom prepared for you from the foundation of the world; for I was hungry, and you gave Me to eat; I was thirsty, and you gave Me to drink. . . . As long as you did it to one of these, My least brethren, you did it to Me." [78]

This infinite mercy of God is the foundation of our hope, and is a most remarkable example for us of mercy and compassion toward our neighbor, being in agreement with the Gospel, which says: "Blessed are the merciful, for they shall obtain mercy." [79] "This is My commandment, that you love one another as I have loved you." [80]

Finally, how are infinite mercy and justice intimately reconciled? There is inexorable justice as regards the damned, who, besides, do not ask for forgiveness. It is only by directly seeing the eminent Deity in which all the divine perfections are so united as not to be in the least destructive of one another, that we shall know how justice and mercy are reconciled. Hence Pius IX says: "When, freed from the trammels of this corporeal life, we see God as He is, we shall certainly understand how close and beautiful is the interrelation between divine mercy and justice." [81] Then, as stated farther on, we shall clearly understand the teaching of the Church when it says that "the gifts of heavenly grace are by no means wanting to those who sincerely will and ask to be directed anew by this light." [82] Thus, although the elect are by God's mercy more loved and helped than others,[83] yet for all it is true to say that God does not command impossibilities, but by commanding both admonishes us to do what we are able, and to ask for what we are not able to do.[84] Thus in the obscurity of faith, especially in infused contemplation, the reconcilia-

[76] Matt. 20: 1–16.
[77] Ibid., 10: 42.
[78] Ibid., 25: 34, 40.
[79] Ibid., 5: 7.
[80] John 15: 12.
[81] Denz., no. 1647.
[82] Ibid., no. 1648. See also no. 1677.
[83] This follows from what St. Paul says (I Cor. 4: 7): "For who distinguisheth thee? Or what hast thou that thou hast not received?" Cf. Ia, q.23, a.4, 5. If it is because of a special act of God's mercy that one of two sinners is converted, far more so is this the reason why the just person is continually preserved from falling into sin, especially so if it is the case of one who was baptized in infancy.
[84] Cf. Denz., no. 804.

tion of infinite mercy, justice, and supreme liberty in the eminence of the Deity is in a certain manner attained. Yet as long as we are in this life we always make use of limited analogical concepts, and these represent God's spiritual attributes after the manner of a mosaic, the little colored stones of which cannot express its charm of appeal. Our concepts of mercy, justice, and liberty are too much disconnected, and not enough united that we may know what properly constitutes the Deity.

CHAPTER XXII

QUESTION 22

THE PROVIDENCE OF GOD

HAVING considered all that relates to the will, we must proceed to those things which have relation to both intellect and will. Of this kind, however, is providence, and predestination is its more exalted part. There is resemblance, by way of analogy, between providence and our virtue of prudence, to which providence belongs with reference to the future as fully explained elsewhere by St. Thomas when he says: "Providence (as the name signifies) implies a certain relation of one who is distant from things that occur in time and that must be directed to their ends." [1] For providence is an orderly direction in the mind, the direction to their ends of those things that are to be done.

The doctrine of St. Thomas on providence has been explained at length by us in other works.[2] Therefore we now make some brief observations only about the principal points. St. Thomas' division of this question is in four articles. (1) Whether providence can suitably be attributed to God, in which the questions as to the existence and nature of providence are solved. (2) Whether everything is subject to the providence of God, or what the scope of providence is. (3) Whether God has immediate providence over everything, the answer to which will be in the affirmative, and thus there is a difference between providence and divine government. (4) Whether providence imposes any necessity on things foreseen. The solution of this doubt will be the corollary to the doctrine as already set forth on this point.[3]

State of the question. The difficulty arises from the following facts: (1) "Providence" denotes a certain part of our prudence in which there is always imperfection, that is, doubt and uncertainty; (2) providence is concerned with existing things that are not eternal. Therefore it does not appear to be anything eternal. There are other difficulties arising especially from the existence of physical and moral

---

[1] *Summa theol.*, IIa IIae, q.49, a.6.

[2] Cf. *Dictionnaire de théologie catholique*, art. "Providence," and also *Providence* (Eng. tr., Herder Book Co.).

[3] Cf. *Summa theol.*, Ia, q.19, a.8.

evil in the world. These difficulties are pointed out by St. Thomas at the beginning of the second article, for he says: "We see many evils existing. Either, then, God cannot prevent these, and thus is not omnipotent, or else He does not have care for everything." This objection belongs properly to the question of the scope of providence, and is explained more fully in another work.[4]

It is affirmed in this article that providence is to be attributed to God, and very many passages from Holy Scripture and the declarations of the Church show that this doctrine is of faith.

In the Old Testament, Judith prays as follows: "All Thy ways are prepared, and in Thy providence Thou hast placed Thy judgments. . . . The prayer of the humble and the meek have always pleased Thee. O God of the heavens, Creator of the waters, and Lord of the whole creation, hear me a poor wretch making supplication to Thee, and presuming of Thy mercy." [5] The Book of Wisdom says: "God made the little and the great, and He hath equally care of all." [6] "Wisdom reacheth from end to end mightily, and ordereth all things sweetly." [7] "Thou has ordered all things in number, measure, and weight." [8] "There is no other God but Thou, who hast care of all." [9] Of those crossing the sea in ships, it says: "Thy providence, O Father, governeth it; for Thou hast made a way even in the sea, and a most sure path even among the waves, showing that Thou art able to save out of all things." [10]

The prayer of petition presupposes faith in divine providence, which extends to the least of our free acts. Hence Mardochai prays in the following manner: "O Lord, Lord almighty King, for all things are in Thy power, and there is none that can resist Thy will, if Thou determine to save Israel." [11] It is in this way, too, that Queen Esther prays and is heard.[12] Never did even the nobler minded among the Greek philosophers reach such a degree of certainty about divine providence, which extends even to the least details. Again, in Ecclesiasticus we read: "As the potter's clay is in his hand, . . . so man is in the hand of Him who made him; and He will render to him according to His judgment." [13] And Isaias says: "The Lord of hosts

---

[4] *Contra Gentes,* Bk. III, chaps. 64, 71–79, 89–97.
[5] Jdth. 9: 5–17.
[6] Wis. 6: 8.
[7] *Ibid.,* 8: 1.
[8] *Ibid.,* 11: 21.
[9] *Ibid.,* 12: 13.
[10] *Ibid.,* 14: 1–5.
[11] Esther 13: 9.
[12] *Ibid.,* 14: 12–19.
[13] Ecclus. 33: 13.

hath decreed, and who can disannul it? And His hand is stretched out, and who shall turn it away?" [14]

The psalms declare the wonders of God's providence toward the Israelites, freeing them from captivity. Thus we read: "When Israel went out of Egypt." [15] "Direct me in Thy truth, and teach me; for Thou art God my Savior." [16] "The Lord ruleth me: and I shall want nothing. He hath set me in a place of pasture. . . . He hath led me on the paths of justice, for His name's sake. For though I should walk in the midst of the shadow of death, I will fear no evils, for Thou art with me." [17] "But I have put my trust in Thee, O Lord. I said: Thou art my God. My lots are in Thy hands. Deliver me out of the hands of my enemies, and from them that persecute me. Make Thy face to shine upon Thy servant: save me in Thy mercy." [18]

There is a certain aspect of God's providence that is most manifest from the order prevailing in the world. Thus the psalmist says: "The heavens show forth the glory of God: and the firmament declareth the works of His hands." [19] But on the other hand, as shown in the Book of Job, there are certain and indeed most sublime ways of Providence that are unsearchable, such as the dispositions of Providence toward Joseph, the son of Jacob, when God permits him to be sold by his brothers. Then the purpose of these ways is made clear, when Joseph says to his brothers: "Not by your counsel was I sent hither, but by the will of God: who hath made me . . . governor in all the land of Egypt." [20] The inaccessible height of Providence is also apparent in the following text: "Thy justice is as the mountains of God: Thy judgments are a great deep." [21] But this greater obscurity is owing to the fact that He is far too luminous for our intellect; for God's providence in itself is light inaccessible, and under the guidance of this light all things co-operate unto good. Hence the Scripture says: "Thou art great, O Lord, forever, and Thy kingdom is unto all ages. For Thou scourgest and Thou savest: Thou leadest down to hell, and bringest up again, and there is none that can escape Thy hand. . . . He hath chastised us for our iniquities: and He will save us for His own mercy." [22] The whole history of the Israelites is ordained by God's providence to prepare them for the coming of

---

[14] Isa. 14: 27.
[15] Ps. 113.
[16] *Ibid.*, 24: 5.
[17] *Ibid.*, 22: 1.
[18] *Ibid.*, 30: 15–17.
[19] *Ibid.*, 18: 2.
[20] Gen. 45: 8.
[21] Ps. 35: 7.
[22] Tob. 13: 1.

the promised Savior. The history of Susanna is for this same end.[23]

God's providence together with His goodness and omnipotence is frequently mentioned in the New Testament. Thus our Lord says: "Behold the birds of the air: for they neither sow nor do they reap nor gather into barns; and your heavenly Father feedeth them. Are not you of much more value than they?" [24] It is an a fortiori argument, the implication being that if God's care extends to the smallest things, far more so is He concerned with the life of the soul. Hence our Lord concludes: "For your Father knoweth that you have need of all these things. Seek ye therefore first the kingdom of God and His justice, and all these things shall be added unto you." [25] And again: "The very hairs of your head are all numbered." [26] The parables of the laborers in the vineyard [27] and of the talents [28] contain this same doctrine. "If you then, being evil, know how to give good gifts to your children, how much more will your Father from heaven give the good Spirit to them that ask Him!" [29] St. Peter says: "Be you humbled, therefore, under the mighty hand of God, that He may exalt you in the time of visitation; casting all your care upon Him, for He hath care of you." [30]

All these texts declare that providence is evident by reason of the order prevailing in the world and the life of the just. On the other hand, there remains the profound mystery expressed by St. Paul in the following words: "How incomprehensible are His judgments and how unsearchable His ways!" [31] This mystery applies especially to the tribulations the just endure, and the iniquity perpetrated by evil persons, both of which are permitted by God for a greater good and which in this life often remain hidden.

Some of the Fathers [32] wrote especially about providence. Thus St. John Chrysostom wrote a number of treatises concerning the providential purpose and advantage of suffering in the lives of the just.[33]

[23] Cf. Dan. 13: 42.

[24] Matt. 6: 26.

[25] *Ibid.*, 6: 33.

[26] *Ibid.*, 10: 30.

[27] *Ibid.*, 20: 1.

[28] *Ibid.*, 25: 14.

[29] Luke 11: 13. Consult also Luke 15: 4 (parable of lost sheep), and John 10: 1 (parable of good shepherd).

[30] I Pet. 5: 6.

[31] Rom. 11: 33.

[32] Cf. Rouet de Journel, *Enchiridion patristicum*, nos. 202, 422, 1014, 1134, 1377.

[33] Cf. *Ad Stagir.*, in which he remarks that we alone are the cause of our spiritual wounds, and one of his treatises concerns those who are scandalized on account of adversities. Consult also St. Leo's *Ep. ad Thuribium*, and St. Gregory Nazianzen's *Oratio 16*.

St. Augustine wrote a book explaining the action of divine providence in its dealings with human beings.[34] There are two cities in the world, which at present are intermixed, but which at the end will be separated. There is the city of evil in which love of self finally leads to hatred of God, and there is the city of God, in which the love of God finally leads to contempt of self.[35]

From the definitions and declarations of the Church it is evident that God certainly foreknew from eternity, and immutably preordained, all future things;[36] yet it does not therefore follow that this makes it absolutely necessary, for all things that come into being.[37] God governs by His providence both visible and invisible things,[38] truly acting upon the world and man.[39] He does not will evil things just as He wills good things,[40] only permitting sin.[41] He does not have to obey the devil,[42] neither does He communicate His omnipotence to us, nor is He subject to us,[43] and He ordains all things for the manifestation of His goodness.[44] Hence the course of man's life is not under the controlling influence of the stars,[45] nor is man ruled by fate.[46]

Among these definitions, the following declaration of the Vatican Council deserves special mention: "God protects and governs by His providence all things which He has made, reaching from end to end mightily, and ordering all things sweetly. For all things are naked and open to His eyes, even those which are yet to be by the free action of creatures." [47]

In the body of the article St. Thomas proves the existence of providence, which is a revealed doctrine. This he does by means of a theological argument, and at the same time he defines providence. He presupposes its quasi-nominal definition, according to which providence is a part of prudence, which orders different things to

[34] *De civitate Dei.*
[35] Cf. *ibid.*, Bk. VII, chap. 29. This chapter must be read since it treats especially of Providence. Consult also *Dict. de théol. cath.*, art. "Providence" (section concerning St. Augustine).
[36] Denz., nos. 300, 316, 321 f., 1784.
[37] *Ibid.*, nos. 321, 607, 3026.
[38] *Ibid.*, nos. 421, 1784.
[39] *Ibid.*, no. 1702.
[40] *Ibid.*, no. 514.
[41] *Ibid.*, no. 816.
[42] *Ibid.*, no. 586.
[43] *Ibid.*, nos. 1217 f.
[44] *Ibid.*, no. 1783.
[45] *Ibid.*, nos. 35, 239.
[46] *Ibid.*, no. 607.
[47] Denz., no. 1784; cf. Wis. 8: 1; Heb. 4: 13.

the attainment of their end. Thus the common saying is that it belongs to the governor of the state to provide for its grain supplies, and to the father of the family for necessities of life.[48] This common notion of providence can be attributed to God only analogically; but now the question is whether it is to be attributed to Him analogically and in the strict sense, or only analogically and metaphorically.

The answer is that providence is predicated analogically and properly of God, and it is proved as follows.

In every effect produced by an intellectual agent, the type or idea of this effect pre-exists in such agent. But God is the cause of all created good by His intellect and hence of the order of things to their end, particularly their ultimate end. Therefore the type of the order of things to their end, which is called providence, in accordance with its nominal definition, pre-exists in God. Thus providence is suitably attributed to God analogically and properly, as it implies no imperfection.

The major of this argument is self-evident and, moreover, is equivalently revealed. But the minor is revealed, and is also proved by philosophy. Thus this argument, by reason of its twofold aspect, belongs to either theology or philosophy.[49] Therefore providence is suitably attributed analogically and properly to God, just as intelligence, will, and the free act of creating are. To deny God's providence would be to deny that He is intelligent, or that He is God.

This proof is quasi a priori, since it presupposes that God is the cause by His intellect; quasi a priori, I say, because providence is not immediately deduced from God's nature, but presupposes that God most freely willed to create.

A philosophical a posteriori proof can also be given of providence, reasoning from the order prevailing in the world. This proof corresponds exactly to the fifth way by which St. Thomas proves God's existence, especially as the supreme Designer.[50] This proof is reduced to the following syllogism: things which lack intelligence do not tend toward their end unless they are directed to it by some intelligent being, as the arrow is shot to its mark by the archer; but we see that things which lack intelligence act for an end, and this is evident from their acting always, or nearly always, in the same way, so as to obtain the best result; therefore some intelligent being exists by whom all natural things are directed to their end, and this being we call God.

It must be remarked that St. Thomas in this fifth proof, just as in

---

[48] Cf. *Summa theol.*, IIa IIae, q.49, a.6.

[49] Cf. *supra,* q.14, a.8: Whether God's knowledge is the cause of things; also q.19, a.8: Whether God's will is the cause of things.

[50] Cf. *ibid.,* Ia, q.2, a.3.

our argument, insists that the order of things toward their end pertains to the good of the universe, of which God is the author. As we stated above,[51] Aristotle splendidly formulated and explained the minor of this fifth proof, namely, that natural agents operate for an end, but he did not grasp the concept of creation, especially of a most free creation from nothing for the manifestation of the orderly direction of divine goodness. Hence he did not acquire the right idea of divine providence.

In the Middle Ages the Averroists, who deny a free action, reduced providence to some general preordination that extends only to the general laws of the world, but not to particulars.[52]

COFIRMATION OF THIS CONCLUSION BY THE SOLUTION OF THE DIFFICULTIES PRESENTED IN THIS ARTICLE

Reply to first objection. Although to take counsel about doubtful matters does not belong to God, nevertheless to give a command as to the ordering of things toward an end does belong properly to God, because it implies no imperfection.

Reply to second objection. Providence is, properly speaking, the reason of order (or the ordering) of things to their end, whereas divine government is the execution of this order. Thus providence is eternal, whereas divine government is predicated of God in time, since it implies a relation to already existing things.[53]

Reply to third objection. Providence, as the word denotes, as being an ordering of things, is in the divine intellect, but it presupposes the willing of the end. "Nobody gives a precept about things done for an end, unless he wills that end, as St. Thomas remarks in this reply. Thus human prudence presupposes the moral virtues, which direct the appetite aright concerning the end. In this reply it is already evident that for St. Thomas, God, like every wise person, first wills the end before He wills the means for the end. This does not mean, indeed, that there are two acts of the will in God, for as stated above, "He wills this to be as means to that, but He does not will this on account of that." [54]

The solution of the objection arising from the existence of evil in the world is given in the following article of this question.[55]

First doubt. In what act of the intellect does providence, strictly speaking, or at least principally, consist? What acts of the will does it presuppose?

[51] *Com.* on q.2, a.3.
[52] Cf. *Contra Gentes*, Bk. III, chaps. 75 f.
[53] Cf. *Summa theol.*, Ia, q.13, a.7, c. et ad 3um; q.103, a.1; q.110, a.1.
[54] *Ibid.*, Ia, q.19, a.5.
[55] Cf. ad 2um.

The replies to the first and second objections of this article make it clear that providence consists, at least principally, in the act of the intellect that is called commanding or giving orders, as prudence does in us. It presupposes two acts of the will, namely, the intention of the end and the choice of means for the end.[56]

There are virtually several acts that concur in divine providence, just as there are really several acts that concur in human providence. (1) God's will, directed by His wisdom, intends as the end in view the manifestation of His goodness *ad extra;* (2) the divine intellect judges concerning the most fitting means for the attainment of the end. On this point, the Salmanticenses correctly state [57] that among all possible dispositions of things, this one is known as possible by God's knowledge of simple intelligence, namely, the disposition in which there is subordination of nature, grace, and glory along with permission of original sin to the hypostatic union (for this constitutes some possible world); (3) this will accepts or chooses the means for the manifestation of divine goodness; (4) in virtue of this efficacious intention and choice, the intellect eternally commands that these means be made use of in time. Providence consists formally in this efficacious command, for, as St. Thomas says in this article, "it orders and gives a command as to the ordering of things toward an end," and "nobody gives a precept about things done for an end, unless he wills that end." [58] This statement demands the attention of those who say that Scotus was the first among theologians who, on the subject of predestination, said that he who wills in an orderly manner, wills the end before willing the means to the end.

Objection. Once there is a choice of something by the divine will, then there is no difficulty in its execution, for nobody resists God's will. Therefore command is superfluous, and hence providence finds its ultimate explanation not in command but in choice.

Reply. I deny the consequent: for we do not posit command in God because of some difficulty to be overcome, but because the means as eligible and the means as possible of execution are objects different in concept. The means actually chosen never would be made use of, unless the command were present to direct the execution of the means. Hence there are two virtually distinct acts in God. In fact, whereas deliberation in the descendent order starts from the intention of the ultimate end to choice of the least of means, command, in the reverse order, by directing the execution of the means, rises from the choice of the least of means to the attainment of the ulti-

---

[56] Cf. *ibid.,* IIa IIae, q.47, a.8; Ia IIae, q.17, a.1: Whether command is an act of the reason.

[57] *Com. in IIIam,* q.1, a.3.

[58] *Summa theol.,* Ia, q.22, a.1 ad 1um et 3um.

mate end; for the end is first in intention and last in execution.

Divine government, however, is the execution in time of the order-ing of things under the direction of the aforesaid command which is eternal. Thus St. Thomas said that the reason of order in things is eternal, whereas the execution of this order is temporal.[59]

Second doubt. Whether God's practical knowledge, which is the cause of things,[60] is distinct from His providence.

Reply. St. Thomas shows that God's providence is distinct from His practical knowledge, because knowledge concerns the end and the means, but providence concerns the means in so far as they are ordered to the end.[61] Providence is also distinct from the eternal law, just as the conclusion is distinct from its principle; for it is by the eternal law that God's providence orders and governs all things. Similarly prudence in us presupposes practical or moral knowledge and the law.

Third doubt. What does providence presuppose on the part of God's will?

Reply. As we already said, it presupposes the willing of the end and the choice of the means. It follows from this that providence presupposes God's love for creatures and two virtues of uncreated love, namely, mercy and justice. Wherefore St. Thomas said in his reply to the third objection of this article that, just as "prudence presupposes the moral virtues, by means of which the appetitive faculty is directed toward good," so it is distinct from art.

Hence the provident God is not only the supreme artificer, or the architect of the universe, but He is also the most holy ordainer of all things and minds to their ultimate end, which is the most holy and most liberal manifestation of His goodness. Thus providence is more than divine art, since it presupposes mercy and justice, just as a man cannot be prudent unless he is just and benevolent toward other men. But providence, since it presupposes justice and mercy, directs the execution of the works of mercy and justice, just as prudence, since it presupposes the moral virtues, directs the acts of these virtues.[62]

Fourth doubt. Does providence presuppose the antecedent and consequent wills of God?

Reply. It presupposes both wills; for the antecedent will, as stated above,[63] concerns what is good in itself, on first consideration inde-pendently of actual circumstances. But since good is not in the mind

[59] Cf. *ibid.*, ad 2um.
[60] Cf. *ibid.*, Ia, q. 14, a. 8.
[61] Cf. *De veritate*, q. 5, a. 1, c. et ad 2um.
[62] Cf. *Summa theol.*, Ia, q. 103, a. 2, 3; *Contra Gentes*, Bk. III, chap. 97.
[63] *Ibid.*, Ia, q. 19, a. 6 ad 1um.

but in things, and things exist only as they actually are, this antecedent will rests on the condition that it is because of some greater good that the defect in the thing is permitted. On the contrary, the consequent will is concerned with good when all its particular circumstances are considered, and therefore only this will is efficacious. Thus by the antecedent will the merchant in a storm at sea would will to save all his merchandise, but to save his life he *de facto* and simply wills to cast it into the sea.

Likewise, God wills antecedently that all the fruits of the earth become ripe, unless some greater good prevents this. In like manner, He wills that all animals find what is necessary for their sustenance, and far more so He wills all men to be saved. But God does not will consequently and efficaciously that all the fruits of the earth become ripe, that all animals actually have what is necessary for their sustenance, that all human beings *de facto* be saved; but, for a greater good not always known to us, He permits that what is defectible may at times be defective.

Thus we have the answer to the doubt, as to whether providence presupposes both antecedent and consequent wills in God. For it presupposes the efficacious intention of the end of all things in the universe, which is the manifestation of divine goodness by way of liberality, mercy, and justice, and moreover the choice of the most fitting means to this end, namely, the disposition of things in accordance with the orders of nature, grace with permission of original sin, and the hypostatic union. But all this implies God's antecedent will to save all men, inasmuch as "God commands not impossibilities but, by commanding both admonishes you to do what you are able, and to ask for what you are not able (to do)," [64] as St. Augustine says.[65] It also implies God's consequent will of effectively leading some, although not all, to their ultimate end. And so we find St. Thomas saying farther on that predestination is a part of providence.[66]

Similarly, as regards the infallibility of divine providence, it follows from what has been said that providence is absolutely infallible even as to the attainment of the end, inasmuch as it presupposes God's consequent or efficacious will; and it is infallible only as regards the ordering of the means to the end and not as regards the attainment of the end, inasmuch as it presupposes only His antecedent will.[67] The Thomists are generally agreed that this consti-

[64] Denz., no. 804.
[65] *De natura et gratia, PL,* XLIV, 271.
[66] *Summa theol.,* Ia, q. 23, a. 1.
[67] This point will be made clearer in the next article.

tutes the difference between providence and predestination, which is the teaching of St. Thomas.[68] For it is evident that the efficacy of providence, in the act of command, depends, in the attaining of the end, on the efficacy of the willing or intending of the end.

Fifth doubt. How does natural providence differ from supernatural providence?

Reply. There is only one providence in God; nevertheless it can be considered under different aspects on the part of its objects. (1) There is providence in its most universal or complete aspect, which consists in the ordering of all beings to the end for which the universe was created, which is the manifestation of God's goodness. (2) Providence may be considered in its relation to particular ends, and thus it is called either natural or supernatural, the supernatural being either ordinary or extraordinary. Thus providence is called natural in so far as it is concerned with natural things, which are ordered by providence in its most universal aspect to supernatural things and to Christ.

But such particular ends are not always efficaciously willed, and thus, although all human beings are by God's providence destined for eternal life, yet not all are saved. On the contrary, the most universal end in the creation of the universe is efficaciously intended by God.

From this it does not follow that we must admit a certain antecedent and inefficacious providence. There is but one providence, which presupposes, for many things, a consequent will, and for other things, an antecedent will. This applies proportionately so to human prudence. Thus there is but one prudence in the merchant who, when a storm is threatening, efficaciously commands the casting of his merchandise into the sea for the saving of his life, although at the same time he may will antecedently or conditionally to save his merchandise; in fact, this merchant prudently does all in his power to save it, but afterward he casts it into the sea. Hence it is not surprising that divine providence likewise for many things presupposes a consequent or efficacious will, and for other things an antecedent or conditional and inefficacious will.

Sixth doubt. How does providence differ from fate?

Reply. As St. Thomas says in explanation of this: "The order given by divine providence to things is called fate by Boethius (*De consol.*, Bk. IV, prosa. 6). Hence as the idea is to the species of the thing, so is providence to fate," [69] in which fate is taken in a good sense, and

---

[68] Cf. *De veritate*, q.6, a.1.

[69] *Ibid.*, q.5, a.1 ad 1um. By the *species rei*, St. Thomas is here referring to the intelligible species that is representative of the object known. By the idea,

not as implying fatalism or absolute determinism, which is a denial of both divine liberty and human liberty.

St. Thomas also remarks [70] that several ancient philosophers were of the opinion that fate is a disposition of the stars under which each one is begotten or born, inasmuch as this disposition of the stars has an influence also on our human actions in things that take place by luck or by chance. To this St. Thomas replies: "It is manifest that a heavenly body acts after the manner of a natural principle," [71] which is determined to one thing. Hence it does not cause those things that are altogether accidental, such as those things that happen by luck or by chance. Previous to this he had said that "human actions (as being spiritual and free acts) are not subject to the action of heavenly bodies, unless accidentally and indirectly," as proved above,[72] that is, according to the influence they have upon the organism. But the indifference of judgment remaining intact, or the free judgment of reason, this influence of the stars on our choice, just as the attraction for us of sensible things, is not necessitating. Otherwise fate would have to be taken in the sense of absolute physical determinism.

But, as St. Thomas says, fate can be taken in a good sense, and then it signifies "the very disposition or order of second causes," [73] to the production of some effects foreseen and ordered by God. Thus we speak nowadays of the physical determinism of the laws of nature, in accordance with a series of connected causes, and besides these laws there is the possibility of miracles, and of various things happening by accident, such as those that happen by luck or chance.[74] "Consequently it does not follow that whatever is subject to the divine will or power, is subject to fate." [75] Thus we are free in our choices.

So then, in establishing the existence of divine providence, its analogical notion is sufficiently determined by saying that it is "the type of the order of things toward their end, or the type existing in the divine mind of things ordered toward an end. It is already apparent in what the infallibility of providence consists, and this will be more clearly shown in the next article.

---

he has in mind the mental type or exemplar according to which things are made or produced. [Tr.]

[70] *Summa theol.*, Ia, q.116, a.1.

[71] *Ibid.*

[72] *Ibid.*, q.115, a.4.

[73] *Ibid.*, q.116, a.2 ad 1um.

[74] *Ibid.*, a.1 ad 2um; q.105, a.7.

[75] *Ibid.*, a.4 ad 2um.

SECOND ARTICLE

WHETHER EVERYTHING IS SUBJECT TO THE PROVIDENCE OF GOD

State of the question. This article is concerned with the scope of providence, whether it extends to all things, even to the least detail and to the moral law. Whether it extends immediately to all things is the point of inquiry in the following article.

St. Thomas also discusses this subject of providence in other works,[76] directing his arguments especially against the Averroists, who were of the opinion that providence does not extend to particulars, but only to general laws.

This article begins by setting forth the state of the question and the many problems it presents. It seems that everything is not subject to divine providence: (1) because many things happen either by hazard or chance; but what happens by chance is not foreseen; (2) because there are many evils in the world, and it seems to follow from this that the omnipotent God does not have care for everything. One meets with this objection throughout the Book of Job and in the ninth chapter of Ecclesiastes. This difficulty made many say that God wills things only in a general way, and that His providence does not extend to details. So said the Deists and to some extent Malebranche. (3) Moreover, many things happen of necessity, and therefore they do not need to be directed by providence. (4) On the other hand, many things happen freely, and, as the Scripture says: "God made man from the beginning, and left him in the hand of his own counsel." [77] Thus Cicero, for the safeguarding of human liberty, denied the infallibility of God's foreknowledge and providence. Among modern philosophers, the Socinians and J. Lequier were of this opinion. (5) Finally, the Deists said that material individual things in their smallest details do not come within the scope of providence. All other objections can be reduced to these.[78] Some ancient philosophers admitted three subordinated providences, the highest of which was divine, and did not extend to things in their least detail.

Yet the answer is in the affirmative and is of faith, namely, that all things, even those of least value, are subject to divine providence, so that nothing happens by chance on God's part.

1) That this conclusion is of faith is evident from many texts of

---

[76] Cf. *Ibid.*, q.103, a.5; *De veritate*, q.5, a.3–7; *Contra Gentes*, Bk. III, chaps. 1, 64, 75, 89, 90, 98.

[77] Ecclus. 15: 14.

[78] Read the beginning of the argumentative part of this article, in which the errors of the ancient philosophers about providence are recounted. See also *De veritate*, q.5, a.3–10; *Contra Gentes*, Bk. III, chaps. 64–75; 89, 90, 94, 95, 149, 164.

Holy Scripture and several definitions of the Church quoted in the preceding article. It suffices for present purposes to recall the following words of the Vatican Council: "God protects and governs by His providence all things which He has made, *reaching from end to end mightily, and ordering all things sweetly*" (Wis., 8: 1). "*For all things are naked and open to His eyes* (Heb. 4: 13), even those which are yet to be by the action of creatures." [79] In like manner, Pope Adrian I says: "God, in His eternal unchangeableness prepared works of mercy and justice. . . . He therefore prepared merits in the justification of human beings . . . and rewards; for the wicked, however. He did not prepare that their wills and deeds be wicked, but He prepared for them just and eternal punishments." [80]

This doctrine concerning the scope of divine providence, which includes even all particular things, is expressed in many texts of Holy Scripture that have already been quoted in the preceding article. Thus Christ teaches that the birds of the air, the lilies of the field, the grass of the field, and the hairs of our head are all subject to divine providence, so that not one of them will fall without our Father's leave.[81] Similarly, concerning our free acts, the Scripture says: "As the potter's clay is in his hand . . . so man is in the hand of Him that made him." [82] And again: "For it is God who worketh in you, both to will and to accomplish, according to His good will." [83] It is foolish for the Christian to say that even some most insignificant act escapes God's providence, and that it happens independently of His will or permission.

Likewise, what we think happens merely by chance is subject to divine providence, for Holy Scripture says: "Lots are cast into the lap, but they are disposed of by the Lord." [84] Also when Joseph, Jacob's son, was sold by his brothers, then cast into prison, and finally was raised to a high position, these things seem to have happened very much by chance; yet they are said to have been according to God's plan. If the merchants who bought Joseph had passed by one hour earlier or later, then this would have changed the entire course of events. But this happened according to the infallible design of Providence, for as Joseph said to his brothers: "Not by your counsel was I sent hither, but by the will of God," [85] and so it is of several other events recorded in Scripture.[86]

79 Denz., no. 1784.
80 *Ibid.*, no. 300. See also nos. 316, 321 f.
81 Matt. 6: 26–31; 10: 19, 28; Luke 12: 22 f.
82 Ecclus. 33: 13.
83 Phil. 2: 13.
84 Prov. 16: 33.
85 Gen. 45: 8.
86 Cf. *ibid.*, chaps. 4, 5.

The Church Fathers always understood these texts of Holy Scripture as applying to God's universal providence that extends even to the least detail. Thus true Christians, especially the saints, see providence and the finger of God even in the many insignificant things that happen.

The answer is proved by a theological proof, although it is apart from this revealed. The reasoning of this proof is theological if at least one premise is considered as revealed, and it is philosophical if both premises are considered as evident from the natural light of reason.

Since every agent acts for an end, the ordering of effects toward that end extends as far as the causality of the first agent extends. But the causality of God, who is the first agent, extends to all things, down to particulars and the least details. Therefore it necessarily follows that, inasmuch as all things participate in existence, in so far they are subject to the divine ordination or to providence.

The major is, in the philosophical order, the corollary of the principle of finality, or of the relation of agent to end, for "every agent acts for an end"; every action tends toward an end that is either known or is not known but attained, as the arrow is shot to its mark. This corollary of the principle of formality is indirectly confirmed in this article by the following statement: "Whence it happens that in the effects of an agent something takes place which has no reference toward the end, because the effect comes from a cause other than and outside the intention of the agent." But no created agent can act without being moved to act by God.[87]

The minor. God's causality extends to all things, even particulars and the least details; and since God produces and conserves matter for the multiplication of individuals of every species, it follows that God by His providence just as by His knowledge knows things not only in general but also in particular.[88] As St. Thomas said in this last article just quoted: "God's knowledge extends as far as His causality extends. Hence, as the active power of God extends not only to forms, which are the source of universality, but also to matter (q. 44, a. 2), the knowledge of God must extend to particular things, which are individualized by matter." [89] With far more reason it includes within its scope particular spiritual things.

This proof is most universal, and it includes God's providence concerning our choices, which positively wills those that are good, and permits those that are evil, as will be more clearly explained.[90]

---

[87] Cf. *Summa theol.*, Ia, q.2, a.3; q.19, a.4, 8.
[88] Cf. *ibid.*, Ia, q.14, a.6, 11.
[89] *Ibid.*, a.11.
[90] Cf. *ibid.*, q.22, a.2 ad 4um; a.4.

Nevertheless there is no reference in this proof to what we find Molina afterward calling the *scientia media* by which God would foresee certain conditionally free acts of the future, whose positively free determination would be independent of Him. But there can be nothing external to God that is not in a relation of causality to God or dependence on Him, except the evil of sin, which is the privation of a good that one ought to have, and which is only permitted by God.

Almost the same proof is given of the universality of providence that extends to particulars even in their least details, for the divine government.[91] Thus, on the part of the agent, for the same reason God is the ruler and cause of things. But God is the cause of the total entity of all beings. Therefore there can be nothing which is not subject to His government. This universality of providence can also be proved from the nature of the end of government. The end of the divine government is the manifestation of divine goodness. But all things have as their end the manifestation of divine goodness. Therefore nothing escapes from the divine government, not even sin, which includes the incurring of punishment. But punishment is a manifestation of God's justice.[92]

THE SOLUTION OF THE DIFFICULTIES CONFIRMS THIS PROOF

PROVIDENCE AND CHANCE

The first difficulty was: Things that happen by chance do not seem to be subject to providence.

The reply to this first difficulty was: Things are said to happen by chance with reference to secondary causes. Thus the finding of a treasure in digging a grave is said to happen by chance to the one who digs, that is, it is beyond what was intended and foreseen. But this was not beyond what God foresaw and provided for. So also the meeting of two servants, although to them it appears a chance circumstance, was foreseen nevertheless by their master who purposely sent them to meet at the one place, in such a way that the one did not know about the other. Thus God sent the Ismaelite merchants on a certain day and hour to that place where they bought Joseph, sold to them by his brothers. The reason given here is the same as in the argumentative part of the article, and it is thus enunciated: "Since, then, all particular causes are included under the universal cause, it could not be that any effect should take place outside the

---

91 *Ibid.*, q. 103, a. 5.
92 Cf. *De veritate*, q. 5, a. 3.

range of that universal cause." This statement applies with equal truth to the free determination, which is the effect of our free will; for it is impossible that this determination should escape the order of the most universal cause, or that it should not be produced by God inasmuch as it is an entity and a good.

Moreover, as St. Thomas remarks farther on: "The very fact that an element of chance is found in those things (that are generated and corrupted) proves that they are subject to government of some kind. For unless corruptible things were governed by a higher being, they would tend to nothing definite (not to anything), especially those which possess no kind of knowledge. So nothing would happen unintentionally, which constitutes the idea of chance." [93] Expressed more briefly: if there were no natural laws and tendencies, then nothing would happen by chance outside the scope of these natural tendencies.

PROVIDENCE AND EVIL

The second difficulty was that the existence of both physical and moral evil seems to show that God does not have a care for all things in particular.

St. Thomas replies to this objection as Plato,[94] Chrysippus the Stoic, and St. Augustine did,[95] by considering the good of the universe.

The solution of the problem of evil is given in this reply by quoting these words of St. Augustine: "God would in no wise permit evil to exist in His works, unless He were so almighty and so good as to produce good even from evil." [96] Thus, unless the lion killed animals, it could not live; and there would be no heroic constancy in the martyrs unless they were persecuted.[97]

St. Thomas says in various parts of his works that good and evil are subject to divine providence as foreknown and ordained; but it is the good that is intended, and not the evil. In fact, moral evil cannot even indirectly and accidentally be willed by God.[98] It is only permitted, and by God's permission it is made to serve a greater good. It is in this sense that St. Thomas says evil is foreknown and ordained by God, yet not intended. "Whatever pertains to the right order of providence comes under providence not only as ordered to

[93] *Summa theol.*, Ia, q.103, a.5 ad 1um.

[94] *De legibus*, 903.

[95] *De civitate Dei*, Bk. XI, chap. 22.

[96] *Enchir.*, chap. 11.

[97] On the advantage of sufferings for Christians and of Christ suffering patiently for us, cf. IIIa, q.46-49; also on patience consult IIa IIae, q.136.

[98] Cf. *Summa theol.*, Ia IIae, q.79, a.1.

the other, but as that to which the other is ordered; but that which departs from the right order, comes under providence, inasmuch as it is ordered to the other but not as the other is ordered to it." [99] Thus evil is permitted for a greater good, and so it is declared that all things are "for the sake of the elect." [100]

In like manner, St. Thomas says: "It is lawful to make use of an evil for the sake of good, as God does, but it is not lawful to lead anyone to do evil." [101]

Thus evil and errors are permitted by providence only that goodness and truth may be more clearly made manifest; just as in a painting the purpose of the darker colors is to bring out the lighter colors in bolder relief, and just as the malice of several actors in a tragedy is for the purpose of showing more clearly the heroism of the famous actors. [102]

There is no contradiction in the chiaroscuro effect of this mystery, but in it these certain principles are preserved intact: moral evil cannot even indirectly be willed by God; God commands not impossibilities, but by commanding admonishes you to do what you are able, and to ask for what you are not able (to do), as said by St. Augustine, whom the Council of Trent quotes. [103] But, on the other hand, no one would be better than another, unless he were loved more by God. [104] But the intimate reconciliation of these principles can be seen only in the immediate vision of the Deity, in whose eminence infinite justice, mercy, and supreme liberty are reconciled. [105]

OTHER SPECIAL DIFFICULTIES

The third objection was: Many things happen in the world from necessity, and these do not need the direction of providence. It is the objection of Democritus.

Reply. That these do not need the direction of man, this I concede; that they do not need the direction of the Author of nature, this I deny. Thus God made the eye for seeing, the ear for hearing, the feet for walking, wings for flying. This ordering, to be sure, inasmuch as it is natural, is necessary and is determined to one effect; but it is so determined by the Author of nature, for all ordering to an end is from the supreme Ordainer, inasmuch as every agent acts

---

[99] *De veritate,* q.5, a.4. See also *I Sent.,* d.39, q.2, a.2 (about the end).
[100] Matt. 24: 22.
[101] *Summa theol.,* IIa IIae, q.98, a.4 ad 4um.
[102] Cf. *De veritate,* q.5, a.4 ad 4um, 5um, 10um, 11um.
[103] Denz., no. 804.
[104] Cf. *Summa theol.,* Ia, q.20, a.3, 4.
[105] See q.22, a.3; q.23, a.5.

for an end, tends to some end, and the order or subordination of agents corresponds to the order of ends.[106]

The fourth objection was: "God left man in the hand of his own counsel." [107] Therefore man, inasmuch as he is free, is not subject to divine providence, as Cicero thought.

Reply. I distinguish the antecedent: God left man to himself, inasmuch as He gave him the operating force that is not determined to only the one effect, this I concede; inasmuch as the very act of free will is not traced to God as to a cause, this I deny. And I deny the consequent.

St. Thomas furthermore remarks: "God extends His providence over the just in a certain more excellent way than over the wicked, inasmuch as He prevents anything happening which would impede their final salvation. "For to them that love God, all things work together unto good" (Rom. 8: 28).[108] In this sense it is said that "all things are for the sake of the elect." [109]

Fifth Objection. It has its foundation in this query of St. Paul: "Doth God take care for oxen?" [110] This was the objection raised by Maimonides (Rabbi Moses).

Reply. God does not show His care in the same way for oxen as for men; but His providence extends even to oxen. As St. Thomas remarks farther on: "Irrational creatures are only acted upon (by God) and do not act. So, when the Apostle says that it is not for the oxen that God has care, he does not wholly withdraw them from the divine government, but only as regards the way in which rational creatures are governed." [111]

Thus the answer of the article is established, namely, that God's providence is most universal, reaching down to the least of individual corruptible things, which is contrary to what Maimonides thought. Thus divine providence disposes all things most wisely, firmly, and suavely, subordinating the lower to the higher. Hence divine providence wills in some manner for their own sake those things that are honorable in themselves or deserving of honor, and likewise those things that are permanent either as individual beings (such as the angels), or specifically so (such as sensible singular things, which serve as means for something higher).[112]

[106] See *supra*, Ia, q.2, a.3: fifth way of proving God's existence.

[107] Ecclus. 15: 14.

[108] *Summa theol.*, Ia, q.22, a.2 ad 4um.

[109] Cf. Matt. 13: 20, 22; 24: 22; Rom. 8: 33; II Tim. 2: 10. See article 4 of this question, and Ia, q.103, a.5 ad 2um, 3um.

[110] I Cor. 9: 9.

[111] *Summa theol.*, Ia, q.103, a.5 ad 2um.

[112] Cf. *Contra Gentes*, Bk. III, chaps. 111–13; *De veritate*, q.5, a.3. See also *Tabula aurea*, under the word "Providentia," nos. 22, 28, 32, 33, 40.

THIRD ARTICLE

WHETHER GOD HAS IMMEDIATE PROVIDENCE OVER EVERYTHING

State of the question. It seems that God has not immediate providence over all things. For: (1) it belongs to the dignity of a king to have ministers by whom he provides for his subjects. Therefore this likewise belongs to the dignity of God; (2) because it appertains to every cause to direct its effect to good; (3) because St. Augustine says: "It is better to be ignorant of some things than to know them, for example, vile things." [113] Aristotle says the same, in fact he seems to declare this of God Himself.[114]

Yet the answer is in the affirmative, and it is of faith.

1) According to revelation, from previously quoted texts,[115] it is evident that divine providence, like divine knowledge, is not ignorant of anything, but orders all things down to the least detail, and even immediately. St. Thomas quotes in this article a text from the Old Testament.[116] Many other texts can be quoted, especially those which make it clear that God knows the prayers addressed to Him by the faithful, and hearkens to them. Our Lord also says: "Are not five sparrows sold for two farthings? And not one of them is forgotten before God. Yea, the very hairs of your head are all numbered." [117] This means that they are numbered directly by God Himself.

The definition of the Vatican Council must be understood in the same sense: "God protects and governs by His providence all things which He has made, reaching from end to end mightily and ordering all things sweetly. (Wis. 8: 1). For all things are naked and open to His eyes (Heb. 4: 13), even those which are yet to be by the free action of creatures." [118] This means that divine providence of itself without any intermediary, reaches to all things and orders them from end to end, even what we do of our own free will, inasmuch as He wills efficaciously our actually accomplished good deeds, and wills to reward them. He also permits evil deeds, either ordaining a just punishment for them or else mercifully pardoning them.

2) The theological proof in the argumentative part of the article results in two conclusions, the first of which belongs to providence and the second to divine government, or to the execution of the providential order.

---

113 *Enchir.*, chap. 17.
114 See *Metaph.*, Bk. XII, chap. 9.
115 See a. 1, 2.
116 Job 34: 13.
117 Luke 12: 6.
118 Denz., no. 1784.

The first conclusion is: As regards the type of the order of things foreordained toward an end, God has immediate providence over everything.

The reason is that He has in His intellect the type of everything, even the smallest, and He has assigned to all causes certain effects, from inanimate things, such as the gravitation required for the cohesion of the universe, even to the lives of the saints. Thus according to God's plan the grain of wheat is for the production of wheat, just as grace, which is the seed of glory, is for this very glory. Likewise God has ordained from all eternity that our prayers of petition are for the purpose of obtaining those things that are either necessary or useful for our salvation and sanctification. This constitutes the dogmatic foundation for the efficacy of prayer, which is very well explained by St. Thomas in the following passage: "For we pray, not that we may change the divine disposition, but that we may impetrate that which God has disposed to be fulfilled by our prayers; in other words, that by asking, men may deserve to receive what Almighty God from eternity has disposed to give, as St. Gregory says" (*Dial.*, Bk. I, chap. 8).[119]

But if God's knowledge did not immediately extend to all things, then it would remain only general and confused, and therefore imperfect, just as is the knowledge of a king, who is incapable of supervising all the particular things of his kingdom. Hence for a king the complete centering of all things in himself would be a practical error, but it would not be so for God.[120]

Second conclusion. As regards the execution of the order, God governs things inferior by superior things, or through these as intermediary.

It is not because of any defect in His power that He does so, but, on the contrary, because of His abundant goodness, so that He may impart the dignity of causality even to creatures.[121]

So also Christ in His mystical body imparts to the Blessed Virgin Mary the dignity of causality, so that, for example, she may be the coredemptress. He also imparts to the saints that in Him and with Him and for Him they may save souls, by carrying their cross, preaching, and being merciful to others.

Thus the error of Plato or of several of the Platonists is excluded, who admitted three subordinated providences.[122] According to a number of Platonists, the providence of the supreme God is con-

---

119 *Summa theol.*, IIa IIae, q.83, a.2.
120 Cf. *ibid.*, Ia, q.14, a.11, 13; q.103, a.6.
121 Cf. *ibid.*, Ia, q.103, a.6.
122 Cf. *ibid.*, Ia, q.103, a.6 ad 1um; q.110, a.1; *Contra Gentes*, Bk. III, chap. 76; *I Sent.*, d.39, q.2, a.2, 2a.

cerned with spiritual things and the whole world in a general way; the providence of the inferior gods is concerned with individual things that can be generated, and the "demons" in a certain manner direct human affairs, as the demon of Socrates does.

The error of the Averroists is likewise excluded, who admitted only a general providence that extends merely to the species and necessary individual things, to the sun and moon, for instance, but not to individual corruptible things.

THIS ANSWER CONFIRMED BY THE SOLUTION OF THE OBJECTIONS

Reply to first objection. "It pertains to a king's dignity to have ministers who execute his providence. But the fact that he has not the plan of those things which are done by them arises from a deficiency in himself. For every operative science (both prudence and providence) is the more perfect, the more it considers the particular things with which its action is concerned."

Reply to second objection. "God's immediate provision over everything does not exclude the action of secondary causes, which are the executors of His order." Thus God provides immediately for all things, and as regards the execution of the plan of providence, He governs the lower creation through the higher, as St. Thomas says farther on: "Therefore God so governs things that He makes some of them to be causes of others in government as a master who not only imparts knowledge to his pupils, but gives also the faculty of teaching others." [123]

Reply to third objection. "It is better for us not to know low and vile things, because by them we are impeded in our knowledge of what is better and higher . . . , and because the thought of evil sometimes perverts the will toward evil. This does not hold with God, who sees everything simultaneously at one glance, and whose will cannot turn in the direction of evil."

First doubt. Does it follow from this conception of divine government through intermediaries that God does not operate immediately in all things?

It does not, for God immediately produces those effects that belong properly to Him, by the immediate contact both of His being and His power. Thus God alone creates things and immediately preserves them in being, even inferior things. [124] So also God alone enters into the soul and moves interiorly our intellect and will. But through the mediation of creatures He produces the effects that belong properly to these creatures. Thus He objectively illumines men

[123] *Ibid.*, Ia, q. 103, a. 6.
[124] Cf. *ibid.*, q. 45, a. 5; q. 104, a. 2; q. 105, a. 3–5.

by means of angels and human teachers, although it is only He who can move interiorly the intellect and will to the performance of their acts.[125] Hence, stated more briefly: Only God can produce and preserve in everything, being absolutely as such or being inasmuch as it is being; but any creature can produce and preserve in another creature of a lower order, a modification of being, for instance, that it be hot or luminous, or this particular kind of being.

Second doubt. Is divine providence always infallible, not only as to the ordering of the means to the end, but also as to the attainment of the end?

Reply. From what has been said,[126] providence is not always infallible. For the efficacy of providence, which consists in the act of command concerning the means for the attainment of the end, depends on the efficacy of the willing or intending of the end. Hence providence is absolutely infallible even as regards the attainment of the end, in so far as it presupposes God's consequent or efficacious will, which is concerned with good here and now to be produced, for as previously stated: "Whatever God simply wills takes place; although what He wills (only) antecedently may not take place." [127]

On the contrary, God's providence is infallible only as regards the ordering of the means to the end, and not as regards the attainment of the end; in so far as it presupposes only His antecedent will. This means that God's providence is infallible in so far as it prepares the means necessary for the salvation of all adults, making the fulfillment of His commands really possible for them, even when they do not actually comply with these commands.

So then in the most general ordering of all things to the end for which God created the universe, this being His glory and the manifestation of His goodness, providence is absolutely infallible even as regards the attainment of the end, which is efficaciously or consequently willed by God.

But as regards certain particular ends, providence is infallible concerning the ordering of the means, but not concerning the attainment of these particular ends, because such ends are not efficaciously willed by God. Thus, although all men are ordered by God's providence to eternal salvation, yet not all are saved, because God does not efficaciously will the salvation of all. Yet all the particular ways of providence, whether they result in the attainment of the end or not, concur in the attainment of the most universal end, for they are

---

[125] Cf. *ibid.*, q.104, a.2; q.105, a.3–5.

[126] See a.1, third doubt: What does providence presuppose on the part of the divine will? See also fourth doubt: Whether God's providence presupposes His consequent and antecedent wills.

[127] *Summa theol.*, Ia, q.19, a.6 ad 1um.

subordinated to it. Thus he who by the act of final impenitence departs from the way of salvation, concurs in God's glory through the manifestation of His justice.[128]

By means of these principles the various texts of St. Thomas about the infallibility of providence are thereby reconciled. Thus he says: "The order of divine providence is unchangeable and certain so far as all things foreseen happen as they have been foreseen, whether from necessity or from contingency." [129] And again: "Divine providence does not fail to produce its effect, nor in the way foreseen." [130] These statements make it certain that God's providence presupposes His consequent or efficacious will.[131]

St. Thomas says in another of his works: "In all ordering of things to their end there are two points to be considered; namely, the order (to the end) and the result or consequence of this order; for not all things that are ordered to their end attain their end. Therefore providence (inasmuch as it depends on God's antecedent will) regards only the order to the end. Hence by God's providence all men are ordered to eternal happiness; but predestination regards also the result or consequence of this order, so that it therefore refers only to those who attain to the glory of heaven." [132] Predestination presupposes God's consequent will as regards the salvation of the elect, and it orders and commands the means that are efficacious for salvation.

From what has just been said it is evident that no good ever actually takes place in the world unless God efficaciously willed from all eternity that it should take place, and unless He efficaciously arranged that it should take place, whether this good is natural or supernatural, whether this good is an act easy or difficult of performance. For as stated above, "whatever God simply wills takes place, although what He wills (only) antecedently may not take place." [133] But the absolute or consequent divine will is concerned with good that will take place when all particular circumstances are considered, and it is only in this way that anything takes place.[134] Likewise no one actually commits a sin, unless God permitted it from all eternity.

Third doubt. Is the infallibility of divine providence only an infallibility of foreknowledge, as some in more recent times have contended, or is it also an infallibility of causality?

---

128 Cf. *ibid.*, q.22, a.2 ad 4um.
129 *Ibid.*, a.4 ad 2um.
130 *Ibid.*, ad 3um.
131 Cf. *ibid.*, q.103, a.7, 8; also *Contra Gentes*, Bk. III, chap. 94.
132 *De veritate*, q.6, a.1; see also *I Sent.*, d.40, q.1, a.2.
133 *Summa theol.*, Ia, q.19, a.6 ad 1um.
134 Cf. *ibid.*

Reply. As regards sin, considered purely as such, of which God cannot be the cause either directly or indirectly, providence is only an infallibility of foreknowledge, on the supposition, however, of God's permissive decree, to which is added His positive decree concerning the physical entity of sin. But with reference to all that is real and good, the infallibility of providence is also an infallibility of causality; for God is the cause of all being and goodness of whatever kind. As St. Thomas says: "Since all particular causes are included under the universal cause, it could not be that any effect should take place outside the range of that universal cause." [135]

WHETHER PROVIDENCE IMPOSES ANY NECESSITY ON THINGS FORESEEN

State of the question. It seems to be so: (1) because the effect follows of necessity from eternal providence, for divine providence cannot be frustrated. (2) God is both provident and almighty. Therefore He imposes the stability of necessity to things provided. Nevertheless the answer is that divine providence imposes necessity upon some things, not upon all.

1) This conclusion is of faith, it being declared in very many texts of Holy Scripture, which affirms that our free choices, our prayers and merits, are subject to divine providence. Therefore the Vatican Council declares: "God protects and governs by His providence all things which He has made . . . even those which are yet to be by the free action of creatures." [136]

The following theological argument is also given in proof of this conclusion.

It pertains to providence to produce every grade of being for the perfection of the universe. But, that every grade of being be produced, there must be both necessary and contingent effects, in fact, free effects. Therefore divine providence has prepared for some effects necessary causes or those that are determined to one particular thing; but for certain other effects providence has prepared contingent causes, so that they may happen contingently, and for some effects free causes or the power of choosing, with indifference of judgment and choice. This argument is but a summary of the complete proof on this point given in a previous article.[137]

The major is evident because the perfection of the universe de-

135 *Ibid.*, Ia, q.22, a.2 ad 1um. Consult also Ia, q.19, a.6; *Contra Gentes*, Bk. III, chap. 94.
136 Denz., no. 1784.
137 Cf. *Summa theol.*, Ia, q.19, a.8.

mands a subordination of beings. For the universe would not be perfect if there were only one grade of goodness in things, a point that is more clearly explained farther on.[138]

The minor is likewise evident inasmuch as the species of things are necessary; and individuals which preserve the continuity of the species (for instance, of plants and animals) are contingent. There must also be necessary effects, that is, those that proceed from a proximate cause that is determined to one particular thing, and contingent effects, in fact, free effects, which proceed from a proximate cause that is not determined to one particular thing. There is a special fitness in this so that in created things there may be a certain reflection of the divine liberty. Therefore the conclusion is established, and it is also revealed, as already stated.

THIS CONCLUSION CONFIRMED BY THE SOLUTION OF THE DIFFICULTIES

Reply to first objection. "The effect of divine providence is not only that things should happen somehow, but that they should happen either by necessity or by contingency." Hence, as St. Thomas says: "God foresaw that it (for example, the conversion of St. Paul) would happen contingently.[139] It follows then infallibly that it will be, contingently and not of necessity."

Reply to second objection. "Thus all things foreseen happen as they have been foreseen by God, whether from necessity or from contingency." For, as stated above, "since the divine will is perfectly efficacious, it follows not only that things are done which God wills to be done, but also that they are done in the way that He wills." [140] Thus the divine will extends even to the free mode of our choices; by actualizing our liberty, He does not interfere with it. As Bossuet remarks, nothing is more absurd than to say that our choice cannot be free because God efficaciously wills it to be free.[141]

Reply to third objection. "The unchangeableness of providence does not fail to produce its effect, and that in the way foreseen." St. Thomas also says in another work: "It belongs to God's providence sometimes to allow defectible causes to fail and sometimes to preserve them from failing." [142]

We should note what Cajetan says on this point. He writes: "I suspect that just as to be foreseen posits neither contingency nor

---

138 Cf. *ibid.*, q.47, a.1.
139 *Contra Gentes*, Bk. III, chap. 94, no. 11.
140 *Summa theol.*, Ia, q.19, a.8.
141 *Traité du libre arbitre*, chap. 8.
142 *Contra Gentes*, Bk. III, chap. 94, no. 14.

necessity in the event that is foreseen . . . , so God, by reason of His excellence, that is far beyond our power of conception, thus provides for things and events, that to be foreseen by Him is the consequence of something more exalted than anything either avoidable or unavoidable." [143]

But Francis Silvester (Ferrariensis) censures Cajetan, not referring to him by name, however, and he shows that the way St. Thomas speaks is better, who says: "God foresaw that it (a particular effect) would happen contingently. It follows then infallibly that it (a particular effect) will be, contingently and not of necessity." [144] It follows infallibly as foreseen, and contingently as proceeding from a proximate cause that is not determined to one particular thing. Thus both the certitude of providence and the true contingency of things are preserved intact. Such is the general teaching of the Thomists.

But Cajetan expressed himself more clearly on this point in another of his commentaries.[145] He had also very well said concerning contingent futures: "The divine ideas . . . represent the existences of things and their contingent characteristics, it being presupposed that the divine will is freely determined as regards the other term of the contradiction." [146] But the divine will is perfectly efficacious, as stated above,[147] and it extends to the free mode of our choices.

First corollary. The unchangeableness of divine providence does not thereby render our prayers useless, but is the very reason why we should pray, because God from all eternity willed and disposed things for our prayers. As St. Thomas says: "For we pray, not that we may change the divine disposition, but that we may impetrate that which God has disposed to be fulfilled by our prayers." [148]

Second corollary. The great mystery connected with God's providence is not so much its reconciliation with human liberty as its permission of sin, especially the sin of final impenitence, which pertains to the mystery of predestination and reprobation.

In fact, the reconciliation of the infallible efficacy of the decrees of providence with the liberty of our choices, although this is in itself profoundly obscure, yet it clearly enough follows from God's nature and the omnipotence of His will. If God is God, He certainly can move created liberties interiorly, firmly, and suavely, and especially so to the performance of salutary and holy acts. Moreover, it is suf-

---

[143] *Com. in Iam*, q. 22, a.4, no. 8.
[144] *Contra Gentes*, Bk. III, chap. 94, no. 11.
[145] *Com. in Ep. ad Rom.* 9: 23.
[146] *Com. in Iam*, q.14, a.13, no. 17.
[147] Cf. *Summa theol.*, Ia, q.19, a.8.
[148] *Ibid.*, IIa IIae, q.83, a.2; see *Contra Gentes*, Bk. III, chaps. 95, 96.

ficiently clear that the divine actualization of our liberty cannot destroy or interfere with this liberty.

But God's permission of sin is a great mystery, especially the sin of final impenitence. It is the mystery of the intimate reconciliation of infinite mercy, justice, and supreme liberty in the eminence of the Deity. Of two sinners (for instance, the two thieves dying on Mt. Calvary) one is efficaciously called, the other is not. As St. Thomas says, quoting St. Augustine, "To whomsoever help is given by God, it is mercifully given; and from whom it is withheld, it is justly withheld, in punishment of a previous sin." [149] There is in this a most profound mystery, which we must now discuss in the following question.

[149] *Ibid.*, IIa IIae, q.2, a.5 ad 1um.

CHAPTER XXIII

QUESTION 23

PREDESTINATION

THERE are three parts to this question: (1) The nature of predestination; (2) its cause; (3) the certainty of it.

The first part, which concerns the nature of predestination, consists of three articles. What its name implies and its reality (a. 1); its real definition and whether it posits anything in the predestined (a 2); what its opposite is, which is reprobation (a. 3).

The second part concerns the cause of predestination. On God's part, whether the predestined are chosen by Him (a. 4); on our part, whether the foreknowledge of merits is the cause of predestination (a. 5).

The third part concerns the certainty of predestination: Whether it is a certainty (a. 6); whether the number of the predestined is certain (a. 7); whether predestination can be furthered by the prayers of the saints (a. 8).

We have discussed this question at length in a special work, to which we refer the reader.[1] In the beginning of this work we treated of the significance and reality of predestination according to Holy Scripture, and of the teaching of the Church on this subject. The principal difficulties of this problem and the method of procedure, as also the classification of the theological systems, were then considered. In this same work the teaching of St. Thomas was compared with that of St. Augustine and with the theories of several modern theologians, especially of Molina and the congruists.

This question is connected with the preceding question. The gratuity of predestination is a disputed point among theologians, in so far as they admit or do not admit the intrinsic efficacy of the divine will as regards the merits of the predestined. For St. Thomas,[2] the Thomists, the Scotists, and the Augustinians, these decrees are of themselves efficacious, so that the merits of the predestined are the effects of predestination and therefore cannot be the cause of predestination, as will be stated in the fifth article. For the Molinists and the congruists, the divine decrees as regards the merits of the

[1] *Predestination* (Eng. tr., Herder Book Co.).
[2] Cf. *Summa theol.*, Ia, q.19, a.4, 6, 7, 8; q.14, a.8; q.20, a.3, 4.

predestined are not of themselves efficacious; but their efficacy depends on our consent foreseen by means of the *scientia media,* and therefore Molina says: "To the foreknowledge, which is included in predestination on the part of the intellect, there is attached the condition of the use of free will without which there would have been no preordaining by God."[3] Something similar is to be found in the congruism of St. Robert Bellarmine and of Suarez, in so far as they retain the theory of the *scientia media;* nevertheless they agree with St. Augustine and St. Thomas in defending the absolute gratuity of predestination to glory.

As we shall see, what clarifies this entire question is the principle of predilection as formulated by St. Thomas in a previous article, in which he says: "Since God's love is the cause (efficacious of itself) of goodness in things, no one thing would be better than another, if God did not will a greater good for one than for the other."[4] And again: "The reason why some things are better than others, is that God wills for them a greater good."[5] This means that no one would be better than another unless loved and helped more by God. This principle presupposes that God's will or His love is the cause that is of itself efficacious of the goodness of our salutary choices and of our merits in accordance with the following text: "For who distinguisheth thee? Or what hast thou that thou hast not received?"[6] It follows from this, as will at once be seen, that as merits are the effects of God's predilection and predestination, they cannot be its cause, as will be stated in the fifth article of this question. This teaching on the divine causality constitutes what there is of clarity, and the permission of the sin of final impenitence constitutes what there is of obscurity in this chiaroscuro.

In other words, St. Thomas preserves the principle of predilection absolutely intact in this question, whereas Molina says: "Of two that are called and equally aided by grace, it can happen that one of them is converted and the other not. It is possible for one who has received a less grace to rise again, when another who has received a greater grace does not rise again, and remains obdurate."[7] Nevertheless, so as not to deny the mystery of predestination and at least defend the extrinsic validity of the principle of predilection, Molina says that it depends entirely on God's good pleasure that Peter was placed in those circumstances in which God, by the *scientia media,* had foreseen his good consent, and that Judas was placed in different

---

[3] *Concordia,* q.23, a.4, 5, disp. I, membr. 11, p. 516.
[4] *Summa theol.,* Ia, q.20, a.3.
[5] *Ibid.,* a.4.
[6] I Cor. 4: 7.
[7] *Concordia,* pp. 51, 565. See also index to this work, under the word "Auxilium."

circumstances in which God, by this same knowledge, had foreseen his sin.[8] Thus the solution of this entire question on predestination is to be sought in the preceding questions on God's knowledge and will. The Thomists reject the *scientia media* completely, for it posits a passivity in God with reference to our conditionally meritorious free acts of the future. They always appeal to this most exalted principle, namely, that no good is actually done by this particular man rather than by another unless God efficaciously willed it, and no one actually commits sin without God's permission.[9]

If these principles are borne in mind, it will be easier to understand what must now be said on this subject.

Let us see what is the general condition of this question from the standpoint of Holy Scripture, what are the principal conflicting errors and the classification of the Catholic theological systems. The explanation of the articles of St. Thomas will thus be much simplified. Many appeal to him as their authority, yet their appeal does not always rest on solid grounds.

TESTIMONY OF HOLY SCRIPTURE

There is already indeed in the Old Testament frequent reference to the gratuitous election by which God chose the people of Israel from among all nations. Thus Seth was elected by God, and not Cain; then Noe was chosen, and Sem in preference to his two brothers; Abraham and Isaac, too, in preference to Ismael, and then Jacob was preferred to Esau. Similarly, in the New Testament we read that God freely calls the Gentiles to salvation, whereas He permits the crime committed by Israel.[10]

Thus it is often said in the Old Testament that God's free election does not conflict with justice. There is no evidence that this divine election presupposes the divine foreknowledge of man's merits. Hence St. Paul says of Jacob and Esau: "When the children were not yet born, nor had done any good or evil (that the purpose of God might stand), not of works but of Him that calleth, it was said to her (Rebecca): the elder shall serve the younger; as it is written: Jacob I have loved, but Esau I have hated," [11] that is, but I loved Esau less. Thus the mystery of salvation was announced "as a type" [12] in the Old Testament.

Does the Gospel declare the mystery of predestination? It cer-

8 *Ibid.*, p. 513.
9 *Summa theol.*, Ia, q. 19, a.6 ad 1um.
10 Rom. 11: 11–25.
11 *Ibid.*, 9: 11.
12 Cf. I Cor. 10: 6, 11.

tainly does, inasmuch as it speaks of the elect and the divine election. The Gospel announces indeed to all the mystery of redemption and the possibility of salvation, as in the following text: "Going therefore, teach ye all nations, baptizing them in the name of the Father and of the Son and of the Holy Ghost, teaching them to observe all things whatsoever I have commanded you." [13] St. Paul likewise says: "God will have all men to be saved and to come to the knowledge of the truth. For there is one God, and one Mediator of God and men, the man Christ Jesus, who gave Himself a redemption for all." [14]

Most certainly God does not command what is impossible, but makes the fulfillment of His precepts really possible at the very moment that they are of obligation, and in so far as they are known by men.

Nevertheless there are men and angels who, through their own fault, have strayed from the path of salvation or have perished, even men who knew Christ the Savior and followed Him, such as "the son of perdition." [15]

Others, who in the Gospel are called the elect, are saved. If they are adults, they not only can keep God's commandments, but they actually do, and they persevere until the end. Of these Christ says: "My sheep hear My voice, and I know them and they follow Me. And I give them life everlasting; and they shall not perish forever, and no man shall pluck them out of My hand. That which My Father hath given Me is greater than all; and no one can snatch them out of the hand of My Father. I and the Father are one." [16] Similarly He says farther on: "Those whom Thou gavest Me have I kept; and none of them is lost but the son of perdition, that the Scripture may be fulfilled." [17] There is reference in these texts not only to God's foreknowledge, but especially to His most efficacious omnipotence. [18]

It is likewise declared that "many are called, but few are chosen." [19] Also in the prophecy concerning the fall of Jerusalem and the end of the world, we read: "Unless those days had been shortened, no flesh should be saved. But for the sake of the elect those days shall be shortened." [20]

[13] Matt. 28: 19.
[14] I Tim. 2: 4.
[15] John 17: 13.
[16] *Ibid.*, 10: 27 f.
[17] *Ibid.*, 17: 12.
[18] Consult St. Augustine's *Com. in Joannem,* 10: 27, tr. 48. Also St. Thomas' *Com. in Joannem (ibid.).*
[19] Matt. 22: 14.
[20] *Ibid.*, 24: 22.

Therefore the Gospel treats of the mystery of the divine election, which is the same as the mystery of predestination. In fact, as St. Robert Bellarmine shows, there are three certain propositions which we conclude from the Gospel.[21]

1) God has chosen several among all classes of men. In the parable of the laborers in the vineyard and in the other of those that were invited to the marriage feast, we read: "Many are called, but few are chosen." [22] And again, there is the following text: "God shall send His angels with a trumpet and a great voice, and they shall gather together His elect from the four winds, from the farthest parts of the heavens to the utmost bounds of them." [23]

2) God efficaciously chose those to be saved that they may infallibly attain to eternal life. Thus we read: "There shall arise false Christs and false prophets, and shall show great signs and wonders, insomuch as to deceive, if possible, even the elect," [24] that is, if this were possible. And again: "This is the will of the Father who sent Me: that of all that He hath given Me I should lose nothing, but should raise it up again in the last day." [25] "My sheep . . . shall not perish forever, and no man shall pluck them out of My hand." [26] This text seems to point to the intrinsic efficacy of the divine election and grace, and that this efficacy does not depend on our foreseen consent. For this text does not speak of God's knowledge, but of His omnipotent will that preserves the elect and leads them to salvation.

3) God's choice of the elect was gratuitous, for we can in no way conclude from the Gospel that God chose them on account of their foreseen merits. Thus in the text: "Fear not, little flock, for it hath pleased your Father to give you a kingdom," [27] the verb "hath pleased" expresses God's good pleasure and mercy. The text does not say: "Fear not, because your merits were foreseen." Likewise, we read: "I have called you friends. . . . You have not chosen Me,

---

[21] *De gratia et libero arbitrio,* Bk. II, chaps. 9 f.

[22] Matt. 20: 16; 22: 14.

[23] *Ibid.,* 24: 31. See also Luke 12: 32.

[24] *Ibid.,* 24: 24. John Maldonatus in his commentary on this text remarks: "When he says, 'if possible,' he indicates that it is not possible. But it is not possible, posited the fact of divine predestination, as the theologians admit in discussing this text. From this passage they conclude the stability and, as they call it, the certainty of predestination. Christ is not speaking of any kind of straying away, but of the kind that is called final separation. For the elect can often be led astray, but they cannot die in that state." Consult also Matt. 24: 40: "Then two shall be in the field: one shall be taken, and one shall be left. Two women shall be grinding at the mill: one shall be taken, and one shall be left."

[25] John 6: 39.

[26] *Ibid.,* 10: 28. Consult St. Thomas' commentary on this text.

[27] Luke 12: 32.

but I have chosen you, and have appointed you that you should go and should bring forth fruit, and your fruit should remain." [28]

These words are uttered, indeed, directly to the apostles, but they concern indirectly all those who must labor in the Lord's vineyard and all God's friends. St. Thomas says: "Many attribute to themselves the cause of divine friendship, in that they attribute the principle of good works to themselves and not to God. And the Lord excluding this, says: 'You have not chosen Me' (namely, that I should be your friend); 'but I have chosen you' (that I should make you My friends), and He is not speaking here only of the grace of the apostolate." [29] St. Thomas explains the whole of this passage as referring to the gratuity of predestination, and he concludes: "It is the good already present in the thing that influences our choice, but the divine election is the cause of greater good in one thing than in another. . . . This shows clearly God's mercy to some, whom He prepares for grace without their having previously merited it." [30]

The gratuity of the divine election is likewise intimated in the following words of our Lord: "I confess to Thee, O Father, Lord of heaven and earth, because Thou hast hid these things (the mysteries of the kingdom of heaven) from the wise and prudent, and hast revealed them to little ones. Yea, Father, for so hath it seemed good in Thy sight." [31] This means, as we read in one of the epistles: "God resisteth the proud, and giveth grace to the humble," [32] and even makes them humble; for humility is God's gift. Hence St. Thomas explains this text from St. Matthew by referring it to predestination, saying: "Why God is merciful to this one rather than to a certain other, is to be attributed solely to His will . . . His will of good pleasure." [33] Therefore, Jesus says: "Yea, Father, for so hath it seemed good in Thy sight." [34]

The deep humility of the saints has its foundation in this, that when great saints see a criminal condemned to death, they say to themselves: "If this man had received all the graces which I received, perhaps he would not have been so unfaithful; and if God had permitted me to commit the sins which He permitted him to commit, this man would be in my place and I would be in his." Thus Christian humility has its foundation in the mystery of creation from nothing and in the mystery of grace or divine election.

Hence already in the synoptic Gospels and in the Gospel of St.

[28] John 15: 16.
[29] Com. in Joannem, 15: 16.
[30] Ibid.
[31] Matt. 11: 25.
[32] Jas. 4: 6.
[33] Com. in Matt. 11: 25.
[34] Matt. 11: 25.

John the mystery of the divine election is declared, as well as its efficacy and gratuity. It must be noted that, just as in the principle of predilection enunciated by St. Thomas,[35] so the gratuity of election follows from its efficacy, which extends even to the merits of the elect, for our Lord says: "Without Me you can do nothing." [36]

What is stated more clearly about this mystery in the epistles of St. Paul? It is called predestination, a name that properly applies to it. The efficacy and gratuity of this predestination are more clearly presented.

Now, in truth, St. Paul frequently declares the principle of predilection, which virtually contains the doctrine of predestination. He says: "For who distinguisheth thee? Or what hast thou that thou hast not received? And if thou hast received it, why dost thou glory as if thou hadst not received it?" [37] This is a quasi-commentary on our Lord's words: "Without Me you can do nothing" [38] as regards salvation. That is, no one thing would be better than another if God did not will greater good for one than for another. St. Paul also says: "It is God who worketh in you, both to will and to accomplish, according to His good will." [39] The efficacy and gratuity of predestination, which is asserted in the following texts, already follows from this principle of predestination.

Such texts are: "Blessed be the God and Father of our Lord Jesus Christ, who hath blessed us with spiritual blessings in heavenly places, in Christ: as he chose us in Him before the foundation of the world, that we should be holy and unspotted in His sight in charity. Who hath predestinated us unto the adoption of children through Jesus Christ unto Himself: according to the purpose of His will: unto the praise of the glory of His grace, in which He hath graced us in His beloved Son." [40] St. Thomas, like his predecessor, St. Augustine, commenting on this passage in his commentary on this epistle, says: "He chose us, not because we were saints, for we were not; but He chose us that we might become saints by leading a virtuous life and one free from vices. . . . But when the Apostle says that God predestinated us unto adoption, these words may be referred to the imperfect likeness of adoptive sonship realized here on earth by sanctifying grace; yet it is better to say they refer to the perfect likeness to God that will be realized in our heavenly home, and it is of this adoption that St. Paul says: 'We ourselves groan within ourselves, waiting

[35] *Summa theol.*, Ia, q.20, a.3.
[36] John 15: 5.
[37] I Cor. 4: 7.
[38] John 15: 5.
[39] Phil. 2: 13.
[40] Eph. 1: 3-7.

for the adoption of the sons' (Rom. 8: 23). But there are two causes assigned . . . for the divine predestination. One is the simple will of God, denoted by the words, 'according to the purpose of His will.' . . . The other cause is final, which is, that we may praise and know God's goodness, and this is denoted by the words, 'unto the praise of the glory of His grace.' " [41] This interpretation of St. Thomas is confirmed by the fact that adoptive sonship in this life is willed by God on account of the perfect adoption realized in heaven. This interpretation also brings out clearly both the gratuity and the efficacy of predestination.

And again St. Paul says: "We know that to them that love God, all things work together unto good, to such as, according to His purpose, are called to be saints. For whom He foreknew ($\pi\rho o\acute{\epsilon}\gamma\nu\omega$) he also predestinated ($\pi\rho o\acute{\omega}\rho\iota\sigma\epsilon\nu$) to be made conformable to the image of His Son; that He might be the firstborn amongst many brethren. And whom He predestinated, them He also called. And whom He called, them He also justified. And whom He justified, them He also glorified." [42]

With St. Augustine, St. Thomas, and St. Robert Bellarmine, [43] we must remark that in this last text the words, "whom He foreknew He also predestinated," the meaning is: "Those whom God has foreknown, looking favorably upon them, He has also predestined. These words do not refer to the divine foreknowledge of our meritorious acts, for such interpretation would imply that there is some good not produced by God Himself. Nowhere in St. Paul's epistles would we find any foundation for this interpretation; and it would contradict the texts just quoted and the ones we are about to quote. The meaning is: Those whom He has foreknown, looking favorably upon them (and among these are children who will die immediately after being baptized, before they performed any meritorious act). This is the frequent acceptation in Holy Scripture of the verb ($\pi\rho o\gamma\iota\gamma\nu\acute{o}\sigma\kappa\omega$) "I foreknow." Thus we read: "God hath not

---

[41] Com. in Eph., 1: 3–7; see also ibid., 1: 11, 12. Consult Estius, Com. in Ep. ad Eph., 1: 11, 12. Concerning the words, "having been predestined in the purpose of Him who works all things according to the counsel of His will," Estius says: "And so the Apostle is of the opinion that our salvation and the whole process of our sanctification is the result of God's efficacious operation in us, just as He operates in all things by a causality that in the strict sense of the term is called physical, which is rashly denied by some who in other respects are learned. It follows, moreover, from this that we are predestined not on account of our merits, but simply because it was God's will. St. Thomas, too, clearly adverts to this fact in his commentary on this passage." See also Father J. M. Vosté, O.P., Com. in Ep. ad Eph., pp. 99–121.

[42] Rom. 8: 28–30.

[43] De gratia et libero arbitrio, Bk. II, chaps. 9 f.

cast away His people, which He foreknew." [44] The Gospel speaks of
the Lord as saying to the wicked: "I never knew you: depart from Me,
you that work iniquity." [45] And St. Paul says: "But now, after that
you have known God, or rather are known by God." [46] "If any man
love God, the same is known by Him." [47] "Then I shall know even as
I am known." [48] "The Lord knoweth who are His." [49] "The Lord
knoweth the way of the just, and the way of the wicked shall perish." [50]
This exegesis of St. Thomas and St. Robert Bellarmine is upheld at
the present day by Lagrange, Allo, Zahn, Julicher, and others.

In the previously quoted passage,[51] the gratuity of predestination is
clearly seen since it depends on God's gratuitous purpose, which is
there referred to.[52] St. Paul also says in another epistle: "In whom
we also are called by lot, being predestinated according to the purpose of Him who worketh all things according to the counsel of His
will, that we may be unto the praise of His glory." [53]

Likewise, in this previously quoted passage, the efficacy of predestination is made clear in its effects, which are vocation, justification, glorification.

Finally, St. Paul sets forth God's supreme independence or liberty
in the distribution of His graces.[54] For God had chosen Israel, which
is now rejected because of its unbelief; and God announces salvation to the Gentiles, but the future conversion of the Jews is also
foretold. The principle of predilection is proclaimed, which is applied to nations and individuals in the following words: "What then
shall we say? Is there injustice with God? God forbid. For He saith
to Moses: I will have mercy on whom I will have mercy, and I will
show mercy to whom I will show mercy. So then it is not of him
that willeth nor of him that runneth, but of God that showeth
mercy." [55]

Father Lagrange, O.P.[56] shows that these words are indeed primarily said of the Gentile nations, but the principles enunciated
therein are also applied, according to St. Paul, in a secondary sense

---

[44] Rom. 11: 2.
[45] Matt. 7: 23.
[46] Gal. 4: 9.
[47] I Cor. 8: 3.
[48] *Ibid.*, 13: 12.
[49] II Tim. 2: 19.
[50] Ps. 1: 6. Cf. Estius *in Ep. ad Rom.*, 8: 29.
[51] Rom. 8: 28–30.
[52] Cf. *ibid.*, v.28.
[53] Eph. 1: 11. See also II Tim. 1: 9; Tit. 3: 5.
[54] Rom. chaps. 9–12.
[55] *Ibid.*, 9: 14 f.
[56] *Epitre aux Romains*, chap. 9, p. 244.

to individuals; in fact, strictly speaking, only persons are predestined. The meaning of these words is that God freely chooses, without offending against justice. Therefore there is no injustice on His part. For God does not command what is impossible and deprives nobody of his due, when He freely grants a greater grace to some as we shall find St. Thomas stating farther on.[57]

St. Paul concludes: "Oh, the depth of the riches of the wisdom and of the knowledge of God! How incomprehensible are His judgments and how unsearchable His ways! For who hath known the mind of the Lord, or who hath been His counselor? Or who hath first given to Him, and recompense shall be made him? For of Him and by Him and in Him are all things. To Him be glory forever, amen." [58]

We shall explain several of these texts again in our commentary on the articles of St. Thomas. At present, however, we must show, with St. Robert Bellarmine,[59] that the three propositions which we have formulated from the Gospel, which concern the divine election, are more clearly deduced from what St. Paul says in his epistles concerning predestination which follows the divine election. They are:

1) God has chosen and predestined some among all classes of men.[60]

2) God efficaciously chose and predestined those to be saved that they may infallibly attain to eternal life. "Those whom He predestinated, them He has also called . . . and justified . . . and glorified." [61]

3) God has freely chosen and predestined the elect. "Those whom He foreknew (looking favorably upon them) He also predestinated." [62] "Who shall accuse against the elect of God?" [63] "There is a remnant saved according to the election of grace." [64] "In Him, in whom we also are called by lot, being predestinated according to the purpose of Him who worketh all things according to the counsel of His will, that we may be unto the praise of His glory." [65]

The gratuity of election is also inferred when St. Paul says that "God is able to make him stand," [66] which means, as the Council of Trent explains, "that he stand perseveringly (and that He is able) to restore him who falleth." [67] This implies that it is by a special

[57] Summa theol., Ia, q.23, a.5 ad 3um (the end).
[58] Rom. 11: 33 f.
[59] De gratia et libero arbitrio, Bk. II, chaps. 9–15.
[60] Cf. Rom. 8: 30–33; Eph. 1: 4.
[61] Ibid., 8: 30.
[62] Ibid., 8: 29.
[63] Ibid., 8: 33.
[64] Ibid., 11: 5.
[65] Eph. 1: 11.
[66] Rom. 14: 4.
[67] Denz., no. 806.

act of God's mercy that he who falls is restored or converted, and it is just as much God's predilection that is made manifest, if one is always preserved from sin and never loses baptismal innocence.

From all these texts of Holy Scripture, St. Augustine deduced the following definition quoted by all theologians: "Predestination is the foreknowledge and preparation of the benefits by which most certainly are liberated whoever are liberated." [68] and St. Augustine says more explicitly: "By predestination God knew what He Himself will do." [69] It is not the foreknowledge of our merits that is assigned as the cause of predestination in this definition, but the merits of the elect are clearly seen to be the effects of this predestination, which is therefore gratuitous. Thus St. Augustine frequently says that God, in rewarding our meritorious acts, crowns His own gifts.[70]

THE TEACHING OF THE CHURCH AGAINST MUTUALLY CONFLICTING HERESIES

The teaching of the Church on this subject was formulated in the condemnations of Pelagianism and Semipelagianism. It is subsequently declared against the absolutely contradictory errors of predestinarianism as also against those of Protestantism and Jansenism. The teaching of the Church is thus like the mountain peak of truth that towers above and between these conflicting errors.

THE DECLARATION OF THE CHURCH AGAINST PELAGIANISM AND SEMIPELAGIANISM

The Pelagians said: "Without grace we can keep the commandments . . . and grace is not necessary except for making it easier to keep them." This proposition was condemned in the fifth canon of the Council of Carthage (418).[71] The Semipelagians said that man does not need grace for the beginning of faith and good will, spoken of as the "beginning of salvation," and that he can persevere until death without a special grace. This statement was condemned by the Second Council of Orange.[72] The Semipelagians held that God wills equally the salvation of all, although certain special graces are granted to some, such as the apostles. Consequently the Semipelagians identified predestination with God's foreknowledge of the beginning of salvation and of merits by which man perseveres until

---

[68] *De dono persever.*, chap. 14.
[69] *De praed. sanct.*, chap. 10.
[70] Cf. Denz., nos. 810, 842; see also no. 141.
[71] *Ibid.*, no. 105.
[72] *Ibid.*, nos. 178, 183.

the end in doing good without any special help. Negative reprobation was identical with the foreknowledge of demerits. Thus predestination and negative reprobation followed human election, whether good or bad. Hence this eliminated the element of mystery in predestination spoken of by St. Paul. Hence God was no longer the author but merely the spectator of that which singles out the elect from the rest of mankind. Hence in Pelagianism and Semipelagianism the elect are not loved and helped more by God.

Concerning children who die before the age of reason, the Semipelagians said that God predestines or reprobates them, foreseeing the good or bad acts they would have performed if they had lived longer. Thus already the Semipelagians admitted, previous to any divine decree, a foreknowledge of the conditionally free acts of the future or of the futurables, which in later times was called by Molina the *scientia media*. The opponents of Pelagianism replied that such interpretation would mean that children are marked for reprobation on account of sins they did not commit, which is unjust.

Toward the end of his life St. Augustine wrote especially two treatises [73] against Semipelagianism, in which he shows from the testimony of Holy Scripture particularly three things: (1) that, without a special and gratuitous grace, man cannot have the beginning of salvation, and that he cannot persevere until the end without a special and gratuitous grace; (2) that God does not will equally the salvation of all, but that He wills more the salvation of children who die immediately after being baptized. He likewise wills more the salvation of believers than of those who *de facto* do not receive the faith, and He wills more the salvation of those who persevere until the end; (3) that the elect, as their name indicates, are loved more and helped more, and that their merits are not the cause but the effect of the divine election. Even in one of his earlier works,[74] St. Augustine had already said, speaking of the angels who were of the elect, that they were "helped more" than the others.

The Council of Orange (529), in condemning Semipelagianism, took many of its formulas from the writings of St. Augustine and of his disciple St. Prosper. All historians agree that it disapproved of the Semipelagian denials of the gratuitousness of grace and of its necessity for the beginning of salvation and for final perseverance.[75]

Hence, on account of the declarations of the Council of Orange, all Catholic theologians admit three propositions, although they do not all interpret them in the same sense. They are: (1) predestination to grace is not because of God's foreseeing our naturally good works.

[73] *De praed. sanct.; De dono persever.*
[74] *De civitate Dei*, Bk. XII, chap. 9.
[75] Denz., nos. 176, 177, 179, 183. See also no. 806.

nor is the beginning of salutary acts due to natural causes; (2) predestination to glory is not because of God's foreseeing we would continue in the performance of supernaturally meritorious acts apart from the special gift of final perseverance; (3) complete predestination, in so far as it comprises the whole series of graces from the first up to glorification, is gratuitous or independent of foreseen merits.

Nevertheless not all Catholic theologians interpret these three propositions in the same sense. There is particularly a difference between the Molinists who deny the intrinsic efficacy of grace, and others who admit it. The latter find this efficacy obviously stated in the declarations of the Council of Orange.

Thus, in the first proposition, for the actual grace that is required for the beginning of salvation, the Molinists understand this grace to be extrinsically efficacious, because our consent was foreseen by God. Hence they differ on this point from the Thomists, the Augustinians, and the Scotists.[76] This does not safeguard so well the gratuity of grace as asserted by the Council of Orange.[77]

Similarly, contrary to the above-mentioned theologians, the Molinists understood the second proposition as meaning that the actual grace of final perseverance is extrinsically efficacious, inasmuch as God foresaw our consent by means of the *scientia media*. St. Augustine said of the grace of final perseverance: "It is a grace that is spurned by no one whose heart is hardened, and it is therefore given that the hardness of heart may first be eliminated." [78] Contrary to this, Molina says: "It may happen that two persons receive in an equal degree the interior grace of vocation; one of them of his own free will is converted and the other remains an infidel. It may even happen that one who receives a far greater prevenient grace when called, of his own free will is not converted, and another, who receives a far less grace, is converted." [79]

It is not so easy to reconcile this statement with what the Council of Trent says: "of this great and special gift of perseverance . . . which cannot be derived from any other than from Him who is able to establish him who standeth [80] that he stand perseveringly, and to restore him who falleth." [81] Likewise, from what the Council of Trent teaches, it is commonly admitted that we cannot merit *de condigno* the grace of final perseverance, for the continuance of the

[76] Consult Molina's *Concordia*, pp. 43, 564.
[77] Denz., nos. 176–78, 199, 200.
[78] *De praed. sanct.*, chap. 8.
[79] *Concordia*, pp. 51, 230, 231, 548.
[80] Rom. 14: 4.
[81] Denz., no. 806; see also no. 826.

state of grace up to the moment of death is the principle of merit, and therefore cannot be merited." [82] Hence, if the Molinists wish to admit predestination to glory after foreseen merits, then they must say that predestination to glory is independent of our foreseen supernatural merits which, without the special gift of final perseverance, would continue until the end. This is expressed in the third proposition, which we are now going to explain.

The third proposition is: "Complete predestination, in so far as it comprises the whole series of graces from the first up to glorification, is gratuitous or independent of foreseen merits." The Molinists differ from St. Thomas in the interpretation of this proposition.

Molina admits it, but he adds: "To the foreknowledge, which is included in predestination on the part of the intellect, there is attached the condition of the use of free will without which there would have been no preordaining by God." [83]

Contrary to this, Augustinians and Thomists understand complete predestination as it is explained by St. Thomas: "It is impossible that the whole of the effect of predestination in general should have any cause as coming from us; because whatever is in man disposing him toward salvation, is all included under the effect of predestination; even the preparation for grace." [84] Thus even the free determination disposing one toward salvation is entirely included in the effect of predestination. "There is no distinction," says St. Thomas, "between what flows from free will and what is of predestination; as there is no distinction between what flows from a secondary cause and from a first cause." [85] They are two total causes that are not co-ordinated, but subordinated. But the effect of predestination cannot be its cause.

The import of these three propositions seems to be that they express the very teaching of St. Augustine and are obvious inferences from the canons of the Council of Orange.

This is especially made clear from the following canons of this same council. Canon 9 reads: "As often as we do good it is God who works in us and with us enabling us to act." [86] Thus efficacious grace

---

[82] The Council of Trent says: "The just man can truly merit eternal life, and the attainment of eternal life itself (if he dies in the state of grace)." (Denz., no. 842). See no. 809. This means that a man can merit the attainment of eternal life, if he retain his merits, however, until the end, and they are retained by the gift of final perseverance.

The Council of Trent, likewise says: "God's goodness toward all men is so great that He will have the things which are His own gifts (see no. 141) to be their merits (canon 32)."

[83] Concordia, p. 516.
[84] Summa theol., Ia, q.23, a.5.
[85] Ibid.
[86] Denz., no. 182.

not only makes it possible for us to do what is good, but by it we actually do what is good. It effectively works in us, as St. Paul says: "It is God who worketh in you both to will and to accomplish." [87] Also canon 12 says: "God so loves us, as we shall be by the gift of His grace, not as we are by our own merit." [88] It follows from this that "God so much the more loves us, as we shall be better by the gift of His grace." [89] This means that no one would be better than another if he were not loved more by God. In the quotation of this last canon,[90] there is reference to the "Indiculus" on the grace of God, which expresses the same doctrine.[91]

Hence ancient theologians, namely, Augustinians and Thomists, noted that this Second Council of Orange expresses in equivalent terms this principle of predilection, which is already enunciated by St. Paul in the following words: "For who distinguisheth thee? Or what hast thou that thou hast not received?" [92] It was this great truth which the Pelagians and Semipelagians denied in maintaining that God wills equally the salvation of all. Thus those who are saved would not be more loved and helped by God, who would be rather the on-looker than the author of what singles out the just from the im-pious.

We must now consider the declarations of the Church against the errors of those who deny God's universal will to save.

Predestinarianism (ninth century) denied God's universal will to save, and taught predestination to evil. Several said that these errors are to be found in the writings of Gottschalk. This was the occasion of much controversy. On this point must be quoted especially the declarations of the councils of Quierzy (853), Valence (855), Toul (859), and Thuzey (860). It was in this last council that the bishops of France came to an agreement on this difficult matter.[93]

There are particularly two declarations which we get from these provincial councils. They are: (1) God wills in a certain way to save all men; (2) there is no predestination to evil, but God decreed from all eternity to inflict the penalty of damnation for the sin of final impenitence, a sin which He foresaw and in no way caused, but permitted.

The meaning and scope of these declarations are clearly seen es-pecially from the third canon of the Council of Quierzy, which says:

[87] Phil. 2: 13.
[88] Denz., no. 185.
[89] St. Prosper's fifty-sixth sentence.
[90] Denz., no. 185.
[91] *Ibid.*, nos. 131, 133–35, 137, 141; see also nos. 189, 193.
[92] I Cor. 4: 7.
[93] Cf. Denz., nos. 316 f.

"Almighty God wills, without exception, all men to be saved,[94] though not all are saved. That some are saved, however, is the gift of Him who saves; if some perish it is the fault of them that perish." [95] This canon is taken from the writings of St. Prosper, who was a disciple of St. Augustine. This canon makes it clear to us that God does not will equally the salvation of all, as the Pelagians thought; for that some are saved, is the gratuitous gift of Him who saves. Moreover, predestination to evil is excluded. Therefore the two extreme aspects of this mystery are declared in plain language, but we fail to perceive the mode of their intimate reconciliation. The fourth canon of the Council of Quierzy affirms that Christ died for all men.

The Council of Valence insists more strongly on the gratuity of predestination to eternal life. This council declared "that God absolutely foreknew that the good will be so by His grace, and that the wicked will be so through their own fault. Nor do the wicked therefore perish, because they could not be good, but because they refused to be good. . . . In the election of those to be saved, God's mercy precedes their merits; but in the damnation of those who will perish, their demerits precede God's judgment. The malice of the wicked was foreknown but not predestined by God, since He is not the cause of this." [96]

Finally the Council of Thuzey (860) very plainly formulates the higher principles that elucidate this question. The first declaration is: "Whatsoever the Lord pleased He hath done in heaven and on earth.[97] For nothing is done in heaven or on earth except what He Himself is pleased to do or justly permits to be done." [98] The bishops who accepted the teaching of St. Augustine demanded nothing more, and so they all agreed. This meant that no good deed is actually performed by this man rather than by a certain other, unless God Himself graciously wills and effects it; and no bad deed is actually performed by this man rather than by a certain other unless God justly permits it. Countless consequences are included in this absolutely general principle. The Thomists see in it the principle of predilection, that no one would be better than another, unless such person were loved more by God.

In the synodal letter approved by the Council of Thuzey all the other declarations proceed from this first one. The fifth declaration

[94] Cf. I Tim. 2: 4.
[95] *Ibid.*, no. 318.
[96] *Ibid.*, nos. 321, 322.
[97] Ps. 134: 6.
[98] *PL*, CXXVI, 123.

reads: "Hence it is because of God's grace that the world is saved; and it is because man has free will that the world will be judged." Thus the two extreme aspects of this mystery are declared: God's universal will to save and the gratuity of predestination.

In the sixteenth and seventeenth centuries, this teaching of the Church was confirmed by the decisions of the Council of Trent against the errors of Protestantism and by the condemnation of Jansenism. The Council of Trent says: "But, though He died for all [99] yet not all receive the benefit of His death, but those only to whom the merit of His passion is communicated." [100] And again: "If anyone says that it is not in man's power to make his ways evil, but that the works that are evil God worketh as well as those that are good, not permissively only, but also *proprie* and *per se,* so that the treason of Judas is no less His own proper work than the vocation of Paul, let him be anathema." [101] Also the following: "If anyone says that the grace of justification is attained only by those who are predestined to life, but that all others who are called, are called indeed, but do not receive grace, as being by the divine power predestined unto evil, let him be anathema." [102]

It is likewise affirmed against the Jansenists that Christ did not die only for the predestined, or only for the faithful, but for all men; [103] that there is a grace which is truly sufficient, and which makes it possible for adults to observe God's precepts according as these can be known by them.

The Church, quoting the words of St. Augustine, affirms against the reformers: "God commands not impossibilities, but, by commanding, both admonishes thee to do what thou art able, and to pray for what thou art not able (to do)." [104]

The Church, however, though asserting that God by a sufficient grace makes the fulfillment of His precepts possible for all, nevertheless affirms the efficacy of grace that actually is productive of good works. Thus the Council of Trent declares that "God, unless men are themselves wanting to His grace, as He has begun the good work, so will He perfect it, working in them the will and the performance." [105]

From all these declarations of the Church against conflicting heresies, we get, by way of summary, the following four propositions.

---

[99] II Cor. 5: 15.
[100] Denz., no. 795. See also no. 797.
[101] *Ibid.*, no. 816.
[102] *Ibid.*, no. 827; cf. no. 200.
[103] *Ibid.*, nos. 1096, 1380 f., 1294.
[104] *Ibid.*, no. 804; see also nos. 806, 807, 816, 827, 1647, 1677.
[105] *Ibid.*, no. 806; Phil. 2: 13.

A. AGAINST PELAGIANISM AND SEMIPELAGIANISM

1) The cause of predestination to grace is not the foreknowledge of naturally good works performed, nor is it on account of any preliminary acts of the natural order that are supposed to prepare for salvation.

2) Predestination to glory is not on account of foreseen supernatural merits that would continue to be effective apart from the special gift of perseverance.

More briefly: "That some are saved, is the gift of Him who saves." [106]

B. AGAINST PREDESTINARIANISM, CALVINISM, AND JANSENISM

1) God (in a certain way) wills to save all men.

2) There is no predestination to evil, but God has decreed from all eternity to inflict eternal punishment for the sin of final impenitence which He foresaw, He being by no means the cause of it, but merely permitting it.

More briefly: "That some perish, is the fault of those who perish." [107]

Hence the two truths that must by all means be held as of faith on this subject are these two propositions declared by the Council of Quierzy: "That some are saved, is the gift of Him who saves. That some perish, however, is the fault of those who perish." Pelagianism denied the first statement, predestinarianism the second. Between these two precipices of error the revealed truth towers like a mountain whose peak cannot be seen. It will be seen only in heaven, for it is the intimate reconciliation of infinite mercy, justice, and supreme liberty in the eminent Deity. Long ago Holy Scripture expressed the two extreme aspects of the mystery, which must be reconciled in these words of the prophet: " Destruction is thy own, O Israel; thy help is only in Me." [108]

These two truths are most certain and the assent of the Christian mind has always been given to them; but their intimate reconciliation can be clearly seen only in the beatific vision.

THE CLASSIFICATION OF THE THEOLOGICAL SYSTEMS

The revealed doctrine of predestination and of the will to save mankind is, as we have remarked, like a mountain peak towering

---

[106] *Ibid.*, no. 318. The Council of Quierzy is quoting from the writings of St. Prosper.

[107] *Ibid.*, no. 318. Again the Council of Quierzy is quoting from St. Prosper.

[108] Osee 13: 9.

above and between the two precipices of Pelagianism on the one hand, and predestinarianism on the other.

This representation makes it easy to see how the theological systems are at variance with one another. There are two contrary systems, each situated about half way up on opposite sides of the mountain. On one side above Semipelagianism is Molinism, and a little farther up the congruism of Suarez. On the other side we have the more rigid interpretations of Augustinianism and Thomism, which modify, so it seems, God's universal will to save, saying that negative reprobation, which is previous to foreseen demerits, consists not only in the permission of sins that are not forgiven, but in the positive exclusion from heavenly glory as from a favor to which one is not entitled.[109]

Midway between the two sides, however, we find the eclecticism of the congruists of the Sorbonne, who with the Molinists admitted the extrinsic efficacy of grace for salutary acts easy of accomplishment, and who with the Thomists and the Augustinians admitted the intrinsic efficacy of grace for difficult salutary acts. This view, which seems to be practically applicable, has in its speculative aspect all the difficulties of Molinism or of the *scientia media* for acts easy of performance, and almost all the difficulties of Thomism for difficult salutary acts. Hence it does not set the mind at rest.

Higher up is the mountain peak, which is, indeed, inaccessible for pilgrims here on earth, this being the Deity just as it is, in whose eminence infinite mercy, justice, and supreme liberty are intimately reconciled. But before we reach this peak, it is possible for us in this life to formulate most certain principles, in which we clearly see the equilibrium or harmony of the revealed doctrine, and which enable us to determine in this life the exact location of this inaccessible peak. These principles are: (1) God does not command impossibilities, but makes it possible for all to be saved. (2) One person would not be better than another, unless such person were loved more by God. "What hast thou that thou hast not received?" [110] But these two principles stem from one more sublime, namely, "God's love is the source of all good," that is, of grace by which we can keep God's commandments, and of grace by which we actually do keep them.

But these two higher principles are the ones that were so famously formulated by St. Augustine and St. Thomas, both of whom admitted their universal validity.

Thus we can now come to the methodical classification of the Catholic systems:

109 See next page, § 1.
110 I Cor. 4: 7.

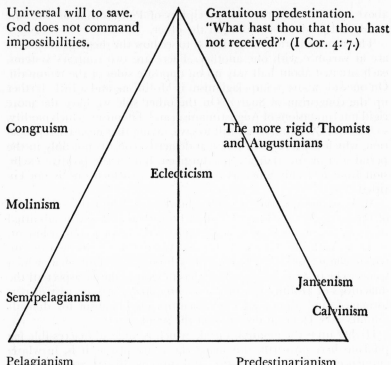

Universal will to save.
God does not command
impossibilities.

Gratuitous predestination.
"What hast thou that thou hast
not received?" (I Cor. 4: 7.)

Congruism

The more rigid Thomists
and Augustinians

Eclecticism

Molinism

Jansenism

Calvinism

Semipelagianism

Pelagianism
Negation of gratuitous
predestination

Predestinarianism
Negation of universal will
to save

The systems have been classified in three ways. The first classification, which is the one more commonly proposed, considers not so
much the principles as the conclusions of the theologians. The second, proposed by Father Billot, S.J., is from the Molinist point of
view and considers rather the principles. The third, proposed by
Father del Prado, O.P., is from the Thomist point of view and likewise considers not so much the conclusions as the principles.

1) According to the commonly proposed classification there are
two principal tendencies. Some say the predestination of adults to
glory is the result of foreseen merits; these are sponsors of the purely
Molinist view, such as Vasquez and Lessius. Others say that the predestination of adults to glory is previous to foreseen merits, and that
negative reprobation or non-election is previous to foreseen demerits. Such is the view of the Thomists, the Augustinians, the
Scotists, and, even among congruists, it is the view of St. Robert
Bellarmine and Suarez.

Nevertheless there is considerable difference of opinion between the theologians of this second category, of those, namely, who admit the absolute gratuity of predestination to glory. Almost all of the old school, namely, the Thomists, the Augustinians, and the Scotists, hold that this gratuitous predestination has its foundation in the divine predetermining decrees. St. Robert Bellarmine and Suarez, however, deny these decrees and retain the Molinist theory of the *scientia media* so as to explain the distribution of "congruent" grace and God's certain knowledge of the consent given by the elect to this grace.

2) The second classification, which is the one proposed by Father Billot,[111] has its foundation not so much in the conclusions as in the principles. For some, he says, the foundation of foreknowledge, which implies predestination, is in the divine predetermining decrees; for others, however, it is in the *scientia media*. Among these latter, there are some who, like Vasquez and Lessius, admit the predestination of certain adults to glory after foreseen future merits, and the non-election of certain ones after foreseen future demerits. But there are others who, like Suarez, hold that the predestination of adults to glory is even before conditionally future foreseen merits, and that negative reprobation or non-election is even before conditionally future foreseen demerits. Finally, others will have it that predestination of adults to glory is after foreseen merits as conditionally future, but not as future. Father Billot admitted this last opinion, which he thinks is the one Molina taught. Thus, for Father Billot, what is absolutely gratuitous is the divine choice of circumstances in which God places a certain person, after having foreseen by the *scientia media* that in these circumstances the consent would be freely given. But as for negative reprobation or non-election, Father Billot's view does not differ much from that of Vasquez, which latter is very difficult to maintain.

Lastly, there is a third classification proposed by Father N. del Prado, O.P.[112] He also takes into consideration not so much the conclusions as the principles of the theologians, according as they admit as the foundation for their doctrine predetermining decrees, or the *scientia media*. But he insists that only the theologians admitting the divine predetermining decrees are faithful followers of St. Thomas, who wrote: "Whatsoever is in man disposing him toward salvation is all included under the effect of predestination, even the preparation for grace." [113] This includes, therefore, even the free determination of the salutary act in so far as it is in this one rather

111 *De Deo uno*, p. 290 (last ed.).
112 *De gratia et libero arbitrio*, III, 188.
113 *Summa theol.*, Ia, q.23, a.5.

than the other, for example, in the good thief on Mt. Calvary rather than in the other. The absolute gratuity of predestination to glory is thus clearly seen; for, since the merits of the elect are the effects of predestination, they cannot be its cause. This is truly what was meant by St. Thomas, who previously in the article just quoted had written: "Now there is no distinction between what flows from free will, and what is of predestination; as there is no distinction between what flows from a secondary cause and from a first cause." For they are two total subordinated causes, so that the entire effect is from God as the first cause, and the effect is entirely from our will as the secondary cause moved by God. They are not two partial co-ordinated causes, as when men are pulling a boat.[114]

It must also be remarked that only the theologians who admit the intrinsic efficacy of the divine decrees and of grace recognize the absolute and universal validity of the principle of predilection formulated by St. Thomas in these words: "Since God's love is the cause of goodness in things, no one thing would be better than another, if God did not will greater good for one than for another." [115] Similarly St. Thomas says: "He who makes a greater effort does so because of a greater grace; but to do so he needs to be moved by a higher cause." [116] This principle of predilection presupposes that the divine decrees concerning our future salutary acts are intrinsically and infallibly efficacious. If, on the other hand, this intrinsic efficacy of grace is denied, the case might arise in which, of two persons who are loved and helped to the same extent by God and who are placed in the same circumstances, one would correspond with the grace received and the other would not. Thus without having been loved and helped more by God, one would prove to be better than the other by doing something either easy or difficult to perform, whether this is the first or final act. This is indeed what, in opposition to St. Thomas, Molina maintains. He reduced the principle of predilection to the divine choice of favorable circumstances in which God places those whom He foresaw will consent to make good use of the grace in such circumstances.

Conclusion. Hence a comparison of the different systems about predestination brings us back to the question of the value of the principle of predilection, namely, that one thing would not be better than another, unless it were loved more by God. Is this principle of absolute and universal validity, as the early theologians thought, especially the Thomists, or has it merely a relative value and one

---

[114] Cf. *ibid.*, Ia IIae, q.112, a.4.
[115] *Ibid.*, Ia, q.20, a.3.
[116] *Com. in Matt.*, 25: 15.

that is restricted to favorable circumstances, as the Molinists and the congruists think, who admit the *scientia media?*

As we shall see when we come to explain the doctrine of St. Thomas in the articles of this twenty-third question, this principle of predilection, in the philosophical order, is the corollary of the principle of causality applied to God's love which is the cause of all good. Hence St. Thomas says: "Since God's love is the cause of goodness in things, one thing would not be better than another, if God did not will greater good for one than for another." [117]

In the supernatural order, however, this principle of predilection has been revealed by St. Paul in these words: "For who distinguisheth thee? Or what hast thou that thou hast not received?" [118] He finds this principle expressed in the Old Testament writing: "For He saith to Moses: I will have mercy on whom I will have mercy, and I will show mercy to whom I will show mercy." [119]

This principle of predilection, as we stated above, was admitted by St. Augustine even for the angels. He says, concerning the good and the bad angels: "If both were created equally good, then, while some fell by their evil will, the others were more abundantly assisted, and reached that high degree of blessedness from which they became certain that they would never fall." [120] It is evident, of course, that the following text applies even to the angels: "For who distinguisheth thee? Or what hast thou that thou hast not received?" [121] St. Augustine also says, speaking of predestination: "Why He draweth one and not another, seek not to judge, if thou dost not wish to err." [122] We must now explain the articles of St. Thomas.

As we said, this twenty-third question consists of three parts. The first part contains the first three articles: (1) What is meant by the

---

[117] *Summa theol.,* Ia, q.20, a.3.

[118] I Cor. 4: 7.

[119] Rom. 9: 15.

[120] *De civitate Dei,* Bk. XII, chap. 9.

[121] I Cor. 4: 7.

[122] On St. John, *hom.* 26. Consult Rouët de Journel's *Enchiridion patristicum,* Index theologicus, p. 850, nos. 127–40. See also *ibid.,* what is meant by the "predestination of the saints," doctrine of St. Augustine: There are some whom God "has predestined to eternal life, He being most merciful in the bestowal of His graces" (nos. 1882, 1951, 1985, 1988, 2002). Predestination to the faith and to justification is absolutely gratuitous. Predestination is "the hidden work of God." Those who are damned, are damned through their own fault. The teaching of other Fathers: Predestination is "God's secret plan" (St. Fulgentius), nos. 2246, 2254, 2255, 2286. Rouët de Journel quotes these words of St. Ambrose: "God predestined to reward those whose merits He foreknew" (no. 1272). *De fide ad Gratianum, PL,* XVI, 665. But these words refer to glory inasmuch as it is the reward in the order of execution; and inasmuch as it is the reward, it is evi-

name predestination and whether persons are predestined. (2) The real definition completes this inquiry: Does it place anything in the predestined? (3) What is meant by its opposite, reprobation? The second part concerns the cause of predestination (a. 4, 5); the third part treats of the certainty of predestination (a. 6, 7, 8).

FIRST ARTICLE

WHETHER MEN ARE PREDESTINED BY GOD

State of the question. The difficulty is (1) that St. John Damascene says: "God foreknows all that is in us, but does not predetermine it all." [123] (2) Other creatures are directed to their end by Providence and are not said to be predestined. Then why would men be predestined?

The answer is: It is fitting that God should predestine men; and predestination, as regards its objects, is a part of providence.

1) The conclusion is proved on the authority of St. Paul, who says: "Whom He predestinated, them He also called." [124]

The word "predestined" (προώρισεν, from the verb προορίζω) signifies to predefine, to decree.[125] The word *praedestinavit*, which St. Thomas quotes from the Latin Vulgate, is a good translation of the Greek verb, though it denotes something that is sent on in advance. There is another foundation for this idea in the Old Testament, for we read: "He hath made me as a chosen arrow. In His quiver He hath hidden me." [126] Likewise in the New Testament: "As many as were ordained to life everlasting, believed." [127]

Moreover, the Fathers and Councils make use of this word "predestination." Thus the Council of Quierzy (853) says: "God, who is good and just, chose from the same mass of perdition (descendants of Adam), according to His foreknowledge, those whom He has predestined by grace for life,[128] and He has predestined eternal life for them. But the rest, whom by His just judgment He left in the mass of perdition, He foreknew will perish, though He did not predestine

---

dently given to adults in the order of execution only on account of merits. Hence, as pointed out farther on, the Thomists generally agree in saying that "God (in the order of intention) freely wills to give glory to the elect, but He does not will to give it freely (in the order of execution)."

123 *De fide orthod.,* Bk. II, chap. 30.
124 Rom. 8: 30.
125 See Eph. 1: 11.
126 Isa. 49: 2. See also Ps. 126: 4.
127 Acts. 13: 48.
128 Rom. 8: 29; Eph. 1: 11.

that they should perish. But because He is just He predestined eternal punishment for them." [129]

This dogma of predestination is affirmed also by the Council of Trent, which says: "No one, moreover, so long as he is in this mortal life, ought so far to presume as regards the secret mystery of divine predestination as to determine for certain that he is assuredly in the number of the predestinate." [130] It likewise says, speaking of the gratuity of the gift of final perseverance: "Which gift indeed cannot be derived from any other but Him who is able to establish him who standeth, that he stand perseveringly, and to restore him who falleth." [131]

The proof from reason is as follows: "Just as there is a type in the divine mind of the ordering (disposition and direction) of all things to their end, which is called providence, so there must be a type of the ordering of those who are to be transmitted to their end, which is supernatural happiness. But the type of the transmission of the rational creature is called predestination, for to destine is to send. Therefore it is fitting that God should predestine men, and predestination is, as regards its objects, a certain part of providence.

This argument means the end of all difficulties. In the reply to the first objection it is remarked that where Damascene says that God "does not predetermine what is in us," he means that "He does not predetermine by an imposition of necessity." This is evident from the context in which Damascene says: "God does not will malice, nor does He compel virtue." Hence predestination is not excluded by Him.

Reply to second objection. Irrational creatures cannot properly be said to be predestined, because they are not capable of attaining to eternal life.

Reply to third objection. Predestination applies to angels, just as it does to men. Thus St. Augustine says: "Who made the good will in the angels, if not He who created them with their good will, that is, with their chaste love, by which they adhered to Him, at the same time establishing them in their nature and endowing them with grace?" [132] A little farther on St. Augustine says that the good angels "were more abundantly assisted and attained to their eternal happiness, whereas the others fell by reason of their evil will." [133]

From this article we get the definition of predestination, which is: "the type of the ordering of some persons toward eternal salvation,

---

[129] Denz., no. 316.
[130] *Ibid.*, no. 805.
[131] *Ibid.*, no. 806.
[132] *De civitate Dei*, Bk. XII, chap. 9.
[133] *Ibid.*

existing in the divine mind." [134] This means that it is the ordering, preconceived in the divine mind, of some to salvation. On this point St. Thomas is completely in agreement with St. Augustine, who defined predestination as "the foreknowledge and the preparation of those gifts whereby they who are delivered are most certainly delivered." [135]

In this definition St. Augustine by "foreknowledge" does not have in mind merely speculative knowledge, or the *scientia media* by which God before any decree foresaw what we of ourselves will do; but he is referring to that practical and effective knowledge by which God foresees what He Himself will do. It is therefore dependent on His executive decree. Wherefore it is said that predestination is "the foreknowledge and preparation of the gifts, whereby they who are delivered, are most certainly delivered." St. Augustine had also said: "By predestination God knew what He will do." [136]

St. Thomas likewise says: "Although knowledge as such does not concern things to be done, nevertheless practical knowledge does, and it is to this knowledge that predestination refers." [137] This means that predestination refers to God's knowledge, "which has the will joined to it, and is the cause of things." [138]

Thus St. Thomas [139] explains St. Paul's words: "Whom He foreknew, He also predestinated," [140] as meaning that He foreknew by the practical knowledge that regulates the choice, and the choice of the will precedes predestination as will be stated farther on; [141] for predestination, as St. Thomas declares,[142] is an act of the intellect, which means that it is an efficacious command concerning the means, concerning the execution of the means already chosen.

To predestine, indeed, means the ordering of the means that are efficacious for the salvation of the elect. But ordering is an act of the intellect, and the ordering of the efficacious means for the attainment of anything is a command that directs the execution of a preconceived and chosen thing. Also providence, of which predestination is an objective part, is an act of prudence, or a command that presupposes choice.

---

[134] Yet it is in a.2 of this question that St. Thomas gives us this definition of predestination. [Tr.]

[135] *De dono persever.*, chap. 14.

[136] *De praed. sanct.*, chap. 10.

[137] *De veritate*, q.6, a.1 ad 7um.

[138] *Summa theol.*, Ia, q.14, a.8.

[139] *De veritate*, q.6, a.1.

[140] Rom. 8: 29.

[141] *Summa theol.*, Ia, q.23, a.4.

[142] *De veritate*, q.6, a.1.

First doubt. In what sense is predestination an objective part of providence?

Reply. It is not to be understood as constituting a subjective part of providence. This means that it is not subordinated to providence as the species is subordinated to its genus. Some said that there are four kinds of providence: (1) providence that concerns the order of nature; (2) general providence that concerns the salvation of all human beings; (3) special providence that concerns the salvation of the predestined, or predestination; (4) providence that concerns the order of the hypostatic union. The distinction between them would be virtual.

St. Thomas says at the end of the argumentative part of this article: "Predestination, as regards its objects, is a part of providence." This means that predestination constitutes some part of the material object of providence. Thus it is that one and the same divine providence concerns the three orders of nature, grace, and the hypostatic union, there being no virtual distinction between these kinds of providence, and it is only because of the different objects that this divine providence receives different names. In this respect it resembles the divine knowledge, which in itself is only of one kind, yet because of its different material objects it is called the knowledge of simple intelligence, of vision, and of approbation.

The reason why divine providence is one and undivided is because its object is one, namely, the universe, which consists of three subordinated orders, and there is one end to which all these orders are ordained, which is God's glory. The Salmanticenses clearly show, in discussing the motive of the incarnation, that God by one and the same decree willed to manifest His goodness by means of the universe in which the subordination between the three orders is as follows: first comes the order of nature, which is subordinated to that of grace with permission of original sin, both of which are subordinated to the hypostatic union.

Second doubt. Does predestination add anything to providence in general?

Reply. It adds the efficacy of the means and the infallible attainment of the end.[143] In other words, as Alvarez explains,[144] by divine providence the end directly intended by God's consequent will is always attained, namely, the good of the universe; but for the attainment of this end certain evils are permitted, and thus certain things are indirectly intended; these are willed by God's antecedent

[143] Cf. *De veritate*, q.6, a.1, and what we said in treating of providence (q.22, a.1).

[144] *De auxiliis*, p. 242.

will, such as that all the fruits do not become ripe, that all human beings are not saved. Contrary to this, since predestination depends solely on God's consequent will, it always obtains its effect, in this sense that the predestined are always saved. Nevertheless, that the predestined in the course of their lives here on earth are permitted to fall into sin is more probably the effect of predestination, so as to make the elect more humble, as will be stated farther on.

SECOND ARTICLE

WHETHER PREDESTINATION PLACES ANYTHING IN
THE PREDESTINED

This article completes the definition of predestination, a point that is particularly evident from the fourth objection, which states that if predestination places anything in the predestined, such as grace, then it is something temporal, and is not eternal and uncreated.

The reply of St. Thomas is: Predestination is not anything in the predestined, but only in the person who predestines. But the execution of predestination is in a passive way in the predestined.

The first part is proved from the fact that predestination, as it was stated, is a part of providence. Now providence is not anything in the things provided for, but is a type of the ordering of those things that exist in the divine mind.

The second part is proved from the fact that, just as the execution of providence, which is the divine government, is actively in God, as an action that is formally immanent and virtually transitive, but is passively in the things governed; so the execution of predestination is passively in the predestined.

First doubt. But what is this execution of predestination, or what are its effects?

St. Thomas replies at the end of the argumentative part of this article that these effects are the calling and magnification, for St. Paul says: "And whom He predestinated, them He also called; and whom He called, them He also justified; and whom He justified, them He also glorified." [145]

Several Thomists, comparing what St. Thomas says in this article with other passages in his various works, define the effect of predestination by saying that it is whatever God does by reason of His efficacious intention of saving some in preference to others. Hence four conditions are required for anything to be the effect of predestination: (1) that the thing is caused by God; (2) that it is the result

[145] Rom. 8: 30.

of God's efficacious intention to save; (3) that it leads one certainly to eternal life, for, since it is the result of God's efficacious intention, it cannot be frustrated; (4) that it is the result of Christ's merits, inasmuch as we are concerned here with the predestination of men in the state of fallen nature.

These four conditions are verified primarily in the proper effects of predestination, which result from it by an elective process. Such are the efficacious call, justification not interrupted by sin and continuing up to the moment of death, and finally glorification. But besides these proper effects there are others that are not a matter of choice, but are imperative only by reason of predestination. Such are the good disposition of the predestined and their natural endowments, which depend by way of choice on the general direction of providence in the natural order. Thus in our human life we distinguish between acts elicited by charity and those commanded by this virtue, which are, of course, elicited by a virtue that is subordinated to charity.

Having posited these conditions, Thomists are generally enough agreed, from a consideration of the various texts of St. Thomas, in arranging the effects of predestination according to the following schema:

Effects of predestination

Elective
- Glorification.
- Good use of grace in the life of the elect (a.5). This is against Molina's theory.
- Uninterrupted justification ending in final perseverance. Also interrupted justification inasmuch as the remembrance of this results in a life of penance by the predestined, and inasmuch as lost merits are restored.
- Especially the efficacious call in the predestined; also the inefficacious call, inasmuch as its remembrance by the predestined leads them to give thanks to God.

Imperative
- Poverty, diseases, misfortunes, death in such circumstances as assure one of being saved.
- Naturally moral good acts, or the good use of natural qualities, such as moral rectitude, meekness.
- Good disposition of the predestined, natural endowments, such as being born of good parents.

It is also more probable that the permission of sin in the predestined, inasmuch as it is the means of greater sanctification for them, is the effect of predestination. This last statement must be understood in the right sense. Indeed it is not sin but the permission of sin that is the effect of predestination, inasmuch as this permission is meant to be the occasion of leading the elect to greater humility and more fervent charity, as is seen in the life of St. Mary Magdalen, or in St. Peter's life after his repentance for having denied the Lord. This doctrine has its foundation in these words of St. Paul: "To them that love God (until death), all things work together unto good"; [146] and St. Augustine adds: "all things, even sins," inasmuch as they serve as the occasion to make one more humble.[147]

Second doubt. How are the natural gifts of the elect the effect of predestination, and how are they conducive to their salvation?

It is easy to see that natural gifts are conducive to salvation, since the natural inclination to fortitude is the foundation for stability in the life of the Christian. But it is more difficult to say how these natural gifts of the elect are the effect of predestination, because the order of nature is presupposed by the order of grace, to which predestination belongs. Hence there is not absolute agreement among Thomists in the explanation of this point, for they arrange in different orders the ordaining of the divine decrees concerning nature, grace, and the hypostatic union.

Some say: (1) God, intending to manifest His goodness, willed the order of nature; (2) He ordained intellectual creatures to a supernatural end; (3) having foreseen Adam's sin and original sin, He decreed the reparation of the human race through Christ the Redeemer; (4) in Christ, God chose some in a more special manner and effectively, leaving the rest alone. According to this order, it is difficult to conceive how the very being of the predestined, native endowments, and other natural qualities, are the effect of predestination, and are thus conducive to salvation. For, according to this view, all these natural qualities, which will be realized in course of time, are supposed as already present in the previous signs. These Thomists seem to multiply excessively the number of virtually distinct divine decrees, nor do they answer the question why God permitted Adam's sin and original sin. This order was followed by John of St. Thomas and Billuart in discussing the motive of the incarnation.

Other Thomists, however, such as the Salmanticenses, Godoi, and Gonet, differ, and with good reason, from John of St. Thomas and Billuart. In discussing the motive of the incarnation, they say that God permits sin only for a greater good. We cannot, of course, say a priori for what greater good He permitted Adam's sin; but after the incarnation this good is clearly seen, as St. Thomas remarks, who says: "God allows evils to happen in order to bring a greater good therefrom. Hence it is written (Rom. 5: 20): 'Where sin abounded, grace did more abound.' Hence, too, in the blessing of the paschal candle we say: 'O happy fault, that merited such

[146] *Ibid.*, 8: 28.
[147] See St. Thomas' *Com. in Ep. ad Rom.*, 8: 28.

and so great a redeemer.' " [148] Thus God permitted Adam's sin on account of the redemptive incarnation that was first willed in the genus of final cause, but not in the genus of material cause that is to be perfected, just as He wills the matter as capable of being actuated by its form, and the form as actuating the matter. Thus God permitted Adam's sin and the abounding of the offense in order that grace might abound yet more. Nor is there any need for a multiplicity of decrees, but by one and the same decree God willed that the natural order should be subordinated to the supernatural order (with permission of Adam's sin), and that the supernatural order should be subordinated to the hypostatic union.[149] In this way it is more readily shown how the natural gifts of the elect serve to promote the salvation of the predestined. Thus the natural intelligence with which St. Augustine and St. Thomas were endowed, helped them in their theological studies. Likewise, in the elect the inclination to prudence is subordinated to infused prudence, just as the natural inclination to fortitude is subordinated to the Christian virtue of fortitude in the martyrs.

Not only do the natural gifts and temperament of the elect promote their salvation, but also their misfortunes and sicknesses do, inasmuch as "to them who love God all things work together unto good," [150] since there could be no heroic patience without suffering.

THIRD ARTICLE

WHETHER GOD REPROBATES ANY MAN

Since opposites have their foundation in the same principle, reprobation must be defined by its opposite, which is predestination.

Reply. It is of faith that there is such a thing as reprobation, which does not mean, however, predestination to evil. The Council of Quierzy says against Gottschalk: "God, who is good and just, chose from the same mass of perdition, according to His foreknowledge, those whom He has predestined for life,[151] and He has predestined

---

[148] *Summa theol.* IIIa, q. 1, a. 3 ad 3um.

[149] This means that God, by His knowledge of simple intelligence, contemplated first of all several possible worlds, and among these was the world of sinners with the redemptive incarnation. In this possible world, the natural order is subordinated to the supernatural order with permission of original sin, and the supernatural order is subordinated to the redemptive incarnation.

Thereupon, just by one decree, God willed this possible world together with all its parts. Thus the architect does not first intend the foundation of the house and then the roof; but he first intends to construct a suitable dwelling and the whole house together with all its parts.

[150] Rom. 8: 28.

[151] *Ibid.*, 8: 29; Eph. 1: 11.

eternal life for them. But the rest, whom by His just judgment He left in the mass of perdition, He foreknew will perish, though He did not predestine that they should perish. But because He is just, He predestined eternal punishment for them." [152]

Holy Scripture speaks of the reprobates, of the son of perdition.[153] St. Paul says: "I chastise my body . . . lest . . . I myself should become a castaway." [154] Christ Himself reveals to us the sentence of judgment: "Depart from Me, you cursed, into everlasting fire." [155]

Theological proof. The following answer is given to those who inquire about the definition and fitness of reprobation: It is the part of providence which permits the failure of some through their own fault to attain glory; and because it was their own fault, the penalty of damnation is inflicted on them. Thus reprobation is the opposite of predestination. It is a question of sin which *de facto* is not forgiven, especially the sin of final impenitence.

That it is fitting for God to reprobate some is proved as follows: It belongs to God's providence, as universal provider, to permit for the general good of the universe the failure among defectible things that are subjected to this providence. But intellectual creatures, who are destined for glory, are of their nature defectible. Therefore it belongs to God's providence to permit that some through their own fault fail to attain their end, and to inflict the penalty of damnation for their sin. The motive, however, of this divine permission will be discussed farther on [156] along with the motive of predestination.

First doubt. Does reprobation imply only foreknowledge?

Reply. It does not, but as St. Thomas says: "It includes the will to permit a person to fall into sin, and to impose the punishment of damnation on account of that sin." This negative reprobation is the will to permit sin which *de facto* will not be forgiven; and, as we shall see,[157] this negative reprobation is previous to foreseen demerits that are not to be forgiven, which are not infallibly foreseen as future without this divine permission.

Positive reprobation, however, is the will to inflict the penalty of damnation for sin, and this is the result of foreseen demerits; for every just punishment presupposes a sin, on account of which the punishment is inflicted.

Second doubt. What must be said of the opinion of certain Thomists who maintain that negative reprobation, which is prior to the

152 Denz., no. 316.
153 John 17: 12.
154 I Cor. 9: 27.
155 Matt. 25: 41.
156 See q.23, a.5 ad 3um.
157 See a.5.

foreseeing of demerits, consists in the positive exclusion from glory, as a gift to which they are not entitled? Such was the opinion of Alvarez, the Salmanticenses, John of St. Thomas, Gonet, and Contenson.

Reply. It is more difficult to reconcile this opinion with God's universal will to save, and there seems to be no foundation for this theory in the present article of St. Thomas, or in any other passage of his works. All that St. Thomas says in this article and elsewhere is: "Reprobation includes the will to permit a person to fall into sin," especially into the sin of final impenitence and other sins that dispose one for it. He does not speak of the positive exclusion from glory as from a gift to which one is not entitled.

St. Thomas says, indeed, in the reply to the first objection of this article: "To some God does not wish this good which is eternal life," which means that He wills eternal life to them only antecedently and not consequently or efficaciously. But to exclude them from glory as from a gift to which they are not entitled would be not only not to will, but to be unwilling; it would be an act of positive exclusion from glory. This seems, however, too harsh a view, and by this very fact, these men, before their demerits were foreseen, would be excluded not only from their ultimate supernatural end, but also from their ultimate natural end.

Similarly, in the reply to the second objection it is stated that "reprobation is the cause of abandonment by God," that is, after sin and on account of sin.

In the reply to the third objection it is explained that the reprobate can be saved, although *de facto* he will not be saved. This point is better explained, however, if we bear in mind that before foreseen demerits such a person is not excluded from glory as from a gift to which one is not entitled.

Therefore this opinion of certain Thomists seems scarcely reconcilable with God's universal will to save. For God, to the utmost extent, sincerely wills by His antecedent will that all be saved, so that it is their own fault if they are damned. But He would not will all to be saved if, before having foreseen any sin on the part of the reprobate, He had decreed positively to exclude such a person from eternal salvation as from a gift to which one is not entitled.

Confirmation of proof. God wills whatever there is of good in anything. But that a person, who is ordained to an ultimate end that is both natural and supernatural, before the foreseeing of sin, be excluded from this end as from a gift to which one is not entitled, is not in itself anything good. Therefore God, before the foreseeing of sin, does not exclude a person from the ultimate natural and supernatural end as from a gift to which one is not entitled.

Hence negative reprobation is simply God's will to permit one through one's own fault to fail to reach the ultimate end. Therefore Thomist theologians generally distinguish between the permission of sin and the denial of efficacious grace; for this latter is an evil that implies a penalty and it therefore presupposes sin; whereas, on the contrary, the permission of sin precedes the sin, and is not a penalty, but something that is not good; for privation is more than a simple denial. There is a great difference, indeed, between not giving something that is gratuitous and refusing to give it.

Objection. Since God proceeds according to order, He first intends the end before the means. But in the case of reprobation, exclusion from glory is the end, and the permission of sin is the means. Therefore God first intends exclusion from glory, and then the permission of sin.

Reply. I concede the major, and deny the minor; for the exclusion from glory as from a gift to which one is not entitled is the end in the case of reprobation; for in the order of execution, the end is that which is attained. But God in the order of execution excludes no one from glory as from a gift to which one is not entitled, but only as a punishment for sin.

Moreover, we must not look for absolute parallelism between reprobation and predestination, because divine providence is not related to good and evil in the same way. It directly intends good things, because these are in themselves appetible; but it does not indirectly intend, but only permits, evil things, because these are not in themselves appetible; and having permitted them, it orders them to some good, and it permits them only because of some good.

Hence, because God first intends the general good of the universe, which demands the manifestations of His justice, He at once and directly wills simply to permit sin, and then He ordains the punishment of the sin which has been permitted and foreseen, which is a good thing; for it is just that sin should be punished, and in this we see the splendor of God's justice.

Third doubt. What is meant by God's permission of sin?

Reply. God's permission of sin means that the will, which by its nature is defectible, is not maintained by Him at that particular time in the performance of good; for if this will were maintained by Him in the performance of good at that particular time, sin would be prevented and would not be permitted.[158]

But that the will is not maintained in the performance of good requires careful consideration. There is a mystery in this, and we must avoid contradiction. Three principles must be noted.

1) That the will, which by its nature is defectible, is not main-

---

158 Cf. *Summa theol.*, Ia IIae, q. 79, a. 1; q. 109, a. 2 ad 2um.

tained by God in the performance of good is not yet an evil, because it is not the privation of a good to which one is entitled.

God is not bound always to maintain in the performance of good the will which by its nature is defectible; whereas, on the contrary, He is bound always to maintain it in existence along with the immortal soul.

Similarly, on the part of the creature, the will, which by its nature is defectible, is not bound always to be maintained in the performance of good, but only in being. If it were entitled to the former, then it would be impeccable.

Hence it is not an evil that the will, which by its nature is defectible, is not maintained by God in the performance of good. Nevertheless we do not say that it is a good. Thus the lack of greater perfection in a less fervent act of charity is not a good; neither is it an evil, because it is not the privation of a good that is due to one. Thus there is a great difference between the lack of greater perfection, and the smallest venial sin, which already is purely a moral evil.

2) Also the first sin that is committed is a moral evil, or the privation of that rectitude required of anyone. But sin follows inevitably the divine permission of sin which, as was stated, implies that one is not maintained by God in the performance of good. Thus the divine permission of sin is good because of the end in view; whereas that one is not maintained by God in the performance of good is neither a good nor an evil. But sin which infallibly follows therefrom, as a necessary consequence not of causality but of inference, is simply a moral evil or a sin.

The denial of God's efficacious grace is not indeed a moral evil, but it is a just punishment which presupposes the guilt of sin. To be without grace is a privation of good, and is not a moral evil but a punishment. Thus this denial of grace differs from the non-maintenance by God of anyone in the performance of good, which precedes even the first sin, and which is neither a moral evil nor a punishment.

Calvin confuses the first principle with the third, namely, God's permission of sin with His denial of grace, whereas St. Thomas plainly distinguishes between them.[159] Similarly, in the reply to the second objection of this article he says: "Guilt proceeds from the free will of the person who is reprobated and deserted by grace. In this way the word of the prophet is true, "Destruction is thy own, O Israel." Thus there is a difference between God's permission of sin, which precedes it and which is only its indispensable condition (not

159 Cf. *I Sent.*, d.40, q.4, a.2.

being at all its cause, either direct or indirect),[160] and being abandoned by Him, which is the result of sin.[161]

WHETHER THE PREDESTINED ARE ELECTED BY GOD

State of the question. In this title the word "elected" as Cajetan observes, is taken strictly in the sense as expressing an act of the will by which, when the choice is offered to one, a person prefers or pre-elects one thing to another.

The principal difficulty is that to which reference is made in the third objection, which is: Election implies some discrimination. But God wills all men to be saved (I Tim. 2: 4). Therefore predestination, which preordains men toward eternal salvation, is without election.

The reply is in the affirmative, however, and is as follows: all the predestinate are objects of election and love, so that love precedes election in the order of reason, and election precedes predestination.

1) It is proved on the authority of Holy Scripture, for St. Paul says: "He chose us in Him (Christ) before the foundation of the world, that we should be holy and unspotted in His sight in charity. Who hath predestinated us unto the adoption of children through Jesus Christ unto Himself: according to the purpose of His will." [162] As St. Thomas explains: "He chose us, not because we were saints, for we were not; but He chose us that we might become saints and be without blemish." [163] This is what St. Augustine had already said.[164]

St. Paul clearly indicates election in the following passage: "For when the children were not yet born, nor had done any good or evil (that the purpose of God, according to election, might stand), not of works, but of Him that calleth, it was said to her: The elder shall serve the younger." [165] And again: "Even so then at this present time also, there is a remnant saved according to the election of grace. And if by grace, it is not now by works: otherwise grace is no more grace." [166]

This election that precedes predestination is expressed by St. Paul in the following words: "Whom He foreknew, He also predestinated," [167] that is, whom He has foreknown looking favorably upon

160 Cf. *Summa theol.*, Ia IIae, q. 79, a. 1, 2. See also *infra:* the motive of negative reprobation.
161 See also Ia, q. 23, a. 3 ad 3um.
162 Eph. 1: 4 f.
163 *Com. in Ep. ad Eph.*, 1: 4.
164 *De praed. sanct.*, chap. 18, no. 36.
165 Rom. 9: 11 f.
166 *Ibid.*, 11: 5.
167 *Ibid.*, 8: 29.

them or with predilection. There are several similar passages in Holy Scripture concerning the elect.[168]

Theological proof. The conclusion is proved by means of two syllogisms. (Some have said recently that Scotus was the first who said: "God first wills the end before willing the means for the end." [169] It is at once evident that this doctrine is to be found in the works of St. Thomas, and it belongs to the very notions of both providence and prudence.)

Nothing is directed toward an end unless the will for that end already exists. But predestination is a part of providence which, like prudence, is the ordering of some things toward an end. Therefore the predestination of some to eternal salvation, presupposes that God wills their salvation; and to this latter belong both election and love.

In the second syllogism it is shown that in God, though not in ourselves, love precedes election. It is proved as follows: God's will, by which He wishes good to someone, is the cause of that good possessed by some in preference to others. But God by His love wills for some the good of eternal salvation, and by His election wills this good for them in preference to others. Therefore God's love precedes election in the order of reason, just as election precedes predestination.

The case is the reverse with our will which, in loving anyone, does not cause good in the person loved, but is incited to love because of the good pre-existing in the person. Hence we choose someone whom we love, and thus in us election precedes love.

This means, as stated above: "God's love infuses and creates goodness in things." [170] Therefore God loves before He elects. Also: "God's will is the cause of goodness in things; and the reason why some things are better than others is that God wills a greater good for them. Hence it follows that He loves the better things more." [171] And again: "Those are the better and the better loved who have more grace." [172] This is the principle of predilection that has already been explained.[173]

This principle is denied by Molina, who says: "Given an equal grace or even a less grace, it can happen that one of two persons

---

[168] Cf. Matt. 24: 22; I Tim. 5: 21; II Tim. 2: 10. See also Denz., no. 316 (Council of Quierzy).

[169] *The Divine Foreknowledge According to Duns Scotus and His First Followers* by Dr. Schwamm, Innsbruck, 1934.

[170] *Summa theol.*, Ia, q.20, a.2.

[171] *Ibid.*, Ia, q.20, a.4.

[172] *Ibid.*, ad 4um.

[173] Cf. *ibid.*, q.20, a.3.

called is converted, and the other not." [174] Hence it is not surprising that Molina wrote: "Election did not precede predestination. . . . Others affirmed the opposite. . . . And this seems to be the opinion of St. Thomas (Ia, q. 23, a. 4). . . . But I never found it acceptable." [175]

In Molina's opinion, predestination to glory is because of at least conditionally future foreseen merits. Thus, as he himself acknowledges, he departs essentially from the teaching of St. Thomas.

Nevertheless, even Molina has to admit that God freely chose to place Peter in those particular circumstances in which He foresaw that he would give his good consent, and He chose to place Judas in other circumstances.

Hence, not even does Molina believe that God wills equally the salvation of all men. If he affirmed this, then he would be denying the very mystery of predestination, for the Council of Quierzy says: "That some are saved, is the gift of Him who saves; that some perish, is the fault of those who perish." [176]

St. Thomas points out in his reply to the third objection of this article that God's universal will to save is His antecedent will, which means that it is His conditioned, but not His consequent, will. This means that God wills all men to be saved, unless higher ends prevent this.

FIFTH ARTICLE

WHETHER THE FOREKNOWLEDGE OF MERITS IS THE CAUSE OF PREDESTINATION

State of the question. On this subject we must recall the principal systems according to the names given them by modern theologians. They have, indeed, already been stated in the prologue to this question.

Predestination to glory

- Not because of foreseen merits
  - Independently of the *scientia media:* St. Augustine
  - Dependent on the *scientia media* for the distribution of congruent grace: congruism of St. Bellarmine and of Suarez
- Because of foreseen merits
  - At least conditionally future: Molina, Billot
  - Absolutely future: Vasquez

[174] *Concordia,* pp. 51, 565.
[175] *Ibid.,* p. 429.
[176] Denz., no. 318.

St. Thomas in his state of the question of this article shows that he is aware of the arguments of his adversaries. He says: (1) it seems that foreknowledge of merits is the cause of predestination, for the Apostle says: "Whom He foreknew He also predestinated"; [177] (2) because otherwise there would be no reason for predestination or it would be unreasonable; (3) because it is unjust to give unequal things to equals.

Yet St. Thomas replies in the counterargument by saying that foreknowledge of merits is not the cause or reason of predestination. It is his principal conclusion, Suarez and St. Bellarmine agreeing with him on this point.

St. Thomas means that foreknowledge of merits is not the cause of predestination to glory, which was already defined by him as "the type of the direction of a rational creature to the end of eternal life." [178] Moreover, predestination only to grace, which is common both to the elect and the reprobates, is not predestination in the strict sense of the word.

St. Thomas in a few words proves this conclusion on the authority of Holy Scripture in the present article, and more at length in his other works. [179]

St. Paul says: "Not by the works of justice, which we have done, but according to His mercy, He saved us." [180] Similarly we read: "I will have mercy on whom I will; and I will be merciful to whom it shall please Me." [181] "He saved me, because He was well pleased with me." [182] "I confess to Thee, O Father, Lord of heaven and earth, because Thou hast hid these things from the wise and prudent, and hast revealed them to little ones. Yea, Father, for so hath it seemed good in Thy sight." [183] That some receive greater helps than others, as stated in these texts, is to be attributed to God's predilection and good pleasure. There are also other texts from St. Paul, which we already quoted in proof of election. These are: "He chose us in Him before the foundation of the world that we should be holy." [184] "So then it is not of him that willeth nor of him that runneth, but of God that showeth mercy." [185] "Who hath first given to Him, and recompense shall be made him? For of Him and by Him and in Him are all

---

[177] Rom. 8: 29.
[178] See q. 23, a. 1.
[179] Cf. *Com. in Ep. ad Rom.* et *ad Eph.* See also the prologue to this question: Testimony of Holy Scripture.
[180] Tit. 3: 5.
[181] Ex. 33: 19.
[182] Ps. 17: 20.
[183] Matt. 11: 25.
[184] Eph. 1: 4.
[185] Rom. 9: 16.

things." [186] "For who distinguisheth thee? Or what hast thou that thou hast not received?" [187] This is tantamount to saying that our merits are the effect of God's predilection, and therefore they cannot be its cause. "O the depth of the riches of the wisdom and of the knowledge of God! How incomprehensible are His judgments and how unsearchable His ways!" [188]

Moreover, that St. Augustine understood these texts in this sense,[189] is recognized by St. Bellarmine and Suarez, even by Molina, for he departs from the opinion of St. Augustine when he says: "And this opinion of St. Augustine alarmingly disturbed the minds of many of the faithful, as also of the learned, and it was even the occasion that their salvation was placed in jeopardy. . . . But the divinelike Thomas, and subsequently many of the Scholastics, followed St. Augustine's opinion." [190] Farther on, when Molina is again explaining his opinion, which is the theory of the *scientia media,* he says: "If these principles had always been given and explained, perhaps neither the Pelagian heresy would have sprung up . . . , nor would so many of the faithful have been disturbed in their mind, and joined the ranks of the Pelagians, because of Augustine's opinion." [191] As if God finally revealed to Molina alone what to Augustine, the holy Fathers, and the most learned of theologians for countless centuries He has not at all made known.[192]

In the prologue to this question we have already seen that this argument derives its greatest force from the texts of Holy Scripture and the writings of St. Augustine.[193]

The principle of predilection as already formulated by St. Thomas elucidates this whole question: "Since God's love is the cause of goodness in things, no one thing would be better than another, if God did not will greater good for one than for another." [194] The equivalent of this principle is declared by St. Paul when he says: "For who distinguisheth thee? Or what hast thou that thou hast not received?" [195]

In the argumentative part of the article, St. Thomas first reminds

[186] *Ibid.,* 11: 35.
[187] I Cor. 4: 7.
[188] Rom. 11: 33. See St. Thomas' *Com. in Ep. ad Rom.,* lect. 2 (the end).
[189] See prologue to this question.
[190] *Concordia,* pp. 546 f.
[191] *Ibid.,* p. 548.
[192] On this point consult Salmanticenses, *De gratia efficaci,* disp. VII, dub. 1 et 3.
[193] On this point consult also St. Albert the Great. *Summa theol.,* Ia, q.63, m.3, a.1.
[194] *Summa theol.,* Ia, q.20, a.3.
[195] I Cor. 4: 7.

us of the condemned heresies, which he arranges and passes judgment on in accordance with the principle of predilection as above enunciated.[196] He begins by remarking:

1) "Nobody has been so insane as to say that merit is the cause of divine predestination as regards the act of the predestinator"; for this is the uncreated act by which God does not will this on account of that, but wills this to be as means to that. This implies that by one uncreated act He wills all things, and His willing the end is not the cause of His willing the means, but He wills the ordering of the means to the end.[197]

But the question is: "Whether, as regards the effect, predestination has any cause; or, what comes to the same thing, whether God preordained that He would give the effect of predestination to anyone on account of merits."

On this point there were three errors:

Predestination is because of foreseen merits	**In a former life**	This was the opinion of Origen, who thought that souls were created in the beginning.		But this contradicts St. Paul, who says: "For when the children were not yet born nor had done any good or evil . . . not of works but of Him that calleth, it was said to her: 'The elder shall serve the younger.' " [198]
	In this life	Before justification, that is, because of the beginning of salvation made by one.	So said the Pelagians and Semipelagians.	But this contradicts St. Paul, who says: "Not that we are sufficient to think anything of ourselves as of ourselves." [199]
		After justification, that is, God predestined some to grace, because He foreknew that they will make good use of it.		St. Thomas replies: "There is no distinction between what flows from free will and what is of predestination; as there is no distinction between what flows from a secondary cause and from a first cause.

It must be observed that the refutation of this third error holds good against Molina, even against all who admit the *scientia media,* which supposes that there is a distinction between what flows *f*rom

---

196 *Summa theol.,* Ia, q.20, a.3, 4.
197 Cf. *ibid.,* Ia, q.19, a.5.
198 Rom. 9: 11 f.
199 II Cor. 3: 5.

free will and what is of predestination (that is, from either indeterminate grace or even a congruent grace).

The first and second causes, indeed, are two causes that are not co-ordinated but subordinated, such that the second cause acts only inasmuch as it is moved by the first cause. This doctrine of St. Thomas holds good, too, against all who admit a simultaneous concurrence, or even an indifferent physical premotion, as Pignataro, S.J.,[200] and others admit. For even these latter theologians maintain that there is a distinction between what flows from the first cause, namely, the being of the act, and what flows from the free second cause, namely, the determination of the free will foreseen by the *scientia media*. Willingly or unwillingly, they have to admit a certain passivity or dependence on God's knowledge, in Him who is pure Act; for of two men equally tempted and helped, according to their opinion, one could be converted and the other not. Thus man would single himself out, and this differentiation would come from the man and not from God, who in His foreknowledge would be a passive onlooker.[201]

In the second part of the body of this article St. Thomas posits two conclusions, and two more in the reply to the third objection.

First conclusion: "There is no reason why one effect of predestination should not be the reason or cause of another; a subsequent effect being the reason of a previous effect, as its final cause; and the previous effect being the reason of the subsequent as its meritorious cause, which is reduced to the disposition of the matter. For the end is first in intention and last in execution. Thus causes mutually interact from different points of view, as God made the matter for the form, and the form as actuating the matter. Thus glory is the final cause of merits, and merits dispose one for the attainment of glory.

Thus "God preordained to give glory on account of merit" (for in the order of execution, contrary to what the Protestants say, God does not give glory gratis, but according to merit); and "He preordained to give grace (efficacious, as a result of His consequent will) to merit glory."

Thus God predestines to glory before He predestines to grace, for the wise man first intends the end before the means to the end, because, as stated in the preceding article, "nothing is directed toward an end unless the will for that end already exists." Scotus, St. Robert Bellarmine, and Suarez agree with St. Thomas and the Thomists on this point.

200 *De Deo Creatore*, p. 519. See also what we said about this opinion in *Predestination*, pp. 248 f., 267, 358 f.

201 See the last and weakest reply of Father d'Ales in his book entitled, *Providence et libre arbitre* (last chapter).

In this first conclusion St. Thomas does not mean that God pre-ordained to give extrinsically efficacious grace to anyone to merit glory. This is excluded by what he has already said about God's consequent will,[202] and concerning predestination in this article, he says: "There is no distinction between what flows from free will, and what is of predestination." The proof of the following conclusion likewise excludes this intention of giving extrinsically efficacious grace for the meriting of glory.

Second conclusion. "It is impossible that the whole of the effect of predestination in general should have any cause as coming from us."

This proposition is admitted by Molina, though in a restricted sense, inasmuch as it implies that the whole of the effect of predestination includes the first grace, which cannot be merited by us. But St. Thomas attaches a much deeper meaning to this proposition, as is evident from the reason he gives.

The reason is: "Whatever is in man disposing him toward salvation is all included under the effect of predestination, even the preparation for grace. For neither does this happen otherwise than by divine help, according to the prophet Jeremias (Lam. 5: 21): Convert us, O Lord, to Thee, and we shall be converted."

This means that even the free determination of our salutary act disposing us to justification and afterward the meritorious acts of the elect, are all included under the effect of predestination. Therefore no cause or reason can be given for predestination, and hence it is not because of foreseen merits. This is against what Molina says, even against congruism, which states that the congruous grace is not of itself efficacious. Thus in this system of congruism the free determination of the merits of the elect is not properly the effect of predestination.

The reason given by St. Thomas is therefore the corollary to the principle of predilection, which states that, "since God's love is the cause of goodness in things, no one thing would be better than another if God did not will greater good for one than for another." [203] "What hast thou that thou hast not received?" [204] Hence, more briefly: The merits of the elect are the effect of predestination, and hence they cannot be its cause.[205]

---

202 *Summa theol.*, Ia, q. 19, a. 6 ad 1um.

203 *Ibid.*, Ia, q. 20, a. 3.

204 I Cor. 4: 7.

205 St. Augustine said: "When God crowns our merits, He crowns His own gifts." Thus in the *Indiculus on the Grace of God*, it is said: "So great is God's goodness to men, that what are His gifts He wills that they shall be our merits; and for those things which He has bestowed upon us, He will reward us with

Therefore St. Thomas adds at the end of the argumentative part of this article: "Yet predestination has in this way, in regard to its effect, the goodness of God for its reason; toward which the whole effect of predestination is directed as to an end; and from which it proceeds, as from its first moving principle." This manifests God's goodness,[206] and is explained in the reply to the third objection.

In the reply to the third objection there are two conclusions.

The third conclusion is: "God willed to manifest His goodness in men; in respect to those whom He predestines, by means of His mercy, in sparing them; and in respect to others whom He reprobates, by means of His justice, in punishing them. This is the reason why God elects some and rejects others." Hence this mystery is both most charming and terrible.

St. Paul proves this by saying: "God, willing to show His wrath (that is, His vindictive justice) . . . , endured (that is, permitted) with much patience vessels of wrath, fitted for destruction, that He might show the riches of His glory on the vessels of mercy, which He hath prepared unto glory." [207]

This finds its explanation in the fact that God made all things in order to manifest His goodness, and indeed in many ways, because created things cannot attain to the simplicity of God. Thus God allows some evils lest many good things may not happen. But God's goodness, inasmuch as it is self-diffusive, is the foundation for His mercy; and inasmuch as He has an indisputable right to be loved above all things, this constitutes the foundation for His justice. Thus this mystery is a fitting manifestation not only of God's mercy, but also of the splendor of His justice, and both express His goodness.[208]

The fourth conclusion is: "But why He chooses some for glory and reprobates others, has no reason except the divine will."

Two proofs are given for this statement: (1) There is the authority of St. Augustine, who says: "Why He draws one, and another He draws not, seek not to judge, if thou dost not wish to err." [209] (2) From the analogy prevailing between natural things and those made by art: thus, too, it depends on the simple will of God that this particular part of matter is under the form of earth, and that other part under the nobler form of fire. Similarly, from the simple will of the artificer it depends that this stone is in the lower part of the

---

eternal life" (Denz., no. 141). See also no. 810, and *Summa theol.*, Ia IIae, q.110, a.1 (the end).

[206] See a.5 ad 1um et 2um.

[207] Rom. 9: 22. See also II Tim. 2: 20.

[208] Cf. *De civitate Dei*, Bk. XII, chap. 12.

[209] *Hom. 26 in Joan.*

wall, and that other stone (which is absolutely the same in size and material) is in the upper part of the wall.

The analogy holds good, for the different goodness that is found in men is not theirs in their own right; because, since God's love is the cause of goodness in things, no one thing would be better than another if God did not will greater good for one than for another." [210] "What hast thou that thou hast not received?" [211]

The **objection** was: It is unjust that unequal things be given to equals.

The **reply** to this objection is: "In things which are given gratuitously a person can give more or less, just as he pleases (provided he deprives nobody of his due), without any infringement of justice. This is what the master of the house said: 'Take what is thine and go thy way. . . . Is it not lawful for me to do what I will?' " [212] But in the elect, efficacious grace is the effect of predestination, not theirs by right, but gratuitously given to them. Yet sufficient grace is given to all adults, which makes it possible for them to keep God's commandments. But the one who resists sufficient grace deserves to be deprived of efficacious grace.

The doctrine of this article was distorted by Calvin, but in itself it is a most beautiful and perfect expression of the traditional teaching on predestination.

This conclusion is confirmed by the teaching of Trent on the gratuitousness of the gift of final perseverance, which is freely given to the good thief on Calvary rather than to the other, and to Peter in preference to Judas. The Council of Trent says: "As regards the gift of perseverance, of which it is written: 'He that shall persevere unto the end, he shall be saved,' [213] it cannot be derived from any other but Him who is able to make him stand [214] that he stand perseveringly, and to restore him who falls." [215]

Hence the common teaching is that the just person cannot merit the gift of final perseverance; for this gift is no more than the continuance of the state of grace up to the moment of death, and the state of grace is the principle of merit, and this latter cannot be merited.[216] If, therefore, some will have it that predestination is because of foreseen merits, they must at least add that these merits do not continue up to the moment of death without the gratuitous gift of final perseverance, which is granted only to the elect.

210 *Summa theol.*, Ia, q.20, a.3.
211 I Cor. 4: 7.
212 Cf. q.23, a.5 ad 3um; also Matt. 20: 15.
213 Matt. 10: 22.
214 Rom. 14: 4.
215 Denz., no. 806.
216 Cf. *Summa theol.*, Ia IIae, q.114, a.9.

Thus St. Thomas in teaching the absolute gratuity of predestination retains the doctrine of Holy Scripture, especially of St. Paul, who says: "What hast thou that thou hast not received?" [217] This also is the conclusion reached by St. Robert Bellarmine and Suarez, who taught the absolute gratuity of predestination to glory, although they retained the theory of the *scientia media* in order to explain the distribution of congruous grace and to explain that the effect of this grace may be infallibly known by God.

Therefore all this teaching of St. Thomas on predestination is virtually contained in the principle of predilection: "Since God's love is the cause of goodness in things, no one would be better than another, unless such person were loved more and helped more by God." [218]

This principle applies even to the angels. Hence St. Augustine says of them: "If both were created equally good, then, while some fell by their evil will, the others were more abundantly assisted, and reached that high degree of blessedness from which they became certain they would never fall." [219]

Finally, there is the statement of the Council of Quierzy, which is taken from the writings of St. Prosper. It reads as follows: "Almighty God wills, without exception, all men to be saved, though not all are saved. That some are saved, however, is the gift of Him who saves; if some perish, it is the fault of them that perish." [220]

This doctrine eliminates systems founded on motives that are too human, and there is left the revealed mystery of predestination as the object of contemplation.

THE MOTIVE FOR NEGATIVE REPROBATION

First doubt. What is the motive for negative reprobation taken absolutely, not as yet considering it as it is the reprobation of this particular person rather than of a certain other?

In the explanation of the third article we said that negative reprobation, according to St. Thomas' opinion, consists in "the will to permit a person to fall into sin," whereas positive reprobation is "the will to impose the punishment of damnation on account of that sin." [221]

[217] I Cor. 4: 7.
[218] Cf. *Summa theol.*, Ia, q.20, a.3.
[219] *De civitate Dei*, Bk. XII, chap. 9.
[220] Denz., no. 318.
[221] Cf. *Summa theol.*, Ia, q.23, a.3. Against predestinarianism, as also against Wyclif, John Hus, Jerome of Prague, Luther, and Calvin, all Catholics hold that God, the just judge, punishes only the one who is guilty. In fact, the Lord says: "I desire not the death of the wicked, but that the wicked turn from his way and live" (Ezech. 33: 11). See also Council of Orange, Denz., no. 200.

Now the doctrine concerning the motive for negative reprobation must be carefully formulated, so that the disadvantages mentioned above (a. 3) may be avoided. These disadvantages follow from the opinion of those who maintain that this reprobation is the positive exclusion from glory as from a gift to which one is not entitled, and it is difficult to reconcile this view with God's universal will to save.

First of all, it is evident that the motive for negative reprobation or for the permission of the sin of final impenitence and of sins that lead to this impenitence cannot be the foreseeing itself of this sin; for God could not foresee the sin of final impenitence, for instance, the impenitence of Judas, as something not only possible but future, if He did not permit it. Likewise, the sins that precede this final sin could not *de facto* dispose one for that sin if God did not permit it; for God can come to the aid of hardened sinners, and He frequently does. The question is why God permitted sins not to be forgiven in others, either original sin or personal sins.

There is a great difference, indeed, between the permission of a sin, such as Peter's sin, so that one may become more humble, at the same time intending that one's salvation be assured, and, on the other hand, the permission of a sin that will not be forgiven, such as the sin of Judas, not intending that one's salvation be assured.

From what has been said, however, it is evident that God permits some to fall into sin before having foreseen their demerits. By the very fact that some in preference to others are predestined to glory before the foreseeing of their merits, it necessarily follows that those are permitted to fall into sin who are not included in the number of the elect.[222]

More briefly: since negative reprobation is the will to permit some to fall into sin and fail to attain the glory of heaven, and since the permission of sin in the reprobates precedes this sin, this sin cannot be its motive.

We must always return to those higher principles, by which in the ninth century the controversy on predestination between the Augustinian bishops of Gaul and others was terminated. The Council of Thurzey (860) formulated these principles in the following words: "Whatsoever the Lord pleased He hath done in heaven and on earth

---

[222] Contrary to this, there are Molinists such as Lessius (*De div. perf.*, Bk. 14, chap. 2, no. 15). Franzelin (*De Deo uno*, th. 55), Pesch (*De Deo uno*, prop. 61–62), and others, who maintain, according to the principles of Molinism as they understand them, that there is no negative reprobation before foreseen demerits. On this point they differ from all Thomists, and even from Suarez, Bellarmine, and Ruiz.

(Ps. 134). For nothing is done in heaven or on earth except what He Himself is pleased to do (such as the conversion of Peter and of the good thief), or justly permits to be done (such as the sin of Judas and of the bad thief)." [223]

Therefore, what is the motive for the permission of the sin of final impenitence, and of sins which *de facto* are not forgiven and which lead to the sin of final impenitence?

The general answer to this question is that God wills a thing only in so far as it is good. Hence it is only on account of some good to be obtained that He wills to permit some, through their own fault, to fail to attain the glory of heaven. Therefore St. Augustine says: "God by no means would permit any evil in His works unless He were powerful enough and good enough to bring good out of evil." [224] More briefly: God permits evil only for a greater good.

But for what greater good does God permit the final impenitence of many men and angels? St. Thomas answers this in his reply to the third objection of this article: "God willed to manifest His goodness in men; in respect to those whom He predestines, by means of His mercy, in sparing them; and in respect of others, whom He reprobates, by means of His justice, in punishing them. This is the reason why God elects some and rejects others." We find this already declared somewhat differently by St. Paul, who says: "God, willing to show His wrath (that is, His vindictive justice) and to make His power known, endured (that is, permitted) with much patience vessels of wrath fitted for destruction, that He might show the riches of His glory on the vessels of mercy, which He hath prepared unto glory." [225]

Therefore the reason for negative reprobation, taken absolutely, is the manifestation of God's goodness by means of His justice. God's goodness, inasmuch as it is self-diffusive, constitutes the foundation for His mercy, and inasmuch as He has an indisputable right to be loved above all things, this constitutes the foundation for His justice.

This holds good as regards the end.

But it must furthermore be said that, as regards the creature or as regards the material cause, the natural defectibility of the creature or its disposition to fail, is the indispensable condition for negative reprobation. For if the creature, either human or angelic, were not by its nature defectible, God, who is the source of all goodness, could not permit it to fail. But, if anything is by nature defectible, the consequence is that it may sometimes fail.

Yet this defectibility is not, strictly speaking, the motive for repro-

223 *PL*, CXXVI, 123.
224 *Enchir.*, Bk. II, chap. 24.
225 Rom. 9: 22 f.

bation, for God does not permit the defect on account of the defectibility of the nature, as being the motive for reprobation, but He
permits the defect on account of some good to be derived therefrom.
Therefore the natural defectibility is rather the indispensable condition, or the aptitude and disposition on the part of the matter.

In this whole question there is no proposition more obscure than
that God permits the final impenitence of some (for instance, of the
bad thief rather than of the other) as a punishment for previous sins
which *de facto* will not be forgiven and for a greater good, which
includes the manifestation of infinite justice. Indeed this proposition is most obscure. But that our firm assent to this proposition
should be made easier for us, we may consider the fact that its contradictory cannot be upheld, or that the aforesaid proposition cannot be proved false. In this proposition we see clearly the application
of the most exalted principle of predilection, which is a corollary to
the principles of causality and finality, which state that all good
comes from the supreme good and is ordered to it. The principle of
predilection was revealed to Moses: "I will have mercy on whom I
will; and I will be merciful to whom it shall please Me." [226] St. Paul
says: "For who distinguisheth thee? What hast thou that thou hast
not received?" [227] No one would be better than another without being
loved more beforehand by God. And among the nobler good things
on account of which God can permit sin, are to be included either
the splendor of His justice or the manifestation of His infinite goodness, which has an indisputable right to be loved above all things.

Thus God wills to permit sin for a greater good. For this reason
He wills to permit that what is defectible may sometimes fail. This
permission is the indispensable condition for sin, but it is neither its
direct nor its indirect cause, because the universal Provider, who
directly sees the higher ends, is not bound to prevent these sins, not
even the sin of final impenitence.

The defectible creature, which by its nature is apt to fall into sin,
cannot justly complain of not having received these more abundant
graces, by which it would have been preserved from falling into sin.
As St. Paul says: "O man, who art thou that repliest against God?
Shall the thing formed say to him that formed it: Why hast thou
made me thus? Or hath not the potter power over the clay, of the same
lump, to make one vessel unto honor, and another unto dishonor?
What if God, wishing to show His wrath (that is, the splendor of His
justice and His mercy) . . . ?" [228] This symbolism was already employed in the Old Testament. Thus we read: "As the potter's clay is

[226] Ex. 33: 19.
[227] I Cor. 4: 7.
[228] Rom. 9: 20 f.

in his hand . . . so man is in the hand of Him that made him; and
He will render to him according to His judgment." [229]

Jeremias also said: "Behold as clay is in the hand of the potter,
so are you in My hand, O house of Israel." [230] And again Isaias said:
"I, the Lord, that do all these things. . . . Drop down dew, ye
heavens, from above. . . . Woe to him that gainsayeth his maker.
. . . Shall the clay say to him that fashioneth it: What art thou
making, and thy work is without hands? Woe to him that saith to
his father: Why begettest thou? And to the woman: Why dost thou
bring forth?" [231]

On the one hand, that is, in respect of those not chosen, the splendor of God's justice is particularly made manifest, yet not without
manifestation of His mercy. On the other hand, that is, in respect of
those chosen, God's mercy is particularly made manifest, yet not
without manifestation of His justice. As St. Thomas says: "Certain
works are attributed to justice, and certain others to mercy, because
in some justice appears more forcibly, and in others mercy. Even in
the damnation of the reprobate mercy is seen, which, though it does
not totally remit, yet somewhat alleviates in punishing short of
what is deserved. In the justification of the ungodly justice is seen,
when God remits sin on account of love though He Himself has
mercifully infused that love. So we read of Magdalen: 'Many sins
are forgiven her because she hath loved much' " (Luke 7: 47).[232]

Moreover, as stated by St. Thomas in this same article just quoted:
"Justice and mercy appear in the punishment of the just in this
world, since by afflictions lesser faults are cleansed in them, and they
are the more raised up from earthly affections to God. As to this
Gregory says: (Moral., XXVI): "The evils that press on us in this
world force us to go to God." [233]

Corollary. Hence there is great inequality either of natural or of
supernatural conditions. But sometimes the inequality of graces
compensates for the inequality of natural conditions. As our Lord
says: "Blessed are the poor in spirit. . . . Blessed are the meek. . . .
Blessed are they that mourn. . . . Blessed are they that hunger and
thirst after justice." [234] This means that many are the tribulations of
the just and that those of the just who are loved more by God, such
as Christ and the Blessed Virgin Mary, must suffer for the others as
victims offered up in complete sacrifice. It was so with all the martyrs
and great servants of God, who always suffered much. Thus there

229 Eccli. 33: 13.
230 Jer. 18: 6.
231 Is. 45: 9 f.
232 Summa theol., Ia, q.21, a.4 ad 1um.
233 Ibid., ad 3um.
234 Matt. 5: 3 f.

is effected a most wonderful compensation, which to some extent is pointed out by Christ in the parable of the wicked rich man and the good beggar, in which we read that Abraham said to the wicked rich man who was condemned to hell: "Son, remember that thou didst receive good things in thy lifetime, and likewise Lazarus evil things; but now he is comforted, and thou art tormented." [235]

We find this compensation most beautifully described in a passage of the Old Testament which expressed the dogma of predestination in these words: "The souls of the just are in the hand of God, and the torment of death shall not touch them. In the sight of the unwise they seemed to die and their departure was taken for misery. And their going away from us, for utter destruction; but they are in peace. And though in the sight of men they suffered torments, their hope is full of immortality. Afflicted in few things, in many they shall be well rewarded; because God hath tried them, and found them worthy of Himself. As gold in the furnace He hath proved them, and as a victim of a holocaust He hath received them (especially so the martyrs). . . . The just shall shine, and shall run to and fro like sparks among the reeds. They shall judge nations and rule over people, and their Lord shall reign forever . . . for grace and peace is to His elect." [236] Thus the dogma of predestination is already clearly expressed in the Old Testament.

This great mystery of divine predestination is of itself more an object of contemplation than of theological discussion. For it is the nature of theological investigation to enable one to acquire a certain more sublime understanding of the mysteries of faith. As the Vatican Council declares: "Reason, indeed, enlightened by faith, when it seeks earnestly, piously, and calmly, attains by a gift from God some, and that a very fruitful, understanding of mysteries . . . ; but reason never becomes capable of apprehending mysteries as it does those truths which constitute its proper object. For the divine mysteries by their own nature so far transcend the created intelligence . . . that they remain shrouded in a certain degree of darkness, so long as we are in this mortal life exiled from the Lord; for we walk by faith, and not by sight." [237]

This statement is particularly true concerning predestination, which is the sublimer part of providence.

Second doubt. What is the motive for negative reprobation taken in the selective sense, namely, as it is the reprobation of this particular person rather than that other?

The answer of St. Thomas is that negative reprobation, taken in

---

[235] Luke 16: 25.
[236] Wis. 3: 1 f.
[237] Denz., no. 1796; cf. II Cor. 5: 6.

the selective sense, has no reason except the divine will. He says: "Yet why He chooses some for glory, and reprobates others, has no reason except the divine will." [238] He gives two proofs for this: (1) The authority of St. Augustine, who says: "Why He draws one, and another He draws not, seek not to judge, if thou dost not wish to err." [239] (2) From the analogy prevailing between natural things and those made by art. He remarks: "Why this particular part of matter is under this particular form, and that under another, depends on the simple will of God; as from the simple will of the artificer it depends that this stone is in this part of the wall, and that (equal in size) in another; although the plan requires that some stones should be in this place, and some in that place." [240]

In this argument founded on the analogy prevailing between natural things and those made by art, there is an unexpressed but implied major, namely: in those who are alike as regards defectibility, no reason can be assigned why one rather than another is permitted to fall into some defect that is not willed by the one foreseeing it. Then the minor is subsumed. But all creatures that are destined for a supernatural end are alike as regards defectibility, and it is only by God's help that they do not fall into some defect; for the very fact of not falling into some defect is a good that comes from the source of all good. Therefore it depends solely on God's will that these particular persons rather than certain others are permitted to fall into some defect. This truth is expressed by the Council of Trent which, in discussing the gift of perseverance, says: "which cannot be derived from any other but Him who is able to make the one stand who stands (Rom. 14: 5), so that such a one stand perseveringly, and to restore the one who falls. . . . Let him who thinks he stands take heed lest he fall (I Cor. 10: 12) and work out his salvation with fear and trembling (Phil. 2: 12)." [241]

The foundation of Christian humility consists in this, namely, the twofold mystery of creation from nothing and the gratuitousness of grace. This humility does not degenerate into pusillanimity and despair, because God does not command impossibilities, and He gives His grace to those who humbly pray for it.

The following principal objections are raised against this doctrine of the motive for reprobation, considered either in a general way or in particular cases. We must show that on this point there is no severity on God's part.

First objection. Without anyone being reprobated, God's justice

[238] See q.23, a.5 ad 3um.
[239] *Hom. 26 in Joan.*
[240] *Summa theol.*, Ia, q.23, a.5 ad 3um.
[241] Denz., no. 806.

would be made manifest in the elect, both by rewarding them, and by punishing them for a time on account of sins they committed.

Reply. Such a procedure would be but an imperfect manifestation of God's infinite justice. For the rewarding of the just is more an illustration of God's mercy than of His justice, and, moreover, it is not at all a manifestation of His vindictive justice. This latter is to some extent made manifest in temporal punishments, but these do not make us realize what it ought to be by reason of the infinite malice of sin, which does all it can to rob God of His dignity of being the final end of creatures. Likewise, God's mercy would be very feebly manifested if He were to reward the elect with the beatific vision only for a time.

Moreover it has been revealed that some are reprobated on account of their sins, which God permitted; and the only possible reason for this permission is the greater good that is intended.

But I insist. The will to manifest vindictive justice before having foreseen the sin, is to will the punishment before the sin. But this is an injustice which leads to the predestinarianism of Gottschalk and Calvin. Therefore this view must be rejected.

Reply. I deny the major, which confuses God's infinite justice with His finite chastisement. For God does not will the permission of sin because of His love and intention to impose finite chastisement, for that would be repugnant to justice. But because He wills the permission of sin for the manifestation of His infinite justice, or the inalienable right of sovereign goodness to be loved above all things, He first wills the permission of sin, and then wills to inflict the punishment for the sin in manifestation of His justice. The punishment is but a means of manifesting infinite justice, and it is a means that is not an intermediate end with reference to the permission of sin. Punishment cannot be, indeed, an intermediate end, for to punish is a good only on the previous supposition of sin. Hence God most certainly does not will the permission of sin because of His love to punish, for this would be cruelty; but He wills it from love of His infinite justice, or from love of His goodness which has a right to be loved above all things. But it is easy to depart from the orthodox teaching on this point, and a slight error in the beginning will be great in the end.

Thus God could cause the great persecutors of the Church to be converted at the last moment of their lives, but He can permit, too, their final impenitence from love of His infinite justice that must forever be made manifest; but He cannot permit this impenitence from love of punishment.

Again I insist. To will the permission of sin for the manifestation of justice, is to will the permission of sin so that it be punished. But this is a hard saying and savors of inclemency. Therefore to will the permission of sin for the manifestation of justice savors of inclemency.

Reply. I deny the major, for it would mean to will the punishment before the sin, which would not be the manifestation of justice, but its contrary. Punishment is not the immediate end, but only the means for the manifestation of justice; for punishment is good only when it presupposes sin, whereas, on the contrary, the manifestation of God's infinite goodness and justice is good even before the foreseeing of the sin; the knowledge of the possibility of sin is sufficient.

It is essentially good that God's inalienable right to be loved above all things as the sovereign good be made manifest; and eternal punishment proclaims this truth, as Dante says in his *Inferno:*

> Through me you pass into the city of woe:
> Through me you pass into eternal pain:
> Through me among the people lost for aye.
> Justice the founder of my fabric moved:
> To rear me was the task of power divine,
> Supremest wisdom, and primeval love.[242]

Second objection. But then we would have to admit the rigorous opinion of certain Thomists, namely, the positive exclusion of reprobates from glory as from a gift to which they are not entitled, before the foreseeing of their sins. For at the same moment in which God chose those who are predestined for glory, He excluded all the others from it. Therefore the more rigorous opinion that was previously rejected follows from this reasoning.

Reply. I distinguish the antecedent. That at the same moment in which God chose those who are predestined to glory, He positively excluded all the rest from it, this I deny; that He permitted them to be excluded, this I concede. Similarly I distinguish the consequent: that the permission of the reprobates to be excluded from glory precedes their foreseen demerits, which will not be forgiven, this I concede; that they are positively excluded from glory, this I deny.

God, in predestining some, does not intend to do the opposite of this, saying: "I will the rejection of the others from glory," but He says: "I will to permit that the others, through their own fault, fail to attain the glory of heaven." This act means, indeed, the exclusion of some from being efficaciously chosen for the glory of heaven, but it does not mean their positive exclusion from this glory. Nevertheless the reprobates are always destined for glory, so that this glory would be attained by them unless they themselves prevented it.

Hence God does not repel them from the glory of heaven, but He

242 *Inferno*, Canto III, verses 1–6.

permits that they fail to attain the glory of heaven, and this through their own fault. As Billuart rightly observes,[243] it is one thing to be excluded positively from glory before sin, and it is another matter to be excluded from being efficaciously chosen for the glory of heaven. The first proposition we deny, but we concede that those not among the elect are excluded, before the foreseeing of their sin, from being efficaciously chosen for the glory of heaven; nor is this efficacious election to glory due to them in virtue of God's antecedent will to save all men, otherwise all would be saved, and God's universal will to save would not only be His antecedent will, but also His consequent will, and it would be infallibly fulfilled.

In truth, those not among the elect, before their sin was foreseen, are excluded from being efficaciously chosen for the glory of heaven, as from a gift to which they are not entitled; and this is accomplished by leaving them to their weakness. This is also in some measure accepted by Molina when he says that God of His own gratuitous love decreed to place the elect in circumstances in which He had foreseen their salvation as a conditioned future, and He decreed to place others in circumstances in which He had foreseen their final impenitence.

Again I insist. But from this permissive exclusion the same effect infallibly follows as in the case of positive exclusion from glory. Therefore it is useless to deny this positive exclusion.

Reply. I distinguish the antecedent. That the same effect follows on the part of the reprobates, this I concede; on God's part, this I deny. For it seems to follow from positive exclusion that God is the cause that some would not be saved, since He would refuse to save them. On the other hand, the only effect that follows from permissive exclusion is that those not among the elect, through their own fault, fail to persevere; and God merely permits this.

There is a considerable difference between these two exclusions. Just as God is not the cause of sin, which contradicts what Calvin asserted; so also He is not the cause of perdition, or of exclusion from the glory of heaven. But He is the cause of our salvation. Hence the Council of Quierzy says: "That some are saved, is the gift of Him who saves; but that some perish, is the fault of those who perish." [244]

Still I insist. Yet the Council of Trent declared: "God forsakes not those who have been once justified by His grace, unless He is first forsaken by them." [245] But the will to permit that some through their own fault fail to attain the glory of heaven is to forsake them

---

[243] *Cursus theol.*, Vol. I, De motivo reprobationis, § 2, Solv. objectiones.
[244] Denz., no. 318.
[245] *Ibid.*, no. 804.

before they separate themselves from Him. Therefore God cannot permit the failure of some to attain the glory of heaven.

Reply. Several theologians interpret these words of the Council of Trent as meaning:

1) That God takes sanctifying grace away from any of the just only on account of a previous mortal sin. And this is most certain.

2) Granted that this being forsaken by God is to be understood as meaning the withdrawal of actual grace, still I distinguish the major: that God is not, strictly speaking, the first to forsake the just by taking away from them His common helps and ordinary protection which He extends toward them, this I concede; for this withdrawal of common helps is a punishment, which presupposes sin. But God permits sin before it is committed; and so it is only in an improper sense that He forsakes one. It is true, indeed, as Billuart says,[246] that God by leaving a man to his defectibility, does not keep him from falling into sin by means of a special and efficacious help. But this special and efficacious help, although it is in some way due to human nature in general, yet it is not due to this individual rather than to a certain other.

It is most evident that God's permission of sin must precede the commission of the sin that is permitted, not indeed as the cause but as the indispensable condition. For if God did not permit this sin, it certainly would not happen to be committed, and nothing happens unless it is either willed or permitted by God. Hence this permission of sin by God does not mean, strictly speaking, that He forsakes anyone, concerning which the Council of Trent says: "God forsakes not those who have been once justified by His grace, unless He is first forsaken by them." [247] If it were said that God forsakes anyone by the very fact that He permits him to fall into sin, then this would be the same as saying that God cannot permit the first sin before it happens to be committed.

The Council of Trent maintains,[248] indeed, that every sin presupposes the divine permission, for it declares that God's part is permissive with reference to sin, for example, to the betrayal of Judas. We also pray in the Mass: "Permit me not to be separated from Thee." [249]

Final objection. Even the Thomists admit that no one is deprived of efficacious help except through his own fault. Therefore it is false to say that God in an improper sense forsakes a person by the withdrawal of His efficacious help.

246 *Cursus theol.*, Vol. I, De motivo reprobationis, § 3.
247 Denz., no. 804.
248 Cf. Denz., no. 816.
249 Prayer before the priest's communion.

Reply. I distinguish the antecedent: that the refusal of efficacious grace is a punishment, which presupposes at least a first sin, this I concede; but the simple permission of sin by God is not, strictly speaking, the refusal of efficacious grace, and this permission evidently precedes the sin.

God in conferring the sufficient grace wills antecedently to confer the efficacious grace, unless a man deliberately and wickedly resists the sufficient grace. God could, indeed, by giving more abundant help, prevent this resistance and this wicked act of the will; but as universal Provider He is not bound to prevent this, and with higher ends in view He wills by His consequent will to leave a man to his defectibility. Thus it is true that a man is deprived through His own fault of efficacious grace which God, in the bestowal of sufficient grace, willed by His antecedent will to give him.

Third doubt. Is original sin a sufficient motive for positive reprobation?

We answer this question as several Thomists do. We distinguish and say that it is a sufficient motive in those who have not been freed from original sin, especially in infants who die without being baptized. These children, inasmuch as they have no other sin, are thus deprived of the beatific vision, without having to suffer, however, the punishment of the senses. But I deny that it is a sufficient reason in those who have been freed from original sin. In these, the effects of original sin (such as concupiscence and a weakening of the will in the performance of good) are conditions that contribute to their greater defectibility, and this latter shows itself in actual sins, and ultimately in the sin of final impenitence, for which they are positively reprobated.

But if it is a question of negative reprobation, since original sin is the same in all, both in the predestined and the reprobates, this sin cannot be in the reprobates the reason why God permits the sins that will not be forgiven. Therefore St. Thomas does not speak of original sin in this article, but says: "Why He chooses some for glory, and reprobates others, has no reason except the divine will." [250] So say the Salmanticenses, Alvarez, and John of St. Thomas.

The effects of reprobation. By the effect of reprobation is meant whatever God does with the efficacious intention of manifesting His justice by means of those whom He reprobates.

Hence the proper effects of reprobation are: (1) the permission of a sin that will not be forgiven; (2) the refusal of grace; (3) blinding of the intellect; (4) hardening of the heart; and finally (5) condemnation to eternal punishment.

[250] Cf. ad 3um.

Sin itself is not the effect of reprobation, for God is in no way the cause of sin, not even indirectly, when He permits it.[251]

The signs of reprobation, however, are too great an attachment to the transitory things of this world, the sin of lust persisted in even to old age, a rebellious attitude toward the teachings of the Church, aversion for the reception of the sacraments, and great pride.

According to the Salmanticenses,[252] reprobation is the effect resulting from the predestination of the elect, because it shows more clearly God's greater mercy toward the elect. Hence St. Paul says: "God . . . endured with much patience vessels of wrath, fitted for destruction, that He might show the riches of His glory on the vessels of mercy, which He hath prepared unto glory." [253] Thus all things are for the sake of the elect, who realize the splendor of God's justice in the very restoration of this order of justice and in the triumph of God's goodness over evil.[254] Angels do not grieve either for sins or

---

[251] Cf. *Summa theol.*, Ia IIae, q.79, a.1, 2. St. Thomas says (*ibid.*, a.1): "Neither can He cause sin indirectly. For it happens that God does not give some the assistance whereby they may avoid sin, and if He gave them this assistance they would not sin. But He does all this according to the order of His wisdom and justice, since He Himself is wisdom and justice: so that if someone sin it is not imputable to Him as though He were the cause of that sin; even as a pilot is not said to cause the wrecking of the ship, through not steering the ship, unless he cease to steer while able and bound to steer." But God is not bound always to preserve from defect that which is naturally defectible. If anything is by its nature defectible, however, the consequence is that sometimes it is defective. And this is permitted by God for a greater good.

St. Thomas says (*ibid.*, a.3), in explaining the blinding of the intellect and the hardening of the heart, which are a punishment of previous sins: "God, of His own accord, withholds His grace from those in whom He finds an obstacle." And again he says (*ibid.*, a.4): "Blindness, of its very nature, is directed to the damnation of those who are blinded; for which reason it is accounted an effect of reprobation. But, through God's mercy, temporary blindness is directed medicinally to the spiritual welfare of those who are blinded. This mercy, however, is not vouchsafed to all those who are blinded, but only to the predestined, to whom *all things work together unto good* (Rom. 8: 28)."

[252] *Cursus theol., De praedestinatione,* tr. V, disp. V, dub. unicum, no. 25. See also *ibid.*, disp. VIII, dub. 2, § 2. Concerning reprobation, their conclusion is: "We must say of reprobation, as regards the first permission of the first sin that leads efficaciously to the damnation of the reprobate, that the cause of this permission is not any demeritorious act of this same reprobate." The reason is that, as regards the permission of this first sin, there can be no question of a previous sin that is the cause of this permission. We are not concerned here with sins that will be forgiven, as happens in the case of many of the elect. We are concerned here with the permission of the first sin that will not be forgiven; whereas, contrary to this, God permits the elect to commit sins that afterward will be forgiven. This is, strictly speaking, an inscrutable mystery, and it is verified both in the angels and in human beings.

[253] Rom. 9: 22 f. It is what St. Thomas says in his Com. in Ep. ad Rom., 9: 24.

[254] Cf. *Summa theol.*, Ia, q.113, a.7.

for penalties inflicted upon men, although sin is displeasing to them as it is to God. They will the fulfillment of the ordering of divine justice in this matter.

Thus too, as the same theologians of Salamanca say,[255] we see more clearly with what liberality God chose the predestined for glory without any obligation on His part, and thus the riches of His mercy toward them are made more manifest. Likewise we see more clearly from reprobation the defectibility of the created free will and at the same time the powers conferred on us by grace. Thus all things are directed "unto the praise of the glory of His grace." [256] St. Augustine frequently said about the same, though more concisely, when he declared that the wicked are in this world either that they be converted or that they afflict the good.[257]

[255] De praedestinatione, disp. VIII, dub. 2, § 2.
[256] Eph. 1: 6.
[257] Cf. Bossuet, Défense de la tradition, Bk. XI, chap. 5. In this work (chap. 4), he says: "There is this difference between God and man, that man is not innocent if he allows himself to commit the sin which he can prevent, and that God, who is able to prevent the sin without this costing Him anything but the will to prevent it, and who allows man to repeat the sins even to the exceeding number seen by us nowadays, is nevertheless just and holy; although He is allowed to do, says St. Augustine (Op. imp., III, chaps. 23, 24, 27), that which, if done by man, would be unjust. Why is this, says this same Father (ibid., chap. 27), unless it is because there is a great difference between the rules of God's justice and those of man's justice? God, he goes on to say, must act as God; and man, as man. God acts as God, when He acts as first cause, omnipotent and universal, which subordinates to the common good what particular causes will and do either of good or of evil; but man, whose weakness cannot make the good triumph in him, must prevent all the evil that he can prevent.

"Such is then the profound reason why God is not bound to prevent the evil of sin. It is because He can draw a greater good from it, even an infinite good. Thus in the crime committed by the Jews in the sacrifice of God's Son, whose merit and perfection are infinite . . . it suffices for us to know, as St. Augustine again says (ibid., chap. 24), that the more exalted is His justice, the more impenetrable are the rules which it makes use of."

Bossuet (ibid., chap. 5), in the height of contemplation, says: "Men wish indeed to understand the purpose in the permissions of sins that turn out to their advantage; for example, of the sin committed by the Jews, the purpose of which was to give men a Savior; of the sin committed by Peter, the purpose of which was to make him more humble; of all sins, whatsoever they may be, whose purpose is to make grace more conspicuous. But when they are told that God permits their sins to show the splendor of His justice, since this permission tends to make them suffer, their self-love turns them against His justice. We must stress just as much this fifth truth, namely, that God permits sin, because if He did not permit it, then there would be no avenging justice, and God's severity would not be known, which is equally adorable and holy as His mercy is. . . . This is what God said to Pharaoh, speaking through Moses (Ex. 9: 13), at the same time announcing to him the punishment for his sins, and we know how forcibly this utterance was repeated by the Apostle (Rom. 9: 17). In this text indeed,

Molina [258] admits that the manifestation of justice is one of the ends for which God permits sin.

PREDESTINATION AS A MYSTERY OF MERCY

The whole of this doctrine on gratuitous predestination may be summed up finally by what we may call an a posteriori observation. It is one that has already been made by us, and it is this: if, of two sinners who are equally obdurate, one is converted rather than a certain other, this is the effect of God's special mercy toward such person. A fortiori, it is the effect of God's special mercy, if any just person perseveres in doing good for many years, and especially if anyone is preserved in the state of grace from the time when he was baptized as a child until death. Thus the mystery of gratuitous predestination is a posteriori made manifest, so to speak, to those who are Christian in sentiment, just as God's universal will to save is also manifested to such as these in many ways. The intimate reconciliation of these truths is hidden in the obscurity of faith, but the light of life, which is the object of contemplation, is found in this obscurity.

The author of the *Imitation of Christ* in his treatise on the spiritual life said about predestination: "I am He who made all the saints, I gave them grace, I brought them glory. I know what every one hath deserved; I led them with the blessings of My sweetness.[259] I foreknew My beloved ones before the beginning of the world. I chose them out of the world; [260] they chose not Me first. I called them by grace, I drew them by mercy, I led them safely through sundry temptations. I poured into them glorious consolations, I gave them perseverance, I crowned their patience.

"I acknowledge both the first and the last; I embrace all with love inestimable. I am to be praised in all My saints; I am to be blessed above all things, and to be honored in all whom I have thus gloriously exalted and predestined without any merit of their own." [261]

St. Paul says to us: "Therefore He hath mercy on whom He will, and whom He will He hardeneth."

In this same work (chap. 6), Bossuet quotes again this saying of St. Augustine, which serves as a principle for every school of theology: "God hardens the heart of anyone, not indeed by bestowing malice, but by not bestowing mercy. (Ep. 194)." In this same chapter Bossuet points out that it is a calumny to say: Therefore, according to St. Augustine, God is the cause of sin; for times without number he plainly said the contrary.

[258] *Concordia*, p. 480.
[259] Ps. 20: 4.
[260] John 15: 19.
[261] *Imitation of Christ*, Bk. III, chap. 58.

Farther on, this same author says: "They glory not in their own merits, inasmuch as they ascribe no goodness to themselves but attribute all to Me who of Mine infinite love have given them all things." [262]

Hence this same author says: "When a certain person who was in anxiety of mind, often wavering between fear and hope, said within himself, 'O, if I knew that I would yet persevere,' he presently heard within him an answer from God, which said: 'If thou didst know it, what wouldst thou do? Do now what thou wouldst do then, and thou shalt be secure.' And being immediately comforted and strengthened, he committed himself wholly to the will of God, and his anxious wavering ceased." [263]

SIXTH ARTICLE

WHETHER PREDESTINATION IS CERTAIN

State of the question. It seems that predestination is not certain: (1) because the crown, which is the effect of predestination, can both be acquired and be lost; (2) because it is possible that one predestined, such as Peter, may sin and then be killed; (3) because God, who most freely predestined this particular man, has it in His power not to predestine him.

Yet the answer is that the effect of predestination is certainly attained. It will at once be seen from the argument that St. Thomas has in mind not only certainty of foreknowledge but also of causality. This latter is denied, however, by Molina.

The certainty of predestination is clearly established from texts in Holy Scripture. Thus we read: "No one can snatch them (My sheep) out of the hand of My Father." [264] This text points to the certainty not only of foreknowledge but also of causality on the part of divine omnipotence, which preserves and leads the elect to salvation. Our Lord says: "There shall arise false Christs . . . insomuch as to deceive, if possible, even the elect." [265] If possible means: unless they had been specially preserved from falling into sin by God.

The certainty of God's foreknowledge and causality is likewise pointed out in St. Augustine's definition of predestination, who says that it is "the foreknowledge and preparation of those gifts whereby whoever are liberated are most certainly liberated." [266]

[262] *Ibid.*, no. 8.
[263] *Ibid.*, Bk. I, chap. 25, no. 2.
[264] John 10: 29.
[265] Matt. 24: 24.
[266] *De dono persever.*, chap. 14.

Theological proof. Predestination is a part of providence, which includes God's absolute and consequent will concerning the elect. But this absolute and consequent will of God is always or infallibly fulfilled. Thus predestination differs from simple providence, which is not fulfilled in the case of those who are included only in God's consequent will. God wills antecedently the salvation of all, but He permits the perdition of many, and wills consequently or absolutely the salvation of the elect.

Yet this consequent will does not interfere with created liberty, because God efficaciously wills also that the elect freely merit eternal life. The divine causality extends even to the free mode of our choices; it actualizes our liberty, and in doing so most certainly does not destroy it, a point which has already been explained.[267]

St. Thomas excludes Molina's opinion, when he writes: "It cannot be said that certainty of foreknowledge is the only thing superadded to providence by predestination. This is tantamount to saying that God ordains the one predestined to salvation as He does anyone else, but that in the case of the one predestined He knows that he will not fail to be saved. In such a case, to be sure . . . , predestination would not be because of the choice of the one predestining, which is contrary to the authority of Holy Scripture and the sayings of the saints. Hence in addition to the certainty of foreknowledge, there is infallible certainty (of causality) in this order of predestination." [268]

Nevertheless this certainty is not injurious to created liberty because, since God's will is most efficacious, it follows not only that the elections of the predestined take place, but that they take place freely, as God wills.

THE SIGNS OF PREDESTINATION

The following signs of predestination, which give one conjectural or at most moral certainty about it, have been taken by the theologians from various passages in the writings of St. Augustine, St. Gregory, St. Anselm, St. Bernard, and St. Thomas. These are: (1) A good life until the end; (2) the testimony of a conscience that is free from serious sins, and especially if one is prepared rather to die than offend God grievously; (3) patience in adversities endured for the love of God; (4) readiness to hear the word of God; (5) compassion for the poor; (6) love of one's enemies; (7) humility; (8) a special devotion to the Blessed Virgin, of whom the Church chants: "He

[267] See commentary on Ia, q. 19, a.8.
[268] *De veritate,* q.6, a.3.

that shall find me shall find life, and shall have salvation from the Lord." [269]

Hence the author of *The Imitation* says: "If thou didst know it (that thou art predestined), what wouldst thou do? Do now what thou wouldst do then, and thou shalt be secure." [270]

These signs are such as to give one particularly a feeling of security under the special inspiration of the Holy Spirit, concerning whom St. Paul says: "The Spirit Himself giveth testimony to our spirit that we are sons of God," [271] through the filial affection we have toward Him, which He inspires in us, as St. Thomas points out in his commentary on St. Paul's Epistle to the Romans. Nevertheless, as the Council of Trent says: "Except by special revelation, it cannot be known whom God has chosen unto Himself." [272] And again: "If anyone saith that he will for certain, with absolute and infallible certainty, have that great gift of perseverance unto the end, unless he shall have learned this by special revelation; let him be anathema." [273]

Thus the fact itself of being saved at the end of one's life still remains an uncertainty; yet "hope tends to its end with certainty, as though sharing in the certainty of faith which is in the cognitive faculty." [274] Thus the certitude of hope is not certainty of salvation, but a tendency to salvation, which is more and more deepened in one as one approaches the end of life.

SEVENTH ARTICLE

WHETHER THE NUMBER OF THE PREDESTINED IS CERTAIN

The answer is that the number of the predestined is certain, and this not only formally but also materially; for God knows how many will be saved, and who will be saved. Thus our Lord says: "I know whom I have chosen"; [275] and St. Paul remarks: "The Lord knoweth who are His." [276]

The Church says that God alone knows the number of the elect

---

[269] Prov. 8: 35; cf. *Summa theol.*, Ia IIae, q.112, a.5; *Contra Gentes*, Bk. IV, chaps. 21, 22, concerning the signs of the state of grace.
[270] *Imitation*, Bk. I, chap. 25, no. 2.
[271] Rom. 8: 16.
[272] Denz., no. 805.
[273] *Ibid.*, no. 826.
[274] *Summa theol.*, IIa IIae, q.18, a.4.
[275] John 13: 18.
[276] II Tim. 2: 19.

who are destined for the happiness of heaven.[277] When this number is completed, the end of the world will come and the generations of men will cease.

Is there a great number of the elect? Absolutely speaking and not comparing them with the number of the reprobates, we can state that the number is very great, for the Apocalypse says: "I heard the number of them that were signed, a hundred forty-four thousand. . . . After this I saw a great multitude which no man could number." [278]

But if we compare the number of the elect with the number of reprobates, then St. Augustine and St. Thomas think that there are not so many elect as reprobates, for our Lord says: "How narrow is the gate and strait is the way that leadeth to life! And few there are that find it." [279] And again: "Many are called, but few are chosen." [280] We are concerned here with "the good that exceeds the common state of nature." [281] But if we include among the saved both angels and men, then St. Thomas is of the opinion that the number of the elect is probably greater than the number of reprobates.[282] Several theologians think it more probable that, among Christians who are Catholics, the number of the predestined is greater than the number of reprobates. It seems possible for us to reach this conclusion from the intention of Christ in instituting His Church and from the efficacy of His Passion and the sacraments.

EIGHTH ARTICLE

WHETHER PREDESTINATION CAN BE FURTHERED BY THE PRAYERS OF THE SAINTS

The answer is that no one is predestined by the prayers of the saints. Predestination, as St. Thomas declares,[283] depends solely on God's good pleasure. But the prayers of the saints can obtain certain effects of predestination; just as the good works of the elect are the meritorious cause of their glory in heaven. Thus "whatever helps that person toward salvation, falls under the order of predestination,

---

277 Secret of Mass for the dead.

278 Apoc. 7: 4.

279 Matt. 7: 14.

280 *Ibid.*, 20: 16; 22: 14. This text is disputed. Many exegetes say it refers to the call of the Jews to accept our Lord as the Messiah. [Tr.]

281 Cf. q.23, a.7 ad 3um, ad 4um.

282 Cf. *I Sent.*, d.39, q.2, a.2.

283 Cf. q.23, a.5 ad 3um.

whether it is one's own prayers, or those of others." [284] Thus the saints by praying for others, are God's assistants.[285]

[284] *Ibid.*, a.8, c.

[285] To present the mystery of predestination in more concrete form, we may quote the following extract from Father J. P. Caussade's beautiful work, entitled: *Absolute Surrender to Divine Providence* (Bk. III, chap. 12): "God assures to faithful souls a glorious victory over the powers of earth and hell":

"If the divine action is veiled here below by an exterior of weakness, it is that the merit of faithful souls may be increased; but its triumph is no less sure. The history of the world is simply the history of the struggle maintained from the beginning by the powers of the world and hell with souls humbly submissive to the divine action. In the conflict all the advantage seems to be on the side of the proud; yet humility is always victorious.

"This world is represented to us under the form of a statue of gold, brass, iron, and clay. This mystery of iniquity, which was shown in a dream to Nabuchodonosor, is but the confused assemblage of all the acts, interior and exterior, of the children of darkness. These are again represented by the beast coming up out of the abyss from the beginning of all ages, to make war upon the interior and spiritual man; and this war still continues. The monsters succeed one another; the abyss swallows them and vomits them forth again. . . . The combat begun in heaven between Lucifer and St. Michael still wages. . . . Lucifer is the chieftain of those who refuse obedience to the Almighty; this mystery of iniquity is but the inversion of the order established by God. . . . All these impious persons who have declared war against God . . . have been seemingly great and powerful princes, famous in the world and adored by men. They are but the beasts which rise from the abyss . . . and God has always resisted them with men truly powerful and great, who give the deathblow to these monsters; and even as hell vomits forth new monsters, heaven raises up new heroes to battle with them. . . . Were the powers of earth and hell arrayed against one single soul, that soul would have nothing to fear in abandoning itself to God's order. That apparent might and irresistible power of iniquity, that head of gold, that body of silver, brass, and iron, is but a phantom of glittering dust. A pebble overthrows it and makes it the sport of the winds. . . .

"All these monsters are sent only to exercise the courage of the children of God; and when the latter's virtue has been sufficiently tried, God gives them the pleasure of killing the monster, and He summons new warriors to the battlefield. . . .

"Thus all opposition to God's order serves but to render it more adorable. All servers of iniquity are the slaves of justice, and from the ruins of Babylon the divine action builds the heavenly Jerusalem."

CHAPTER XXIV

QUESTION 24

THE BOOK OF LIFE

FIRST ARTICLE

In Holy Scripture "the book of life" is a metaphorical expression for "the knowledge of God by which He firmly remembers that He has predestined some to eternal life."

SECOND AND THIRD ARTICLES

Primarily those are said to be written in the book of life who are predestined to glory; but, in a secondary sense, the expression applies to those who are justified, and then fall from grace, dying in that state.

This completes the question of predestination, which is clarified by these two principles: (1) God does not command impossibilities; [1] hence it is really possible for all adults to keep God's commandments, as these are known by them. (2) But, on the other hand, "since God's love is the cause of goodness in things, no one would be better than another, without being loved more by God." [2] St. Paul says: "Who distinguisheth thee? Or what hast thou that thou hast not received?" [3] But in heaven the blessed see how God's infinite justice, mercy, and the supreme liberty of His good pleasure are intimately reconciled in the eminence of the Deity. As our Lord says: "Yea, Father, for so hath it seemed good in Thy sight." [4]

Dante, in his *Paradiso*,[5] speaks of predestination. There, in poetic language, he declares that the mystery of predestination is beyond the ken even of the saints in heaven.

[1] Denz., no. 804.
[2] Cf. Ia, q.20, a.3.
[3] I Cor. 4: 7.
[4] Matt. 11: 26.
[5] Canto 20, 130 f.; canto 21, 80 f.; Cary's translation:

> "O how far removed,
> Predestination! is thy root from such
> As see not the first Cause entire."

718

"But not the soul
That is in heaven most lustrous, nor the seraph,
That hath his eyes most fixed on God, shall solve
What thou hast asked: for in the abyss it lies
Of the everlasting statute sunk so low,
That no created ken may fathom it."

This means that not even the blessed, without a special revelation, know with certainty who of those still on this earth are among the elect; nor can they know the ultimate reason for predestination, which is hidden in the Deity and in God's most free good pleasure. See Ia, q.12, a.8, and what we said on this subject in the *Dictionnaire de théologie catholique*, art. "Predestination" (end): "The culminating point of this mystery and its spiritual fruits."

CHAPTER XXV

QUESTION 25

THE POWER OF GOD

FIRST ARTICLE

WHETHER THERE IS POWER IN GOD

WHAT has already been said permits us to dismiss this question with a few brief comments.

Passive power cannot be attributed to God, who is pure act; active power, however, can rightly be attributed to Him. For it is manifest that everything, according as it is in act and is perfect, is the active principle of something.

It must be observed that the idea of active power is retained in God, inasmuch as it is the principle of an effect *ad extra*; not, however, as it is a principle of action, for God's action is His essence, which is His *esse* and His *agere*.

Reply to second objection. Hence "God's action is not distinct from His power," and God's action *ad extra* is formally immanent and virtually transitive, inasmuch as it produces the effect *ad extra*.

Reply to fourth objection. Active power in God is the divine command itself, inasmuch as this latter is the principle of His works *ad extra*.

SECOND ARTICLE

WHETHER THE POWER OF GOD IS INFINITE

It is of faith that God's power is infinite. The Second Council of Constantinople says: "If anyone says or thinks, either that God's power is finite, or that He has done all the things that He was able to have in mind, let him be anathema." [1]

Proof. The more perfectly an agent has the form by which it acts, the greater is its power to act, for instance, in giving heat. But God's essence, by which He acts, is infinite,[2] or His power is infinitely perfect.[3]

[1] Denz., no. 210.
[2] Cf. *Summa theol.*, Ia, q.7, a.1.
[3] Cf. *ibid.*, q.25, a.2 ad 1um.

Reply to second objection. "Even if it were to produce no effect, the power of God would not be ineffectual; because a thing is ineffectual which is ordained to an end to which it does not attain. But the power of God is not ordered toward its effect as toward an end; rather it is the end of the effect produced by it."

St. Thomas in this reply observes that "the power of a univocal agent is wholly manifested in its effect. The generative power of man is not able to do more than beget man. But the power of a non-univocal agent does not wholly manifest itself in the production of its effect," just as the power of the sun is not wholly manifested, for instance, in the ripening of the fruits of the earth. But God evidently is not a univocal agent. "Hence His effect is always less than His power." Nevertheless His infinite power is manifested in the mode of producing things, inasmuch as He produces something out of nothing, or from no presupposed subject.

Analogically we say that men of great genius are superior to the works they produce; but it is, nevertheless, in the way they produce these works that their superiority is seen. On the contrary, men of ordinary ability are, so to speak, univocal agents, and the whole of their power is manifested in the effect produced. They could not do more.

THIRD ARTICLE

WHETHER GOD IS OMNIPOTENT

It is of faith that God is omnipotent [4] as His power is infinite. God is said to be omnipotent, inasmuch as He can do whatever is absolutely possible, that is, whatever is not repugnant to existence, whatever is capable of existing, or whatever can be conceived as real being.

Proof. "The divine existence, upon which the nature of power in God is founded, is infinite, and is not limited to any genus of being; but it possesses within itself the perfection of all being. Therefore whatever has or can have the nature of being, is numbered among the absolute possible beings, in respect of which God is called omnipotent."

Reply to third objection. "God's omnipotence is particularly shown in sparing and having mercy . . . , and in that He freely forgives sinners, thus leading them on to the participation of an infinite good."

Reply to fourth objection. "The wisdom of the world is deemed foolish because what is impossible to nature, it judges to be impossible to God."

[4] Denz., no. 1783.

FOURTH ARTICLE

WHETHER GOD CAN MAKE THE PAST NOT TO HAVE BEEN

The answer is that God cannot make the past not to have been, because what implies contradiction does not come within the scope of God's omnipotence. But that the past should not have been implies a contradiction. Thus God cannot remove from the sinner the fact of his having sinned, and of having lost charity. God removes sin, indeed, by justification, but He cannot remove from the sinner the fact of his having sinned.

FIFTH ARTICLE

WHETHER GOD CAN DO WHAT HE DOES NOT

The Council of Sens condemned the following proposition of Abelard: "It is possible for God to do only those things which He has done, and not to do only those things which he has not done; and to do things only in the manner and at the time in which He does them, and not otherwise." [5]

St. Thomas recalls two erroneous opinions: (1) That God acts from natural necessity in such a way as the sun illumines. So said the Neoplatonists and subsequently Spinoza. (2) That God acts indeed by His will, but by His will determined by reason of the necessity of His knowledge. Thus, among modern philosophers, Leibnitz says that God by reason of a moral necessity was bound to create the best among possible worlds, otherwise He would not have been either infinitely wise or infinitely good. Rosmini said practically the same.[6]

These errors deny the dogma of divine liberty, which is expressed by the Vatican Council in these words: "God, of His own goodness and almighty power, not for the increase of His own happiness, nor to acquire but to manifest His perfection by the blessings which He bestows upon creatures, with absolute freedom of counsel, created out of nothing from the beginning of time, both the spiritual and corporeal creature, to wit, the angelic and the mundane; and afterwards the human creature . . . , consisting of both spirit and body." [7]

St. Thomas explained the divine freedom in a previous article,[8] and he now recalls the principal argument as set forth by him in that article, saying: "The whole idea of order which a wise man puts into

---

[5] *Ibid.*, no. 374.
[6] *Ibid.*, no. 1908.
[7] *Ibid.*, no. 1783. Cf. *ibid.*, no. 428 (Fourth Lateran Council).
[8] *Summa theol.*, Ia, q. 19, a. 3.

things made by him is taken from their end. . . . But the divine goodness (that must be manifested) is an end exceeding beyond all proportions things created. Therefore the divine wisdom is not so restricted to any particular order that no other course of events could happen."

Thus the apparent movement of the sun could be in the reverse direction; likewise there could be other species of plants and of animals, God could create angels of a higher order, and many other things similar to these.

Reply to first objection. Whatever is not in itself a contradiction in terms is absolutely possible, or is possible by God's absolute power, such as the annihilation even of all spiritual creatures. But this annihilation of souls and angels is not possible by God's power as ordained by His wisdom, whether this power be ordinary or extraordinary, because there can be no motive for this annihilation.

SIXTH ARTICLE

WHETHER GOD CAN DO BETTER THINGS THAN WHAT HE DOES

The answer is given in the words of St. Paul: "God is able to do all things more abundantly than we desire or understand." [9] St. Thomas enunciates and proves three propositions:

1) God cannot make a thing essentially better than it is itself; because the specific difference, by which it is constituted in its essence, does not admit of increase or decrease. Thus He cannot make the number four greater than it is, or man essentially better, because man is essentially and immutably a rational animal.

2) God can make accidentally better the things He made. Thus He can make a thing brighter, a man wiser or more virtuous; also God, by His absolute power, could increase the light of glory in the most holy soul of Christ.[10]

3) Absolutely speaking, God can make something else better than each thing made by Him. Thus He can always create more perfect angels, who would be loftier in intellect and who would have a better knowledge of created and possible things. Hence there is no limit to what is possible for God, because His infinite omnipotence is inexhaustible.

Reply to first objection. Nevertheless God cannot make a thing better, if the word "better" is taken as an adverb, and not as a substantive. Thus God cannot make a thing from greater wisdom and

[9] Eph. 3: 20.
[10] Cf. *Summa theol.*, IIIa, q. 7, a. 12 ad 2um; IIIa, q. 10, a. 4 ad 3um.

goodness; but He can always make something better, in this sense, that He can always make a better thing. Thus the animal is better than the plant, but it has not a better arrangement of its parts than the plant has, for even in the plant there is the best arrangement of its parts to its end.

Reply to third objection. "The universe (the present creation being supposed) cannot be better, on account of the most beautiful order given to things by God. . . . For if any one thing were bettered, the proportion of order would be destroyed; as if one string were stretched more than it ought to be, the melody of the harp would be destroyed."

This orderly arrangement is true not only as regards the subordination of essences, but also as regards singulars and their characteristics; it even applies to good on account of which evils are permitted, as in the permission of persecution to try the patience of the martyrs. But, as St. Thomas says at the end of his reply to the third objection: "Yet God could make other things, or add something to the present creation, and thus there would be another and a better universe," which means it would be better, but not disposed better, taking the word "better" as an adverb.

The above reply is the answer that must be given to the objections of Leibnitz, who wanted to prove that the present world is the best possible world. There is, indeed, a highest created nature, this being the highest angel, but there can be no limit to what is possible for God, because "He can always make something else better than each thing made by Him."

Reply to fourth objection. "The humanity of Christ from the fact that it is attributed to the Godhead, and created happiness from the fact that it is the fruition of God, and the Blessed Virgin from the fact that she is the mother of God, all these have a certain dignity from the infinite good, which is God. And on this account there cannot be anything better than these; just as there cannot be anything better than God." Nevertheless, by His absolute power, God could increase the light of glory in the most holy soul of Christ, and likewise in the Blessed Virgin Mary and the other saints.[11]

What we have said suffices for God's omnipotence, and it confirms the teaching of St. Thomas, who declared in a previous article: "Since the divine will is perfectly efficacious, it follows not only that things are done, which God wills to be done, but also that they are done in the way that He wills. Now God wills some things to be done necessarily, some contingently, to the right ordering of things, for the building up of the universe."[12]

11 Cf. *ibid.*
12 *Ibid.*, Ia, q. 19, a.8.

CHAPTER XXVI

QUESTION 26

OF THE DIVINE BEATITUDE

AFTER considering all that pertains to God's operation, namely, to His knowledge, His will, and His power in its relation to external effects, we must treat of the divine beatitude, for beatitude is the perfect good of an intellectual creature. By so doing, we complete what pertains to the unity of the divine essence. There are four articles to this question.

1) Whether beatitude belongs to God; (2) whether God is called blessed in regard to His intellect; (3) whether God is essentially the beatitude of each of the blessed; (4) whether all other beatitude is included in the beatitude of God.[1]

FIRST ARTICLE

WHETHER BEATITUDE BELONGS TO GOD

The answer is in the affirmative and it is of faith. St. Paul says of God: "Who is the Blessed and only Mighty, the King of kings and Lord of lords." [2] The Vatican Council says that God is "of supreme beatitude in and from Himself." [3]

Theological proof. "Beatitude is the perfect good of an intellectual nature." The irrational animal finds its pleasure indeed in the possession of its good, but it has not beatitude, "because it does not know that it has a sufficiency of the good which it possesses." Only an intellectual nature knows what is meant by good and evil, and so it alone is formally capable of beatitude, and it alone can "control its own actions" for the attainment of this beatitude. In other words, it is only an intellectual agent that knows the end as such, not merely the thing which is the end. In this it differs from the irrational animal, and thus it alone is capable of possessing the end as such. Thus this article gives us a complete idea of beatitude, making it clear to us that beatitude as thus defined belongs in a most excellent way to

---

1 *Contra Gentes*, Bk. I, chap. 100.
2 I Tim. 6: 15.
3 Denz., no. 1782.

God, inasmuch as God is the most perfect Being, possessing intelligence in the highest degree. For God possesses the supreme Good with fullness of intelligence.

Reply to second objection. As God has being, though not begotten; so He has beatitude, although it is not acquired by merit.

SECOND ARTICLE

WHETHER GOD IS CALLED BLESSED IN RESPECT
OF HIS INTELLECT

St. Thomas follows St. Augustine and Aristotle on this point. The former said: "Vision is the whole of the reward." [4]

The answer of St. Thomas is: "Beatitude must be assigned to God in respect of His intellect, as also to the blessed."

The reason is that "beatitude is the perfect good of an intellectual nature. . . . Now that which is most perfect in an intellectual nature is the intellectual operation, by which in some sense it grasps everything." Thus God adequately comprehends Himself and understands all things in Himself as the cause.

Reply to second objection. "Since beatitude is a good, it is the object of the will; now the object is understood as prior to the act of a power. Hence, in our manner of understanding, divine beatitude precedes the act of the will at rest in it. This cannot be other than the act of the intellect," by which God perfectly possesses His infinite goodness. Delight or fruition in the divine will follows from this perfect knowledge. This fruition is therefore the complement of beatitude, and is not its essence, which consists in the perfection of perfect good.

Scotus attacked this conclusion. He considers that formal beatitude consists principally in love, giving three reasons for this view: (1) that beatitude is a good, which is the object of love; (2) that we must know God in order to love Him, but not love Him in order to know Him; (3) that what we love more is beatitude, and the will loves its act of love more than the act of the intellect.

Cajetan replies to this by making three observations: (1) Objective beatitude is indeed a good, which is the object of love; but the will in loving is not an apprehensive faculty, and the possession of God is accomplished by seeing, from which follows fruition in the will. (2) In this life, of course, we must know God to love Him, and not vice versa, because in this life it is better to love God than to know Him, for love tends toward God as He is in Himself, whereas our

---

[4] *De civitate Dei,* Bk. XXII, chap. 26. See also Aristotle's *Metaphysics,* Bk. XII, chap. 7; *Ethics,* Bk. X, chap. 7.

knowledge of God in this life draws Him to us, according to the limitation of our concepts. But in heaven the vision of God is immediate, and so it is superior to love, which necessarily follows from it as a property from its essence. (3) The will, by an elicited appetitive act, prefers what is better not for itself, but for the individual who wills. Therefore, if the act of the intellect is a greater perfection of the individual than volition, then the correct attitude in the will is for it to prefer intellection to volition.

THIRD ARTICLE

WHETHER GOD IS THE BEATITUDE OF EACH OF THE BLESSED

The answer is that God is objectively the beatitude of all the blessed, but He is not formally their beatitude, for this consists in the beatific vision, which admits of different degrees.

FOURTH ARTICLE

WHETHER ALL OTHER BEATITUDE IS INCLUDED IN THE BEATITUDE OF GOD

The answer is: "Whatever is desirable in whatever beatitude, whether true or false, pre-exists wholly and in a more eminent degree in the divine beatitude. As to contemplative happiness, God possesses a continual and most certain contemplation of Himself and of all things else; and as to that which is active, He has the governance of the whole universe."

Thus we finish the treatise on *The One God*, or the divine essence, in which three things have been considered: (1) Whether God exists (q. 2); (2) How God exists, or rather how He does not exist (q. 3–13); (3) His operations, namely, His knowledge, will, and power (q. 14–25). Thus the question on the divine beatitude (q. 26) completes what pertains to the unity of the divine essence, and prepares for the treatise on the Trinity of the divine Persons and on God the Creator.

Praise be to God, who, as the Vatican Council says, "is of supreme beatitude in and from Himself, and ineffably exalted above all things besides Himself which exist or are conceivable." [5] For He is the self-subsisting Being, self-subsisting Intellection, essential love. Thus "He is absolutely simple and unchangeable, and thus He is really and essentially distinct from the world," which is essentially composite and changeable.[6]

[5] Denz., no. 1782.
[6] *Ibid.*

Thus in the whole of this treatise on *The One God,* we find verified the words spoken by God to Moses, which may be considered as
the definition of God: "I am who am," [7] which is tantamount to saying that, compared to Him, creatures are non-existent. Of themselves,
indeed, creatures are non-existent, but for God they are something,
because they are loved by Him. In fact, "God so loved the world
as to give His only begotten Son." [8]

[7] Ex. 3: 14.
[8] John 3: 16.

INDEX